P9-BXY-645

STUDENT SERVICES

STUDENT SERVICES

A Handbook for the Profession, Fourth Edition

Susan R. Komives, Dudley B. Woodard, Jr.,
and Associates

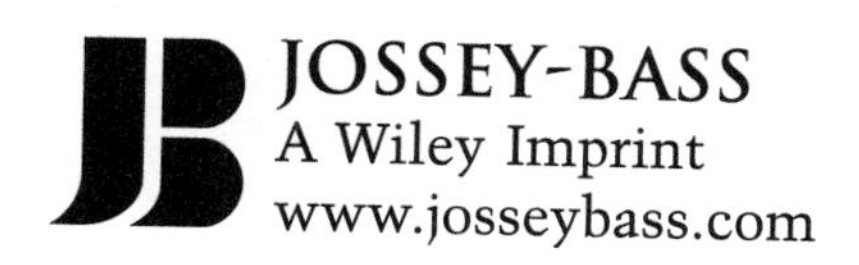

JOSSEY-BASS
A Wiley Imprint
www.josseybass.com

Published by Jossey-Bass
A Wiley Imprint
989 Market Street, San Francisco, CA 94103-1741 www.josseybass.com

Jossey-Bass books and products are available through most bookstores. To contact Jossey-Bass directly call our Customer Care Department within the U.S. at 800-956-7739, outside the U.S. at 317-572-3986, or fax 317-572-4002.

Jossey-Bass also publishes its books in a variety of electronic formats. Some content that appears in print may not be available in electronic books.

Library of Congress Cataloging-in-Publication Data
Komives, Susan R., 1946–
Student services : a handbook for the profession / Susan R. Komives, Dudley B. Woodard, Jr., and associates.— 4th ed.
p. cm. — (The Jossey-Bass higher and adult education series)
ISBN 0-7879-6050-0 (alk. paper)
1. Student affairs services—United States—Handbooks, manuals, etc. 2. College student development programs—United States—Handbooks, manuals, etc. 3. Counseling in higher education—United States—Handbooks, manuals, etc. I. Woodard, Dudley, 1940– II. Title. III. Series
LB 2342.92 .K65 2003
378.1'94—dc21

2002153386

Printed in the United States of America
FIRST EDITION
HB Printing 10 9 8 7

THE JOSSEY-BASS HIGHER AND ADULT EDUCATION SERIES

CONTENTS

FIGURES & EXHIBITS

Figures:

Exhibits:

PREFACE

One hundred years after the first dean of students appeared in American higher education, the field of student affairs can claim a proud tradition of supporting and enriching millions of college students' personal and academic lives. In that time, postsecondary institutions have repeatedly affirmed the need for traditional student affairs functions, and they have continually added new challenges to the student affairs portfolio in response to societal shifts as well as institutional and student needs.

The study and practice of student affairs has developed over time to encompass a broad theoretical base, extended graduate-level preparation, a strong commitment to service rather than personal gain, and a community of practitioners with high standards for ethical practice and conduct. We must, however, continue to meet our professional and ethical obligations to challenge, revitalize, and expand both our study and our practice. We must know more next year than we did this year. We must share what we know. Finally, we must expect the highest standards of quality in our colleagues' work.

As members of a broad and diverse professional field, we continue to face the challenge of achieving a common understanding. This book is intended to promote a common language about students and higher education, to help ground our practice and inform the many professionals who work in student services functions.

The "Green Book"

In 1980, Ursula Delworth, Gary Hanson, and their associates provided a great service to our field when they published the first edition of *Student Services.* At that time, no single publication covered the breadth and depth of student affairs practice and the principles that guide it. The second edition of *Student Services,* published in 1989, was eagerly awaited and immediately embraced as a valuable update. The "Green Book," as it was called, quickly became a fixture in the student affairs field, helping scores of master's and doctoral degree students become oriented to the profession. The decision to carry *Student Services* into a third edition in 1996 was a tribute to the visionary thinking of Ursula Delworth, Gary Hanson, and each of their authors. We were pleased to edit the third edition and to find new generations of student affairs professionals learning foundational material and new material on such topics as identity theory, student learning, leadership, multiculturalism, and the philosophy of the field. The Green Book is indeed organic. It grows, changes, and expands with the complexity of the field of student affairs work and the complexity of students' experiences. This edition continues the updates on foundational topics and expands to include chapters on student success, advising, community building, professionalism, and collaborations.

A Note on the Title

What term best applies to the profession described in this book? Our field has been called many things: student personnel, student services, student development, student affairs. While some find the appellation "student services" too limiting, believing that it describes only a portion of what we do or one philosophical approach to practice, we have decided to honor the history and tradition of the previous three editions of this book by keeping the same title for the fourth edition.

Focus of the Fourth Edition

This edition, like the first three, focuses on enhancing students' experience with postsecondary education through the development of student affairs professionals' knowledge, skills, and attitudes. We hope that as you read this book, you will ask yourself, How does this information enhance my work with students?

The fourth edition focuses on the new student affairs professional, calling upon a wealth of strong literature in the field to establish a solid foundation for student affairs practice. It also targets graduate students studying to become student affairs professionals as well as individuals entering the field from other professions, such as nurses, campus child-care center directors, and faculty taking on academic advising roles. In addition, we hope other professionals working in postsecondary education will also find numerous sections of interest in their work with students.

This book presents a scholarly review of the foundations of the student affairs profession, including its history, context, values, and theoretical base. It outlines the core competencies required of student affairs professionals, assesses desired outcomes of student affairs practice, and explores future directions for the field. The content of each chapter is not only updated but also transformed, viewing each topic through multiple lenses or frames reflecting the wide diversity of institutional types, student characteristics, and developmental experiences. Just as the future will benefit from curricular transformation around multiple frames, the study of student affairs must model that practice.

This edition has been designed as a comprehensive text. While many sections and chapters stand alone, the reader will note that many chapters build on and assume knowledge of information presented in previous chapters. Readers are also encouraged to turn to other books, web sites, and associations for the depth that now exists in so many of these topics.

This edition includes major updates of chapters in all sections. In addition to updated scholarship that has appeared since the 1995 writing cycle for the third edition, our authors have focused on the diversity of types of educational settings and have expanded their thinking to include groups of students underrepresented in our practice such as graduate students and distance learners. Five totally new chapters are included: theories influencing student success (in Part Three); processes of advising (in Part Five); processes of community building and programming (in Part Five); reflections on professionalism (in Part Five); and strategies for collaborations (in Part Six).

Contents of the Fourth Edition

This edition is divided into six sections, addressing the historical and philosophical foundations of student affairs, the professional principles underpinning practice in the field, theoretical understandings of student development, organizing and delivering student affairs and educational interventions, professional competencies that facilitate student learning and the broader collegiate experience, and future challenges.

Specifically, Part One explores our historical and philosophical roots and the contemporary context of American higher education. It presents the history of American postsecondary education and provides a foundation for understanding the many different types of institutions and diverse characteristics of college students.

In Chapter One, John Thelin offers a succinct history of American higher education as a whole, tracing the events and movements that have influenced or reflected the student experience in the United States. In Chapter Two, Sylvia Hurtado describes the foundations of the diversity we see today in American postsecondary institutions. She provides a historical overview of these institutions and portrays the current context, emphasizing institutions that have often been often overlooked in the literature, such as Black colleges and universities and women's colleges. In Chapter Three, Elaine El-Khawas explores the diversity of college students. She examines the demographic and social trends that have produced the student body of today, investigating how these trends will affect who will go to college in the future.

Part Two presents the professional principles essential to student affairs practice. These chapters build on the history of student affairs and the needs and characteristics of American institutions and students, enumerating the core values of the field, the ethical principles that guide our professional behavior, and the legal foundations that serve as a context for our professional work.

In Chapter Four, Elizabeth Nuss updates the history of the student affairs field, tracing the evolution of the profession and its key functions. Nuss includes the movement in the 1990s for campus collaborations around student learning and the role the student affairs profession has had in that movement. In Chapter Five, Robert Young presents the philosophies and values guiding the profession. He identifies common themes from historical documents, tracing the evolution of these key ideas into the shared professional vision, values, and philosophy of today's student affairs practitioner. Understanding the beliefs and values that undergird our profession is central to our work in times of rapid change. In Chapter Six, Jane Fried presents ethical and moral guidelines for practice and illustrates how ethical actions provide a foundation for professional behavior in a cultural context. Ethics and standards are such an important aspect of this profession that the entire ethics statements from both the American College Personnel Association (ACPA) and the National Association of Student Personnel Administrators (NASPA) are included in the Resources section at the back of the book. In Chapter Seven, Margaret Barr updates her discussion of the essential legal principles affecting student affairs practice, applying them to such important topics as speech codes, campus safety, and domestic partners.

Part Three examines the theoretical bases essential to the profession. These bases are changing as the field of student affairs becomes more complex. Student affairs is a proudly interdisciplinary field, integrating theories from such fields as psychology, sociology, anthropology, and public policy and applying them to the student experience in the academic environment. The theoretical frames are expanded from the third edition to reflect this growing base of theory and perspective. Each of the chapters in this section makes intentional theory-to-practice applications for diverse students.

In Chapter Eight, Marylu McEwen discusses the nature of theory in student affairs and how theory can guide practice. In Chapter Nine, Nancy Evans presents an overview of classic domains of student development theory—focusing on psychosocial, cognitive, and typological models—reframed around social construction theory and updated with new theoretical material such as spirituality development. This chapter also includes career development theory and includes a critique of the limitations of existing theoretical frames to teach the reader how to use multiple lenses.

In Chapter Ten, Marylu McEwen applies perspectives to understanding identity development. She presents the student's life in a personal context, including the social construction of such frames as race, gender, class, ability, and sexual orientation and explores the concepts of multiple identities. Chapter Eleven, by Patricia King, explores cognitive-structural theory and focuses on student learning. King emphasizes the responsibility of student development educators to enhance student learning. George Kuh has updated his chapter on organizational theory. In Chapter

Twelve he describes several inclusive, flexible organizational models for times of rapid change. In Chapter Thirteen, Carney Strange presents an understanding of the collegiate environment and discusses theories on interaction between individuals and their environment. Strange traces the history of this theoretical line and addresses limitations on its development. He emphasizes current theories and research, including ecological models and the concepts of student cultures and climate. In Chapter Fourteen, a new chapter, John Braxton explores theoretical and research frames for retention and student success. He presents classic and current critiques of these frames and their application.

Part Four presents the foundations of student affairs practice and how student services are organized to meet student and institutional needs. The contributors to this section focus on functional areas and the key administrative awareness needed to lead student affairs programs and services.

In Chapter Fifteen, Gwen Dungy presents student affairs organization, functions, and standards of practice. The chapter offers an overview of traditional functional areas and gives special attention to emerging functional areas. In Chapter Sixteen, John Schuh offers an updated discussion of planning and finance, with greater emphasis on revenue sources like activity fees and issues such as fee-based structures, downsizing, and outsourcing. In Chapter Seventeen, Will Barratt challenges us to make creative and effective use of technology and information systems. Jon Dalton again discusses human resources in Chapter Eighteen, presenting a practical foundation for selecting, hiring, developing, supervising, and evaluating staff.

Part Five presents the essential competencies and techniques for skillful professional practice in student affairs. As the contributors to this section demonstrate, professional practice is informed by theory and research and implemented through key roles (such as administrator, counselor, educator), with each role drawing on the practitioner's knowledge, skills, and attitudes to guide his or her practice.

Donna Talbot discusses multicultural and diversity competencies in Chapter Nineteen. This chapter leads the competency section to emphasize the centrality of this perspective and how important the skill of being multicultural is in understanding diverse frames, world views, and experiences of all on campus. Talbot stresses the importance of developing the knowledge, skills, and attitudes required to effectively work with diverse students and to create and sustain multicultural communities on campus. In Chapter Twenty, Judy Rogers writes again on leadership. This chapter presents an inclusive, empowerment-based model of leadership. This model represents a paradigm shift in the profession to collaborative, process-oriented leadership designed to aid effective change in flexible systems. In Chapter Twenty-One, Larry Roper discusses teaching and training in support of the student development educator's role with groups and individuals. In Chapter Twenty-Two, Roger Winston offers an updated version of his discussion of personal counseling including cross-cultural counseling strategies. The advising portions of the previous chapter in the third edition have been expanded into a new chapter in this edition. In the new Chapter Twenty-Three, Patrick Love presents the breadth and scope of individual, group, and organizational advising with an emphasis on academic advising, career advising, and organizational consulting. Saunie Taylor explores the competencies of intergroup dialogue, mediation, and conflict resolution in new chapter Twenty-Four. Student affairs staff have long been community-builders on campus, and in new chapter Twenty-Five, Denny Roberts explores the concepts and skills of community building and the role of programming in supporting community and personal development. Assessment of student outcomes has a central role in student affairs practice and in Chapter Twenty-Six, assessment expert Lee Upcraft outlines competency in assessment and evaluation. The competency section concludes with new Chapter Twenty-Seven by Stan Carpenter on professionalism. Carpenter explores professional expectations, identity, and professional development as central to this way of being.

Part Six seeks to lay a new foundation for the future by clarifying the impact of student affairs on students. This section also presents issues, trends, and challenges that deserve attention as student affairs professionals continue to enhance the student experience in the future.

In Chapter Twenty-Eight, Leonard Baird discusses the overall impact of the college experience on students. These outcomes include central, general findings and findings that are salient for diverse specific groups by institutional type. In Chapter Twenty-Nine, another new chapter, Charles Schroeder challenges us to operationalize these findings in collaborative ways with diverse partners particularly with those in academic affairs. In Chapter Thirty, we identify trends and developments in higher education, student characteristics and needs, and professional knowledge bases and competencies. We conclude the chapter by presenting advice for the conceptualization and delivery of student services for the new millennium.

Dedication: Ursula Delworth

We dedicate this fourth edition to our friend and colleague, Ursula Delworth, whose legacy with this book we seek to emulate. Ursula's forty-year career in higher education included her work as a counseling psychologist and educator at Colorado State and the University of Iowa as well as work at the Western Interstate Commission for Higher Education (WICHE) in understanding campus ecology. She was an active contributor to the American College Personnel Association serving as chair of the counseling commission and as chair of Division 17 of the American Psychological Association among many other contributions. She and Gary Hanson founded this book and with Allen Jossey-Bass they started the now famous New Directions in Student Services series. Ursula was bright, candid, informed, generative, challenging, and visionary. She truly cared for all creatures. Her passion for her cats was well known and led her to work with cats and the elderly and support for abused and neglected animals. Her heartfelt laugh and her pensive nod have motivated and inspired many. She is missed, but her legacies live on in all of her students, staff, and those who ever knew her—and with thousands of professionals who have read her books, including early editions of the Green Book.

In Appreciation

Any book this comprehensive represents the hard work of the graduate students and colleagues on the campuses of all our authors. We all benefit by the shared wisdom of so many who read chapters and brainstormed ideas with us and with these fine authors. We are both exceptionally grateful to George McClellan, a wise doctoral student at the University of Arizona who served as our colleague in the process of this book. We were blessed by George's scholarly reading, excellent editing, and skilled management of us and of the process! We both also appreciate the support of the Vice President for Student Affairs at Arizona. Dr. Saunie Taylor's office provided us financial support for the lengthy phone calls, massive amounts of paper, and urgent overnight mailings that go into the editing of such a volume. This support was critical.

Doug is grateful to his wife, Karen, for her wisdom and encouragement during good times as well as difficult ones. He and Karen offer a special thanks to their children, who have enriched their lives in so many ways. Doug appreciates the work of Quanhua Zhou, a doctoral student and graduate associate of Doug's who provided particularly helpful support in the final editing and administrative aspects of preparing this book for publication. Doug is grateful to the many other graduate students who contributed directly or indirectly to the development of the third and fourth editions—truly outstanding students who have or will become successful practitioners and faculty. Moreover, Doug has been blessed with world-class colleagues. Thank you Larry Leslie, John Levin, Gary Rhoades, and Shelia Slaughter for your support, insights, and encouragement for the past fifteen years. Finally, Doug hopes by the time this book is published, he will be teaching part-time and finding new ways to be generative!

Susan is grateful to her husband, Ralph, who continues to amaze her with all the ways he shows his support, and to the inspiration of new granddaughters, Mary and Molly. Most authors wrote these chapters in the fall of 2001 filled with the shared concern of September 11, 2001. Granddaughter Molly was also born that day, reminding all of us of the circle of life that does go on. Susan is also blessed with the wisdom of her many recent alums and graduate students who read various versions of the book and assisted with chapter editing: special thanks to Craig Alimo, Penny Asay, Renee Baird Snyder, Dee Campanella, John Dugan, Wallace Eddy, Amy Ginther, Jeff Greene, Laura Irwin, Susan Longerbeam, Felicia Mainella, Cara Meixner, Laura Osteen, Julie Owen, Richard Stevens, Kristin Vogt, Rhondie Voorhees, and Jennifer Weisman.

The student affairs field brings constant change, constant renewal, and a rich opportunity to learn from many scholarly people. In the process of developing this edition of *Student Services,* we have learned from each of our authors, from our graduate students who assisted in reviewing the contributions, and from each other. We continue to feel exceptionally lucky that we chose a career in student affairs work and in that process have worked with many people of character, people devoted to the student experience, and people passionate about helping their institutions be empowering environments for students and all who work there. It is up to each person reading this book to create space around you where people learn, are valued, and are engaged in meaningful work in ethical environments. Generations of college students to come will continue to find the college experience to be joyous, threatening, growth producing, upsetting, expanding, and capacity building. Student affairs professionals continue to be the guides to our students in this journey and to our institutions in the design of those pathways. We hope you will find these chapters rich with foundational material to help you in this journey.

October 2002

Susan R. Komives
University of Maryland, College Park
Dudley B. Woodard, Jr.
University of Arizona

THE AUTHORS

Leonard L. Baird is a professor in the higher education and student affairs program at the Ohio State University and editor of the *Journal of Higher Education.* His B.S. and M.A. degrees are in psychology, and his Ed.D. degree is in higher education and measurement. All were received from the University of California, Los Angeles. The author of numerous articles and books, Dr. Baird's chief research interests are the impact of college on students, college quality, and the social psychology of higher education. He has over thirty years' experience assessing students and institutions in higher education, first as a researcher at the American College Testing Program and then at the Education Testing Service, conducting studies on a variety of aspects of higher education.

Margaret J. Barr is professor emeritus at Northwestern University. Her degrees include a B.S. in elementary education from the State University of New York College at Buffalo, an M.S. in college student personnel from Southern Illinois University Carbondale, and a Ph.D. in higher education administration from the University of Texas at Austin. Dr. Barr served as vice president for student affairs at Northwestern University prior to her retirement and previously served as vice chancellor for student affairs at Texas Christian University and vice president for student affairs at Northern Illinois University. She is the author of over thirty-five books, book chapters, and monographs. A former president of the American College Personnel Association (ACPA), Dr. Barr has also served as president of the National Association of Student Personnel Administrators (NASPA) Foundation. She has received the Contribution to Literature Award from both ACPA and NASPA, the Professional Service Award from ACPA, and the Contribution to Higher Education Award from NASPA.

William Barratt is associate professor and master's program coordinator in the Department of Counseling at Indiana State University where he also served as associate dean of the School of Graduate Studies. His B.A. degree is in history and philosophy from Beloit College. His M.S. degree is from Miami University in personnel counseling, and his Ph.D. degree is in student development in postsecondary education from the University of Iowa (1983). Dr. Barratt authored several articles on information technology in higher education. He has served on the directorate for ACPA Commissions VI, IX, and XII and chaired the ACPA Information Technology Task Force. Dr. Barratt is active in developing web sites and in promoting creative uses of information technology for student learning and student affairs.

John M. Braxton is professor of education and coordinator of the Higher Education Program in the Department of Leadership and Organizations at Peabody College, Vanderbilt University. Dr. Braxton has over fifty refereed journal articles, book chapters, and books. He edited *Reworking the Student Departure Puzzle* (2000) as well as *Perspectives on Scholarly Misconduct in the Sciences* and *Faculty Teaching and Research: Is There Conflict?*. He has also authored, with Alan E. Bayer, *Faculty Misconduct in Collegiate Teaching* and serves as a consulting editor for the *Journal of Higher Education* and *Research in Higher Education*. Dr. Braxton serves as a member of the National Review Panel of the ASHE-ERIC Higher Education Report Series. In addition, he is the general editor of the Vanderbilt University Press "Studies in Higher Education" book series. One of Dr. Braxton's areas of research focuses on the structure and processes of the college student experience.

Stan Carpenter is professor of educational administration and director of the Center for Leadership in Higher Education at Texas A&M University. He holds a B.S. degree in mathematics from Tarleton State University (1972), an M.S. degree in student personnel and guidance from Texas A&M-Commerce (1975), and a Ph. D. degree in counseling and student personnel services from the University of Georgia (1979). Dr. Carpenter has served as the executive director of the Association for the Study of Higher Education (ASHE) and as editor/chair of the ACPA Media Board, as well as the NASPA board of directors. He has received awards for teaching (Texas A&M's College of Education), scholarship (Senior Scholar of ACPA, 2000; SACSA's Melvene Hardee Award), and service (Distinguished Service Award from ASHE; National Distinguished Service Award from Alpha Phi Omega National Service Fraternity).

Jon C. Dalton is associate professor and director of the Center for the Study of Values in College Student Development at Florida State University. He earned a B.A. degree in philosophy from Franklin College, an M.Div. degree in religion from Yale University, and an M.S. degree in student personnel services and an Ed.D. degree in higher education from the University of Kentucky. Dr. Dalton was previously vice president for student affairs at Florida State University and Northern Illinois University and served as president of the National Association of Student Personnel Administrators. He has authored four monographs, twelve book chapters, and numerous articles. He directs the annual *Institute on College Student Values,* edits the online *Journal of College and Character,* and serves as senior editor of *About Campus.* Dr. Dalton has received professional leadership and service awards from ACPA and NASPA.

Gwendolyn Jordan Dungy is the executive director of the National Association of Student Personnel Administrators. Her degrees include a B.S. in English from Eastern Illinois University, an M.S. in counseling from Eastern Illinois University, an M.A. in

English from Drew University, and a Ph.D. in policy and administration from Washington University in St. Louis. Dr. Dungy's previous professional association work was at the Association of American Colleges and Universities. Her campus work as an administrator has been at a number of community colleges as both an academic and a student affairs dean.

Elaine El-Khawas is professor of education policy at George Washington University. She also is director of the ERIC Clearinghouse on Higher Education. Previously she served as professor of higher education at the University of California, Los Angeles, and as vice president for policy analysis and research at the American Council on Education. A sociologist, with master's and doctoral degrees from the University of Chicago, she is a former president of the Association for the Study of Higher Education, a member of the board of trustees of Emmanuel College, and currently serves on the editorial boards of the *Review of Higher Education, Higher Education Management,* and other academic journals.

Nancy J. Evans is a professor in the Department of Educational Leadership and Policy Studies and coordinator of the Higher Education Program at Iowa State University. Her degrees include a B.A. in social science from Potsdam State College, an M.A. in higher education/college student personnel from Southern Illinois University, an M.F.A. in theatre from Western Illinois University, and a Ph.D. in counseling psychology from the University of Missouri. Dr. Evans has edited or authored five books, including *Student Development in College: Theory, Research, and Practice,* along with numerous book chapters and journal articles. She served as president of the American College Personnel Association in 2001–02, is a member of the editorial board of the *Journal of College Student Development,* received the Contribution to Knowledge Award from ACPA, and is an ACPA Senior Scholar. Dr. Evans' research is focused on the impact of the college environment on student development, particularly with regard to the experiences of lesbian, gay, bisexual, and transgender students.

Jane Fried is a professor in the Department of Counselor and Family Therapy Education at Central Connecticut State University, where she is the coordinator of the master's degree program in Student Development in Higher Education. She holds a B.A. degree in American and world literature from Harpur College, SUNY Binghamton, an M.A.Ed. degree in student personnel from Syracuse University, and a Ph.D. degree in counseling and human development from the Union of Experimenting Colleges and Universities. Dr. Fried is the coauthor of *Understanding Diversity: A Learning in Practice Primer,* author of *Shifting Paradigms in Student Affairs,* and author/editor of *Ethics for Today's Campus.* Her most recent publication is "Civility and Spirituality in Student Affairs," a chapter in *Transforming Campus Life: Reflections on Spirituality and Campus Pluralism.* Dr. Fried has served as chair of the ACPA Standing Committee on Women, the Ethics Committee, and the Affirmative Action Committee.

Sylvia Hurtado is associate professor and director of the Center for Study of Higher and Postsecondary Education at the University of Michigan. She received her B.A. degree in sociology from Princeton University, master's degree in education from Harvard, and Ph.D. degree in education from UCLA. Dr. Hurtado has numerous publications on diversity in higher education focusing on the success of diverse college students in diverse institutional contexts. She is lead author of *Enacting Diverse Learning Environments: Improving the Climate for Racial/Ethnic Diversity in Higher Education (1999)* and coeditor with David Schoem of *Intergroup Dialogue: Deliberative Democracy in School, College, Workplace, and Community* (2001). Dr. Hurtado has served on the Board of AAHE and the accrediting body, the Higher Learning Commission, and has previous administrative experience in undergraduate and graduate admissions. Her recent research is focused on the preparation of students' cognitive, social, and democratic skills to participate in a diverse democracy.

Patricia M. King is a professor in the Center for the Study of Higher and Postsecondary Education at the University of Michigan. She earned her B.A. degree in English at Macalester College in St. Paul, Minnesota, and her Ph.D. degree in educational psychology at the University of Minnesota. Dr. King is the author of numerous articles and book chapters on student learning and development and is the coauthor (with Karen Strohm Kitchener) of *Developing Reflective Judgment* (1994). She was a founding editor of *About Campus* and serves as its executive editor. Dr. King previously served as chair of the Department of Higher Education and Student Affairs at Bowling Green State University, as assistant vice president for student services at The Ohio State University, and as senior research psychologist to the vice president for student services at the University of Iowa. She has received the ACPA Contribution to Knowledge Award and Senior Scholar Diplomate, and NASPA's Robert Shaffer Award.

Susan R. Komives is associate professor of counseling and personnel services and faculty associate for the Division of Student Affairs at the University of Maryland, College Park. She earned her B.S. degree in mathematics and M.S. degree in higher education at Florida State University, and doctorate degree in educational administration at the University of Tennessee, Knoxville. Dr. Komives is a member of the editorial board for the *Journal of College Student Development*, publications and research editor of the National Clearinghouse for Leadership Programs, and coauthor of *Exploring Leadership* (1998) and *Management and Leadership Issues for a New Century* (2000). She has served as vice president for student development at the University of Tampa, as vice president and dean of student life at Stephens College, and in various student affairs positions at Denison University and the University of Tennessee, Knoxville. Dr. Komives is a former president of the American College Personnel Association, a recipient of that association's Esther Lloyd-Jones Professional Service Award, and is a Senior Scholar Diplomate of ACPA.

George D. Kuh is chancellor's professor of higher education at Indiana University Bloomington. He holds a B.A. degree from Luther College, an M.S. degree from St. Cloud State University, and a Ph.D. degree from the University of Iowa. Dr. Kuh has written extensively about student engagement, assessment, institutional improvement, and college and university cultures. He directs the College Student Experiences Questionnaire Program and the National Survey of Student Engagement, an annual survey of first-year and senior students that is funded by Lumina Foundation for Education and The Pew Charitable Trusts, and cosponsored by The Carnegie Foundation for the Advancement of Teaching and the Pew Forum on Undergraduate Learning. A past president of the Association for the Study of Higher Education,

Dr. Kuh has consulted with more than 150 educational institutions and agencies in the U.S. and abroad.

Patrick Love is an associate professor of higher education at New York University. He earned his B.A. degree in political science and M.S./C.A.S. degree in counseling psychology and student development from the State University of New York at Albany, and his Ph.D. degree in higher education and student affairs from Indiana University. Dr. Love is the coauthor, with Anne Goodsell Love, of *Enhancing Student Learning: Intellectual, Social, and Emotional Integration* (1995), with Vicki Guthrie of *Understanding and Applying Cognitive Development Theory* (1999), and with Dudley Woodard and Susan Komives of *Leadership and Management Issues for the New Century* (2000).

Marylu K. McEwen is associate professor with the College Student Personnel program in the Department of Counseling and Personnel Services, University of Maryland, College Park. Her degrees include a B.S. in mathematics and a Ph.D. in counseling and personnel services from Purdue University and an M.S.Ed. in college student personnel from Indiana University. Dr. McEwen is coeditor of *Working with Asian American College Students,* has served as associate editor of the *Journal of College Student Development,* and has directed more than thirty doctoral dissertations. Her teaching and research interests are in multiculturalism in student affairs and higher education; student development theory, particularly the applicability and enhancement of psychosocial theories for students of color; and White racial identity development. Dr. McEwen is the recipient of NASPA's 2001 Outstanding Contribution to Literature or Research Award as well as awards from Purdue University, Indiana University, and ACPA's Committee on Multicultural Affairs.

Elizabeth M. Nuss retired as vice president and dean of students from Goucher College in Baltimore, Maryland, in 2001. She earned her B.A. degree from the State University of New York at Albany, her M.Ed. degree from The Pennsylvania State University, and her Ph.D. degree from the University of Maryland. Prior to Goucher College, Dr. Nuss served as executive director of the National Association of Student Personnel Administrators (NASPA) from 1987–95 where she played a key role in establishing the association's presence in Washington, D.C. The first twenty years of her career in student affairs were spent at Penn State, the University of Maryland College Park, and Indiana University. Dr. Nuss received NASPA's Dissertation of the Year Award in 1982 and the Fred Turner Award for Outstanding Service to NASPA in 1996. She has authored numerous publications and is a frequent presenter and consultant.

Dennis C. Roberts is assistant vice president for student affairs at Miami University in Oxford, Ohio, and assistant professor in the Educational Leadership Department at Miami. His degrees include a B.A. in music and an M.Ed. in student personnel administration from Colorado State University, and a Ph.D. in college student personnel from the University of Maryland. Dr. Roberts is the author of numerous articles and chapters in books, as well as the editor for *Student Leadership Programs in Higher Education,* the first book advocating and providing an explicit model for leadership development in higher education, and *Designing Campus Activities to Foster a Sense of Community.* Dr. Roberts held several leadership positions in ACPA, including serving as its president in 1985–86. He currently serves on the board of directors of the

LeaderShape Institute and is the founding convener of the International Leadership Association's Leadership Educators' section.

Judy Lawrence Rogers is an associate professor and director of graduate studies in the College Student Personnel master's program in the Department of Educational Leadership at Miami University (at Oxford, Ohio). Her undergraduate degree in history was earned at St. Mary College (Kansas), and she received both her Master's degree in counseling and guidance and her Ph.D. degree in higher education administration from The Ohio State University. Dr. Rogers' teaching and writing interests focus on leadership, leadership development, and organizational transformation. Most recently her publications and professional presentations have explored the spiritual dimension of leadership. Dr. Rogers has served on the *NASPA Journal* editorial board and also as book review editor for the *NASPA Journal.* She currently serves on a Strategic Planning Team for the International Leadership Association.

Larry D. Roper has served as vice provost for student affairs and professor of ethnic studies at Oregon State University since 1995. He received his A.B. degree in history from Heidelberg College, his M.A. degree in college student personnel from Bowling Green State University, and his Ph.D. degree in college student personnel administration from the University of Maryland, College Park. Dr. Roper's publications and presentations reflect interests in topics such as individual and institutional racism, diversity issues, and leadership and community development. He teaches courses in speech communications, ethnic studies, college student services administration, and the doctoral program in community college leadership. Dr. Roper's involvement in professional associations includes serving as editor of the *NASPA Journal,* as a senior scholar with the American College Personnel Association, and as director of the Richard F. Stevens Institute.

Charles C. Schroeder is a professor in the educational leadership and policy analysis program at the University of Missouri-Columbia. His B.A. and M.A degrees are in psychology and history from Austin College, and his Ed.D. degree is in college student personnel administration from Oregon State University. Dr. Schroeder has authored more than seventy articles, chapters, monographs, and books. During the past thirty years, he has served as chief student affairs officer at Mercer University, Saint Louis University, Georgia Institute of Technology, and the University of Missouri-Columbia. Dr. Schroeder has been very active in the American College Personnel Association, serving twice as president, as executive editor of *About Campus: Enriching the Student Learning Experience,* and as president of the ACPA Educational Leadership Foundation as a senior scholar. He has received awards from ACPA for professional service and contributions to knowledge.

John H. Schuh is professor and chair of the Department of Educational Leadership and Policy Studies at Iowa State University. He earned his B.A. degree at the University of Wisconsin, Oshkosh, and his M.C. and Ph.D. degrees at Arizona State University. Previously, Dr. Schuh held administrative and faculty appointments at Wichita State University, Indiana University, and Arizona State University. He is the editor in chief of the New Directions for Student Services sourcebook series and associate editor of the *Journal of College Student Development.* Dr. Schuh has received the Contribution to

Knowledge Award, the Presidential Service Award, the Annuit Coeptis Award, and the Senior Scholar Diplomate Award from the American College Personnel Association. He also received the Contribution to Literature or Research Award from the National Association of Student Personnel Administrators. Dr. Schuh recently received a Fulbright Award to study higher education in Germany.

C. Carney Strange is professor of higher education and student affairs in the Higher Education Administration and college student personnel graduate programs at Bowling Green State University (Ohio). A graduate of St. Meinrad College in Indiana (B.A. degree) and the University of Iowa (M.A. and Ph.D. degrees), he is the lead author, with James Banning, of *Educating by Design: Creating Campus Learning Environments that Work*. Dr. Strange has been an active teacher-scholar for twenty-four years, researching and writing on college student development, campus environments, and multicultural pedagogy. He currently serves on the board of trustees of Saint Xavier University, Illinois. The American College Personnel Association selected Strange for an Annuit Coeptis Senior Professional Award in 1996 and recognized him as an ACPA 75th Anniversary Diamond Honoree in 1999.

Donna M. Talbot is an associate professor in the Counselor Education and Counseling Psychology Department at Western Michigan University where she also coordinates the Student Affairs in Higher Education graduate programs. She received a B.A. degree in sociology from Amherst College, an M.Ed. degree in special education from Lesley College, an Ed.S. degree in counselor education from the University of Florida, and a Ph.D. degree in college student personnel administration from the University of Maryland. Previously, Dr. Talbot has had experience with residence life research, college counseling and HIV counseling, multicultural affairs, leadership development, judicial affairs, the Peace Corps, and teaching high school mathematics. She has been an active member of ACPA and NASPA, having held several leadership roles nationally and regionally. In 1993, Dr. Talbot received the Melvene Hardee Dissertation of the Year Award from NASPA and the Annuit Coeptis Award from ACPA. Since then she has received several ACPA commission awards for service, research, and scholarship.

Saundra Lawson Taylor is vice president for campus life and a tenured faculty member in the Center for the Study of Higher Education at the University of Arizona. She received her B.A. in psychology from DePauw University, an M.A. degree in clinical psychology from Bowling Green State University, and a Ph.D. degree in clinical psychology from Ohio University. Dr. Taylor previously served at Western Washington University as vice president for student affairs, interim vice president for university advancement, and tenured faculty member in psychology. Dr. Taylor is active in the National Association of Student Personnel Administrators (NASPA), having served as a member of the national board and of the *NASPA Journal* board. Dr. Taylor also was national coordinator of NASPA's Minority Undergraduate Fellows Program (MUFP) from 1999 to 2002.

John R. Thelin is professor of the history of higher education and public policy at the University of Kentucky. In 2000, the board of trustees and faculty selected Dr. Thelin to be University Research Professor. A 1969 alumnus of Brown University, he concentrated in European history and was elected to Phi Beta Kappa. As a graduate student at the University of California, Berkeley, he received an M.A. degree in American history and a Ph.D. degree in the history of education. Dr. Thelin is the author of six books and numerous articles on higher education, public policy, and history. At the College of William and Mary in Virginia from 1981 to 1993 he was chancellor professor, director of the Higher Education Doctoral Program, president of the university senate, and received the Phi Beta Kappa Award for Faculty Scholarship. Before joining the faculty at the University of Kentucky in 1996 he was professor of higher education and philanthropy at Indiana University. Dr. Thelin served as president of the Association for the Study of Higher Education (ASHE) in 1999–2000. He has received two major research grants from the Spencer Foundation.

M. Lee Upcraft is an assistant vice president emeritus for student affairs, affiliate professor emeritus of higher education, and a senior research scientist in the Center for the Study of Higher Education at the Pennsylvania State University. He received his B.A. degree in history and his M.A. degree in guidance and counseling from SUNY Albany, and his Ph.D. degree in student personnel administration from Michigan State University. Dr. Upcraft is the author or editor of nine books and seventy-five book chapters and refereed journal articles on topics such as residence halls, the first-year experience, academic advising, student affairs administration, and assessment. During his nearly forty years in higher education, he has served in various student affairs administrative and faculty positions. Dr. Upcraft has received recognition for his professional accomplishments from several national and regional professional organizations and is a Senior Scholar Diplomate of the American College Personnel Association.

Roger B. Winston, Jr. is professor emeritus of college student affairs administration at the University of Georgia where he taught for over twenty-five years. His degrees include a B.A. in history from Auburn University, an M.A. in philosophy, and Ph.D. in counseling and student personnel services from the University of Georgia. Dr. Winston is the author or editor of thirteen books in student affairs. His most recent books include: *Supervising New Professionals in Student Affairs: A Guide for Practitioners* with Steven M. Janosik, Joan B. Hirt, Don G. Creamer, Sue A. Saunders, and Diane L. Cooper (in press); *Learning Through Supervised Practice in Student Affairs* with Diane L. Cooper, Sue A. Saunders, Joan B. Hirt, Don G. Creamer, and Steven M. Janosik; *The Professional Student Affairs Administrator: Educator, Leader, and Manager* with Don G. Creamer and Theodore K. Miller; and *Improving Staffing Practices in Students Affairs* with Don G. Creamer. Dr. Winston is also author of over 100 professional journal articles and book chapters and is coauthor of the *Student Developmental Task and Lifestyle Assessment* (with T. K. Miller). He is a Senior Scholar Diplomate of the American College Personnel Association.

Dudley B. Woodard, Jr. is professor of higher education in the Center for the Study of Higher Education at the University of Arizona. He holds a B.A. degree in psychology from MacMurray College, and an M.A. degree in human relations (college student personnel) and Ph.D. degree in counseling, guidance, and student personnel from Ohio University. He served as the director of the University of Arizona's Center for the Study of Higher Education and was vice president of student affairs at the State University of New York, Binghamton, and the University of Arizona. He is a past president of National Association of Student Personnel Administrators and past chair of the NASPA Foundation Board. His most recent publication with Love and Komives is *Leadership and Management Issues for the New Century* (2000).

Robert B. Young is professor, chair of the Department of Counseling and Higher Education, and director of the Center for Higher Education at Ohio University. He earned an A.B. degree in history from the University of Rochester, an M.S. degree in counseling from California State University at Los Angeles, and a Ph.D. degree in higher education from the University of Illinois. Dr. Young is the author of *No Neutral Ground: Standing by the Values We Prize in Higher Education* and the editor of five books. He has authored many chapters, articles, and other publications dealing with student affairs administration, general higher education issues, and community college education. Dr. Young has served on the executive councils of NASPA and ACPA and is currently a senior scholar for ACPA. His awards include the Contribution to Knowledge award of ACPA.

STUDENT SERVICES

PART ONE

HISTORICAL ROOTS AND CONTEMPORARY CONTEXT

Every profession has a history. In student affairs, as in all other professions, we have a collective sense of how we came to be what we are—our values, customs, traditions, and beliefs. Our history forms our identity, serves as an anchor, provides direction. The contemporary context of higher education and student affairs is very much influenced by our understanding of historical events and by the meaning we attach to them. An appreciation of history and context helps the student affairs practitioner understand the ideas, values, and events that shape her or his practice. The chapters in this part describe the history of American postsecondary education, the diversity of our institutions of higher education today, and the characteristics of contemporary and future college students.

American higher education was distinctive from the beginning in that it was based on the belief that the student's character as well as scholarship must be developed. In Chapter One, John Thelin takes us quickly through over three hundred years of higher education history. Throughout this odyssey, he reminds us that the American system was founded on the principles of student learning and character development. He begins with a discussion of colonial colleges, transitioning into the emergence of a distinctive "American Way" in higher education. He then traces the development of the modern university including an excellent description of higher education during the "Golden Age" and the "Era of Accountability" and concluding with an analysis of the cumulative changes of the twentieth century and how these changes will influence our work as professionals. In concluding, he reminds us that "each generation of college officials, students, donors, and legislators has wrestled with the perennial issue of who shall be educated and how." This theme is central to this edition of the "Green Book."

In Chapter Two, Sylvia Hurtado describes the breadth and diversity of American higher education institutions with a focus on the distinctive features that shape the learning environment for the nation's college-going population. She describes the development and mission of various types of institutions of higher education and institutions that traditionally have been underrepresented in the literature. She further discusses the diversity of institutions in the context of understanding that higher education is not bounded by walls like a building, and posits faculty and student affairs professionals need to find ways to facilitate student learning in a variety of contexts as a way of addressing access and enhancing learning.

In Chapter Three, Elaine El-Khawas concludes this part with an informative discussion of the diversity and pluralism of today's college students. Her multifaceted consideration of who our students are will help the reader gain an appreciation of the present and future diversification of student bodies and the necessity for understanding one of the major founding principles of our profession—each student is unique. She concludes with advice and suggestions on ways to understand who our students will be tomorrow.

After reading Part One, the reader should have an appreciation for the historical events which have helped to shape our profession and the diversity of our institutions and students. An appreciation of context is a necessary prerequisite in developing the knowledge base for successful practice.

CHAPTER ONE

HISTORICAL OVERVIEW OF AMERICAN HIGHER EDUCATION

John R. Thelin

During a visit to the Midwest in 1910, an editor researching the growth of American colleges and universities noted that "the University of Chicago does not look its age. It looks much older. This is because it has been put through an artificial aging process, reminding one of the way furniture is given an 'antique oak finish'" (Slosson, 1910, p. 429). Indeed, American universities' fondness for Gothic spires and Georgian-revival brick quadrangles reveals an essential feature about higher education in the United States: the American public expects its colleges and universities to be historic institutions, with monumental architecture that invokes a sense of continuity and heritage. In fact, a historical profile of U.S. higher education is in large part a story of structures, not just bricks and mortar but also the legal and administrative frameworks—products of U.S. social and political history—that have made colleges and universities enduring institutions.

Our concern is with higher education's history, not its archaeology, so we need a theme to bring these skeletal structures to life. The key is provided by historian Frederick Rudolph's account of a Williams College alumni banquet in 1871. James Garfield, later president of the United States, praised his own alma mater's president by proclaiming, "the ideal college is Mark Hopkins on one end of a log and a student on the other" (Rudolph, 1962, p. 243). His tribute reminds us that despite the proliferation of magnificent buildings and elaborate facilities in American colleges and universities, ultimately the history of colleges and universities in this country is about teaching and learning. Although their relationship has continually evolved, students and faculty remain the central characters in the higher education drama, without which the structures are nothing but inanimate stage props. Whether in the eighteenth, nineteenth, or late twentieth century, the American tradition in higher education espoused a strong commitment to undergraduate education. Maintaining this tradition requires vigilance, however, as established and aspiring universities have emphasized advanced programs, research centers, and other activities far afield from the bachelor's degree curriculum. From time to time highly publicized commentaries, such as the 1993 report of the Johnson Foundation's Wingspread Conference, have urged higher education leaders to reclaim the American education heritage by rediscovering the importance of "putting student learners first" (Wingspread Group on Higher Education, 1993, p. 1).

Structures and Students

A good way to chart the history of higher education in the United States is to keep in mind that quantitative changes have signaled qualitative changes. For example, from 1700 to 1900, less than 5 percent of Americans between the ages of eighteen and twenty-two enrolled in college. Between World Wars I and II, this figure increased to about 20 percent, rising to 33 percent in 1960, and dramatically expanding to more than 50 percent in the 1970s. These numbers define the transformation of American higher education from an elite to a mass activity, a trend that continued during the final decades of the twentieth century as the prospect for universal access to postsecondary education emerged as part of the American agenda (Trow, 1970). According to one estimate, in 2000 more than 15 million students enrolled in postsecondary education in the United States. (Chapters Two and Four detail this development.) Furthermore, as shown in Chapter Three, expansion has been characterized by variety, both in the addition of new kinds of institutions and in the changing demographic composition of students. Hence, tracing the history of American higher education involves no less than the interesting task of interpreting this blend of continuity and change.

To attempt to grasp the 300-year history of American higher education in a single glimpse is both unwieldy and unwise. Therefore the following pages first consider the legacy of the English influence on colonial colleges and then shifts to how America wrestled with the question of creating a distinctive "American Way" in higher education during the new national period. Next, the discussion highlights the emergence of the "university" model from 1880 to 1914, with the reminder that other institutional forms also flourished during this period. After considering higher education in the three decades between World Wars I and II, the historical analysis moves to the problems of abundance and prosperity in the 1960s, whereas the decades of 1970 to 1990 are analyzed as an era bringing further adjustment and accountability. Finally, analysis of some of the demographic and structural trends since 1990 provides a way to make sense out of the transition into the twentieth-first century. Having completed this narrative account, the chapter then aims to bring coherence to the history of American higher education by considering the implications for professional practice and policies brought on by trends in research and scholarship within a variety of related disciplines.

The Colonial Period: Sorting Out the English Legacy

Although the ideal of an intense undergraduate education by which young adults are prepared for leadership and service is a distinctively American tradition, it owes much to the example set by the English universities of Oxford and Cambridge in the sixteenth and seventeenth centuries. These institutions earned a reputation for their unique practice of arranging several residential colleges within a university structure, all located in a pastoral setting. This so-called "Oxbridge" model departed from the patterns of academic life and instruction found in the urban universities of the late middle ages at Paris, Salerno, and Bologna, where scholars banded together for protection and in order to set standards for teaching, pay, and tuition but gave little attention to building a permanent campus or supervising student life (Haskins, 1923). In sharp contrast, by the seventeenth century Oxford and Cambridge had developed a formal system of endowed colleges that combined living and learning within quadrangles. This model consisted of an architecturally distinct, landscaped site for an elaborate organizational culture and a pedagogy designed to build character rather than produce expert scholars. The college was an isolated, "total" institution whose responsibilities included guiding both the social and academic dimensions of undergraduate life. The Oxford-Cambridge model not only combined these elements, it integrated them within a coherent philosophy of residential education. This approach eventually influenced college builders in the New World.

Rudolph (1962) called this adopted educational tradition the "collegiate way" (pp. 86–109). Even when the realities of the American wilderness set in or college officials ran out of money for building, it persisted as an aspiration in the national culture. The most telling legacy of the early college founders is their combination of optimism and caution in their quest to create what historian Axtell (1974) has called the "school on a hill." The American colonists built colleges because they believed in and wished to transplant and perfect the English idea of an undergraduate education as a civilizing experience that ensured a progression of responsible leaders for both church and state. Their plans reflected a deliberate attempt to avoid the problems and mistakes associated with a loss of control over curriculum and governance, problems that sometimes characterized their European counterparts. Ironically, this meant that the two groups most central to their plan—students and teachers—were from the start restricted from holding official authority in matters of external institutional governance. Ultimate power was vested in a college lay board to maintain discipline and accountability—an antidote to the sloth and indulgence attributed to autonomous masters and scholars at the English universities. By incorporating a tight connection between the college board and its host civil government, the colonial colleges fostered both responsible oversight and a source of government funding from taxes, tolls, and lotteries. The importance of colleges to colonial life is suggested by their proliferation and protection—starting with Harvard, founded in the Massachusetts Bay Colony in 1636, and followed by The College of William and Mary in Virginia in 1693, Yale in Connecticut in 1701, and six more colleges by the start of the Revolutionary War.

Tensions between students and faculty characterized colonial college life. Indeed, the residential college was as much a recipe for conflict as for harmony. Numerous consumer complaints ranging from bad food in the dining commons to dissatisfaction with the curriculum often sparked student riots and revolts. Although relatively homogeneous, the student body still institutionalized the nuances of social class. College rosters listed students by social rank. Furthermore, following the Oxford tradition, academic robes reflected socioeconomic position, delineating the "commoners" (those who dined at college commons) from the "servitors" (those who waited on tables).

Religion, of course, was an important part of the fabric of American culture, including its colleges. Religious concerns and sectarian competition often fueled the creation of colonial colleges. A majority of these institutions developed denominational ties, and most college presidents were men of the cloth. However, emphasis on Christian values and discipline did not preclude preparation for secular life. As relatively young students matriculated, colleges often embraced the role of in loco parentis, with the faculty and president offering supervision of student conduct and moral development. While colonial colleges did train future ministers that purpose was only one of many among the undergraduate bachelor of arts curriculum (Handlin & Handlin, 1974).

Few written records are available to help reconstruct the colonial curriculum. The best estimate is that oral disputations provided the most rigorous hurdles, subject to the immediate critical evaluation of both masters and fellow undergraduates. The motivation to study classical texts or to solve complex mathematical problems was to avoid the ridicule and jeers from classmates that greeted a student's poor public speaking, flawed logic, or faulty Latin translations. One puzzling characteristic of the colonial colleges is that there was little emphasis on completing degrees. Many students matriculated and then left college after a year or two, apparently with none of the stigma now associated with dropouts. Enrollments were modest, seldom as much as a hundred students. At William and Mary, so few undergraduates petitioned for graduation that the new governor of Virginia put up commencement prize money as an incentive for students to complete their degree requirements.

American higher education in the eighteenth century did include some precedents for diversity—and the associated challenges. Periodically colonial colleges attempted to expand their missions but often encountered only weak, or even disastrous results. For example, attempts to extend collegiate education beyond the White population of the British colonies reflected noble intentions, but relied on limited planning, and thereby generated extremely limited results. One of these episodes caused Franklin (1784) to recount how after a group of Native American students returned from their scholarship studies, their chieftain fathers complained that the sons had become unhealthy, lazy, and unable to make good decisions. As a result, tribal elders politely refused the college's offer to renew the scholarship program, suggesting instead that perhaps the colonial leaders would like to send *their* sons to the Native Americans for an education that would make the Anglo boys into strong and wise men.

The novelty (and high failure rate) of such experiments underscores the fundamental limits of the colonial colleges' scope and constituency. Enrollment in college courses was confined to White males, mostly from established, prosperous families. College attendance tended to ratify or confirm existing social standing rather than provide social mobility. The curriculum primarily provided an analytic or intellectual edge in the discourse and writing associated with public life or the practice of law (Handlin & Handlin, 1974). In plain terms, the college mission was to ensure the preparation and disciplined seasoning of a future leadership cohort. Certainly this was an "elite" student group. This exclusiveness, so contrary to contemporary notions of equity and social justice, does not negate the important fact that in the eighteenth century a college education served the serious, albeit limited, societal function of transforming a potential indolent, indulgent group of privileged young men into a responsible, literate elite committed to serving their colony and, later, the nation.

The aim of the colonial college, then, was the rigorous education of the "gentleman scholar." If the colonial colleges were limited in their constituency and mission, they were at least remarkably effective in their education of an articulate and learned leadership group, as suggested by the extraordinary contribution of their alumni (including Thomas Jefferson and James Madison) to the political and intellectual leadership of the American Revolution and the creation of the new United States.

Creating the "American Way" in Higher Education: The New National Period

During the new national period following American independence in 1776 and extending into the mid-nineteenth century, the small college persisted as the institutional norm, despite scattered attempts to create a modern comprehensive university. On closer inspection, continual innovations and experimentation in American higher education existed, as evidenced by the curriculum developed by Thomas Jefferson at the University of Virginia. An undeniable fact of American life well into the late nineteenth century was that going to college was not necessary for "getting ahead" economically, although a college degree did confer some prestige. Colleges had to compete incessantly for the attention of both donors and paying students. Campaigns to create a truly "national" university were unsuccessful. However, the establishment of the West Point Academy in 1802 did provide the new nation with an educational institution attractive to students from every state and a school that would prepare generations of America's leaders.

New state governments showed relatively little inclination to fund higher education, although granting college charters was a popular and easy way for legislators to repay political debts. State universities in Georgia, North Carolina, and South Carolina were chartered by the early nineteenth century, but they enjoyed only sparse support from their respective legislatures and often took years to get around to the business of actually enrolling students and offering instruction. That the American college was not universally supported—either by legislators, donors, or paying students—did not mean it was unimportant. Letters from fathers corresponding with their college sons in the early 1800s indicate that established families took college education very seriously. Parents wanted assurance that their sons were acquiring the values and skills requisite for responsible, effective participation as adults in public affairs and commerce (Wakelyn, 1985). Also, the fervor generated by the Second Great Awakening seemingly caused every religious group to want to build its own college for propagating its doctrines and for reinforcing its distinctive orthodoxy among members who were growing from adolescence into adulthood. The interesting result was a boom in college building in the first half of the nineteenth century. Whereas in 1800 there were probably twenty-five colleges offering instruction and conferring degrees, by 1860 this number had increased almost tenfold to 240—not including numerous institutions that had opened and then gone out of business (Burke, 1982). Though clearly a growth industry, higher education relied heavily on continual efforts at student recruitment and fundraising. Thus, college marketing and student recruitment were peculiar during the new national period. The impoverished colleges often scrounged to survive by lowering their charges to attract more students as the start of the autumn term approached. This typically disastrous strategy, however, perpetuated the idea that pursuing a college education was not necessarily a worthwhile endeavor. Today's historians, with the benefit of hindsight, emphasize two reasons colleges lacked qualified students during the period 1800 to 1860. First, American education was top-heavy and overextended; there were literally hundreds of colleges, but most of them had inadequate operating funds or endowments. Second, the country lagged in providing secondary education, the obvious and necessary source for college applicants. In a display of American ingenuity, however, colleges responded to this void by creating preparatory programs to serve the dual purpose of providing sources of operating income and students who could pass the college entrance examination.

The typical image of early nineteenth century higher education revolves around the notion of the "old-time college"—an institution thought of as at best moribund and locked into an archaic curriculum of classical texts and daily recitations and usually tightly connected to a particular religious denomination (Axtell, 1970). Consequently, scholars have depicted the early nineteenth century as the "false dawn of the state university." And in fact, the influential Yale Report of 1828, a statement responding to the threat of curricular change in the traditionally prescribed course of study, affirmed commitment of American colleges to a classical curriculum as the essence of the bachelor of arts course of study. Nevertheless, it would be a misnomer to claim that American higher education of the nineteenth century was monolithic or that the institutions were impervious to innovation or change (Geiger, 2000). A revised interpretation recognizes the activities within the college campus of the time as actually quite varied and substantive. For instance, reforming presidents, including Frances Wayland at Brown University in Rhode Island and Philip Lindsley at the new University of Nashville, urged colleges to offer a modern, utilitarian course of study for which students and their parents would be eager to pay a fair price. However, the quest for a curriculum that would attract more students often remained sluggish and sporadic. Even the 1862 Morrill Act, which provided federal support to promote advanced study in the mechanical arts and agriculture, proved slow in bringing about change, even though it is usually cited for introducing "useful" fields into the college curriculum.

The image of a stagnant campus has also been modified by evidence of considerable curricular innovation at many colleges, as the pragmatic will to survive led some presidents and boards to approve new courses in engineering, the sciences, and modern languages while also experimenting with dual-track curricula. The public did not always respond favorably to such useful innovations, however. The result is an erratic record of survival and mortality among new curricula and programs in the first half of the nineteenth century. Novel programs may not have always succeeded, but claiming there were no attempts at innovation has proven quite incorrect.

In addition, historians have looked beyond the formal course of study of these universities to their extracurricular activities, such as literary societies, debating clubs, and service groups and found dramatic innovations and the foundations of lasting change. Here scholars identified the roots of the extensive university library of today, with readings in modern fiction, journalism, and such new fields as political economy and the natural sciences. Furthermore, even though most college presidents were drawn locally from the ranks of ordained ministers, the scholarly and intellectual life of the faculty and students frequently included connections with the Scottish Enlightenment, as found in the works of Adam Smith, David Hume, and John Locke, and the popular philosophical and academic trends of Europe. In addition, analysis of extracurricular activities of the time shows that students exerted great influence on the life of their college and determined which activities and values were emphasized (Rudolph, 1962). This leverage required tenacity and strong fellowship, as college officials, who feared activities that departed from the formal curriculum, often attempted to discourage or even prohibit the various student literary and social groups.

Although attending college remained impractical for most Americans, a gradual change in the socioeconomic makeup of many student bodies occurred. A mix of students from a wide range of family incomes replaced the more homogeneous group in what has been called a convergence of "paupers and scholars." What this meant was that at some of the newly established "hilltop colleges" such as Amherst, Williams, Bowdoin, and Dartmouth, first-generation college students came from modest farming families, and many were older than the customary seventeen- to twenty-one-year-olds (Allmendinger, 1975). Typically they worked their way through college, often taking time out to teach elementary school or perform a variety of subsistence jobs. Furthermore, the creation of a number of charitable trusts and scholarship funds helped colleges provide financial aid for able yet poor young men who looked forward to joining the clergy or teaching (Peterson, 1963).

Elsewhere, some colleges innovated by affiliating themselves with freestanding professional schools of medicine, law, and commerce, most of which (contrary to contemporary assumption) did not require any undergraduate education or a bachelor's degree for admission. Despite the popularity of the new "scientific" courses of study at some colleges in the nineteenth century, a certain intellectual snobbery marked the traditional curriculum. At daily chapel, for example, students from the "scientific school" were required to sit in the rear pews, conspicuously apart from the liberal arts students.

Between 1860 and 1900, such historically excluded constituencies as women, African Americans, and Native Americans gained some access to higher education. (See Chapter Three for a detailed discussion of the diversification of American higher education.) By the mid-nineteenth century, women in particular had become formal participants in advanced studies. One educational innovation was the founding of the "female academies" and "female seminaries"—institutions that offered a range of courses and instructional programs beyond elementary and secondary schooling. In part, curricula included home economics and, at some institutions, the social graces and deportment associated with a "finishing school." Important to keep in mind is that the curriculum also included formal instruction in the sciences, mathematics, foreign languages, and compositions—subjects associated with undergraduate collegiate curricula. Even though such studies did not officially lead to the bachelor's degree for women, they often rivaled the academic excellence of the men's colleges of the era. Over time, especially by the 1860s and 1870s, many of the female seminaries became degree-granting colleges in their own right (Horowitz, 1984; Solomon, 1985). In the late nineteenth century a few colleges, such as Oberlin and, later, Cornell, pioneered coeducation, enrolling both men and women—a policy that would soon gain a wide following in the Midwest and on the Pacific Coast (Gordon, 1990).

Between 1865 and 1910 some provisions were made for African American students to pursue higher education, with the founding of Black colleges in the South. The first impetus for financial support for these colleges came from Northern philanthropic groups such as the Peabody Foundation, funds from Black churches and finally a mix of federal and state appropriations. Many of these institutions, such as Booker T. Washington's Tuskegee Institute, began as secondary schools that eventually offered a college-level curriculum. In this respect, newly established institutions for African Americans followed familiar patterns of America's nineteenth century colleges. The Land Grant Act of 1890 also provided funding for Black colleges offering studies in agriculture and the mechanical arts. An often overlooked fact is that federal monies and private foundations also supported higher education for Native Americans—whether as part of such campuses as Virginia's Hampton Institute or at distinct institutions such as Pennsylvania's famous Carlisle School for Indians.

The cumulative impact of the innovations and experiments in American higher education in the nineteenth century generated an interesting social change: by 1870, "going to college" had come to capture the American fancy. As one brash, ambitious undergraduate candidly told historian Henry Adams in 1871, "A degree from Harvard is worth money in Chicago" (Adams, 1918, pp. 305–306). More precisely, to be a "college man"—or a "college woman"—lifted one to a social standing that had both prestige and "scarcity value" (Canby, 1936, pp. 23–56). Around 1890, popular national magazines started to run profiles of selected colleges and universities as a regular feature. The growing number and diversity of students and institutions illustrated the variety of American higher education. There were multiple models, ranging from comprehensive institutions with a diverse student body to special-purpose colleges serving a separate, distinct group. (See Chapter Two for a more thorough discussion of institutional type.)

University Building and More: 1880 to 1914

As higher education became more and more popular, the emergence of the modern university in America dominated press coverage. At one extreme, the ideal of advanced, rigorous scholarship and the necessary resources of research libraries, laboratories, and Doctor of Philosophy programs were epitomized by the great German universities. Emulating and transplanting the German model to the United States became the passion of the Johns Hopkins University in Baltimore, Clark University in Massachusetts, and the University of Chicago. At the same time, a commitment to applied research and utility gained a following at the emerging land grant institutions, ranging from the University of Wisconsin to the urban Massachusetts Institute of Technology. Between 1870 and 1910 America witnessed a dramatic "university movement," which created a hybrid institution undergirded by large-scale philanthropy and widespread construction of new campus buildings (Veysey, 1965). As Slosson (1910) wrote, "the essential difference between a college and university is how they look. A college looks backward, a university looks forward" (p. 374). But when historians examined the situation, they found complications and exceptions to Slosson's typology. Although the university was news, the ideal of the undergraduate college also soared in popularity. Even in the age of university building, the undergraduate—not the doctoral student or professor—became the object of praise, even envy. On balance, the building of great universities in America contributed to the advancement of cutting edge scholarship. At the same time, however, this "cutting edge" remained marginal to the central purpose of undergraduate education. Although the ideals of research and utility were conspicuous, they were tempered to varying degrees by the value traditionally placed upon a liberal education and piety. The best evidence of this claim is that no American university, including the pioneering examples of Johns Hopkins and Clark, was able to survive without offering an undergraduate course of study. Furthermore, in contrast to higher education in the twenty-first century, American universities of 1910 remained relatively underdeveloped and small. Only a handful of institutions, such as the urban universities of Harvard, Columbia, and Pennsylvania, enrolled more than five thousand students.

Sponsored research and graduate programs were limited in size and in resources. One of the more substantial achievements of the university-building era was the annexation of such professional schools as medicine, law, business, theology, pharmacy, and engineering into the academic structure of the university. Equally important, American undergraduates displayed ingenuity and perseverance by creating a robust extracurricular world of athletics, fraternities, sororities, campus newspapers, and clubs, which vied successfully for attention with the official curriculum. Observers likened the student culture to a "primitive brotherhood" or, drawing an analogy from political science, a "city-state within a campus" (Canby, 1936, pp. 23–36). The strength of the undergraduate culture gained added support from a new entity: organized alumni associations, which created an alliance of old and new students who worked tirelessly to ensure that presidents and professors did not encroach upon the precious traditions of undergraduate life. The result was a compromise of sorts, in which the emerging American campus of 1900 tried to minimize conflicts by accommodating a wide array of programs and priorities.

Even thirty years after passage of the 1862 Morrill Land Grant Act, public higher education remained relatively underdeveloped. After 1900, however, public higher education ballooned in prominence along with the burgeoning of the private universities. Legislatures in the Midwest and West started to embrace and financially support the idea of a great university as a symbol of state pride. Applied research, a utilitarian and comprehensive curriculum, not to mention the public appeal of spectator sports and the availability of federal funds for such fields as agriculture and engineering, led to the growth and maturation of the state university. Many states also utilized funding provided by the Second Land Grant Act of 1890, which created the historically Black land grant institutions along with agricultural extension services (Wright, 1988). In addition, by World War I, the move to increase the accessibility of study beyond high school was further signaled by the founding of a distinctive American institution: the junior college (Diener, 1986).

Higher Education after World War I: 1915 to 1945

Historian Levine (1986) charted the rise of American colleges and the concomitant "culture of aspiration" (p. 13) in the three decades between World Wars I and II. The most salient feature of this period was the stratification of American higher education into institutional layers, indicating that distinctions were drawn between prestige and purpose in pursuing a college education. The emergence of public junior colleges, an increase in state normal schools (or teachers' colleges), and the creation of new technical institutes all revealed this trend (Diener, 1986; Levine, 1986). The great state universities of the West and Midwest finally started to fulfill the promise of the Morrill Act to serve the broad public, with enrollment at typical large campuses reaching fifteen thousand to twenty-five thousand. However, depictions of popular access to state universities must be analyzed carefully and not exaggerated. Many institutions regarded today as large state universities were still relatively limited in size and curricular offerings in the first half of the twentieth century. As late as 1940, many state universities had a total enrollment of less than five thousand and offered little in the way of advanced programs or doctoral studies.

Enrollments rose during the Great Depression due, in part, to widespread unemployment. Universities received relatively little federal support, although some government involvement in selected scientific research programs existed. A few campuses, especially those with strong scientific and engineering departments, pioneered working relations with corporations and industry in research and development. But these exceptional ventures remained something of a rehearsal; they did not flourish in any sustained way until the emergence of government-sponsored projects during World War II.

Perhaps the greatest puzzle facing American higher education in the early twentieth century is what may be termed the dilemma of diversity. Individuals at the most heterogeneous institutions often encountered the most glaring conflicts and hostilities. Coeducation, for example, deserves to be hailed as a positive change in promoting equity and access for women. At the same time, however, such celebration needs to be tempered with careful historical analysis of how women students were treated. Gordon (1990) found that at the University of California, the University of Chicago, and Cornell, women undergraduates encountered discrimination both academically and in student activities. A comparable pattern of discrimination occurred at those universities that enrolled ethnic, racial, and religious minorities. Historian Horowitz (1987) traced the effects of this discrimination, noting how student subcultures developed over time, with "insider" groups tending to dominate the rewards and prestige of campus life. Nerad's (1999) historical case study of the University of California, Berkeley, from the 1890s into the 1960s documented a lamentable feature of coeducation in the twentieth century: gender equity was seldom achieved and women as students, faculty, and administrators tended to be confined to what was called the "academic kitchen." Conversely, Horowitz's (1984) account of the founding of new women's colleges from 1860 to 1930 suggests that special-purpose colleges provided distinctive educational benefits for their students and alumni.

In the 1920s some colleges enjoyed the luxury of choice. For the first time they had more applicants than student places, allowing administrators to implement selective admission policies. They looked to the testing programs of the United States military for models and inspiration of how to administer and process standardized tests. Ultimately, the Educational Testing Service was developed as an appendage of the College Entrance Examination Board. Creation and refinement of the Scholastic Aptitude Test (universally known as the "SAT") gained both stature and infamy among education-minded young Americans as a rite of passage from high school to college. Unfortunately, these policies were used to exclude some students on the basis of race, ethnicity, gender, or other criteria unrelated to merit. On balance, American higher education's capacity to provide access ran ahead of its ability to foster assimilation and parity within the campus. The result was a complex dilemma for campus officials and policy analysts: how to best serve minority groups and new participants in higher education? The customary American response was to provide no single answer or consistent policy, relying instead on a laissez-faire arrangement of student choice and institutional autonomy, predicated on the availability of a mixture of comprehensive and special-purpose institutions. More often than not, American higher education achieved diversity through colleges dedicated to serving a special constituency, whether defined by race, ethnicity, gender, or religious affiliation.

Higher Education's "Golden Age": 1945 to 1970

Oscar Wilde noted that nothing is so permanent as a temporary appointment. Certainly this describes the dramatic changes in student enrollments after 1945. The Federal Government intended that The Servicemen's Readjustment Act, popularly known as the G. I. Bill, provide a short-term measure by which the federal government could mitigate the pressure of loosing scores of returning war veterans on a saturated labor market by making federal scholarships for postsecondary education readily available. But the G. I. Bill had unexpected long-term consequences: it set a precedent for making portable government student aid an entitlement, and it provided a policy tool for increasing the diversity of American universities.

The popularity of the G. I. Bill underscored the importance of higher education to the nation's long-term adjustment to a new economy and postwar democracy. A 1947 report authorized by President Harry S. Truman brought to Congress and the American public the bold proposition of permanently expanding access and affordability to higher education. This egalitarian impulse coincided with effective lobbying for the expansion of government- and foundation-sponsored research grants for university scholars. The convergence of the two trends resulted in what has been called higher education's "golden age," one marked by an academic revolution in which colleges and universities acquired unprecedented influence in American society (Freeland, 1992; Jencks & Riesman, 1968). Growing states such as California faced the attractive problem of whether they could build sufficient classrooms to accommodate the influx of new students. Some decisions made in these years would have long-term consequences on student learning and retention. For example, in his landmark study *Four Critical Years,* psychologist Astin (1977) noted that after 1950 most states tended to favor the construction of new commuter institutions such as community colleges and junior colleges. Although this approach succeeded in accommodating growing enrollments, the new institutions made little provision for full-time residential education—a significant departure from the traditional notion of "the collegiate way."

The emergence of the multicampus university system also developed during this era of expanding enrollments. In place of one or two flagship universities, many states now joined numerous branches into a centrally administered network. Although the seventy-five great research universities commanded the most attention in this era, equally noteworthy were the growth and curricular changes in numerous branch campuses and teachers' colleges, most of which added master's and graduate professional programs. In addition, public community college systems became partners with the state universities; the community colleges offered the first two years of undergraduate education and provided a smooth transfer to the state university for upper-level work. Such were the coalitions and compacts that characterized this era of state coordinating commissions, master plans, and accrediting agencies, with campus officials working to build in a measure of coherence and quality to accompany the system's growth. The most significant change in the 1960s was the large, enduring presence of the federal government through a complex cluster of programs ranging from the 1964 Civil Rights Act to the accompanying funding for student financial aid and the assistance provided by the Higher Education Facilities Act. All institutions, public and private, were cognizant of the growing federal presence of incentives and penalties.

Problems During a Time of Prosperity: The 1960s

Ironically, the prosperity of the 1960s actually created new problems for higher education. Freeland's study (1992) of universities in Massachusetts during the years 1945 to 1970 recounted an era of ruthless competition among colleges and universities in the pursuit of students, research grants, and external funds. Most troubling for those concerned with the quality of undergraduate education was the strong temptation for all universities to use undergraduate enrollments as a convenient means of subsidizing new graduate programs and research institutes. Policy proposals included discussions between university officials and state legislatures over teaching strategies. For example, faculty and administration haggled over issues such as the efficiency and legitimacy of teaching in large lecture halls as opposed to the value of personalized instruction in small class sections.

The prestigious title used to describe the idealized institutions of the era was "multiversity," which described what Kerr (1964) entitled the "federal grant university" (p. 46). These institutions consisted of a flagship campus with advanced degree programs, whose enrollment often exceeded twenty thousand students and whose budget relied heavily on the "soft money" of research and development projects funded by the federal government and private foundations. Despite the predominance of these schools, enrollment in other kinds of institutions—small colleges, religious colleges, private universities, community colleges, regional campuses, and technical institutes—were also healthy, even beyond enrollment capacity. As sociologist Clark (1970) documented, at the same time that the "multiversity" gained prominence, the private and distinctive liberal arts college also flourished. Curricular innovations at all of these types of institutions included honors programs and freshman seminars. Testimony to the strength of the historical "collegiate ideal" for American educators of the late twentieth century was that even the large public universities came full circle to ponder ways in which mass higher education might provide a modern equivalent of the old New England hilltop college. Kerr (1964) of the University of California summed up the challenge for undergraduate education in the early 1960s with the question, "How do we make the university seem smaller as it grows larger?" (pp. 104–105). He attempted to answer his own query by supporting an interesting innovation known as the "cluster college"—separate residential units within a large university, which restored the colonial ideal of bringing living and learning together within an Oxford-Cambridge model of higher education. However, such experiments were exceptional and expensive; despite their best efforts, Americans still had not resolved the dilemma of how to ensure expansive access, high retention, and personalized attention in higher education.

Expansion of such relatively young institutions as community colleges, state systems, regional campuses, and tribal colleges created a complex umbrella system of "postsecondary education" in the three decades of growth after World War II. The ledger sheet around 1960 suggested that American postsecondary education demonstrated remarkable success in providing access to higher learning but remained uncertain about perfecting the process and experience of a college education. Ultimately this gap between ideal and reality fanned a growing discontent among undergraduates. A landmark event, both for higher education and for student services, was the publication in 1962 of an interesting volume edited by psychologist Nevitt Sanford, *The American College.* It was a significant work on two counts: first, its research findings by behavioral and social scientists provided an early warning of problems that would surface later in the decade; second, it marked the emergence of higher education as an increasingly systematic field of study with implications for campus administrators and planners.

The history of higher education is often the story of unexpected consequences. For college and university administrators of the 1960s, the boom in construction and enrollments tended to mask problems and tensions among students that would emerge between 1963 and 1968 and violently erupt between 1968 and 1972. Two distinct yet related sources of undergraduate discontent existed. First, discontented students complained of large lecture classes, impersonal registration, crowded student housing, and the psychological distance between faculty and students caused by booming campuses. Second, student concern about external political and societal events—notably the Vietnam War, the draft, the counter-cultural movement, and the Civil Rights movement—kindled a visible and eventually widespread student activism. This activism not only preoccupied but also strained the real and symbolic foundations of higher education, and it affected universities' internal and external conduct. By 1970 the national media portrayed the American campus less as a sanctuary and more as a battleground in a protracted generational war between college students and the established institutions associated with adult society. Outspoken student activists became symbols of a new popular culture and acquired high visibility in both television and newspaper coverage.

An Era of Adjustment and Accountability: 1970 to 1990

Years of student unrest contributed to several negative effects on American higher education, not the least of which was declining confidence on the part of state governments and other traditional sources of support. No longer did public officials assume that a university president or a dean of students could keep his or her "house in order." By 1972 the federal government exerted its presence within higher education by dictating an increased commitment to social justice and educational opportunity on university and college campuses. The national government's action emerged with large-scale entitlements for student financial aid—an alphabet soup of funding including Basic Educational Opportunity Grants (BEOG) and Supplementary

Educational Opportunity Grants (SEOG), later known as Pell Grants. These generous programs embodied the ideal that affordability should not circumscribe students' choice in making college plans. Enactment of further loan programs and work study opportunities combined with increased institutional funds for scholarships to create a formidable change in access to higher education from 1972 to 1980. The traditional image of the student as "Joe College" was supplemented by women, Native Americans, African Americans, Asian Americans, and Hispanics. During the same years, new legislation prohibiting discrimination in educational programs (Title IX) allowed women to gradually gain access to extracurricular activities such as intercollegiate athletics and to academic fields such as business, law, medicine, and a host of Ph.D. programs. By 1990, Section 504 of the Vocational Rehabilitation Act had further encouraged diversity and access by providing guidelines for educational institutions to serve students with disabilities.

How did these new programs and policies shape campus life? The best way to approach that question is to fuse historical analysis with sociology and anthropology. Anthropologist Moffatt's (1989) account of undergraduate life at Rutgers in the 1980s, *Coming of Age in New Jersey,* suggested that students had become increasingly resourceful at navigating the complexities of large institutions. Cohesion, however, was an increasingly uncertain dimension of the campus and curriculum. Critics continually asked whether academic standards were becoming diluted as the number of students attending college grew. Obviously, no definitive answer to that complex question existed. However, Moffatt's study included a historical analysis comparing student life in 1880 to that of a century later. His surprising finding was that undergraduates of the earlier era did not necessarily study more hours than the students of 1980. Rather, they simply devoted more entries in their daily logs and journals commenting on their intention to study or expressing their remorse over not having studied more!

The history of higher education during the 1970s and 1980s included other puzzles and uncertainties. For example, economists of the early 1970s accurately predicted to college presidents and trustees a forthcoming "new depression" in funding. By 1978 the financial hard times were even worse than had been anticipated. Campuses and other nonprofit institutions encountered ten consecutive years of double-digit inflation along with soaring heating-oil prices. Rounding out the gloomy picture, demographers projected a substantial decline in the number of high school graduates. All of this signaled a future marked by campus closings and cutbacks.

The early 1980s also witnessed a succession of commission reports, including *A Nation at Risk,* criticizing American public education as uncertain and incoherent. Initially the focus revolved around primary and secondary schooling giving higher education a temporary reprieve. However, this changed in 1984 when the Study Group on the Conditions of Excellence in American Higher Education (sponsored by the National Institute of Education) released its report, *Involvement in Learning: Realizing the Potential of American Higher Education.* Its call for scrutiny and reform in higher education was reinforced by numerous other reports, especially the periodic studies on the college curriculum, the college as a community, and reconsideration of scholarship that the Carnegie Foundation for the Advancement of Teaching published under the leadership of Ernest Boyer. Consequently, by 1985 colleges and universities, especially public institutions, were increasingly expected by governors and state legislators to demonstrate efficiency and effectiveness. One state strategy was to tie a portion of state appropriations to performance measures, as part of a larger assessment movement that caught on in numerous states, including Tennessee, Arizona, Kentucky, and New York.

The problems were real, and the concerns were warranted, but American higher education demonstrated a great deal of innovation and resiliency. Enrollment declines were muted as colleges recruited new constituencies, including older students and more students from such traditionally underserved constituencies such as women and minorities. Campus administration underwent a managerial revolution in two ways. First, administrators increasingly relied on systematic data analysis from national and institutional sources, which helped colleges make informed decisions that promoted budget accountability. Second, new government incentive programs prompted colleges to shift resources to marketing, fundraising, and student recruitment in order to seek and retain new student constituencies (and develop new programs to serve them). Thus the period 1979 to 1989, which was supposed to have been a grim winter for American colleges and universities, turned out to be an extended summer of unexpected abundance.

History, however, always includes seasonal change, and ultimately American colleges and universities could not evade financial problems. By 1990, reports from virtually every governor's office in the country indicated severe shortfalls in state revenues, in addition to other sustained indications of a depressed economy. At the same time, federal support for university-based research waned, making even the most prestigious universities vulnerable to cutbacks. If an apt motto existed for the situation facing higher education in the last decade of the twentieth century, it was to "do more with less." Paradoxically, going to college remained a valued experience in American life, with rising enrollment and student demand at the very time that adequate funding for higher education was uncertain. The rub was that the increased demand for higher education coincided with increased government obligations for road construction, health services, prison reform, and other reforms such as primary and secondary education, all during a period of scarce resources. Parents worried that their children might not have access to the same quality of higher education that they enjoyed in the prosperous decades after World War II. By 1990, changing financial and demographic circumstances prompted educational leaders and critics to consider the need for a fundamental shift in attitudes toward higher education and the collegiate structure in the United States. The optimism of the early 1960s had waned. Higher education no longer necessarily aimed for unlimited diversity and choice. Perhaps one consolation in this continuous dilemma is the fact that the present still reflects the past—colleges and universities remain integral to the significant issues of American life and have often developed innovative solutions to deal with seemingly unsolvable financial and practical dilemmas.

From the Twentieth to the Twenty-First Century, 1990 to 2001

Between 1990 and 2000 most colleges and universities were prosperous and had robust enrollments that erased the harsh memories of declining state appropriations and dismal endowment portfolios of 1989. This good fortune, however, did not spare colleges—including student affairs officers—from persistent concerns about how to rethink the college campus and the college experience to acknowledge the qualitative and quantitative changes of the recent past. Cross (1981), a pioneering dean of students and researcher, forewarned her colleagues of a generation of "new learners" and "adults as learners." Realities at the end of the twentieth century reaffirmed her research findings from the 1970s and 1980s. Furthermore, even though both parents and institutions enjoyed the prosperity of the 1990s, concerns about rising college costs persisted (Ehrenberg, 2000). Deans of student affairs had to face the fact that the services for which they are responsible accounted for a substantial portion of these higher costs. History suggests that skyrocketing costs could be partially explained by the demands and expectations of undergraduates and their parents a few decades ago. Whatever luxuries American higher education of 1950s or 1960s claimed, closer inspection finds them lacking by contemporary standards with regard to such obvious services as career planning, campus security, residence hall wiring to accommodate computers and equipment, health and wellness programs, and a myriad of new, expanded programs for students. Nevertheless, in making sense out of the nation's investment in higher education, it is important to note that while costs of student services increased in actual dollars in the 1980s and 1990s, it remained fairly constant as a percentage of an institution's total annual operating budget—that is, about 4 to 6 percent (Woodard, Love, & Komives, 2000, pp. 73–75).

By 2000 the certainty and coherence of the undergraduate campus experience had been diffused and diluted. The diversity of students in American higher education eventually influenced the shape and structure of institutions. One intriguing doctoral dissertation charted the ways in which a public comprehensive university altered its student services and assumptions about who was attending college—resulting in the designation "the commuter's Alma Mater" (Mason, 1993). However, for some higher-education analysts the effort to include all students at all institutions as part of the "college experience" ceased to make good sense. Alexander Astin, for example, opted to exclude community college students from his 1993 research on the college experience, *What Matters in College?* This categorical determination was bold but troubling, given that about 40 percent of freshman enrollments were in the nation's two-year community colleges.

Also during this time, women became a decisive majority of student enrollments at numerous independent and public institutions, and the character and composition of women's intercollegiate sports and other activities reflected this change. Despite these gains, it appears that women in coeducational institutions still received less than their fair share of resources and opportunities in all activities. Still, changes in access and admissions altered student organizational life. At several state universities, for example, first-generation college students, including women and students of color, participated in student government and campus elections. This resulted in the emergence of new leadership groups among students—and signs of a relative decline of the influence of such traditionally powerful groups as fraternities in campuswide activities. Adults as college students at all levels continued to gain in numbers and as a percentage of enrollments; likewise, women and minority students in graduate and professional programs continued to increase diversity. This not only changed configurations within institutions but increased options among campuses. Some women's colleges that resisted the invitation to coeducation in the 1970s now enjoyed resurgence of enrollments and revitalization of special missions and constituencies. Tribal colleges, especially in the Far West, gained autonomy and funding after numerous deliberations with state and federal governments. Finally, American consumerism combined with technological advances provided a generation of students with opportunities to study via distance learning courses, Internet curricula, "virtual universities," and off-campus sites—all of which could be mixed and matched with the more traditional setting of the residential campus. This led to nontraditional students and adults showing inordinate interest in a segment of postsecondary education often overlooked and underestimated by established colleges and universities: namely, the emergence of a flourishing for-profit sector. These proprietary institutions gained substantial momentum by securing federal financial aid for eligible students and legitimizing electronic credit courses—both of which were tied to the right to confer course credit and offer degree programs.

The net result of these cumulative changes was a continued decline of a dominant, discernible "collegiate culture." And, to the extent that this diffusion reflected the respective contributions and influences of new or previously underserved student constituencies, it was healthy. Perhaps one troubling sign was that older forms of American undergraduate life no longer had much ability to shape and elevate the standards and tastes of young Americans. Whereas in 1910 or 1950 high school students could look forward and aspire to being part of "college life," by the 1990s there had been a cultural reversal: the student culture of junior high school and high school now set the tone for college life—reversing the customary pattern. The dilemma for student affairs leaders, then, was not so much how to accept and work with change, but rather how to embrace changes in the national culture yet still provide a campus experience that was substantive and distinctive.

Conclusion

Any attempt to present a brief survey of American higher education over three centuries risks superficiality. A good resolution to carry away is to see the history of American colleges and universities less as a compendium of facts and more as a description of the lively process by which each generation of college officials, students, donors, and legislators has wrestled with the issue of who shall be educated and how. Central to this is the idea of a "useful past," in which the history of higher education is understood as essential and can be applied to one's work in campus administration and other professional roles in higher education. Recently the most interesting historical research on higher education has incorporated concepts from the related disciplines of sociology, anthropology, economics, and political science (Goodchild & Wechsler, 1989). Sociologist Clark (1970), for example, developed the notion of a "campus saga" to explain how some colleges acquired over time a sense of heritage and mission that they effectively transmit to new students and faculty, as well as alumni. Much work remains to be done in order to apply Clark's concept to numerous understudied and unexamined colleges and universities. Intensive case studies of individual institutions are a good way for higher education administrators to make sense of their own experience and institution in terms of preceding generations and national trends. The great issues of access, accountability, social justice, and excellence are pressing, but they are not new. Higher education professionals must recognize that understanding the history of distant eras remains an unfinished task. Today we take for granted readily available statistical data on such aspects of student life as retention and degree completion and sophisticated analyses of university budgets. Unfortunately this knowledge does not extend back very far; too often we rely on sparse anecdotes for our estimates of institutional performance in the eighteenth and nineteenth centuries. Scholars need to compile fresh historical data to supplement contemporary information for policy making. Statistics and other compilations from the past, linked with present data, can be integral to thoughtfully analyzing whether colleges are changing—and if so, how much—in matters of efficiency and effectiveness. At the same time, we have not given much attention to the fiction and memoirs of student life from our own era. The ultimate challenge for a lively history of higher education, then, is to be aware of landmark events and to draw from precedents some information and inspiration to consider the complexities of significant issues dealing with student life, university governance, and the all-too-familiar task of trying to fulfill educational ideals with scarce resources.

References

Adams, H. (1918). *The education of Henry Adams: An autobiography.* Boston: Houghton Mifflin.

Allmendinger, D. (1975). *Paupers and scholars: The transformation of student life in nineteenth-century New England.* New York: St. Martin's Press.

Astin, A. W. (1977). *Four critical years.* San Francisco: Jossey-Bass.

Astin, A. W. (1993). *What matters in college? Four critical years revisited.* San Francisco: Jossey-Bass.

Axtell, J. (1970). The death of the liberal arts college. *History of Education Quarterly, 4,* 339–352.

Axtell, J. (1974). *The school upon a hill: Education and society in colonial New England.* New Haven, CT: Yale University Press.

Burke, C. B. (1982). *American collegiate populations: A test of the traditional view.* New York: New York University Press.

Canby, H. S. (1936). *Alma mater: The gothic age of the American university.* New York: Farrar and Rinehart.

Clark, B. R. (1970). *The distinctive college.* Chicago: Aldine.

Cross, K. P. (1981). *Adults as learners.* San Francisco: Jossey-Bass.

Diener, T. (1986). *Growth of an American invention: A documentary history of the junior and community college movement.* New York: Greenwood Press.

Ehrenberg, R. G. (2000). *Tuition rising: Why college costs so much.* Cambridge, MA: Harvard University Press.

Franklin, B. (1784). *Remarks concerning the savages of North America.* London.

Freeland, R. (1992). *Academia's golden age: Universities in Massachusetts, 1945–1970.* New York: Oxford University Press.

Geiger, R. L. (Ed.). (2000). *The American college in the nineteenth century.* Nashville, TN: Vanderbilt University Press.

Goodchild, L., & Wechsler, H. (1989). *ASHE reader on the history of higher education.* Needham, MA: Ginn.

Gordon, L. (1990). *Gender and higher education in the progressive era.* New Haven, CT: Yale University Press.

Handlin, O., & Handlin, M. (1974). *The American college and American culture.* New York: McGraw-Hill.

Haskins, C. (1923). *The rise of the universities.* Ithaca, NY: Cornell University Press.

Horowitz, H. L. (1984). *Alma mater: Design and experience in the women's colleges from their nineteenth-century beginnings to the 1930s.* New York: Knopf.

Horowitz, H. L. (1987). *Campus life: Undergraduate cultures from the end of the eighteenth century to the present.* New York: Knopf.

Jencks, C., & Riesman, D. (1968). *The academic revolution.* New York: Doubleday.

Kerr, C. (1964). *The uses of the university.* Cambridge, MA: Harvard University Press.

Levine, D. (1986). *The American college and the culture of aspiration, 1915–1940.* Ithaca, NY: Cornell University Press.

Mason, T. (1993). *The commuters' alma mater: Profiles of college student experiences at a commuter institution* Unpublished doctoral dissertation, The College of William and Mary.

Moffatt, M. (1989). *Coming of age in New Jersey: College and American culture.* New Brunswick, NJ: Rutgers University Press.

Nerad, M. (1999). *The academic kitchen: A social history of gender stratification at the University of California, Berkeley.* Albany, NY: SUNY Press.

Peterson, G. (1963). *The New England college in the age of the university.* Amherst, MA: Amherst College Press.

Rudolph, F. (1962). *The American college and university: A history.* New York: Knopf.

Sanford, N. (Ed.). (1962). *The American college.* New York: Wiley.

Slosson, E. (1910). *Great American universities.* New York: Macmillan.

Solomon, B. M. (1985). *In the company of educated women.* New Haven, CT: Yale University Press.

Trow, M. (1970). Reflections on the transition from mass to elite higher education. *Daedalus, 99,* 1–42.

Veysey, L. R. (1965). *The emergence of the American university.* Chicago: University of Chicago Press.

Wakelyn, J. L. (1985). Antebellum college life and the relations between fathers and sons. In W. J. Fraser, R. F. Sanders, & J. L. Wakelyn (Eds.), *The web of Southern social relations: Women, family, and education* (pp. 107–126). Athens: University of Georgia Press.

Wingspread Group on Higher Education. (1993). *An American imperative: Higher expectations for higher education.* Racine, WI: Johnson Foundation.

Woodard, D. B., Love, P., & Komives, S. R. (2000). *Leadership and management issues for a new century* (New Directions for Student Services No. 92). San Francisco: Jossey-Bass.

Wright, S. (1988). Black colleges and universities: Historical background and future prospects. *Virginia Humanities, 14,* 1–7.

CHAPTER TWO

INSTITUTIONAL DIVERSITY IN AMERICAN HIGHER EDUCATION

Sylvia Hurtado

Compared to systems of higher education across the globe, American higher education is unparalleled in its achievement of near universal access, its decentralized nature of organization, and the variety of institutions that offer opportunities for postsecondary education. Moreover, today's students may enter and exit higher education through many "portals" based on skills, career aspirations, and financial or personal time constraints across different stages of their lifespan. Another distinguishing aspect of postsecondary education (and elementary and secondary education as well) in the United States is that it is the prerogative of the individual states and not of the federal government. These features contribute to the diversity of institutions that have evolved over time in the United States, each in service to an increasingly diverse student population. The sheer number and variety of institutions is testimony to the entrepreneurial spirit and value placed upon higher education for many in the United States. Across the fifty states and the District of Columbia, 9,485 postsecondary institutions report information to the U.S. Department of Education (Brown, 2001). The Secretary of Education recognizes approximately 4,500 of these as accredited, degree-granting higher education institutions that are distinguished by their mission, structure, the types of students they enroll, and their distinct cultures defined by history and tradition. Many of these institutional distinctions may have been determined at the time of the establishment of a college or university, but other features have evolved at historical turning points.

There is a link between the diversity of students in higher education and the diversity of higher education institutions. Chapter Three by El-Khawas will present a discussion of student diversity; this chapter presents an overview of the diversity of American higher education institutions with a focus on the distinctive features that shape the learning environment for the nation's college-going population. In many cases, these features represent both challenges and opportunities as places of employment for higher education professionals. They also sometimes represent different frames for understanding modes of operation, the students who attend a particular institution, and the need for specific kinds of academic support and student service programs.

Institutional Type and Mission

In a report on the advancement of teaching, the Carnegie Foundation for the Advancement of Teaching (CFAT) (2001) concluded that "one of the greatest strengths of the higher education system in the United States is its diversity of institutions" (p. viii). The diversity of institutional types in American higher education is most frequently discussed using the Carnegie Classification framework, but the use of that descriptive system is limiting in some important ways. This section will discuss the Carnegie Classifications, offer a word of caution about their use, and note other frames for consideration of the diversity of institutional types.

Carnegie Classification of Institutions of Higher Education

In the early 1970s, the Carnegie Commission on Higher Education sought to make sense of the tremendous diversity in American higher education. Because not all institutions are alike in terms of degree offerings, emphasis on function (research, teaching, and service), and mission, the Commission developed a taxonomy of higher education institutions that could be used for a variety of purposes. "We sought to identify categories of colleges and universities that would be relatively homogeneous with respect to functions of the institutions as well as with respect to characteristics of students and faculty members" (Carnegie Commission, 1973, p. v). Using empirical data on types and numbers of degrees conferred, academic fields of emphasis (liberal arts fields versus specialized or technical fields), and amount of federal research dollars reported to the U.S. Department of Education by each institution, the Carnegie Foundation for the Advancement of Teaching developed and revised what is now known for over three decades as the Carnegie Classification of Institutions of Higher Education (Carnegie Foundation for the Advancement of Teaching [CFAT], 2001). Another revision of the classification system is scheduled for 2005 and may include additional flexibility for users to review institutional differences that may indicate emphasis on teaching, engagement in public service, and further differentiate institutions within each of the major categories.

The 2000 edition of the Carnegie Classification categorizes a total of 3,941 institutions into six major types of institutions: Doctoral/Research Universities, Master's Colleges and Universities, Baccalaureate Colleges, Associate's Colleges, Specialized Institutions, and Tribal Colleges and Universities. The Tribal Colleges and Universities may confer both baccalaureate and associate's degrees but differ significantly from other institutions in that they are typically tribally controlled, are members of the American Indian Higher Education Consortium, and may be located on reservations. Further distinctions are made between Research Universities in terms of *Extensive* awarding of doctoral degrees in at least 15 disciplines or *Intensive* focus on doctoral education in select fields; and Master's institutions in terms of conferral of master's degrees at levels *I* (averaging forty or more per year across at least three disciplines) and *II* (averaging twenty or more per year). Baccalaureate Colleges fall into three main subcategories:

- Liberal Arts colleges, awarding at least half of all baccalaureate degrees in selected liberal arts fields. Selected liberal arts fields include English, language, literature, the sciences, social sciences, arts and humanities, and multi- or interdisciplinary studies; (see the technical notes at the end of this chapter for information on the Classification of Instructional Programs (CIP) used to classify these baccalaureate-granting institutions [Carnegie Foundation for the Advancement of Teaching, 2001])
- General colleges, awarding fewer than half their degrees in liberal arts
- Baccalaureate/Associate's Colleges, where the majority of degrees conferred are below the baccalaureate level but still confer bachelor's degrees to at least 10 percent of all graduates.

Although the Carnegie Classification system has yet to distinguish among the vast number of Associate's Colleges, a recent report released by the National Center for Education Statistics begins to distinguish between this large number of institutions by categorizing public two-year colleges into:

- Community Connector Institutions, targeting job- and career-related skills and offering some general education to facilitate transfer to four-year institutions
- Community Mega-Connector institutions, large multipurpose institutions with a well-developed transfer function (Phipps, Shedd, & Merisotis, 2001).

Figure 2.1 shows the distribution of institutional categories across American higher education. This provides an overview of the predominance of institutions that may be quite different from the perspective developed while working or receiving an education in only one or two of these categories of institutions. In slight contrast, Figure 2.2 illustrates where students are enrolled in accredited higher education institutions. Each of the institution types may require a slightly different approach to both academic support and student service programs and may have slightly different organizational configurations to deliver student services. Furthermore, since emphasis on fields and degree awards differ, it stands to reason that outcomes may differ for students. For example, long-term earnings typically increase with each level of education attained (Pascarella & Terenzini, 1991) but students who begin at a community college are less likely to eventually obtain a baccalaureate degree (Astin, 1979; Baker & Velez, 1996). Such information gathered on student outcomes has served as a basis for the development of community college transfer programs between two-year and baccalaureate-granting colleges.

FIGURE 2.1. DISTRIBUTION OF INSTITUTIONAL TYPES/MISSION BY CARNEGIE CLASSIFICATION.

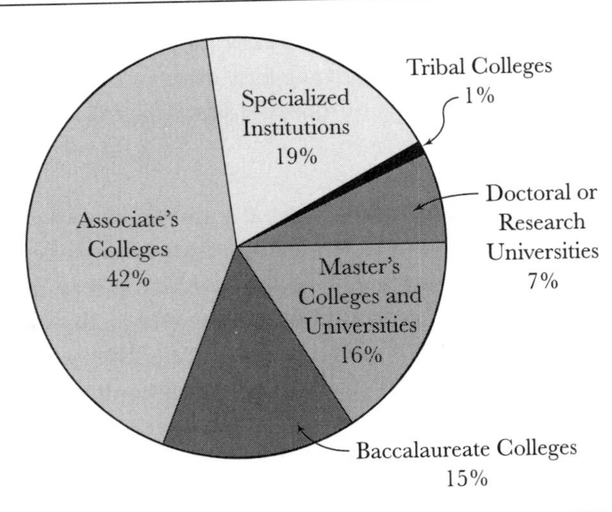

Source: The Carnegie Foundation for the Advancement of Teaching (2001). Reprinted with permission.

FIGURE 2.2. STUDENT ENROLLMENT BY INSTITUTIONAL TYPES/MISSION.

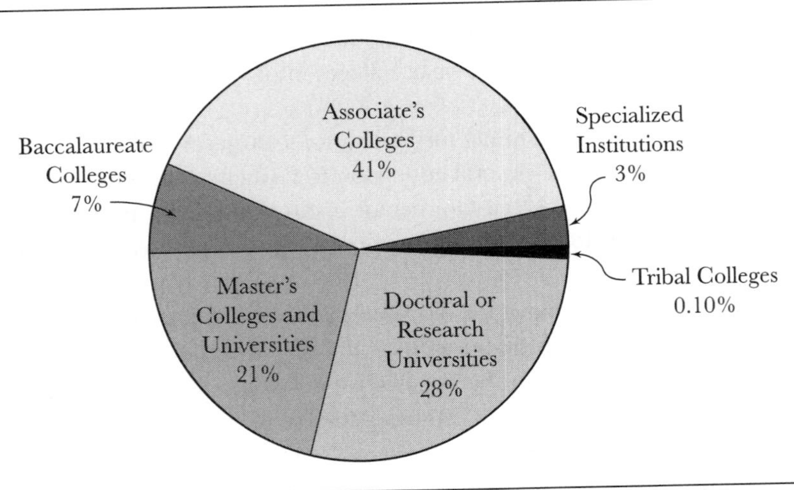

Source: Adapted from the Carnegie Foundation for the Advancement of Teaching (2001).

Doctoral and Research Universities. Although doctoral and research universities make up only 7 percent of all institution types, they enroll 28 percent of all students in accredited higher education institutions. Understandably, the more degrees offered in various fields of study, the larger the student enrollment at the institution. This is especially true of the research universities that can be segmented into many schools for both professional and graduate education (such as schools of medicine, engineering, education, and social work), in addition to undergraduate education. A developing trend is for many individual schools within large research universities to hire professional advisors, recruiters, and their own student service personnel in addition to their own admissions and fundraising staff. This duplication of professional and administrative roles suggests that there are many units and departments where skilled higher education professionals can be employed, gain experience, and advance their careers.

Research universities have come under recent criticism, however, for a perceived lack of attention to undergraduate education (Boyer Commission, 1998). In fact, undergraduate education at the doctoral-granting institutions helps to fund the research and graduate education enterprise through the employment of graduate students who must also learn how to teach undergraduates. Graduate students are often used to assist faculty in grading and leading small discussion groups to minimize the impersonal nature of learning in large lectures. To circumvent criticisms and improve the undergraduate experience, it is not unusual to see additional attention at research universities focused on the development of new undergraduate programs that require linkages across academic and student services units. These have included the development of first year seminars, living-learning communities, and honors programs.

Master's Colleges and Universities. Master's colleges and universities are also typically large, enrolling 21 percent of all students in higher education, but not as bureaucratically complex as major research universities (see Figure 2.2). Identifying ways to make the most out of the undergraduate experience at these types of institutions that are large in size, or contain many specializations and student communities, is a challenge addressed in a subsequent section on institution size.

Baccalaureate Colleges and Specialized Institutions. In contrast, there are many baccalaureate colleges (15 percent) and specialized institutions (19 percent), which together constitute over one third of all institutional types but remain quite small in terms of student enrollment (7 percent and 3 percent of all higher education students, respectively). From early higher education almost until the 1950s, small four-year colleges were the norm, and these were established in a manner similar to the establishment of settlements and communities across America. The spirit of the college movement captured an era of entrepreneurship: "College-founding in the nineteenth century was undertaken in the same spirit as canal-building, cotton-ginning, farming, and gold-mining. . . . All were touched by the American faith in tomorrow, in the unquestionable capacity of Americans to achieve a better world" (Rudolph, 1965, p. 9). Much of the early theory development in student affairs was developed in studies of students attending baccalaureate colleges, leading to narrow perspectives in terms of who students are and how they develop.

Although some of these initial baccalaureate colleges have evolved into more complex higher education organizations, some have closed due to financial problems; still others remain strong liberal arts colleges where students acquire the values of a liberal education. Students attending liberal arts colleges are also more likely than students at other types of institutions to realize the value of intrinsic occupational rewards (Pascarella & Terenzini, 1991). In contrast to a broad liberal arts curriculum, the small Specialized Institutions provide a focus on specific careers and vocations. The continued coexistence of many liberal arts colleges, as well as the more career-specific development of Specialized Institutions, is testimony to the spirit of an entrepreneurial era in education that persists until today. Each institution type provides distinct educational experiences for students in relatively close-knit communities.

Associate's Colleges. Associate's colleges constitute 42 percent of all accredited higher education institutions and served approximately 40 percent of all students enrolled in accredited, degree-granting higher education institutions in 1998 (see Figures 2.1 and 2.2). A recent report on two-year colleges indicates that they may now enroll up to half of all students in postsecondary education (Phipps, Shedd, & Merisotis, 2001). Given the additional features of open access (addressed in the next section), two-year colleges continue to be viewed as places of opportunity that are focused on teaching and learning of classic subjects, learning for leisure, learning for specialized employment and vocational areas, as well as coursework in newly emerging topics essential to the job market. Thus the mission of two-year colleges is much broader than the goal of awarding associate's degrees that may meet the same general education requirements of baccalaureate-granting institutions. Many two-year institutions perceive themselves in service to local community learning needs—often duplicating missed opportunities at previous levels of education as well as introducing new subject matter that is practically oriented or technical in nature. Because of these diverse educational goals, their sheer numbers, low cost, and convenience, the community colleges attract the most diverse student bodies in terms of age, race and ethnicity, and career aspirations. They seek to deliver their student services and academic support programs in a way that serves a highly mobile and diverse population.

Specialized Institutions. Specialized institutions in the Carnegie Classification are further differentiated into many categories that include theological seminaries, medical schools, separate health profession schools, schools of engineering and technology, schools of business and management, schools of law, teachers colleges, schools of art, music, and design as well as a generic category of other specialized institutions. Many of these institutions enroll students in professional or graduate programs, and student affairs practice in service to students enrolled in such programs is an emerging area of growth and research.

Tribal Colleges and Universities. The American Indian Movement in the 1960s and its goals for "self-determination" gave birth to organized efforts to counter problems associated with education for Native Americans, including attempts to eradicate native cultures and assimilate students in schools and colleges. The goal of preserving culture and pride in identity remains central at Tribal Colleges. Founding leaders believed that postsecondary education could be a primary vehicle for improving conditions on reservations that have high rates of poverty, sustaining native culture and advancing the progress of Native Americans without assimilation (Boyer, 1997). The first tribally controlled college, now called Diné College, was established by the Navajo Nation in 1968 (AIHEC, 1999). The American Indian Higher Education Consortium (AIHEC) was founded by the presidents of the first six tribal colleges and is jointly governed by the participating tribal colleges. AIHEC recognizes thirty-one tribal colleges—twenty-eight of which are tribally chartered and managed locally, and three of which are federally chartered and governed by national boards. The primary mission of tribal colleges is to offer culturally based education, addressing the whole person (mind, body, spirit, and family), and advance local economic and other pressing needs of the native community (White House Initiative on Tribal Colleges and Universities, 1996).

Today the tribal colleges, enrolling students from over 250 tribal nations, are located in twelve states. Compared to other institution types, they are typically small with an average of 530 students per institution (Carnegie Foundation for the Advancement of Teaching, 2001). Tribal colleges offer degrees and certificates in more than 350 areas of study and 180 vocational programs. All offer two-year degree programs, several offer baccalaureate degrees, and a few offer master's degrees. The colleges offer courses on tribal languages and culture that could disappear if not preserved, their libraries serve as repositories for cultural artifacts and oral histories with Indian elders, and American Indian role models constitute 30 percent of the teaching faculty and 79 percent of the full-time staff (AIHEC, 1999). They provide technical assistance vital to rural communities and meet community needs by offering adult education and distance education for nontraditional students, and as a result do not typically provide a residential college experience. These institutions focus on assisting students to meet their goals in overcoming social and economic barriers, foster a family-like atmosphere, and build strong relations between students and faculty (Tierney, 1992).

They are relatively young institutions, some established in the late 1980s and early 1990s, and they often face financial challenges because they receive little or no state funding. Federal legislation intending to provide funds for core operations, the 1978 Tribally Controlled and University Assistance Act, has only provided half of the funds committed. In 1994, a new land-grant act awarded *land-grant status* to tribal colleges along with fifty-five public institutions and seventeen historically Black colleges and universities (HBCUs) (AIHEC, 1999). In addition, these institutions were recently made eligible for funds under Title III of the Higher Education Act, an initiative to strengthen minority-serving institutions that include HBCUs and Hispanic-serving Institutions. Given chronic funding problems, President Clinton also issued an executive order to strengthen the infrastructure of tribal colleges, encourage partnerships, and strengthen and sustain quality education in these culturally based institutions (White House Initiative on Tribal Colleges and Universities, 1996). Contrary to popular assumptions, only five of the tribal colleges are eligible to receive a small and unstable income from casinos—very few tribes actually operate gaming facilities (American Indian College Fund, 2002). These colleges serve areas in extreme poverty and require improved facilities and technology to accomplish their educational mission of preserving a culture and advancing the economic progress of Native American communities. As the majority of Native American students (55 percent) in higher education are enrolled in two-year colleges, finding ways to increase access to other levels of higher education and support their success in baccalaureate institutions may require higher education professionals to develop partnerships with Tribal Colleges in the future.

Uses and Consequences of the Carnegie Classification System

Researchers in higher education have made great use of the Carnegie Classification system to examine institutional differences, study the effects of different types of environments on student development and long-term outcomes, describe the enrollment of students in higher education, and select similar types of institutions that may be regarded as "peer institutions" for further study or program comparison. However, many unintended uses of the classification system have also occurred over the years. It was not intended as a ranking system, or as a motivator for institutions to shift from one category to another, and yet many in higher education have viewed it as such. For example, researchers have documented a marked increase in research emphasis among faculty working at many institutional types over the years, indicating that institutions may seek to emulate the mission and reputation of the Research University (Dey, Milem, & Berger, 1997). By deemphasizing institutional resources, providing less differentiation within categories, as well as searching for alternative sources of information about institutional differences, the developers of the Carnegie Classification system seek to make the information less vulnerable to interpretation as a ranking system and more amenable to wide use for understanding American higher education in the future (CFAT, 2001).

The Land-Grant Mission

Although the 2000 Carnegie Classification System attempts to distinguish institutions by institutional mission using curricular focus and function (research and teaching emphasis), they have yet to more directly distinguish institutions by their commitment to a mission of public service. Fortunately some of these institutions can be identified by their historic development as land-grant institutions, or what President Abraham Lincoln called "the public's universities" (Kellogg Commission on the Future of the State and Land-Grant Universities, 2000). Institutions that were created or benefited from an infusion of funds from the sale of public lands through the Morrill Act of 1862, introduced by Vermont legislator Justin Morrill Smith, and the second Morrill Act of 1890 are still identified today as land-grant institutions. The original Morrill Act was intended for the support of at least one higher education institution that would be dedicated to the advancement of agriculture, the mechanical arts (for example, mining and engineering), and instruction in more practical or utilitarian curricula in addition to classic subjects and military studies (Nidiffer, 1998). The lasting legacy of the land-grant mission was a democratization of higher education, including: increased access for the sons and daughters of the industrial class and farming communities, a shift to utilitarian subjects for study intended to support the development of communities and regions, and government support for low-cost public higher education (Lucas, 1994; Nidiffer, 1998). The extension of knowledge and training for public service also became an important part of the mission of land-grant institutions.

There are sixty-nine land-grant universities located in each of the fifty states, the District of Columbia, and Puerto Rico; and seventeen states have two land-grant institutions primarily due to their historical legacy of segregated systems of education (Nidiffer, 1998). Today, land-grant institutions are largely responsible for many of the agricultural and technological advancements that have resulted in increased productivity in specific regions of the country as well as many areas of the globe. It is not surprising, therefore, to see land-grant institutions become outstanding research universities at the same time that they continue to attract students from rural areas who seek careers in modern agricultural techniques. Public institutions are actively seeking renewal of the original intent of the land-grant mission in an effort to become more engaged with the needs of society in the twenty-first century (Kellogg Commission on the Future of State and Land-Grant Universities, 2000). A revitalization of the public service goals of institutions is occurring with initiatives that target student programming and curriculum development to include service learning, provide access to underserved populations, develop partnerships with communities to extend and transfer resources, promote the public's effective use of natural resources, and encourage civic engagement among students and faculty. Understanding the historic mission of the public land-grant institution provides insight into institutional priorities and modes of operation where higher educational professionals may seek successful careers. Further information about the activities of land-grant institutions can be followed through the work of the National Association of State Universities and Land-Grant Colleges (NASULGC), the nation's oldest higher education association founded in 1887 (see www.nasulgc.org).

Serving Specific Populations in Higher Education

Other than the identification of tribal colleges as relatively unique institutions, the Carnegie Classification does not differentiate institutions according to institutional missions that address the goal of educating specific student populations. There are several other types of colleges that are dedicated, as an explicit part of their historic mission, to advancing the education of a specific population of students. Although these institutions do not constitute a large segment of higher education, they are important in their distinct mission because they continue to serve specific populations that were often excluded from higher education in an earlier era. These institutions today include approximately 80 women's colleges, 118 historically Black colleges and universities (HBCUs), 203 Hispanic-serving institutions (HSIs), and 3 institutions serving the differently abled (CFAT, 2001; Harwarth, Maline, & DeBra, 1997; National Association for Equal Opportunity in Higher Education, 2000).

Women's Colleges. The female academy or seminary became the early nineteenth century prototype of the women's college, which emerged at a time when women had virtually no choice or opportunity to attend higher education. These institutions prepared their students for teaching in the nation's rapidly expanding school systems and presented curriculum rigorous enough to often include subjects available at men's colleges (Solomon, 1985). Contrary to prevailing beliefs, the success of the female seminaries had proven that women could handle the intellectual rigor associated with a college-level curriculum and actually expand their roles in service to society—without harming their ability to bear children. Increasing interest in establishing educational institutions at all levels across the nation contributed to the natural "upward extension" of the female seminary to the development of the women's college (Rudolph, 1965).

The majority of women's colleges were established between 1850 and the beginning of the twentieth century; fewer than 10 percent were founded since World War II (Pepin et al., 1982). The women's colleges flourished as result of the Civil War casualties and the need for labor, including the need for women to support themselves financially to assist in rebuilding communities, and the expansion of educational institutions. Since the late 1880s, three main types of women's colleges had evolved, each determining their own approach to the education of women: independent private colleges (including the "Seven Sister" colleges that attempted to parallel the elite men's colleges in the east, southern women's colleges, southern Black women's colleges, and Roman Catholic colleges for the education of religious teachers), where single-sex education was a tradition, and less than a handful of public women's colleges (Harwarth, Maline, & DeBra, 1997).

Women's colleges proliferated in those states where there was high resistance to coeducation—primarily states in the east with private education for men and fewer in the west with the rapid expansion of public institutions (Rudolph, 1965). From the close of World War II, American higher education experienced accelerated growth, with the highest number of women's four-year colleges (214) reported in 1960 (Tidball, 1977). Various social movements increased awareness and demands for equal opportunity, equal pay, and equal status during the 1960s and early 1970s. Coupled with landmark federal legislation for women, minorities, and low-income students, these events lowered resistance to coeducation and opened the doors for entry of these diverse groups of students into higher education. Finding themselves in competition with many coeducational institutions recruiting the best students and attempting to meet costs, many women's colleges closed, merged, or became coeducational. Many of the prestigious colleges for men (such as Yale, Princeton, and University of Virginia) also relented to the pressure to become coeducational. Although there were only 125 women's colleges by 1976, it was a historic turning point. Many women's colleges that chose to reaffirm their role "asserted their autonomy and their inherent value as entities distinct from other forms of higher education and unique in their concerns for the education of women" (Tidball, 1977, p. 397). They created new methods to assist in the development of women, provided opportunities for many women to return to college for training, initiated cross-registration opportunities to take advantage of resources from neighboring institutions, and stimulated scholarship on gender-related topics. Some institutions were also able to maintain their historic mission because of large endowments and active alumnae—an important benefit of student satisfaction with the educational environment. Women's colleges found ways to strengthen their goals and no longer sought to replicate men's education.

Most of the research on college students indicates that women's colleges have been successful in their mission because they can count many women leaders and professionals among their alumnae. This success is not only demonstrated in terms of the accomplishments of their students but also in the special environment of support they manage to create for students (Smith, 1989). Women's college students are more satisfied than students at other institutions with the faculty, academic requirements, individual support services, and with the overall quality of instruction (Astin, 1993). Moreover, their satisfaction with college persists five years after graduation (Langdon, 1999). This may be because, compared with other institutions in the same Carnegie Classification category (that is, Baccalaureate and Master's institutions), women's colleges are more likely to employ women at substantially higher rates. Depending on institution type, they employ women role models in 65–75 percent of their professional staff, over 70 percent of their executive and managerial staff, and 55–69 percent of their total faculty (Harwarth, Maline, & DeBra, 1997). Women's colleges were also found to have positive effects on students' overall academic development, baccalaureate completion, cultural awareness, writing skills, critical thinking ability, and foreign language skills (Astin, 1993). A relatively higher proportion of students from women's colleges eventually complete doctoral degrees compared to other institutions and entering students' academic credentials (Tidball, 1999). These outcomes attest to the relative success of women's colleges in achieving key liberal education goals.

Historically Black Colleges and Universities. The earliest of the HBCUs were established in 1830 when the education of Blacks was prohibited, as most were still slaves and considered the property of White landowners. A few colleges were established before the Civil War by Black communities for self-education, but organized efforts to educate former slaves occurred primarily after the Civil War with the work of the Freedmen's Bureau (a federal assistance program), the Black community, and philanthropic and religious organizations (Hoffman, Snyder, & Sonnenberg, 1996). Most of the public support for the establishment of Black colleges, as well as the general growth in the public sector of institutions, came in the form of funds to states from the sales of public lands in the National Land-Grant Colleges Act (the First Morrill Act of 1862). In the post–Civil War era, these grants were distributed on the stipulation they be used "to create educational opportunity for all students, including the newly freed blacks" (Hoffman, Snyder, & Sonnenberg, 1996).

However, many states in the South chose to build educational institutions only for White students. In 1896, the Supreme Court ruled in *Plessy v. Ferguson* that southern laws that prohibited the sharing of facilities by Blacks and Whites (known as Jim Crow laws) were legal under the constitution if they met a "separate but equal" standard. To counter resistance to the education of African Americans and sustain the development of public higher education nationally, Congress passed the Second Morrill Act (1890) requiring states with dual systems of higher education to provide land-grant assistance to both Black and White institutions, which eventually led to the development of 19 public institutions for Black students (Hoffman, Snyder, & Sonnenberg, 1996). The "separate but equal" doctrine was not overturned in education until a series of cases questioned whether separate educational facilities could constitute an equal education and eventually led to the landmark decision of *Brown v. Board of Education* in 1954. The Supreme Court declared that the "separate but equal" standard did not ensure equal opportunity for education, and the nation was urged to desegregate public education at all levels.

To overcome the effects of discrimination and strengthen institutional capacity, several generations of American Presidents have each signed Executive Orders in support and recognition of the work of HBCUs. In addition, further litigation persisted well into the 1980s in an attempt to correct inadequate funding of public HBCUs, increase minority student access to predominantly White institutions, and to desegregate eighteen states with a history of dual systems of higher education. States continued to receive pressure to equalize the facilities and educational opportunities across predominantly Black and predominantly White public institutions. In the 1992 *U.S. v. Fordice* case, the Supreme Court ruled that the states had not done enough to rectify the effects of segregation and must justify or revise their current practices. While there was some initial concern that the ruling does not preserve the HBCUs, the states appear to be planning to provide more choice and opportunities for Black and White students to encourage more diverse student bodies both at public HBCUs and predominantly White institutions.

These institutional origins, with an unusual mix of private and public support, resulted in many different types of HBCUs that span all six different Carnegie Classification categories today. With the infusion of land-grant funds, some private HBCUs eventually became public institutions and some private colleges remained private but continued to receive public funds. Unlike any institution in the country, Howard University is the only private research university that continues to receive direct appropriations from the federal government almost since its support by the Freedmen's Bureau began in 1866. However, most HBCUs remain rather small relative to their institution type, have lower tuition, and continue to attract a relatively high percentage of disadvantaged students who view these institutions as a place of opportunity for African Americans. Most of the HBCUs offer baccalaureate degrees and have residential facilities. Students entering with disadvantages in academic preparation find support for their educational goals at these institutions, and the results of education here are impressive: HBCUs enrolled only 16 percent of Black college students nationwide but granted 48 percent of bachelor's degrees in agriculture and natural resources, 44 percent of the bachelor's degrees in the physical sciences, 45 percent of the mathematics degrees, 40 percent of the degrees in biological sciences, 38 percent of the education degrees, and 37 percent of the degrees in computer sciences and information sciences earned by African Americans in 1994 (Hoffman, Snyder, & Sonnenberg, 1996). HBCUs awarded about one fourth of engineering degrees earned by African Americans (AAUP, 1995). In addition, some of the most prominent African Americans today were educated at an HBCU. Impressive alumni include many famous political leaders, scholars, writers, judges, and entertainers (such as Martin Luther King, Jr., former Supreme Court Justice Thurgood Marshall, Jesse Jackson, Andrew Young, Spike Lee, Oprah Winfrey, Toni Morrison, and Alice Walker) in addition to many Black professionals, faculty, and military personnel (see eric-web.tc.columbia.edu/hbcu/appendix.htm for a list of prominent HBCU alumni).

Research across many studies indicate that Black college attendance is significantly associated with students' cognitive development, baccalaureate attainment, and level of educational attainment; the occupational status among Black women; and relatively higher academic and social self-concepts among African American students (Pascarella & Terenzini, 1991). Allen (1992) reported in the National Study of Black College Students that African American students who attended historically Black public universities reported more favorable relations with professors, more support and concern for their welfare, better academic performance, greater social involvement, and higher occupational aspirations than did Black undergraduates at predominantly White universities. In contrast, Black students reported more concerns with the racial climate at predominantly White universities and a lack of integration. However, some of these climate issues may also be the result of impersonal environments and a lack of a student-centered focus at some predominantly White universities. Students reported favorable racial climates at predominantly White institutions where there was a high concern for students and their development, regardless of size or type of institution or the race or ethnicity of the student (Hurtado, 1992). Lessons learned from education at an HBCU suggest that a student-centered environment, high expectations for students, affirmation for racial or ethnic identity, and interactions with faculty make a positive environment for learning and student development (Hurtado, Milem, Clayton-Pederson, & Allen, 1999; Smith, 1989).

Hispanic-Serving Institutions. Unlike the previous institutions that have a historic mission in serving a specific population that has been excluded from higher education, the majority of Hispanic-Serving Institutions (HSIs) began as predominantly White institutions located in regions that have experienced significant demographic growth in terms of Hispanic births and immigration over time. Only a few institutions were established with the express purpose of responding to the educational needs of Hispanic/Latino students, including Hostos Community College and Boricua College (both located in New York), and St. Augustine in Illinois that offers bilingual higher education. Instead, HSIs are institutions defined primarily by enrollment: at least 25 percent of their full-time equivalent, undergraduate student enrollment must be of Hispanic or Latino ethnicity (see White House Initiative on Excellence in Education for Hispanic Americans, www.ed.gov/offices/OIIA/Hispanic). The Hispanic Association of Colleges and Universities (HACU) began in 1986 as a group of higher education leaders interested in overcoming persistent educational barriers and recognizing their special role as institutions responsible for educating large numbers of Hispanic/Latino students. It was not until 1992, however, that Congress formally recognized the role of HSIs as minority-serving institutions, allowing campuses to become eligible for federal appropriations to support the educational progress of their Hispanic students.

There are 203 Hispanic-serving institutions, located in 12 states and Puerto Rico, which serve over 46 percent of all Hispanic full-time equivalent students in higher education. The majority of HSIs are public (68 percent) and are located near urban areas where large increases in the college-age, Hispanic/Latino population have occurred. Although there is much more variety in terms of institutional type compared to Tribal Colleges, approximately 53 percent of the HSIs are two-year institutions that enroll large numbers of Hispanic students, 14 percent offer bachelor's degrees, about 18 percent offer master's degrees, and 12 percent offer doctorates as their highest degree. Many first generation college students are of Hispanic origin (Horn & Nunez, 2000), and HSIs have a large share of these students. It is important to note that there are over twice as many proprietary institutions (for-profit institutions with specialized academic programs) that have Hispanic enrollments over 25 percent, but these institutions are not officially recognized as HSIs.

It will remain important to increase outreach initiatives among the four-year institutions to provide access, assist in improving transfer from two-year colleges, and offer supportive environments for Hispanic students once they arrive on campus. Attending to the climate for diversity is key to successful Latino student adjustment at four-year colleges, as is providing sensitive support staff and peer support (Hurtado, 1994; Hurtado, Carter, & Spuler, 1996). As HSIs and other institutions become more attuned to their growing Latino student population, we are likely to learn more about factors that contribute to the success of these students in the future.

Institutions Serving Students Who Are Deaf/Blind. In addition to institutions serving students who are members of historically underrepresented and underserved ethnic minorities, there is also a well-known institution that was established for deaf and blind students, Galludet University, that began in 1817 as a for-profit college. It is now one of three nonprofit higher education institutions dedicated to the education of deaf students. The other two institutions for deaf students are the National Technical Institute for the Deaf, part of the Rochester Institute of Technology, and the Southwest Collegiate Institute for the Deaf (a community college).

It is important to note that institutions that began with a history of service to underserved populations in higher education did not restrict their admission of other groups, but the majority of students continue to be from the population group for whom the institution was established. For example, historically Black colleges and universities (HBCUs) never engaged in race-exclusive policies and, although they have faculty and students of all races, they continue to serve a unique function in primarily educating Black students. The majority of HBCUs and women's colleges today enroll many other types of students as part-time or evening students, as well as students who come to obtain degrees in unique academic programs.

The Paradox of Structure

Institutions do not simply differ by type and historic mission; there is also wide variation between institutions within the same Carnegie classification categories. Structural features such as institutional selectivity, size, and control including for-profit versus nonprofit status often represent paradoxical challenges and opportunities. At first glance, the structural features of institutions may represent obvious ways in which institutions differ, but the implications for the nature of interactions on campus that are shaped by institutional structure may be less obvious to prospective students or members of the community. Fortunately, years of research on college students help us to understand the impact of structural differences and the need for programming to overcome those that pose a barrier to institutional goals for student learning and development.

Access and Selectivity

Through financial assistance provided to students and opportunities at a variety of postsecondary institutions, the federal government and states have made at least two years of postsecondary enrollment almost universally accessible. Moreover, almost 90 percent of high school seniors indicate they expect to attend some type of postsecondary education in the future (Hurtado, Inkelas, Briggs, & Rhee, 1997). However, institutions vary substantially in terms of the level of access afforded to students as determined by established admissions policies. The level of institutional selectivity is often referred to as the proportion of admitted students relative to applicants. In educational research articles, the average SAT or ACT score of entering students at an institution often serves as a proxy for selectivity when comparing educational effects. Through differing levels of selectivity, American higher education offers access to some type of postsecondary opportunity for all who desire it, but all colleges are not available to anyone who applies. Institutions may determine the criteria they will use to select students based on academic qualifications, leadership qualities or personal characteristics, or representation of state high school graduates.

In some cases, states may provide guidelines for institutional selection criteria to be used at public colleges and universities, as in the example of the California Master Plan for public higher education. This legislative document specified in 1960, and in subsequent revisions, the proportion of the state's high school graduates that could be admitted based on rank in class to the University of California (top eighth), the California State College (top third), and California Community colleges (all who apply) (the original Master Plan legislative documents and subsequent revisions are available at www.ucop.edu/acadinit/mastplan). The plan also differentiates public institutions by function (their relative emphasis on research and teaching) and specifies degrees that can be awarded by each institution type, indicating clear distinctions in state-supported institutions. Additional changes to the Plan are in development as California prepares for twenty-first century projections of demographic growth and continuing high demand for access to postsecondary education.

Institutions that are relatively open access often serve more diverse populations (in age, race or ethnicity, and career aspirations) and are more dependent on local economic conditions and the overall quality of the local school systems, which determine the level of preparation of high school graduates. Greater variation in student preparation may suggest the need for innovative academic support strategies, as well as variety in student services (such as staff availability and delivery of programs) to achieve the educational goals of institutions that offer opportunities for students from a variety of socioeconomic backgrounds. For example, finding ways to improve student retention often becomes a key focus at less selective institutions because students enter with different levels of preparation, self-confidence, and aspirations. Ensuring adequate and accessible academic and social support for a wide range of students becomes an important part of the role of higher education professionals working in institutions that offer access to nearly all who apply. In some institutions, staff may be working with traditional-aged students in residence halls as well as commuting, working adults.

In contrast, due to relative uniformity in the level of student academic preparation and competition for admission that assures that students have a strong desire to attend a particular college, more selective institutions typically tend to have higher retention rates. Selective institutions also often cater to a more traditional population of recent high school graduates and offer fewer remedial courses. Students from selective institutions are also more likely to be satisfied with their undergraduate experience than students attending less selective institutions (Astin, 1979), which may be due to the academic reputation and resources available at the nation's most selective institutions. Moreover, the research suggests that selective institutions not only recruit ambitious students but also nurture their ambitions, as evidenced by their graduates' level of occupational attainment, attendance of graduate and professional schools, and the choice of sex-atypical careers among women (Pascarella & Terenzini, 1991). This is all to say that the level of selectivity of an institution determines both the student population and shapes the nature of services and resources offered for these different student populations.

Institutional Size

American higher education affords students great variety in terms of the size of the college or university community where students can choose to study. The size of an institution is often calculated as actual headcount of part-time and full-time enrollments or more frequently calculated as full-time equivalent enrollment (FTE), where three part-time students are equivalent to one full-time enrollment. The institution's size typically affects such issues as the student-faculty ratio, size of classrooms, and bureaucratic organization or complexity of the institution. It is a key element of institutional structure that shapes the nature of interactions on campus, although both higher education professionals and students themselves have been able to implement many activities to overcome impediments to learning and development that might be hindered by institutional size.

Research on college students found that those enrolled at large institutions were less likely to interact with faculty, get involved in student government, participate in athletics or honors programs, and have opportunities to speak-up during class; and as a result, are also much less satisfied with faculty relationships or classroom instruction than students attending smaller campuses (Astin, 1979). However, students on large campuses are more satisfied than students on smaller campuses with the social life, the quality of science programs, and variety in the curriculum. Although students who attended small colleges typically have good records of educational attainment and positive self-images relative to those students who attended large campuses, successful students at the latter campuses had relatively higher long-term earnings and occupational status (Pascarella & Terenzini, 1991). There is also some evidence to suggest that students on large campuses are able to adjust (socially, academically, and emotionally) to college well, once they learn to navigate the social and physical geography of a campus (Hurtado, Carter, & Spuler, 1996). These results indicate significantly different types of educational experiences and outcomes for students but it appears to be a matter of student preference in judging what would be the best place to gain a higher education.

An interesting paradox as it relates to size is that at the same time that large campuses can hinder individual involvement in particular activities, these are places of tremendous activity with hundreds of student organizations that address a variety of social and academic interests. Students use organizational memberships to achieve personal goals, make sense of large environments, and engender a sense of belonging to the campus community (Hurtado & Carter, 1997). Campus administrators are also employing many initiatives to make large campuses operate like small college environments through residence hall programming, undergraduate research programs where students develop relationships with faculty, first-year seminars with limited enrollments, and orientation programs that help students navigate complex environments. The size of an institution, therefore, has implications for individuals seeking employment at large versus relatively small institutions. First, higher education professionals are likely to work in more highly specialized units or programs at large institutions, and coordinating efforts can be a challenge across units, while those at smaller institutions are more likely to wear a variety of "hats" as they perform multiple roles in support of student learning and development. Second, finding ways to create greater campus community becomes an implicit goal on campuses where it is not possible for everyone to know each other. This has been achieved through campus traditions and rituals that integrate members in a common purpose. However, major events programming and planning will inevitably involve considerations for the security, safety, and control of crowds on the largest campuses, particularly in the wake of the September 11th terrorist attacks and necessary precautions. These may become issues to consider in determining whether the size of an institution is important in selecting a campus for employment or study.

Control

To gain a full sense of the higher education enterprise in the United States, one must take into account the variety of choices that all students have available to them in public and private for-profit and nonprofit sectors. Governing board structures, sources of funding, revenue management methods, and systems arrangements are ways to make distinctions within sectors. The irony in funding differences lies in the fact that what we typically call nonprofit higher education actually has many enterprises that are designed to produce a profit for the general institutional fund or for specific academic or service units. Nonprofit institutions typically refer to institutions that are exempt from the payment of taxes (Ruch, 2001). In the case of public institutions, they also obtain an average of 50 percent of their operating budgets in the form of federal, state, or local government subsidies. However, the level of dependence on such tax subsidies varies even among public institutions in the same state depending on other primary sources of revenues that include tuition, endowment funds, and the profits of key services. Changes in state funding for the general operating budget, and federal funding of student aid and support for research, can have a tremendous impact on what public institutions do in terms of seeking alternative sources of revenue to carry out their educational mission, including setting the price of tuition and the development of revenue-producing programs. There may be less distinction today between some of the private and elite public institutions than there were many years ago, as many launch major campaigns to build endowments, seek donors, and identify new streams of revenue.

Private, nonprofit colleges and universities are also tax exempt but may receive, on average, about 17 percent of their budget from tax subsidies and typically rely more on tuition and fees and private gifts, grants, and contracts than public institutions (Ruch, 2001). Private higher education has an extremely long tradition in the United States—since the founding of the first colleges—and today these outnumber the public institutions by approximately 345 degree-granting institutions (see Figure 2.3). Among the four-year institutions, they are twice as likely to offer residential facilities and typically charge higher tuition and fees than public institutions (Brown, 2001). More than half of all the private, nonprofit institutions remain affiliated with religious organizations. In terms of student outcomes, researchers conclude that students at private institutions are more likely to enhance their aesthetic, cultural, and intellectual values, increase educational aspirations, and attain a degree than students attending public institutions (Pascarella & Terenzini, 1991).

The private, for-profit sector of higher education does not receive tax subsidies (except in the form of student aid for eligible students) and are essentially tax-paying institutions. Their distinguishing feature is that they operate much like a business: faculty deliver the curriculum but are not involved in management (reappointment depends

FIGURE 2.3. NONPROFIT AND FOR-PROFIT INSTITUTIONS BY DEGREE-GRANTING STATUS.

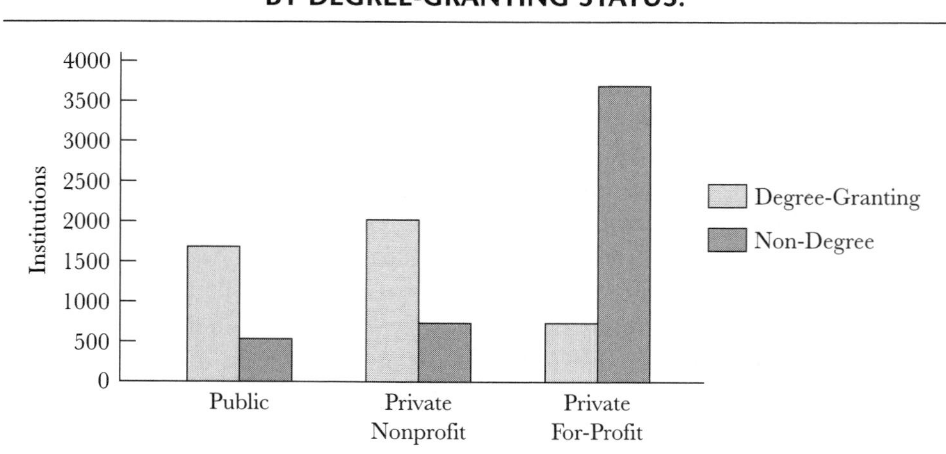

on job performance), the institutions are accountable to stockholders, and they have a strong customer service orientation (Ruch, 2001). Some of the successful for-profit universities (such as the University of Phoenix, DeVry Institutes of Technology) have come to be viewed as competitors for traditional higher education, although the for-profits have typically offered courses in areas that nonprofits would not specialize in and contend that their students have been ignored by nonprofit higher education.

Figure 2.3 shows there are an estimated 759 for-profit institutions recognized as accredited, degree-granting institutions; the larger sector of (nondegree) proprietary schools is composed of over 3,700 schools whose main mission is to deliver education in some specialized area where they believe there is a student market or demand for employees (Brown, 2001). These numbers continue to change as more institutions seek accreditation and become eligible to participate in Title IV, meeting requirements to receive disbursements of student aid. Although almost the size of the entire nonprofit sector, most of the proprietary schools offer very little in the way of student services. Instead, the for-profit degree-granting institutions offer a good deal in the way of academic advising (and tutorial services) as well as career and personal counseling because these activities are viewed as central to student retention, completion, and placement rates (Ruch, 2001), making student success a key selling point for the institution. The for-profit institutions typically attract students whose goal is to "get in, get out, and get a job"; they are older undergraduates, a majority work thirty-five or more hours per week, and a high proportion are women and minority students (Ruch, 2001, p. 134). Student participation in organizations exists but is limited, and students must adhere to strict attendance policies to ensure student-aid disbursement to the institution. There are lessons to be learned from the success of the for-profit sector in recent years, including the need for institutional adaptation to technology (offering convenience in program delivery) and institutional responsiveness in terms of meeting the demands of the marketplace, making teaching central to the operation with a focus on student outcomes, and serving students effectively as the highest priority. These features of the for-profit institutions make them interesting places to work for higher educational professionals who may feel constrained by traditional academic culture in the nonprofit sector.

Another emergent trend is the "virtual university." The early model of free-standing for-profit virtual universities has recently been copied by private and public not-for-profit institutions who have created within themselves not-for-profit virtual colleges. Whether virtual universities or virtual colleges, many of these ventures have faltered or failed while only a few to date have performed as anticipated or desired. Nonetheless, it is likely that in the future increasing numbers of students will use synchronous and asynchronous technology in meeting some or all of their educational objectives.

Choice and Opportunity in American Higher Education

The diversity of American institutions and their international reputation for quality remains a key advantage for the social and economic development of our society. The diversity in mission and function, also in size and resources, among institutions permits them as a group to target areas of specialization to advance knowledge in their unique ways as well as join together in consortia to achieve common goals. In times of national need and priority, the federal government has provided funds to motivate those institutions with specific research expertise to advance the necessary knowledge base and its practical application as others focus on nurturing the development of students' values, skills, and knowledge. Institutional diversity ensures great stability in sustaining time-honored traditions at institutions that can exist alongside "experimental" institutions. From one perspective, there is a great deal of "institutional imitation" going on in higher education, and quality assurances through the accreditation process provide uniformity in terms of educational standards. However, it should be noted that institutions also strive for unique identities that will attract students, faculty, and professionals. The friendly "competition" among peer institutions not only ensures a continued focus on institutional improvement, but also emphasis on each institution's unique history, traditions, and culture. More importantly, comparison with peer institutions on key issues (such as student retention, public service, and technology use) can lead to innovation in programs and initiatives. There is much to be learned from the different institutions that have developed their own approach to serving American college students and the continuing needs of society today.

Students seeking opportunities for study in higher education have many choices, due primarily to an unshakable belief among Americans that everyone should have the opportunity to advance the development of their values, skills, and knowledge to desired levels. However, based on the development and success of the variety of institutions described in this chapter, one can say that American higher education has been characterized by an ongoing dynamic of educating an elite citizenry and a countervailing force to develop institutions more responsive to the needs of a diverse society. Public policy has historically played an important role in not only shaping public higher education but also in providing the impetus to increase broad access to higher education. This was especially noted when policymakers laid the groundwork for student aid programs that enabled students to select and attend any kind of institution for which they were eligible regardless of family income. However, it is important to note that not every college is for everyone—perceptions of access, convenience to work and family, career goals, and affordability remain prime considerations for students in selecting when and which college to attend. On a positive note, the implementation of technology for curricula and service delivery in many institutions promises to close the perceived gaps in distance, time, and convenience for various populations of students at an accelerated rate. Students are increasingly likely to acquire part of their learning through online venues at many types of institutions, including those that continue to use classrooms and residence halls. It is well known that student learning and development is not bounded by the walls of a building, and so the challenge for faculty, student services personnel, and other higher education professionals is to work together to identify ways to facilitate student learning and development in these many contexts.

References

Allen, W. R. (1992). The color of success: African-American college student outcomes at predominately White and historically Black public colleges and universities. *Harvard Educational Review, 62,* 26–44.

American Indian College Fund. (2002). Retrieved July 16, 2002, from http://www.collegefund.org/main.shtml

American Indian Higher Education Consortium. (1999). *Tribal colleges: An introduction.* Retrieved July 16, 2002, from http://www.aihec.org/intro.pdf

Astin, A. W. (1979). *Four critical years.* San Francisco: Jossey-Bass.

Astin, A. W. (1993). *What matters in college? Four critical years revisited.* San Francisco: Jossey-Bass.

Baker, T. L., & Velez, W. (1996). Access to and opportunity in postsecondary education in the United States: A review. *Sociology of Education,* 82–101.

Boyer, P. (1997). *Native American colleges: Progress and prospects.* Princeton, NJ: Carnegie Foundation for the Advancement of Teaching.

Boyer Commission on Education Undergraduates in the Research University. (1998). *Reinventing undergraduate education: A blueprint for America's research universities.* Stony Brook, NY: Carnegie Foundation for the Advancement of Teaching. (See also www.sunysb.edu/boyerreport.)

Brown, P. Q. (2001). *Postsecondary institutions in the United States: 1993–94 and 1998–99.* Report No. 2001–176. Washington, DC: U.S. Department of Education.

The Carnegie Commission on Higher Education. (1973). *A classification of institutions of higher education.* Berkeley, CA: The Carnegie Commission on Higher Education.

The Carnegie Foundation for the Advancement of Teaching. (2001). *The Carnegie Classification of Institutions of Higher Education, 2000 edition: A technical report.* Menlo Park, CA: The Carnegie Foundation for the Advancement of Teaching.

Dey, E. L., Milem, J. F., & Berger, J. B. (1997). Changing patterns of research productivity: Accumulative advantage or institutional isomorphism? *Sociology of Education, 70,* 308–323.

Harwarth, I., Maline, M., & DeBra, E. (1997). *Women's colleges in the United States: History, issues, and challenges.* Washington, DC: U.S. Department of Education.

Hoffman, C. M., Snyder, T. D., & Sonnenberg, B. (1996). *Historically Black colleges and universities 1976–1994.* Washington, DC: National Center for Education Statistics.

Horn, L., & Nunez, A. M. (2000). Mapping the road to college: First generation college students' math track, planning strategies and context of support, Report 2000–153. Washington, DC: U.S. Department of Education.

Hurtado, S. (1992). The campus racial climate: Contexts of conflict. *Journal of Higher Education, 63,* 539–569.

Hurtado, S. (1994). The institutional climate for talented Latino students. *Research in Higher Education, 35,* 21–41.

Hurtado, S., & Carter, D. F. (1997). Effects of college transition and perceptions of campus racial climate on Latinos' sense of belonging. *Sociology of Education, 70,* 324–345.

Hurtado, S., Carter, D. F., & Spuler, M. (1996). Latino student transition to college: Assessing difficulties and factors in successful college adjustment. *Research in Higher Education, 37,* 135–157.

Hurtado, S., Kurotsuchi Inkelas, K., Briggs, C., & Rhee, B. S. (1997). Differences in college access and choice among racial/ethnic groups: Identifying continuing barriers. *Research in Higher Education, 38,* 43–75.

Hurtado, S., Milem, J. F., Clayton-Pederson, A., & Allen, W. (1999). *Enacting diverse learning environments: Improving the climate for racial/ethnic diversity in higher education* (ASHE-ERIC Report Series). San Francisco: Jossey-Bass.

Kellogg Commission on the Future of State and Land-Grant Universities. (2000). Renewing the covenant: Learning, discovery and engagement in a new age and different world, Sixth Report. (See www.nasulagc.org)

Langdon, E. (1999). Who attends a women's college today and why she should: An exploration of women's college students and alumnae. In I. B. Harwarth (Ed.), *A closer look at women's colleges.* Washington, DC: U.S. Department of Education. (See also www.ed.gov/pubs/WomensColleges)

Lucas, C. J. (1994). *American higher education: A history.* New York: St. Martin's Press.

National Association for Equal Opportunity in Higher Education (2000). (See www.nafeo.org)

Nidiffer, J. (1998). Morrill Land-Grant Act of 1862. In L. Eisenmann (Ed.). *Historical dictionary of women's education in the United States* (pp. 275–277). Westport, CT: Greenwood Press.

Pascarella, E., & Terenzini, P. T. (1991). *How college affects students.* San Francisco: Jossey-Bass.

Pepin, A., et al. (1982). *Trends and patterns, A study of enrollment in higher education, 1970–79.* Washington, DC: American Council on Education.

Phipps, R. A., Shedd, J. M., & Merisotis, J. P. (2001). *A classification system for 2-year postsecondary institutions. Methodology report* (Postsecondary Education Descriptive Analysis Reports). Washington, DC: National Center for Educational Statistics.

Ruch, R. S. (2001). *Higher ed, inc.: The rise of the for-profit university.* Baltimore, MD: Johns Hopkins University Press.

Rudolph, F. (1965). *The American college and university: A history.* New York: Knopf.

Smith, D. G. (1989). *The challenge of diversity: Involvement or alienation in the academy?* (ASHE-ERIC Higher Education Report Series, No. 5). Washington, DC: George Washington University.

Solomon, B. M. (1985). *In the company of educated women: A history of women and higher education in America.* New Haven, CT: Yale University Press.

Tidball, E. (1977). Women's colleges. In *The International Encyclopedia of Higher Education,* p. 4395.

Tidball, M. E. (1999). What is this thing called institutional productivity? In I. B. Harwarth (Ed.), *A closer look at women's colleges.* Washington, DC: U.S. Department of Education. (See also www.ed.gov/pubs/WomensColleges)

Tierney, W. G. (1992). Official encouragement, institutional discouragement—minorities in academe: The Native American experience. Norwood, NJ: Ablex.

White House Initiative on Tribal Colleges and Universities. (1996). Retrieved July 16, 2002, from http://www.ed.gov/offices/OPE/TribalColleges/index.html

CHAPTER THREE

THE MANY DIMENSIONS OF STUDENT DIVERSITY

Elaine El-Khawas

We live in an age where the settings in which we live, the type of work we do, and the demands on our time all seem to have multiple and complex dimensions. Many of us encounter a diverse range of people in our daily lives as well. Although pluralism and diversity are important values in America's communities and educational settings, it can be difficult for us, as individuals, to have sufficient perspective about the many dimensions of diversity. The task is especially complex when we encounter new settings and new people who don't neatly fit with what we have already learned to recognize. College and university administrators, counselors, and faculty certainly try to recognize many aspects of difference among their students, and they increasingly use inclusive thinking and terminology with respect to them. Yet there is probably more to understand, a deeper awareness that awaits.

The population of college students today is enormous. In the United States alone, about fifteen million students are formally enrolled for degree study in a year's time. These students, found at close to 5,000 different institutions of higher education, include traditional-age as well as adult learners; they include two million students who are pursuing graduate or professional study, more than five million students who are enrolled at two-year colleges, three million students who attend private four-year institutions, and about six million students who attend public four-year institutions (National Center for Educational Statistics, 2000).

Historically, the United States has steadily evolved toward increased diversity of students enrolled in higher education. This trend has accelerated since the 1950s, accompanied by a long-term increase in student numbers and broad gains in access to postsecondary education, which allowed previously underserved individuals to attend college (Eaton, 1992; Nettles, 1991). As part of the trend toward greater student diversity, many groups of students emerged that have articulated their concerns and called for appropriate responses by institutions of higher education. Over several decades, certain types of students increased in number and awareness, found their voice, and sought group-conscious forms of assistance. In most cases institutions responded slowly and unevenly, though some acted more quickly than others (Nettles, 1991; Richardson & Skinner, 1991). Thus, increasing diversity and continuing institutional response are part of a long-term process of increasing access, its ramifications only gradually unfolding. The dimensions of diversity today are more complex than several decades ago, but probably will develop further in the future. University administrators, counselors, staff, and faculty can benefit from trying to anticipate how they will respond to future student populations that are even more diverse than those enrolled today.

One implication of this long-term dynamic is that educators should be open to changing definitions and groupings of students. The various dimensions of diversity reflected in current discussions represent just a few of the aspects by which students differ. A continuing challenge for educators is to use broad and inclusive language in speaking about students. Another challenge is to acknowledge distinctive subgroupings while paying attention to broad student needs. Educators must also be reflective, willing to consider ways in which changing student interests and experiences may help identify institutional practices that are outmoded or narrowly conceived.

This chapter discusses some characteristics essential to understanding the diverse needs of today's students. In much of the literature, demographic or personal background factors are given the most attention. To spur broader thinking and to help anticipate the future, this chapter is organized according to a two-part framework of student characteristics. It includes two separate dimensions: diversity of background and varying situational differences. Examples shown within each of these categories are meant to help draw attention to the many characteristics that affect learning as well as personal development and academic accomplishment. Some may not have been a central part of recent campus discussions, but all are relevant to understanding students and their needs. Examples of characteristics in each category are shown in Exhibit 3.1.

EXHIBIT 3.1. SOME CHARACTERISTICS RELEVANT TO UNDERSTANDING STUDENTS AND THEIR NEEDS.

Diversity of Background	Situational Differences
Race, ethnicity	Full- or part-time study
Religion	Working while enrolled
Socioeconomic origin	Differences by degree objective
Gender	Residential or commuter students
Sexual orientation	Intermittent students
Older or younger students	Transfer students
Generational cohorts	Students with multiple enrollments
Students with disabilities	Differences by type of institution
International students	Online students

The first dimension, diversity of background, includes key background factors. The second dimension, situational differences, draws attention to other factors that are temporary or could change, including systematic differences related to the degree sought or the type of institution attended. Both are analytical categories, meant to organize our awareness of relevant dimensions of student diversity. Readers will also find it useful to make use of somewhat different categories used by Woodard, Love, and Komives (2000) in their own analysis of significant trends affecting our understanding of students. In any situation, only certain dimensions of these approaches to categorization may be relevant; some will be more meaningful than others for different students and at different times. The goal is to keep in mind these and other aspects of diversity.

Background Factors

Many background factors arising from students' family or personal circumstances affect their ability to accomplish their educational goals. These may involve basic rights, including the obligation that universities and colleges protect civil rights and pursue affirmative action procedures. Other background factors help universities or colleges understand different learning styles or anticipate the developmental issues salient to their students.

Awareness of student diversity is much higher today than several decades ago, when college students were typically described by a few background characteristics. Today, age, ethnicity, and gender are only a starting point for understanding student populations; many other factors are now considered pertinent.

Men and Women

In 1950, 32 percent of college students were women; in 1978, half were women. By 1982, women received as many baccalaureate degrees as men. Today, women also earn at least half of all master's degrees and about 42 percent of doctoral and professional degrees (The Chronicle of Higher Education, 2001, p. 25).

This aspect of higher education's recent history illustrates the profound ways in which increasing numbers generate other effects. The increased number of women students brought about many changes in curriculum and campus programs. Majors in education dropped as fewer women students sought teaching careers, which had traditionally been considered especially appropriate for women students. Business, law, and communications programs have expanded, in part due to the increased number of women studying these subjects. Older women students have spurred new child-care centers as well as special counseling and career placement services. Other far-reaching changes (notably in collegiate athletics) were prompted by federal law prohibiting discrimination against women.

Increased numbers, along with a growing social and political consciousness among women students, have led to increased attention to subtle forms of bias and the cumulative effect of implicit, sometimes inadvertent, behaviors. Advocates for women have contributed to higher education's understanding of the way such behaviors, taken together, can create a negative, discouraging atmosphere—a "chilly" climate (Sandler & Hall, 1982)—that hampers the full educational achievement of female students. Many of the most egregious problems of the past—ranging from sexual harassment to restrictive admissions policies or quotas—have been addressed or reforms introduced to address them. However, substantial concern remains that a "level playing field" has not been achieved for women students. For example, there is some evidence of limited access for women students to opportunities for developing leadership skills. Issues of personal safety for women students still need to be addressed on many campuses. In short, there is a need for continued awareness of issues of a potentially "chilly climate" for women; this powerful image helps focus attention on the many subtle but powerful environmental effects that can hamper the personal and academic development of women students.

Recently, attention has turned to the way that the college environment affects men students; here too, the concern is that college and university climates are hostile and unsupportive to male students in some systematic ways. Some data have suggested that men are less likely than women to enroll and to make progress toward successful degree attainment. Recent research on the experiences of African-American men has been especially troubling. As several studies, including Cuyjet (1997), Hopkins (1997), and Polite and Davis (1999) have shown, Black men are less likely than Black women to enroll and more likely to experience a hostile, negative climate on campus. Fries-Britt (1997) found that a negative climate also affects highly able and ambitious African-American men. New approaches are needed to provide support and advising to offset the negative factors and to help these students move ahead in their academic and social development.

Race and Ethnicity

Racial and ethnic background are fundamental factors in monitoring and understanding diversity. (See Chapter Two in this volume.) Receiving the most attention in the United States are three categories of persons—African Americans, Hispanics, and Native Americans—that fall under the protection of federal laws. Compared to several decades ago, progress has been made. In 1982, 2.1 million students from these racial and ethnic categories were enrolled; by 1999, 4 million were enrolled. Seen as a proportion of overall enrollment, however, a pattern of underrepresentation continues to exist (National Center for Education Statistics, 2000).

There has been progress in degree attainment, but it is nevertheless clear that the broader policy objective of achieving equal representation in academic achievement has not been attained (Harvey, 2001). African American, Hispanic, and Native American students remain underrepresented in most degrees awarded. Recent data (for 1997 and 1999) show that African-American students comprised 11.5 percent of undergraduates, but only 8.6 percent of those awarded baccalaureates. This pattern holds for other groups: Hispanics were 9.2 percent of undergraduates but 5.8 percent of those graduating, and Native American students were 1.1 percent of undergraduates but only 0.7 percent among graduates (The Chronicle of Higher Education, 2001). Analysts have pressed campuses to undertake closer monitoring of degree progress, for example by reporting annual comparisons between one indicator and another (such as number enrolled compared to number graduating or number of high-school graduates in a state compared to number enrolled) to show what remains to be achieved (Richardson & Skinner, 1991, pp. 227–254).

In some parts of the country, ethnic subgroupings are important. Many campuses distinguish between Puerto Ricans, Cuban Americans, Mexican Americans, and students from Central and South America. Other campuses have found that Asian American students are best served when different subgroups are recognized: Vietnamese students, for example, have different concerns than Korean or Japanese students. Looking ahead, campuses should expect that steadily increasing numbers of students will be multiracial or of bicultural heritage. In general, increasing numbers of students will not identify with a single racial or ethnic group; this trend will reflect changing demographics as well as new attitudes by many individuals about ways they wish to describe their cultural identity.

America's diversity extends far beyond the legally protected groups that receive direct attention. Numerous other groups can point to discriminatory treatment or to special aspects of their history that have left them at a disadvantage. In some parts of the country, distinctive concerns have arisen from historical patterns of discrimination against Irish, Italian, or other groups. Contemporary world events can have an unpredictable impact on student experiences and perceptions. Many individuals of Eastern European background have recently developed a stronger sense of their heritage and mistreatment, following the collapse of communism. Since the terrorist attacks of September 11, 2001, students from Middle Eastern background (or others, such as Sikhs, who are mistaken for Middle Eastern) have been subject to bigotry or harassment (Kantrowitz & Naughton, 2001). In the near future, academic institutions may face difficult issues in supporting students who are not U.S. citizens—including undocumented students or international students on student visas—who may face new government restrictions.

Religion

It is also important that campuses be aware of the religious backgrounds of students, in part to be cognizant of the religious traditions and practices that should be respected as college or university activities and calendars are planned. Established religious traditions on campus may need to be adapted to respect new ideas and customs among religious groups, or newly emerging groups may need to have their own opportunities for expressing aspects of their religious identity. On some campuses, fundamentalist Christian denominations are of growing importance (Mooney, 1995). In recent years, many campuses have hosted increasing numbers of Muslims and Buddhists whose religious traditions are not well understood by other students.

At times, universities and colleges need to stand ready to protect certain religiously based groups if problems develop. Religious intolerance, a significant part of America's history, can certainly be expected to surface, often in new guises or in response to new issues. Following the September 11th terrorist attacks, many campuses have increased their efforts to educate campus communities and to support religiously based groups in practicing their customs (Kantrowitz & Naughton, 2001).

Socioeconomic Origin

Much research documents that socioeconomic background continues to affect the academic and social progress of students. Although financial aid is intended to allow students to enroll for college study regardless of economic circumstances, low-income students continue to face difficulties that other students do not (Levine & Nidiffer, 1996). Supportive services other than financial aid are often needed.

Problems related to socioeconomic background are often commingled with other characteristics, especially race and ethnicity. Among Native American students, for example, where a substantial proportion are from low-income circumstances, negative stereotypes and past injustices complicate their progress with college study. Many low-income students are "first-generation" students, without the information and resources that other students receive from parents (Warburton, Bugarin, & Nunez, 2001).

Family circumstances also have become more complex. A student's parents often are divorced or remarried. Many students are constrained by their own family situation (whether a spouse is working, number of dependents, etc.) more than the circumstances of their parents, as many, although young and unmarried, are financially independent.

Other aspects of family background need to be recognized. As an example, the number of students who have been "home schooled" for their primary and secondary education is growing. For international students, events affecting their families in their own countries can create the need for new adjustments or, sometimes, may precipitate a sudden loss in their financial support.

Sexual Identity

The importance of a supportive learning environment has been salient in the issues facing gay, lesbian, bisexual, and transgender students. Distinctive issues among these students, estimated to involve as many as one in six students (Sherrill & Hardesty, 1994), have been addressed at a number of colleges and universities over the last decade, although typically in limited ways. Basic rights to safety and to protection from harassment are paramount, as some of these students have faced both physical assaults and psychological intimidation because of their sexual orientation. Most schools have trained police and security forces to raise their awareness about hate crimes and other acts of intolerance.

Beyond basic protections are the complex issues of ensuring an effective learning environment for gay, lesbian, bisexual, or transgender students (Lark, 1998). Such students often feel uncomfortable on college campuses, sometimes reluctant to live in residence halls and participate in routine college activities, or find it difficult to negotiate a process of "coming out" to their friends and fellow students. Under these circumstances, otherwise promising students are likely to drop out or interrupt their studies. In addition to preventing discriminatory treatment, college administrators and counselors should also reach out to students in ways that support them in achieving their developmental and learning goals (Engstrom & Sedlacek, 1997).

Age

Another consequential change is greater diversity in the age of those enrolled for college study, affecting all degree levels. Workplace changes, including cutbacks and dislocations as well as new opportunities, continually spur adults to undertake job retraining or change careers. By 1997, a majority of undergraduate students (51 percent) were over twenty-one and about 25 percent of undergraduates were over thirty (National Center for Education Statistics, 2000). Growing enrollments for graduate and professional degrees, or for postbaccalaureate certificates, have also dramatically boosted the number of older students. On many campuses, growing numbers of older students are undertaking master's degrees that they see as preparation for professional careers, not as a step toward a doctorate degree.

Older students are generally distinctive because of their workplace, family, or other life experiences. Issues in serving older students also intersect with issues concerning part-time students. Although such students may have little interest in traditional campus services, they often need assistance in learning about options for registration, financial aid, or library services, or in developing a coherent academic program that builds on their prior experience and courses. Planning for campus activities and academic programs should also recognize that adults bring relevant experience of their own. Indeed, older students have helped sensitize many instructors to the "age-specific" focus of some undergraduate programs and textbooks targeted to younger audiences.

Generational Cohorts

Also important are generational differences among students. Several authors have recently emphasized how different generations of students bring distinctive perspectives to campus. Arthur Levine has analyzed the hopes and fears of several cohorts of college students, documenting much change in a short time (Levine, 1980; Levine & Cureton, 1998). Adelman (1994) added to this perspective by offering a close look at how those who had reached their thirties looked back on their educational experiences.

Strauss and Howe (1990; Howe & Strauss, 2000) vividly demonstrated the value of monitoring patterns of generational change, especially by looking to the distinctive attitudes and world views of each new generation of Americans coming to maturity. Young people, they argue, experience the world differently than older students; they encounter different political and social debates. They share many cultural phenomena, from aspects of pop culture to their understanding of history and even to the distinctive beliefs of their parents about child rearing. Consider the way that today's twenty-year-olds have experienced the world of electronic media, with its strong visual imagery, fast pacing, and interactive features. The effect of such experiences on students—and on how information directed to them should be organized and transmitted—may be seriously underestimated.

Howe and Strauss argue that each generation is shaped by distinctive cultural themes, political events, and moral conflicts. Their most recent work (2000), describing the "millennial" generation, points to the experiences that have led to distinctive "can-do" attitudes and a readiness to think of collective and community concerns in the generation now entering the nation's colleges and universities. Already these students are raising issues and pressing for new activities and programs that respond to their special perspectives and values.

Administrators, counselors, and faculty should be mindful that different generations of students may give new meaning to what otherwise appear to be the same objects or attitudes. In UCLA's annual survey of incoming freshmen, for example, more students now say they want to be well off financially (Sax, Astin, Korn, & Mahoney, 2000). The actual meaning may have changed, however. The survey began in the 1960s, a time of national prosperity. Students back then may have interpreted being well off as meaning extravagant, or wealthy beyond conventional needs. Today's students, having grown to maturity during a time of greater economic uncertainty, rising college costs, and rising student loan burdens, may see "being well off" as just being able to make it in life.

Students with Disabilities

Students who have physical or other disabilities that affect their learning represent another growing campus constituency. Since the 1970s, the percentage of freshmen who report having a disability has tripled. In 1998, about 9 percent of entering freshmen reported a disability; in 1978, 3 percent did so. The trend could continue, given federal legislation upholding the rights of persons with disabilities.

Assisting students with disabilities involves more than assuring physical access and safety. As Belch and colleagues (2000) and Vickery and McClure (1998) have emphasized, college enrollment has been a revolving door for too many students with disabilities. Needed support may involve a range of services, such as helping students with disabilities become involved with clubs, organizations, internships, and leadership opportunities that allow them to develop a range of skills and to participate as valued members of the campus community. Career development is another important need (Aune & Kroeger, 1997).

As with other student groupings, new patterns can arise over time. Many campuses are working with an increasing number of students with hidden disabilities such as health impairments or learning disabilities that, while not noticeable, still require accommodation or assistance. Some campuses have developed strong programs to assist a growing number of students with a range of learning disabilities. Mental health issues and health-related disabilities, including AIDS and chemical sensitivity, are receiving increased attention. A recent report (Henderson, 1999) indicates that students with hidden disabilities now make up more than half of all freshmen with disabilities.

International Students

Students from other countries are another important constituency for American colleges and universities. In fall 2000, a record 547,000 international students attended U.S. institutions (Institute for International Education, 2001). Most enroll for degree study (split almost evenly between undergraduate and graduate degrees), but increasing numbers (22 percent in 2000–2001) enroll in practical training, intensive English, or other nondegree programs.

Although international students account for only 3 percent of enrollment, their presence is substantial at many institutions. International students are more than 10 percent of enrollment at about forty U.S. institutions, including universities, small baccalaureate colleges, and community colleges. On some campuses, international students comprise 20 to 25 percent of enrollment (Institute for International Education, 2001). Many of these institutions offer models for assisting international students in adjusting to the academic requirements of American institutions and to cultural practices that may be quite different from what they have experienced.

Summary

As this brief review of nine factors demonstrates, background characteristics can dramatically shape the barriers and opportunities that students face as they enroll for college study. Many factors, such as socioeconomic background, gender, and race or ethnicity, have long been the focus of research and intervention efforts to help students overcome barriers. Other factors, often just as problematic for students, have received systematic attention more recently. An institution's objectives should be to help students overcome the barriers they face and, more generally, to create an environment in which students of any background can benefit from their college experience to the fullest extent possible.

Situational Factors

Another set of factors that affect student opportunities are temporary or could change. Student diversity on these factors—such as studying part-time, enrolling in some semesters and not others, or transferring between institutions—has been increasing and is likely to grow in the future. Situational factors also include systematic differences related to the degree sought or the type of institution attended. Each of these factors are briefly discussed below, emphasizing ways that they may impinge on student opportunities or create special needs for support and guidance by campus officials. Often, too, they help to define distinctive contributions that students bring to their academic life. Many of these factors may increasingly shape student circumstances and, in many settings, may require a new definition of who is a typical student.

Degree Objectives

Much planning still focuses on full-time undergraduates pursuing a baccalaureate degree, but many students have other objectives. At some universities, significant numbers of students are undertaking doctoral study. Other schools have had a sizable expansion in master's degree and professional-degree students over the past three decades. At some community colleges, most students enroll for practical, job-oriented courses, while at other community colleges, enrollments have increased in degree courses, including transfer programs.

Increased master's degree enrollment has been especially significant at liberal arts colleges and four-year comprehensive universities. At independent institutions, more than 682,000 students were enrolled for graduate study in 1998, more than double the 1972 number. These institutions have had to adapt and redirect their overall culture and the structure of their support services, which had been shaped in the past by the needs of baccalaureate students.

Also growing is the number of students who enroll for certificate programs that last less than two years (for example, in practical nursing, police training, and health and medical technology specialties). Usually they enroll at community colleges and at private, for-profit institutions. In 1998, 249,355 certificates were awarded, including 112,340 for programs lasting less than one year. Many such students already hold a college degree. About one in five of them are minority students (National Center for Education Statistics, 2000).

The influence of overlapping characteristics can be illustrated with degree objective and international status. An increasing share of postbaccalaureate enrollment is accounted for by international students. This can be seen, for example, in the rising share of doctoral degrees awarded to international students. In 1998, one-fifth of all doctorates were awarded to non-U.S. citizens on temporary visas. Another 4.5 percent were awarded to non-U.S. citizens on permanent visas (Sanderson, Dugoni, Hoffer, & Selfa, 1999).

Part-Time Study

Part-time enrollment has grown steadily for decades and is substantial in almost all sectors of higher education. In 1997–98 there were five million part-time undergraduates, or about 40 percent of all undergraduates. There also were one million graduate students studying part-time, accounting for 60 percent of graduate enrollment.

This created a need for new campus awareness and services. Today many institutions primarily serve part-time students, especially at two-year and four-year schools in urban areas. Also, increasing proportions of students at public research universities and other public universities are enrolled part-time. Similarly, the expansion of master's degree programs has taken place mainly in part-time evening programs, including off-campus locations.

As institutions have gained experience, they have become aware that part-time students (especially those who are older) have distinct needs and expectations. Students typically have specific learning goals and serious constraints on their time. They may find that various institutional services—such as the registrar, financial aid office, library reference desk, and campus bookstore—are not available at convenient hours.

Working Students

As a result of several trends, it has become increasingly the norm that students are working while pursuing college study. Most students (both full-time and part-time) are working, and the trend is toward students working for a considerable number of hours each week. In 1995–96, 79 percent of all undergraduates worked. Even among full-time students who reported employment, about one in five worked full-time, and another one-quarter worked between twenty-one to thirty-four hours per week (National Center for Education Statistics, 1998).

College and university administrators should monitor this trend and encourage formal discussions about its implications. What does it mean for students to have a "full-time" academic course load when they are also working thirty or forty hours per week? It is important to monitor the proportion of such students on each campus. If the proportion is large, many campus policies might need to take this reality into account. Introduction of internships or service learning requirements would be affected, for example, as might other expectations for student participation in campus programs. Urban institutions have often found that they must make adjustments in requirements and practices. Many, for example, schedule lab sessions or discussion sections with close links to course lectures so that students do not need to come to campus at separate times for the two components of a course. Other implications should be anticipated, especially if this situational characteristic grows in importance.

Online Students

A new category of students includes those who enroll for distance-based or online courses. Today this may include a substantial proportion of students who are simultaneously taking courses both on campus and online. Another group, those who study entirely online, can be expected to grow in the future, yet many campuses have just begun to adjust their services to such students.

How will universities recognize and address the needs of students who may never set foot on campus, who may have their entire academic experience via a TV screen or computer three hundred miles from their instructors, and who may accumulate online courses from several institutions? The number of students in such situations will grow in the future, even if appropriate support services have not been adequately identified and developed. One issue that has arisen is the extent to which students studying online should pay certain general fees normally imposed on all students (Carnevale, 2001). Other issues will certainly arise as more students study entirely online.

Because completion rates have sometimes been low with distance-based courses, assisting online students with study habits and advice may be necessary. Perhaps academic advising should be provided in a different way, especially for students who take online courses from several institutions.

Transfer Students

Transfer students also have distinctive needs for information and advice, both at "sending" and "receiving" institutions. They often need special advising to help them mesh their previous academic work with the requirements of their new school, especially when terminology differs between the old one and the new. They are liable to encounter initial difficulties with a new environment that are not addressed by orientation programs for freshmen.

Although information is not regularly reported on the number of students who transfer, some trends are known. For example, estimates are that about one-quarter of students at community colleges will transfer at some point, often before completing an associate degree. Of those who move to four-year institutions, most will earn a baccalaureate degree. Longitudinal studies suggest that as many as one in four students at any type of school transfer to a new institution at some point (National Center for Education Statistics, 1999).

Intermittent Study

An increasing number of students are what might be called intermittent students, those who enroll for one semester and then return to their studies after some lapse of time. NCES reported recently that almost 30 percent of first-year students left school before the beginning of their second year; however, a majority of these students returned to some type of postsecondary education within the next five years (National Center for Education Statistics, 1999). Several trends—higher college costs, more students combining employment with study or having family obligations, and so on—suggest that the numbers of students in such situations will grow.

Advising and adjustment problems for these students resemble, in some respects, those faced by transfer students. Curriculum and degree requirements may have changed during the time they were not enrolled, so academic planning and advising must consider both old and new requirements to define what remains to be completed. As college and university administrators review their services for transfer students, they should also explore the needs that arise among intermittent students.

Especially in urban areas, some students "stop out" at one institution while they take courses at another institution, whether because of course availability, scheduling convenience, or other reasons. Students may also have multiple enrollments (that is, at more than one institution) during the same term. A particular danger, however, is that such courses may not complement each other or move the student toward degree completion. Campus advisors need to be aware of such situations; other campus offices may also need to offer assistance.

Institutional Type

Another situational factor involves differences between types of institutions. In many respects, higher education enrollments can be divided into four quite distinctive subpopulations (National Center for Education Statistics, 2000):

- Students at community colleges (about one-third of enrollment)
- Undergraduates at public four-year institutions (another one-third of enrollment)
- Undergraduates at independent institutions, primarily four-year universities (about 15 percent of enrollment)
- Graduate students, mostly at the master's level (about 10 to 15 percent of enrollment)

Each is distinctive. Students at community colleges are mainly part-time, more than half are over twenty-five years of age, and at least one-quarter are people of color. In contrast, three-quarters of undergraduates at public four-year institutions and independent institutions are less than twenty-five years of age and are studying full-time. Graduate students have a different profile: most are part-time, at least twenty-five years old, and working.

It is important to understand just how deeply ingrained these differences are. Hurtado makes it clear in Chapter Two of this book that such patterns of stratification among students (in which students of certain socioeconomic and/or racial and ethnic backgrounds are found to be concentrated in certain types of institutions) have been a fundamental fact in American higher education for decades. Policy attention has been rarely directed to this de facto stratification, although campus administrators, counselors, and faculty routinely address such realities as they work with students.

Another institutional type relevant to student needs are urban universities (Dietz & Triponey, 1997). While overlapping with other institutional categories, a focus on urban institutions is still warranted if it brings power to understanding the special needs of students. Urban universities have distinctive student clienteles, typically based largely on graduates of local high schools, often mainly commuter students who have many other obligations. For many urban universities, their locations offer tremendous cultural, educational, and other resources, but universities need to find ways to bridge what is often a wide gap between the resources available and the limited use of these resources by students.

Summary

Situational factors have a different origin than do the background characteristics discussed earlier. Yet, they still may create problems for students and make it difficult for them to succeed with their studies. Many of these situational factors, and undoubtedly others not addressed here, need to be monitored by campus officials.

Understanding Tomorrow's Students

Both background and situational characteristics help define today's students and will certainly remain important in the future. It is likely that new categories will emerge as well. Some distinctions will emerge in response to further demographic and economic changes affecting the entire country or certain regions. No single set of categories can adequately reflect the full array of students, so new categories are bound to arise. On some campuses, for example, graduate teaching assistants have emerged as an important grouping in recent years, in part due to efforts to develop unions of teaching assistants. Another subpopulation that may be increasingly salient for campuses are those who are in the military reserves; these students sometimes find that their academic schedules are disrupted on short notice. In some settings, being aware of the number of students who hold considerable student debt may be important. Further aspects of diversity have been highlighted by Woodard et al. (2000) in regard to student background and situational differences as well as distinctive aspects related to developmental issues faced by today's students.

The task, then, is clear: educators must adopt a stance of openness, expecting that continuous learning is necessary. Test assumptions. Look for what's new. Continually explore who your students are. The following section offers five maxims to underscore this general theme—the essential necessity of continually exploring and redefining the nature of any student population and its needs.

Continually Observe

University administrators must be good observers, good investigative reporters, and good detectives. They should continually scan their immediate surroundings for clues to important changes within the student populations they serve. Sharing information among different campuses can be valuable for monitoring trends. The data-sharing and peer networks that are possible with the new National Survey of Student Engagement (Kuh, 2001) offer a convenient mechanism for staying apprised of student reactions to their college environment. Other ad hoc, informal networks or email exchanges can be readily established.

Currently enrolled students are a special resource. Observe what students are reading, what video games they play, or what music they enjoy. Listen to their stories and perspectives. Keep up with their favorites, whether in video games and television programs or in books and teachers. Be aware of what news events and media stories best capture the dreams and fears of students. Organize regular sessions with high schools as another way to stay alert to the changing needs, interests, and expectations of soon-to-be college students.

Turn to formal resources, including journals, books, and conference presentations as well as reports on demographic, economic, and social trends found in the popular media. Especially seek out and listen to the views of analysts and experts who have demonstrated a keen ability to characterize change. The greatest payoff to such listening and observing comes from being alerted to those trends and indicators that signal fundamental, long-term change in student populations.

Define and Define Again

We all need a hedge against complacency, a habit of not assuming that we understand the meaning of events, objects, or remarks from the perspective of students. As a university president recently cautioned, administrators should always try to see the "shades of gray" in a situation (Sample, 2001). Defining again and again may also mean rethinking what devices are effective in communicating with students. Today's students, whatever their age and background, have such wide media awareness that they are more sophisticated than past generations. They have had significant exposure to sarcastic humor and are quick to poke fun at pious, high-minded statements. This means that colleges and universities must use an acceptable, believable vocabulary that fits with student perceptions. Educators must be aware that, in many aspects of communication with students, time-honored approaches may have lost their meaning.

Look to the Pioneers

Although this chapter has emphasized the continually evolving nature of student populations, the overall pace of change is sometimes quite gradual. Subgroups of students that receive special attention in one decade were generally present a decade earlier although probably in smaller numbers and without formal organizations or only in certain locations.

Because distance learners will be a more important component of student populations in the future, for example, it is important to listen to their views today. Much can be learned from the experiences of a pioneer such as the National Technological University, which has already had considerable experience with distance learners. So too, because two important and rapidly growing groups of students are Asian Americans and Hispanics, much can be learned from the experience of colleges and universities in California, Arizona, Florida, and other locations that have already enrolled substantial numbers of Asian and Hispanic students. Similarly, learning from the experience of Hispanic-serving institutions would be valuable.

Watch the Scale

In this context, scale refers to the relative size of groupings of students. Although the specific timing is uncertain, a natural evolution takes place for many student groups in which, as their numbers increase, they develop their own group identity and their ability to give voice to their needs. University and college administrators can anticipate the dimensions of new student voices by paying attention to the underlying numbers, such as the growth in numbers of students with certain characteristics, the introduction of additional clubs, and the like.

Issues of scale—having sufficient numbers of students with certain characteristics so that they have a general effect—have been raised recently in trying to describe the broader benefits that accrue when campuses gain a significant degree of racial and ethnic diversity (Chang et al., 1999; Madhere, 1998; Smith, Gerbick, & Figueroa, 1997).

Compare Notes and Be Open to Different Views

The reality of student diversity is too complex for any one person to comprehend. A pooling of experience will yield a richer, more accurate view of salient changes in student populations. Sessions at national conferences offer opportunities for such exchange, but many less formal exchanges of insights should be sought as well. Cross-institutional polling can be useful, especially to gain a base of comparison for understanding changes occurring on one's own campus. Increased use of mental illness services on one campus, for example, might be interpreted differently when it becomes evident that other campuses have had similar increases.

Every institution offers its own opportunities for comparing notes. Faculty have many insights drawn from their classroom teaching that add to the perspectives available to student affairs personnel. Officers in admissions, in student financial aid, even in the parking office have still other perspectives to share. The office of institutional research, the alumni office, and the career placement office are other useful sources of perspective.

Conclusion

Diversity and pluralism have made American life richer. To recognize and deal with the complexity of student characteristics may seem a difficult task, but the growing sense of diversity can also be understood as an exercise in facing up to important realities. In many ways, previous generations operated with substantial perceptual blinders that made it difficult for them to understand patterns of student behavior. Educators today have an advantage: they have already become comfortable with an expanded awareness of difference and its effect on student achievement. The skills learned today in thinking about diversity will surely be put to much further use in the future.

References

Adelman, C. (1994). *Lessons of a generation: Education and work in the lives of the high school class of 1972.* San Francisco: Jossey-Bass.

Aune, B. P., & Kroeger, S. A. (1997). Career development of college students with disabilities: An interactional approach to defining the issues. *Journal of College Student Development, 38* (4), 344–56.

Belch, H. A. (Ed.). (2000). *Serving students with disabilities* (New Directions for Student Services No. 91). San Francisco: Jossey-Bass.

Carnevale, D. (2001, September 14). Should distance students pay for campus-based services? *The Chronicle of Higher Education,* A35–36.

Chang, M., Witt, D., Jones, J., & Hakuta, K. (Eds.). (1999). *Compelling interest: Examining the evidence on racial dynamics in higher education.* Palo Alto, CA: Stanford University Center for Comparative Studies in Race and Ethnicity.

Chronicle of Higher Education (2001, August 31). *Almanac Issue, 2001–2.*

Cuyjet, M. J. (Ed.) (1997). *Helping African-American men succeed in college* (New Directions for Student Services No. 80). San Francisco: Jossey-Bass.

Dietz, L. H., & Triponey, V. L. (Eds.). (1997). *Serving students at metropolitan universities: The unique opportunities and challenges* (New Directions for Student Services No. 79). San Francisco: Jossey-Bass.

Eaton, J. S. (1992). The evolution of access policy: 1965–1990. In Aspen Institute (Ed.), *American higher education: Purposes, problems and public perceptions* (pp. 141–158). Queenstown, MD: Aspen Institute.

Engstrom, C. M., & Sedlacek, W. (1997). Attitudes of heterosexual students toward their gay male and lesbian peers. *Journal of College Student Development, 38*, 565–76.

Fries-Britt, S. (1997). Identifying and supporting gifted African-American men. In M. J. Cuyjet (Ed.), *Helping African-American men succeed in college* (New Directions for Student Services No. 80, pp. 65–78). San Francisco: Jossey-Bass.

Harvey, W. (2001). *Minorities in higher education: Eighteenth annual status report.* Washington, DC: American Council on Education.

Henderson, C. (1999). *College freshmen with disabilities: A biennial statistical profile.* Washington, DC: American Council on Education.

Hopkins, R. (1997). *Educating black males: Critical lessons in schooling, community and power.* Albany: SUNY Press.

Howe, N., & Strauss, W. (2000). *Millennials rising: The next great generation.* New York: Vintage Books.

Institute for International Education. (2001). *Open doors, 2000–2001: Report on international educational exchange.* New York: Institute for International Education.

Kantrowitz, B., & Naughton, K. (2001, Nov. 12). Generation 9–11. *Newsweek*, pp. 46–56.

Kuh, G. D. (2001). Assessing what really matters to student learning. *Change* (May/June), pp. 10–17, 66.

Lark, J. S. (1998). Lesbian, gay, and bisexual concerns in student affairs: Themes and transitions in the development of the professional literature. *NASPA Journal, 35*, pp. 157–68.

Levine, A. (1980). *When dreams and heroes died: A portrait of today's college students.* San Francisco: Jossey-Bass.

Levine, A., & Cureton, J. S. (1998). *When hope and fear collide: A portrait of today's college students.* San Francisco: Jossey-Bass.

Levine, A., & Nidiffer, J. (1996). *Beating the odds: How the poor get to college.* San Francisco: Jossey-Bass.

Madhere, S. (1998). Cultural diversity, pedagogy, and assessment strategies. *Journal of Negro Education, 67*, pp. 280–95.

Mooney, C. J. (1995, May 19). Religious revival grips students at church colleges. *Chronicle of Higher Education*, A39.

National Center for Education Statistics. (1998). *The condition of education.* Washington, DC: Author.

National Center for Education Statistics. (1999). *Stopouts or stayouts? Undergraduates who leave college in their first year.* Washington, DC: Author.

National Center for Education Statistics. (2000). *Digest of educational statistics.* Washington, DC: Author.

Nettles, M. T. (1991). Assessing progress in minority access and achievement in American higher education. In Education Commission of the States (Ed.), *State policy and assessment in higher education* (pp. 1–43). Working papers. Denver, CO: Education Commission of the States.

Polite, V. C., & Davis, J. E. (Eds.). (1999). *African-American males in school and society.* New York: Teachers College Press.

Richardson, R. C., & Skinner, E. T. (1991). *Achieving quality and diversity: Universities in a multicultural society.* New York: American Council on Education/Macmillan.

Sample, S. B. (2001, Oct. 19). When the buck stops, think contrarily. *Chronicle of Higher Education*, B11–13.

Sanderson, A. R., Dugoni, B., Hoffer, T., & Selfa, L. (1999). *Summary report 1998: Doctorate recipients from United States universities.* Chicago: National Opinion Research Center.

Sandler, B. R., & Hall, R. M. (1982). *The classroom climate: A chilly one for women?* Washington, DC: Association of American Colleges.

Sax, L. J., Astin, A. W., Korn, W. S., & Mahoney, K. M. (2000). *The American freshman: National norms for fall 2000.* Los Angeles: Higher Education Research Institute, UCLA.

Sherrill, J., & Hardesty, C. A. (1994). *The gay, lesbian, and bisexual students' guide to colleges, universities, and graduate schools.* New York: New York University Press.

Smith, D. G., Gerbick, G. L., & Figueroa, M. A. (1997). *Diversity works: The emerging picture of how students benefit.* Washington, DC: Association of American Colleges and Universities.

Strauss, W., & Howe, N. (1990). *Generations: The history of America's future, 1584 to 2069.* New York: Morrow.

Vickery, L. J., & McClure, M. D. (1998). *The 4 P's of accessibility in post-secondary education: Philosophy, policy, procedures, and programs.* Muncie, IN: Ball State University.

Warburton, E. C., Bugarin, R., & Nunez, A. M. (2001). *Bridging the gap: Academic preparation and postsecondary success of first-generation students.* Washington, DC: National Center for Education Statistics.

Woodard, Jr., D. B., Love, P., & Komives, S. R. (2000). Students of the new millennium. In D. B. Woodard, P. Love, & S. R. Komives, *Leadership and management issues for a new century* (New Directions for Student Services No. 92, pp. 35–47). San Francisco: Jossey-Bass.

PART TWO

PROFESSIONAL FOUNDATIONS AND PRINCIPLES

Part One described the historical and contemporary context of higher education, demonstrating how changing societal needs have affected the shape of higher education and the context of student affairs. The roots of our profession begin with the development of higher education in America. Although formal student affairs roles did not develop until the late nineteenth century, the concept of student development was born in the early days of American higher education. Individuals engaged in student affairs work are guided by the common values and philosophies of the profession. They are responsible for high ethical standards and have a legal obligation to uphold a proper professional relationship with students and one another. It is impossible for any graduate or staff development program to identify or outline what a practitioner should do in every possible scenario. Thus practitioners must be capable of making wise decisions in unpredictable situations. They must learn, practice, and model professional behavior and develop a professional perspective based on the foundational elements of the student affairs field. These basic principles serve as frames for professional practice.

In Chapter Four, Elizabeth Nuss traces the development of the profession, from the university's in loco parentis role to the development of the contemporary student affairs practitioner, a professional role grounded in theory and practice. She reviews the founding years of the profession and discusses recent developments, including professional preparation and associations, theory and research, standards, and issues influencing the evolution of the profession.

As Nuss clarifies, the philosophy underlying the core principles of the field has roots that go back to the changing nature of higher education at the turn of the century. In Chapter Five, Robert Young illustrates the evolution of the key philosophies and values that ground individual student affairs practice and have become cultural norms within the profession.

As the student affairs field evolved, a recognized set of ethical standards of practice emerged. These tenets guide practitioners' behavior toward students, their expectations of other higher education professionals, and their understanding of their responsibilities to their host institution. In Chapter Six, Jane Fried describes ethical standards in student affairs and stresses their importance in addressing difficult dilemmas faced by student affairs professionals. Fried challenges readers to think of the cultural framing and assumptions that support and challenge ethical practices. Ethical practices are so indispensable to sound practice that we have included the ethical standards of both the American College Personnel Association and the National Association of Student Personnel Administrators in the Resource section at the back of this book.

In addition to ethical standards, the law has increasingly prescribed how student affairs professionals and institutions must treat students. Thus it is essential for the student affairs practitioner to understand legal principles, legal thinking, and the broader culture's expectations regarding how he or she relates to others, individual practitioner rights and responsibilities, and the legal boundaries that provide a context for practice. In Chapter Seven, Peggy Barr presents key legal principles, concepts, and terms that guide professional decision making and illustrates their application in student affairs practice.

We need to understand institutional expectations, whether those of an individual office, a division, an entire college or university, or society. We must concurrently examine our individual character as it intersects with these expectations. All student affairs practitioners must examine their practices for congruence with these professional principles. Further, professionals must examine the tension points between institutional expectations due to mission or purpose and obligations for practice based on professional ethics. It is essential that we intentionally model these high standards in our care and work with each other as colleagues.

CHAPTER FOUR

THE DEVELOPMENT OF STUDENT AFFAIRS

Elizabeth M. Nuss

The development of student affairs in the United States parallels that of American higher education. Influenced by changing religious, economic, social, and political forces, the practice of student affairs has evolved and developed. An understanding of this evolution provides an essential context for understanding today's student affairs programs, services, events, and tensions.

This chapter traces the evolution of the profession from the faculty role of in loco parentis to the creation of the specialized roles of deans of women and deans of men and finally to the organizational patterns and roles seen in student affairs today. The evolution of key concepts and components such as extracurricular and cocurricular activities, integration of student affairs with the academic mission, student development theory, professional standards, student learning and assessment, quality assurance, and student affairs in graduate and professional education are also discussed. Critical historical points are marked and recorded by key documents and events. The establishment and evolution of professional student affairs associations and the roles they played in the history of the profession are also discussed.

As you consider the history of student affairs, please note two enduring and distinctive concepts. The first is the profession's consistent and persistent emphasis on and commitment to the development of the whole person. In spite of the dramatic changes that have occurred in higher education, the profession's adherence to this fundamental principle should not be overlooked or underestimated. Second, student affairs was originally founded to support the academic mission of the college, and one

Note: The author acknowledges the research assistance provided by Julie E. Owen, Coordinator of Service, Leadership, and Assessment, University of Maryland, College Park.

of the characteristic strengths of American higher education is the diversity among the missions of these institutions (see Chapter Two for a discussion of institutional diversity). Student affairs' sustained commitment to supporting the diversity of institutional and academic missions over time is a hallmark of the history of the profession. The commitment of student affairs to these two fundamental principles should be viewed as evidence of the professional nature of student affairs work rather than as a limitation or shortcoming.

The Founding and Early Years: 1636 to 1850

The roots of today's comprehensive student affairs programs in American colleges can be traced to the founding of the colonial colleges (Leonard, 1956). Dormitories and dining halls were an essential aspect of collegiate life in the early colonial colleges. Rudolph (1965) described the collegiate way of life as one based on the "notion that a curriculum, a library, a faculty, and students are not enough to make a college" (p. 87). The dormitory made it possible for the faculty to exercise supervision and parental concern for the well being of the students. Students were viewed as immature adolescents requiring counsel, supervision, vocational guidance, and, frequently, remedial classes (Leonard, 1956). Colonial colleges were empowered to act in loco parentis and were therefore free to develop and enforce rules and regulations as if they were the parents. The doctrine of in loco parentis persisted in some form until the 1960s. The system of discipline was paternalistic, strict, and authoritarian. Unlike their British faculty counterparts, the faculty at the colonial colleges was responsible for enforcing all disciplinary regulations (Brubacher & Rudy, 1976).

By the middle of the nineteenth century, the concept of the extracurriculum was emerging. Extracurricular activities were a student response to the traditional, strictly classical course of study. They reflected the desire for the development of the whole student—mind, personality, and body. Early activities included literary societies, debate clubs, and campus publications (Geiger, 2000).

Athletics and physical education in the early American colleges were spontaneous and informal and intended for recreation and enjoyment. Some denominational colleges frowned on sports as a distraction from the spiritual atmosphere of the college (Brubacher & Rudy, 1976).

The first Greek-letter organization, Phi Beta Kappa, was founded in Virginia at the College of William and Mary in 1776, essentially as a literary and debating society (Brubacher & Rudy, 1976; Jackson, 2000). Social fraternities began in 1825 with the founding of Kappa Alpha. By 1840, the Greek-letter fraternity had been widely introduced in New England colleges. By the 1850s, the first Greek-letter societies for women had been established, and both fraternities and sororities were providing housing for their members (Brubacher & Rudy, 1976). Throughout history, fraternities and sororities have been criticized as antidemocratic, exclusive, and anti-intellectual. They have, however, demonstrated "remarkable resiliency and staying power" (Brubacher & Rudy, 1976, p. 129).

Student rebellions in the late 1700s and early 1800s were usually the result of dissatisfaction with the prevailing methods of teaching, the intrusive forms of discipline imposed by the faculty, and, on occasion, dissatisfaction with the food (Cowley & Williams, 1991; Rudy, 1996). Jackson (2000) observed that student life at Harvard and elsewhere seemed to take on a less combative tone after the 1840s.

Increasingly, education was viewed as a means of obtaining social and economic mobility. As the idea of higher education for the common man developed, the country witnessed the introduction of women and, in a few instances, African Americans to colleges and universities (Leonard, 1956).

Diversification: 1850–1900

The first appointments of designated personnel to handle student problems coincided with several events. Growing demands on college presidents, changing faculty roles and expectations, and the increase in coeducation and women's colleges are among the reasons most frequently cited (Boyer, 1990b; Leonard, 1956; Rudolph, 1965). By the mid-nineteenth century American higher education, once devoted primarily to the intellectual and moral development of students, was shifting from the shaping of young lives to the building of a nation (Boyer, 1990b). One of the most significant events was the passage of the Morrill Act of 1862, which created the land grant colleges. Ingrained in the land grant ideal was the concept of a collegiate education for all at public expense—the beginning of the contemporary concept of equal access.

The passage of the second Morrill Act in 1890 led to the establishment of publicly funded, but segregated, Black colleges in seventeen states (Rudolph, 1965). Unfortunately, the legislation continued to sanction the doctrine of "separate but equal." However, it did increase opportunities for African Americans to pursue higher education at a time when very few opportunities were available. During this time period, the participation of women in higher education also increased dramatically (Geiger, 2000; Leonard, 1956; Nidiffer, 2001; Rudolph, 1965).

As enrollments of both sexes increased in the mid-1800s, the search for housing accommodations on and off campus intensified. There was also a shift from "the absolute and unquestioning obedience expected of students in Colonial days" (Leonard, 1956, p. 92) to a more positive tone, in which good conduct was expected rather than imposed.

By the 1860s, the German university movement was influencing American student life in many ways. With the introduction of the gymnasium, American colleges and universities saw expanded athletic activities and a new emphasis on health, physical activity, and life adjustment tasks (Leonard, 1956; Rudolph, 1965). In 1869 the first intercollegiate football game—soccer as we know it today—was played between Rutgers and Princeton (Brubacher & Rudy, 1976). Also, physicians began to join college faculties, marking the beginning of health services for students (Leonard, 1956). German university education reinforced a trend away from "the collegiate way of living" (Cowley & Williams, 1991, p. 148). German universities viewed responsibility related only to the training of the student's mind. They had little interest in how students spent their time outside of class. By the late 1800s, the paternalism associated with the colonial colleges and the collegiate way of life had given way to almost complete indifference (Cowley & Williams, 1991). Evidence of this was detected in the diminished interest in residence halls, the decline in compulsory chapel, and the reduced involvement of faculty in student discipline.

In 1870, Harvard University appointed Professor Ephraim Gurney its first college dean in higher education. His main task, in addition to teaching, was to release the president from his responsibilities as disciplinarian (Stewart, 1985). With the appointment of Dean LeBaron Briggs at Harvard in 1891, the role of dean was expanded to include personal counseling. Thomas Arkle Clark, commenting on his appointment in 1901 as the first dean of men at the University of Illinois, observed, "I relieved the President of some very unpleasant duties" (Williamson, 1961, p. 6). (For a more detailed description of student life in these early years, see Sheldon, 1901/1969.)

While this period witnessed many significant events in higher education, there were problems that influenced the development of student affairs. Prior to 1900, the principal function of a college was to provide an education that emphasized mental discipline, religious piety, and strict rules governing student behavior (Bok, 1982). A countervailing view developed among some educators after 1900. They warned against departing from the traditional commitment to intellectual, vocational, and moral education and allowing development of the intellect to become the dominant concern (Williamson, 1961). Cowley (1940) noted that three influences—secularism, intensive scholarship and research, and specialization—threatened higher education's previous commitment to preparing young adults for citizenship. Although the intellectualists of the late 1800s and early 1900s were not able to eliminate the early personnel services, they were "put on a starvation ration" (p. 158).

Charles William Eliot, president of Harvard, led another aspect of reform influencing the changing role of faculty and the development of student affairs from 1869 to 1909. Eliot advocated a broadly elective course of study to replace the prescribed classical curriculum (James, 1930). Recognizing individual differences, the elective course of study eventually required more attention to academic advising programs.

Emergence of the Profession: 1900 to 1945

The student personnel movement is a twentieth-century phenomenon. By the turn of the century, the participation of faculty in student personnel matters (what is now referred to as student affairs) had changed. As the burden of disciplining and regulating students shifted from faculty, there was greater recognition of student responsibility. Student councils and other forms of student government were widespread during the first decade of the twentieth century. By 1915, at least 123 colleges and universities were employing some variant of the honor system. Brubacher and Rudy (1976) concluded that "in the years following 1918 the student personnel movement gained national recognition and professional stature; it was becoming self-conscious, confident, and widely influential" (p. 336). Williamson (1961) observed that the program of student affairs had been evolving slowly for many years. Then, in the latter half of the nineteenth century, accelerated changes in the character of institutions of higher education and their students produced conditions that made the greater development of these services both possible and urgent. Following World War I, the organizational patterns of modern student affairs evolved, assuming many of the forms we recognize today (Brubacher & Rudy, 1976; Rentz, 1994; Williamson, 1961). Yoakum (1919/1994) outlined one of the earliest plans for personnel bureaus in educational institutions. Their primary functions were associated with vocational guidance, including obtaining accurate data on each student, codifying the requirements of different professions, and supervising the use of ability and interest inventories.

Distinct student personnel functions had developed by 1925. For example, organized placement bureaus supervised by staff specialists were set up on many large college campuses and were beginning to appear at small and midsized colleges as well (Brubacher & Rudy, 1976). A sufficient number of colleges and universities were providing student health services, leading to the establishment of the American Student Health Association in 1920. The most significant trend in college health work after 1918 was the growing concern with mental health and psychological services (Brubacher & Rudy, 1976).

A variety of professional titles described student personnel workers (Cowley, 1957/1994a; Lloyd-Jones & Smith, 1938): director of personnel, dean of students, social director, and vocational counselor, among others. While such titles were used at different institutions, as though the duties involved were synonymous, diversity rather than conformity was the norm for the organization of student affairs. Two factors—the personalities and idiosyncrasies of individuals and the unique history and mission of each institution—contributed to the diversity of student affairs organizations and job titles (Williamson, 1961). As Lloyd-Jones and Smith (1938) pointed out, the personnel aspect of the educational program was "not a simple, unitary thing any more than . . . the curriculum [was]" (p. 19).

Professional Preparation

The first formal program of study in vocational guidance for student affairs practitioners began at Columbia University's Teachers College. The first professional diploma for an "Adviser of Women" was awarded in conjunction with the Master of Arts degree in 1914 (Bashaw, 1992; Gilroy, 1987; Teachers College, 1914). In 1929 Esther Lloyd-Jones was the first recipient of a doctorate in the field, and the program began to admit men in 1932 (C. Johnson, personal correspondence, August 12, 1993). The number of preparation programs remained relatively stable through the 1990s. Over eighty master's and doctoral degree programs in student affairs are listed in the *Directory of Graduate Preparation Programs in College Student Personnel* (American College Personnel Association, 1999).

Professional Associations

Once student affairs emerged as a distinct organizational entity and deans of men and women had become more prevalent, professional associations were established to articulate the shared concerns of student affairs practitioners. The fact that student affairs in the early 1900s were organized by gender and race influenced the development of these associations.

The jobs of the early deans of women varied among colleges and regions of the country (Bashaw, 1992). At most coeducational colleges, the dean of women was the highest-ranking woman on campus (Bashaw, 1992). There were few other women on campus with whom the dean of women could consult or collaborate. Many found it useful to have an opportunity to gather to discuss issues related to their job (Sturdevant & Hayes, 1930). In 1910, a group of deans of women came together at the American Association of University Women (AAUW) meeting and concluded that it would be useful to have their own organization. The National Association of Deans of Women (NADW) was organized in 1916. Approximately 70 percent of the early membership came from the Northeast and Midwest; only about 14 percent were from southern schools (Bashaw, 1992). Since its founding, the organization focused on serving the needs of women in education. In 1956, the NADW became the National Association of Women Deans and Counselors (NAWDC). By the early 1970s, there were fewer deans of women on campus and advocates for women had assumed new roles and titles (Bashaw, 1992). As a result, in 1973 the organization became the National Association of Women Deans, Administrators, and Counselors (NAWDAC) (Bashaw, 2001). In 1991, the organization's name was changed to the National Association for Women in Education (NAWE), to more accurately reflect its contemporary scope and focus (Hanson, 1995; Nuss, 2000). While several of its publications and programs were well regarded, membership and conference attendance declined (Gangone, 1999). The board and membership voted to dissolve the association in 2000.

In January 1919, a meeting referred to as the Conference of Deans and Advisers of Men was held at the University of Wisconsin. That meeting is now recognized as the founding of the National Association of Deans and Advisers of Men (NADAM). After two earlier attempts (in 1948 and 1949) failed, the organization officially adopted the name National Association of Student Personnel Administrators (NASPA) in 1951. This broadened the association's base, and for the first time NASPA began to recruit members (Rhatigan, 2001).

As NASPA's organizational mission broadened, a few women began to join. The first woman to attend a NADAM/NASPA conference did so in 1926 (Rhatigan, 2001). In 1958, Mary Ethel Ball, acting dean of students at the University of Colorado, became the first female "institutional representative" of NASPA. Not until the period 1965–1975 did women begin to hold office and participate actively in NASPA. K. Patricia Cross, then of Cornell University, was the first woman appointed to the NASPA executive committee in 1966. In 1971, NASPA established its women's network, and in 1976 it elected its first woman president—Alice Manicur of Frostburg State University. Today women play a significant role in the governance and leadership of NASPA, and approximately half of its membership are women.

The American College Personnel Association (ACPA) traces its founding to 1924, when it began as the National Association of Appointment Secretaries (NAAS) (Bloland, 1983; Johnson, 1985; Sheeley, 1983). (Appointment secretaries assisted in placing teachers and other college graduates.) NAAS's first meeting in 1924 was held jointly with the NADW. In 1929, NAAS's name was changed to the National Association of Placement and Personnel Officers (NAPPO) to reflect its broader professional role. In 1931 the name was changed again, to the American College Personnel Association (ACPA) (Bloland, 1983; Johnson, 1985). In 1952 ACPA helped form the American Personnel and Guidance Association (APGA); Robert H. Shaffer, an ACPA leader, became its first president. Johnson (1985) observed that only a few years later ACPA members were questioning their affiliation and threatening to withdraw. The issue was discussed numerous times until 1991, when the ACPA voted to disaffiliate from what was by then known as the American Association for Counseling and Development (AACD). ACPA became an independent organization in 1992 (M. Nellenbach, personal communication, May 17, 1995).

By 1945, other professional organizations had been established to address the specialized student affairs roles developing on campus, including the Association of College Unions International (ACUI), established in 1910; the American Association of Collegiate Registrars and Admissions Officers (AACRAO), established in 1910; the American College Health Association (ACHA), established in 1920; and the National Orientation Directors Association (NODA), established in 1937 (Cowley, 1964/1994b; Nuss, 2000).

Racial barriers and discrimination prevented the full participation of minorities in these professional associations. African American student affairs deans were unable to attend conferences held in segregated hotels or restaurants. In 1954, two minority professional organizations—the National Association of Deans of Women and Advisers of Girls in Colored Schools (DOWA) founded in 1929 and the National Association of the Deans of Men in Negro Educational Institutions founded in 1935—met to plan, organize, and develop the National Association of Personnel Workers (NAPW) (Barrett, 1991; Traylor, 1998). Founded a few months before the historic Supreme Court decision barring "separate but equal" educational programs, the NAPW's common interests focused on the "hopes, aspirations, and goals of 'Negro' education" (Barrett, 1991, p. 2). Dr. Sadie Yancey, dean of students at Florida A&M and dean of women at Howard University, was the first president. In 1994, the NAPW changed its name to the National Association of Student Affairs Professionals (NASAP) (S. Whittaker, personal communication, May 19, 1995). More information about NASAP is available at their website (http://www.angelfire.com/ga/NASAP/).

The Student Personnel Point of View

As mentioned earlier, the *Student Personnel Point of View* (SPPV) has shaped the core values of the profession for the past sixty-five years. The landmark report was the result of several years of activity, culminating in a committee appointed by the American Council on Education (ACE) to study personnel practices in colleges and universities (American Council on Education, 1937/1994a). The final paper acknowledged that a long and honorable history stood behind the student affairs point of view. The report recommended, "in addition to instruction and business management adapted to the needs of the individual student, an effective educational program [should include]—in one form or another—the following services adapted to the specific aims and objectives of each college and university" (American Council on Education, 1937/1994a, p. 69). The report emphasized the importance of understanding the individual student, the importance of coordinating the major functions of instruction and management, and the notion that student services should be offered and organized in ways that support the unique mission of each college. It included a list of twenty-three specific functions that should be included in a comprehensive student personnel program. In 1949, E. G. Williamson chaired another ACE committee, which revised the 1937 report (American Council on Education, 1949/1994b). "The concept of education is broadened to include attention to the student's well rounded development—physically, socially, emotionally, and spiritually, as well as intellectually" (p. 109). The 1949 *Student Personnel Point of View* outlined conditions and goals for student growth, the fundamental elements for a student personnel program, and the administrative organization and governance. (The report is also discussed in Chapter Five.) The principles outlined in both the 1937 and 1949 *Student Personnel Point of View* influenced the philosophical development of the profession and persist today as guiding assumptions.

Expansion: 1945–1985

Several significant events during this period shaped the development of the student affairs profession. These included increased federal support and involvement in higher education, landmark legal challenges resulting in the end of in loco parentis and changing relationships between students and institutions, the beginning of student development research and theory, and the development of professional standards.

Federal Involvement

By the conclusion of World War II, the concept of providing universal access to higher education was firmly established (Cowley & Williams, 1991). Partially motivated by peacetime economic and employment prospects, the Serviceman's Readjustment Act, commonly referred to as the G. I. Bill, was passed in June 1944. This legislation had dramatic consequences for higher education and student affairs. The massive enrollment buildup from the late 1950s through the 1970s was the direct result of the increased interest in higher education generated by the G. I. Bill.

In 1947, the Truman Commission Report—*Higher Education for American Democracy*—called for dramatically expanded access to postsecondary education, increased financial aid, and a broader curriculum emphasizing world perspectives. The report also influenced and stimulated the development of community colleges (Cowley & Williams, 1991).

The passage of Title IV of the Housing Act of 1950 fueled a massive program of housing construction. The act's goal was to house and feed large numbers of returning students in an economical fashion. This led to the construction of high-rise residence halls still found on many college campuses today. Increasingly, colleges and universities recognized that a student's academic performance was affected in important ways by his or her surroundings—particularly housing. Student residence halls were viewed as an effective way to reintegrate the curriculum and extracurricular activities (Brubacher & Rudy, 1976).

The 1960s marked the beginning of increased federal support and hence increased federal interest and involvement in higher education. This increased involvement has led over time to volumes of regulations that influence student affairs policies and practices. It is beyond the scope of this chapter to enumerate or analyze the significant federal legislation enacted that has affected the student affairs profession. However, when one considers just a sample of the major legislation, the impact becomes clear. In 1963 alone, Congress passed the Vocational Education Act, the Higher Education Facilities Act, and the Health Professions Act. In 1965, Congress passed the Higher Education Act, designed to expand opportunities for higher education. Other examples include Title VI of the Civil Rights Act of 1964, Title IX of the Education Amendments of 1972, and Section 504 of the Rehabilitation Act of 1973. Much of this legislation mandated the elimination of discrimination and required equal access and treatment for educational and other programs receiving federal financial assistance. The legislation influenced the development of increasingly specialized roles for student affairs practitioners, particularly in the area of financial aid and student support services for previously underrepresented groups. It also created new expectations for student and institutional relationships. Staff were either retrained or hired to provide support and services in these areas, and new codes of conduct and grievance procedures were developed.

As a result of legislation and other societal changes, higher education and student affairs began experiencing what was to become a major shift in student demographics, as increasing numbers of previously excluded or underrepresented groups gained access to higher education. Patterns of enrollment also began to change, with increasing numbers of adult and part-time students enrolling in evening and weekend degree programs. (Elaine El-Khawas discusses these and other significant changes in Chapter Three.)

Legal Challenges and Changing Relationships

The following labels often characterize the 1960s: the age of student activism, the downfall of in loco parentis, the sexual revolution, and the years of civil disobedience. Speaking at a NASPA meeting in 1956, W. H. Cowley, former president of Hamilton College and a faculty member at Stanford, warned that the campus was a likely setting for agitation and destruction if social conditions galvanized students (Cowley, 1957/1994a).

The assassinations of President John F. Kennedy and the Reverend Martin Luther King, Jr., urban rioting, concerns about the military industrial complex, and the civil rights movement were among the signature events of the decade that impacted students. During this period, special rules and regulations for female students were abolished, coed student housing developed, and the nature of the relationship between the student and the institution changed dramatically.

In the late 1950s and early 1960s, questions about the civil liberties of college students were raised, and the long-standing doctrine of in loco parentis was challenged and eventually abolished. In 1961, in *Dixon* v. *Alabama State Board of Education* (294 F.2d 150), the Supreme Court declared that due process requires notice and some opportunity for a hearing before students at a tax-supported college could be expelled for misconduct (Ardiaolo, 1983; Ratliff, 1972). Following *Dixon,* the Supreme Court rendered a series of student-rights decisions that reflected the recognition that, for the most part, persons above the age of eighteen are legally adults and that students at public colleges do not relinquish their fundamental constitutional rights by accepting student status (Bickel & Lake, 1994).

Activist students protested the Vietnam War, racial injustice, and the shortcomings of higher education. Disruptions at Santa Barbara, Kent State, and Jackson State College resulted in injury and death (Cowley & Williams, 1991; Rudy, 1996). Public pressure and impatience increased, and student affairs professionals' skills at conflict resolution and mediation became essential.

The nature of the relationship between students and their colleges and universities changed significantly during this period. After in loco parentis was eliminated, the emphasis on the student affairs professional's role as disciplinarian or authority figure declined and the role of coordinator and educator increased (Garland & Grace, 1993). The role of student participation in institutional governance also changed. Students began to play more influential roles on academic committees, and many institutions appointed student representatives to their governing boards. As Boyer (1990a) lamented, however, "while old rules were abolished, changes were made more out of compromise than conviction, and few colleges had the imagination or the courage to replace abandoned rules with more creative views of campus life" (p. xii).

One way to view the changing relationship between students and institutions in the 1960s is from a rights and responsibilities perspective. In June 1967, a committee composed of representatives from the American Association of University Professors (AAUP), the United States National Student Association (USNSA), the American Association of Colleges (AAC), NASPA, and NAWDAC met in Washington to draft the *Joint Statement on Student Rights and Freedoms.* The statement, endorsed by each of the five national sponsors as well as a number of other higher education associations, outlined the minimal standards of academic freedom necessary for student learning. The principles embodied in the statement have persisted over time and continue to guide student affairs practice. On the occasion of its twenty-fifth anniversary in 1992, "an interassociation task force met in Washington, D.C., to study, interpret, update, and affirm (or reaffirm) the joint statement. Members of the task force agreed that the statement has stood the test of time quite well and continues to provide an excellent set of principles for institutions of higher education" (National Association of Student Personnel Administrators, 1992, p. 1). The 1992 task force also developed interpretive notes to reflect changes in the law and higher education that have occurred since 1967.

Others saw the relationship between students and their institutions as essentially contractual, implying that if students pay tuition and meet the academic and social requirements outlined in college publications, they will receive a degree (Gehring, 2000). More recently, the relationship has been cast in terms of a consumer model. The consumer model requires colleges and universities to provide a wide range of information to students on subjects such as tuition refund policies, the release of educational records and information, alcohol and substance abuse policies, graduation rates, campus safety and security networks, and sexual assault policies so that the consumer—both student and parent—can make informed decisions about which institution to attend.

Continued expansion of higher education resulted in increased numbers of specialized student affairs professionals, for example, in admissions, financial aid, students with disabilities, and an increased reliance on paraprofessionals and peer advisors. As the roles of student affairs professionals became more specialized and the relationship between students and institutions changed, professional names and titles changed as well. Increasingly, "student affairs" or "student development" replaced the expression "student personnel."

Student Development Theory and Research

An increasingly diverse and complex student affairs profession sought to establish its theoretical base at a time when many believed the gap between academics and extracurricular activities was widening (Boyer, 1987). The debate over the purpose of higher education intensified, and it appeared to some that the concept of the development of the whole student was in jeopardy (Brown, 1972). The Council of Student Personnel Associations (COSPA) emerged at least partially in response to this diversity and specialization. Established in 1963 to develop cooperation among the student affairs professional associations, COSPA's goal was to initiate programs that would do for all groups what no single association could do for itself (Cowley, 1964/1994b; Rentz, 1994). One of COSPA's most important contributions was the publication in 1975 of *Student Development Services in Postsecondary Education* (1994). The paper noted the "purpose of student development services in postsecondary education was to provide affective and cognitive expertise in the processes involved in education" (Council of Student Personnel Associations, 1975/1994, p. 429). The paper outlined common assumptions of student development specialists; noted that their clientele included the individual, the group, and the organization; and summarized the competencies and functions of student development specialists. The three broad functions of student affairs were described as administration, instruction, and consultation. COSPA dissolved in 1975.

A significant amount of published research on the impact of college on students began to appear in the late 1950s and 1960s. In 1969, Feldman and Newcomb published *The Impact of College on Students,* which reviewed and synthesized the findings of more than fifteen hundred studies conducted over four decades. In the intervening decades, both the number of empirical studies and the major areas of inquiry have increased dramatically. The contribution of early theories of student development as well as that of more recent developments is discussed in detail in Part Three. ACPA launched its response to the prospect of changes in the profession with its Tomorrow's Higher Education (THE) project. Robert Brown (1972) was commissioned to write *Student Development in Tomorrow's Higher Education: A Return to the Academy.* The monograph focused attention on the changing roles of student affairs professionals and noted that having an impact on student development meant having an awareness of and involvement in the "total environment of the student—not just where he lives or what organization he belonged to" (Brown, 1972, p. 38). Brown also called for student affairs staff to work as partners with faculty in the educational process and argued that the concern for student development needed to move from the extracurricular to the curricular.

Since the introduction of the concept of student development, professional leaders have debated whether there is a difference between the concept of student affairs and that of student development (Garland & Grace, 1993; Rhatigan, 1974/1994). Questions about the influence of 1970s student development theory on the profession are also being raised today. Bloland, Stamatakos, and Rogers (1994) questioned the premises of the student development movement and its effect upon the field of student affairs. In their critique of student development, they attempted to resolve the question as to whether the *Student Personnel Point of View* or the 1975 COSPA document *Student Development Services in Postsecondary Education* represented a professional philosophy for the student affairs profession. They concluded that the *Student Personnel Point of View* more adequately fulfills the four components of a philosophy and that the purpose of higher education "is not student development per se but the development of the whole person including, of course, intellectual ability and educational achievement" (p. 112). Strange (1994) and Upcraft (1994) also provide useful analysis and critique of student development theory and the difficulties inherent in translating theory into professional practice.

Professional Standards

Over the years, student affairs gained stature, vision, and recognition as an essential part of higher education's mission. But until 1979 one important element—comprehensive standards for program development, evaluation, self-study, and accreditation—was missing (Mable, 1991; Miller, 1991). A meeting of student affairs professional associations was held in June 1979 to "consider the desirability and feasibility of establishing professional standards and accreditation programs in student affairs" (Mable, 1991, p. 11). Later that year an invitational conference for interested student affairs associations was held. The conference provided strong support for an interassociation entity, which eventually became the Council for the Advancement of Standards in Higher Education (CAS). A consortium of higher education professional associations, the CAS has grown to include thirty-four member organizations. The first *CAS Standards and Guidelines* were published in 1986 and addressed nineteen functional areas of higher education programs and services. The most recent "Blue Book" of standards addresses twenty-nine functional areas (Council for the Advancement of Standards in Higher Education, 2001). The CAS standards provide direction and strategy for professional practice in higher education programs and services and for promoting quality services and programs. They enable institutions to assess, study, evaluate, and improve their student services. Standards for campus information and visitor services, college health programs, educational services for distance learners, and lesbian, gay, and transgender programs were included in the latest edition and point to emerging areas of professional practice (http://www.cas.edu).

The Contemporary Scene: 1985 to Present

Kerr (1990) characterized the 1980s as a "status quo" decade. Callan (1993) however noted that the seeds of important change might be sown in such normal periods. He noted that one of the most significant changes of the 1980s was the resurgence of the states and greater influence of governors and state legislators in higher education. Economic development and educational reform were a centerpiece of the new state policy agendas. The 1986 National Governors' Association report, *Time for Results,* called on states to "define institutional missions clearly, emphasize the importance of undergraduate education, see that colleges and universities implemented systematic approaches to the assessment of student learning, provide incentives for the improvement of quality, and emphasize the importance of commitment to access" (Callan, 1993, p. 5). Edgerton (1997) noted that higher education in the 1990s confronted at least six new realities. These included new enrollment demands, public shock over rising college costs, new competitors for public funds, a weakening of support for access, growing concerns for quality, and a view that higher education was no longer seen as having a central role in addressing the nation's most pressing problems. Increasingly higher education commentators urged that new standards for determining the quality of higher education be considered (Boyer, 1990b; Edgerton, 1997). Edgerton argued that retention (the extent to which students who began actually completed a course of study), student learning as evidenced by "understanding," and the extent to which students were developing the ability to act on their values and ideas were essential elements of quality. These debates led to increased emphasis on making connections between learning inside and outside the traditional classroom, to a new emphasis on the assessment of student learning, and on experiential learning through community service and service-learning.

Annual data from the UCLA freshman surveys and Levine and Cureton (1998) indicated that more students were coming to college with psychological and emotional problems. As a result counseling and mental health programs were expanded to assist students in achieving their academic goals.

These issues form the context within which to consider several important and recent developments in student affairs. Foremost of the developments were increased student diversity, shifts in public policy perspectives, campus climate, attention to graduate and professional students, student learning initiatives, internationalization, and a contemporary critique of the profession.

Increasing Student Diversity

While the total enrollment in the 1980s and 1990s remained virtually unchanged, the student population became more diverse in all aspects than at any other time in American higher education (Altbach, 1993; Baxter Magolda & Terenzini, 1999). The needs and interests of gay, lesbian, and transgender students began to receive increased attention during the contemporary period. The diversity and complexity of the student body presented a formidable array of new challenges for instructors and administrators. See Chapter Three for an extensive discussion of diversity in higher education.

Shifts in Public Policy

Public policy initiatives in the past twenty years have produced evidence of what might be described as a pendulum swing or at least a change of emphasis. The Drug Free Schools and Communities Act, the 1990 Student Right-to-Know and Campus Security Act, the Americans with Disabilities Act of 1990, and the Higher Education Amendments of 1992 and subsequent modifications continued the emphasis on the consumer's need for information on issues such as graduation rates and campus safety. There has also been evidence of a shift toward less privacy and confidentiality of student discipline records (Blimling, 1999) and less tolerance on the part of federal and state lawmakers to award financial aid to students who are violating laws or making less than satisfactory progress to earning their degrees. The Americans with Disabilities Act and the Higher Education Amendments of 1992 mandated greater access for persons with disabilities and others. Later in the 1990s, state policy in Texas, California, and Florida challenged the concept of affirmative action and set-asides (Kolling, 1998). These shifts in public policy were evidence of the changing nature of the relationship between the institution and its students and expectations for changes in campus climate.

Campus Climate

Boyer (1990a, 1993) noted that students in the 1980s seemed to enjoy high degrees of freedom in personal and social matters. There seemed to be confusion or ambivalence among parents, legislators, the media, and others about what should be the appropriate level or degree of institutional responsibility for student conduct expectations. Highly publicized cases such as the drug overdose death of Len Bias at the University of Maryland in 1986, the murder of Jeanne Clery at Lehigh University in 1986, and incidents of sexual assaults and alcohol and drug abuse received increased public scrutiny. The Carnegie Foundation for the Advancement of Teaching issued a report *Campus Life: In Search of Community* (1990) which called for higher education to pay greater attention to the nature of undergraduate experience and to find ways to help students put their own lives in context (Boyer, 1993). The concern about campus climate and student conduct was evident as colleges and universities continued to face considerable public scrutiny about race relations, alcohol and substance abuse, and mounting concern about the regulation of campus protests, celebrations, and other forms of disruption (Blimling, 1999).

Graduate and Professional Students

Graduate deans and student affairs professionals were urged to focus greater attention on enhancing the learning environment for graduate students (Pruitt-Logan & Isaac, 1995). The developmental needs of graduate students are considerably different from those of traditionally aged college students. Growing participation in graduate and professional degree programs (Baxter Magolda & Terenzini, 1999) and concerns about the collective bargaining efforts of graduate assistants also contributed to changing expectations for institutional services and programs for graduate and professional students. As universities argued that graduate assistants were students and not employees, it was no surprise that deans of graduate schools and student affairs officers began to examine the type and level of services provided to graduate and professional students. Increasingly, the out-of-class experiences and quality of life issues for graduate students became a matter of concern. Graduate student housing, health and counseling services, childcare, and orientation programs were either instituted or enhanced. Graduate schools and student affairs divisions created positions and programs designed to extend services previously offered exclusively or primarily to undergraduate students. Consideration was also being given to determining the appropriate scope, level, and delivery methods to offer services to students enrolled in distance education programs and other nontraditional programs.

Student Learning

Earlier in this chapter two enduring and distinctive concepts—the development of the whole person and the fact that student affairs' role was to support the academic mission of colleges and universities—were noted. Student affairs' support for the academic mission is most evident in the recent efforts to enhance the quality of undergraduate education and student learning.

Student affairs and higher education have struggled with the need to affirm the fundamental principles and research that guide the profession as well as with the need to integrate in-class and out-of-class activities to strengthen the quality of the collegiate experience. Attention is currently focused on ways in which student affairs professionals and academic planners can collaborate to enhance the overall educational experience for an increasingly diverse student clientele.

The Carnegie Foundation for the Advancement of Teaching issued a report on undergraduate education in America that noted "conflicting priorities and competing interests that diminish the intellectual and social quality of the undergraduate experience" (Boyer, 1987, p. 2). Eight tension points were identified, most notably the "great separation, sometimes to the point of isolation, between academic and social life on campus" (p. 5). Concerns about what some referred to as "an unhealthy separation between in-class and out-of-class activities" (Carnegie Foundation for the Advancement of Teaching, 1990, p. 2) promoted more research, recommendations, and insights into the conditions that facilitate and enhance student learning.

In commemoration of the fiftieth anniversary of the *Student Personnel Point of View,* NASPA appointed a "plan for a new century" committee, which issued *A Perspective on Student Affairs* (National Association of Student Personnel Administrators, 1987). This report presented a perspective on what the higher education community could expect from student affairs. It outlined the profession's fundamental assumptions and beliefs, including the preeminence of the academic mission and the uniqueness, worth, and inherent dignity of each student. It also emphasized that bigotry cannot be tolerated, feelings affect thinking and learning, student involvement enhances learning, personal circumstances affect learning, and out-of-class environments affect learning.

Kuh, Schuh, Whitt, and their associates (1991) described how "institutional factors and conditions work together in different colleges and universities to promote learning and personal development through out-of-class learning experiences" (p. 4). Pascarella and Terenzini's *How College Affects Students* (1991) was a landmark summary of research on the impact of college on individual students. They explored several fundamental questions: Do students change in various ways during the college years? To what extent are their changes attributable to the college experience? What college characteristics and experiences tend to produce desired changes?

The major professional associations—NASPA, ACPA, and AAHE (American Association of Higher Education)—engaged in studies and projects designed to stimulate discussion on how student affairs professionals and others can create conditions that will enhance student learning and personal development (American College Personnel Association, 1994) and what students and institutions can reasonably expect from each other in terms of enhancing learning productivity (Kuh, Lyons, Miller, & Trow, 1995). ACPA published the *Student Learning Imperative* (1994), and NASPA produced *Reasonable Expectations* (Kuh et al., 1995).

Discussions at regional and national conferences and on individual campuses about the themes and ideas in both *Reasonable Expectations* and the *Student Learning Imperative* led to the development of the *Principles of Good Practice for Student Affairs* (ACPA & NASPA, 1997) and *Powerful Partnerships: A Shared Responsibility for Learning* (Joint Task Force, 1998). There was an increasing appreciation and understanding that "only when everyone on campus—particularly academic affairs and student affairs staff—shares the responsibility for student learning will we be able to make significant progress in improving it" (p. 1). Student learning was not a new initiative for the profession.

Evans and Reason (2001) noted that student affairs professionals were urged to advise faculty about learning and student characteristics as early as 1937. However, these documents prepared by faculty and academic and student affairs leaders called for an interweaving of students' academic, interpersonal, and developmental experiences as a critical institutional role and brought renewed attention and focus to the topic. All those involved with higher education were called upon to view themselves as teachers, learners, and collaborators in service to learning (Joint Task Force, 1998). As evidenced in conference presentations and programs, there were increasing examples of greater collaboration among academic affairs and student affairs staff on campus. Examples of programmatic priorities involving joint leadership and contributions from academic affairs and student affairs include service learning and community service programs, enhanced new student orientation and first-year programs, diversity programming and curriculum transformation efforts, leadership transformation efforts, and senior capstone seminars and programs, among others.

Associations not typically associated with student affairs also issued reports and guidelines to encourage greater integration of academic and student services. For example, the Association of American Colleges and Universities, an organization for liberal arts colleges, designed programs to mobilize collaborative leadership for educational and institutional effectiveness. Its web page announced that AAC&U believes that the most important outcomes of a college education result from purposeful, engaged, and cumulative learning. The curriculum as a whole and the institution as a whole are the most powerful teachers. The National Association of State University and Land-Grant Colleges (NASULGC) also issued a report calling for renewed attention on the student experience (Kellogg Commission, 1997). The language describing the curriculum as a whole and the institution as a whole reinforces the concepts outlined in the *1937 Student Personnel Point of View.*

Internationalization

While the Association of College Unions (ACU-I) added International to its name in 1961 and the Association of College and University Housing Officers became ACUHO-I in 1981, student affairs professionals became increasingly involved in international programs throughout the 1980s and 1990s and began to incorporate a more global perspective into their work. The American student affairs models were also of increasing interest to educational leaders in Latin America, Europe, Africa, Asia, and the Pacific (Dalton, 1999). Kruger and Dungy (1999) noted that in 1995 there were five conference programs dealing with international issues at the annual NASPA conference and twenty-seven of the twenty-six hundred attendees were from outside the United States. By 1998, there were over twenty conference programs including a two-day preconference workshop, and eighty-seven of the thirty-four hundred registrants were international participants. Increasingly student affairs professionals were participating in Fulbright Scholar Programs and other exchange programs such as those sponsored by NASPA with France, Germany, and Mexico.

Critique of the Profession

There have been debates in the student affairs profession about whether it meets the definitions of a profession (Stamatakos, 1981) and whether there is a difference between the concept of student affairs and student development. Critical analysis of the profession continues today. Woodard, Love, and Komives (2000) explored what they labeled the assumptions, myths, and heresies of the profession. In exploring "the dark corners of student affairs" they urged professionals to consider a "self-transformation, transforming how we see our world—ourselves, our students, our roles and our institutions" (Woodard et al., 2000, p. 3). They challenged the self-marginalization of the profession, the fact that our emphasis has not been sufficiently on the whole student but rather on the psychosocial experiences of students, and that the profession focuses almost exclusively on the "traditional" undergraduate college student. Their analysis was constructive and also described the skills they believed would be essential in the future. These skills included entrepreneurship, resource attraction, organizing around the assessment of student learning and developmental outcomes, employing multiple forms of reference, technology adaptation and application, and future forecasting. These skills complement the traditional competencies such as listening, oral and written communication skills, multicultural competencies, administrative skills, conflict and crisis management, and leadership skills. Carpenter (2001), Young (2001), and others called for serious self-examination about student affairs work and whether or not our work can legitimately be considered as a form of scholarship. In Chapter Twenty-Seven, Carpenter discusses the efforts to develop quality assurance and professionalism in student affairs graduate preparation programs.

Other Developments

The 1990s also saw colleges and universities enjoying the results of the completion of successful fundraising campaigns and increased state authorizations for facility renovation and new construction. The renovation and construction of residence halls, student unions and centers, and recreation and fitness centers were prevalent around the country. George Mason University and Princeton University opened campus centers that combined academic and student life functions.

Public-private partnerships and outsourcing of student life has not flourished as had been predicted by some. Changes in emphasis on health education and managed care may have contributed to slowing down the privatization of student health services. While campuses have increasingly engaged with private companies for the construction of new residence halls, institutional student life personnel staff many of these halls. While Blimling (1999) predicts that the number of for-profit companies specializing in student services will increase, this author believes it is too soon to conclude that private contractors can provide the level and quality of service expected by many consumers and still be considered "profitable" for investors. Crozier (2001) notes "the effects of commercial activities on university campuses are garnering increased scrutiny from both scholars and activists" (p. 45).

An Uncertain Future

While many argued in the early 1990s that student affairs as a profession was in jeopardy as a result of reorganizations and downsizing, this does not appear to have occurred. Membership in professional associations such as ACPA and NASPA continued to grow through the 1990s, and conference attendance was also high. There has however been greater attention placed on the role of student affairs in the assessment of student learning, in providing students with the tools and the habits to engage as life-long learners, and in developing students' ability to translate their educational experiences into the habits of effective citizens (Boyer, 1993; Edgerton, 1997).

As the twentieth century came to a close higher education continued to grapple with its ability to document or attest to student learning, waning public confidence, rising costs, access questions, and the most effective use of technology, among other issues. The economic boom times that enabled colleges and universities to complete successful capital campaigns and increase state appropriations appeared to be coming to an end.

Edgerton's *Education White Paper* (1997) and ACPA's *Higher Education Trends for the Next Century* (Johnson & Cheatham, 1999) are examples of documents outlining what were at the time considered to be the major issues and challenges facing higher education and student affairs in the twenty-first century. Events occurring while this chapter was being completed make additional predictions more difficult.

On Tuesday, September 11, 2001, the nation and the world experienced a previously unimaginable act of terrorism in New York City and Washington, D.C. Faculty and student affairs staff suspended normal operations for several days to grapple with the enormity of the situation and to provide comfort and support to one another and to the family and friends of victims and survivors. Immediately following the attacks it was apparent that the previously established domestic and foreign policy agendas would be altered. It is still too early to speculate on the precise implications for educational agendas except to say that the nation's short- and long-range attention has shifted to the priority of responding to the crisis caused by these events. Resources and priorities shifted to homeland security, national defense, and public health concerns related to outbreaks of anthrax-induced illness and death. For example, tuition increases for fall 2002 were higher than previously anticipated due to the shortfall in private philanthropic support and state appropriations. Legislation to tighten scrutiny on foreign students was introduced. Colleges that relied heavily on the enrollment of international students anticipated enrollment shifts and additional administrative requirements (Hebel, 2002).

Rudy (1996) traced campus involvement and reactions during four crucial periods in American history from the American Revolution to the conflict in Vietnam. He concluded that the academic community was closely involved in each of the crises and, while not the ultimate decision makers, colleges and universities played important roles in determining what those decisions would be. As mentioned earlier, Edgerton (1997) observed that higher education was seen by many as not playing a central role in addressing the nation's pressing problems. It remains to be seen what role higher education and student affairs will play as events around the world unfold after September 11, 2001.

At the beginning of this chapter, two enduring and distinctive concepts were noted: the development of the whole person and the fact that student affairs was established to support the academic mission of institutions of higher education. Adherence to these principles is expected to continue to play a dominant role in the future evolution of the profession. But just as accelerated changes in higher education made the development of student affairs possible in the late nineteenth century, so will the changes of the twentieth-first century influence the profession's future course, both in the United States and throughout the world.

References

Altbach, P. G. (1993). Students: Interests, culture, and activism. In A. Levine (Ed.), *Higher learning in America: 1980–2000* (pp. 203–221). Baltimore: Johns Hopkins Press.

American College Personnel Association. (1999). *Directory of graduate preparation programs in college student personnel.* Alexandria, VA: Author.

American College Personnel Association. (1994). *The student learning imperative: Implications for student affairs.* Washington, DC: Author.

American College Personnel Association & National Association of Student Personnel Administrators. (1997). *Principles of good practice for student affairs.* Retrieved from http://www.acpa.nche.edu/pqp/principles.html

American Council on Education. (1994a). The student personnel point of view. In A. L. Rentz (Ed.), *Student affairs: A profession's heritage* (American College Personnel Association Media Publication No. 40, 2nd ed., pp. 66–77). Lanham, MD: University Press of America. (Original work published 1937)

American Council on Education. (1994b). The student personnel point of view. In A. L. Rentz (Ed.), *Student affairs: A profession's heritage* (American College Personnel Association Media Publication No. 40, 2nd ed., pp. 108–123). Lanham, MD: University Press of America. (Original work published 1949)

Ardiaolo, F. P. (1983). What process is due? In M. J. Barr (Ed.), *Student affairs and the law.* (New Directions for Student Services No. 22, pp. 13–26). San Francisco: Jossey-Bass.

Barrett, B. N. (1991). The presidential issue. *NAPW Journal III,* 1, 1–35.

Bashaw, C. T. (1992). We who live "off on the edges": Deans of women at Southern coeducation institutions and access to the community of higher education, 1907–1960. Unpublished doctoral dissertation, University of Georgia, Athens.

Bashaw, C. T. (2001). Reassessment and redefinition: The NAWDC and higher education for women. In J. Nidiffer & C. T. Bashaw (Eds.), *Women administrators in higher education* (pp. 157–182). Albany, NY: SUNY Press.

Baxter Magolda, M. B., & Terenzini, P. T. (1999). Learning and teaching in the 21st century: Trends and implications for practice. In C. S. Johnson & H. E. Cheatham (Eds.), *Higher education trends for the next century: A research agenda for student success* (pp. 20–27). Washington, DC: ACPA.

Bickel, R. D., & Lake, P. T. (1994). Reconceptualizing the university's duty to provide a safe learning environment: A criticism of the doctrine of *in loco parentis* and the restatement (second) of torts. *Journal of College & University Law, 20,* 261–293.

Blimling, G. S. (1999). Accountability for student affairs: Trends for the 21st century. In C. S. Johnson & H. E. Cheatham (Eds.), *Higher education trends for the next century: a research agenda for student success* (pp. 51–56). Washington, DC: ACPA.

Bloland, P. A. (1983). Ecumenicalism in college student personnel. In B. A. Belson & L. E. Fitzgerald (Eds.), *Thus we spoke: ACPA-NAWDAC, 1958–1975* (pp. 237–254). Alexandria, VA: American College Personnel Association.

Bloland, P. A., Stamatakos, L. C., & Rogers, R. R. (1994). *Reform in student affairs: A critique of student development.* Greensboro, NC: ERIC Counseling and Student Services Clearinghouse.

Bok, D. C. (1982). *Beyond the ivory tower: Social responsibilities of the modern university.* Cambridge, MA: Harvard University Press.

Boyer, E. L. (1987). *College: The undergraduate experience in America.* New York: Harper & Row.

Boyer, E. L. (1990a). Foreword. In Carnegie Foundation for the Advancement of Teaching, *Campus life: In search of community* (pp. xi–xiii). Princeton, NJ: Princeton University Press.

Boyer, E. L. (1990b). *Scholarship reconsidered: Priorities of the professorate.* Princeton, NJ: Carnegie Foundation for the Advancement of Teaching.

Boyer, E. L. (1993). Campus climate in the 1980s and 1990s: Decades of apathy and renewal. In A. Levine (Ed.), *Higher learning in America: 1980–2000* (pp. 322–332). Baltimore: Johns Hopkins Press.

Brown, R. D. (1972). *Student development in tomorrow's higher education: A return to the academy* (Student Personnel Series No. 16). Washington, DC: American Personnel and Guidance Association.

Brubacher, J. S., & Rudy, W. (1976). *Higher education in transition: A history of American colleges and universities, 1636–1976.* New York: Harper & Row.

Callan, P. S. (1993). Government and higher education. In A. Levine (Ed.), *Higher learning in America: 1980–2000* (pp. 3–19). Baltimore: Johns Hopkins Press.

Carnegie Foundation for the Advancement of Teaching. (1990). *Campus life: In search of community.* Princeton, NJ: Princeton University Press.

Carpenter, S. (2001). Student affairs scholarship (re?)considered: Toward a scholarship of practice. *Journal of College Student Development, 42*, 301–318.

Council for the Advancement of Standards in Higher Education. (2001). *CAS standards and guidelines.* Washington, DC: Author. (Standards originally published 1986)

Council of Student Personnel Associations. (1994). Student development services in postsecondary education. In A. L. Rentz (Ed.), *Student affairs: A profession's heritage* (American College Personnel Association Media Publication No. 40, 2nd ed., pp. 428–437). Lanham, MD: University Press of America. (Original work published 1975)

Cowley, W. H. (1940). The history and philosophy of student personnel work. *Journal of the National Association of Deans of Women, 3* (4), 153–162.

Cowley, W. H. (1994a). Student personnel services in retrospect and prospect. In A. L. Rentz (Ed.), *Student affairs: A profession's heritage* (American College Personnel Association Media Publication No. 40, 2nd ed., pp.150–155). Lanham, MD: University Press of America. (Original work published 1957)

Cowley, W. H. (1994b). Reflections of a troublesome but hopeful Rip Van Winkle. In A. L. Rentz (Ed.), *Student affairs: A profession's heritage* (American College Personnel Association Media Publication No. 40, 2nd ed., pp. 190–197). Lanham, MD: University Press of America. (Original work published 1964)

Cowley, W. H., & Williams, D. (1991). *International and historical roots of American higher education.* New York: Garland.

Crozier, J. L. (2001). Can this campus be bought? Commercial influence in unfamiliar places. *Academe, 87* (5), 44–48.

Dalton, J. C. (1999). The significance of international issues and responsibilities in the contemporary work of student affairs. In J. C. Dalton (Ed.), *Beyond borders: How international developments are changing student affairs practice* (New Directions for Student Services No. 86, pp. 3–11). San Francisco: Jossey-Bass.

Edgerton, R. (1997). *Education white paper.* Retrieved Aug. 28, 2001, from http://www.pewundergradforum.org/wp1.html

Evans, N., & Reason, R. (2001). Guiding principles: A review and analysis of student affairs philosophical statements. *Journal of College Student Development, 42,* 359–377.

Feldman, K., & Newcomb, T. (1969). *The impact of college on students.* San Francisco: Jossey-Bass.

Gangone, L. (1999). *Navigating turbulence: A case study of a voluntary higher education association.* Unpublished doctoral dissertation, Columbia University Teachers College, New York.

Garland, P. H., & Grace, T. W. (1993). *New perspectives for student affairs professionals: Evolving realities, responsibilities, and roles* (ASHE-ERIC Higher Education Report No. 7). Washington, DC: George Washington University, School of Education and Human Development.

Gehring, D. D. (2000). Understanding the legal implications of student affairs practice. In M. J. Barr & M. K. Desler (Eds.), *The handbook of student affairs administration* (2nd. ed., pp. 347–376). San Francisco: Jossey-Bass.

Geiger, R. L. (2000). College as it was in the mid-nineteenth century. In R. L. Geiger (Ed.), *The American college in the nineteenth century* (pp. 80–90). Nashville, TN: Vanderbilt University Press.

Gilroy, M. (1987). *The contributions of selected teachers of college women to the field of student personnel.* Unpublished doctoral dissertation, Columbia University Teachers College, New York.

Hanson, G. S. (1995). The organizational evolution of NAWE. *Initiatives, 56* (4), 29–36.

Hebel, S. (2002, April 22). Senate passes bill to tighten security of foreign students. *The Chronicle of Higher Education.* Retrieved April 24, 2002, from http://www.chronicle.com/daily/2002/04/2002042201n.html.

Jackson, L. (2000). The rites of man and the rites of youth: Fraternity and riot at 18th century Harvard. In R. L. Geiger (Ed.), *The American college in the nineteenth century* (pp. 46–79). Nashville, TN: Vanderbilt University Press.

James, H. (1930). *Charles W. Eliot.* Boston: Houghton Mifflin.

Johnson, C. S. (1985). The American College Personnel Association. *Journal of Counseling and Development, 63,* 405–410.

Johnson, C. S., & Cheatham, H. E. (Eds.). (1999). *Higher education trends for the next century: A research agenda for student success.* Washington, DC: ACPA.

Joint Task Force on Student Learning. (1998). *Powerful partnerships: A responsibility for learning.* Retrieved from http://www.aahe.org/teaching/tsk_frce.html

Kellogg Commission on the Future of State and Land-Grant Universities. (1997). *Returning to our roots: The student experience.* Washington, DC: NASULGC.

Kerr, C. (1990). Higher education cannot escape history: The 1990s. In L. W. Jones & F. A. Nowotny (Eds.), *Agenda for the new decade* (New Directions for Higher Education No. 70, pp. 5–17). San Francisco: Jossey-Bass.

Kolling, A. T. (1998). Student affirmative action and the courts. In D. Gehring (Ed.), *Responding to the new affirmative action climate* (New Directions for Student Services No. 83, pp. 15–31). San Francisco: Jossey-Bass.

Kruger, K. W., & Dungy, G. J. (1999). Opportunities for international travel and professional exchange for student affairs professionals. In J. C. Dalton (Ed.), *Beyond borders: How international developments are changing student affairs practice* (New Directions for Student Services No. 86, 3–11). San Francisco: Jossey-Bass.

Kuh, G. D., Lyons, J., Miller, T. K., & Trow, J. (1995). *Reasonable expectations.* Washington, DC: National Association of Student Personnel Administrators.

Kuh, G. D., Schuh, J. H., Whitt, E. J., & Associates. (1991). *Involving colleges: Successful approaches to fostering student learning and development outside the classroom.* San Francisco: Jossey-Bass.

Leonard, E. A. (1956). *Origins of personnel services in American higher education.* Minneapolis, MN: University of Minnesota Press.

Levine, A., & Cureton, J. S. (1998). *When hope and fear collide: A portrait of today's college students.* San Francisco: Jossey-Bass.

Lloyd-Jones, E. M., & Smith, M. R. (1938). *A student personnel program for higher education.* New York: McGraw-Hill.

Mable, P. (1991). Professional standards: An introduction and historical perspective. In W. A. Bryan, R. B. Winston, Jr., & T. K. Miller (Eds.), *Using professional standards in student affairs* (New Directions for Student Services No. 53, pp. 5–18). San Francisco: Jossey-Bass.

Miller, T. K. (1991). Using standards in professional preparation. In W. A. Bryan, R. B. Winston, Jr., & T. K. Miller (Eds.), *Using professional standards in student affairs* (New Directions for Student Services No. 53, pp. 45–62). San Francisco: Jossey-Bass.

National Association of Student Personnel Administrators. (1987). *A perspective on student affairs.* Washington, DC: Author.

National Association of Student Personnel Administrators. (1992). *Student rights and freedoms: Joint statement on rights and freedoms of students.* Washington, DC: Author.

Nidiffer, J. (2001). Crumbs from the boys' table: The first century of coeducation. In J. Nidiffer & C. T. Bashaw (Eds.), *Women administrators in higher education* (pp. 157–182). Albany, NY: SUNY Press.

Nuss, E. M. (2000). The role of professional associations. In M. J. Barr & M. K. Desler (Eds.), *The handbook of student affairs administration* (2nd ed., pp. 492–507). San Francisco: Jossey-Bass.

Pascarella, E. T., & Terenzini, P. T. (1991). *How college affects students: Findings and insights from twenty years of research.* San Francisco: Jossey-Bass.

Pruitt-Logan, A. S., & Isaac, P. D. (1995). Looking ahead. In A. S. Pruitt-Logan & P. D. Isaac (Eds.), *Student services for the changing graduate student population* (New Directions for Student Services No. 72, pp. 123–128). San Francisco: Jossey-Bass.

Ratliff, R. C. (1972). *Constitutional rights of college students.* Metuchen, NJ: Scarecrow Press.

Rentz, A. L. (Ed.). (1994). *Student affairs: A profession's heritage* (American College Personnel Association Media Publication No. 40, 2nd ed.). Lanham, MD: University Press of America.

Rhatigan, J. J. (1994). Student services vs. student development: Is there a difference? In A. L. Rentz (Ed.), *Student affairs: A profession's heritage* (2nd ed., pp. 438–447). Lanham, MD: American College Personnel Association & University Press of America. (Original work published 1974)

Rhatigan, J. J. (2001). NASPA history. In *NASPA member handbook* (pp. 6–8). Washington, DC: National Association of Student Personnel Administrators.

Rudolph, F. (1965). *The American college and university: A history.* New York: Knopf.

Rudy, W. (1996). *The campus and the nation in crisis.* Teaneck, NJ: Fairleigh Dickinson University Press.

Sheeley, V. L. (1983). NADW and NAAS: 60 years of organizational relationships (NAWDAC-ACPA: 1923–1983). In B. A. Belson & L. E. Fitzgerald (Eds.), *Thus we spoke: ACPA-NAWDAC, 1958–1975* (pp. 179–189). Alexandria, VA: American College Personnel Association.

Sheldon, H. D. (1969). Student life and customs. In L. A. Cremin (Ed.), *American education: Its men, ideas, and institutions.* New York: Arno Press. (Original work published 1901)

Stamatakos, L. (1981). Student affairs progress toward professionalism: Recommendations for action. *Journal of College Student Development, 22,* 105–113.

Stewart, G. M. (1985). *College and university discipline: A moment of reflection, a time for new direction.* Unpublished manuscript, Catholic University of America, Washington, DC.

Strange, C. C. (1994). Student development: The evolution and status of an essential idea. *Journal of College Student Development, 35,* 399–412.

Sturdevant, S. M., & Hayes, H. (1930). *Deans at work: Discussion by eight women deans of various phases of their work.* New York: Harper.

Teachers College. (1914). Columbia University School of Education Announcement. New York: Author.

Traylor, J. G. (1998). *A heritage of service: The history of the National Association of Student Affairs Professionals (NASAP).* Jackson, MS: NASAP.

Upcraft, M. L. (1994). The dilemmas of translating theory to practice. *Journal of College Student Development, 35,* 438–443.

Williamson, E. G. (1961). *Student personnel services in colleges and universities.* New York: McGraw-Hill.

Woodard, D. W., Love, P., & Komives, S. R. (2000). *Leadership and management issues for a new century* (New Directions for Student Services No. 92). San Francisco: Jossey-Bass.

Yoakum, C. S. (1994). Plan for a personnel bureau in educational institutions. In A. L. Rentz (Ed.), *Student affairs: A profession's heritage* (American College Personnel Association Media Publication No. 40, 2nd ed., pp. 4–8). Lanham, MD: University Press of America. (Original work published 1919)

Young, R. B. (2001). A perspective on the values of student affairs and scholarship. *Journal of College Student Development, 42*, 319–337.

CHAPTER FIVE

PHILOSOPHIES AND VALUES GUIDING THE STUDENT AFFAIRS PROFESSION

Robert B. Young

This chapter concerns the philosophies and values that guide student affairs practice. Philosophy does not create new knowledge; it deepens "our understanding [of] the experiences, thoughts, concepts, and activities that make up our lives and that ordinarily escape notice because they are so familiar" (Nagel, 2002, p. 74). In this chapter, philosophy is explored to deepen our understanding of our thoughts and activities as student affairs administrators and educators. The values of practice are explored as well. Values are essences of philosophy that guide our actions in important ways. They provide acorns of understanding while philosophies provide the oaks.

The chapter is organized into three major sections. First, the topic of philosophy is introduced. Four philosophies are described and explored in relationship to higher education and student affairs. None of the philosophies sustains a complete conception of student affairs. In the second section of the chapter, the central values of student affairs are explored. Values of individuation, community, equality, justice, and caring are described. The final section of the chapter concerns the future of student affairs as seen through the lenses of philosophy and values.

Philosophies Relevant to Student Affairs

The entire subject of philosophy could not be addressed in any single chapter, nor need it be. Student affairs is part of higher education, and higher education is focused on just one of the three great interests of philosophy, the truth. The others are beauty and virtue. At one point, truth and virtue were inseparable. During a "premodern" era of philosophy, truth was found in the absolute principles of one's religious faith.

In some religiously oriented colleges, they are still inseparable, but most of higher education has separated the questions of truth from the certainty of faith.

Most of higher education involves "modern" and "postmodern" philosophy. Modern philosophy focuses on logic and evidence. It idealizes objectivity and vilifies subjectivity. Its advocates say that "seeing is believing." Postmodern philosophy emphasizes the subjective context of any object. Its advocates argue that "believing is seeing" (Whitt, Carneghi, Matkin, Scalese-Love, & Nestor, 1990).

Four philosophies are especially important to student affairs practice: rationalism, empiricism, pragmatism, and postmodernism. They are presented in chronological order, from the oldest to the newest.

Rationalism

The rationalist believes that mental ability differentiates humans from other animals. Therefore, the best thinkers are the best human beings, and the sole aim of education is to cultivate reason (Taylor, 1952). Rationalism is rooted in the teachings of Plato and Aristotle, who believed that people must use their reasoning skills to understand moral issues as well as material ones. However, over many centuries, reason has become separated from emotion and morality. The intellect, all by itself, has become the rationalist's definition of being. As Descartes said, "I think, therefore, I am."

Assumptions. Hutchins (1967) summarized the assumptions of rationalist higher education when he wrote: "Education implies teaching. Teaching implies knowledge. Knowledge is truth. The truth is everywhere the same. Hence, education should be everywhere the same" (p. 66). The rationalist believes that universal truths exist, and time reveals which truths endure. The best source of eternal truths, then, is classical literature, because it has passed the test of time.

In the rationalist college, the three Rs are reading, writing, and deductive reasoning. Deduction is the first form of logic and some people think it is the essence of higher learning (Conant, 1964). Eternal truths help us differentiate permanent from transient reality and, thereby, make better decisions.

Institutional Identity. The liberal arts college embodies the purposes and principles of rationalist philosophy. It is a teaching institution and a "community of scholars" that resembles a nuclear family. Scholars hand down the lessons of the ages to youngsters who, when the time comes, will hand down the same knowledge to those who succeed them. The academy is unified in this single purpose.

Practices and Roles. The rationalist college is a teaching and teacher-centered institution, not a learning and learner-centered one. The classical truths are revealed through classical methods of teaching. Faculty have the authority for determining and protecting the truth. Lectures are the means for transmitting information, and Socratic dialogues are the means for debating it. Good students learn how to think better this way; weak students do not. The intellectual elite is supposed to prevail in this kind of higher education and, eventually, in life itself.

Relationship to Student Affairs. Faculty in rationalist colleges want student affairs administrators to identify capable students, attract them to campus, help them read better, and discipline any "who may cause ripples in the academic serenity that is so necessary to the study of universal truths and values" (Lloyd-Jones, 1952, p. 215). In the rationalist institution, student affairs administrators are subservient to faculty, and student services are extracurricular and, therefore, unessential (Knock, Rentz, & Penn, 1989).

However, the classical liberal arts also embrace many of the purposes of student affairs practice. Boyer (1995) declared that student affairs maintained the ideals of the colonial teaching college within the modern research university, and, by implication, it provided the general education that research faculty had abandoned. Boyer (1987) believed that student affairs helped students learn how to "become personally empowered and also committed to the common good" (p. 69). In Boyer's conception of the teaching college, the development of reason goes hand in hand with the development of ethical behavior. Discipline in this college is not just punishment, but a means to develop character (Rhatigan, 1978).

Empiricism

Empiricism has shattered the myth that scientific knowledge is fundamentally whole and one. This was the first "truth" of rationalist higher education, this wholeness of knowledge that a university stands for (Conant, 1964). Empiricism has focused on the acquisition of knowledge in many different specialized areas. As the term "empirical" means "under test," truth is attached to statements that agree with the observed facts of sensory life. The value of any truth is proportionate to the amount of evidence that supports it.

Assumptions. Empirical higher education emphasizes inductive instead of deductive reasoning. Induction forms principles from collections of facts and calls them probable instead of certain. Two kinds of truths are considered empirical, those that can be verified by experience and those that help analyze experience. The first involve sensory data while the second involve theories, mathematical formulae, and the like. The first led to scientific research. The second led to logical positivism. Logical positivism holds that all metaphysical, ethical, and poetic concepts are meaningless because they cannot be verified through science. They are pseudoconcepts that arouse emotion but lack cognitive significance. Subjectivistic, relativistic, and ultimately arbitrary, these pseudoconcepts cannot be validated, only asserted (Sloan, 1980).

Institutional Identity. Empiricists believe that the classical, liberal arts curriculum belongs in schools or in colleges, whereas true "higher" education is only found in the research university. In a commentary about colleges, character, and jazz, Martin (1982) compared the empirical university to trumpeter Miles Davis and the rationalist college to pianist Oscar Peterson. The empirical university is like Miles Davis, bent on discovering new modes of expression that might be on the outer edge of musical taste. In contrast, the rationalist college is like Oscar Peterson, who does not invent music;

he interprets it. The rationalist college interprets the classics but it does not change them in any fundamental way.

Practices and Roles. "Pure" scientific research is the most prized role for faculty to perform in the research university. Teaching takes a back seat. It supports research by training incoming generations of scholars and scientists; teaching for other purposes is best done elsewhere. As in the rationalist college, good students are those who reason logically, observe carefully, and make good decisions about what they find. However, the content of instruction is much less certain, not time-tested, and seldom universal in its message.

Relationship to Student Affairs. During the early 1950s, the term "neohumanism" was used to describe the empirical philosophy of higher education as applied to student affairs. Lloyd-Jones (1952) noted, "How vastly extended is personnel work in institutions dominated by neo-humanists beyond the scope of such work in institutions dominated by the rationalists!" (p. 218). But Lloyd-Jones was concerned: student affairs programs might be quantitatively greater, but their educational function was fragmented. Faculty cultivated intelligence in the classroom and left everything else to be tilled by student affairs specialists. The aggregation of intellectual and nonintellectual focuses was supposed to yield "inner unity and harmony" (Lloyd-Jones & Smith, 1954, p. 11), but what resulted instead was excessive organization and specialization. Student affairs programs became elaborate, extensive, and independent of the curriculum (Lloyd-Jones, 1952).

Empiricism supports a functional point of view of student affairs, a philosophy of student services or what Blimling (2001) called an "administration orientation." Hundreds of articles about student affairs management and at least one philosophical treatise, the *Perspective on Student Affairs* (Plan for a New Century Committee, 1987), have supported an empirical approach to student affairs. This has spawned new administrative practices and scientific accountability. Services are specialized, and their value is measured by their size as well as their purpose. The advocates of specialized, large, administrative services acknowledge that their efforts might be ancillary in the empirical academy, but they also argue—and with accuracy—that student services are given greater support when scientific means are used to justify their existence.

Pragmatism

Pragmatic truth is what works. William James said, "True ideas are those that we can assimilate, validate, corroborate, and verify. False ideas are those that we cannot" (Boller, 1980, p. 263).

Pragmatism is the child of empiricism and it shares its parent's distrust of thought without observation. But traditional empiricism looks backward, for the causes of ideas, while pragmatism looks forward, to their impact on experience. Dewey (1938/1971) wrote: "To know the meaning of empiricism we need to understand what experience is" (p. 25). The origin, logic, and elegance of an idea are secondary to its practical outcomes.

The character of this forward thinking, results-oriented philosophy is profoundly American. The key philosophers of pragmatism, Charles Peirce, James, and Dewey were Americans who took ideas from other Americans, such as Benjamin Franklin and Ralph Waldo Emerson. Dewey said that the roots of pragmatism might be European, but the philosophy was raised in American soil, in the context of our society.

Pragmatism contends that people deserve respect for what they are and will become; concepts, facts, aims, and values are validated by their practical consequences; knowledge is whole and dynamic; and people have the potential for growth "toward cooperative ways of living, thinking, and acting" (Taylor, 1952, p. 37)

Assumptions. Pragmatic education is individually constructed. The learner's experience is the center of the educational process, but experience by itself is not necessarily educational; it has to be contemplated and reconstructed in order to increase a person's ability to direct subsequent experiences (Brubacher, 1962). Dewey (1938/1971) wrote that there was no tenet of pragmatic, progressive education that was "sounder than its emphasis upon the importance of the participation of the learner in the formation of the purposes which direct his activities in the learning process, just as there is no defect in traditional education greater than its failure to secure the active cooperation of the pupil in construction of the purposes involved in his studying" (p. 67). Experience became educational when it met the conditions of interaction and continuity. Experience had to interact with a person's inner thoughts and social behavior, and it had to have an impact on the good life. Lifelong learning is implicit in this conception of educational experience (Border, 1999).

Institutional Identity. Pragmatic philosophy is the foundation of the state university, where the curriculum is no longer bound to the liberal arts and participation no longer restricted to intellectuals (Taylor, 1970). Pragmatism supports the comprehensive community college, as well. At both institutions, people are taught what they must know in order to live in modern society. The curriculum contains those studies and fosters those experiences that are significant to individual lives and, at the same time, relevant to the needs of society. This does not exclude the classics, but it demands a test of their impact on human betterment.

Practices and Roles. In the pragmatic institution, empirical knowledge is no longer an end in itself; knowledge is measured by its benefits to students and the social order. The preferred form of research is "applied" instead of "pure," because it offers tangible rewards for institutions and society (Bahm, 1980).

The student in the pragmatic institution is no longer a passive receptacle of knowledge, but the central factor in a learner-centered environment. Faculty are supposed to provide courses that students want to take, instead of the courses that they want to teach. Likewise, teaching focuses on learning instead of the activities of the instructor.

Relation to Student Affairs. Pragmatism has been widely accepted in our field. Lloyd-Jones and Smith (1954) wrote: "The [pragmatic] philosophy, much more than that of rationalism or neo-humanism, seems to represent the principles in which student personnel workers have protested they believe (p. 12).

The acceptance of this philosophy was a matter of place and timing as well as principle. Pragmatism was ascending in American thought just as student affairs practice was becoming a specialization in higher education. Cowley (1936) called pragmatism the "torch" that student affairs professionals brought back to the academy, to enlighten rationalist faculty who valued only the student's mind. The torch was lit by two of the primary philosophers of pragmatism, William James and John Dewey. Each had direct contact with many pioneers of student affairs administration. James influenced several prominent deans of men, including LeBaron Russell Briggs, the first Dean of Men at Harvard. Dewey influenced many deans of women when he taught at the University of Chicago and Columbia University.

The tenets of pragmatism were written into the seminal documents of student affairs. The 1937 Student Personnel Point of View [SPPOV] (American Council on Education, 1937) confirmed the ideas that the student was whole, that each was a unique individual, and that programs should be based on student needs instead of those of rationalist professors. The 1949 SPPOV (American Council on Education, 1949) asserted that the central concern of student affairs work was "the development of students as whole persons interacting in social situations" (p. 122). In 1954, Lloyd-Jones and Smith (1954) offered four "common beliefs" about student affairs: belief in the worth of the individual; belief in the equal dignity of thinking and feeling and working; belief that the world has a place for everybody; and belief that what an individual gathers from his experiences continues on in time—"it is not what is imposed, but what is absorbed that persists" (p. 5). The fourth belief restates Dewey's concept of continuity.

Postmodernism

Postmodernism is a term that has been applied to existentialism, phenomenology, structuralism, deconstruction, poststructuralism, and other philosophies that became popular in the twentieth century. "Continental Philosophy" is another name for them, because French and German philosophers have dominated postmodern thinking. Some of these philosophies differ significantly from others, but all question the assumptions of modernism. They challenge established forms of thinking, objectivity, and concepts of progress.

Like pragmatists, postmodernists center experience in the human context, but they contend that individuality is deeply related to social power, and "one of the privileges of dominant group status is the luxury to simply see oneself as an individual . . . [whereas] those in subordinated groups . . . can never fully escape being defined by their social group memberships" (Adams, Bell, & Griffin, 1997, p. 9).

Some of the tenets of postmodernism are:

1. There is no objective, permanent world "out there"; everything is subjective and relative.

2. Therefore, knowledge does not exist without context.
3. Because everything is contextual, caring is an essential characteristic of the human condition, and caring can range from simple interest in others to deep solicitude for them.
4. The repetition of words, structures, and actions creates a false sense of their objectivity and universality.
5. This false objectivity sustains economic, political, and social hegemony.
6. The apparent structures built by repetition need to be deconstructed to reveal their subjective essence.
7. This revelation cannot come through purely intellectual means; truth is revealed intuitively.

Postmodernism is very attractive to members of subcultures, because no group has objective superiority over another. Derrida (1982) created the term *différance* to capture his belief that absolutes do not exist in language (or in culture); one must defer to the basic reality of differences.

Assumptions. In 1971, Illich summarized the premises of postmodernist education. It "should provide all who want to learn with access to available resources at any time in their lives; empower all who want to share what they know to find those who want to learn it from them; and, finally, furnish all who want to present an issue to the public with the opportunity to make their challenge known" (p. 76). Illich added, "Learners should not be forced to submit to an obligatory curriculum, or to discrimination based on whether they possess a certificate or a diploma. Nor should the public be forced to support, through a regressive taxation, a huge professional apparatus of educators and buildings, which in fact restricts the public's chances for learning to the services the profession is willing to put on the market. It should use modern technology to make free speech, free assembly, and a free press truly universal and, therefore, fully educational" (p. 76). Although Illich was writing about deschooling society, it can be assumed that he wanted to decollege it as well.

Postmodernism favors socially constructed education (over societal systems of education), lifelong learning (over time-bound classes), informal experiences (over formal ones), and multicultural education (over melting-pot education). Group reflection and activity are important. Relationships within and across groups are raised to consciousness, deconstructed, and reconstructed, often with the goal of political and social transformation.

Institutional Identity. For more than thirty years, futurists (such as Ferguson, 1980; Naisbitt, 1990; Toffler, 1970) have predicted a revolution in information technology that would demand an equivalent revolution in leadership and relationships. Today technology has made knowledge available to almost anyone, anytime, anywhere. Computers cost a few hundred dollars; the home, the library, and the residence hall are wired to the Internet, and the virtual university has arrived.

In the virtual university, students and faculty can be partners in a knowledge culture that does not have to be located on any ivied campus. Consumer-students take a course here and a course there and sum the aggregate into a degree program. Professor-entrepreneurs might have no regular contract at any institution. Students take courses at their convenience, fitting study around the demands of the rest of their lives, and professors post notes on-line and at their convenience.

Roles and Practices. Since faculty no longer own knowledge and form a superior culture of intellect in postmodern higher education, learning is emphasized instead of teaching, the educational process begins from the ground up instead of the top down, and peer-based learning communities become the ideal.

The revolution in learning relationships profoundly affects activities and roles on residential campuses. Faculty and students do not identify with the institution, but with subcultures instead. The institution is anarchical—fluid, with unclear goals, and an absence of leadership, goals, and rationality (Birnbaum, 1988)—and symbolic, appearing to be whole only on football weekend or when a tragedy occurs (Bolman & Deal, 1991).

Subcultures prevail. Sometimes they build respect for each other. At other times, they war with each other, and no super-ordinate Truth can rein them in. Faculty unite against administrators, chemistry professors against English faculty, Asian American students against Latinos: "it's a ___ thing, you wouldn't understand," because "you" are the "other" and cannot understand the norms and history of "my" context.

Relation to Student Affairs. Postmodernist assumptions have affected student affairs since the new majority of Americans entered the academy in the 1960s. Those students were legal adults, no longer children to be formed by Alma Mater. In loco parentis was out; students consumed higher education and were ready to judge the benefits they got from the learning they bought.

Legal rights have meant that the roles of students and staff have been put into contracts; every right and responsibility has been defined in logical and linear terms. Distinctions between educational discipline systems and legal proceedings have been blurred, and professional actions have been tempered by an ever-present threat of litigation.

In the early 1960s, inclusion meant the integration of African American students on predominantly White campuses. In contrast, postmodern programming emphasizes the distinctive identities of women, GLBT students, Latinos, and other cultural groups. Programming decisions are not made on the basis of financial control or even majority rule. These are artifacts of oppression instead of symbols of democracy in action.

Universities have lured students with the promise of technology, and students are using it in unanticipated ways. Chat rooms have replaced late evening bull sessions, and "you've got mail" substitutes for sticky notes on the door of one's room. Communities are forged across campuses and cultures that have no connection to the enrollment of any student. Ivy still clings to the brick of old buildings, but students are aggregating, not congregating, inside them. The ideal of residential life is jeopardized. So are the other models of human interaction that our practice tries so hard to implement.

Where Does Student Affairs Fit?

Student affairs identifies most with pragmatism and postmodernism, philosophies that are grounded in the human experience. However, it is impossible to position a complete student affairs philosophy within any one of these four philosophies, just as it is impossible to find all of higher education in one and only one of them. Each of the philosophies has influenced higher education and student affairs. Research and student services are justified using empirical, scientific methods. Teaching, learning, and advising reflect rationalistic, pragmatic, and postmodern ideas.

Perhaps it is impossible to find—or create—an entire philosophy or higher education and student affairs within these conceptions of knowledge because philosophies of knowledge relate to the *idea* of the institution and student affairs, but they do not address higher education and student affairs as *temporal* entities, as political, social, and economic institutions and functions. Only pragmatism and postmodernism seem very engaged with human contexts that extend beyond the ivory tower. Thus, philosophies of higher education and student affairs might never be complete without engaging the philosophies connected to the economic, political, and social contexts that they are part of.

The next section looks at specific values for more information and guidance about the student affairs profession. The intention is to deconstruct the philosophies, examine the values that seem most important, and then reconstruct the values into systems of meaning and action.

Values

Values are abstract ideals that are centrally located within our belief system and tell us how we ought to behave (Rokeach, 1976). They can be instrumental or intrinsic. Instrumental values govern how people make decisions and take action. Intrinsic values represent desirable end-states, the goals of a good life. Higher education and student affairs are instruments of society; therefore their values are instrumental more than intrinsic.

Some values are recognized consciously; they serve as personal mission statements, but many values lie beneath the surface of knowing, guiding activities such as teaching, counseling, and administration through a subconscious ideology (Rogers, 1989). To illustrate: a resident assistant might provide counseling to a student at three in the morning because she values caring more than getting good grades. However, she might not be aware of this priority until she is asked why she missed class the next day. The purpose of this section is to bring some of those values into consciousness.

Two topics will be explored here: the values revealed in the discussion of philosophies, and the values that seem to be most important to the field of student affairs.

Values in the Philosophies

Rationalism, empiricism, pragmatism, and postmodernism concerned the value of truth, but they described it in very different ways. Rationalism viewed truth as unitary, abstract, and absolute. Empiricism and pragmatism found truth through temporal facts, facts about the causes of things or about the consequences of action. Postmodernism viewed truth as fragmented, subjective, and relativistic.

Rationalism values freedom, intellectual excellence, deductive reasoning, tradition, teaching, and individual responsibility. Empiricism advocates freedom, tolerance, research, and inductive powers. Both are confident that objective truth can be known, either through revelation or through an indisputable preponderance of evidence.

Pragmatism and postmodernism relate the search for truth to the human context, to individuals in relation to knowledge and each other. Pragmatism begins with the individual, and postmodernism begins with subjective contexts—others and differences before selves and similarities. The development of the individual in society is central to pragmatism, as is the service that higher education can perform by building human experience. Action is as important as insight; pragmatism values the integration of knowledge over mere intellectual apprehension. Postmodernism takes a more active social stance, calling for mutual empowerment and caring through an understanding and reconstruction of contextual experience.

All these values affect student affairs practice and some are embraced by it, primarily the values found in pragmatism and postmodernism. Other values seem to oppose student affairs practice while guiding academic behaviors, primarily the values that are central to rationalism and empiricism. What follows next is a discussion of the central values of student affairs.

Examining the Values of Student Affairs Practice

The values of student affairs practice have been derived from reviews of practices, surveys of practitioners, and studies of historical documents (such as Barr, 1987; Brown & Krager, 1985; Dalton & Healy, 1984; Evans & Reason, 2001; Sandeen, 1985; Upcraft, 1988; Young, 1993; Young & Elfrink, 1991). The resulting values usually focus on individuals, their context, and caring. The values of individuals include wholeness, uniqueness, experience, and responsibility. Values of the context include community, equality, and justice. Caring links individuals to their context. Caring is an instrumental value as well as a goal of practice.

Individuation: Human Dignity Growing

Sometimes referred to as human dignity (Young & Elfrink, 1991), individuation is respect for the person growing. It is the understanding that a college student is supposed to find a meaningful identity. Gardner (1961) has summarized the traditional conception of this value: "What we must reach for is a conception of . . . one's best self, to be the person one could be. This is a conception that far exceeds formal education in scope. It includes not only the intellect but also the emotions, character, and personality. It involves not only the surface, but deeper layers of thought and action" (p. 136). Individuals are whole, unique, and responsible; their experience is the measure of their education and the source of student affairs programs.

The Whole Individual. In an analysis of major student affairs documents, Evans and Reason (2001) found that the most prevalent and foundational concept was "the notion that the 'whole' student must be considered in every educational endeavor" (p. 370). In 1924, the first Dean of Men at Columbia, Herbert Hawkes, said that his college "should educate the whole [student] . . . the physical, the social, the aesthetic, the religious, the intellectual aspects, each in its appropriate manner" (Fley, 1980, p. 42). Thirteen years later, the 1937 SPPOV included the attributes of intellectual capacity, emotions, physical condition, social relationships, vocational skills, moral and religious values, economic resources, and aesthetic appreciations. Cowley created the word "holoism" to capture this conviction that an individual reacts in any situation as a totally integrated person (Lloyd-Jones, 1952).

The Unique Individual. Uniqueness is built on difference, and Evans and Reason (2001) remarked, "respect for individual differences is a second long-standing value of the profession" (p. 370). Clothier (1931) said that individual differences were a major tenet of the profession, but he did not invent this idea. Differentiation is a fact of science and a dictum of philosophy (Lloyd-Jones & Smith, 1938). Each student is a being in the process of becoming, a singularity, someone who cannot be duplicated.

The Experiencing Individual. This might be the fundamental value of pragmatic philosophy, and it has been affirmed in many documents about student affairs work. For example, the authors of the 1937 SPPOV claimed that student programming must reflect the needs of students to *do* and to *be.* An adequate student affairs program must be "fully as concerned with the art of living as it is with the more utilitarian aspects of education. It must concern itself with the student as he is at present, with the sort of design for living that he is working out for himself *right now*" (Lloyd-Jones & Smith, 1954, p. 8).

The Responsible Individual. Evans and Reason (2001) wrote that the third most important, student-oriented value of student affairs was "assisting students to develop a sense of agency" (p. 372). The 1949 SPPOV declared that students are responsible participants in their development instead of passive recipients of knowledge and skills. Individual development was linked to responsibility; freedom must be disciplined for the fulfillment of human dignity. Thomas Arkle Clark was blunt about this. He thought that there was no place in college for loafers. Character was developed by "doing things difficult enough to cut lines in a [person's] soul" (Fley, 1979, p. 32).

Contextual Values

In 1954, Lloyd-Jones and Smith decried the ways that student affairs was emulating large, impersonal, specialized organizations: "The problem becomes one of how students and staff can work together to improve their community . . . to examine together how their human relationships may be improved and strengthened so as to contribute to total growth for each member" (p. 340). One of the eleven student needs listed in the 1949 SPPOV was "a sense of belonging to the college" (p. 128). Students must find a role in relation to others that will make them feel valued, contribute to their feelings of self-worth, and contribute to a feeling of kinship with others.

Community. Community is explored in depth in Chapter Twenty-Five, so it is described only briefly here. As a value, community is an organic conception of social relationships, a few steps up from the family. The organic academy involves students with each other, faculty, and administrators; it is a reflection of students, an extension of students, and a resource for their self-realization (Fisher & Noble, 1960). Early conceptions of community were homogeneous, reflecting the hegemony of elite, private, liberal arts education, but in recent years, the conceptions have embraced diverse communities on campuses and within the totality of American society (Martin, 1994).

No matter its size, an educational community must be mutually empowering, and the 1949 SPPOV reminded everyone on campus, especially faculty, of the need to *mutually* empower students. In their review of historical documents, Evans and Reason (2001) noted that student affairs professionals were supposed to collaborate with faculty and to "serve as co-instructors and program providers to carry out learning initiatives and to build *learning communities*" [emphasis added] (pp. 373–374).

Equality. Early conceptions of the value of equality involved individual talents. Educating the whole student meant that character was as important as the mind. During the past fifty years, however, the value of equality has stressed the status of groups in colleges and the broader culture. Thus, it is presented as a contextual value of student affairs.

Unfortunately, in its own history, the field of student affairs did not treat women and men equally. Deans of Women had to fight for equal recognition with Deans of Men; they fought even harder for the rights of women students. However, the field came to embrace the rights of women as well as equal rights for other disadvantaged groups. The civil rights movement had a major impact on the student affairs profession (Hammond, 1981; Sandeen, 1985). Student affairs professionals bore responsibility toward the "broad spectrum of persons who can profit from post- secondary education" (p. 392), presumably without bias, because "the potential for development and self-direction is possessed by everyone" (Council of Student Personnel Associations, 1975, p. 393).

Justice. Justice is intertwined with equality. Vlastos (1962) wrote: "The great historic struggles for social justice have centered about some demand for equal rights: the struggle against slavery, political absolutism, economic exploitation, the disfranchisement of the lower and middle classes and the disfranchisement of women, colonialism, racial oppression" (p. 31). To illustrate, in 1991, Evans and Wall wrote *Beyond Tolerance: Lesbians, Gays, and Bisexuals on Campus.* The title of the book was a declaration; equality required action if LGBT students were to be treated fairly. Nine years later, Wall and Evans (2000) wrote *Toward Acceptance: Sexual Orientation Issues on Campus.* The title reaffirmed the need for action as much as insight about equal rights.

Justice means fairness, which can be achieved by procedural, distributive, or corrective means. The first type relates to laws, the second to opportunities, and the last to the redress of social inequities. Procedural justice is easiest to implement because it is based on specific legal processes. Distributive justice takes more effort, for example, revising general education courses to be more representative. Corrective justice involves the sacrifice of some goods for the benefit of others who need them. It is much more difficult to implement, and prone to charges of reverse discrimination, but "rectification is the chief task of the fair and the just or at least of those who are institutionally constrained to be so. It is the least one can do, and far less than most of humanity can hope for" (Shklar, 1984, p. 31).

While it has been convenient to separate justice and caring in developmental psychology, the values are connected, especially in the case of corrective justice. Sanford (1980) wrote, without some "minimum of caring and being cared for, justice will not become an important value" (p. 202). Corrective justice is a way of caring above and beyond the strictures of law, for example, to provide affirmative programs for oppressed minority groups.

Caring. The value is called caring in this chapter, in recognition of its role and definition in postmodernist philosophy. Postmodernist philosophy includes two notions of caring, and while both are evident in student affairs, the field has emphasized caring as concern for human betterment over benign attention to one's context. Altruism is another name for this sort of caring, and Sandeen (1985) and Young and Elfrink (1991) have called altruism an essential value of the student affairs profession. Altruism is defined as primarily selfless service to others; thus "service" is another name for the value of caring.

Caring is a means for action and a goal for living. The value is manifested through student affairs functions and ethical behavior. It is something we do, but caring is also a value that student affairs professionals try to develop in students. For example, service to society has been a traditional focus of the field.

Service and Services. Caring underlies the fundamental mission of student affairs and of institutions of higher education: to serve. Many faculty view truth as the highest value of higher education, but some administrators argue that society supports institutions of higher education because seeking and sharing truth are important social services. In a democratic society, the truth "shall make you free." Service makes scholarship a moral enterprise instead of an amoral one; it makes truth an instrumental value instead of an abstract ideal.

Service is the value behind the provision of student services. In 1954, Lloyd-Jones and Smith extolled *Student Personnel Work as Deeper Teaching.* The authors assailed the way that student affairs had come to be thought of as a collection of services and they wanted "to set forth the view that student personnel workers should not so much be expert technicians as they should be educators in a somewhat unconventional and new sense" (p. 7). Summarized, that sense was a collaborative service function, to provide "teachers of subject matter" (p. 13) with information about their students—when, where, and how they find significant experiences inside and outside the classroom.

Caring-Based Ethics. Canon and Brown (1985) have promoted the development of caring-based ethics in student affairs practice. Caring-based ethics is sometimes called *virtue ethics,* to differentiate it from approaches based only on logic. Those approaches emphasize the rules or outcomes of ethical behavior. Caring-based ethics require information about the context and care for the parties involved in the context, exploring the values, situation, and characteristics of the parties involved (Fried, 1997). In addition, caring-based ethics "relies on the character and judgment of the agent in addressing particular problems in specific contexts" (Fried, 1997, p. 14). Personality is at least as important as principle. Caring-based ethics are intuitive instead of normative, ethnically persistent (Cortese, 1990), and consistent with postmodern theories (Lisman, 1996).

Students Caring for Society. Evans and Reason (2001) determined that the historical documents of our field supported the value of student service to society. This value was promoted "most adamant[ly]" (p. 374) by the authors of the 1949 SPPOV, but it was reaffirmed as recently as 1997 in the ACPA/NASPA *Principles of Good Practice.*

What's Next?

No one can step outside personal experience to describe an objective philosophy or set of values, and no one can step outside time to construct a permanent one. Morrill (1981) said that "there are no enduring and general, no absolute or universal, standards for human conduct. Whatever standards exist are tied to special conditions, relative to particular times, places, and cultures" (p. 59). The philosophies and values of student affairs represent the social context in which administrators have practiced their craft. Future social priorities will alter our ideas and beliefs as surely as they alter our work.

The temporary and subjective nature of philosophy has led some to argue that student affairs does not need to develop a definitive philosophy. Whitt et al. (1990) noted the continuing quest for student affairs to develop its own philosophy, and they questioned the validity of the quest to find a unified philosophy in postmodern times. The same conclusion was reached by Blimling (2001) who argued: "Student affairs is no longer a unitary concept. It has matured into four distinct communities of practice that overlap, at times conflict, but coexist. . . . I challenge student affairs practitioners to understand and use aspects of all communities of practice, but to find a home and a professional center by adopting one" (p. 395).

If postmodernism is adopted as the center of the profession's philosophy, even temporarily, then student affairs will be challenged as much as it is comforted by this choice. Postmodernism is a "paradigm [that] embodies chaos, context, unpredictability and irreversibility of change" (Fried, 1997, p. 9); thus it is difficult to tell how it might shape our field. Postmodernism might promote dynamic social agency or it might be a mere mélange of ideas that "assumes a transgressive role only in its disquieting excess, and not because it has established the grounds for a project based on the referents of social justice and cultural struggle" (Kanpol & McLaren, 1995, p. 3).

Some student affairs practitioners will work to develop a "praxis of emancipation" (Kanpol & McLaren, 1995, p. 4), a philosophy to support social reform within the institution and beyond it. Perhaps they will attain their goal, or perhaps they will become dispirited by the atomism, nihilism, and chaos that postmodernism carries with it (Tierney, 1989). At this point, no one knows. Eventually, however, all professionals will have to decide how much student affairs should try to promote the philosophical and scientific traditions of higher education and how much it should try to win "the minds and hearts of people to a different set of goals for education—an education that is explicitly linked to the transformation of the social and cultural reality in which we live" (Shapiro, 1995, p. 33).

The Future of Values

What do we do in the meantime? It is hard to imagine that the values of community, individuation, and caring will disappear even if their philosophical foundations are transformed. Any period of time might focus more on the individual or the community (Levine, 1980), but the focus is never exclusionary; ultimately, each value nurtures the other. The educational importance of the individual or the community is not reduced, even if postmodernism has changed the appearance of each value from a unitary and permanent concept to something that is more diverse and open ended (Kanpol & McLaren, 1995).

Earlier, the analogy was made that philosophies provide the oaks of understanding, and values, the acorns. It might be equally apt to say that philosophies are the roots, and values, the flowers. One of the definitions of values is as desired end-states (Rokeach, 1976). The flower is the end-state of the root, its visible expression above the surface, while the roots struggle in the soil below.

St. Exupery (1939) bemoaned the fact that there were gardeners of flowers but no equivalent gardeners of human potential, who would isolate the roses of humanity, tend them, and foster them. Student affairs serves this purpose on college campuses. It tends to the flowers, the human values and valued humans that stand above the roots of thought. By nurturing the flowers, it invigorates the roots. As Dewey (1934) wrote: "Ours is the responsibility of conserving, transmitting, rectifying, and expanding the heritage of values we have received that those that come after us may receive it more solid and secure, more widely accessible and more generously shared than we have received it" (p. 87).

References

Adams, M., Bell, L. A., & Griffin, P. (Eds.). (1997). *Teaching for diversity and social justice: A sourcebook.* New York: Routledge.

American College Personnel Association/National Association of Student Personnel Administrators. (1997). *Principles of good practice.* Retrieved May 1, 2002, from http://www.acpa.nche.edu/pgp/principle.htm

American Council on Education. (1937). The student personnel point of view. Reprinted in G. Saddlemire & A. Rentz (Eds.) (1986), *Student affairs: A profession's heritage* (pp. 74–88). Media Publication, 40. Alexandria, VA: American College Personnel Association.

American Council on Education. (1949). The student personnel point of view. Reprinted in G. Saddlemire, & A. Rentz (Eds.) (1986), *Student affairs: A profession's heritage* (pp. 122–136). Media Publication, 40. Alexandria, VA: American College Personnel Association.

Bahm, A. (1980). *Axiology: The science of values.* Albuquerque, NM: World Books.

Barr, M. J. (1987). Individual and institutional integrity. *NASPA Journal, 24,* 2–6.

Birnbaum, R. (1988). *How colleges work: The cybernetics of academic organization and leadership.* San Francisco: Jossey-Bass.

Blimling, G. (2001). Uniting scholarship and communities of practice in student affairs. *Journal of College Student Development, 42,* 381–396.

Boller, P. (1980). William James as an educator: Individualism and democracy. In D. Sloan (Ed.), *Education and Values* (pp. 255–269). New York: Teachers College Press.

Bolman, L. G., & Deal, T. E. (1991). *Reframing organizations: Artistry, choice, and leadership.* San Francisco: Jossey-Bass.

Border, L. L. (1999). Taking diversity seriously: New developments in teaching for diversity. In M. Svinicki (Ed.), *Teaching and learning on the edge of the millennium: Building on what we have learned* (New Directions for Teaching and Learning No. 80, pp. 83–89). San Francisco: Jossey-Bass.

Boyer, E. L. (1987). *College: The undergraduate experience in America.* New York: Harper & Row.

Boyer, E. L. (1995). *Scholarship reconsidered: Priorities of the professorate.* Teleconference: National University Telecommunications Network.

Brown, R., & Krager, L. (1985). Ethical issues in higher education. *Journal of Higher Education, 56,* 403–418.

Brubacher, J. (Ed.). (1962). *Eclectic philosophy of education: A book of readings.* Englewood Cliffs, NJ: Prentice-Hall.

Canon, H., & Brown, R. (1985). How to think about professional ethics. In H. Canon & R. Brown (Eds.), *Applied ethics in student services* (New Directions for Student Services No. 30, pp. 81–87). San Francisco: Jossey-Bass.

Clothier, R. C. (1931). College personnel principles and functions. Reprinted in G. Saddlemire & A. Rentz (Eds.) (1986), *Student affairs: A profession's heritage* (pp. 9–20). Media Publication, 40. Alexandria: American College Personnel Association.

Conant, J. (1964). *Two modes of thought: My encounters with science and education.* New York: Trident Press.

Cortese, A. (1990). *Ethnic ethics: The restructuring of moral theory.* Albany, NY: SUNY Press.

Council of Student Personnel Associations. (1975). Student development services in post-secondary education. Reprinted in G. Saddlemire & A. Rentz (Eds.) (1986), *Student affairs: A profession's heritage* (pp. 390–401). Media Publication, 40. Alexandria: American College Personnel Association.

Cowley, W. H. (1936). The nature of student personnel work. Reprinted in G. Saddlemire & A. Rentz (Eds.) (1986), *Student affairs: A profession's heritage* (pp. 47–73). Media Publication, 40. Alexandria: American College Personnel Association.

Dalton, J., & Healy, M. (1984). Using values education activities to confront student conduct issues. *NASPA Journal, 22,* 19–25.

Derrida, J. (1982). *Différance.* In J. Derrida (Ed.), *Margins of Philosophy* (pp. 3–27). Chicago: The University of Chicago Press.

Dewey, J. (1934). *A common faith.* New Haven, CT: Yale University Press.

Dewey, J. (1971). *Experience and education.* New York: Collier. (Original work published 1938)

Evans, N., & Wall, V. (Eds.). (1991). *Beyond tolerance: Gays, lesbians, and bisexuals on campus.* Washington, DC: American College Personnel Association.

Evans, N. J., & Reason, R. D. (2001). Guiding principles: A review and analysis of student affairs philosophical statements. *Journal of College Student Development, 42,* 359–377.

Ferguson, M. (1980). *The aquarian conspiracy.* Los Angeles: Tarcher.

Fisher, M. B., & Noble, J. L. (1960). *College education as personal development.* Englewood Cliffs, NJ: Prentice Hall.

Fley, J. (1979). Student personnel pioneers: Those who developed our profession. *NASPA Journal, 17,* 23–39.

Fley, J. (1980). Student personnel pioneers: Those who developed our profession. *NASPA Journal, 17,* 25–44.

Fried, J. (1997). Changing ethical frameworks for a multicultural world. In J. Fried (Ed.), *Ethics for today's campus: New perspectives on education, student development, and institutional management.* (New Directions for Student Services No. 77, pp. 5–21). San Francisco: Jossey-Bass.

Gardner, J. (1961). *Excellence.* New York: Harper & Row.

Hammond, E. (1981). The new student-institutional relationship: Its impact on student affairs administration. *NASPA Journal, 19,* 17–21.

Hutchins, R. M. (1967). *The higher learning in America.* New Haven, CT: Yale University Press.

Illich, I. (1971). *Deschooling society.* New York: Harper & Row.

Kanpol, B., & McLaren, P. (1995). *Critical multiculturalism: Uncommon voices in a common struggle* (pp. 1–13). Westport, CT: Bergin & Garvey.

Knock, G., Rentz, A., & Penn, R. (1989). Our philosophical heritage: Significant influences on professional practice and preparation. *NASPA Journal, 27,* 116–121.

Levine, A. (1980). *When dreams and heroes died: A portrait of today's college students.* San Francisco: Jossey-Bass.

Lisman, C. D. (1996). *The curricular integration of ethics: Theory and practice.* Westport, CT: Praeger.

Lloyd-Jones, E. (1952). Personnel work and general education, In *Yearbook on general education* (pp. 214–229). Chicago: National Society for the Study of Education.

Lloyd-Jones, E. M., & Smith, M. R. (1938). *A student personnel program for higher education.* New York: McGraw Hill.

Lloyd-Jones, E. M., & Smith, M. R. (1954). *Student personnel work as deeper teaching.* New York: Harper and Brothers.

Martin, W. B. (1982). *A college of character.* San Francisco: Jossey-Bass.

Martin, W. B. (1994). *Complex choices, cultural pluralism and college values: An essay on diversity and vitality in higher education.* Nashville, TN: United Methodist Board of Higher Education and Ministry, Occasional papers, *91.*

Morrill, R. (1981). *Teaching values in college.* San Francisco: Jossey-Bass.

Nagel, T. (2002, April 11). In the stream of consciousness. *The New York Review,* pp. 74–76.

Naisbitt, J., & Aburdene, P. (1990). *Megatrends 2000: Ten new directions for the 1990s.* New York: Morrow.

Plan for a New Century Committee. (1987). *A perspective on student affairs.* Washington, DC: National Association of Student Personnel Administrators.

Rhatigan, J. (1978). There was almost no chapter on discipline. In J. Appleton, C. Briggs, & J. Rhatigan (Eds.), *Pieces of eight: The rites, roles, and styles of the dean by eight who have been there* (pp. 99–104). Portland, OR: NASPA Institute for Research and Development.

Rogers, W. (1989). Values in higher education. In D. Mitchell (Ed.), *Values in teaching and professional ethics* (pp. 1–14). Macon, GA: Mercer University Press.

Rokeach, M. (1976). *Beliefs, attitudes, and values: A theory of organizational change.* San Francisco: Jossey-Bass.

St. Exupery, A. (1939). *Wind, sand, and stars.* New York: Reynal & Hitchcock.

Sandeen, A. (1985). The legacy of values education in college student personnel work. In J. Dalton (Ed.), *Promoting values development in college students* (Monograph Series, No. 4, pp. 1–16). Washington: NASPA.

Sanford, N. (1980). *Learning after college.* Orinda, CA: Montaigne Press.

Shapiro, S. (1995). Educational change and the crisis of the left: Toward a postmodern educational discourse. In B. Kanpol, & P. McLaren (Eds.) *Critical multiculturalism: Uncommon voices in a common struggle* (pp. 25–38.). Westport, CT: Bergin & Garvey.

Shklar, J. (1984). Injustice, injury, and inequality: An introduction. In F. Lucash (Ed.), *Justice and equality here and now* (pp. 13–33). Ithaca, NY: Cornell University Press.

Sloan, D. (1980). *Education and values.* New York: Teachers College Press.

Taylor, H. (1952). The philosophical foundations of general education. In *Yearbook on general education* (pp. 20–45). Chicago: National Society for the Study of Education.

Taylor, H. (1970). Progressive philosophy. In G. Smith (Ed.), *1945–1970: Twenty-five years.* (pp. 111–116). San Francisco: Jossey-Bass.

Tierney, W. (1989). *Curricular landscapes, democratic vistas: Transformative leadership in higher education.* New York: Praeger.

Toffler, A. (1970). *Future shock.* New York: Random House.

Upcraft, M. L. (1988). Managing right. In M. L. Upcraft, & M. Barr (Eds.), *Managing student affairs effectively* (New Directions for Student Services No. 42, pp. 65–78). San Francisco: Jossey-Bass.

Vlastos, G. (1962). Justice and equality. In R. Brandt (Ed.), *Social justice* (pp. 31–72). Englewood Cliffs, NJ: Prentice-Hall.

Wall, V., & Evans, N. (Eds.). (2000). *Toward acceptance: Sexual orientation issues on campus.* Lanham, MD: University Press of America.

Whitt, E., Carneghi, J., Matkin, J., Scalese-Love, P., & Nestor, D. (1990). Believing is seeing: Alternative perspectives on a statement of professional philosophy for student affairs. *NASPA Journal, 27*, 178–184.

Young, R. (1993). Essential values of the profession. In R. Young (Ed.), *Identifying and implementing the essential values of the profession* (New Directions for Student Services No. 61, pp. 5–14). San Francisco: Jossey-Bass.

Young, R., & Elfrink, V. (1991). Essential values of student affairs. *Journal of College Student Development, 32*, 47–55.

CHAPTER SIX

ETHICAL STANDARDS AND PRINCIPLES

Jane Fried

Ethical beliefs and standards represent a community's most deeply held and widely accepted values. Therefore, these standards and beliefs are inseparable from the communities that create them. Aristotle (1941 version) emphasized the connection between community values and ethics when he wrote that the purpose of ethical inquiry was to determine the good which most benefits both the individual and the society. Ethical discourse addresses both private virtue and public behavior. An ethical citizen is expected to behave habitually in a manner that contributes to the public welfare. Similarly a discussion of ethical standards and principles for the profession of student affairs requires a conversation about the obligations that individual members of the profession have to each other, to the profession at large, and to the range of communities that the student affairs profession serves. The complexity of these relationships provides a backdrop to the complexity of ethical decision making in twenty-first century higher education.

Higher education likes to consider itself a community, but it is often split between faculty and administration and between the professional staff and the clerical and maintenance staffs. Student groups are also split in a process that Levine and Cureton (1998) call *mitosis,* a phenomenon that involves groups splitting into increasingly smaller segments based on increasingly narrower definitions of what members have in common. In addition to internal interest groups there are also external groups that have a strong interest in what goes on in colleges and universities—the families of students, alumni, donors, corporate sponsors and, in the case of public universities, state legislators. In every college community there is a local government that is also concerned about the ways in which the institution does business and the ways in which it handles disruptions of community order. Some of these groups may have codes of ethics. Many do not. All have members who try to advance their own individual and collective ideas about the good at the point where their interests intersect with that of some element of the university.

Ethics can be considered a continuing discussion that explores questions about the highest good to be achieved in particular situations. Ethical inquiry is divided into three levels: principles, theories, and codes of conduct (Kitchener, 1985). Principles are the most fundamental, articulating a set of ideas about "the good," which are considered binding on their face or *prima facie.* Emphasis on different fundamental principles such as love, justice, duty, or caring can lead to differing ethical approaches. Ethical theories provide the rationale for making decisions when two or more ethical principles come into conflict. When ethical principles conflict in a particular situation, this is called an ethical dilemma. Ethical codes are the most specific and provide the clearest guidelines for behaving ethically and resolving ethical dilemmas when they occur. Professions generally have ethical codes and expect their members' behavior to conform to the code. The American College Personnel Association (ACPA) and the National Association of Student Personnel Administrators (NASPA) have both published ethical codes which are discussed later in this chapter and appear in their entirety at the end of this book. Ethical codes apply only to members of the profession that subscribes to them and more specifically to members of the association that has published each code. This chapter will discuss ethical principles, virtues that are considered characteristic of ethical practitioners, ethical codes, and a new approach to ethical analysis that incorporates many of the traditional approaches and adds several new dimensions. Vignettes are inserted throughout the chapter to illustrate the various frameworks and principles.

Knowing Right from Wrong: Principles and Virtues

A college admissions office is mandated to increase enrollment by 2 percent a year for the next five years. The university makes additional scholarship money available to help recruit more students. The admissions and financial aid offices develop a policy that awards substantial aid to 30 percent of the entering class and then cuts the number of students who receive the large awards to 25 percent in the second year and 10 percent in the third and fourth years. They intend to implement this policy but not to tell students who receive the aid packages that they are on a declining scale of assistance.

Principles

Student affairs has based its ethical frameworks on a set of five principles: respecting autonomy, doing no harm, benefiting others, being just, and being faithful (Kitchener, 1985). In this chapter, the additional principle of veracity, or truth telling, is also suggested. Principles provide the fundamental elements of ethical decision-making. They are presumed to reflect universal values and to remain consistent across time and place. The study of ethics in student affairs has consisted of applying principles to specific cases, balancing the relative significance of each principle to the particular case, and then deciding on the most ethical response to the problem. These six principles are considered equal in overall significance. Deciding which principles are most relevant to a specific situation is the task of the decision maker.

Respecting Autonomy. Autonomy involves respecting the right of each person to make his or her own choices with as little interference from outside influences as possible. The principle of respecting autonomy is fundamental to American values and is closely connected to First Amendment rights such as freedom of speech and assembly and the right to self-determination. The principle of respecting autonomy has become difficult to apply in dealings with students who come from cultures that are more collectivist and less individualistic than the United States. Southeast Asian, Native American, African American, and Latino students often understand freedom of choice differently from the ways that Anglo-Americans understand it. Student affairs professionals must first understand how students see themselves as decision makers in their own lives and what responsibilities families expect those students to fulfill. After making the effort to understand a student's worldview, the notion of autonomy must be fully explored as we help students from collectivist cultures decide how to make life choices.

This caveat also applies to the general management of student affairs policies in relating to the entire student body. Professionally, student affairs no longer works in loco parentis with students. We are responsible for maintaining a safe, civil, and educationally supportive environment on our campuses, but we are not necessarily responsible for controlling student life so completely that students do not have the opportunity to learn from their own mistakes, either personal errors or errors made by student organizations. Walking this line is a delicate balance, particularly in an era of heightened security when families may wish to keep their college students in a cocoon of apparent safety.

Doing No Harm. Doing no harm is generally considered the fundamental principle of all helping professions. "Above all, hurt no one" is the foundation of the Hippocratic Oath. Doing no harm has become as complex as respecting autonomy. It is relatively easy to avoid hurting people physically. We put up barriers to keep people out of areas that are physically unsafe. We conduct fire inspections and drills. We interfere with or stop harassment and punish harassers. However, what kind of harm do we do when we tell a student from a collectivist culture to make their own decisions and "follow your dream"? We may well be setting that student up for a serious, potentially harmful conflict with their family.

It is the end of the year and you are planning the annual awards banquet for student leaders. Your most outstanding student leader is a young woman of Chinese heritage. As student government president, she has pushed the group to wonderful achievements because of her skills in working with groups and helping people resolve conflicts. You plan to award her "Student Leader of the Year." As recipient, she must give a speech in which she explains her accomplishments to the audience. Most students are thrilled to receive this award and pleased to make a short speech at the ceremony. Chia Li turns pale when you tell her that she will receive this award. She declines to accept and says that she could never make such a speech. The achievements were accomplished by the group. Her family would be humiliated if she made such a speech.

Benefiting Others. Student affairs professionals typically choose this career because they want to help other people. Once again, it is very important to be sure that the help is perceived as helpful and can be accepted as such. Benefiting others can best be carried out in the context of understanding how a student or group of students defines good. It is also important to examine one's motivation and to be sure that your understanding of what might be good for somebody does not emerge from an excess of well-intentioned authoritarianism. For example, a student activities advisor might suggest that a student group choose a date for its event that does not conflict with several other events that appeal to the same population, but that advisor should not tell the group when to hold their event.

Being Just. Justice implies fairness, impartiality, quality and reciprocity. Equals are to be treated equally and unequals may be treated unequally if the source of the inequality is relevant to the circumstances (Fried, 2001). During registration, residence hall staff, athletes, and members of various traveling groups are often permitted to choose courses before the rest of the student body. Is this unfair or is it a reflection of groups being unequal because of unequal responsibilities and therefore eligible for different treatment? A huge area of debate around the justice principle is affirmative action. Is this redress for past injustices? Are African Americans still disadvantaged, or is that a historical remnant? Is justice served when people of non-European heritage are given extra points in the admissions process? Is there such a thing as reverse discrimination? All these questions go to the issue of unequal circumstances justifying unequal treatment.

The Black Student Union has invited a prominent member of the Nation of Islam to speak on your campus. This individual provokes conflict wherever he speaks. The director of the Student Union states that the nation of Islam is not welcome on campus and refuses to grant permission to hold the event. He says that the college can't afford all the protection that would be required. He knows that this speaker would draw protest groups, that additional security staff would have to be hired, and that the publicity in the area would probably be bad for the college. As a student activities advisor, you disagree with this decision.

Being Faithful. Fidelity "is at the core of relationships between people. If people were not faithful to each other, no meaningful human bonds could exist" (Kitchener, 1985, p. 25). The foundation of the student affairs profession, as all other helping professions, is the creation of bonds of trust between people (Fried, 2001). Being faithful means keeping promises, stated or implied. It means keeping appointments and commitments with students and colleagues. It means being honest when we don't completely understand how to answer a question or present a policy to students. It means honoring confidentiality and not gossiping. It means living up to the ethical codes of our profession by confronting colleagues when we believe that they are not keeping their promises. Being faithful also carries some caveats. If we believe that we are keeping our promises flawlessly, we run the risk of arrogant condescension with people whose promise keeping is flawed. The most important promise we can ever keep is to respect the dignity of others and treat them with compassion. The Golden Rule is represented in most of the world's religions, and it contains the most significant promise we can make—to treat others as we wish to be treated. Keeping that promise protects us from an excess of virtue in keeping the others.

Veracity. Truth telling is quite problematic in a postmodernist era that has learned to respect multiple perspectives. We now know that what one person thinks is true (small "t") is often a function of that person's perspective, which always limits what each person can see or understand. Multiple truths coexist whenever multiple persons are involved in a situation. Nevertheless, operational understandings of truth can usually be agreed upon in the context of respectful listening, honest speaking, and nondefensive understanding. Student affairs professionals should honor the principle of speaking accurately and making clear distinctions between reporting facts and making inferences.

> You are a staff member in the career development office. You have overheard one of your colleagues talking about the way she grabbed a job announcement off the fax as it came in because it was exactly the kind of job her partner is looking for. She gave him the original announcement, and now she's trying to decide if she should post a copy for others to see. This woman is your colleague and you believe her behavior is unethical.

Virtues

Virtues complement principles. While principles are presumed to remain constant across time and context, virtues vary with the situation. Every culture and most contexts have slightly different ideas of what type of behavior and what personality characteristics are considered virtuous. "A virtue is a trait of character that is socially valued and a *moral virtue* is a trait that is morally valued" (Beauchamp & Childress, 1994, p. 63). The research on counselors, psychologists, and other helping professionals suggests that there are four essential virtues for anyone in the helping professions: prudence, integrity, respectfulness, and benevolence (Meara, Schmidt, & Day, 1996). Virtues are elements of a person's typical ways of behaving and thinking. Rather than serving as principles that one thinks about as a guide to action, virtues are predispositions or habits that tend to shape one's responses to specific situations. A person could think through an ethical dilemma on the basis of principles. That person might know what to do but still be unable to carry out the ethical response to the problem. A person who had developed ethical virtues would not have that split between analysis and action.

Self-Regarding Virtues: Prudence and Integrity. Self-regarding virtues primarily benefit the person who acquires and demonstrates them. They are marks of the character strength of people who possesses them. Prudence suggests a habitual tendency to think carefully and act cautiously when faced with ethical conflicts. Prudent people do not leap into action as soon as one side of the problem becomes apparent. They consider all sides, taking time to reflect and consider potential outcomes before making a decision or taking action. Other, more impulsive, persons may find prudence very aggravating, especially in emergencies. Nevertheless, prudence leads to better decisions over time. The habit of prudence also leads to development of integrity. Integrity suggests internal consistency and wholeness. People of integrity are what they appear to be and are generally consistent in behavior and decision making. People of integrity live according to their professed values and cannot be accused of unfairness or bowing to political pressure. Needless to say, developing integrity is the work of a lifetime.

Other-Regarding Virtues: Respectfulness and Benevolence. Other regarding virtues are "oriented toward producing moral good for others or providing for the good of the community in general" (Meara et al. 1996, p. 37). They are intertwined with the self-regarding virtues. If a person is characteristically prudent, it is easier to treat others with respect. Many Americans of European descent are now challenged to become more respectful of their Arab and Muslim neighbors. When the United States became the target of terrorist attacks, the imprudent response was to attack persons in the immediate environment who appeared to be connected in some way to the perpetrators. Fortunately, political, religious, and civic leaders spoke out immediately and presented a more prudent response. Anger is an understandable response to assault. Prudent people do not respond with uncontrolled anger. Much more thought must be given to the situation before a response can be crafted that doesn't make the situation worse. Respectfulness generally leads to benevolence. If one treats another with respect, taking a person's welfare into account becomes habitual. "True compassion is not just an emotional response but a firm commitment founded on reason. Therefore a truly compassionate attitude toward others does not change even if they behave negatively" (Dalai Lama, 1998, p. 40).

Patterns of Meaning and Ethical Perspective

College campuses and the world around them have become incredibly complex places where people from all over the world study, work, and interact socially on a daily basis.

FIGURE 6.1. ETHICS WHEEL.

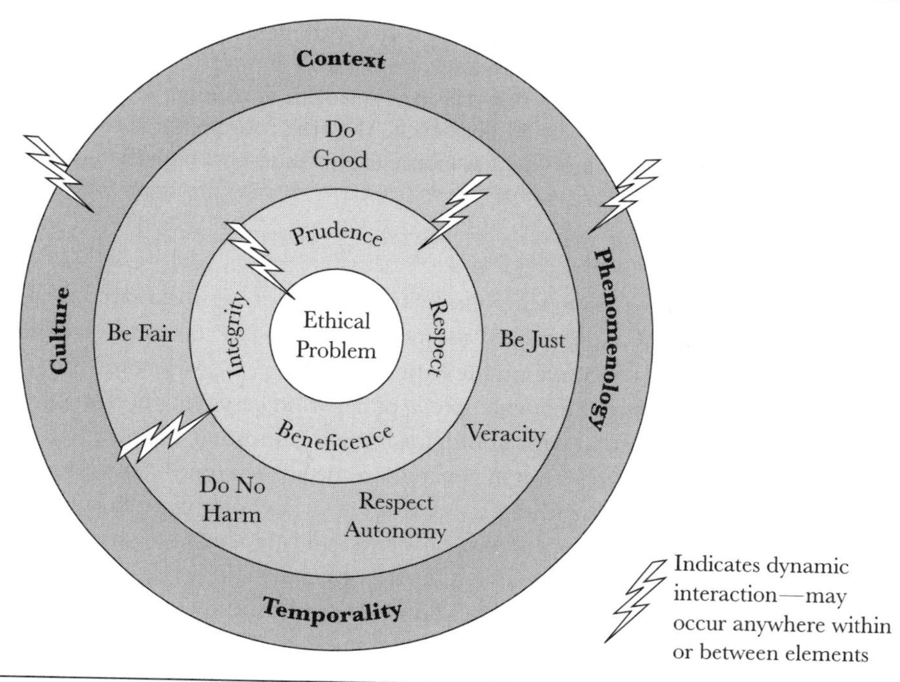

Source: Fried & Malley (2002). Not to be reproduced without permission.

Principles provide consistency when making ethical decisions. Virtues describe patterns of behavior that are considered exemplary in particular settings. There remains a need for a broader framework that brings coherence to these two dimensions and integrates them with a sense of context. Fried and Malley (unpublished manuscript) have created a three-dimensional model, the Ethics Wheel, that incorporates consideration of virtues and principles in a broader context that includes culture, phenomenology, time frame, and dynamic interaction among all segments of the three dimensions (see Figure 6.1).

Cultural Values

Values that pertain to any specific ethical dilemma include the cultural perspectives and values of individuals from various ethnic groups as well as nonethnic cultures such as GLBT (gay, lesbian, bisexual, transgender) persons, athletes, persons with disabilities, and so forth. Campus culture and the culture of the surrounding community are also relevant. A racial incident that occurs on a public urban campus in the Northeast, for example, might have different ramifications than a similar incident that occurs in a private college in a rural area. Students from different cultures may have dramatically different reactions to the same event.

A White male student whose great grandfather fought for the Confederacy hangs up a Confederate flag in his residence hall room. Several of the African American students on the floor ask him to remove it. At a staff meeting, the RA brings up the problem with the hall director and the area coordinator. They are all concerned that the continued presence of the flag might lead to a violent encounter. The hall director is concerned about autonomy and free speech. The area coordinator is concerned about doing no harm. Is there a prudent response to this issue—or more than one?

Phenomenology

Phenomenology refers to individual points of view that are based on the interaction of cultural and personal perspectives. These perspectives are developed by talking about and reflecting on life experience. Every person's individual phenomenology is slightly different. For example, a patient and easygoing person might not get too upset about having to wait in line for forty-five minutes to check out at the bookstore. A less patient person might get angry or decide to come back tomorrow or buy the books online. A student with an anti-authoritarian bent might become very angry if a professor calls on her in class and makes a sarcastic comment if she can't answer the question. A student with a different phenomenology might react to the same put down by admitting that he hadn't done the reading and couldn't really blame the professor for getting upset with him. Phenomenology shapes the kinds of reactions people have to events that contain ethical dilemmas and influences what kinds of events to which people choose to react.

Your mom is the minister in your church. You've been active in this church all your life. You're a youth group advisor, do maintenance work around the buildings, and sing in the choir. Your mom has a different last name than you do. She has written one of your reference letters. Everything she says about you is true, but you ask her not to mention that she's your mom.

Temporality

Temporality refers to all the timing elements that are relevant to any particular dilemma. Has the situation been going on for months or did it just develop recently? Are there deadlines for resolving this issue? Has a major event occurred while this problem was in process to change the perspectives of those involved? Has the event occurred among friends who have known each other for a long time or among strangers who don't know each other very well? Phases of the academic calendar are also relevant to some situations—whether an event occurred at the beginning of the year or midwinter may change the outcome. Finally, the spirit of the times in which a dilemma arises can also influence the resolution of that dilemma. Campus attitudes changed drastically after September 11, 2001. There was less criticism of government policy, more patriotic symbols displayed, and more students walking around campus in fatigues. Student "pranks" like setting off firecrackers might have been treated more severely because people on campus were more frightened of anything that sounded like an explosion—or less severely because campus officials understood the student need to relieve tension. Attitudes continue to evolve as this chapter is being written.

Dynamic Interactions

Dynamical considerations involve the elements of a situation that are in flux. The Ethics Wheel in Figure 6.1 is intended to convey a picture of a fluid system where all of the elements interact and co-evolve as time goes on and perspectives shift. The lightening bolts around the wheel signify the dynamic elements of the ethical process. Dynamical systems are "open to the environment, exchanging matter, energy and information" (Caine & Caine, 1997, p. 58). Universities are dynamical systems in which information circulates. Information may attract or repel resources at any given time. Energy can move into the system when people are hopeful and flow out of the system when people are depressed, such as in times of budget cuts or campus crises like fires and floods. When systems are close to equilibrium, in times of little change and adequate resources, small problems do not provoke big changes. When systems are far from equilibrium, in times of great change and social disruption, any small event may provoke enormous and unanticipated consequences. A swastika spray-painted on the side of a building may simply be painted over in times of stability. The day after a threat is made to kill all Jews and Americans, that event will provoke a very different reaction.

The Ethics Wheel can be used to analyze ethical dilemmas. The reader should imagine that each circle turns independently of the others and that the key issues can be lined up in order to imagine which elements interact and their relative importance in the situation. Some suggested questions to consider are as follows:

1. Are there cultural concerns involved in this situation? Are there values held by specific groups that are being challenged? Are there considerations that affect various cultural groups on campus differentially?
2. What is the time frame that is relevant to this situation? Do we have months to investigate or does something have to be done in the next few hours or days? Is anyone or anything in danger?
3. Are there radically different individual perspectives about the importance of the problem? Does the vice president for student affairs see things very differently from the vice president for academic affairs?
4. Do the people who have to address this problem share an ethical framework that guides their thinking or are there conflicting ethical perspectives in the decision-making group? Are these people open to listening to each other or attempting to gain advantage for their approach?
5. The Ethics Wheel suggests many of the dimensions that should be considered when investigating potential responses to ethical dilemmas, but does not suggest any particular sequence of questions or set of priorities. The Wheel should be used in an atmosphere of community engagement and authentic dialogue.

Processes for Ethical Decision Making

There is no universally accepted set of procedures to follow in addressing an ethical dilemma. Several approaches are suggested in the paragraphs that follow. All of these approaches have common characteristics—careful data gathering, analysis, consultation, and decision making. Resolutions of ethical dilemmas are rarely noncontroversial. Use of the ethical virtues of prudence and integrity are essential in the review process. In all cases the person who is concerned about a possible ethical violation is obligated to speak with the person or persons believed to be in violation of a professional code. A discussion of professional codes follows.

The Interactive Process for Social Construction of a Response

Cottone (2001) suggests that ethical decision making cannot yield objective decisions based on absolute values. The decision-making process must be built on the construction of a social consensus among the concerned parties about what ethical concerns exist and the relative priority of standards in deciding on a course of action. Ethical decisions should be consensualized if possible and arbitrated if necessary. This process involves:

1. Gathering information from all involved in the problem, determining who is involved. Who is potentially affected may provide an additional dilemma.
2. Assessing the nature of the relationships among the parties involved. Are there conflicting opinions and adversarial relationships, or do the persons basically share similar values?
3. Consulting with valued colleagues and experts in the community and reviewing the pertinent ethical standards and codes.

After these steps are taken a social process must occur in which meaning and values are discussed and negotiated in order to achieve a consensus. If consensus building fails, interactive reflection is suggested in order to determine if arbitration is necessary. Interactive reflection is "a process of conversation with trusted individuals to come to an agreement as to whether arbitration should be sought or whether a position needs to be modified to reenter negotiations" (p. 43).

Rion's Six Question Guidelines

Rion (1996) suggests that developing answers to six questions will guide the process of ethical decision making. While the social constructivist model discussed above is useful in public situations that involve several segments of the campus community, Rion's approach is one of interior dialogue intended to lead to "ethically sensitive and well-considered judgment" (p. 13) by individuals. Rion's six questions are:

1. Why is this bothering me?
2. Who else matters? Are there stakeholders in this situation?

3. Is it my problem? Have I caused the problem and am I responsible for resolving it?
4. What is the ethical concern? What principles, virtues, laws, cultural, temporal, or phenomenological considerations should I take into account?
5. What do others think? Would discussing this with a person who might disagree with me help me think more clearly?
6. Am I being true to myself? What are my personal beliefs about this issue, beyond consideration for the relevant ethical codes and guidelines? (pp. 13–14).

Community as Context for Dialogue

In the information-saturated environments where most student affairs work is accomplished, all three dimensions of the ethical analysis model interact constantly. Creating a culture in which ethical concerns can be discussed is a project that must be undertaken by the entire campus community, not simply the division of student affairs (Brown, 1985). In this context, community is best considered a process rather than a place or a group. A sense of community emerges from an attitude of respect rather than simply from physical proximity. Parker Palmer considers community a place where the person you never want to see again moves in next door and the subsequent work that developing a relationship with that person involves (personal communication, March, 1995). Peck (1987) describes community as a safe place where a "group can fight gracefully" (p. 70). The community process focuses on dialogue, the exchange of perspectives for the purpose of creating shared meaning on subjects of mutual concern. Community is not easily achieved in this period of global tension. It must be created constantly in response to the endless conflicts that seem to make consensus a hypothetical goal beyond a constantly receding horizon. Unless community is seen as a value and a practice, addressing ethical dilemmas becomes a process of resolving conflicts among competing interests with few if any agreed upon priorities and principles.

Communities must be committed to dialogue if they wish to create frameworks within which ethical dilemmas can be addressed. Dialogue is a sustained process that allows all participants to express their perspectives, listen openly to the perspectives of others, suspend judgment, and finally come to a common understanding of the meaning of the events in which they are all involved. Dialogue is "thinking together in a coherent way . . . . (it) does not require people to agree with each other. Instead it encourages people to participate in a pool of shared meaning that leads to aligned action" (Jaworski, 1998, p. 111). Dialogue encourages the development of prudence, benevolence, respect, and integrity within a community. Brown (1985) considered community as fundamental to the creation of ethical practice in student affairs. He suggested that establishment of an ethical environment in which dialogue could occur as essential to the mission of education for student development and citizenship. Developmentally, students are in the midst of often conflicting personal needs—to make friends, to choose majors and pursue careers, to learn group and leadership skills, and to achieve academically. Students are attempting to make sense out of their lives and learn how to live in relation to others in ways that are meaningful and satisfying.

Student affairs administrators help students learn ethical behavior, not by talking about it, but by modeling it in conversation and behavior. This practice exposes students to increasing levels of cognitive complexity, necessary for the comprehension and resolution of ethical dilemmas. We now know that cognitive development occurs in a social context and that "individual, social partners and the cultural milieu are inseparable contributors to the ongoing activities in which cognitive development takes place" (Love & Guthrie, 1999, p. 54). If students do not experience the real-life struggles with problems that have no simple solutions, we will all remain trapped in the dualistic mind set described by Perry (1970). We will continue to hear slogans like "America—love it or leave it." We will be trapped in situations where students, and possibly colleagues, continue to think in "us and them" terms that make conflict resolution extremely difficult using zero-sum perspectives. We must continually attend to our own ethical practice, to the creation of communities that support ethical dialogue, and to the process of ethics education that we conduct with students on a daily basis. None of this can be divided.

Professional Codes and Communities

Professional communities bring practitioners together to advance their scholarship and practices. Chapter Twenty-Seven discusses the nature of professional practice in student affairs. Student affairs has two profession-wide organizations and numerous smaller associations that focus on specific areas of practice such as activities, housing, career development, academic advising, and so forth. The two generalist organizations are the National Association of Student Personnel Administrators (NASPA) and the American College Personnel Association (ACPA). Both have well-developed ethical codes, each of which reflects the history and the emphasis of the association. Professional associations are discussed elsewhere in this book. This chapter will address the major elements of the ACPA and NASPA ethical codes.

ACPA has been associated with counseling and the provision of services and education for individuals and small groups of students. The code of ethics reflects a strong emphasis on student development and the connections between professional competence and responsibilities to students, the institution, and the society at large. The ACPA Statement of Ethical Principles and Standards is preceded by Kitchener's (1985) five ethical principles. The code also includes a description of the process for using the statement in relationship to colleagues (NASPA, 1993). The entire code is quite specific about obligations and prohibitions including such issues as avoidance of dual role relationships, institutional loyalty, refraining from actions that impinge on personal privacy, representing one's institution and one's competencies accurately, supporting student development, avoiding discrimination and harassment, and preparing students for the responsibilities of citizenship.

NASPA's historical origins are connected to administration and organizational leadership. Its ethical statement emphasizes the relationship between the student affairs professional and the institution that employs him or her. It is composed of eighteen brief statements that stipulate expectations for ethical behavior addressing such issues as management of institutional resources, agreement with institutional mission and goals, hiring practices, job evaluations, responsibility for promoting a sense of community on campus, obligations for continuing professional development, and accurate representation of personal competence. NASPA's (1993) statement also mandates respect for confidentiality, integrity of information and research, and fostering responsible student behavior. More attention is paid to institutional obligations in the NASPA statement and more to student development and education in the ACPA statement, but both statements cover similar areas of practice.

All of the vignettes and issues that have been described in this chapter come from the author's experience and may happen to someone who reads this book. Since college students, institutions of higher education, and the larger social context continue to change, the ethical dilemmas we face also change endlessly. No one knows how to handle every issue that she or he confronts as a professional. Once again, the role of community in understanding and addressing these issues is paramount. Just as it is important to create a sense of ethical community on each campus, professional associations also provide ethical communities for their members. ACPA has a formal Ethics Committee that provides programs at national conferences, conducts research about ethical practices, and supports columns in *Developments,* the ACPA newsletter. This Ethics Committee also is available for consultation with members about specific concerns. NASPA has no formal ethics committee but has published a monograph called *Mountains and Passes: Traversing the Landscape of Ethics and Student Affairs Administration* (Lampkin & Gibson, 1999).

Ethical Themes and Fundamental Principles

As soon as student affairs professionals begin to integrate the ethical framework of the profession into their work, ethical dilemmas become visible. I urge readers to consider ways this multidimensional exploration of ethics can provide guidance in addressing dilemmas. I have chosen three overarching questions that I consider especially significant: (1) How shall we treat each other, both as colleagues and as people who have fiduciary responsibilities for students? (2) How and what shall we help our students learn? (3) How shall we steward the resources we are responsible for managing?

How Shall We Treat Each Other?

The ethics of relationship constitutes one school of ethical thinking (Gilligan, 1982; Noddings, 1984). *Caring* is the fundamental principle that guides this approach. The principle of caring asserts that taking the well being of the other person into account should be the supreme consideration in ethical relationships. The notion of caring in specific situations becomes complex. Guthrie (1997) refers to Noddings' concept of "ethical affect" (Noddings, 1984), which "acknowledges the interaction of cognition and feeling in the creation of an ethical response to the other" (Guthrie, 1997, p. 33).

Thinking about a relationship or a problem that has occurred within it serves the higher goal of understanding how to care about a particular person in a specific situation. Gilligan, who writes descriptively about moral development, struggles with the same type of integration. Her model of female moral development has three stages: (1) caring about self, (2) caring about others, and (3) balancing care for self with care for others (1982). Although Gilligan discusses moral rather than cognitive development, it is clear that increasingly complex thinking capacities are necessary for people to think through moral dilemmas when they are trying to take the needs of both people into account, as they do in stage 3 of her framework.

Cultural and institutional complexity highlight some of the challenges an ethical person faces when trying to understand how to demonstrate caring for another person. These challenges are particularly difficult for Americans from the dominant culture, given the historical American belief in the melting pot approach and general unwillingness to adapt to the expectations of members of nondominant cultures in the United States (Fried & Associates, 1995). A simple American gesture of caring, a hug for example, can be considered incredibly rude to a Japanese person. A hug from an American woman to a Moslem man is a violation of prescribed behavior between unrelated males and females. Direct feedback about behavior to many persons from East Asia is insulting although such feedback often represents a gesture of caring to Americans. Directness, which is valued in American culture, is considered tactless in many other cultures. These same cultures often prefer to send messages of distress through a third party in a very subtle way, assuming that the message will get to the person for whom it is intended. An American might receive such a message with confusion or see it as a request to spread gossip.

How and What Shall We Help Students Learn?

The traditional "curriculum" of student affairs is widely understood among members of our profession but does not resemble a formal academic curriculum. The student affairs approach to teaching and learning tends to be less formal than traditional academic instruction. Teaching methods tend to have strong behavioral and affective components. We often call our teaching "training," because our responsibilities include training students to do specific kinds of jobs on campus, including paraprofessional work in residence halls and career centers and leadership in student organizations. Our teaching combines counseling, training, and coaching. We help people learn to live their own lives and get along with others in one-to-one conversations that occur in counseling and disciplinary discussions. Much of the teaching that student affairs professionals do on campus does not carry academic credit and is not part of any academic department.

Nevertheless, the curriculum of student affairs is central to the mission of most colleges. It includes interpersonal communication, conflict resolution, personal life planning, financial planning, career planning, leadership and participation in small and large groups, public speaking, and developing the necessary skills to live and work in a culturally diverse democracy (Fried, 2002). In some cases, it also includes guiding students through the process of deepening and personalizing their faith and their capacity to behave ethically. Academically this learning is below the radar screen although it is integrated into every segment of student life. These skills and capacities represent the glue that allows college graduates to use whatever else they have learned in college to create productive and satisfying lives for themselves and their families.

Ethically we are obligated to provide whatever types of training and education in these areas that the policy makers on each campus expect us to provide or that we believe students need. If a college president asked a dean of students to create a career development office, the dean would not be at liberty to refuse. In times of crisis, such as the death of a student, a hate crime, or a national catastrophe, student affairs professionals are ethically obligated to participate in or lead the effort to help students understand and respond. If we handle these responsibilities well, our students finally resume their daily lives with some sense of equanimity. If we handle these situations effectively, students also learn about the situation, themselves, others in their community, and the world in which the agonizing incident occurs. We help students learn powerful lessons often under excruciating circumstances. Ethically, we are obligated to do this. The ACPA code of Ethics is quite clear: "Student development is an essential purpose of higher education and the pursuit of this aim is a major responsibility of student affairs. Development is complex and includes cognitive, physical, moral, social, career, spiritual, personal and educational dimensions. Professionals must be sensitive to the variety of backgrounds, cultures and personal characteristics evident in the student population and use appropriate theoretical perspectives to identify learning opportunities and to reduce barriers that inhibit development" (ACPA, 1993, p. 91).

In addition, student affairs professionals also teach in more formal settings such as new student orientation and college survival courses, many of which carry academic credit.

The ethical issue that arises in this discussion is about integrity. If the type of learning that student affairs professionals are responsible for is so significant in student life, how have we, as a profession, let this work be ignored by our academic and administrative colleagues for so long? Why is student development a marginalized function even though it is highly visible in the mission statements of most colleges and universities? What ethical mandates must our profession honor in order to move the work of student affairs from the margin of our educational institutions to the center, where students live and learn as integrated human beings?

Apocryphal comments from graduating seniors:[1]

Q: What were the most important things you learned in college?

A: How to plan my time, get along with my roommates, keep a boy/girlfriend, control my temper, speak in front of groups, take care of myself, and get along with some very weird people (from my point of view).

Q: Who did you learn the most from?

A: Hard to answer. Lots of people—a professor who took time to help me figure out my major and career possibilities, a residence hall director who taught

> me how to stay out of fights, the advisor to my fraternity who helped me learn how to handle chapter meetings. Mostly I learned just by meeting different people and learning to get along with them.

The ethics of discussing and carrying out the educational role of student affairs presents us with a conundrum, a two-sided issue with no unambiguous resolution. If people are learning but nobody is teaching, how do we describe that phenomenon? This kind of learning is very important to students, but the faculty responsible for provoking and structuring it, guiding it and reinforcing it, are not considered part of the educational staff of the institution. What ethical precepts are relevant to the remediation of this misrepresentation?

How Shall We Steward the Resources We Are Responsible for Managing?

The ethical issues present in this huge area of responsibility are sometimes obvious, sometimes subtle. They often involve use of funds, oversight of facilities, responsible attention to the details of planning, and supervising events. All of our ethical guidelines address the issues which responsible stewardship raises. Stealing and mishandling funds is obviously a violation of trust. Failure to provide for proper security at a campus event is unfair to the students who plan and attend the event and involves the possibility of permitting harm to these people. On a somewhat more subtle level, consider these dilemmas:

> You are the supervisor of the maintenance staff of the student center. You have two janitors who aren't doing their jobs very well. You come in and see the bathrooms dirty, trash cans full, and both of them sleeping in cleaning closets on different floors of the building. One person is a refugee from Bosnia. The other is a Puerto Rican who has lived most of his life on the mainland. You arrange a meeting with the Puerto Rican janitor to explain that you're putting him on probation because of his poor work performance. You don't speak to the Bosnian employee because you have trouble understanding him and he's had a horrible life.
>
> You are the coordinator of the intramural program and schedule the use of the basketball courts for the intramural leagues. There are so many teams using the facilities that some of the games are played at 1:00 A.M., which nobody likes. Your supervisor's child plays on an intramural team. You give them the 7:00 P.M. slot every time they play.

In many ways, our responsibilities for managing the physical and fiscal elements of our work are the easiest and most obvious ones to analyze when it comes to making ethical choices. In these cases the biggest challenge may be determining the difference between ethical behavior and common practice. Much of the time, common practice falls in the domain of the ambiguous-subtle, apparently not harming anyone, yet not quite right. Learning how to tell the difference is one of the most difficult challenges a new professional faces. As Harry Canon (personal communication, 1992) has often remarked, the hardest thing about untangling an ethical dilemma is knowing that you are in one. Stealing has become "misappropriation." Lying has become "misrepresenting." Not getting caught seems to have replaced doing the right thing. "Everybody does it" and "I didn't hurt anybody" seem to have replaced our sense of right and wrong in many situations.

Today's Ethical Issues

Ethical issues on today's campuses reflect the complexity of the world in which we live. The dilemmas flow from many sources that were unanticipated even twenty years ago. A few of the major dilemmas are described below:[2]

Access

Access is primarily a financial issue. Public financial support for higher education has been decreasing for at least a decade. More debt is assumed by individual students and less nonloan aid is available. How do we maintain access for students who do not want to burden the first half of their lives with debt, keep our costs manageable, and still provide quality experiences in the student affairs domain? How high should private institutions raise their tuition in order to fund scholarships for students with fewer financial resources?

On the boundary between financial and academic access, we find the question of allocation of institutional resources. How does a vice president for student affairs manage faculty relations when members of the faculty have decided that too much money is being spent on student affairs programs at the expense of academic priorities? In the gap between both sides of this boundary is an especially explosive issue—how do we define eligibility for "affirmative action" programs and scholarships? Is diversity a function of race and ethnicity or class? Finally, who pays for academic support programs for underprepared students? This question cuts to the heart of the university's mission—what is higher education? Is remediation part of the mission of colleges and universities or should that mission be served by community colleges and special preparatory "academies"?

Personnel

There have always been serious ethical dilemmas in the domain of hiring and supervising staff. How are an applicant's ethical standards and past behavior assessed during the process of hiring and checking references? How does a supervisor convey the ethical standards of the institution to new staff members? What are the ethics of "caring confrontation" between two staff members when one of them thinks that the other has violated some element of professional ethics? What is a reasonable time lapse between the moment when a supervisor discovers that a staff member has done something inappropriate, committed an ethical lapse, or simply behaved incompetently, and the moment when the supervisor confronts that individual? What ethical issues arise when a supervisor cannot reduce staff responsibilities even though the staff has been "downsized"? How does a department head balance the need to produce good results for the institution and the need to protect staff members from working such long hours that they become ill or short-tempered? This is a fine line to walk, and judgments made in this domain must be supported by an understanding of the ethical guidelines of the profession.

Crisis Intervention and Threats to the Community

Student affairs divisions are generally responsible for the physical and emotional health and well-being of students on their campuses. Crises have become less predictable and seem to be more frequent. In our wired universe, a riot in Rwanda or an earthquake in Turkey can provoke a disturbance on campus in a matter of hours. Psychological pressure has increased on our campuses. Students in the military reserves are being called to active duty. Muslim students, including but not limited to those whose ancestry may be traced to the Middle East, Pakistan, or Afghanistan have become targets of hostile and dangerous behavior. Some of these students have also exhibited this kind of behavior. Students continue to become infected with AIDS and spread it to others. We have no way of knowing how people will handle these stresses and who will act out their fears in dangerous ways. Student affairs divisions are ethically obligated to review crisis protocols on a regular basis and to imagine what new crises might develop. Albert Einstein is quoted on bumper stickers as believing that "Imagination is more important than knowledge." This is one area where we must use our imaginations to meet our ethical obligations.

Information Oversight

Information is not a thing but a process, and the process presents us with ethical dilemmas every day, both electronically and interpersonally. Wheatley (1994) calls information "a dynamic element . . . that gives order, that prompts growth, that defines what is alive" (p. 102). She calls information "the key source of structuration—the process of creating structure" (p. 104). Organizations thrive when information flows freely. The ethical dilemmas we face with information are what to communicate and how to determine credibility. When do we choose to use the information we have to work with colleagues to solve institutional problems, and when do we hold our information close to the chest in order to look like heroic problem solvers or to protect privacy? In the domain of electronic communication on campus, information oversight becomes a policy issue similar to the one raised by crisis protocols. Are the institutional policies related to abuse of information on the web current, responsive to the endless creativity of web-users, some of whom use this vehicle to harass, intimidate, steal, or lie?

Ethical Management of External Financial Resources

In a time of diminished budgets, numerous opportunities for partnering with external agencies appear. Money comes into budgets from external vendors, auxiliary services, companies who recruit on campus and provide in-kind or financial support for programs in career development, and other organizations that benefit from doing business on campus. Grants carry formulas for determining overhead costs, and some of this money can be channeled to questionable purposes. Privatized housing and other facilities may not appear as costs on the budget of university departments, but long-term maintenance remains a responsibility of the institution. Even when there is allegedly "no money" there is some discretionary money in a budget someplace. Determining how to manage financial resources remains a constant ethical challenge.

Athletics and Other Independent Power Centers

Relationships between the athletic department and the division of student affairs on campuses where athletics play an important role is a serious challenge to ethical decision making. In almost any situation where student athletes violate university policy, there is some hidden or obvious source of pressure to be more lenient with athletes than with other students. The more money the athletic program generates, the more difficult this problem can become. Major private donors, whether they support athletic or other personal projects within the institution, cannot be easily ignored. Donors can also be the source of vague pressure to ignore the rules for student behavior, to change a room or grant a single room to a student not ordinarily eligible for one, to pay for damage but not punish the vandal. In public institutions, this pressure may also come from members of local or state government. When the president receives a phone call requesting a favor from a member of the state legislature who will vote on the university budget, the president listens. When the president listens, the staff may be expected to listen as well.

Ethical Presentation of the Value of Student Affairs in the Institution

Student affairs is considered an auxiliary function, focusing on management of student behavior rather than contributing to learning. Student affairs positions typically have lower pay scales than faculty or other administrative positions. While behavior management remains an important part of student affairs work, the field has expanded its responsibilities dramatically. In terms of our responsibilities to attend to the welfare of the "whole student," it remains very important that senior student affairs officers and any relevant designees describe the work of student affairs and the level of responsibility that student affairs staff members carry whenever appropriate or whenever it appears that these contributions are being overlooked in policy decisions.

This brief review of ethical themes and current issues illustrates the complexity of the ethical environment in which student affairs professionals work. Professional codes provide one very valuable source of guidance in ethical decision making. Each code was written by a different professional association, and each springs from a community of values that forms the foundation for the different associations. Although both groups share a great deal in common, each has a slightly different area of professional emphasis.

Conclusion

The days when professionals could confidently and easily resolve ethical dilemmas are long gone, if indeed they ever existed. Ethical standards, values, norms, and codes are created by communities that share certain beliefs about good and bad and the relative importance of the individual and the community of which that person is a member. Our campuses are populated by people who represent ethnic communities from all over the globe, all of the major religious traditions, and dozens if not hundreds of different professions and societies, each of which has its own code of ethics. In addition, there are numerous belief systems about acceptable behavior that students, faculty, and administrators hold on a personal level as well as dozens of other less formal group identities that shape personal perspective. When ethical issues arise, they almost automatically evoke ethical perspectives from many different groups. In most cases, no person and no single point of view dominates. The process by which we resolve ethical dilemmas must incorporate elements of the approaches described throughout this chapter. Individuals must reflect on their own personal ethics and the ways they adapt to both the ethical codes of their professions and the ethical expectations of the institutions where they work. Each of us must identify the stakeholders in these dilemmas and decide how to construct solutions to our problems that all can live with. We must learn to listen carefully and accurately to all persons involved so that we stretch to understand perspectives and values that we have never before considered. Finally, each of us must decide how many and what kinds of risks we are willing to take in order to conduct ourselves with integrity personally and professionally. None of this is easy or simple. However, unless we continually review our own ethical standards and behaviors, we will undermine our ability to call ourselves a profession. Ethics provides the foundation for a coherent approach to professional practice and continuing ethical dialogue is essential.

Endnotes

1. Thanks to my young relatives (Becky, Matt, Brian, and Jim) who have had versions of this conversation with me during their college years.
2. Many of the dilemmas in this section were gleaned from conversations with colleagues including Dr. Linda Kuk, Angela Rolla, Dr. Joanne Lewis, Cynthia Jones, and Dr. Carol Henry.

References

American College Personnel Association (1993). Statement of ethical principles and standards. *Journal of College Student Development, 34,* 89–93.

Aristotle (1941). In R. McKeon (Ed.). *The basic works of Aristotle.* New York: Random House.

Beauchamp, T., & Childress, J. (1994). *Principles of biomedical ethics.* (4th ed.) New York: Oxford University Press.

Brown, R. (1985). Creating an ethical community. In H. Canon & R. Brown (Eds.), *Applied ethics in student services* (New Directions for Student Services No. 30, pp. 67–79). San Francisco: Jossey-Bass.

Caine, R., & Caine, G. (1997). *Education on the edge of possibility.* Alexandria, VA: Association for Supervision and Curriculum Development.

Cottone, R. (2001). A social constructivism model of ethical decision-making in counseling. *Journal of Counseling and Development, 79,* 39–45.

Dalai Lama. (1998). *The path to tranquility.* New York: Penguin Books.

Fried, J. (September 2001). Keeping our promises. *Developments.* Washington, DC: American College Personnel Association.

Fried, J. (April 30, 2002). Transforming higher education: Learning how we really learn. *NetResults.* Retrieved from http://www.naspa.org/netresults/article.cfm?ID=643.

Fried, J., & Associates. (1995). *Shifting paradigms in student affairs: Culture, context, teaching and learning.* Lanham, MD: American College Personal Association/University Press of America.

Gilligan, C. (1982). *In a different voice: Psychological theory and women's development.* Cambridge, MA: Harvard University Press.

Guthrie, V. (1997). Cognitive foundations of ethical development. In J. Fried (Ed.), *Ethics of today's campus: New perspectives on education, student development and institutional management.* (New Directions for Student Services No. 77, pp. 23–44). San Francisco: Jossey-Bass.

Jaworski, J. (1998). *Synchronicity: The inner path of leadership.* San Francisco: Berrett-Kohler.

Kitchener, K. (1985). Ethical principles and ethical decisions in student affairs. In H. Canon & R. Brown (Eds.), *Applied ethics in student services.* (New Directions for Student Services No. 30, pp. 17–30). San Francisco: Jossey-Bass.

Lampkin, P., & Gibson, E. (1999). *Mountains and passes: Traversing the landscape of ethics and student affairs administration.* Washington, DC: National Association of Student Personnel Administrators.

Levine, A., & Cureton, J. (1998). *When hope and fear collide.* San Francisco: Jossey-Bass.

Love, P., & Guthrie, V. (1999). *Understanding and applying cognitive development theory.* (New Directions for Student Services No. 88). San Francisco: Jossey-Bass.

Meara, N., Schmidt, L., & Day, J. (1996). A foundation for ethical decisions, policies and character. *The Counseling Psychologist, 24,* 4–77.

NASPA (1993). Standards of professional practice. *Member Handbook 1993–1994.* Washington, DC: National Association of Student Personnel Administrators.

Noddings, N. (1984). *Caring: A feminine approach to ethics and moral education.* Berkeley, CA: University of California Press.

Peck, S. (1987). *The different drum: Community making and peace.* New York: Simon & Schuster.

Perry, W. G. (1970). *Forms of intellectual and ethical development in the college years: A scheme.* Austin, TX: Holt, Rinehart and Winston.

Rion, M. (1996). *The responsible manager.* Amherst, MA: Human Resources Press.

Wheatley, M. J. (1994). *Leadership and the new science: Learning about organization from an orderly universe.* San Francisco: Berrett-Koehler.

CHAPTER SEVEN

LEGAL FOUNDATIONS OF STUDENT AFFAIRS PRACTICE

Margaret J. Barr

Knowledge of the law is an essential element of the professional practice of any student affairs administrator, for it shapes policies, practices, and decisions on a daily basis. The legal environment of higher education and student affairs has changed rapidly in recent decades, and the legal ramifications for student affairs practice have grown even more pronounced.

The law, however, is not something to be feared. Instead, it provides a framework for guiding student affairs practice. Student affairs practitioners must be aware of both fundamental legal constraints and newly emerging areas of the law to effectively serve both their students and their institution.

This chapter provides an overview of the most salient legal issues influencing student affairs. One caveat is in order: this discussion is not intended as a substitute for competent legal advice, and each student affairs professional is strongly urged to seek appropriate legal assistance when dealing with such matters. Rather, the chapter provides an overview of those points of law that most directly influence professional practice in student affairs. Topics covered are the legal differences between public and private institutions, the sources of the law, constitutional issues, federal and state statutes, contracts, liability issues, the Family Educational Rights and Privacy Act, working with legal counsel, and emerging legal issues of concern to student affairs professionals.

The legal framework for higher education reflects the values of the greater society and always evolves and changes over time. As society changes so does the law, for it reflects the principles that bind the society together. Understanding of the law is predicated on understanding of the issues and forces at work in society when a judicial decision is rendered, a law is passed, or an executive order is issued (see Chapter Five and Chapter Six in this volume for a broader discussion of these issues).

Private Versus Public Institutions

The differences between public and private institutions of higher education have become increasingly blurred. Financial support from the state and federal government for research or student aid has led many to believe that there are essentially no differences between such institutions. This is not the case.

A public institution's authority is derived from its statutory or constitutional entitlement. In private institutions the authority to act is derived from the institution's articles of incorporation, charter, or license. The differences between private and public institutions are most marked in regard to federal constitutional questions. The First, Fourth, Fifth, and Fourteenth Amendments to the United States Constitution provide the basis for the application of constitutional law to higher education. Kaplin and Lee (1997) note that public institutions and their officers are fully subject to constitutional constraints, whereas private institutions and their officers are not. For private institutions, a clear relationship must be demonstrated between any activity alleged to be governed by constitutional mandates and the action of the state. A finding of state action by a private institution requires that the private institution (1) acted as an agent of the state, or (2) performed a function that is considered the responsibility or government, or (3) obtained substantial resources from a governmental entity (Kaplin & Lee). For example, if a private institution provides a course exclusively for the social security administration staff in the district office, it could be found to be engaging in state action, and constitutional protections apply for the students enrolled in that specific class.

Most private institutions have, however, adopted guarantees similar to constitutional protections as part of their contract of enrollment with students, even though they are not bound to do so. In addition, although private institutions are technically free from federal constitutional constraints, students attending such institutions do have protection. Many individual rights are protected by statutes or by the applicable state constitution, and other rights are protected by precedent in case law (Barr, 1988). It should be noted that the "government does retain substantial authority to regulate private education" (Kaplin & Lee, p. 387).

Sources of the Law

The law has nine sources that can influence practice in student affairs in both public and private institutions; however, the degree of influence varies from one type of institution to another. The nine sources of the law are the federal Constitution; the applicable state constitution; federal, state, and local statutes; judicial decisions; the rules and regulations of administrative agencies; contracts; institutional rules and regulations; academic tradition; and foreign or international law.

The U.S. Constitution

As Kaplin and Lee (1997) explain, "Constitutions are the fundamental source for determining the nature and extent of governmental powers. Constitutions are also the fundamental source of the individual rights guarantees that limit the power of government and protect citizens generally, including members of the academic community" (p. 14). The federal Constitution is the highest source of law in the country. As noted above, however, the influence of the Constitution in private institutions is limited to certain circumstances.

State Constitutions

Provisions of the applicable state constitution can influence both public and private institutions. Through the residual powers of the Constitution, all powers not specifically reserved for the federal government are ceded to the states and their citizens (Alexander & Solomon, 1972). Thus, higher education comes primarily under state control. Private institutions are also subject to some provisions of state constitutions. In some states, the constitution provides even greater protection for civil rights than the federal Constitution (*State v. Schmid,* 1980; *Commonwealth of Pennsylvania v. Tate,* 1981). In both of these cases, the court found a constitutional right of access to the property of private institutions by nonaffiliated persons. Careful review of the state constitution is needed to determine the influence of specific provisions at private institutions.

Statutes

A statute, at any governmental level, is a specific law passed by the legislative body and signed into law by the executive branch of the government. Three levels of statutes influence higher education: federal, state, and local. Federal statutes govern all citizens of the United States and must be consistent with the powers reserved for the federal government under the Constitution. Most public institutions are created by state statutes and are subject to all provisions of the state constitution and state laws. Both public and private institutions must conform to the general laws of the state and submit to regulation by state agencies whose primary function is not education. Although private institutions are shielded from much state regulation, they are not immune from regulations derived from the general police power of the state. Private institutions also come under state control through statutes governing trusts, chartering, licensing, and coordinating bodies.

The influence of local ordinances on a given institution is determined by the legal status of the institution, the statutory entitlement of the municipality or county where the institution is located, and the facts of a particular situation. In general, both public and private institutions are subject to local ordinances regarding health and safety, such as fire codes and zoning laws. A public institution, however, as an arm of the state, has authority over local government unless such powers are restricted by state or federal constitutional provisions (Thompson, 1976).

Judicial Decisions

As Gehring (2000) explains, "The function of the judicial system is to settle controversies, decide the constitutionality of laws and interpret laws" (p. 348). The force of any judicial decision depends on the jurisdiction of the deciding court. The federal court systems include the Supreme Court, the courts of appeals, special federal courts, and district courts. In matters related to federal constitutional issues and federal statutes, only the decisions of the U.S. Supreme Court are "binding precedents throughout the country" (Kaplin & Lee, 1997 p. 21). Eleven federal districts, or circuits, constitute the courts of appeals and serve as appellate courts in the federal system. In addition, the District of Columbia has a federal court of appeals. The circuit courts each have a specific geographic jurisdiction, and their decisions are only binding within that jurisdiction. Cases may be appealed as a matter of right from a district court to the appropriate circuit court. Appeals may also be heard by the U.S. Supreme Court, but the court does not agree to hear all cases. Finally, each federal district court is a one-judge trial court; its decisions are binding only in the district where the judgment is rendered.

Each state court system is unique; however, most state court systems are structured like the federal courts. State district courts are usually courts of general jurisdiction and have judicial responsibilities for a geographic area within the state. Most states have separate district and appellate courts for civil and criminal matters.

Although court decisions are binding only within a given court's jurisdiction (at both the state and federal levels), all decisions should be carefully reviewed. The reasoning of one court with a limited jurisdiction may be persuasive and therefore adopted by other jurisdictions.

Administrative Rules and Regulations

Kaplin and Lee (1997) indicate that the most rapidly expanding sources of higher education law are the directives of state and federal agencies. Like statutes, administrative regulations at both the state and federal levels carry the force of law and must be consistent with applicable state and federal laws and constitutional provisions. Proposed implementing regulations for federal statutes are published in the *Federal Register* with an invitation to comment. After the specified public comment period, the regulations, which have the status of law, are issued. Student affairs administrators should read the *Federal Register* and comment, within institutional guidelines, on proposed regulations. Experience with the proposed regulations governing the Student-Right-To-Know and Campus Security Act of 1990 illustrate that thoughtful comments can influence the final regulations.

Contracts

A contract creates a binding legal arrangement between the contracting parties, enforceable by either party if one party fails to comply with its terms. Four elements must be present in a contract: a promise or set of promises, an offer and an acceptance, an agreement of what is to be gained or given up, and an agreement between the parties that each has the same understanding (Gehring, 2000). In recent years, courts at all levels and jurisdictions have defined the relationship between the student and the institution as that of a contract. As a result, almost every oral and written statement between a student and an institutional representative has the potential to become part of a mutually binding contract (*Johnson v. Lincoln Christian College,* 1986). When disputes arise the first source of law to be checked is the elements of the contract between the parties.

Institutional Rules and Regulations

Although institutional rules and regulations are subject to the sources of the law already described, they are also a source of law in and of themselves. Often the question in litigation is whether an institution has followed its own rules. The key to sound institutional rules is to ensure that they are consistent with other sources of the law, are specific, are enforceable, are known, and are consistently enforced.

Academic Tradition

Academic tradition, custom, and usage represents the expectations members of the academic community hold for the behavior of the institution and its members and is the most diffuse source of law influencing higher education. Academic tradition is much more informal than other sources of the law; it may be documented through speeches, correspondence, media releases, and other interpretations of how the college or university conducts its business. The use of academic tradition as a source of law has been recognized under specific circumstances by the courts (*Krotkoff v. Goucher College,* 1978). Academic tradition has been used to interpret the elements of a contract between an employee and an institution by defining what the widely held expectations of members of the community are for the general institution and each other. *Perry v. Sinderman* (1972) involved a faculty member's expectation for receiving tenure based on what had traditionally happened at the institution and wording of the faculty handbook. It is the leading case in this area of the law.

Foreign or International Law

The increase in study abroad programs, research consortiums, and professorial exchanges requires awareness that the laws of other countries may influence the work of student affairs. For example, students studying abroad must comply with the law in the country where they are studying. Failure to do so could have severe consequences. Study abroad handbooks and orientation sessions should emphasize the need for compliance with the law when in other nations. If problems arise involving students, faculty, or staff involved in study programs, appropriate legal counsel should be immediately consulted.

Constitutional Issues

All of the sources of law described have great potential to influence the practice of student affairs professionals, but constitutional issues are often a major part of the daily practice of student affairs.

Freedom of Religion

The First Amendment to the U.S. Constitution states in part that "Congress shall make no law respecting the establishment of religion or prohibiting the free exercise thereof." The Supreme Court in *Lemon v. Kurtzman* (1971) established a three-pronged test to determine if the separation clause has been violated: (1) Does the activity have a clearly secular purpose? (2) Does the activity have a primary effect of neither advancing nor inhibiting religion? (3) Does excessive entanglement exist between the church and the state? If so, the action may be unconstitutional.

In *Widmar v. Vincent* (1981), the Supreme Court held that the neutral accommodation of student religious groups, in accordance with institutional policies, is not a violation of the First Amendment. *Rosenberger v. Rector and Visitors of the University of Virginia* (1995) involved a denial of an allocation of student fees to a religiously oriented magazine. The Supreme Court held that denying funding constituted "viewpoint discrimination" (p. 256) which is impermissible under the Constitution. In *Linnemeier v. Board of Trustees of Purdue University* (2001) a public institution made an auditorium available for a play that some citizens saw as anti-Christian and blasphemous. Three citizens sought to restrain the university from making the space available. The plaintiffs argued that such use was a violation of the establishment clause of the First Amendment. That argument was rejected by the court.

Private institutions are free to establish a religion or prohibit the free exercise of religion that is not consistent with their stated policies or mission. They must, however, be consistent in applying such criteria.

Freedom of Speech

The freedom of speech clause of the First Amendment also raises a number of issues of concern to student affairs administrators. While freedom of speech is not absolute (*Schenk v. United States,* 1919), it is an essential element in the marketplace of ideas of higher education. In *Siegel v. Regents of the University of California* (1970), the court held in part that "utterances in the context of violence, involving a definite and present danger, can lose significance as an appeal to reason and become part of an instrument of force . . . unprotected by the Constitution" (at 838).

Many cases regarding freedom of speech have focused on outside speakers, and most courts have agreed that neither a public nor private institution is obliged to open its doors to outside speakers. However, if a college or university allows outside speakers and "opens its lecture halls, it must do so nondiscriminately" (*Stacy v. Williams,* 1969).

Tinker v. Des Moines Independent School District (1969), although a secondary school case, established the right of students to symbolic free speech and declared that their "constitutional rights were not shed at the schoolhouse gate" (at 736). Wright's three principles (1969) are still valid today regarding free speech. First, expression cannot be prohibited because of disagreement with the content expressed. Second, expression is subject to reasonable regulations of the institution regarding its time, place, and manner. Third, expression can be prohibited if it can be proved that such expression will materially and substantially disrupt the primary educational mission of the institution.

The question of commercial free speech has also been litigated. *American Futures Systems, Inc. v. Pennsylvania State University* (1979/1980/1982/1983) is a series of cases dealing with this issue. In the case, the company sought to sell products in residence hall rooms through telephone solicitation and arranged demonstrations in residents' rooms. The university took the position that such solicitation violated the privacy of students and that commercial enterprises did not have absolute free speech rights in university residence halls. The university prevailed under the condition that its regulations were reasonable and alternate forms of expression existed for the commercial vendor.

Hate speech has resulted in some institutions introducing speech codes to regulate such behavior. This approach has been less than successful. The University of Michigan's policy prohibiting "any behavior, verbal or physical, that stigmatizes or victimizes an individual on the basis of race, ethnicity, religion, sex, sexual orientation, creed, national origin, ancestry, age, marital status, handicap or Vietnam-era veteran status" was declared unconstitutional because it was overly broad and vague (*Doe v. University of Michigan,* 1989). The Supreme Court also rejected portions of the Communications Decency Act (CDA) as an unconstitutional infringement on free speech on the Internet (*Reno v. American Civil Liberties Union,* 1997). Hate speech remains a vexing problem, and it is clear that more creative ways must be found to address the issue rather than more regulation.

Freedom of the Press

Freedom of the student press has been vigorously upheld by the courts. In *Dickey v. Alabama State Board of Education* (1967), the courts declared that an institution could not exercise prior restraint by removing an editorial critical of the state governor. Furthermore, funding cannot be removed due to a disagreement or potential institutional embarrassment regarding a student newspaper's content (*Minnesota Daily v. University of Minnesota,* 1983). Obscenity is not a reason for dismissal of a student editor or for using the campus discipline system against the editor (*Papish v. Board of Curators of the University of Missouri,* 1973). Removal of editorial advertisements has also not been upheld (*Lueth v. St. Clair County Community College,* 1990). Student newspapers must, however, conform to applicable statutes governing libel and slander (*Mazart v. State University of New York,* 1981).

Rosenberger, supra, held that funding of a Christian student newspaper does not violate the establishment clause of the First Amendment and also held that public universities, as centers of free expression, should not deny religious expression through withholding funding. Administrators at public institutions should seek legal advice on the implications of this case for specific funding approaches to the student press on their campus.

Freedom of Association

Private institutions may prevent, limit, or refuse to authorize the peaceful assembly of any group, including student organizations. Public institutions may not. However, both public and private institutions must follow their own published rules, and such rules should be reasonably specific, neither too vague nor too broad. In *Healy v. James* (1972), the Supreme Court upheld the right of a chapter of the organization Students for a Democratic Society to be recognized on a college campus. The institution claimed that the organization's philosophy espoused overthrowing the U.S. government. The Court held that there was a difference between advocacy and action and declared that nonrecognition was thus unconstitutional. The *Healy* decision has been tested in the last decades in cases involving gay and lesbian organizations seeking recognition by colleges and universities (*Gay Lib v. University of Missouri*, 1977; *Gay Student Services v. Texas A&M University*, 1984; *Gay Lesbian and Bisexual Alliance v. Pryor*, 1997); the courts upheld the rights of free association by students on the campuses of state colleges and universities. It should be noted, however, that in general, colleges and universities can deny recognition based on the record of conduct of the group (*Pi Lambda Phi Fraternity, Inc. v. University of Pittsburgh*, 2000).

Freedom of Assembly

Restrictions on the use of campus facilities have been upheld by the courts as long as the regulations are fair, reasonable, and enforced in an equitable manner. If student organizations follow institutional rules and regulations regarding time, place, and manner of assembly, they are free to use campus facilities for meetings. Restrictions on the use of campus facilities by outside groups have been upheld by the courts, if the restrictions are enforced in a fair and reasonable manner (*American Civil Liberties Union of Virginia v. Radford College*, 1970). The prime educational mission of the institution must also be protected by facility use policies (*State v. Jordan*, 1972). Once an institution has opened its doors to outside groups such as political parties, however, it must make facilities equally available to all, regardless of the content of the proposed event (*National Socialist White People's Party v. Ringers*, 1973). Furthermore, due process must be provided for denial of the use of facilities by outside groups (*Watson v. Board of Regents of the University of Colorado*, 1973). In addition, "state and local governments have trespass and unlawful entry laws that limit the use of postsecondary facilities by outsiders" (Kaplin & Lee, 1997, p. 483), and the courts have generally upheld these statutes and ordinances.

Search and Seizure

The Fourth Amendment provides protection against unreasonable search and seizure. Although *Moore v. Student Affairs Committee of Troy State University* (1976) permitted warrantless searches, another line of cases (*Smyth v. Lubbers*, 1975) has held such searches to be unlawful. Housing agreements must explicitly define the circumstances under which entry and search may occur (*State v. Hunter,* 1992). Although officials at public institutions can enter a room of a student under two conditions, the purposes for such entry are clearly stated as part of the housing contract with the student or if there is reason to believe an emergency exists. In either case, however, caution should prevail. When possible, administrators should seek to notify the student involved and obtain specific permission for the search and consent to enter the premises. Many times, however, that is not possible and good judgment must be used in the situation. In *Washington v. Chrisman* (1982), the Supreme Court heard a residence hall search and seizure case and affirmed that the "plain view" doctrine applied to warrantless searches. *New Jersey v. T.L.O.* (1985) also has implications for higher education. In this case, the Court held that a warrantless search was permissible because the secondary school official had reasonable suspicion that contraband was present. Private institutions should also carefully review their various contractual relationships with students and state law in this important area. Current issues, such as mandatory drug testing for student athletes, forecast more Fourth Amendment challenges of unreasonable search and seizure on the campuses of both public and private institutions.

Due Process

The Fourteenth Amendment provides, in part, for due process protection. The courts have held that students have a right to at least minimal due process standards in disciplinary hearings. Minimal standards include: notice of the charges, an opportunity to respond to the charges, having a hearing before an impartial person or board, and having an appropriate hearing for the type of alleged offense (*Dixon v. Alabama State Board of Education,* 1961). Gehring (2000) explains "the process that is due depends on the nature of the right that is deprived. Thus, a minor noise violation in a residence hall would not demand the same amount of due process as if the student faced expulsion" (p. 368). Private institutions do not need to adhere to the same due process standards as their public counterparts, but they must follow their own rules once they are established (*Harvey v. Palmer School of Chiropractic,* 1984), and they must treat students fairly (*Clayton v. Trustees of Princeton University,* 1985).

In general, the courts have also not interfered in academic matters. In *Ewing v. Board of Regents of the University of Michigan* (1985), the Supreme Court declared in part that courts may not interfere in a genuine academic decision unless "it is such a departure from accepted academic norms as to indicate that the faculty member or committee did not exercise professional judgment" (p. 507). Student affairs administrators, if they have institutional authority to do so, can take immediate action to suspend a student who poses a real and genuine threat to the welfare of the community. Such summary suspensions can be made on an interim basis, but a hearing must follow, and the institution must follow its own rules in taking such a serious step (*Swanson v. Wesley College,* 1979).

Equal Protection

The Fourteenth Amendment also provides that no person shall be denied equal protection under the law. This clause applies to private institutions when they are acting under "color of state law." Gehring (2000) indicates "the equal protection clause means that if an institution is engaged in state action, similarly situated individuals must be treated equally. Unless a fundamental right is denied to a class of people or a 'suspect class' is created, only a rational relationship between the classes of people created by the different treatment and the legitimate interests of the state must be demonstrated" (p. 370). To illustrate, a requirement that all women but only freshman men must live on-campus was found to be in violation of the equal protection clause (*Mollere v. Southeastern Louisiana College,* 1969). In combination with civil rights legislation, the Fourteenth Amendment provides powerful protection to students and others.

Civil Rights Issues

The various civil rights laws, which prohibit discrimination against certain protected classes of individuals, can influence all aspects of a student affairs division. This section reviews applicable federal statutes; the reader is cautioned to review state civil rights laws as well.

Seven broad statutes exist that prohibit discrimination for certain classes of individuals and require affirmative actions on the part of colleges and universities. The statutes include Section 1981, Section 1983, Title VI, Title VII, Title IX, Section 504, and the Americans with Disabilities Act.

Section 1981

The Civil Rights Act of 1866 (*U.S. Code,* Vol. 42. sec. 1981) is a broad statute regarding racial discrimination linked to the Thirteenth Amendment and applying to both public and private acts. Under Section 1981, a showing of state action is not required for the law to apply to private institutions, but it has not been widely applied to higher education because the plaintiff must prove that there has been purposeful and intentional discrimination by the defendant (*Williams v. DeKalb County,* 1978).

Section 1983

Unlike claims under Section 1981, claims under Section 1983 of the Civil Rights Act of 1964 are commonly used in litigation involving institutions of higher education. Under Section 1983, a plaintiff must only prove that he or she has been deprived of federally protected rights and that the deprivation occurred under color of state law (*Weise v. Syracuse University,* 1982).

Title VI

In 1954, racial discrimination in public schools was declared unconstitutional by the Supreme Court (*Brown v. Board of Education of Topeka,* 1954). Although *Brown* had far-reaching implications, it did not reach into the private sector. Title VI (*U.S. Code,* Vol. 42, sec. 2000d-1) was enacted to fill this gap. Title VI prohibits discrimination on the basis of race, color, or national origin in programs receiving federal financial assistance. In *Regents of the University of California v. Bakke* (1978), a White male alleged reverse discrimination in the admissions process. Initially four justices relied on Title VI (joined by a fifth justice relying on the Fourteenth Amendment) to hold that the institution discriminated against Bakke when admission was denied. However, a different group of five justices determined that a properly devised admissions program that used race or ethnic origin as one factor could be deemed to satisfy a legitimate and compelling state interest. Although affirmative action and numerical quotas can be used to cure specific cases of prior racial discrimination, race cannot be the only factor in an admission decision.

In *Hopwood v. University of Texas* (1996/2000), the law school at the University of Texas was initially enjoined from using racial data in selection of students for admission. That decision expressly conflicted with the Supreme Court decision in Bakke (*supra*). The university appealed and sought an *en banc* review by the Fifth Circuit Court of Appeals. Although the *en banc* review was denied, a new panel of judges heard the case and reversed the injunction by the district court. The Fifth Circuit panel affirmed the award for damages and attorney's fees and remanded the case back to the district court for findings in support of the injunction consistent with *Bakke.* The United States Supreme Court declined to hear the case.

Gratz v. Bollinger et al (2000) involved a class action challenge to the race conscious admissions policy of the law school of the University of Michigan. The district court issued an injunction stating that the policy was not sufficiently narrow, and further that the desire of the law school to enroll a "critical mass" of minority students was the functional equivalent of a quota. The injunction was stayed by the Sixth Circuit Court of Appeals, and the case is still being litigated as of this writing.

Title VII

The provisions of Title VII apply only to employment and prohibit discrimination on the basis of race, color, national origin, sex, or religion in businesses with fifteen or more employees. Title VII has sweeping implications for the hiring, promotion, termination, and benefits for all employees of the academy. This is a complex and specialized area of the law, and space does not permit full discussion of the issues here. The reader is urged to seek legal advice regarding employment issues from hiring to termination.

Title IX

This statute (*U.S. Code,* sec.1681–1686) applies specifically to education and educational institutions. It prohibits discrimination on the basis of sex. Certain types of institutions are not subject to the provisions of Title IX, including those controlled by religious, military, or merchant marine organizations, although such institutions may be covered under state antidiscrimination laws. *Grove City College v. Bell* (1984) established that Title IX does not cover the entire institution. The Equal Employment Opportunity Commission has prohibited both *quid pro quo* and hostile environment sexual harassment, and the courts have upheld those regulations (*Patricia H. v. Berkley Unified School District,* 1993). In a secondary school case applicable to higher education (*Gebser v. Lago Vista Independent School District,* 1998), the Supreme Court held that an institution could be held liable for the sexually harassing actions of employees noting, however, that someone in power must be notified of the harassment. Student-to-student sexual harassment issues are not as clear with several circuit courts disagreeing over whether the institution can be held liable under Title IX for such harassment. The Title IX doctrine from the Office of Civil Rights is still evolving. It is clear, however, that institutions can be held liable if they fail to act when harassing behavior is reported to institutional officials.

Title IX also includes gender equity in intercollegiate athletics. While it is not impermissible to award separate athletic scholarships for men's and women's teams on the basis of athletic ability, Title IX requires that institutions provide "reasonable" opportunity for men and women to receive athletic financial assistance in proportion to the number of male and female students enrolled in the institution. In addition, the regulations require that men and women participating in intercollegiate athletics receive equal benefits in terms of travel, locker rooms, training opportunities, and the like. It is a complex issue with enormous financial implications for colleges and universities.

Section 504

As part of the Vocational Rehabilitation Act of 1973 (*U.S. Code,* Vol. 29, secs. 791–794), Section 504 prohibits discrimination on the basis of handicap for any otherwise qualified student in any educational program receiving federal financial assistance. The act broadly defines handicaps and the interpretation of what constitutes a handicap. In addition, the implementing regulations focus on physical accessibility for programs on college and university campuses.

The Supreme Court held in *Southeastern Community College v. Davis* (1979) that a qualified person "is able to meet all of the program's requirements in spite of handicap(s)" (pp. 405–406), and under such conditions exclusion does not imply discrimination. Under Section 504, institutions must make reasonable accommodations for students with handicaps in housing, admissions, career counseling, and other services.

The question of what constitutes reasonable accommodation under Section 504 has been tested in the courts. In *Guckenberger v. Boston University* (1998), the court held that blanket decisions regarding course substitutions based on handicap are not permissible. Allowing additional time between medical school clinical clerkships has been deemed to be a reasonable accommodation (*Wong v. Regents of the University of California,* 1999).

Responsibility for payment for auxiliary aids for handicapped students has been answered differently in different jurisdictions. Some courts have said that the responsibility lies with the state rehabilitation agencies, not the institution (Gehring, 2000, p. 359). An Eleventh Circuit case (*United States v. Board of Trustees,* 1990), however, indicated that an institution may require students to seek funding from state agencies or private funding, but if these sources are unavailable the institution must provide the aids and services at no cost. This will continue to be an important area to monitor.

Americans with Disabilities Act (ADA)

While Section 504 deals solely with educational institutions, ADA is a sweeping act that applies to employers, including institutions of higher education, with more than twenty-five employees. The Americans with Disabilities Act (*U.S. Code,* Vol. 42, secs. 12101 et.seq.) covers employment issues but also focuses on physical and program accommodations for people with disabilities, including members of the public who may visit the campus and other places of public accommodation. Examples of institutional compliance with ADA include providing sign language interpreters at all public lectures and programs or providing assistance to visually impaired nonstudents who purchase recreation facility memberships. It is yet unclear what all the implications of ADA will be for higher education. The recent consent decree agreed to by Duke University agreeing to changes in programs and facilities may be a bellwether for other institutions.

Campus Safety and Security

Concern about the safety, security, and general health and well being of college students has been the subject of federal legislation (which is mirrored by similar statutes in many states). The Drug Free Schools and Communities Act of 1989 requires institutions to develop and disseminate information to students regarding substance abuse. The Hate Crime Statistics Act of 1990 requires the U.S. attorney general to collect additional data about crimes that manifest evidence of prejudice based on race, religion, sexual orientation, or ethnicity (Buchanan, 1993).

The Student Right-to-Know and Campus Security Act of 1990 requires colleges and universities to collect data on certain defined crimes; to advise students, faculty, and staff in writing of those crimes; to have a plan for emergency notification of criminal activity; and to publish crime statistics on an annual basis. Data for the prior three years must be included in all reports, and the reports must be available to current students and applicants. Additionally, the act requires that the institution annually publish the graduation rates of all student intercollegiate athletes.

Sexual assault and rape have received both legislative and judicial attention. Colleges and universities have a responsibility to protect student tenants and not assign an individual to a residence hall who presents a foreseeable risk to other students (*Nero v. Kansas State University,* 1993). In *Stanton v. University of Maine System* (2001), the court affirmed that a duty of reasonable care is an imperative responsibility of an institution. Finally, institutions have an obligation to provide appropriate support services to victims of sexual assault and rape and should engage in prevention activities to avoid problems.

Contracts

As indicated above, the contractual relationship between a student and an institution has been the basis of a great deal of litigation. Cases have been litigated regarding admission in both private and public institutions (*Nuttleman v. Case Western Reserve University,* 1981; *Hall v. University of Minnesota et al.,* 1982). The admissions policies of institutions have been upheld by the courts in all cases where the institution included specific language in its publications reserving certain rights for the institution and clearly articulating procedures.

Discipline cases, both academic and behavioral, have also been brought to the courts under contract theory. The courts have been reluctant to interfere in matters involving the judgment of professionals; however, when it could be proved institutional officials acted in an arbitrary and capricious manner, the institutions have been subject to judicial scrutiny for their actions (*McDonald v. Hogness,* 1979).

The right of an institution to alter requirements, change fees, and make other adjustments during a student's period of enrollment have been upheld by the courts, if such changes are reasonable (*Mahavongsanan v. Hall,* 1976). Tuition and fee refunds have also been litigated as a contractual obligation, and as long as the institution included appropriate disclaimers in its publications regarding costs, they have been upheld by the courts (*Basch v. George Washington University,* 1977; *Prusack v. State,* 1986). It would be prudent to place disclaimers in publications to educate staff about the importance of oral statements and to ensure that their regulations are fair, equitable, and consistently enforced.

Liability

Many factors have contributed to administrators' growing concern regarding personal and institutional liability. Litigation has increased, institutional and personal insurance costs have risen, and the number of contractual disputes has grown—all of these developments have contributed to concern about liability.

The question of whether a public institution—or a private institution engaging in state action—is immune from suit is difficult to answer. State law is the primary determining factor. Additional factors include whether the institution was engaged in state action, the charter provisions of the school, and other state statutes.

Tort Liability

Preventing and defending against liability claims in colleges and universities is both difficult and complex. The most common forms of liability actions fall under the doctrine of torts. As Kaplin and Lee (1997) explain, "A tort is broadly defined as a civil wrong, other than a breach of contract, for which the courts will allow a damage remedy" (p. 88). Tort actions may be brought in the event of either a direct invasion of some legal right of a person or a failure to meet a public duty or obligation toward a person.

Negligence. There are three legal prerequisites for pressing a claim of negligence: (1) the defendant owed a duty of care to the claimant, (2) the defendant breached that duty, and (3) the breach of duty was the proximate cause of injury. Courts have held, in regard to persons invited to campus, that institutions of higher education have a duty to take ordinary and reasonable care with respect to the conditions of their premises (*Mead v. Nassau Community College*, 1985). When a person is on the institution's premises for his or own convenience but with the sufferance of the institution, the institution owes the duty of maintaining the property in a reasonably safe condition. A trespasser is on the property without the legal permission of the owner, and under these conditions an institution may have diminished legal responsibility in claims of negligence.

Accidents are also a source of negligence claims. If an institution knows of a dangerous condition and fails to correct it, it can be held liable (*Lumbard v. Fireman's Fund Insurance Company*, 1974). But a person suffering a fall or injury does not by itself establish negligence. When a person has knowingly assumed a risk, liability claims against institutions or their agents have not been upheld in the courts (*Dudley v. William Penn College*, 1974).

Professionals involved in organizing and supervising off-campus trips and activities need to be particularly aware of potential liability issues. Insurance coverage by the bus company or other source of transportation should meet institutional standards and show evidence that it is current. If students are using institutional vehicles other questions come under consideration such as insurance coverage, driver training, emergency procedures, and vehicle maintenance. Many institutions, for example, halted the use of fifteen passenger vans by student groups when highway safety tests demonstrated that the vehicle was difficult to control on the open highway. Policies regarding the use of vehicles by students should be reviewed each year to make sure that all reasonable safety measures have been taken.

Sexual Assault. Cases of sexual assault have also been tried under claims of negligence. Such negligence claims have not been upheld when the assault was not foreseeable, there was not evidence of repeated criminal activity, and adequate security was in place (*Brown v. North Carolina Wesleyan College, Inc.*, 1983). A claim of negligence was upheld, however, in *Mullins v. Pine Manor College* (1983), in which the court declared that there was a special duty of care present, owing to the landlord-tenant relationship between the student and the institution.

Liability and Alcohol. State law is the most important variable in determining liability with regard to alcohol. The institution may be found liable as a supervisor of student conduct, property owner, seller of alcohol, or social host. In *Bradshaw v. Rawlings* (1979), however, an appellate court held there was not duty on the part of a college to keep a student from getting into a car with an intoxicated person.

Unintentional injury is often associated with alcohol, and even when there was no intent to harm, both the institution and its agent may be found liable. State laws vary greatly in this area and should be clearly understood. Residence hall staff members at the University of California (*Zavala v. Regents of the University of California,* 1981) served alcohol to an intoxicated person who subsequently fell and was injured. Although he played a part in his own injury, the institution was held partially liable under California law.

Some institutions have established areas on campus where alcohol is sold. Specific questions of liability may be involved in the operation of such premises, and the scope of state law as well as the criminal and civil penalties that attach under the law vary considerably. Potential liability connected with the sale of alcohol also extends to student organizations. Events, whether on- or off-campus, where alcohol is sold under the sponsorship of student organizations, also involve special issues. Again, state law will prevail, including requirements for a temporary license and insurance. Liability may also attach to an institution in states where statutes or case law establish civil liability for private hosts who furnish intoxicating beverages (*Estate of Hernandez v. Board of Regents,* 1994).

Other Areas of Liability

There are a number of other areas of potential liability of concern to student affairs administrators. These include defamation, civil rights liability, and contract liability. Each is an important area of the law and legal advice should be sought in all cases of potential liability.

Family Educational Rights and Privacy Act (FERPA) of 1974

The Family Educational Rights and Privacy Act of 1974 (FERPA, 34 CFR Part 99) was developed to protect the privacy of student educational records. Initially passed in the fall of 1974, it was amended three months later based on concerns from the educational community.

Generally known as the "Buckley Amendment," FERPA applies to any educational agency or institution (public or private) which is the recipient of federal funds. Under the law, parents (of minors) and students have a right to inspect and review their personal educational records, a right to add explanatory information to the record, and a right to a hearing to challenge the contents of the records. Institutions may not release personally identifiable records or files unless there is written consent for the release of the records. The request to release the records must include the reasons for the release and the parties to whom the records may be released. There are exceptions to the rule of prior written consent for records release including the following:

Directory Information. Directory information may include: name, address, telephone number, date and place of birth, major field of study, participation in officially recognized activities and sports, weight and height of members of athletic teams, dates of attendance, degrees and awards received, and the most recent institution attended by the student. Each institution must define and publicize what information the specific institution will release without prior written consent of the students. Each institution must also provide a reasonable period of time after publicity for students and parents to refuse to release directory information.

Other School Officials. Educational records can be released to other school officials with a legitimate educational interest in the record. This exception includes state and local officials in connection with an audit of any federally funded or state-supported program as well as the state's juvenile justice system.

Financial Aid. This exception allows the use of social security numbers in connection with the application for or receipt of financial aid.

Research. An exception is provided for organizations conducting studies for or on behalf of agencies or institutions in order to develop, validate, or administer predictive tests, administer student aid programs, and improve instruction. All information must be destroyed at the end of the study.

Accrediting Agencies. Educational records may be released to accrediting organizations in order to carry out accrediting functions.

Emergency Situations. Records may be released to appropriate persons to protect the health and safety of the student or other persons.

Victims. An educational institution may disclose to an alleged victim of a crime of violence the final result of any disciplinary proceeding. In 1998, through an amendment to the Higher Education Act (U.S. Code, Title 18, section 16), this concept was broadened to include the final results of any disciplinary hearing involving a crime of violence or nonforcible sex offense to anyone, if the institution determines that the student committed a violation of its rules or policies with respect to the crime.

Parental Notification. The 1998 Higher Education Amendments also added a new exception to FERPA, allowing higher education institutions to disclose to a parent or legal guardian information regarding violation by a student of any law or institutional rule or policy regarding alcohol or other controlled substances if the student is under twenty-one and the institution determines that the student is in violation of the rules of the institution.

Enforcement. Institutional violations of FERPA can result in loss of federal funding to the institution and a student cannot individually sue an institution for a violation of FERPA. As of this writing, however, the United States Supreme Court is considering a case where a student is suing Gonzaga University for a FERPA violation (*Gonzaga and League, Roberta v. Doe*, 2002). The Washington Supreme Court held that the student had a right to sue the university under FERPA, and the state appealed both the decision and the monetary settlement. Readers are urged to follow that case as it has great implications for higher education. Finally, questions regarding compliance with FERPA should be discussed with legal counsel in order to minimize unintentional violations of the law.

Working with Legal Counsel

Throughout this chapter reference has been made to working with legal counsel and seeking legal advice. Whether the attorney is an in-house counsel, on retainer to the institution, or hired to defend a specific case, the administrator must define the relationship with the attorney and determine who is the client. In matters of policy, attorneys should provide competent legal advice; however, it is the administrator's responsibility to determine what action should be taken. Too often, administrators abrogate their decision-making responsibilities to attorneys.

Duncan and Miser (2000) provide cogent advice on working with an attorney when there is a crisis or an administrator is being sued, cautioning that the administrator should: make no assumptions, inform the attorney of all the facts, get approval prior to commenting or writing about the case, and get training for a deposition. They remind practitioners that, although an out-of-court settlement may not be what an administrator wants personally, it may be in the best interests of the institution. Finally, if one is unsure about the quality of legal advice being received, it is worthwhile to engage a private attorney to protect one's personal interests if they may differ from those of the institution.

Emerging Issues

A number of points of law and the relationship of the law to students, institutions, and administrators have not been settled.

Affirmative Action

Institutional admissions and hiring policies continue to be a focus of lawsuits. An important question to be answered is whether or not *Bakke* will continue to stand permitting race to be one factor in admissions decisions or if race can be considered in the award of scholarships.

Alcohol Issues

Although not a new issue, alcohol abuse is one that remains with colleges and universities. Clarification will continue to be sought regarding the duty of an institution to protect students from their own harmful acts.

Antiterrorism Policies

Statutes relating to both changes in the Family Educational Rights and Privacy Act and tracking student visas are currently wending their way through the legislative process. How the emerging antiterrorist legislation will influence the work of student affairs administrators, particularly those associated with records and international students, is yet to be determined.

Auxiliary Aids for Students with Disabilities

Although the courts have been clear that institutions must provide such aids, they have left the door open for institutions to claim an "unreasonable burden." Definition of such unreasonable burden will occur in the years to come.

Students with Long-Term Psychological Issues

Institutions are dealing with increasing numbers of students who enter with long-term psychological problems that may result in behavior disruptive to the community. The question of how to ensure access for such students while also assuring a safe and calm learning environment for all students will continue to be an issue on campus.

Hate Speech

The issue of hate speech will continue as a problem that will need to be addressed on campus. Acts of violence based on bigotry and intolerance and fear are clearly unlawful but speech regulations are still being challenged.

Use of the Internet and Computing Resources

The issue of how the computing resources of the institution, including equipment and Internet access, may be used will continue to vex administrators. Use of computing facilities for criminal activities, hate speech, harassment, copyright infringement, and other matters will continue to pose both administrative and legal questions.

Loan Relief

New legislation regarding relief from loan repayment schedules for victims of terror and those called to active duty in the armed services will create new compliance and tracking burdens for student financial aid officers.

Professional Liability Insurance

Each professional must determine whether or not they have appropriate liability insurance coverage. Although most student affairs professionals are covered by their institution, consideration should be given to purchase of individual professional liability insurance. Such insurance is available through a number of professional organizations and is a good investment for the practitioner. Professional liability insurance provides the freedom to seek personal legal advice if a difficult situation should arise.

Transgendered Students

Transgendered students, faculty, and staff, particularly when they are in the process of change, pose interesting accommodation questions for institutions of higher education (*Cruzan v. Minneapolis Public School System, Special School District No. 1,* September 5, 2001). It is likely that issues regarding housing, athletic participation, and membership in fraternities and sororities will be litigated in the near future.

Conclusion

It is clear that the law is a part of the professional practice in student affairs. Staff training in the legal implications of student affairs is required for sound practice. Publications should be reviewed. Legal assistance should be sought, early and often, and the student affairs administrator should exercise sound judgment when receiving that advice. Administrators should not be afraid to challenge traditional practices if they are inappropriate.

Finally, student affairs officers should exercise the best judgment possible based on the facts, including the educational mission of the institution. The law is one of many tools available to student affairs administrators to meet the goals of honesty, fairness, equity, and responsibility.

References

Alexander, K., & Solomon, E. (1972). *College and university law.* Charlottesville, VA: Michie.

Barr, M. J. (Ed.). (1988). *Student services and the law: A handbook for practitioners.* San Francisco: Jossey-Bass.

Buchanan, E. T. (1993). The changing role of government in higher education. In M. J. Barr & Associates, *The handbook of student affairs administration* (pp. 493–508). San Francisco: Jossey-Bass.

Duncan, M. A., & Miser, K. M. (2000). Dealing with campus crisis. In M. J. Barr & M. K. Desler (Eds.), *The handbook of student affairs administration* (2nd ed., pp. 453–473). San Francisco: Jossey-Bass.
Gehring, D. D. (2000). Understanding the legal implications of student affairs practice. In M. J. Barr & M. K. Desler (Eds.), *The handbook of student affairs administration* (2nd ed., pp. 347–356). San Francisco: Jossey-Bass.
Kaplin, W. A., & Lee, B. A. (1997). *A legal guide for student affairs professionals.* San Francisco: Jossey-Bass.
Thompson, J. (1976). *Policymaking in American public education.* Englewood Cliffs, NJ: Prentice Hall.
Wright, C. A. (1969). The Constitution on campus, *Vanderbilt Law Review, 22,* 1027–1088.

Legal Case References

American Civil Liberties Union of Virginia, Inc. v. Radford College, 315 F. Supp. 893 (W.D. Va. 1970).
American Future Systems, Inc. v. Pennsylvania State University, 464 F. Supp. 1252 (1979), 752 F.2d, 1984).
American Future Systems, Inc. v. Pennsylvania State University, 618 F. 2d 252 (3d Cir. 1980).
American Future Systems, Inc. v. Pennsylvania State University, 688 F. 2d 907 (3d Cir. 1982).
American Future Systems, Inc. v. Pennsylvania State University, 568 F. Supp. 666 (M.D. Pa. 1983).
Basch v. George Washington University, 370 A. 2d 1364 (D.C. Cir. 1977).
Bradshaw v. Rawlings, 612 F. 2d 135 (3d Cir. 1979); cert den. 446 U.S., 909 (1980).
Brown v. Board of Education of Topeka, 347 U.S. 483 (1954).
Brown v. North Carolina Wesleyan College, Inc. 309 S.E. 2d 701 (N.C. App., 1983).
Clayton v. Trustees of Princeton University, 608 F. Supp. 413 (D. N.J. 1985).
Commonwealth of Pennsylvania v. Tate, 432 A. 2d 1382 (Pa. 1981).
Cruzan v. Minneapolis Public School System, W.L. 1173860, September 5, 2001.
Dickey v. Alabama Board of Education, 273 F. Supp. 613 (1967).
Dixon v. Alabama Board of Education, 294 F. 2d 150 (5th Cir. 1961), cert. Denied 368 U.S. 930 (1961).
Doe v. University of Michigan, 721 F. Supp. 852 (E.D. Mich. So. Div. 1989).
Dudley v. William Penn College, 219 N.W. 2d 484 (Iowa, 1974).
Estate of Hernandez v. Board of Regents, 866 P. 2d 1330 (AZ 1994).
Ewing v. Board of Regents of the University of Michigan, 743 F. 2d 913 (6th Cir. 1984), rev'd. (other grounds) 106 S.Ct. 507 (1985).
Gay Lesbian and Bisexual Alliance v. Pryor, 110 F. 3d 1543 (11th cir. 1997).
Gay Lib v. University of Missouri, 58 F. 2d 848 (8th Cir.) 1977.
Gay Student Services v. Texas A&M University, 737 F. 2d 1317 (5th Cir. 1984).
Gebser v. Lago Vista Independent School District, 118 S.Ct. (1989) 1998.
Gonzaga and League, Roberta v. Doe, No. 01–679, argued April 23, 2002, Supreme Court (2002).
Gratz v. Bollinger et al. 122 F. Supp. 2d 811 (E.D. Mich. 2000), No 97–75928, 2001 W.L. 315715 (E.D. Mich. April 3, 2001).
Grove City College v. Bell, 104 S.Ct. 1211 (1984).
Guckenberger v. Boston University, 8 F. Supp. 2d 82 (D. Ma. 1998).
Hall v. University of Minnesota et. al. 530 F. Supp. 104 (D. Minn. 1982).
Harvey v. Palmer School of Chiropractic, 363 N.W. 2d 443 (Iowa, 1984).
Healy v. James, 92 S.Ct. 2338 (1972).
Hopwood v. University of Texas, 78 F. 3d 932, cert denied 518 U.S. 1033 (1996), *on remand,* 999 F. Supp. 872 (W.D. Tex, 1998), *aff'd in part, rev'd in part,* 236 F. 3d 256 (5th Cir. 2000).
Johnson v. Lincoln Christian College, 501 N.E. 2d 1380 (Ill. App. 4th Dist. 1986).
Krotkoff v. Goucher College, 585 F. 2d 675 (4th Cir. 1978).

Lemon v. Kurtzman, 403 U.S. 602 (1971).
Linnemeier v. Board of Trustees of Purdue University, 2001 App. Lexis 17922 (7th Cir. 2001).
Lueth v. St. Clair County Community College, 732 F. Supp. 1410 (E.D. Mich. S.D. 1990).
Lumbard v. Fireman's Fund Insurance Company, 302 So. 2d 394 (Ct. App. La. 1974).
McDonald v. Hogness, 598 P. 2d 707 (Wash. 1979).
Mahavongsanan v. Hall, 529 F. 2d 488 (5th Cir. 1976).
Mazart v. State University of New York, 441 N.Y.S. 2d 600 (Ct. Ct. 1981).
Mead v. Nassau County Community College, 483 N.Y.S. 2d 953 (Sup. Ct. 1985).
Minnesota Daily v. University of Minnesota, 719 F. 2d 279 (8th Cir. 1983).
Mollere v. Southeastern Louisiana College, 304 F. Supp. 826 (W.D. AR, Fayetteville Div. 1969).
Moore v. Student Affairs Committee of Troy State University, 284 F. Supp. 775 (M.D. Ala, 1976).
Mullins v. Pine Manor College, 449 N.E. 2d 331 (1983).
National Socialist White People's Party v. Ringers, 473 F. 2d 1010 (4th Cir. 1973).
Nero v. Kansas State University, 861 P. 2d 768 (1993).
New Jersey v. T.L.O., 469 U.S. 325 (1985).
Nuttleman v. Case Western Reserve University, 560 F. Supp. 1 (N.D. Ohio, 1981).
Papish v. Board of Curators of the University of Missouri, 93 S.Ct. 1197 (1973).
Patricia H. v. Berkley Unified School District, 830 F. Supp. 288 N.D. CA. (1993).
Perry v. Sinderman, 408 U.S. 593 (1972).
Pi Lambda Phi Fraternity, Inc. v. University of Pittsburgh, 229 F. 3d 435 (3rd Cir. 2000).
Prusack v. State, 498 N.Y.S. 455 (A.D. 2Dept. 1986).
Regents of the University of California v. Bakke, 438 U.S. 265 (1978).
Reno v. American Civil Liberties Union, 521 U.S. 844 (1997).
Rosenberger v. Rector and Visitors of the University of Virginia, 115 S. Ct. 2510 (1995).
Schenk v. United States, 249 U.S. 47 (1919).
Siegel v. Regents of the University of California, 308 F. Supp. 832 (Calif. 1970).
Smyth v. Lubbers, 398 F. Supp. 777 (W.D. Mich. 1975).
Southeastern Community College v. Davis, 442 U.S. 397 (1979).
Stacy v. Williams, 306 F. Supp. 963 (N.D. Miss. 1969).
Stanton v. University of Maine System, 773 A. 2d 1045 (Me. 2001).
State v. Hunter, 831 P. 2d. 1033, (Utah App. 1992).
State v. Jordan, 53 Hawaii 634, 500 P. 2d 56 (1972).
State v. Schmid, 423 A. 2d 401 (N.J. 1980).
Swanson v. Wesley College, 402 A. 2d 401 (Del. Sup. Ct. Kent. Co. 1979).
Tinker v. Des Moines Independent School District, 393 U.S. 503 (1969).
United States v. Board of Trustees, 908 F. 2d 740 (11th Cir. 1990).
Washington v. Chrisman, 455 U.S. 1(1982).
Watson v. Board of Regents of the University of Colorado, 512 P. 2d 1161 (1973).
Weise v. Syracuse University, 553 F. Supp. 675 (N.D.N.Y. 1982); 522 F. 2d 397 (2d. Cir. 1975).
Widmar v. Vincent, 103 S. Ct. 269 (1981).
Williams v. DeKalb County, 582 F. 2d 457 (5th Cir. 1978).
Wong v. Regents of the University of California, 166 F. 3d 698 (9th Cir. 1999).
Zavala v. Regents of the University of California, 125 Cal. App. 3d 648 (1981).

PART THREE

THEORETICAL BASES OF THE PROFESSION

Parts One and Two set a foundational context for student affairs practice. As the contributors to those parts made clear, understanding diverse students' experience with postsecondary education requires a thorough grounding in the historical and philosophical foundations of American higher education. But student affairs professionals also need a deep understanding of how students grow, develop, and learn and how the environment influences that change. Therefore, this part presents the developmental, educational, organizational, environmental, and student success theories essential to the work of every student affairs practitioner.

Each edition of this book illustrated the rich and growing theoretical heritage of the student affairs profession covering a span of thirty years. In the first edition, written in the late 1970s, the visionaries Delworth and Hanson included chapters on student development theory as well as environmental interaction theory. They expanded that theoretical frame in the second edition, written a decade later, to include organizational theory. Our third edition further expanded the theoretical perspective to include discussions on what theory is and how it is useful in practice, new perspectives on identity development, and theoretical explorations of how students learn. This edition expands this section with the theoretical and research grounding of the retention of students and the growing body of interest in student success.

In Chapter Eight, Marylu McEwen introduces the role and nature of theory applicable to students and the higher education context, including logical positivism, critical science, and social construction. Her discussion on how and why theoretical applications are useful for one's own development and in one's work with students and the higher education environment reinforces the benefits of putting theory into practice. She has expanded this chapter to discuss the elements of developmental theory and the families of theories that exist in student affairs work. In Chapter Nine, Nancy Evans presents an overview of theories of student development, including psychosocial development theory (emphasizing adult and career development). Her discussion is informed by individual differences that might not have been taken into account in the original development of select theories. In Chapter Ten, Marylu McEwen expands on important aspects of identity development, emphasizing social construction of such dimensions as gender, ability, race, and class with increased attention to how different aspects of identity might develop concurrently. In Chapter Eleven, Pat King presents an overview of how students learn. As a central element in student development, cognitive-structural theory and student learning should be a primary expertise base of student development educators. In Chapter Twelve, George Kuh explores both conventional and alternative views of how organizational systems function. Organizational systems and the expectations of people in various organizational relationships have a direct influence on the student experience. In Chapter Thirteen, Carney Strange reviews the importance of understanding how environments influence learning and development, with a particular focus on understanding campus climate and culture. In the new Chapter Fourteen, John Braxton explores and critiques retention theories and related theoretical frames such as adult transition theory that support the applications leading to student success.

It is encouraging that student affairs professionals are engaging in healthy and critical dialogue about the role and use of theoretical perspectives in practice and research. Part Three contributes to that inquiry by presenting both the breadth and depth of theoretical perspectives that should inform student affairs practice. The challenge for theoreticians today is to reformulate and integrate theory to make it useful in practice, and the challenge for practitioners is to inform their professional actions with appropriate theory and research.

CHAPTER EIGHT

THE NATURE AND USES OF THEORY

Marylu K. McEwen

As an academic advisor to students who have not yet made a decision about their major, it is difficult for you to understand some of the differences among your advisees—why, for example, many of your first-year student advisees, regardless of their background and abilities, seem almost preoccupied with whether they can handle college-level work.

You regularly conduct diversity training with groups of student leaders. You have noticed that some students are open and excited about the training and others seem highly resistant, and you are confused by their different reactions.

As a residence hall director, you supervise resident assistants and undergraduate students in four different buildings. In two units the students seem to possess a true sense of community; in another there are difficulties with discipline, vandalism, and hate speech; in the fourth unit the students seem passive and indifferent. You can't make sense of why this would be the case.

You observe that the administrative division and the academic affairs division in the college where you work always seem to conduct their business differently. When someone from the administrative division wants to meet with you, he or she has always involved, and received permission, from his or her supervisor. But when a faculty member or an assistant academic dean meets with you, it is unusual for either the department chair or the dean to know about it. On the other hand, you usually inform your supervisor but rarely ask for permission. You wonder how and why all these units within the same college function so differently.

Note: I wish to acknowledge the generous assistance of Ralph Komives in the computer design of Figures 8.1 and 8.2.

The differences in the above situations are most likely neither just chance nor random occurrences, and they may be understood through various theories and theoretical perspectives. Theories about how college students develop can help to understand the first two examples. Theories about how people and environments interact and models of the design of environments for educational purposes provide clues about the differences among the four residence hall units. Organizational theory offers perspectives on how different organizations function and what kinds of outcomes might be expected in different situations. More important, however, theory not only helps us to understand what we experience and observe but provides a foundation for practice in student affairs. The use of theory is one way of assisting student affairs professionals to be expert scholar-practitioners.

The six purposes of this chapter are to consider the following: (1) why student affairs professionals need theory; (2) families of theory that inform practice in student affairs; (3) purposes and development of theory and the role of theory in student affairs; (4) theory as social construction; (5) contemporary challenges to theory; and, (6) how one makes individual choices about which theories to use, including the importance of looking at oneself in learning, selecting, and applying theories.

Why Student Affairs Professionals Need Theory

Student affairs professionals should use theory for many reasons. First and perhaps most important, a theoretical basis for knowledge, expertise, and practice serves as a foundation for a profession, which student affairs is and has been for almost a century (see Chapter Four). Second, knowing and understanding theory provides a medium of communication and understanding among student affairs professionals. Third, theory can serve as a "common language" within a "community of scholars" (Knefelkamp, 1982).

A student affairs professional needs theory because it is difficult for one person to hold simultaneously in his or her understanding all the aspects of a particular phenomenon he or she is interested in—for instance, all the characteristics of a student's identity or all the components of a particular environment. Ivey (1986) has suggested that "there is more going on in development than meets the eye of consciousness, and development is too complex for us to be aware of it all" (p. 312). Each one of us has our own informal theories about people, environments, students, human development, and how to work with students, although these theories or perspectives may not always be a conscious or clear part of our awareness. Thus people turn to theory—both formal and informal—to make the many complex facets of experience manageable, understandable, meaningful, and consistent rather than random.

Since the primary goals of student affairs professionals are to facilitate students' development, to understand and design educationally purposeful environments, and to be experts about organizations and how they function, it is our responsibility, both professionally and ethically, to know and understand the individuals, groups, and institutions with whom we work. One important way to do this is through theory. Student affairs professionals are primarily theory users, consumers, and interpreters rather than formal theorists (although they are informal theory developers).

Theories, models, and perspectives used in student affairs come from familiar sources such as the disciplines of human development, developmental psychology, organizational behavior, counseling psychology, and social psychology. Researchers who have studied the development and success of college students and the characteristics of organizations of higher education are other sources. Theories and perspectives also evolve out of our own and others' observations and experiences and from literature and stories. Student affairs professionals can acquire a comprehensive understanding of theory about student and human development, higher education, and organizations in an interdisciplinary fashion, drawing from the literature not only in psychology and education but also in ethnic studies, women's studies, sociology, history, literature, anthropology, philosophy, business, and management, as well as from oral and written stories and from one's own observations.

Families of Theories in Student Affairs

Rich sets of theories and models about students have evolved since the mid-1960s. These theories concern how students develop during college, how they learn, what elements come together to contribute to students' success, and how the dynamics of college environments relate to educational purposes. In Part Three, six authors discuss these perspectives about students and how higher education organizations and environments are constructed and function. The model in Figure 8.1 portrays the families of theories that inform practice in student affairs and the hypothesized relationships among the theory families. Figure 8.2 is an elaboration of developmental theories, representing the relationships among the subsets of developmental theories and how developmental theories come together in developmental synthesis. Brief descriptions of the families of theories are provided below, followed by a narrative portrayal of the dynamic relationships among the theory families and a rationale for the organization of the theory sets. Names and foci of specific theories associated with each family and subcategory of theories are identified in Exhibit 8.1.

Developmental Theories

Development, growth, and change are often used synonymously and interchangeably. Sanford (1967), however, contrasts these three terms, suggesting that they have different meanings. In a general sense, development is about becoming a more complex individual (with, for example, a more complex identity, more complex cognition, or more complex values). A more precise definition is that development represents the "organization of increasing complexity" (Sanford, 1967, p. 47), or an increasing differentiation *and* integration of the self (Sanford, 1962, p. 257). Thus, development involves change, and it may include growth; but more specifically, it represents a qualitative

FIGURE 8.1. WORKING MODEL OF RELATIONSHIPS AMONG FAMILIES OF THEORIES IN STUDENT AFFAIRS.

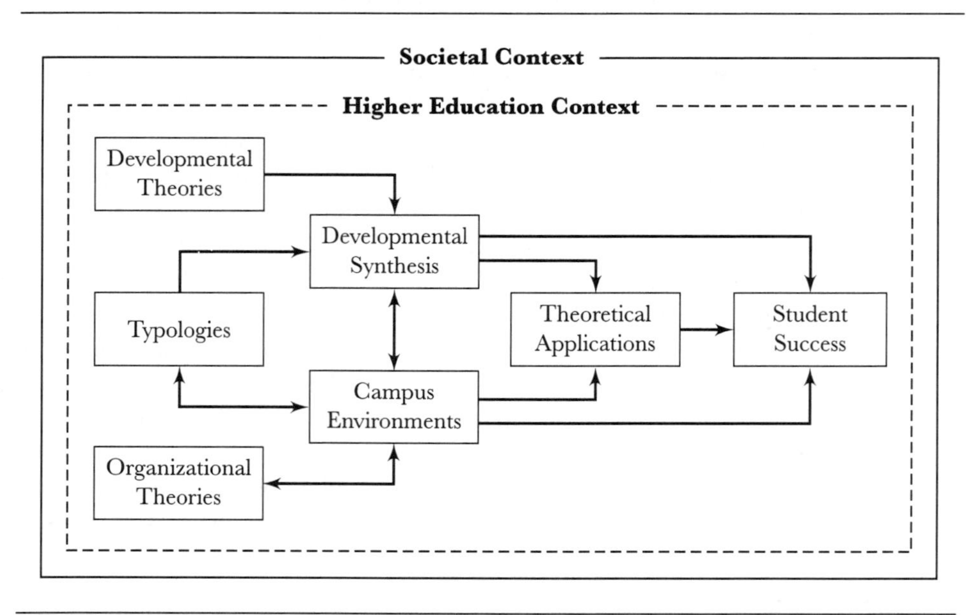

FIGURE 8.2. MODEL OF RELATIONSHIPS AMONG THEORIES ABOUT THE DEVELOPMENT OF COLLEGE STUDENTS.

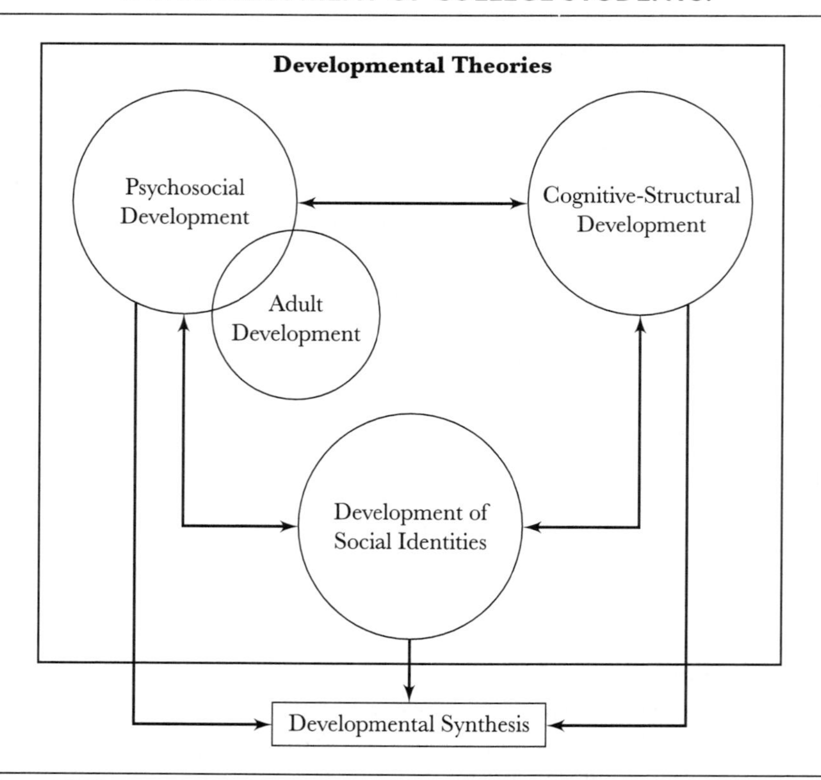

EXHIBIT 8.1. THEORIES ABOUT COLLEGE STUDENTS, ENVIRONMENTS, AND ORGANIZATIONS.

Theory Family	Subcategory	Focus of Theory	Specific Theories
Psychosocial Development (See Chapter Nine for theories of psychosocial development.)	General psychosocial development	Foundational theory	Erikson
		Challenge and support	Sanford
		Vectors of development	Chickering
		Young adults and alienated students	Keniston
		Patterns of continuity versus crisis in personality change	King
		Crisis and commitment	Marcia
		Women's development	Josselson
	Career development	Life-span development and self-concept implementation	Super
	Adult development	Life stage	Erikson; Gould; Levinson; Vaillant
		Life events	Fiske; Schlossberg, Waters, & Goodman; Sugarman; Whitbourne
		Life course	Neugarten; Bengston; Elder; Hughes & Graham
Cognitive-Structural Development (See Chapters Nine and Eleven for theories of cognitive-structural development and student learning.)	General cognitive-structural development	Foundational theory	Piaget
		Perry scheme	Perry
		Women's ways of knowing	Belenky, Clinchy, Goldberger, & Tarule
		Reflective judgment	King & Kitchener
		Epistemological reflection	Baxter Magolda
		Conceptual systems and training environments	Harvey, Hunt, & Schroder

(*Continued*)

EXHIBIT 8.1. THEORIES ABOUT COLLEGE STUDENTS, ENVIRONMENTS, AND ORGANIZATIONS. (*CONTINUED*)

Theory Family	Subcategory	Focus of Theory	Specific Theories
	Moral development	Justice and rights	Kohlberg
		Care and responsibility	Gilligan
		Moral reasoning	Rest, Narvaez, Bebeau, & Thoma
	Faith development	Faith	Fowler
		Spirituality	Parks
		Black womanist ethics	Cannon
		Mujerista theology	Isasi-Díaz
Development of Social Identities (See Chapter Ten for theories of social identity development.)	Contextual analysis		Weber
	Racial identity	Black racial identity	Cross; Helms; Jackson
		White racial identity	Helms; Hardiman
		Asian American racial identity	Kim; Sodowsky, Kwan, & Pannu
		Native American racial identity	Horse
		Latino racial identity	Bernal & Knight; Casas & Pytluk; Ferdman & Gallegos
		People of Color racial identity	Helms
		Biracial identity	Poston; Kich; Kerwin & Ponterotto
		Multiracial identity	Root; Wijeyesinghe
	Ethnic identity	Crisis and commitment	Phinney
		Ethnic identity	Ruiz
		Bicultural orientation	Torres
	Sexual identity	Gay and lesbian identity	Cass; Fassinger; D'Augelli
		Bisexual identity	Klein
		Heterosexual identity	Mueller; Worthington, Savoy, Dillon, & Vernaglia
		General sexual identity	Klein, Sepekoff, & Wolf; Sullivan

EXHIBIT 8.1. (*CONTINUED*)

Theory Family	Subcategory	Focus of Theory	Specific Theories
	Gender identity	Feminist identity	Downing & Roush
		Womanist identity	Ossana, Helms, & Leonard
		Gender role	O'Neil
	Minority identity		Atkinson, Morten, & Sue
	Social class and background		
	Religious identity		
	Abilities and disabilities		
	Multiple identities	Multiple oppressions	Reynolds & Pope
		Multiple identities	Jones & McEwen
Developmental Synthesis		Maturity	Douglas Heath
		Self-evolution	Kegan
Typologies (See Chapters Nine and Eleven for personality and learning typologies.)	Personality	Intercultural maturity	King & Baxter Magolda
		Temperament and development	Roy Heath
		Psychological type	Myers-Briggs
		Vocational personality types	Holland
	Learning	Learning style	Kolb
		Field dependence and independence	Witkin
		Multiple intelligences	Gardner
		Surface and deep approaches	Marton & Säljö
		Self-regulated learning	

(*Continued*)

EXHIBIT 8.1. THEORIES ABOUT COLLEGE STUDENTS, ENVIRONMENTS, AND ORGANIZATIONS. (*CONTINUED*)

Theory Family	Subcategory	Focus of Theory	Specific Theories
Organizational Theories (See Chapter Twelve for theories about organizations and Chapter Eighteen for theories about multicultural organizational development.)	Conventional approaches	Rational-bureaucratic	Weber
		Collegial	Austin & Gamson
		Political	Baldridge
	Postconventional views	Organized anarchy	Cohen & March
		Cultural phenomenon	Kuh & Whitt; Schein; Tierney
		Learning organization	Morgan; Senge
		Multicultural organizational development	Jackson & Holvino; Manning & Coleman-Boatwright; Pope; Tierney; Grieger; Talbot
	Organizational redesign		Eckel, Hill, Green, & Mallon; Kezar & Eckel; Peterson, Dill, Mets, & Associates; Tierney
Campus Environments (See Chapter Thirteen for theories and models about campus environments.)	Physical components		Barker; Dober; Gaines; Moffatt; Michelson; Sommer; Stern
	Human aggregates	Subcultures	Astin; Clark & Trow; Holland; Kolb; Myers
		Person-environment interactions	Holland
	Organized environments	Organizational structures and dynamics	Hage & Aiken
	Constructed environments	Environmental press	Pace & Stern; Moos
		Campus culture	Chaffee & Tierney; Horowitz; Kuh; Kuh & Whitt; Moffatt; Schein

EXHIBIT 8.1. (*CONTINUED*)

Theory Family	Subcategory	Focus of Theory	Specific Theories
	Design for educational success	Inclusion and safety, involvement, community	Strange & Banning
	Environmental impact		Moos; Strange & Banning
Theoretical Applications	Involvement		Astin
	Mattering and marginality		Schlossberg
	Transition theory		Schlossberg
Student Success (See Chapter Fourteen for theories and models about student success.)	Student departure	Economic	Becker
		Organizational	Berger & Braxton
		Psychological	Individual level—Bean & Eaton; student development theories
			Environmental level—Moos; Baird
		Sociological	Cultural capital—Bourdieu
			Student culture—Kuh & Love
			Interactionalist theory—Tinto
	Nontraditional student attrition		Bean & Metzner
	Modified model of student persistence		Berger & Milem

Source: McEwen, 2002.

enhancement of the self in terms of the self's complexity and integration. Positive values are usually attached to the word *development;* for example, highly developed is better than less developed, and greater development represents increased maturity.

Knefelkamp, Widick, and Parker (1978) identified four essential components of theoretical knowledge about student development for student affairs professionals: "Who the college student is in developmental terms; how development occurs; how the college environment can influence student development; and toward what ends development in college should be directed" (p. x). They suggested, "knowledge in these four areas would give specific and concrete meaning to the task of encouraging student development" (p. x).

Psychosocial development theories (see Chapter Nine) are concerned with the *content* of development (Evans, Forney, & Guido-DiBrito, 1998), that is, "*what* students will be concerned about" (Knefelkamp et al., 1978, p. xii). The major issues that students think about and what they are preoccupied with, and how those major issues and preoccupations evolve over time, are at the core of psychosocial development theory. Although these theories generally focus on the individual (the "psychological" part of psychosocial), the environment (the "social" part) also plays a critical role. Included within psychosocial development are *adult development* and *career development theories.*

Cognitive-structural development theories (see Chapters Nine and Eleven) address "how students will think about those [psychosocial] issues and what shifts in reasoning will occur" (Knefelkamp et al., 1978, p. xii), *not* what they think about. These theories propose cognitive structures, which might be thought of as filters or lenses, of increasing complexity through which one takes in information, perceives experiences, and constructs meanings. Cognitive-structural development theories also include those theories specific to moral development and faith development.

Social identity development theories (see Chapter Ten) address the ways in which individuals construct their various social identities, namely, race, ethnicity, gender, and sexual orientation, and the intersection of these multiple identities. Social class, ability and disability, and religion are three other identity dimensions considered within this family. Many of the identity development theories are concerned *both* with *what* students think about their specific social identity *and how* they think about it. Models of multiple identities, because they focus primarily on social identities, are also part of this family of theories.

Developmental synthesis models consider students' development holistically—that is, their psychosocial and cognitive development in interaction with one another. Social identity development, although not incorporated within the few existing models, may be included in future development of integrative models.

Other Theories and Models About College Students

Typology models (see Chapters Nine and Eleven) consider certain persistent characteristics or behaviors of individuals that remain relatively stable over time. Typology models do not describe development, although some of the models' creators have discussed a developmental component underlying the typologies. Many of these models consider learning styles or personality styles. Some of the early typology models

(Clark & Trow, 1966; Holland, 1966; Newcomb, Joenig, Flacks, & Warwick, 1967) concerned person-environment interaction and student subcultures.

Theoretical applications (see Chapters Nine and Fourteen) consider ways in which students' development and their environments come together to affect their college experiences. Theories include those of student involvement (Astin, 1984), mattering and marginality (Schlossberg, 1989), and transition (Schlossberg, Waters, & Goodman, 1995).

Student success theories (see Chapter Fourteen) address what happens to students as they enter and matriculate through colleges and universities. Models and theories concern student departure, attrition, and persistence.

Theories of Organizations and Campus Environments

Organizational theories (see Chapter Twelve) concern the behavior of individuals and groups within complex organizations. *Theories about campus environments* (see Chapter Thirteen) address the dimensions and dynamics of environments and the design and redesign of environments for educational purposes.

Relationships Among Theory Families

Relationships among theory families are presented graphically in Figures 8.1 and 8.2. Let's first address the large grouping of developmental theories in Figure 8.2. Psychosocial and adult development theories are one major subset, represented by two intersecting circles. Although some theories of adult development (life stage) are part of psychosocial development, others (such as life events and life course) extend beyond the constructs of psychosocial development theories. Social identity development and psychosocial development are also closely intertwined and influence one another (indicated by bidirectional arrows). Bidirectional arrows illustrate the cognitive-structural aspect of many social identity theories and the interaction between psychosocial development and cognitive-structural development. Psychosocial, adult, social identity, and cognitive-structural development theories all contribute theoretically to developmental synthesis; this is represented in Figure 8.2 by the arrows from each of these groupings to developmental synthesis.

Let's now return to Figure 8.1. Theories about students and higher education environments and organizations should be considered within environmental, historical, and sociocultural contexts, represented in Figure 8.1 by the two large rectangles. The larger outer rectangle represents the societal context, primarily in the United States but also in the larger global society. The inner rectangle represents the context of a particular institution of higher education; the dashed line of the inner rectangle suggests that higher education institutions do not exist separately from the larger society. All theories must be considered within these two contexts.

The three sets of theories on the left in Figure 8.1, namely, the development of college students, typologies about college students, and theories about the organizations of colleges and universities, are hypothesized to occur simultaneously. Developmental theories and typologies take place concurrently and in interaction with one another to form developmental synthesis, suggested by the unidirectional arrows. Similarly, typologies about students and organizations interact to create campus environments and are also influenced by campus environments, indicated by the bidirectional arrows. The relationship of organizational theories to student development theories is hypothesized to be indirect, and thus there is no arrow connecting the two groupings.

Developmental synthesis and campus environments contribute directly to student success and also indirectly through theoretical applications, that is, students' transitions, to how they feel they matter or how marginalized they feel, and their involvement. Campus environments contribute to students' development (developmental synthesis), and, in turn, students' development can influence campus environments (bidirectional arrow).

It should be noted that college students enter institutions of higher education with certain characteristics, such as race and gender, and previous experiences, for example, academic, social, and family experiences. Who students are and what experiences they have had, then, become part of and shape their development in college.

In addition, although Figure 8.1 represents student success as the ultimate outcome, student success (or lack thereof) also affects students' development and how higher education organizations and environments are structured. Thus, the model in Figure 8.1 suggests dynamic relationships among the theory families and also a feedback mechanism of student success to students' development and higher education organizations and environments.

Rationale for Theory Families

The psychosocial development, cognitive-structural development, developmental synthesis, and typology theory families are congruent with Knefelkamp et al.'s (1978) organization of theories in student development and with others' (Evans et al., 1998; Rodgers, 1980) use of similar categories. Families of career development, adult development, student success, organizational theories, and theoretical applications are included because of their importance to student affairs professionals' knowledge and understanding of students.

The family of social identity development theories is the one not consistently considered as a separate family. For example, Evans et al. (1998) placed identity development theories as a subset of psychosocial development. Evans et al.'s approach is clearly appropriate, because identity is considered a psychosocial construct and because the central developmental task of Erikson's (1968) life-span development theory is the development of identity. I have chosen, however, to place identity development theories as a separate family for three reasons. First, because social identity development is important and encompasses a vast and diverse array of models, a separate category seems necessary. Second, many of the identity development models involve *how* one thinks about one's specific social identity as well as *what* the conceptualization of that identity is; thus, cognitive-structural development is a part of social identity development. Third, and most important, is the political stance in highlighting this group of theories, which have evolved from the oppressed status of certain groups in the United States. These theories then are not so much about a personal or global identity (Deaux, 1993) but an identity that occurs because of sociopolitical environments and conditions.

Theory Definition, Purpose, Evolution, and Role in Student Affairs

What are theories? Why do we need them? How do they come about? What use will theory be in the practice of student affairs? This section addresses these important questions.

Definition and Description

Theory can be thought of as a description of the interrelationships among concepts and constructs. These interrelationships are often represented by a particular set of hypotheses—about human development, about organizations, about the dynamics of environments—developed by an individual or a group of individuals. Some hypotheses are empirical in nature, evolving from the collection and examination of quantitative or qualitative data. Others are rational in nature, based not on formal data but rather on ideas and relationships that attempt to explain a particular phenomenon. Thomas (2001) defined theory as "a proposal about (a) which components or variables are important for understanding such a phenomenon as human development and (b) how those components interact to account for why the phenomenon turns out as it does" (p. 1). Thomas identified model, explanatory scheme, and paradigm as synonyms, but he noted, "some authors assign separate meanings to each of those terms" (p. 1).

Theory frequently serves to simplify the complex—to connect what appears to be random and to organize what appears to be chaotic. Theory is inherently reductionistic; it helps one reduce or organize many difficult-to-manage pieces or dimensions into fewer, simpler parts and an integrated, organized whole. One aspect of theory usually not described or discussed is that theory—whether empirical or rational—is developed through the lenses, or perspectives, of those who create or describe it. Thus theory is not objective, as frequently claimed, but evolves from the subjectivity of the theorist or researchers. L. L. Knefelkamp (personal communication, October 16, 1980) has suggested that all theory is autobiographical—that is, theory represents the knowledge, experience, and worldviews of the theorists who construct it. King (1994) echoes this idea in stating that "we produce ourselves as theorists and remember ourselves at the center(s) of theory building" (p. 29). For example, even if they have completed exhaustive research, scholars developing a theory about human behavior in organizations might observe in their data (and thus reflect in their theory) only those dimensions that reflect their own experience in organizations. Their theory becomes, in essence, an autobiographical account of their own organizational experiences. Thus it is important to be aware of the subjectivity and context of any theory.

Purposes and Elements of Theory

Theory is a framework through which interpretations and understandings are constructed. Theory is used to describe human behavior (Knefelkamp et al., 1978, p. xiii), to explain, to predict, and to generate new knowledge and research. Moore and Upcraft (1990) offer a fifth purpose, based on Harmon's work, that theory provides the tools to "influence outcomes" (p. 3). A sixth use of theory—often not cited—is to assess practice. Presenting the uses of theory in a slightly different way, theory should help us to develop a more comprehensive and precise understanding of students, institutions, and related processes and dynamics, such that we can "inform our practice" and thus "transform it" (Hall, as cited in Apple, 1993, p. 25).

These purposes or uses of theory can be applied to student affairs. For example, different theories may help us do the following: (a) *describe* first-year college students in terms of their concerns and their behavior, (b) *explain or understand* the differences in behavior between students who live in coeducational versus single-sex residence halls, (c) *predict* how staff in an office may act when a supervisor with a collaborative style is replaced by one with an autocratic style, (d) *generate* new research and theory about first-generation college students, (e) *influence* the development of students in an honors program by designing the program in certain ways, and (f) *assess* an institution's practices for creating a positive multicultural environment.

Formal criteria exist for evaluating theories. Patterson (1980) has summarized the following eight criteria for use in considering the adequacy of a theory: it should be (1) important, not trivial; (2) precise and understandable; (3) comprehensive; (4) simple and parsimonious but still comprehensive; (5) able to be operationalized; (6) empirically valid or verifiable; (7) able to generate new research, new knowledge, and new thinking and ideas; and (8) useful to practitioners. It is quite likely that many theories that seem valid and useful do not meet all of these criteria; nevertheless, the criteria provide appropriate goals for further theory development and refinement. For example, a theory may be comprehensive but not parsimonious, or a theory may be precise, understandable, and useful but difficult to put into operation.

Each family of theories usually contains certain elements. For example, among developmental theories, most include stages with corresponding developmental tasks. Each stage represents a predominant developmental issue or a certain quality or complexity of thinking. Whether and how one addresses the developmental task or issue relates to two conditions for development: a readiness within the person and stimuli to challenge the individual, to upset an existing psychological equilibrium within the person (Sanford, 1962, 1967). Further, stages occur in a prescribed order evolving from more simple to increasingly complex. Each successive stage builds on the preceding stages and how well one negotiates, or does not negotiate, the preceding stages. And, although theories about the development of college students address the development of individuals, all the theories incorporate to some degree the role of the environment, an often overlooked aspect of these theories.

Differences also exist within major families. Among psychosocial theories, an order is prescribed but is considered to be variable. In contrast, the order is invariant in cognitive-structural development theories, that is, one *must* progress through the stages in the order prescribed. Within social identity development theories, and similar to cognitive-structural development theories, Helms (1992, 1995) suggests that, as one develops, the individual has access to, and in fact is likely to draw upon, stages or statuses through which one has already passed. For Black racial identity development, Parham (1989) suggests that persons can recycle through the developmental tasks represented within the various stages or statuses. Perry (1981) and Kegan (1982) write about a similar phenomenon in considering development as a helix, in that persons can revisit issues similar to those of earlier stages but in more complex ways.

How Theories Evolve

Scholars present their theories and models through scholarly literature and professional conferences. If a theory meets the criteria of a good theory, then it serves to generate new research and new ideas, which in turn inform new theories. When research disputes theory, theory is either revised or new theory is created. Practice also informs theory, as well as scholarly and public critiques. Theory generates new theory.

Theory development also takes place because of shifts in paradigms. Kuh, Whitt, and Shedd (1987) define a paradigm as a set of "assumptions and beliefs about fundamental laws or relationships that explain how the world works" (p. 2). A dominant paradigm represents the prevailing, overriding set of assumptions about the nature of a given subject (such as human development). Kuh et al. explain, "when paradigms shift, understandings are markedly altered" (p. 2). They elegantly describe the "silent revolution" (p. 1) that takes place when a dominant paradigm gives way to an emergent paradigm, the accompanying theoretical shifts in related disciplines, and the implications of paradigm shifts for student affairs. Conventional views or beliefs about, for example, the goal-directed nature of organizations or the highly individualistic nature of human beings are replaced within the emergent paradigm by alternate perspectives describing the relational and contextual aspects of organizations or individuals. With different or changing beliefs and assumptions now at the core of people's understanding of reality, new theories are developed. (See Chapter Twenty for an extensive discussion of how paradigm shifts have led to new thinking and new theories about leadership.)

Theory generation and development is a constantly evolving, dynamic process. Some theories may stand the tests of time, practice, and research and continue to exist in a minimally changed state. Some theories encounter few challenges from scholars and practitioners; others face many challenges. In general, however, the evolution of a theory follows an identifiable cycle: a new theory leads to research and new forms of practice, which in turn inform the existing theory, which is then modified or changed. Sometimes a theory is changed by a theorist; other times an alternate theory is proposed by others. Examples of theory evolution are Chickering's psychosocial development theory (Chickering & Reisser, 1993), moral development theories, and Helms's (1995) People of Color racial identity development theory.

Chickering's theory of the psychosocial development of college students (1969), described in Chapter Nine, was modified in work by Chickering and Reisser in 1993.

The modifications were based both on new understandings from the original theorists (Thomas & Chickering, 1984) and on research by others. Kohlberg's (1975) theory of moral development (see Chapter Nine) also evolved based on his own work and that of colleagues. However, Gilligan (1982), formerly a student of Kohlberg (Larrabee, 1993), found that a gender-related perspective of care seemed to have been left out of Kohlberg's theory and developed her own perspective on moral development. Kohlberg's and Gilligan's theories of moral development now exist side by side, one theory having provided a partial springboard for the development of the other. These two theories also represent different paradigms; Kohlberg's was the conventional paradigm, Gilligan's the emergent one. Helms (1995) created a theory of People of Color racial identity development (see Chapter Ten) from the confluence of her adaptation of Cross's model of Black racial identity development and Atkinson, Morten, and Sue's minority identity development.

Theory in Student Affairs

Theory, some formal, some informal, has no doubt existed in student affairs from the beginning. Some of the early textbooks on student affairs provide evidence of the use of traditional psychological theories and, to some degree, theories on management, organizations, and administration.

Research specific to college students and their development can be traced to the 1950s and early 1960s, first to Nevitt Sanford and his colleagues at Vassar College (Canon, 1988) and then to the publication of Sanford's classic, *The American College* (1962). The 1960s and early 1970s were a time of much writing and research about college students, primarily by the psychologists Heath (1964), Heath (1968), Keniston (1971), King (1973), Chickering (1969), and Perry (1970), in addition to Sanford. The student affairs profession embraced these theorists and their research. Brown's (1972) call for student development to become central to the profession was enthusiastically answered, and student development theory became a foundation of the student affairs profession in the mid to late 1970s. Parker, Knefelkamp, and Widick, at the University of Minnesota, brought the multiple theoretical and research bases of student development theory together, providing an organized schema of theories for understanding student development and practicing student affairs (Knefelkamp et al., 1978).

Other theories about students are also important to student affairs. Models of person-environment interaction (Walsh, 1973) emerged in the 1960s. Models such as wellness (Hettler, 1980), student involvement (Astin, 1984), and mattering and marginality (Schlossberg, 1989) were added to the rich theoretical foundations of student affairs in the 1980s.

Knefelkamp (1982) has suggested that student development theory provides a common language for both student affairs professionals and faculty in higher education. Contemporary attention to student learning (American College Personnel Association, 1996) and holistic student development emphasizes the continuing value of student development theory for student affairs. Thus, the value and centrality given to theory by the student affairs profession is primarily due to the importance of student development theory to the field, although environmental and organizational theory are also influential.

Theory as Social Construction

Although theories have always been viewed as providing varying perspectives on certain constructs and relationships, within the past decade increasing attention has been given to the contextual basis for theories. That is, theories are developed and considered within certain sociological, historical, and political contexts. Further, these contexts change both with the passage of time and with changing ideas and issues within U.S. and world societies.

Earlier in this chapter, shifts in paradigms, from a dominant, conventional paradigm to an emergent one, were identified as one of many reasons about why and how new theory is developed. Part of the dominant, conventional paradigm, the mode of inquiry that has traditionally been used in both education and psychology is logical positivism, also known as the natural scientific method, which has provided important and significant contributions to the theory and research base of student affairs. It is this mode of inquiry that has produced most of our knowledge to date about the development of college students, how individuals and environments interact, and how organizations function.

Focus on the emergent paradigm in considering the relational and contextual aspects of organizations or individuals has led to closer examination of the logical positivistic mode of inquiry. According to Borg and Gall (1989), some scholars have been rethinking many of the assumptions of logical positivism; much of this reexamination was stimulated by Thomas Kuhn's (1962) book *The Structure of Scientific Revolutions.* Critics of logical positivism have also raised important questions about whether theory and research under the dominant, conventional paradigm can truly be objective and value-free. For example, Isasi-Díaz (1993) suggests that "what is called objectivity [e.g., theory] . . . is the subjectivity of those who have the power to impose it as objectivity" (p. 6).

A contemporary and important perspective is that theories are socially constructed and that objects of theories and constructs incorporated within theories are also socially constructed. This perspective comes from the idea that knowledge is never neutral and "that social scientists are participants [rather than impartial researchers] in the socio-historical development of human action and understanding" (Comstock, 1982, p. 377). Further, Comstock suggests the value of understanding "society as humanly constructed and, in turn, human nature as a collective self-construction" (p. 377).

Many constructs, such as race or sexual orientation, have meaning only when they are viewed or considered within social, political, and historical contexts. For instance, it is not the biological meaning of race that we draw on; rather, it is how this society at this point in history conceives of race. In the United States, *race* refers to skin color, language, cultural traditions, patterns of communication, and values and beliefs. It is surrounded by the context of the civil rights movement and the shared history of specific groups of people. *Race,* therefore, is not an objective term meaning what genetically constitutes different groups of people; rather, it is a subjective term that has been socially constructed.

The objects of theories, including identity, learning, environments, and organizations, are themselves socially constructed. Individuals, organizations, and environments, including students and organizations of higher education, do not exist or develop in a vacuum. Individuals live in social settings, each with historical and political elements. Individuals have their unique family histories, and different cohorts of individuals have varying sociopolitical and historical experiences. The identity that one creates for oneself comes out of one's lived experience. Organizations and environments are composed of people and created by people; organizations and environments also have different heritages and various sociopolitical and historical elements. Even what I, as the author of this chapter, write about here is socially constructed. This chapter is constructed at a certain point in history, and it is influenced by what I know and how I see the world.

Just as concepts and objects of theories are socially constructed, so too are theories. Theories are composed of concepts and interrelationships—concepts that are socially constructed and interrelationships formed from the social constructions of theorists. Theories are therefore extensions of social constructions, informed by the data from which they are developed. Important dimensions of the social construction of theory include who the theorist is, on whom the theory is based, for whom the theory is designed, and in what socio-historical context the theory has been developed. Thus theories are not value-free, they are not objective, and they are not "pure" representations of human development. Sue, Ivey, and Pedersen (1996) suggest, "each [theory] has its own interpretation of reality" (p. 7).

A significant problem with many theories is that the theorists have not put forth their concepts, assumptions, and hypotheses *as* socially constructed. In other words, theorists have not usually stated who they are in terms of socially constructed characteristics, backgrounds, values, and other factors that may influence the development and presentation of their theory. Further, in theories of human development, the basis for the theory—for example, the participants, the nature of the research, where the research was conducted—is often minimally provided, if at all. Not having adequate information about either the theorist or the basis for the theory means that the theory may be applied too broadly or that concepts and hypotheses may be readily accepted without question. Chickering's (1969; Chickering & Reisser, 1993) work can be used to illustrate this issue. To understand and apply Chickering's work, it is important to know that he developed the seven vectors from research conducted at Goddard College between 1959 and 1965 and that he identified the hypotheses related to the key environmental influences from research at thirteen small colleges between 1964 and 1969 (Thomas & Chickering, 1984). The revision of his work (Chickering & Reisser, 1993) incorporated recent research findings of others, but is not based on additional research conducted by Chickering. Illustrative comments within the 1993 edition came from students over a three-year period of time who took classes or workshops taught by Linda Reisser. Too frequently, for example, student affairs professionals can identify

Chickering's theory of seven vectors without being aware of the foundation of the vectors nor understanding the complexity of the theory.

Examining the ways in which a theory is socially constructed means making the invisible social constructions visible, the hidden purposes explicit, and the camouflaged populations for whom the theory is intended known and acknowledged. This challenge also means revealing the social constructions of the concepts included in the theory. Further, it is necessary for us to examine ourselves to make known what lenses and filters we are using to understand, portray, and apply theory.

In understanding the social construction of theories, it may be necessary to undo, or unravel, some of the theory. Sampson (1989) indicates that deconstruction usually becomes "the analysis of language and symbolic practices as the key to be deciphered. Each seriously challenges the Western understanding of the person-society relationship, in particular the centrality and the sovereignty of the individual" (p. 6). The difficulty, Sampson says, is "that the tools used to deconstruct this tradition come from that very tradition" (p. 7). Sampson suggests that the difficulty in deconstructing theory involves using tools that are familiar to try to unravel a theory that is familiar and commonly known (p. 7). So the question is whether, through lenses created out of Western thought and understanding, we can undo and unveil those very structures—the language, symbolism, constructs, and theories—that are at the very heart of the Western tradition. Sampson offers a particularly important caution: that to deconstruct a theory means "to undo, not to destroy" (p. 7). hooks (1994) echoes Sampson's caution in critiquing the sexism in Paulo Freire's work, when she says that "critical interrogation [of a theory] is not the same as dismissal" (p. 49).

Also a part of understanding theory as social construction and emerging from a literature known as critical theory is to identify the dimensions of power and oppression implicit in theory, dimensions that are frequently not addressed. Fine (1992) points out characteristics such as gender, race, and class are usually studied as differences; the power dimensions between or within genders, races, or social classes are usually not addressed. When power is not addressed, then women, people of color, and other oppressed groups appear in the research as "less than," as not meeting the "standards" or norms of the dominant group, as a special case. Fine cautions us against our vulnerability "to the possibilities of *gender essentialism* and *racial/ethnic/class erasure*" (p. 15). (Essentialism means treating a particular characteristic such as gender or race as having an inherent "biological inequality." [Frankenberg, 1993, p. 14.]) Taking an activist stance toward feminist researchers, Fine (1992) offers advice that we in student affairs would do well to heed: If we "do not take critical, activist, and open stances on our own work, then we collude in reproducing social silences through the social sciences" (p. 206). In other words, Fine is suggesting that not to engage in critical inquiry is to perpetuate the errors, omissions, and overgeneralizations residing within the theories that we use in student affairs.

Hill Collins (1991) talks about what theories should be: "Theory and intellectual creativity are not the province of a select few but instead emanate from a range of people" (p. xiii). She also points out that "oppressed groups are frequently placed in the situation of being listened to only if we frame our ideas in the language that is familiar to and comfortable for a dominant group" (p. xiii). Addressing power from the consideration of privilege, Hill Collins encourages us to be cognizant of theory's role "in sustaining hierarchies of privilege" (p. xii).

In summary, to consider theory as social construction means taking a social constructivist view of both the central concepts of the theory and the ways in which the theory has been created. It implies that we need to engage in a "peeling away of the layers" of the theory to uncover and discover its hidden and unstated bases and intentions. How power and oppression function within a theory, its development, and its applications also should be examined. By engaging in self-reflection and critical analysis, we in student affairs can develop deeper and clearer understandings of the theories available to us and of how and why we select certain theories to aid us in practice.

Contemporary Challenges to Theory

It can be easy to accept theory without question and use it in practice without challenge. Yet one of the important components of knowing and using theory is to evaluate it, both within practice and in relationship to new literature and new research. There are also, however, other considerations in using theory.

Sampson (1989) identified six challenges to psychological theory that can be applied to theories used in student affairs: (1) cross-cultural investigation, which points out that a Western worldview is frequently assumed in theory and looks for perspectives that are not part of the dominant literature; (2) feminist reconceptualizations, which challenge patriarchal views and offer alternative perspectives; (3) social constructionism, which proposes that concepts and theories are "social and historical constructions, not naturally occurring objects" (p. 2); (4) systems theory, in which persons and constructs are viewed in relation to an overall whole rather than as separate individual entities; (5) critical theory, which "claims that through self-reflection it reveals the distortions and malformations of social life" (Gibson, 1986, p. 36); and (6) deconstructionism, which challenges "all notions that involve the primacy of the subject (or author)"—or theorist—in order "to undo, not to destroy" (Sampson, 1989, pp. 2, 7). These challenges, although different, are overlapping and not mutually exclusive. Understanding theory as social construction is also closely related to Sampson's challenges.

These challenges suggest six ways in which student affairs professionals need to consider and examine theory. First, theory must be examined in terms of its implicit worldview and those worldviews or cross-cultural perspectives that are absent. In many theories of human behavior, for example, individualism is valued, but how one relates to others (such as seeing oneself as part of a family) is ignored or negated. Second, underlying assumptions about gender (and other individual conditions), patriarchy, dominance, and power should be identified. Theories that embrace personal independence and devalue social interdependence reflect a male orientation. Third, how a theory has been socially constructed—under what social conditions, at what point in history, by whom, and with whom—should be considered. For instance, knowing that many theories and models about college students were developed in the 1950s and 1960s—usually by male psychologists and based on research with male students at private, elite colleges—has a significant impact on one's understanding of how student development has traditionally been conceptualized.

A fourth consideration is whether or not a theory regards the person as part of a whole or as a separate, discrete entity, seemingly without an external context and impervious to the influence of others. Excellent examples are early retention models about underrepresented student groups, in which deficits in the students were identified, but the institutional systems they were recruited into were not considered. Critical theory, a fifth challenge, reminds us to engage people as active participants in theory and research rather than solely as subjects. For instance, studying the involvement of commuter students might mean not only collecting traditional data about their participation but also examining, with their participation, what it means to be involved and creating a dialogue with them about the tentative findings. The sixth challenge is to consider how a theory can be deconstructed (without destroying it). One way to deconstruct a theory of human behavior is to "peel away" the layers of the central constructs and relationships within it. For instance, to deconstruct a theory of identity development, we might first look at how the construct of identity is conceptualized, whose perspectives are reflected in such conceptualizations, what basis exists for the theory, and alternative ways to construct the theory, given that theory base.

King (1994) talks about theory as a political object. She raises a number of questions about theory: What political and personal beliefs are incorporated within a theory? How do formal, generic theories mask or hide informal, specialized ones? On the other hand, what "specialized" theories are really broad and comprehensive? King (1994) adds a question raised by Hill Collins: "When is it important *not* to display under the sign 'theory' and for what reasons?" (p. 29). In considering environmental theories, for example, King might ask the following questions: What is implicit in a theory about what an environment should be? (That is, what is a "positive" environment?) Do formal, generic environmental theories gloss over important information about the college classroom setting or student participation in the campus community? Does a particular environmental theory presented as broad and comprehensive more accurately represent a specialized environment, such as student organizations, than some purportedly specialized theories? And drawing from Hill Collins's (1991) question, what kinds of environments are not addressed by environmental theories, and why not? For example, theories about the culture or environment of a university president's office may not have been created, in part to keep hidden the intimate and innermost workings that may go on in such an office. Or, using an example from Hill Collins (1991), persons who study something such as "cultures of resistance" may choose not to describe their work as "theory." Some researchers or scholars may see theory as antagonistic or contradictory to the liberation or emancipation implied in "culture of resistance" (p. 18).

Choosing Which Theories to Use

A value both explicit and implicit in student affairs is that student affairs professionals should guide and inform their professional practice with appropriate theories. As you will see in the chapters that follow, there are multiple theories for the many phenomena and constructs relevant to student affairs. An important question, often overwhelming, is how do you select which theory or theories to guide your practice? Before choosing theories, however, you should consider the importance and value of looking at yourself.

The Importance of Looking at Self

Knowing and examining oneself is especially important in relation to learning, critiquing, and using theories about student and human development. It is also pertinent to understanding and using other theories, such as organizational and environmental theory. Who each of us is, including the experiences and history we carry within us, creates the filters and frameworks through which we interpret others' experiences and perspectives (including those of organizations) and the theories we use in our work.

Thus each of us must begin by examining who we are and what we believe—our identity and our perspectives or informal theories on human nature, how people change, and the nature and functioning of organizations. For example, we should look at how we see race and how we view sexual orientation, whether we behave in ageist or sexist ways, and if we have anti-Semitic attitudes. We should also examine what we think about organizations and whether we are likely to be more attuned to the structure and processes of an organization or to the individuals and groups within it. Most important, each student affairs professional must see and understand himself or herself as a person with multiple characteristics (a certain race, gender, sexual orientation, ethnicity, social class, place of origin, and so on), which are part of his or her identity.

Examples exist in the literature about how theory is closely connected to one's sense of self. Helms's 1992 book *A Race Is a Nice Thing to Have* implies that White persons' understanding of theories and literature about people of color is inextricably linked with their sense of self as White. Research has shown that encountering a disability in another person elicits feelings about the self, about one's own helplessness, needs, and dependencies (Asch & Fine, 1988), thus hampering one's ability to see beyond the disability and understand the other person as an individual. In speaking about multiculturalism, Taylor (1992) described this effect succinctly: It "is *not* a commitment to learning about *them;* instead, it is a commitment to learning about myself—and ultimately, us" (p. 1).

Student affairs professionals need to ask questions of themselves, such as Who am I, as an able-bodied, middle-class, educated White woman? or a second-generation bisexual Asian man? or an African American woman? or a person with any other combination of characteristics? Such self-reflection will help you discover and understand those frameworks you use in both the consideration and the application of theory.

Thoughtful, insightful, and continuing introspection about oneself is a necessary part of a student affairs professional's journey of learning, understanding, and using theory—about organizations, environments and their interactions with students, and, especially, college students and their development.

Selecting Appropriate Theories

Many perspectives exist about the selection and use of theory. One perspective offers a "purist" approach—that for a particular phenomenon, such as understanding organizational change or students' cognitive development, one should select and use a *single* theory. Proponents of this perspective believe a "true" theory can stand alone—that is, it provides assumptions, defines relationships, and describes how those relationships occur under given conditions. Further, using more than one theory may violate the assumptions of individual theories and thus may invalidate the relationships and beliefs prescribed within any theory.

A second perspective is to adopt an "eclectic" model. Eclectic use of theory means a professional draws on the useful and relevant aspects of multiple theories and combines those aspects into a meaningful whole. Some people believe this permits them to use the best parts of many theories, thus making the combined usage stronger than any one theory. Opponents of such a perspective argue that various assumptions of the individual theories may not be honored or may even be violated. It is also possible that there is little if any consistency, for any one individual, from one usage to another, and little consistency from one individual to another. Thus there is no common language or framework within which professionals can discuss or deal with the phenomena of common interest.

In spite of the challenges to eclectic theory, many persons do not believe that any one theory is comprehensive enough to adequately describe any given phenomenon. And, practically speaking, there are few individuals who adopt one theory exclusive of all others in a similar family or grouping of theories. Thus, what guidelines can a student affairs professional use in selecting theories? I offer the following guidelines.

Select a theory or theories that you understand and that make sense to you. For instance, if a certain theory resonates for you and seems to appropriately describe a certain phenomenon, then you are more likely to internalize that theory, understand it more deeply, and apply it in your practice. On the other hand, if a theory isn't very clear to you or doesn't "come alive," then you may find it more difficult to apply in your practice.

Knowing yourself will help you decide which theories to choose and which ones to "put back on the shelf." For theories that seem to fit you and your understanding of the world, ask yourself what it is about them that fits. Is it because they describe your own experiences? If so, whose experiences do they not describe?

Because theories "operate from both explicit and implicit assumptions that guide their formulations" (Sue et al., 1996, p. 1), Sue et al. recommend an "assumption audit" as a part of using theory. An assumption audit therefore would identify those assumptions both explicit and implicit within a theory. Some implicit assumptions about student development undergird many of the theories and student affairs professionals' application and use of such theories, but they are frequently not articulated. Two assumptions are that development of students is good, and thus that greater developmental complexity is desirable, and that a goal of student affairs professionals is to promote the development of students. A third assumption with some of the student success models, sometimes explicit and sometimes implicit, is that involvement and engagement in the academic community is valued.

As noted earlier, theories are reductionistic—they describe some relationships and concepts but not others. So, what theory or theories do you draw on for *each* phenomenon of interest? In thinking about a student, you may be interested in understanding his or her psychosocial and cognitive development as well as his or her racial identity development. How, then, do you combine a theory or theories for each of these areas with one another? Or, you may want to draw on several theories to describe a single phenomenon. In either case, think about how the theories fit together. Do the assumptions of each theory fit with one another, or do some conflict? If they conflict, how do you understand the conflict, and on what basis could you decide the incongruence is not pertinent? What parts of each theory do you draw upon? What, then, is your own modified version of this melding of certain theories? Be thoughtful, be intentional, and, as Evans says in Chapter Nine, be intelligent about using theory. Be explicit about the theories you use.

Conclusion

The theories available to use in student affairs come from many different sources, and they serve multiple and varied purposes. Theories are evolving, both in their own development and in how we use them in student affairs. Yet we must remember that theories are not pure; they are not perfect; they were not created and do not exist in a vacuum. Sampson's (1989) six challenges about theory and knowing and taking into account our own personal filters and values are important complements to the selection and use of theory. Critical science offers a method by which we can examine how a theory has been socially constructed and how it may need to be deconstructed. Finally, as a student affairs professional, it is necessary that one be thoughtful, intentional, and systematic in selecting which theory or theories to draw upon. It is also important to know why one has selected a theory, to know its strengths and limitations, and to be conscious of how selecting and applying a given theory relates to who you are as a person and as a student affairs professional.

References

American College Personnel Association. (1996). The student learning imperative: Implications for student affairs. *Journal of College Student Development, 37,* 118–122.

Apple, M. W. (1993). Constructing the "other": Rightist reconstructions of common sense. In C. McCarthy & W. Crichlow (Eds.), *Race, identity, and representation in education* (pp. 24–39). New York: Routledge & Kegan Paul.

Asch, A., & Fine, M. (1988). Introduction: Beyond pedestals. In M. Fine & A. Asch (Eds.), *Women with disabilities: Essays in psychology, culture, and politics* (pp. 1–37). Philadelphia: Temple University Press.

Astin, A. W. (1984). Student involvement: A developmental theory for higher education. *Journal of College Student Personnel, 25,* 297–308.

Borg, W. R., & Gall, M. D. (1989). *Educational research: An introduction* (5th ed.). White Plains, NY: Longman.

Brown, R. D. (1972). *Student development in tomorrow's higher education: A return to the academy* (Student Personnel Monograph No. 16). Washington, DC: American College Personnel Association.

Cannon, K. G. (1988). *Black womanist ethics.* Atlanta, GA: Scholars Press.

Canon, H. J. (1988). Nevitt Sanford: Gentle prophet, Jeffersonian rebel. *Journal of Counseling and Development, 66,* 451–457.

Chickering, A. W. (1969). *Education and identity.* San Francisco: Jossey-Bass.

Chickering, A. W., & Reisser, L. (1993). *Education and identity* (2nd ed.). San Francisco: Jossey-Bass.

Clark, B. R., & Trow, M. (1966). The organizational context. In T. M. Newcomb & E. K. Wilson (Eds.), *College peer groups: Problems and prospects for research* (pp. 17–70). Chicago: Aldine.

Comstock, D. E. (1982). A method for critical research. In E. Bredo & W. Feinberg (Eds.), *Knowledge values in social and educational research* (pp. 370–390). Philadelphia: Temple University Press.

Deaux, K. (1993). Reconstructing social identity. *Personality and Social Psychology Bulletin, 19,* 4–12.

Erikson, E. H. (1968). *Identity: Youth and crisis.* New York: Norton.

Evans, N. J., Forney, D. S., & Guido-DiBrito, F. (1998). *Student development in college: Theory, research, and practice.* San Francisco: Jossey-Bass.

Fine, M. (1992). *Disruptive voices: The possibilities of feminist research.* Ann Arbor: University of Michigan Press.

Frankenberg, R. (1993). *The social construction of whiteness: White women, race matters.* Minneapolis: University of Minnesota Press.

Gibson, R. (1986). *Critical theory and education.* London: Hodder & Stoughton.

Gilligan, C. (1982). *In a different voice: Psychological theory and women's development.* Cambridge, MA: Harvard University Press.

Heath, D. H. (1968). *Growing up in college.* San Francisco: Jossey-Bass.

Heath, D. H. (1980). Wanted: A comprehensive model of healthy development. *Personnel and Guidance Journal, 38,* 391–398.

Heath, R. (1964). *The reasonable adventurer.* Pittsburgh, PA: University of Pittsburgh Press.

Helms, J. E. (1992). *A race is a nice thing to have: A guide to being a White person, or understanding the White persons in your life.* Topeka, KS: Content Communications.

Helms, J. E. (1995). An update of Helms's White and People of Color racial identity models. In J. G. Ponterotto, J. M. Casas, L. A. Suzuki, & C. M. Alexander (eds.), *Handbook of multicultural counseling* (pp. 181–198). Thousand Oaks, CA: Sage.

Hettler, B. (1980). Wellness promotion on a university campus. *Journal of Health Promotion and Maintenance, 3* (1), 77–95.

Hill Collins, P. (1991). *Black feminist thought: Knowledge, consciousness, and the politics of empowerment.* New York: Routledge, Chapman & Hall.

Holland, J. L. (1966). *The psychology of vocational choice: A theory of personality types and model environments.* Waltham, MA: Blaisdell.

hooks, b. (1994). *Teaching to transgress: Education as the practice of freedom.* New York: Routledge.

Isasi-Díaz, A. M. (1993, March). *Educating for a new world order.* Presented at the conference of the National Association for Women in Education, Seattle, WA.

Isasi-Díaz, A. M. (1996). *Mujerista theology: A theology for the twenty-first century.* Maryknoll, NY: Orbis.

Ivey, A. E. (1986). *Developmental therapy: Theory into practice.* San Francisco: Jossey-Bass.

Kegan, R. (1982). *The evolving self: Problem and process in human development.* Cambridge, MA: Harvard University Press.

Keniston, K. (1971). *Youth and dissent.* New York: Harcourt, Brace, Jovanovich.

King, K. (1994). *Theory in its feminist travels: Conversations in U.S. women's movements.* Bloomington: Indiana University Press.

King, P. M., & Baxter Magolda, M. (2001, November). *The development of intercultural maturity: Examining how facets of development are interrelated.* Paper presented at the conference of the Association for the Study of Higher Education, Richmond, VA.

King, S. H. (1973). *Five lives at Harvard: Personality change during college.* Cambridge, MA: Harvard University Press.

Knefelkamp, L. L. (1982). Faculty and student development in the '80s: Renewing the community of scholars. In H. F. Owens, C. H. Witten, & W. R. Bailey (Eds.), *College student personnel administration: An anthology* (pp. 373–391). Springfield, IL: Thomas.

Knefelkamp, L. L., Widick, C., & Parker, C. A. (1978). Editors' notes: Why bother with theory? In L. Knefelkamp, C. Widick, & C. A. Parker (Eds.), *Applying new developmental findings* (New Directions for Student Services No. 4, pp. vii–xvi). San Francisco: Jossey-Bass.

Kohlberg, L. (1975). The cognitive-developmental approach to moral education. *Phi Delta Kappan, 56,* 670–677.

Kuh, G. D., Whitt, E. J., & Shedd, J. D. (1987). *Student affairs work, 2001: A paradigmatic odyssey.* Washington, DC: American College Personnel Association.

Kuhn, T. S. (1962). *The structure of scientific revolutions.* Chicago: University of Chicago Press.

Larrabee, M. J. (1993). Gender and moral development: A challenge for feminist theory. In M. J. Larrabee (Ed.), *An ethic of care: Feminist and interdisciplinary perspectives* (pp. 3–16). New York: Routledge & Kegan Paul.

Moore, L. V., & Upcraft, M. L. (1990). Theory in student affairs: Evolving perspectives. In L. V. Moore (Ed.), *Evolving theoretical perspectives on students* (New Directions for Student Services No. 51, pp. 3–23). San Francisco: Jossey-Bass.

Newcomb, T. M., Joenig, K. E., Flacks, R., & Warwick, D. P. (1967). *Persistence and change: Bennington College and its students after 25 years.* New York: Wiley.

Parham, T. A. (1989). Cycles of psychological Nigrescence. *Counseling Psychologist, 17,* 187–226.

Patterson, C. H. (1980). *Theories of counseling and psychotherapy* (3rd ed.). New York: Harper & Row.

Perry, W. G., Jr. (1970). *Forms of intellectual and ethical development in the college years: A scheme.* New York: Holt, Rinehart and Winston.

Perry, W. G., Jr. (1981). Cognitive and ethical growth: The making of meaning. In A. W. Chickering & Associates, *The modern American college.* San Francisco: Jossey-Bass.

Rodgers, R. F. (1980). Theories underlying student development. In D. G. Creamer (Ed.), *Student development in higher education: Theories, practices & future directions.* Washington, DC: American College Personnel Association.

Sampson, E. E. (1989). The deconstruction of the self. In J. Shotter & K. J. Gergen (Eds.), *Texts of identity* (pp. 1–19). Newbury Park, CA: Sage.

Sanford, N. (1962). *The American college.* New York: Wiley.

Sanford, N. (1967). *Where colleges fail: A study of the student as a person.* San Francisco: Jossey-Bass.

Schlossberg, N. K. (1989). Marginality and mattering: Key issues in building community. In D. C. Roberts (Ed.), *Designing campus activities to foster a sense of community* (New Directions for Student Services No. 48, pp. 5–15). San Francisco: Jossey-Bass.

Schlossberg, N. K., Waters, E. B., & Goodman, J. (1995). *Counseling adults in transition* (2nd ed.). New York: Springer.

Sue, D. W., Ivey, A. E., & Pedersen, P. B. (1996). *A theory of multicultural counseling & therapy.* Pacific Grove, CA: Brooks/Cole.

Taylor, K. (1992, March 31). *Remarks.* Presented at the awards luncheon of the annual conference of the National Association of Student Personnel Administrators, Cincinnati, OH.

Thomas, R., & Chickering, A. W. (1984). Education and identity revisited. *Journal of College Student Personnel, 25,* 392–399.

Thomas, R. M. (2001). *Recent theories of human development.* Thousand Oaks, CA: Sage.

Walsh, W. B. (1973). *Theories of person-environment interaction: Implications for the college student.* Iowa City, IA: American College Testing Program.

CHAPTER NINE

PSYCHOSOCIAL, COGNITIVE, AND TYPOLOGICAL PERSPECTIVES ON STUDENT DEVELOPMENT

Nancy J. Evans

Allison recently accepted a new position as an academic advisor at an urban community college. Previously she was a hall director at a small private college, and she is amazed at how different the students are in her new setting. How is Allison to make sense of the differences in age, background, concerns, and interests she sees in these college students?

Student development theory provides a useful guide for student affairs professionals like Allison. It describes how students grow and change throughout their college years; it provides information about how development occurs and suggests conditions that encourage development. In this chapter, three major classifications of student development theory are introduced: psychosocial, cognitive structural, and typology. Highlighted are several specific theories within each category that have particular utility in student affairs practice. Chapters Ten and Eleven introduce theories of identity development and epistemological development, respectively; they also contribute to a comprehensive understanding of student development.

Psychosocial Perspectives

Mary is a nineteen-year-old White sophomore at the private college where Allison previously worked. She is trying to identify a career direction and discover what matters to her as a person. Mary has always looked to her parents for guidance, but now she finds it important to strike out on her own. Shawna, also a second-year student, attends the urban community college where Allison currently works. She is a thirty-five-year-old African American single parent who enrolled in college to create a better life for her family. Her main goal is to be a good role model for her children and to make a positive contribution to her community.

Although they are both sophomores, these two women face very different challenges and look at life from different perspectives. Psychosocial theorists attempt to explain such differences. The major concepts associated with this approach derive primarily from the work of Erikson (1959, 1968). Erikson suggested that development occurs within a series of age-linked, sequential stages that arise during each individual's lifetime. Within each stage, particular issues, called developmental tasks, become preeminent and must be addressed. In our example, Mary is dealing with such developmental tasks as determining a vocational direction and identifying a personal set of beliefs and values. Shawna is revisiting her previous life decisions in these arenas while also focusing on the developmental tasks of actively nurturing her offspring and contributing in a productive way to society.

According to Erikson (1959), each new stage occurs when internal psychological and biological changes interact with external social demands to create a developmental crisis, or turning point, in a person's life. For Mary, the maturation associated with young adulthood, along with the societal expectation that college students must choose a career, has contributed to a developmental crisis: establishing her identity. Each such crisis offers heightened opportunity as well as vulnerability for the individual (Erikson, 1968).

A successful resolution of each developmental crisis leads to the development of new skills or attitudes. A less successful resolution, however, contributes to a negative self-image and restricts the individual's ability to successfully address future crises. Regression to previous stages and recycling of developmental issues frequently occur as individuals attempt to more successfully resolve previous crises. To work through the issues associated with making a contribution to her community, for example, Shawna is revisiting issues associated with earlier stages, such as developing a sense of accomplishment and acquiring skills and knowledge.

Marcia (1966), Josselson (1987, 1996), Chickering and Reisser (1993), and Sanford (1966) each expanded upon Erikson's ideas and focused on the development of college students. Their work is discussed in this section, along with Super's (1957, 1990) psychosocial perspective on career development. Three orientations to adult development, each of which focuses on psychosocial development across the lifespan, are also reviewed. The section concludes with a discussion of the uses of psychosocial theory in student affairs practice.

Identity Development: Marcia and Josselson

Erikson did not specifically discuss college students' developmental issues. However, later theorists applied his ideas to this population. For example, Marcia (1966) examined identity development in late adolescence. He found that identity resolution was based on the extent to which the individual (1) had experienced crises related to vocational choice, political values, and/or religion, and (2) made commitments in these areas. Marcia's work suggests that not all students approach the identity resolution process similarly and that they may need different types of interventions to progress.

Building on the work of Marcia (1966), Josselson (1987, 1996) examined identity development in women, starting during their college years and continuing into their forties. Social, sexual, and religious values, more than occupational and political values, were the significant areas of crisis and commitment for women in young adulthood. According to Josselson, crisis in relationships, more than in any other area, leads to growth and change for women. The degree to which women deviated from or remained connected to the value system of their parents—especially their mothers—largely determined their identity.

Vectors of Development: Chickering and Reisser

Chickering's landmark study of undergraduate students in thirteen small colleges appeared in 1969. His theory expanded upon Erikson's (1968) notions of identity and intimacy and suggested that the establishment of identity is the central developmental issue during the college years. In 1993, working with Linda Reisser, Chickering revised his theory to incorporate new research findings.

Chickering and Reisser (1993) proposed seven vectors of development that contribute to the formation of identity (see Exhibit 9.1). Chickering (1969) chose the term

EXHIBIT 9.1. CHICKERING AND REISSER'S VECTORS OF DEVELOPMENT.

1. *Developing Competence.* This vector focuses on the tasks of developing intellectual, physical and manual, and interpersonal competence. In addition, students develop confidence in their abilities within these arenas.
2. *Managing Emotions.* In this vector, students develop the ability to recognize and accept emotions, as well as to appropriately express and control them. This vector includes a broad range of feelings such as depression, anger, guilt, caring, optimism, and happiness.
3. *Moving Through Autonomy Toward Interdependence.* At this stage, students develop increased emotional independence, self-direction, problem-solving ability, persistence, and mobility, as well as recognition and acceptance of the importance of interdependence.
4. *Developing Mature Interpersonal Relationships.* Tasks addressed in this vector include the development of acceptance and appreciation of differences as well as the capacity for healthy and lasting intimate relationships.
5. *Establishing Identity.* A positive identity includes (1) comfort with body and appearance, (2) comfort with gender and sexual orientation, (3) a sense of one's social and cultural heritage, (4) a clear conception of self and comfort with one's roles and lifestyle, (5) a secure sense of self in light of feedback from significant others, (6) self-acceptance and self-esteem, and (7) personal stability and integration. Chickering and Reisser (1993) acknowledged differences in identity development based on gender, ethnicity, and sexual orientation.
6. *Developing Purpose.* This vector consists of developing clear vocational goals, making meaningful commitments to specific personal interests and activities, and establishing strong interpersonal commitments.
7. *Developing Integrity.* In this vector, students progress from rigid, moralistic thinking to a more humanized, personalized value system that acknowledges and respects the beliefs of others. Values and actions become congruent.

Source: Adapted from Chickering and Reisser (1993).

vectors to describe developmental tasks students experience "because each seems to have direction and magnitude–even though the direction may be expressed more appropriately by a spiral or by steps than by a straight line" (p. 8). Chickering and Reisser noted that students move through these vectors at different rates, that vectors can interact with one another, and that students often find themselves reexamining issues they had previously addressed. Although not rigidly sequential, Chickering and Reisser's vectors do build on each other and lead to greater complexity, stability, and integration. Their work incorporates emotional, social, and intellectual aspects of development.

Chickering and Reisser (1993) argued that educational environments exert a powerful influence that helps students move through the seven vectors of development. Key factors include institutional objectives, institutional size, faculty-student interaction, curriculum, teaching practices, diverse student communities, and student affairs programs and services. Three principles underscore these factors: integration of work and learning, recognition of and respect for differences, and recognition of the cyclical nature of learning and development.

Researchers examining the applicability of Chickering's (1969) theory and its later revision (Chickering & Reisser, 1993) to various populations, including women, African American, Asian American, international, and nonheterosexual students, have found gender and cultural differences in the ordering and importance of various vectors. See Evans, Forney, and Guido-DiBrito (1998) for a summary of this research, as well as recent articles by Jones and Watt (2001), Kodama, McEwen, Liang, and Lee (2001), and Pope (1998). Theories that address specific aspects of identity development are reviewed in Chapter Ten. A discussion of applications of Chickering and Reisser's theory to student affairs practice is found in Evans et al. (1998).

Challenge and Support: Sanford

Sanford's (1962) longitudinal study of Vassar women had a profound impact on the student affairs field in that it provided evidence that change did indeed take place during college and that the college environment significantly influenced development (Canon, 1988). It was also one of the first significant studies of college women. Sanford's concepts of challenge and support were a major contribution to student development theory.

Building on Erikson's (1968) notion that resolution of developmental crises is encouraged by optimal dissonance (that is, a moderate, growth-enhancing level of discomfort with one's current functioning), Sanford (1966) suggested that a balance of challenge and support must be present for development to occur. If there is too little challenge, the individual may feel safe and comfortable, but development will not take place. On the other hand, too much challenge can induce maladaptive responses. According to Sanford, the amount of challenge a person can handle is contingent on the amount of support available. Creating an appropriate balance between challenge and support in the college environment is an important factor in facilitating student development (Sanford, 1966). The amounts of challenge and support needed by each student will vary depending on personality, background, and previous experiences.

An additional concept introduced by Sanford (1966) is readiness. He noted that individuals are unable to demonstrate particular behaviors unless they are physically or psychologically ready to do so. Readiness results either from internal maturation processes or from conditions in the environment that encourage development.

Career Development: Super

Since the 1950s, Super's life-space, life-span approach has been the primary developmental career theory used in most industrialized countries (Herr, 1997). His theory is interactionist in nature, suggesting that personal and societal factors interact in the process of career development over the life span (McDaniels & Gysbers, 1992). McDaniels and Gysbers and Herr provide good summaries of Super's theory.

In 1984, Super introduced the life-career rainbow, a pictorial device for depicting nine overlapping roles that individuals assume across the span of their lives. These include child, student, leisurite, citizen, worker, spouse, homemaker, parent, and retired person. Each role contributes to a person's career and has varying degrees of prominence at different points in the person's life. In 1990, in his Archway model, Super focused more broadly on the "dynamic interaction of the individual and society" (Herr, 1997, p. 240). This model suggests that environmental determinants (including the economy, status of natural resources, family, community, and peer groups) interact with personal determinants (such as needs, aptitudes, values, and interests), influencing the life roles people assume and contributing to their self-concepts. These factors, in turn, contribute to the evolution of careers over the life span.

Super (1957) suggested that career development is a process that continues throughout an individual's life. He identified five stages of development. In the first stage, *Growth* (ages 0–14), children try out various experiences and develop an understanding of work. In the second stage, *Exploration* (ages 14–24), individuals investigate possible career options, become aware of their interests and abilities, and develop the skills necessary to enter a career. Stage three, *Establishment* (ages 25–44), consists of becoming competent in a career and advancing in it. In the fourth stage, *Maintenance* (ages 45–65), persons continue to enhance their skills to remain productive while making plans for retirement. The final stage, *Decline* (age 65+), involves adjusting work to one's physical capability and managing resources to remain independent. Super (1990) suggested that recycling occurs during periods of transition, allowing for additional growth, exploration, and establishment.

Super (1990) believed that individuals were adaptable and could be happy in a variety of occupations. He also saw preferences, situations, and self-concepts evolving over time, leading to varying levels of satisfaction and different choices over the course of the life span. According to Super (1983), career maturity (labeled "career adaptability" in adulthood) contributes to successful adjustment and satisfaction in specific settings. He defined career maturity as "a readiness to engage in the developmental tasks appropriate to the age and level at which one finds oneself" (McDaniels & Gysbers, 1992, p. 48). To enhance career development, Super (1990) believed that individuals need a clear understanding of their abilities, interests, and other personal qualities, as well as opportunities to experience various roles and receive feedback. This knowledge and experience can be gained through self-exploration, career shadowing, internships, and part-time employment.

Adult Development

Because so many college students are beyond the ages of eighteen to twenty-two, student affairs professionals must be aware of developmental issues facing individuals across the entire life span. Theories of adult psychosocial development can be categorized into three major groups: life stage, life events, and life course. Integrative perspectives (such as Baltes, 1987; Magnusson, 1995; Perun & Bielby, 1980), which account for biological, sociological, and psychological aspects of development, are also gaining popularity. A good introduction to adult development theories is provided by Clark and Caffarella (1999).

Life Stage Perspectives. This approach suggests that individuals become more individuated and complex as they progress through life, with later developmental tasks building on earlier tasks in a predictable pattern. Developmental change occurs according to an internal timetable, influenced to some extent by environmental forces. Some theories in this category suggest that development is age-linked (for example, Gould, 1978; Levinson, 1978; Levinson & Levinson, 1996) while others (for example, Erikson, 1959, and Vaillant, 1977) present sequential stages that are not necessarily tied to specific ages.

The life stage perspective is based almost entirely on the experiences of heterosexual men. Research suggests that although women progress through similar developmental stages at roughly the same ages as men, they experience greater conflict in achieving their more complex goals, which involve both relationships and careers (Roberts & Newton, 1987). Levinson and Levinson (1996) identified gender-based differences in how various components of each stage were addressed; for example, marriage roles were separated into the homemaker role for women and the provisioner role for men. (Clearly some bias regarding gender roles is evident in this approach!)

Life Events Perspectives. These theories focus on the timing, duration, spacing, and ordering of life events in the course of human development. Significant events may be individual (such as marriage or death) or cultural (such as war or economic conditions). Unlike the life stage theorists, theorists associated with this perspective do not see life events as necessarily occurring in predictable stages. Life events theorists focus on how individuals make meaning of the events they experience and how they negotiate them. Rather than being a point in time, events are viewed as a process that individuals must address over a period of time (Schlossberg, Waters, & Goodman, 1995). The manner in which they accomplish these tasks is contingent on both internal factors, such as personality and attitude, and external variables, such as available support networks and outside resources. Because of its focus on variability, interconnectedness, and environmental influence, the life events perspective is particularly well suited for explaining women's development across the life span. Tittle (1982), for instance, found that while men make clear distinctions between career, marriage, and parenthood, women see the three as being interrelated. Life events theorists include Fiske and Chiriboga (1990), Schlossberg, et al. (1995), Sugarman (1986), and Whitbourne (1985).

Life Course Perspectives. Also referred to as sociocultural perspectives, theories associated with this approach focus on the social roles that individuals assume during their lives (Elder, 1995; Hughes & Graham, 1990) and the timing of life events (Bengston, 1996; Neugarten, 1979). More so than life stage or life events theorists, theorists in this group stress the variability of human development and the importance of environment in growth and change. Life course theorists examine the socially constructed beliefs that people hold about the roles they assume, such as what it means to be a parent, worker, partner, or friend. Also considered are the impact on the individual of factors such as the modification of roles (such as redefinition of the parent role when a child leaves home), assumption of new roles (such as getting married), and loss of certain roles (such as having a parent die).

The timing of events in a person's life is viewed as particularly important. According to these theorists, people develop "social clocks" that tell them when certain events are supposed to occur in their lives. When events are "off-time" (Neugarten, 1979, p. 888), such as starting college at age thirty-five, stress results. In dealing with life events, Elder (1995) stressed that people have agency—they plan and make choices as to how to respond. Their decisions alter the course of their lives. He also noted that individual lives are linked; a person's actions affect the lives of their significant others. Elder also examined the influence of social forces, place, and historical time, noting that the individual life course exists within the context of the larger society.

Using Psychosocial Theories in Practice

At this point you may be wondering what all these developmental tasks, vectors, and crises have to do with student affairs practice. Revisiting Allison, the new academic advisor at an urban community college, may provide some suggestions. Certainly, psychosocial theories give Allison a better understanding of the issues that may be important to the students with whom she works. For instance, Elder's theory of adult development suggests that lives are linked together, with significant events in one person's life influencing the lives of those around them. As an example, what is happening in the lives of Shawna's children will affect Shawna's ability to function effectively in college. This knowledge can increase Allison's sensitivity as she helps Shawna plan her schedule to allow for attendance at her children's school events. Understanding psychosocial development helps educators to be more proactive in anticipating student issues and more responsive to, and understanding of, concerns that arise as they work with students.

Psychosocial theory is also helpful in program development. Whether planning orientation, educational sessions for Greek chapters, or the staff development program for resident assistants, student affairs professionals can use their knowledge of the timing and content of developmental stages to guide the selection of topics for presentation. For instance, at the private college where Allison previously worked, most first-year students were probably dealing with Chickering's early vectors. Programming in the first-year residence hall, then, might focus on academic and social skills and managing the stresses of college. Examples of programming based on Chickering's (1969) theory include Schuh's (1989) description of a workshop designed for paraprofessional staff and the residence hall wellness programming described by Elleven, Spaulding, Murphy, and Eddy (1997). Intentionally designed academic coursework can also encourage development along Chickering's vectors (Wood, Wood, & McDonald, 1988).

In addition, psychosocial theory can guide the formation of policy. For example, Sanford's (1966) theory suggests that challenge must be balanced with appropriate supports to enhance development. Knowing that most students at the community college are older adults who are working and attending evening classes raises awareness that they may face challenges in accomplishing routine tasks such as registering for classes during regular business hours. Supports might involve adjusting policies to allow for online registration or having offices open during the evening.

Cognitive Structural Perspectives

Allison is facing a dilemma. Ana, a Muslim student who is one of her advisees, has come to her with a concern about her Food Science class. In this class, students are expected to sample foods to assess such qualities as sweetness, texture, and bitterness. However, during the holy month of Ramadan, Muslims must fast from sunrise until sundown. Ana has spoken to her instructor about this problem, but the instructor was not sympathetic, suggesting that Ana drop the class if she can't fulfill the requirements. Ana needs the class to graduate on time and can't afford to stay an extra semester. Allison believes that Ana is being treated unfairly by a professor insensitive to Ana's religious beliefs, and her first impulse is to intervene on Ana's behalf with the department chair. However, Allison has also been cautioned by her supervisor not to "rescue" her advisees and to think twice before criticizing the actions of faculty members.

How both Allison and Ana are processing this dilemma can be better understood through the lenses of cognitive structure theories. Rooted in the work of Piaget (1952), cognitive structural theories examine how people think, reason, and make meaning out of their experiences. The mind is thought to have structures, that is, sets of assumptions people use to adapt to and organize their environments. Structures determine *how* people think, but not *what* they think. Structures change, expand, and become more complex as a person develops. Younger students, like Ana, are less likely to see the complexities of the dilemmas they face than individuals further along in their cognitive development, like Allison.

Cognitive structural stages are viewed as arising sequentially and always in the same order, regardless of cultural conditions. The age at which each stage occurs and the rate of speed with which the person passes through it are variable, however. Each stage derives from the previous one, incorporating aspects of it, and is qualitatively different and more complex than earlier stages (Wadsworth, 1979).

According to cognitive structural theorists, change takes place as a result of assimilation and accommodation. Assimilation is the process of integrating new information into existing structures, rounding them out and contributing to their expansion—a quantitative change. Accommodation is the process of creating new structures to incorporate stimuli that do not fit into existing structures—a qualitative change (Wadsworth, 1979). Disequilibrium, or cognitive conflict, occurs when expectations are not confirmed by experience. When conflict is experienced, the individual first tries to assimilate the new information into the existing structure; if assimilation is not possible, then accommodation occurs in order to regain equilibrium (Wadsworth, 1979). Encountering an instructor who would not adjust his class requirements was a conflict for Ana; trying to decide how to handle her student's problem was likewise a conflict for Allison. Each first attempted to use strategies that were familiar to her: Ana went to an authority for a solution; Allison's first impulse was to intervene on behalf of her student. If these approaches do not work, they will search for new, more effective, approaches.

Piaget (1952) stressed the importance of heredity in cognitive development but also noted the role played by the environment, which presents experiences to which the individual must react. Social interaction with peers, parents, and other adults is especially influential in cognitive development. The interaction between Ana and Allison, for example, has the potential to affect the manner in which each of them comes to understand this and similar situations in the future.

Many theories applicable to college students are based in the cognitive structural tradition. This section examines theories of self-evolution (Kegan, 1982, 1994), moral development (Gilligan, 1982; Kohlberg, 1976; Rest, Narvaez, Bebeau, & Thoma, 1999) and spiritual development (Fowler, 1981; Parks, 1986, 2000). Chapter Eleven includes discussion of theories of intellectual and epistemological development.

Self-Evolution: Kegan

Kegan (1982, 1994) proposed a model of life span development that takes into account both cognitive and affective components. Because he considered himself a neo-Piagetian, he is usually grouped with the cognitive structural theorists. His first work (1982) focused on the evolution of the self and how individuals make meaning of their experiences, especially in relation to "the other." In his later work (1994) he extended his theory and examined the demands of modern life on adult lives. Love and Guthrie (1999) have provided an excellent summary of Kegan's theory and its applicability in student affairs while Ignelzi (2000) did a masterful job of outlining the implications of Kegan's work for teaching and learning.

Kegan (1994) introduced five "orders of consciousness," principles of mental organization that determine how persons construct their experience (see Exhibit 9.2). How they think, feel, and relate to self and others are different at each level. These orders or consciousness are not strictly hierarchical but they do progress from simple to complex ways of making meaning of one's experiences with later orders building on earlier ones. In addition to having a cognitive component, each order has a different way of delineating self-concept and relationships. As consciousness develops,

EXHIBIT 9.2. KEGAN'S ORDERS OF CONSCIOUSNESS.

First Order of Consciousness. Characteristic of young children, thinking at this level is concrete, self-centered, and focused on immediate needs. Objects are viewed as individual entities rather than categorically and behavior is impulsive.

Second Order of Consciousness. This level is exemplified by the ability to form "durable categories"— "lasting classifications in which physical objects, people, and desires come to have properties of their own that characterize them as distinct from 'me'" (Love & Guthrie, 1999, p. 69). It is apparent in late childhood through adolescence or early adulthood. Self-concept develops as children recognize that they have particular qualities and characteristics that separate them from or connect them to others. Ongoing needs and desires now take precedence over momentary ones but individuals are still primarily focused on their own self-interests. A transition from second to third order consciousness takes place between the ages of twelve and twenty as a result of the demands of modern society for abstract thinking and working within the context of a larger community (Kegan, 1994).

Third Order of Consciousness. This level involves the ability to think abstractly, engage in self-reflection, consider the needs and perspectives of others, subordinate one's own interests to the larger good, and intentionally commit to a set of values. Another transition occurs between the third and fourth orders of consciousness that Kegan (1994) identifies as the major transformation of adulthood. Love and Guthrie (1999) described this transition as "attaining self-authorship: the ability to 'write' one's own life" (p. 71). It often occurs when a significant relationship ends and persons realize that they can and do exist and have purpose independent of their relationships.

Fourth Order of Consciousness. The capacity "to construct generalizations from abstractions" (Love & Guthrie, 1999, p. 72) is evident. According to Kegan (1994), less than half of the adult population functions at this level. Individuals who do achieve fourth order consciousness are able to articulate and use a coherent and deeply held set of convictions to guide their behavior. These core beliefs allow them to make choices among their values when those values are in conflict. Individuals at this level have a strong sense of identity and rely on themselves rather than others when faced with difficult decisions. They are able to objectively evaluate the quality of their relationships and take steps to enhance them in ways that will be beneficial to both individuals.

Fifth Order of Consciousness. According to Kegan (1994), this type of thinking is quite rare and only achievable at age forty or older. At this level individuals use systems thinking that transcends the individual and the other. Kegan saw this level as controversial since "it suggests a notion of development beyond the autonomy of establishing one's identity and points to a level of development that relies on the individual being able to experience a sharing or intimacy with others" (Love & Guthrie, 1999, p. 73). At this level, contradictions are accepted as a part of life.

Source: Adapted from Kegan (1994) and Love and Guthrie (1999).

people are more able to reflect on and move beyond their previous ways of making meaning of intrapersonal and interpersonal dimensions of their existence. An important outcome of this process is self-authorship—the ability to "internalize multiple points of view, reflect on them, and construct them into one's own theory about oneself and one's experience" (Ignelzi, 2000, p. 8). Self-authorship results in a stable identity that persists across settings and relationships.

In discussing factors that encourage development of more complex orders of consciousness, Kegan (1994) drew on Sanford's (1966) concepts of challenge and support, suggesting that society is better at introducing challenges than at providing supports. Kegan noted the importance of "sympathetic coaches" who provide "welcoming acknowledgment to exactly who the person is right now" (p. 43) while also introducing dissonance to encourage growth. He saw educators and peers as both playing an important role in providing a bridge for students between old and new ways of making meaning of their worlds.

Moral Development

Moral development is the process by which individuals go about making decisions that affect themselves and others. Kohlberg's (1976) work focusing on moral reasoning, the cognitive component of moral behavior, provided the foundation for later work by Gilligan (1982) and Rest, Narvaez, Bebeau, and Thoma (1999).

Kohlberg. Kohlberg's (1976) research and theory of moral development built upon Piaget's (1932/1977) study of the moral development of children. Kohlberg developed a six-stage model of moral development centered around the concept of justice, which he defined as "the primary regard for the value and equality of all human beings, and for reciprocity in human relations" (Kohlberg, 1972, p. 14). He grouped his stages into preconventional, conventional, and postconventional levels, based on the individual's relationship with the rules of society (Colby, Kohlberg, & Kauffman, 1987; Kohlberg, 1976) (see Exhibit 9.3).

The ability to reason logically and to see the point of view of others is necessary, but not sufficient, to achieve more advanced levels of moral reasoning (Kohlberg, 1976). Moral development occurs in response to cognitive conflict that disrupts one's current way of thinking. It is enhanced by chances to confront situations that have moral implications (Kohlberg, 1972).

Kohlberg's theory has spawned extensive research, which has generally supported his major hypotheses (see Evans et al., 1998; Rest, 1986). Studies suggest that university life, including academic coursework, structured programs, and social networks, can have a significant impact on moral development (Derryberry & Thoma, 2000; Pascarella, 1997; Rest, 1986). Kohlberg's theory has come under attack, however, for being biased against women (Gilligan, 1977, 1982), failing to take into account cultural differences, using hypothetical dilemmas rather than real-life situations, and emphasizing rational aspects of reasoning while neglecting emotional factors (see Arnold, 2000; Rest et al. 1999).

EXHIBIT 9.3. KOHLBERG'S STAGES OF MORAL REASONING.

Preconventional Level. At this level the individual's thinking is concrete and self-focused. Societal rules and expectations are not yet understood. This level has four stages.

Stage 1. Heteronomous Morality. The direct consequences of actions determine right and wrong. The individual acts to avoid being punished. The rights and concerns of others are not recognized.

Stage 2. Individualistic, Instrumental Morality. Decisions are made pragmatically, based on equal exchange. "You scratch my back and I'll scratch yours" sums up this position.

Conventional Level. At this level the rules of society and the opinions of others take precedence in decision-making. Being a good citizen is an important criterion for action. This level also consists of two stages.

Stage 3. Interpersonally Normative Morality. Good behavior is defined as that which pleases those to whom one is close and gains their approval. Individuals adhere to stereotyped images of "right" behavior.

Stage 4. Social System Morality. Actions are based on upholding the system and obeying the rules of society. Showing respect for authority and maintaining the social order for its own sake are seen as important.

Postconventional, or Principled, Level. Reasoning at this level is based on self-determined principles and values. Individuals choose their own directions rather than following a prescribed path. Two stages are included at this level as well.

Stage 5. Human Rights and Social Welfare Morality. Right action is determined by standards that have been agreed upon by society, but an awareness exists that rules can be reevaluated and changed. Individuals are bound by the social contracts into which they have entered.

Stage 6. Morality of Universalizable, Reversible, and Prescriptive General Ethical Principles. Self-chosen ethical principles, including justice, equality, and respect for human dignity, guide behavior. Principles take precedence over laws.

Source: Adapted from Colby, Kohlberg, and Kauffman (1987) and Kohlberg (1976).

Gilligan. Gilligan (1977, 1982) asserted that Kohlberg's theory, with its focus on justice and rights, did not take into account the concern that women have with care and responsibility for others. Based on her findings from several studies involving real-life moral dilemmas such as whether or not to have an abortion, Gilligan proposed an alternative model of moral development with three levels and two transition periods. In the first level, which Gilligan called *Orientation to Individual Survival,* decisions center on the self and one's own desires and needs. In the first transition, *From Selfishness to Responsibility,* the desire to take care of oneself remains but is in conflict with a growing sense that the right thing to do is to take care of others. In the second level, *Goodness as Self-Sacrifice,* acceptance by others becomes the primary criteria. This goal is achieved by caring for others and protecting them; one's own desires are relegated to a secondary position. As persons begin to question the logic of always putting themselves second, the second transition, *From Goodness to Truth,* begins, and the concept of responsibility is reconsidered in an effort to include taking care of oneself as well as others. In the third level, *The Morality of Nonviolence,* the individuals "asserts a moral equality between self and other" (Gilligan, 1977, p. 504) and comes to understand that the prohibition against hurting also includes not hurting oneself. This principle of nonviolence becomes the person's main guiding force.

Gilligan's (1982) work set off much debate and led to a substantial amount of research designed to determine if there are gender differences in moral development. While most studies using the Kohlbergian model found few gender-related differences (see Rest, 1986; Walker, 1984), evidence does suggest that two types of reasoning guide the moral judgments people make—one based on justice and rights and another based on care and responsibility (see Evans et al., 1998). While these styles of reasoning are not gender-*specific,* they do appear to be gender-*related;* that is, while both men and women have been found to use both styles, men use justice and rights arguments more often, while women more frequently base their judgments on responsibility and care (Gibbs, Arnold, & Burkhart, 1984; Jones & Watt, 2001; Liddell, Halpin, & Halpin, 1993).

Gilligan's (1982) theory has been used to guide student affairs practice. For instance, Delworth and Seeman (1984) suggested that institutional policies and organizational structures be examined for underlying assumptions about care and justice. In addition, Gilligan's ideas about the ethics of care have been applied to counseling, residence life, and leadership development (see Evans et al., 1998, for examples).

Rest. Rest and his associates have actively pursued research on moral development for over twenty-five years (Rest et al., 1999). They have recently introduced a neo-Kohlbergian approach to understanding moral reasoning (Rest, Narvaez, Thoma, & Bebeau, 2000). It is similar to Kohlberg's (1976) approach in four ways: (1) it is cognitive structural in nature, (2) it focuses on how individuals attempt to make meaning out of their social experiences, (3) it is developmental (reasoning increases in complexity over time), and (4) it emphasizes the shift from conventional to postconventional thinking in early adulthood.

The theory advanced by Rest et al. (2000) differs from Kohlberg's in five ways: (1) they use the term *schema* rather than *stage* because they "envision development as shifting distributions rather than as a staircase" (p. 384); (2) their schemas are more concrete than Kohlberg's stages; (3) they do not attempt to separate content from structure in their schemas, arguing that such separation, which Kohlberg attempted, is impossible; (4) they reject Kohlberg's claim of universality, regarding "cross-cultural similarity as an empirical question" (p. 385); (5) they assess moral reasoning using a recognition task (a multiple choice test) rather than an interview task to avoid placing restraints on individuals with poor verbal skills. They suggest that people often understand more than they can explain verbally.

Rest et al. (2000) postulated three structures in moral reasoning, based on how the person interprets and responds to societal obligations: the Personal Interest Schema, the Maintaining Norms Schema, and the Postconventional Schema. They defined schemas as "general knowledge structures residing in long-term memory" that develop as individuals "notice similarities and recurrences in experiences" (p. 389). The Personal Interest Schema predominates in childhood and becomes less prominent in reasoning as the person moves into adolescence. This type of reasoning involves analysis of what each individual has to gain or lose and does not acknowledge the importance of society-wide cooperation. The emphasis is on the concerns of the individual and those to whom he or she is close. As can be seen, this schema includes elements of Kohlberg's second and third stages. The Maintaining Norms Schema is similar to Kohlberg's fourth stage. Individuals using this type of reasoning recognize and abide by established societal norms, believe that all norms must be obeyed, and acknowledge the legitimate role of authorities. At this level, individuals believe that "maintaining the established social order defines morality" (Rest et al., 2000, p. 387). Postconventional Schema thinking, in contrast, interprets moral obligations as "based on shared ideals," "fully reciprocal," and "open to scrutiny" (p. 388). This schema contains aspects of Kohlberg's postconventional stages five and six.

Spiritual Development: Fowler and Parks

Spirituality, defined by Parks (2000) as a personal search for purpose and meaning in life, is an important, yet often neglected aspect of student development. Recently, however, attention has been devoted to ways in which students explore and address spiritual issues and how educators can better assist them in their spiritual quests (Jablonski, 2001; Love & Talbot, 1999).

Fowler (1981), the first theorist to address spirituality from a developmental perspective, examined the development of faith over the life span. He saw faith, a process of making meaning out of life's experiences, as being relational in nature, focusing on the interaction of self and others as well as the commitment the individual holds to a larger center of meaning and purpose (God). Fowler described faith as "a universal feature of human living, recognizably similar everywhere despite the remarkable variety of forms and contents of religious practice and belief" (p. 14).

Fowler (1981) drew on the work of Piaget (1950) and Kohlberg (1976); his six stages of faith development parallel their stages of intellectual and moral development, respectively. Fowler's stages focus on how beliefs and values come to be important to the individual, not on the specific beliefs and values the individual adopts. He adhered closely to traditional cognitive structural assumptions, describing his stages as sequential, hierarchical, and universal. Crises in the lives of individuals lead to movement from one stage to the next. Each stage is more complex than the one it follows with later stages being more mature expressions of faith than earlier ones. As with other cognitive structural theories, movement through these stages is influenced both by internal maturational processes and by environmental factors.

Fowler (1981) did not specifically address the faith development of young adults in college. Parks (1986, 2000) attempted to fill this void by proposing a stage between adolescence and adulthood, which she called the "young adult" stage. Grounding her work in both psychosocial and cognitive structural approaches to student development, she emphasized the interconnections of affective, cognitive, and social/cultural factors in faith development. Parks (2000) identified four interacting components of faith:

self, other, world, and "God." The manner in which each of these elements is viewed and relates to the others undergoes change as the person's faith develops.

Parks (2000) suggested that the experiences of young adults in college are shaped by forms of knowing (cognitive processes), dependence (affective aspects focusing on relationships), and community (social and cultural contexts). She presented a four-stage model of development in which each of these forms contributes to a distinctive understanding of faith. In the Adolescent or Conventional stage, the individual's view of the world is dualistic and based on information provided by authorities. One's sense of self is dependent on others and being a part of a community that shares norms and beliefs is crucial. As dissonance occurs when conflicting information is introduced, a loss of faith may be experienced. Parks noted, however, that loss of this type of unexamined faith actually can be developmental. Most college students are in the Young Adult stage, where persons make and learn from tentative commitments. They begin to develop a sense of independence from others. At this point, they need a compatible mentoring community in which to explore. Some college students, particularly older adults or graduate students, may be in the Tested Adult stage, which is characterized by more secure commitment and confident inner-dependence. Individuals in this stage seek out communities that have compatible belief systems. Mature Adult faith is rarely achieved until midlife. It involves "connection to, interaction with, and belonging to the broader world" (Love, 2001, p. 14).

Parks (2000) stressed the role of imagination in faith development, identifying five steps in acts of imagination. *Conscious conflict* involves recognizing that something in one's life is out of balance. *Pause* is a time of reflection and examination. *Image (or Insight)* is the moment when everything comes together. *Repatterning and Release of Energy* consists of letting go of tension and reorganizing the phenomena under consideration. The last step, *Interpretation,* involves openly trying out new perceptions. Parks suggested that colleges are communities of imagination that can affect faith development either positively or negatively. For positive development to occur, students need to be introduced to new ideas and have opportunities to reflect on them and to try out new positions.

Using Cognitive Structural Theories in Practice

Remember our friend Allison? Cognitive structural theories can assist her in her work as an academic advisor. First, knowledge of moral development theories can help Allison understand students' reasoning about the dilemmas they experience. With regard to the conflict she is facing about her Food Science class, Ana's first concern is her religious community's norms and beliefs. She seems to be using stage three thinking in Kohlberg's model or Rest's Maintaining Norms schema. In working with Ana, Allison will want to use reasoning at the same level to insure that Ana understands her. Parks's faith development model is informative to Allison in that the crisis Ana is experiencing seems to be a moment of conscious conflict as her religious commitment is tested. Parks's model suggests that Allison can assist Ana by helping her reflect and evaluate her situation (Pause) in hopes of achieving Insight, Repatterning, and Interpretation.

Understanding the process of cognitive development can also be very helpful to Allison as she designs workshops and classes. Kohlberg's ideas have successfully guided moral education programs in schools and universities (Kohlberg, 1972; Kohlberg & Wasserman, 1980). For instance, a workshop for first-year students on academic integrity might expose students to different stages of reasoning about issues such as cheating and plagiarism. Such exposure would challenge them to think more complexly about these topics. Involving students in policy development is another way to challenge their level of reasoning and create opportunities for their personal involvement in meaningful decision making, which will enhance their moral development. For example, Allison might suggest that students be included on a committee to examine graduation requirements or to establish a policy on academic dishonesty.

Typology Perspectives

Mike and Carla, both paraprofessional student advisors whom Allison supervises, have been selected to put together a program for first-year students on how to choose a major. They are having a hard time working together. Mike prefers to take a relaxed approach; he is constantly throwing out interesting and creative suggestions, but he can't seem to get down to actually making a decision. Carla, on the other hand, would really prefer to develop a detailed written outline of the program so they have time to practice the workshop several times before they give it. She would like time to think about Mike's ideas, but before she can, he moves on to something different.

Typology theories help explain problems such as the difficulty Mike and Carla have working together. These theories examine individual differences in how people view and relate to the world. Unlike psychosocial and cognitive structural theories, typology theories are not truly "developmental" in that they do not consist of stages through which individuals progress.

According to Jung (1923/1971), human behavior does not vary by chance; rather, it results from innate differences in mental functioning. These differences appear in many aspects of life, such as how people take in and process information, how they learn, and the types of activities that interest them. Typology theorists identify factors that create consistent ways of coping with the demands of life. When faced with similar developmental challenges or environmental situations, individuals will respond differently, depending on their type. Mike and Carla, for instance, approach the task of preparing a program in different ways because of their different types. These theories also give us important information about sources of support and challenge for students who are otherwise developmentally similar. Mike thrives on spontaneous activity and the freedom to "do his own thing," while Carla does better when she can plan ahead.

Typology theories are nonevaluative in nature. Various types are viewed as different rather than as good or bad. Each type is seen as making positive and unique contributions to any situation. In our example, Mike and Carla both have something positive to offer to the program. Mike is a great idea person, while Carla is very good at detail.

In this section, two of the best known and most extensively used typology theories are introduced: the Myers-Briggs theory of personality type (Myers, 1980) and Holland's (1985) theory of vocational interest. Kolb's (1976) theory of learning styles, which proposes that individuals have preferred ways of learning, is examined in Chapter Eleven. This section concludes with an examination of the uses of typology theory in student affairs settings.

Psychological Type: Jung and Myers

Jung's (1923/1971) theory of psychological types is concerned with individuals' orientation to the world; how they perceive their environment (become aware of people, things, events, and ideas); how they make judgments, or reach conclusions, about the information they take in; and how they relate to their external environment. Jung suggested that some people prefer the outer world of people and things (Extraversion, or E) while others are more interested in the inner world of ideas and concepts (Introversion, or I). Jung also proposed two ways of perceiving: Sensing (S) and Intuition (N). Sensing involves taking in information directly through the five senses, while Intuition is an indirect method of perceiving through the use of ideas or associations by way of the unconscious (Myers, 1980). When using the Sensing process, individuals report real, observable facts. In contrast, an individual relying on the Intuitive mode of perception will present underlying meanings, connections, and symbolic relationships.

According to Jung (1923/1971), there are also two ways of judging: Thinking (T) and Feeling (F). When using the Thinking process, individuals rely on the logical analysis of causes and effects, pros and cons, and the weight of evidence in support of various positions. Individuals using a Feeling process base their decisions on personal, subjective values. Human relationships are their primary consideration when making decisions (Myers, 1980).

A final preference implicitly suggested by Jung (1923/1971) and more clearly defined by Myers (1980) is the preference for the perceptive or judgment attitude when dealing with the outside world. People who prefer Judging (J) enjoy organization, planning, and making decisions quickly, while those who prefer Perception (P) are curious, flexible, and prefer to gather a lots of information before making a decision (McCaulley, 1990).

Personality type theory, as proposed by Jung (1923/1971), further developed by Myers (1980), and measured by the Myers-Briggs Type Inventory (MBTI) (Myers & McCaulley, 1985), suggests, then, that there are four bipolar scales, EI, SN, TF, and JP. Preferences on each scale are identified and organized into one of sixteen different types (for example, ENTP, ISFJ).

Application of type theory to our understanding of the college environment is discussed in Chapter Thirteen, while its contributions to student learning are reviewed in Chapter Eleven. A particularly interesting example of research on learning involving personality type is a study conducted by Dewar and Whittington (2000). They found that the learning strategies used by online learners varied depending on Myers Briggs type. A summary of research involving the MBTI and the theory upon which it is based can be found in Evans et al. (1998). They also provide an overview of applications of this approach to student affairs practice.

Vocational Personality Types: Holland

Holland's (1985) theory of vocational choice examined both people's interests and the characteristics of work environments. Holland viewed vocation as an expression of personality; as such, individuals pursuing specific careers have similar personalities. They respond to situations similarly and create unique interpersonal environments. People look for environments that will allow them to pursue their interests and use their abilities and that reinforce their attitudes and values. Satisfaction and success are contingent on the interaction between one's personality and the characteristics of one's environment. Holland identified six personality types, along with six corresponding work environments (see Exhibit 9.4). He also introduced several assumptions about his personality types and work environments, having to do with their consistency and differentiation as well as the congruence of personality and environmental types. These are discussed in Chapter Thirteen.

Holland's (1985) theory has been found to be valid for both men and women and for African Americans (Herr & Cramer, 1992). However, recent research suggests that gender differences identified in earlier research continue to exist with regard to personality type preferences and that these differences have implications for choice of

EXHIBIT 9.4. HOLLAND'S PERSONALITY TYPES.

Realistic. This type is characterized by an interest in physical activities requiring motor skills and strength; concrete rather than abstract tasks are preferred. Individuals prefer working with things rather than with people or ideas.

Investigative. These individuals tend to be scholarly, analytic, and inquisitive. They prefer thinking to acting and they enjoy the world of ideas more than working with people or things.

Social. People exhibiting this type are friendly, helpful, cooperative, and sensitive to others. They enjoy close interpersonal contact and prefer to work with people rather than with things or ideas.

Conventional. These individuals like order and structure and work well within a system. They are conscientious, efficient, and practical. They like working with numbers, records, and data.

Enterprising. People in this category are verbally skilled, persuasive, confident, and concerned with status. They like to lead and organize others. They enjoy working with people but in a managerial rather than a helping role.

Artistic. This type is expressive, imaginative, and creative. These individuals dislike structure and prefer innovative assignments. They enjoy work that involves artistic creation.

Source: Adapted from Holland (1985).

major and extracurricular involvement (Murray & Hall, 2001). Feldman, Ethington, and Smart (2001) proposed, though, that socialization is more important than personality type in development of abilities and interests once students are in particular environments. Discussion of other research and application of Holland's theory to student affairs practice can be found in Evans et al. (1998).

Using Typology Perspectives in Practice

Our friend Allison will certainly find typology theories useful in her work as an academic advisor. Understanding personality types can assist Allison in predicting students' likes and dislikes with regard to classes and extracurricular activities, assessing the learning environment in which they will do best, and determining career options they might want to explore. For example, a Realistic student may do extremely well in a major such as welding where he can use his hands and work alone but would be out of his element in a field like social work that involves extensive social interaction.

Typology theories can also help explain interpersonal interactions and provide guidance in working through conflicts (such as the one between Mike and Carla). Individuals can learn to anticipate others' work styles and use the strengths each person brings to a project. Group interactions can also be analyzed using typology theory. For instance, the Advising Center staff might all take the MBTI and process the implications of their results for working more effectively together. Typology theories can also be of great utility in making effective work assignments. For example, Carla would be most effective in a job requiring precision and organization, while Mike would be good at a task requiring creativity.

Typology theories can also provide guidance concerning the design of classes, workshops, training sessions, and other structured educational experiences. These applications are discussed further in Chapter Eleven. In addition, residence hall staff developing room assignment policies might take into consideration similarities and differences in MBTI type or interests suggested by an assessment of students' Holland codes.

Conclusion

As can be seen from the examples presented, each theoretical perspective adds a piece to the puzzle of student development. Theory is useful in helping student affairs professionals such as Allison interpret what they are hearing from students. It provides a framework for understanding students' concerns, attitudes, and thought processes. Theory helps student affairs professionals process information and respond appropriately. Such responses may take the form of suggesting actions to students, challenging their thinking, providing support with a listening ear, creating workshops, or advocating changes in policy.

Theory can also help student affairs professionals become more proactive in their work with students. Theory suggests questions to ask, avenues to explore, and hypotheses to test. It provides shortcuts to exploring students' concerns and analyzing how they are addressing them. It also provides direction in developing appropriate programs and class offerings for particular groups of students.

Theory can help student affairs professionals evaluate their work. First, by suggesting developmental outcomes, theory provides goals to work toward, such as helping students develop a clear sense of purpose in their lives. Then, assessing the extent to which these goals are achieved can determine how student affairs programs are impacting development.

Much work remains to be done, however. As McEwen stressed in Chapter Eight, theories are socially constructed and influenced by the perspectives and biases of their creators. They are also limited in the constructs they explain. While descriptions of developmental stages exist and the issues, attitudes, and behaviors that occur within these stages are apparent, much less is known about how to facilitate students' movement through these stages. What factors lead to cognitive conflict, for example, and how do they propel development? What can be done to ensure that change is positive? Why do some students change but not others? More must be discovered about the forces that work against development and what can be done to intervene. Societal factors such as economic pressures, political attitudes, fear of violence, and other affectively charged concerns may influence students in ways about which very little is known. As researchers study the psychology of development, they must not lose sight of its sociology.

It is important to remember that development is a complex process. Individuals don't fit all stages perfectly or address all issues as they are "supposed" to. No theory can tell any student what to do with his or her life. Only students themselves can determine those answers. Educators must also remember that research is just beginning to provide information about the diversity of student experience. Most of the theories discussed in this chapter were based on White male, middle-to-upper class populations. Theories may suggest directions to explore in advising students from diverse backgrounds, but student affairs practitioners must remain open to hearing different answers than they hear when they talk to students from dominant populations.

As McEwen suggested in Chapter Eight, understanding oneself is important in the process of seeing the benefits and drawbacks of specific theories. One's own background, values, and biases will clearly influence how one interprets theories and makes connections between theories and what is seen and heard when interacting with students. Being able to identify these potential constraints is an important step in using theory intelligently.

Upcraft (1994) cogently stated an often-heard complaint: student affairs practitioners don't use theory as a guide to practice. Hopefully, the examples and connections provided in this chapter have demonstrated ways in which theory can be used effectively in the daily activities of student affairs professionals and have encouraged readers to become theory-based practitioners. But, obviously, reading one chapter on student development theory won't make anyone an expert. Further reading and ongoing study is needed. As Upcraft pointed out, it is easier to learn about theory if it is necessary for some aspect of one's position. Teaching student development theory to peer counselors, developing a program with a theory base, or heading up the staff development committee are all possible ways to gain increased familiarity with student development theory. Another very good way to learn about student development is to talk to students in an intentional way about their experiences, concerns, beliefs, and challenges. Many of the theories presented in this chapter were developed in this way. Perhaps you, too, can add to the profession's knowledge base on student development. At the very least you will become a better informed and more effective student affairs professional.

References

Arnold, M. L. (2000). Stage, sequence, and sequels: Changing conceptions of morality, post-Kohlberg. *Educational Psychology Review, 12,* 365–383.

Baltes, P. B. (1987). Theoretical propositions on life-span developmental psychology: On the dynamics between growth and decline. *Developmental Psychology, 23,* 611–626.

Bengston, V. L. (Ed.). (1996). *Adulthood and aging: Research on continuities and discontinuities.* New York: Springer.

Canon, H. J. (1988). Nevitt Sanford: Gentle prophet, Jeffersonian rebel. *Journal of Counseling and Development, 66,* 451–457.

Chickering, A. W. (1969). *Education and identity.* San Francisco: Jossey-Bass.

Chickering, A. W., & Reisser, L. (1993). *Education and identity* (2nd ed.). San Francisco: Jossey-Bass.

Clark, M. C., & Caffarella, R. S. (1999). *An update on adult development theory: New ways of thinking about the life course* (New Directions for Adult and Continuing Education No. 84). San Francisco: Jossey-Bass.

Colby, A., Kohlberg, L., & Kauffman, K. (1987). Theoretical introduction to the measurement of moral judgment. In U. Delworth & D. Seeman (Eds.), The ethics of care: Implications of Gilligan for the student services profession. *Journal of College Student Personnel, 25,* 489–492.

Derryberry, W. P., & Thoma, S. J. (2000). The friendship effect: Its role in the development of moral thinking in students. *About Campus, 5* (2), 13–18.

Dewar, T., & Whittington, D. (2000). Online learners and their learning strategies. *Journal of Educational Computing Research, 23,* 385–403.

Elder, G. H., Jr. (1995). The life course paradigm: Social change and individual development. In P. Moen, G. H. Elder, Jr., & K. Lüscher (Eds.), *Examining lives in context: Perspectives on the ecology of human development* (pp. 101–139). Washington, DC: American Psychological Association.

Elleven, R. K., Spaulding, D. J., Murphy, S. D., & Eddy, J. P. (1997). Wellness programming: Does student choice relate to recognized development vectors? *College Student Journal, 31,* 228–234.

Erikson, E. H. (1959). Identity and the life cycle. *Psychological Issues, 1,* 1–171.

Erikson, E. H. (1968). *Identity: Youth and crisis.* New York: Norton.

Evans, N. J., Forney, D. S., & Guido-DiBrito, F. (1998). *Student development in college: Theory, research, and practice.* San Francisco: Jossey-Bass.

Feldman, K. A., Ethington, C. A., & Smart, J. C. (2001). A further investigation of major field and person-environment fit: Sociological versus psychological interpretations of Holland's theory. *Journal of Higher Education, 72,* 670–698.

Fiske, M., & Chiriboga, D. A. (1990). *Change and continuity in adult life.* San Francisco: Jossey-Bass.

Fowler, J. (1981). *Stages of faith: The psychology of human development and the quest for meaning.* New York: Harper & Row.

Gibbs, J. C., Arnold, K. D., & Burkhart, J. E. (1984). Sex differences in the expression of moral judgment. *Child Development, 55,* 1040–1043.

Gilligan, C. (1977). In a different voice: Women's conceptions of self and morality. *Harvard Educational Review, 47,* 481–517.

Gilligan, C. (1982). *In a different voice: Psychological theory and women's development.* Cambridge, MA: Harvard University Press.

Gould, R. L. (1978). *Transformations: Growth and change in adult life.* New York: Simon & Schuster.

Herr, E. L. (1997). Super's life-span, life-space approach and its outlook for refinement. *The Career Development Quarterly, 45,* 238–246.

Herr, E. L., & Cramer, S. H. (1992). *Career guidance and counseling through the lifespan: Systematic approaches* (4th ed.). New York: HarperCollins.

Holland, J. L. (1985). *Making vocational choices: A theory of vocational personalities and work environments* (2nd ed.). Englewood Cliffs, NJ: Prentice Hall.

Hughes, J. A., & Graham, S. W. (1990). Adult life roles: A new approach to adult development. *Journal of Continuing Higher Education, 38* (2), 2–8.

Ignelzi, M. (2000). Meaning-making in the learning and teaching process. In M. B. Baxter Magolda (Ed.), *Teaching to promote intellectual and personal maturity: Incorporating students' worldviews and identities into the learning process* (New Directions for Teaching and Learning No. 82, pp. 5–14). San Francisco: Jossey-Bass.

Jablonski, M. A. (Ed.). (2001). *The implications of student spirituality for student affairs practice* (New Directions for Student Services No. 95). San Francisco: Jossey-Bass.

Jones, C. E., & Watt, J. D. (2001). Moral orientation and psychosocial development: Gender and class-standing differences. *NASPA Journal, 39,* 1–13.

Josselson, R. (1987). *Finding herself: Pathways to identity development in women.* San Francisco: Jossey-Bass.

Josselson, R. (1996). *Revising herself: The story of women's identity from college to midlife.* New York: Oxford University Press.

Jung, C. G. (1971). *Psychological types.* (F. C. Hull, Ed.; H. G. Baynes, Trans.). Princeton, NJ: Princeton University Press. (Original work published 1923)

Kegan, R. (1982). *The evolving self: Problem and process in human development.* Cambridge, MA: Harvard University Press.

Kegan, R. (1994). *In over our heads: The mental demands of modern life.* Cambridge, MA: Harvard University Press.

Kodama, C. M., McEwen, M. K., Liang, C.T.H., & Lee, S. (2001). A theoretical examination of psychosocial issues for Asian Pacific American students. *NASPA Journal, 38,* 411–437.

Kohlberg, L. (1972). A cognitive-developmental approach to moral education. *Humanist, 6,* 13–16.

Kohlberg, L. (1976). Moral stages and moralization: The cognitive-developmental approach. In T. Lickona (Ed.), *Moral development and behavior: Theory, research, and social issues* (pp. 31–53). New York: Holt, Rinehart and Winston.

Kohlberg, L., & Wasserman, E. R. (1980). The cognitive-developmental approach and the practicing counselor: An opportunity for counselors to rethink their roles. *Personnel and Guidance Journal, 58,* 559–567.

Kolb, D. (1976). *Learning styles inventory technical manual.* Boston: McBer.

Levinson, D. J. (1978). *The seasons of a man's life.* New York: Ballantine.

Levinson, D. J., & Levinson, J. D. (1996). *The seasons of a woman's life.* New York: Ballantine.

Liddell, D. L., Halpin, G., & Halpin, W. G. (1993). Men, women, and moral orientation: Accounting for our differences. *NASPA Journal, 30,* 138–144.

Love, P., & Talbot, D. (1999). Defining spiritual development: A missing consideration for student affairs. *NASPA Journal, 37,* 361–375.

Love, P. G. (2001). Spirituality and student development: Theoretical connections. In M. A. Jablonski (Ed.), *The implications of student spirituality for student affairs practice* (New Directions for Student Services No. 95, pp. 7–16). San Francisco: Jossey-Bass.

Love, P. G., & Guthrie, V. L. (1999). *Understanding and applying cognitive development theory* (New Directions for Student Services No. 88). San Francisco: Jossey-Bass.

Magnusson, D. (1995). Individual development: A holistic, integrated model. In P. Moen, G. H. Elder, & K. Lusher (Eds.), *Examining lives in context: Perspectives on the ecology of human development* (pp. 19–60). Washington, DC: American Psychological Association.

Marcia, J. E. (1966). Development and validation of ego-identity status. *Journal of Personality and Social Psychology, 3,* 551–559.

McCaulley, M. H. (1990). The Myers-Briggs Type Indicator: A measure for individuals and groups. *Measurement and Evaluation in Counseling and Development, 22,* 181–195.

McDaniels, C., & Gysbers, N. C. (1992). *Counseling for career development: Theories, resources, and practice.* San Francisco: Jossey-Bass.

Murray, J. L., & Hall, P. M. (2001). Gender differences in undergraduate Holland personality types: Vocational and cocurricular implications. *NASPA Journal, 39,* 14–29.

Myers, I. B. (1980). *Gifts differing.* Palo Alto, CA: Consulting Psychologists Press.

Myers, I. B., & McCaulley, M. H. (1985). *Manual: A guide to the development and use of the Myers-Briggs Type Indicator.* Palo Alto, CA: Consulting Psychologists Press.

Neugarten, B. L. (1979). Time, age, and the life cycle. *American Journal of Psychiatry, 136,* 887–894.

Parks, S. D. (1986). *The critical years: Young adults and the search for meaning, faith, and commitment.* New York: HarperCollins.

Parks, S. D. (2000). *Big questions, worthy dreams: Mentoring young adults in their search for meaning, purpose, and faith.* San Francisco: Jossey-Bass.

Pascarella, E. T. (1997). College's influence on principled moral reasoning. *Educational Record, 78,* 47–55.

Perun, P. J., & Bielby, D. D. (1980). Structure and dynamics on the individual life course. In K. W. Back (Ed.), *Life course: Integrative theories and exemplary populations* (pp. 97–119). Boulder, CO: Westview.

Piaget, J. (1950). *The psychology of intelligence.* San Diego, CA: Harcourt Brace Jovanovich.

Piaget, J. (1952). *The origins of intelligence in children.* New York: International Universities Press.

Piaget, J. (1977). *The moral judgment of the child* (M. Gabain, Trans.). Harmondsforth, England: Penguin. (Original work published 1932)

Pope, R. L. (1998). The relationship between psychosocial development and racial identity of Black college students. *Journal of College Student Development, 39,* 273–282.

Rest, J. R. (1986). *Moral development: Advances in research and theory.* New York: Praeger.

Rest, J. R., Narvaez, D., Bebeau, M. J., & Thoma, S. J. (1999). *Postconventional moral thinking: A neo-Kohlbergian approach.* Mahwah, NJ: Lawrence Erlbaum.

Rest, J. R., Narvaez, D., Thoma, S. J., & Bebeau, M. J. (2000). A neo-Kohlbergian approach to morality research. *Journal of Moral Education, 29,* 381–395.

Roberts, P., & Newton, P. M. (1987). Levinsonian studies of women's adult development. *Psychology and Aging, 2,* 154–163.

Sanford, N. (1962). *The American college.* New York: Wiley.

Sanford, N. (1966). *Self and society: Social change and individual development.* New York: Atherton.

Schlossberg, N. K., Waters, E. B., & Goodman, J. (1995). *Counseling adults in transition* (2nd ed.). New York: Springer.

Schuh, J. H. (1989). A student development theory to practice workshop. *Journal of Counseling and Development, 67,* 297–298.

Sugarman, L. (1986). *Life-span development: Concepts, theories and interventions.* New York: Methuen.

Super, D. E. (1957). *The psychology of careers.* New York: Harper & Row.

Super, D. E. (1983). Assessment in career guidance: Toward truly developmental counseling. *Personnel and Guidance Journal, 61,* 555–562.

Super, D. E. (1984). Career and life development. In D. Brown, L. Brooks, & Associates (Eds.), *Career choice and development: Applying contemporary theories to development* (pp. 192–234). San Francisco: Jossey-Bass.

Super, D. E. (1990). A life-span, life-space approach to career development. In D. Brown, L. Brooks, & Associates, *Career choice and development: Applying contemporary theories to development* (2nd ed., pp. 197–261). San Francisco: Jossey-Bass.

Tittle, C. K. (1982). Career, marriage, and family: Values in adult roles and guidance. *Personnel and Guidance Journal, 61,* 154–158.

Upcraft, M. L. (1994). The dilemmas of translating theory to practice. *Journal of College Student Development, 35,* 438–443.

Vaillant, G. (1977). *Adaptation to life.* Boston: Little, Brown.

Wadsworth, B. J. (1979). *Piaget's theory of cognitive development* (2nd ed.). New York: Longman.

Walker, L. J. (1984). Sex differences in the development of moral reasoning: A critical review. *Child Development, 55,* 677–691.

Whitbourne, S. K. (1985). The psychological construction of the life span. In J. E. Birren & K. W. Schaie (Eds.), *Handbook of the psychology of aging* (2nd ed., pp. 594–618). New York: Van Nostrand Reinhold.

Wood, N. L., Wood, R. A., & McDonald, T. D. (1988). Integration of student development theory into the academic classroom. *Adolescence, 23,* 349–356.

CHAPTER TEN

NEW PERSPECTIVES ON IDENTITY DEVELOPMENT

Marylu K. McEwen

Suppose that you are a professional at Millennium University, a traditionally White university located about ten miles from Cleveland. You are responsible for advising students on cocurricular programming for an innovative learning community focusing on community service and social justice. Some of the students with whom you work are Kawezia, Josh, Tiffany, Drew, Maria, and Noel. These are great students and a very diverse group. However, you are puzzled by some of the dynamics within the group and also by what you know about some of their other experiences.

- Kawezia is an African American woman who grew up in Philadelphia and attended racially diverse schools. Her parents are middle-class African Americans, and she has an older sister who is attending Spelman College. Kawezia is a sophomore communications major who lives in the residence halls.
- Tiffany is a White woman who grew up in suburban Atlanta; she lives on campus, is a junior, and majors in women's studies.
- Drew came from Chicago and is biracial; his father is White and his mother Latina. Drew lives on campus, is a senior, and majors in journalism. Drew is highly involved in a Catholic parish close to campus.
- Josh is Cambodian American; his family immigrated to the United States when he was seven. He grew up in a close-knit family that considers itself socioeconomically lower-middle-class. Josh is the first in his family to attend college, is a junior majoring in business, and commutes to the university. He works thirty hours per week at his family's business.
- Noel is a White man who came to the university from Oregon; he is a junior and majors in elementary education. Noel is an activist on campus for a variety of liberal causes, including pro-choice, domestic partner benefits, and racial diversity.

- Maria, a Puerto Rican American woman, was attracted to the university through an offer of a four-year scholarship. She is a first-year student who is undecided about her major. Maria lives off-campus with relatives.

All six of these students have expressed strong interest in working on cocurricular programming for the innovative learning community. At the end of the past semester, Kawezia, Tiffany, and Drew were part of a committee who decided that the group should be involved in community service at a local soup kitchen. Tiffany, however, expressed dissatisfaction with that option and instead recommended volunteering at the university's women's resource center.

Josh, Maria, and Noel have just joined the project. The discussion about community service opportunities continues. Kawezia offers another option and is rather insistent about tutoring at a predominantly Black public school. Maria supports Tiffany in focusing on the women's resource center, because she indicates that she needs to be able to return home every weekend to care for her aging grandmother. Noel really likes the diversity of students involved with the project but thinks that a single community service site should be selected and that any one who chooses to participate in this learning community should be held to the standards of the group. Josh supports Kawezia about tutoring but is concerned about balancing community service with his off-campus work responsibilities. Drew is the natural leader of the group, although for the past two meetings he has not taken that role and doesn't seem to be quite himself. In terms of participation in the soup kitchen, Drew's primary concern is that it not conflict with Sunday responsibilities at his local parish.

You are confused about some of the issues and lack of consensus within the group. You hope that knowledge about the development of social identities will help you understand these students better and advise the group more effectively.

Identity and Development

The illustrations above provide brief snapshots of six college students, their dynamics in working together, and some of their experiences on campus. An understanding of the development of various social identities of college students, along with their psychosocial and cognitive-structural development (described in Chapters Nine and Eleven), is important for student affairs professionals and faculty members.

The major purposes of this chapter are to: (1) define the constructs of identity and development, (2) identify common themes related to race, class, gender, and sexuality, (3) provide an overview of models and theories of identity development for race, sexual orientation, and gender, (4) discuss the three social identities of social class, abilities and disabilities, and religion, and consider geographic region as a context for identity development, (5) present models of multiple social identities, and (6) suggest next steps and future directions toward a more comprehensive conceptualization and understanding of these six social identities and their development in college students.

Identity

Erikson (1959/1980) and Chickering (1969; Chickering & Reisser, 1993) proposed that identity development is a central part of adolescence and early adulthood but also a lifelong task. Achieving identity is the culmination of earlier developmental tasks in the life cycle and a building block for later developmental tasks. Identity is "the accrued confidence that one's ability to maintain inner sameness and continuity . . . is matched by the sameness and continuity of one's meaning for others" (Erikson, 1959/1980, p. 94).

Widick, Parker, and Knefelkamp (1978) defined identity as "the organized set of images, the sense of self, which express who and what we really are" (p. 2) and who we want to become. Widick et al. underscored the psychosocial nature of identity: "[Erikson] places the developing person in a social context, emphasizing the fact that movement through life occurs in interaction with parents, family, social institutions and a particular culture, all of which are bounded by a particular historical period" (p. 1).

The word *identity* is used and interpreted in various ways. Sometimes identity refers to one's global identity, an overall sense of self or sense of being. Both Erikson's (1959/1980) theory of identity development throughout the life cycle and Chickering's (1969; Chickering & Reisser, 1993) seven vectors of identity development refer to identity in this global sense. On the other hand, the word *identity* may be used in a more specific manner to describe either the core essence of self or particular dimensions of identity.

Deaux (1993) helps to unravel some of the puzzle of identity by offering a conceptualization of identity as incorporating both personal identity and social identities. Personal identity refers to the collection of self-descriptive characteristics, such as being genuine, dependable, and energetic. Social identity, however, relates to roles, such as parent or friend, or membership categories, such as Latino or woman, that a person believes is representative of oneself (Deaux, 1993, p. 6).

Identity Development

Identity development is the process of becoming more complex in one's personal and social identities. Sanford (1967) (see Chapter Eight) described development as the "organization of increasing complexity" (p. 47), or increasing differentiation *and* integration of the self (Sanford, 1962, p. 257). Identity development represents a qualitative enhancement of the self in terms of complexity and integration.

Social Identities

Theories and models of social identity development have evolved from the sociohistorical and sociopolitical climate of the United States, in which social groups that are not White, heterosexual, male, able-bodied, and of the privileged class have been oppressed (see Brown, 1970; Chan, 1991; Heyck, 1994; Takaki, 1993; Weber, 1998, 2001;

Zinn, 1995). More recent models also concern the social identities of *dominant* social groups, the primary groups in the United States who *collectively* have power and privilege (McIntosh, 2001; also see Chapter Nineteen) and whose perspectives constitute what society considers normative. Dominant, however, is not necessarily synonymous with a numerical majority.

Weber (2001) provides a useful framework for considering the complexity of race, class, gender, and sexuality, and the interactions among these social identities. According to Weber, race, class, gender, and sexuality are "complex social systems—patterns of social relationships—that are complex—intricate and connected; pervasive, widespread through all societal domains . . . variable . . . persistent—prevailing over time and across places; severe—serious in their consequences for social life; and hierarchical—unequal . . . benefiting and providing options and resources for some by harming and restricting options and resources for others" (p. 17).

Weber (1998) identified six themes in the conceptualization of race, class, gender, and sexuality.

1. *Contextual*—the four constructs are fluid and vary across historical eras as well as national, geographic, and cultural contexts.
2. *Socially constructed*—these constructs are created within social hierarchies of domination and oppression.
3. *Systems of power relationships*—race, class, gender, and sexuality are not simply different ways of being but exist within power relationships.
4. *Social structural (macro) and social psychological (micro)*—the four constructs are embedded within and have meaning in *both* what occurs for individuals psychologically and in their day-to-day experiences *and* what occurs at the systemic levels of society, communities, and social institutions (ideological, political, and economic).
5. *Simultaneously expressed*—all four of these constructs, race, social class, gender, and sexuality, are a part of every experience and social situation.
6. *Interdependence of knowledge and activism*—the study of these four constructs relates both to analyzing oppression and power relationships within the constructs and to "seeking social change and social justice" (pp. 16–25).

Two additional themes underlie the social identities of race, sexual orientation, and gender for which developmental models exist. One theme is that development concerns the awareness and abandonment of internalized racism, heterosexism, and sexism. A second theme is that greater and more complex development is better, is valued as a goal for college students, and is associated with greater mental health (see, for example, Corbett, 1995; Parham & Helms, 1985).

Racial Identity Development

The terms *race* and *ethnicity* represent different constructs with different meanings. Racial identity, according to Helms (1990e), refers to "a sense of group or collective identity based on one's perception that he or she shares a common racial heritage with a particular racial group" (p. 3). Helms (1995) suggests that race is more sociopolitical and less a cultural construction. Sodowsky, Kwan, and Pannu (1995) contrast racial identity and ethnic identity. Racial identity is "based on a sociopolitical model of oppression, . . . a socially constructed definition of race, and concerned with how individuals abandon the effects of disenfranchisement and develop respectful attitudes toward their own racial group" (p. 133). Ethnic identity, however, "concerns one's attachment to, sense of belonging to, and identification with one's ethnic culture; does not have a theoretical emphasis on oppression/racism; but may include the prejudices and pressures that ethnic individuals experience when their ways of life come into conflict with those of the White dominant group" (Sodowsky et al., p. 133). (For ethnic identity development, readers should refer to Phinney [1990, 1992], whose model is one of the most prominent.)

Helms and Cook (1999) describe racial identity models as "psychological models because they intend to explain individuals' intrapsychic and interpersonal reactions to societal racism in its various manifestations. That is, they are descriptions of hypothetical intrapsychic pathways for overcoming internalized racism and achieving a healthy socioracial self-conception under varying conditions of racial oppression" (p. 81).

Racial identity development has been applied frequently to persons of oppressed racial groups, that is, those persons of African, Latino, Asian, and Native American descent (named ALANA by Helms & Cook, 1999). It is also necessary, however, to consider the racial identity development of White people and of those who are biracial, multiracial, or of mixed or "blended" races.

Helms's (1995) models of People of Color (POC or ALANA) racial identity development and White racial identity development are presented here. Although she considers her two models to be stage models of development, Helms replaced the term "stages" with "statuses" to portray that "an individual may exhibit attitudes, behaviors, and emotions reflective of more than one stage" (p. 183) and to reflect the "dynamic interplay between cognitive and emotional processes that racial identity models purport to address" (p. 183). Within each model each status is distinct and qualitatively different and each subsequent status more complex than the previous one. Helms and Cook (1999) suggest that if individuals develop more than one status, then the statuses can exist simultaneously. Further, "most people probably do not express their racial identity in pure forms" (Helms & Cook, 1999, p. 93). Any or all of the statuses a person has developed may affect one's responses to racial stimuli. Helms's use of status emphasizes that, although one may have developed complexity in one's attitudes, feelings, and behaviors in regard to race, at any time one has access to, can, and will likely use a variety of the statuses. Maturity relates not only to whether a person has developed higher level statuses but whether the status "is strong enough to be called upon to assist the person in coping with racial material" (Helms, 1995, p. 184).

People of Color or ALANA Racial Identity Development. Racial identity development of persons of color has received increasing attention in the literature over the past thirty years. Both Cross (1971, 1978, 1991, 1995; Cross & Fhagen-Smith, 2001) and Helms (1990a) have written extensively about the racial identity development of Black persons. Helms's (1995; Helms & Cook, 1999) People of Color (POC) or ALANA

(African, Latino, Asian, and Native American) model has evolved from Cross's nigrescence model and Atkinson, Morten, and Sue's minority identity development model (Helms, 1995). Helms's model is presented because of its broad applicability and extensive research validating this model for racial groups that have been oppressed within the United States (for Asian Americans, see Alvarez, 1997, 2002; Alvarez & Yeh, 1999; Kohatsu, 1993; for Latinos and Latinas, see Canabal, 1996; Miville, 1997). Because all the racial groups that comprise People of Color are subjected to various kinds and forms of discrimination and racism and collectively lack power in relation to the dominant White group, Helms and Cook (1999) believe that these groups share a common developmental task "to overcome or abandon socialized negative racial-group conceptions (that is, internalized racism) . . . in order to develop a realistic self-affirming collective identity" (p. 86).

The People of Color or ALANA racial identity development model is composed of six statuses (see Exhibit 10.1). The developmental process evolves from an implicit

EXHIBIT 10.1. PEOPLE OF COLOR RACIAL IDENTITY STATUSES.

Status 1: *Conformity.* Adaptation and internalization of White society's perspectives of one's racial group(s). Involves either embracing stereotypes of one's group(s), or "attempting to become White and assimilated into White culture" (p. 86). Preference for White group values and devaluing of cultural heritage and upbringing. Depreciating attitude toward self and toward members of one's same group(s).

Status 2: *Dissonance.* Realization that one is not able to be a full part of White society. "Ambivalence and anxiety caused by the lack of familiarity with the nature of one's own group's cultural and sociopolitical battles and accomplishments and the lack of positive material about one's own group with which to replace one's waning idealization of the White group" (p. 86).

Transition: Person begins to resolve conflicts and confusions of dissonance stage and begins to ask why one should feel shame about oneself and one's cultural background and heritage.

Status 3: *Immersion.* Replaces negative information or lack of information about one's own group(s) with positive information. Strong identification with and idealization of everything about one's own group(s), and rejection of everything related to White society.

Status 4: *Emersion.* "Community, communalism, and commitment to one's own group[s]" (p. 88). Primarily an affective state in which one feels solidarity, comfort, and joy with one's own group(s).

Status 5: *Internalization.* Positive commitment to and identification with one's own group, sense of pride and fulfillment. Also able to critically assess and respond both to members and aspects of one's own group(s) as well as to White people and society.

Status 6: *Integrated Awareness.* Positive views of one's own group(s) and racial self. Recognition of and resistance of racism, particularly those practices that "discourage positive racial self-conceptions and group expression" (p. 89). Embracing and integration of other aspects of self related to other social identities. Greater understanding and support, as well as capacity for empathy and collaboration, with other oppressed people.

Source: Helms and Cook (1999), pp. 85–89.

acceptance of White standards and the devaluing of one's own racial group to idealizing one's racial group and dismissing anything perceived as White, eventually to a critical acceptance and commitment toward one's racial group, and ultimately to embracing work against oppressions shared with other groups. Parham (1989) elaborates that, from late adolescence or early adulthood on, Black people may have to repeatedly confront developmental issues connected with their racial identity. He describes this process as "recycling."

Models of racial or ethnic development for Asian Americans (for example, Kim, 2001; Sodowsky, Kwan, & Pannu, 1995), Latinos (for example, Bernal & Knight, 1993; Casas & Pytluk, 1995; Ferdman & Gallegos, 2001; Ruiz, 1990; Torres, 1999), and Native Americans (for example, Horse, 2001) also exist. Kim's (2001), Ferdman and Gallegos's (2001), and Horse's (2001) models are presented in Exhibit 10.2.

Let's return to Kawezia and Josh. You don't know how to interpret Kawezia's insistence on tutoring at a predominantly Black public school, after she initially agreed to work at a soup kitchen. However, the POC or ALANA model suggests that her

EXHIBIT 10.2. MODELS OF LATINO/LATINA, ASIAN AMERICAN, AND AMERICAN INDIAN IDENTITY.

Latino and Latina Racial Identity Orientations (Ferdman & Gallegos, 2001)	**Asian American Identity Development** (Kim, 2001)
	Ethnic awareness
White-identified	White identification (active and passive)
Undifferentiated/Denial	
Latino as other	
Subgroup identified	
	Awakening to social political consciousness
Latino-identified (Racial/Raza)	Redirection to Asian American consciousness
Latino-integrated	Incorporation

Paradigm of American Indian Identity
(Horse, 2001)

- How well one is grounded in native language and culture
- Whether one's genealogical heritage as an Indian is valid
- Whether one embraces a general philosophy or worldview that derives from distinctly Indian ways, that is, old traditions
- The degree to which one thinks of himself or herself in a certain way, that is, one's own idea of self as an Indian person
- Whether one is officially recognized as a member of a tribe by the government of that tribe. (p. 100)

Note: Latino/Latina racial orientations, although *not* a stage model, and Asian American identity development stages parallel one another in the ways listed. Horse's paradigm of Indian identity does *not* represent stages but rather five ways in which American Indian consciousness is influenced.

attitudes may be shifting to the Immersion status, although it is not evident from the example what sort of experiences Kawezia may have had to push her thinking into Immersion. That Kawezia's sister attends Spelman College, a historically Black women's college, provides a clue that her sister and perhaps her family may be Black identified and knowledgeable about the oppression of Black people in the United States. Josh's support for Kawezia with the tutoring project may suggest a more developed status such as Integrated Awareness or a naïveté about race such as Conformity.

Biracial and Multiracial Identity Development. The numbers of persons who are biracial or multiracial are increasing rapidly in the United States, and these people may not identify with a single racial group (Root, 1996a). The general pattern of multiracial development is that individuals develop an initial awareness of racial identity, then experience having to make a choice of one of their racial identities, and, ultimately, integrate their multiple racial identities in a meaningful way. For additional resources on biracial and multiracial identity, refer to Kerwin and Ponterotto (1995), Kich (1992), Poston (1990), Root (1990, 1992, 1996b), and Wijeyesinghe (2001).

White Racial Identity Development. The racial identity of White people has historically been ignored in the United States, essentially because, as the racial group with collective power and privilege (McIntosh, 2001), White people have not had to face or name their race and the various characteristics, attributes, privileges, and power associated with it. Helms and Piper (1994) define White people as "those Americans who self-identify or are commonly identified as belonging exclusively to the White racial group regardless of the continental source (such as Europe or Asia) of that racial ancestry" (p. 126). Helms (1990f, 1992, 1995) has provided the most extensive theoretical and research work to date on White racial identity.

Racism is central to the construction of White racial identity, both in terms of its presence in the United States and White people's role in perpetuating it. Two phases characterize Helms's model of White racial identity development (see Exhibit 10.3). In the first phase, people abandon a racist identity; in the second, they develop a nonracist identity. According to Helms, it is impossible to develop a healthy White identity without acknowledging, understanding, and working to rid oneself of deep, internalized racism.

Helms's model is especially useful in helping White people understand what racial attitudes they hold and how they view and act on racial matters and racial interactions; it can also help one consider how a traditionally White institution of higher education or a predominantly White environment may perceive and handle racial issues. Helms's model provides a blueprint for White persons to help them develop into healthy racial beings and for student affairs professionals to assist White students in developing healthy racial attitudes and behaviors.

From the brief descriptions of Noel and Tiffany, who are White students, we can draw some hypotheses about their racial identity development. They do not seem to understand the different racial and cultural interests of others in the group, which suggests that their White racial identity is not highly developed. Noel's liberal attitudes and his comfort with the racially diverse group suggest racial attitudes that represent the

EXHIBIT 10.3. WHITE RACIAL IDENTITY DEVELOPMENT.

In order to develop a healthy White identity, defined in part as a nonracist identity, virtually every White person in the United States must overcome one or more of these aspects (individual, institutional, and cultural) of racism. Additionally, he or she must accept his or her own Whiteness, the cultural implications of being White, and define a view of Self as a racial being that does not depend on the perceived superiority of one racial group over another. (Helms, 1990f, p. 49)

Phase 1: Abandonment of Racism

Status 1: Contact—"The Happy Racist." One encounters the idea or actuality of ALANAs or Persons of Color. Naive curiosity, obliviousness to racial/cultural issues, cultural-neutral view of world, uses White criteria automatically without awareness that other criteria are possible. Limited interracial interaction. Positive feelings about self and about the "idea" of and fair treatment of ALANAs and People of Color. "A primitive status, primarily characterized by simplistic reactions of denial and obliviousness to the ways in which one benefits from membership in the entitled group and only superficial acknowledgment of one's membership in the White group" (Helms & Cook, 1999, p. 91).

Transition: When enough experiences of seeing differences in how ALANAs and People of Color in the U.S. are treated and "when one can no longer escape the moral dilemmas of race in this country and one's participation in them (Helms & Cook, 1999, p. 91), person enters next stage or status.

Status 2: Disintegration. Conscious but conflicted awareness of one's Whiteness, recognition of moral dilemmas associated with being White. Resulting discomfort reduced by avoiding contact with ALANAs, trying to convince others that People of Color are not so inferior, and/or trying to obtain information from Whites or ALANAs that racism either does not exist or that it is not the White person's fault. Guilt, depression, helplessness, anxiety, distress, confusion.

Transition: Desire to reduce discomfort and anxiety and to be accepted by one's own racial group.

Status 3: Reintegration. Acknowledges a White identity and accepts belief in White superiority and Black inferiority; believes that race-related negative conditions are result of Blacks' inferior qualities, and that Whites' positive conditions come from earning such privileges. Fear and anger toward Blacks, anger covertly or overtly expressed, racist behavior either active or passive. In U.S. society, it is fairly easy for Whites to remain or to fixate at this stage.

Transition: A personally jarring event, direct or vicarious, painful or insightful. One begins to question his or her previous definition of Whiteness and the justifiability of racism in any of its forms.

Phase 2: Development of a Nonracist Identity

Status 4: Pseudo-Independence (often known as "White liberal"). One begins actively to question that Blacks are innately inferior to Whites, begins to acknowledge responsibility of Whites for racism. Redefines White identity often in the form of intellectual acceptance and curiosity about Blacks; intellectual understanding of Black culture and of privileges of being White. Most feelings submerged. Behavior involves helping Blacks to change themselves to function more like Whites on White criteria. Looks to Blacks to explain racism.

(*Continued*)

EXHIBIT 10.3. WHITE RACIAL IDENTITY DEVELOPMENT. (*CONTINUED*)

Transition: If personal rewards are great enough to encourage continued strengthening of a positive White identity, then one may begin to seek positive aspects of Whiteness unrelated to racism.

Status 5: *Immersion/Emersion.* Attempts to redefine a positive White identity by replacing myths and stereotypes with accurate information about being White in the U.S. and in the world in general. Asks questions such as "Who am I racially?" "Who do I want to be?" "Who are you really?" Turns to other Whites in similar journeys through biographies, autobiographies, or consciousness-raising groups. Changing White people is focus, rather than changing Blacks (and other people of color).

Transition: One feels secure enough in his or her White identity to use one's knowledge about being White to eliminate racism, to change Whites, and to acquire new knowledge about being White and about Blacks and other people of color.

Status 6: *Autonomy.* Racially transcendent worldview. Has internalized a positive, nonracist White identity, seeks to acknowledge and abolish racial oppression. Autonomy represents highest level of White racial identity and thus is an ongoing process, where one is continually open to new information and new ways of thinking about race and culture.

Source: Adapted from Helms (1990f, 1992, 1994); Helms and Cook (1999).

pseudo-independent status. But when Noel becomes frustrated with other group members' not behaving and thinking the way he wants them to, then his attitudes suggest the Reintegration status. That Noel as a White person is not examining his own racism implies that his attitudes in this vignette are not at a status of Immersion/Emersion or Autonomy. The few clues about Tiffany suggest lower statuses of racial identity, perhaps Contact, in that she does not demonstrate support for either the soup kitchen nor the tutoring and does not seem to make connections across oppressed groups.

Racial Identity in Race Dialogue. Racial identity development informs the complexity of interactions and dialogues across races. Helms (1990b, 1990c, 1990d, 1995; Helms & Cook, 1999) identified two primary patterns of cross-race interactions: parallel and crossed (progressive and regressive). Parallel interactions occur within or across socioracial groups when persons exhibit similar racial identity statuses. Progressive interactions exist when the individual with more power in the relationship (supervisor, instructor, counselor, or advisor) is more developmentally advanced in terms of racial identity; regressive interactions occur when the person with more power is less developmentally advanced. What these patterns suggest is that student affairs professionals have the potential to enhance (progressive), or support, or maintain (parallel) students' racial identity. If the interaction is regressive for students (if the student affairs professional is less advanced developmentally), then students' development is either hindered, or students become frustrated with or dismiss the student affairs professional in terms of the quality of the racial interaction. In regard to groups, Helms (1990d) discusses dimensions such as perceptions of power, group racial norms, and racial identity coalitions. Tatum (1997) identifies examples of challenges in cross-racial dialogues.

Within the racially diverse group of students, both parallel and crossed (not similar developmentally) racial interactions can occur. The kinds of racial interactions that take place between students depend on each student's racial identity status at the time of the interaction. However, as a student affairs professional, you play a significant role. If your racial identity status is more developed, then you have the potential to contribute to the racial identity development of students in the group. However, if your racial identity status and expression is less developed, then you may contribute to frustration and disengagement of students with more highly developed racial identity statuses.

Sexual Identity Development

Another important dimension of identity relates to the development and affirmation of one's sexual orientation. Sexual identity as a social identity occurs in the context of Western culture (Broido, 2000). Sexual identity is historically and culturally specific, and the relationship of one's culture of origin to the dominant culture can influence the development of one's sexuality (Rust, 1996).

Broido (2000) differentiated among the terms *lesbian, gay, homosexual, bisexual,* and *heterosexual.* She said that *lesbian* and *gay* are *identity* descriptors and that the term *homosexual* is a descriptor of *behavior.* However, "the terms *bisexual* and *heterosexual* are used as both behavioral and identity descriptors" (Broido, 2000, p. 15), since alternate words do not exist to distinguish between behavior and identity. Transgenderism is included in this discussion because of its oppressed status and because transgender identity is frequently grouped with gay, lesbian, and bisexual identities. Transgendered, however, is not a sexual orientation but rather a blending or crossing (*trans*) of gender identity (Carter, 2000).

Kinsey and his associates (Kinsey, Pomeroy, & Martin, 1948; Kinsey et al., 1953) proposed that sexual orientation should be considered along a continuum, ranging from exclusively heterosexual to exclusively homosexual. Others (Keppel & Hamilton, 1992; Klein, Sepekoff, & Wolf, 1990) suggest that sexual orientation is multidimensional, including variables of sexual attraction, sexual behavior, sexual fantasies, emotional preference, social preference, self-identification, lifestyle preference, and political identity. Klein et al. and Keppel and Hamilton indicate that these eight dimensions can be considered on a seven-point scale, with the two extremes representing primarily heterosexual or primarily homosexual, and the middle three points as degrees of bisexuality.

Gay and Lesbian Identity Development. Brown (1989) identified three elements that underlie a gay or lesbian identity: "biculturalism, with its requirements of juggling, balance, and living in and with ambiguity; marginality, with its perspective that is both outside and within the mainstream; and normative creativity, the ability to create boundaries that will work where none exist from tools that may be only partially suited to the task" (p. 452). Biculturalism and normative creativity, albeit difficult and painful outcomes of the gay and lesbian experience, represent desirable goals for any developmental journey.

The developmental literature focuses on how to "come to terms" with one's sexual orientation, particularly for gays and lesbians. Exhibit 10.4 summarizes three models

EXHIBIT 10.4. MODELS OF SEXUAL IDENTITY DEVELOPMENT.

Homosexual Identity Formation (Cass, 1979)	**Lesbian and Gay Identity Formation** (Fassinger & Miller, 1997; McCarn & Fassinger, 1996)		**Life-span Model of Lesbian-gay-bisexual Development** (D'Augelli, 1994)
	Individual Identity	*Group Identity*	
Stage 1: Identity Confusion	Awareness		Exiting heterosexual identity
Marked by a conscious awareness that homosexuality has relevance to themselves and their behavior (either overt, as in kissing, or internal, as in the case of thoughts, emotional, or physiological response) (p. 222)	Aware of feeling or being different	Aware of others who have sexual orientations other than heterosexual and that gay and lesbian communities exist	
Stage 2: Identity Comparison	Exploration		
By the end of Stage 1, if identity foreclosure has not taken place, the person has accepted the possibility that his or her identity may be homosexual (p. 225)	Actively exploring feelings of difference	Seeking knowledge of gays and lesbians and of gay/lesbian communities	
Stage 3: Identity Tolerance			
Increased commitment to the possibility of being gay or lesbian, "commonly expressed in the statement 'I probably am a homosexual'" (p. 229)			

Stage 4: Identity Acceptance			
"Characterized by continued and increasing contacts with other homosexuals" (p. 231). The individual "now accepts rather than tolerates a homosexual self-image" (p. 231)			
Stage 5: Identity Pride	Deepening/commitment		
Utilizes strategies to "revalue homosexual others more positively" (p. 233)	Developing greater self-knowledge and starting to make choices regarding one's sexuality	Greater knowledge and awareness of value and oppression of lesbian/gay community and commitment to community, along with informed knowledge of possible consequences	Developing a lesbian-gay-bisexual intimacy status Developing a lesbian-gay-bisexual social identity
Stage 6: Identity Synthesis	Internalization/synthesis		
Sees both good and bad in other homosexuals as well as heterosexuals. Integrates "homosexual identity with all other aspects of self" (p. 235)	Greater self-acceptance of same-sex feelings, practices, and relationships; synthesis of gay/lesbian identity with overall identity	Identification with community, internalization of group identity, and synthesis with one's overall identity	Becoming a lesbian-gay-bisexual offspring Developing a lesbian-gay-bisexual intimacy status Entering a lesbian-gay-bisexual community

of sexual identity development. Cass's (1979) model, widely cited in the literature (Fassinger, 1991) and one of the most frequently used models of sexual identity development among student affairs professionals, consists of six stages, beginning with a tentative possibility that one is gay or lesbian. Unless one forecloses about one's homosexual identity, the commitment increases and deepens over the six stages as one becomes increasingly certain about and comfortable with an identity as a gay man or as a lesbian. Fassinger and her colleagues (Fassinger & Miller, 1997; McCarn & Fassinger, 1996) separate internal and personal from sociopolitical and group identities, represented by parallel branches each consisting of four phases. D'Augelli (1994), in a life-span human development perspective, proposes six identity processes (see Exhibit 10.4), including exiting heterosexual identity and becoming a lesbian-gay-bisexual offspring. Levine and Evans (1991) and Reynolds and Hanjorgiris (2000) provide excellent summaries of other models of gay and lesbian identity development.

Returning to Tiffany, you find it difficult to understand her recent and strong interest in the women's resource center. You're beginning to get some clues that Tiffany may be struggling with her sexual identity, yet she continues to talk about a boyfriend back home. These clues suggest that she may be in the early phases of sexual identity development. You know that, although many women serve as volunteers at the resource center, a significant number are lesbians. Tiffany may consider this an excellent opportunity to think further about her sexual identity, perhaps identity comparison (Cass) and exploration (Fassinger). Her occasional mention of her boyfriend back home suggests that she may be struggling with exiting her heterosexual identity (D'Augelli).

Bisexual Identity. Bisexuality can be a considered "as a state of being, as a desire, as a behavior, and as a personal identity" (Morrow as cited in Robin & Hamner, 2000, p. 247). Until the past decade, bisexuality primarily has been a neglected topic, viewed only as a confused state (Zinik, 1985), or a transition between heterosexuality and being gay and lesbian (Robin & Hamner, 2000). In a personal essay about being Jewish, bisexual, and differently abled, Reichler (1991) points out the invisibility of each of these dimensions, especially that of bisexuality, which "is not seen as an authentic way of being in almost every community" (p. 79). Two challenges for persons who are bisexual or who are developing a bisexual identity are invisibility in both heterosexual and gay communities and stigma in nonheterosexual identities (Robin & Hamner, 2000).

Understanding bisexuality within different cultures is important. Fox (1996) presents an excellent overview of both historical and cross-cultural aspects of bisexuality. Noteworthy in Fox's discussion is the normality of bisexuality in many cultures. Again, it is the social construction of sexual orientation within the United States that places bisexuality, along with gay and lesbian identity, as not normative in relation to the privileged status of heterosexuality.

Fox (1996) cited Klein's differentiation of transitional, historical, sequential, and concurrent bisexuality. Transitional bisexuality in relationship to gay and lesbian identity is "a stage in the process of coming out as lesbian or gay . . . while for others, a gay or lesbian identity is a step in the process of coming out as bisexual" (p. 22). Historical bisexuality is having had both same- and opposite-sex relationships or attractions in the past. Sequential bisexuality is having relationships with only men or only women at one point in time. Concurrent bisexuality is having relationships with both men and women during the same time period.

Transgender Identity. Transgendered students are often grouped with lesbian, gay, and bisexual students (the T in LGBT students). According to Carter (2000), "the term *transgendered* . . . [means] an individual who bends or blends gender. It encompasses terms such as cross-dresser, transvestite, transsexual, and intersexual" (p. 263). Transgender concerns one's emotional sense of self in terms of gender as male or female. Sexual identity, on the other hand, "concerns the gender of the object of one's affections, such as heterosexual, gay, lesbian, or bisexual" (Carter, 2000, p. 272).

Although gender identity and sexual identity are distinct issues, Carter (2000) identifies three concerns that bring the two identities together: overlapping identities, mistaken identities, and the sexual orientation of transgendered persons (p. 272). "Some transgendered people have identified themselves, or currently identify themselves, as gay, lesbian, or bisexual; transgendered people are also targets of homophobia, and transgender sexual orientation should be included when referring to all minority sexual orientations" (Carter, 2000, p. 274). Fox (1996) indicates that transgendered people have often been presumed to be heterosexual but cites research by Devor which suggests that there is as much variability in sexual orientation and sexual identity of transgendered persons as in the gay, bisexual, and heterosexual populations.

Heterosexual Identity. Literature on heterosexuality is scant. The reason for this lack of examination of heterosexuality is that heterosexuality is the dominant sexual orientation. McIntosh (1995), in discussing White privilege, raises the issue of heterosexual privilege, by which persons of another dominant group hold unearned advantages, and points out an obliviousness about heterosexual privilege as well as White privilege and male privilege.

Herek (1986) suggests that heterosexual masculinity is defined both positively and negatively. He indicates that "as more lesbians and gay men publicly assert their identities . . . more people in the dominant majority must consciously label themselves as heterosexual rather than taking it for granted" (pp. 570–571).

In essays of heterosexual-identified undergraduate students, Eliason (1995) identified six themes: students had never thought about their heterosexuality, they believed society had "made" them heterosexual, gender and gender socialization were the major determinants of their heterosexuality, students viewed sexuality as either innate or a choice, viable options to heterosexuality do not exist, and religion influences sexuality. Eliason concluded, "many heterosexual students were unaware of what it means to be heterosexual in this society" (p. 833).

Models of heterosexual identity development are beginning to emerge. Mueller (2002) and Worthington, Savoy, Dillon, and Vernaglia (2002) offer complex and integrative models of heterosexual consciousness and heterosexual identity development.

Sullivan (1998), drawing on Cass's model and Hardiman and Jackson's dominant identity development model, provides a model of sexual identity development for heterosexual, gay, lesbian, and bisexual persons.

Gender Identity Development

Gender identity development can be defined as how one views oneself in relation to one's own gender group, that is, as a woman or a man, and how these views evolve and become more complex over time. Because of the way in which our society has constructed gender roles, the beginning point of men's gender identity development differs from that of women's. Women's gender identity development emerges from a societal position in which women as a group have been oppressed. Gender identity development for men begins from a position of power and dominance. Gender identity must also be considered within the contexts of sociohistorical, cultural, and racial constructions.

Differences between gender identity models in this chapter and other gender-related models can be confusing. Sexism is at the heart of models concerning the development of gender identity, similar (but not identical) to racism in the racial identity models. The experience and process of becoming aware of sexism, abandoning a sexist identity, and developing a nonsexist identity is different for women, the oppressed group, than it is for men, the dominant group. Three models of gender identity development, two for women and one for both men and women, are outlined briefly in Exhibit 10.5. All begin with an acceptance of traditional gender roles. One's gender identity evolves from an external definition of what it means to be a woman or a man to an internal, personal definition.

In the two models for women, one by Downing and Roush (1985) and the other by Ossana, Helms, and Leonard (1992), the first four stages are similar. Development

EXHIBIT 10.5. MODELS OF GENDER IDENTITY DEVELOPMENT.

Feminist Identity Development for Women (Downing & Roush, 1985)	**Womanist Identity Development** (Ossana, Helms, & Leonard, 1992)	**Gender Role Journey** (O'Neil, Egan, Owen, & Murry, 1993)
Stage 1: Passive acceptance	Stage 1: Pre-encounter	Phase 1: Acceptance of traditional gender roles
Stage 2: Revelation	Stage 2: Encounter	Phase 2: Ambivalence
		Phase 3: Anger
Stage 3: Embeddedness-emanation	Stage 3: Immersion-emersion	Phase 4: Activism
Stage 4: Synthesis	Stage 4: Internalization	Phase 5: Celebration and integration of gender roles
Stage 5: Active commitment		

proceeds from an acceptance of traditional gender roles to a questioning of societal gender constructions, usually as a result of one or more specific experiences. It then progresses to immersion in an exploration, usually with other women, of oneself as a woman, and finally to the fourth stage, which produces a positive sense of self as a woman and an integration of this part of oneself with other aspects of one's identity. Downing and Roush identify a fifth stage, in which the woman takes an activist position in creating a nonsexist world. Both models are based on Cross's (1971, 1978) model of Black racial identity development. (Refer to Moradi, Subich, and Phillips [2002] for a discussion of support for Downing and Roush's model.)

Two major differences exist between these models for women. First, Downing and Roush (1985) identify their model as one of *feminist* identity development while Ossana et al. identify theirs as one of *womanist* identity development (see Walker, 1983, pp. xi–xii, for descriptions of *womanist*). Second, according to Ossana et al. (1992), "the womanist identity model characterizes 'healthy' development as personal and ideological flexibility that may or may not be accompanied by acknowledged feminist beliefs or social activism" (p. 403).

The "gender role journey" is a portrayal of transitions in both men's and women's lives with respect to sexism and gender roles. Much of O'Neil's early work (O'Neil, 1981, 1990; O'Neil & Fishman, 1992; O'Neil, Helms, Gable, David, & Wrightsman, 1986) focused exclusively on men. Notable in O'Neil's model is the Anger phase, which involves both one's negative emotions about sexism as well as the act of expressing those emotions to individuals and groups.

Maria and Tiffany provide examples of gender identity development. Maria's interest in the women's resource center and support for women's issues, yet her commitment to what seems to be a traditional and perhaps unexamined gender role for herself with her boyfriend, suggests that she may be struggling with her role as a woman. Because Maria is a Puerto Rican American woman, it may be more appropriate to apply the womanist identity development model because in that model we can consider Maria's gender identity development separate from feminism, often viewed by women of color as advocacy primarily for and by White women. Maria perhaps is struggling between the Pre-encounter and Encounter stages of this model. Tiffany, however, may be connecting her exploration of her sexual identity with an examination of her role as a woman. Downing and Roush's feminist identity development model provides some clues that Tiffany may be either reflecting Stage 2 Revelation or Stage 3 Embeddedness-emanation.

Ability/Disability, Social Class, Religion, and Geographic Region

Discussions of identity often include discussion of ethnicity, sexual orientation, or gender. There are, however, many more dimensions of identity to be considered. This section will touch on a few of these additional dimensions.

Ability and Disability. Defining, identifying, and understanding disabilities is neither an easy nor a simple process. Considering persons with disabilities as part of an oppressed status has occurred primarily within the past thirty years, beginning with a grassroots movement and then with the Rehabilitation Act of 1973 (Bryan, 2000). In addition to persons with disabilities having other social identities such as race and gender, Bryan pointed out "there are large numbers of disabilities and each one is considered a separate condition within its own group identity" (p. 325).

One guide for university faculty and staff (President's Commission on Disability Issues, 1990) describes three kinds of disabilities: visible disabilities (easily recognizable physical impairments), hidden disabilities (learning disabilities, hearing impairment, psychiatric or seizure disorders), and multiple disabilities. Multiple disabilities may be caused by primary conditions such as multiple sclerosis or cerebral palsy, which "may be accompanied by a second impairment—in mobility, vision, speech, or coordination—which may, in fact, pose greater difficulties" (p. 5). Disabilities are either congenital (blindness, absence of an arm, seizure disorder, learning disability) or acquired (paralysis resulting from an accident, AIDS, blindness, multiple sclerosis). For acquired disabilities, age of onset is an important dimension in how the person views and is affected by the disability. Two approaches are used for defining a disability: one is "to identify specific mental or physical conditions" (Atkinson & Hackett, 1998, p. 9) that can be diagnosed; the other is to "identify the life activity affected" (p. 9). Fine and Asch (2000) underscored the importance of understanding the "*differences* among disabling conditions and their varied impact on the lives of people" (p. 331).

Fine and Asch (2000) identified four assumptions commonly held about persons with disabilities. The assumptions include "the person and the disability are . . . synonymous" (p. 332), the person with a disability is a "victim" (p. 333), problems faced by a person with a disability are caused by the disability, and "disability is central to the . . . person's self-concept, self-definition, social comparison, and reference groups" (p. 334).

Abilities and disabilities should be understood as socially constructed experiences that are also historically mediated (Fine & Asch, 2000; Harris & Wideman, 1988; Jones, 1996; Scheer, 1994): "A disability has a social meaning and it is that indisputable fact that constitutes the major difficulty" for persons with disabilities (Harris & Wideman, 1988, p. 116). In his autobiography about dealing with the effects of a growing tumor inside his spinal column, which eventually resulted in quadriplegia, Murphy (1987) talked about how clear it became to him that illness and impairment are not only related to one's body but also have psychological and social components as well (p. 12).

Excellent illustrations of disability as a social construction exist in the literature. Jones (1996) demonstrates that "to understand disability as socially constructed is to celebrate the uniqueness of individual difference while directing attention toward social change and transformation of oppressive structures. [It] is to distinguish between the biological fact of disability and the handicapping social environment in which the person with disabilities exists" (pp. 50–51). Wise-Mohr (1992), who has multiple sclerosis, described a personal experience in which others did not believe she had a disability because she did not look disabled. Rousso (as cited in Asch & Fine, 1988) described how her mother's efforts to make her appear more "normal"—by having her try to change how she walks—made her feel like she was removing an integral part of her own identity, since she had incorporated her disability into her identity as a child.

For student affairs professionals, two interrelated implications concern the social construction of disabilities; a third implication is about the hidden nature of some disabilities. First, student affairs professionals should learn how an individual with a disability understands and conceptualizes that disability, rather than just relying on the socially constructed definition of it. Second, it is important to understand oneself—specifically in terms of how one views disability. Asch and Fine (1988) suggest that disabilities in others often raise issues about our own helplessness, needs, and dependencies. Thus, if we do not know ourselves, we may act according to our own insecurities and needs rather than in the best interest of a student with a disability. Third, although some physical disabilities are more easily observed, student affairs professionals should consider that some students have learning and psychological disabilities, which are not easily known. Students with disabilities, including hidden disabilities, may need appropriate accommodations in their cocurricular involvement as well as curricular work, and support with self-advocacy and in their campus and career transitions.

From the student portraits, you are not sure what is going on with Drew, since he has been such a vital member of the group but has recently been much less engaged in the past several meetings. What you do not know, however, is that Drew deals with an invisible disability, that of a psychological disability. You learn that Drew has been struggling with the appropriate therapeutic levels of his medication and that this has affected the level of his participation in the group. In terms of Drew's identity, what is important is how he views this disability, whether or not he considers it disabling, and whether he discloses information about this disability. Although we may create our own understanding of what a psychological disability is like, Drew's perceptions and experiences with this disabling condition are the salient considerations. If Drew tells you, as the advisor, about his psychological disability, it is important to attend to your personal thoughts about Drew and his disability and to determine whether those thoughts need to be altered such that your views do not limit your understanding of Drew and his abilities and contributions.

Social Class. One's social class is an important variable that relates to one's identity and interacts with other identity dimensions such as race and ethnicity, ability or disability, gender, and sexual orientation. Dill (1994) pointed out that much of the literature about race and gender tends to omit consideration of social class, just as the class and gender literature tends to ignore race. Similarly, hooks (2000) suggests that class, contrasted with race and gender, is the oppression which is not directly addressed and which makes people uncomfortable. The silencing of class then helps to perpetuate class oppression and to privilege the acquisition of wealth and power.

Langston (2001) addresses the myth of the "classless society" and discusses the effects of power in relation to social class. The myth is that one can pull oneself up by one's bootstraps, that "ambition and intelligence alone are responsible for success" (p. 126).

Social class is important to student service professionals concerned about student development because class concerns economic security of students and their families, choices students perceive and those choices available, and cultural background (including education, language, and behavior) (Langston, 2001).

The example of Josh is useful in thinking about social class. You are frustrated that Josh is involved in this learning community but is concerned about the time commitment he can make to community service. Josh, expecting a college degree, may anticipate a middle-class status, although his family is economically lower-middle-class. But his upbringing and experiences, regardless of his future earnings, may continue to have a strong influence on the choices he perceives and the risks he is willing to take. Further, Josh may have feel strong obligations to his family. So, both his social class and his family obligations may play a significant role in his needing to work thirty hours per week.

It is also important to consider the intersection of Josh's race, gender, and social class. For example, not only are the options Josh perceives likely to be connected to—and perhaps limited by—his socioeconomic class, but they are also affected by the discrimination he may face as a Cambodian and Asian American. His gender, given male privilege, might be a positive factor in relation to his social class, but as an Asian American man he might face greater discrimination and questions of self-esteem than White men.

Religious Identity. Religious identity is an important dimension for those who identify with their religion or religious beliefs. Religious identity is not simply belonging to a religious group or denomination, nor how religious one is, nor to what religious beliefs one ascribes. Rather, religious identity refers to whether or not one views religion as an integral part of one's identity. Faith and spiritual development concern one's way of finding or making meaning (Cannon, 1988; Fowler, 1981; Isasi-Díaz, 1996; Parks, 1986, 2000), but they are different concepts from religion (Love, 2002) or religious identity.

Within the United States there are many different religions, beliefs, and practices. However, it is within this context of a dominant Christian society with a diversity of other religions, beliefs, and practices that many college students develop their religious identity.

Religion is an integral part of some cultures and subcultures. Religious beliefs are interwoven with their traditions and values, and religious rituals play an essential role in daily life, sometimes including the food people eat and the clothes they wear. Particularly in the United States with the marginalization of religions that are not Christian, religious identity may be a significant part of the complex identity issues faced by college students.

Much of the literature on religious identity comes from research on Jewish identity and the development of self-esteem in young Jewish adults. Klein (1980) addresses Jewish identity as ethnic identity, which Gordon (1964) defined as a "sense of peoplehood" (pp. 23–24). This sense of peoplehood, according to Klein (1980), includes both identification with one's past and one's ancestors and a "future-oriented identification" (p. 9) with one's ethnic group. The minority identity development model (MID; Atkinson, Morten, & Sue, 1998) could be applied to religious identity development.

The only information about the religious identity of the six students is the reference to Drew's active participation in a local Catholic parish. We have no real indication of how central religion is to Drew's identity. It may be that Drew has simply accepted his religion from his family and that participation in his church (but not religion) is an expectation and obligation for him. Another possibility is that Drew's move away from home to college may have encouraged a personal examination of religion and that a central part of Drew's identity is who he is as a member and participant in his religion.

Geographic Region. Although geographic region generally is not an identity in terms of sociopolitical oppression and history, where one grows up, forms basic values, currently resides, and envisions oneself in the future are rarely considered in discussions of identity development. Yet if identity is socially constructed, then one's region or place may be a salient part of such social constructions. Place may also reflect the social dimension of urban, suburban, or rural.

Garreau (1981), in identifying and describing nine regions of North America, encourages one to forget traditional notions of region, such as those that are historically, geographically, or politically defined. Rather, Garreau speaks of the sociological and psychological components of region. He indicates, "each nation [or region] has a distinct prism through which it views the world" (p. 2). According to Garreau, a region or geographic entity is limited for individuals by a "certain intuitive, subjective sense of loyalties that unify it" (p. xv). He underscores the importance of a region's feeling "right" to the individual. Although Garreau's work is not explicitly about identity, he does address it: "Your identity is shaped by your origins. Thus, to come away with a new understanding of regionalism is to come away with a better understanding of yourself" (p. xvi).

Considering students' "home" region or place may help student affairs professionals put students' concerns, developmental struggles, and attitudes into a meaningful context that constitutes part of their overall identity. Regional identity may have implications for one's level of comfort or alienation in a given environment, one's ways of talking and interacting with others, the values one holds, and the foods one eats; it may also relate to one's connection with a sense of family.

Region or place may or may not be salient to the six students in the vignettes. Although there may be a strong geographic identity for each of the regions in which these students were raised, they may or may not connect with place as a part of their personal identity. Some of the students, however, may have a heightened awareness of that identity during their time at Millennium University located near Cleveland. Both Josh and Maria may connect strongly with their countries of origin (Cambodia and Puerto Rico) and their cultures, as well as with the communities in which they now live.

Multiple Identities

Multiple oppressions and multiple identities are beginning to be addressed in the psychological literature. Reynolds and Pope (1991) and Jones and McEwen (2000) provide models of how individuals consider and negotiate multiple oppressions and multiple identities.

Weber (1998) pointed out that not only have the intersections of identities not been considered much in the literature but that ignoring the intersections means ignoring groups of people who hold multiple identities, particularly those persons who hold identities that have been marginalized. For example, to examine race without considering gender differences may be dismissive of women's experiences. And, examining issues of social class without considering differences by and intersections with race, gender, and sexual orientation may ignore the unique experiences of People of Color, and gay, lesbian, bisexual, and transgendered persons.

Reynolds and Pope (1991) focus on multiple oppressions from the micro level (Weber, 1998) and challenge the dichotomies or segmentation of identities seen in literature and in society. They also point to the lack of attention to within-group differences. Building on Root's biracial identity model, Reynolds and Pope (1991) in their Multidimensional Identity Model (MIM) identify two dimensions of identity development. One dimension concerns whether an individual chooses to identify with only one aspect of his or her identity or with multiple aspects. A second dimension concerns whether an individual is active or passive in taking on one or more identities.

These two dimensions result in a matrix of four possibilities for negotiating one's identities:

- Identify with one aspect of self (society assigned-passive acceptance).
- Identify with one aspect of self (conscious identification).
- Identify with multiple aspects of self in a segmented fashion.
- Identify with combined aspects of self (identity interaction) (p. 179)

Reynolds and Pope (1991) do not indicate how and under what conditions an individual's pattern may change over time. One of the premises of developmental theory suggests that development involves an interaction between what happens within a person and what takes place in his or her environment. Thus, changing environmental conditions may have an important effect on how an individual's identity develops. An example may be useful. Racial identity theory suggests that a race-related experience or series of experiences may provide a trigger for facing a new racial identity status. Similar kinds of experiences—trigger events—may challenge an individual to address an aspect of his or her identity that has been put aside or has not yet emerged. Such a situation may occur when a person is, perhaps for the first time, one of a few similar persons in a group of "others" and thus feels marginalized.

Jones and McEwen (2000) in their conceptual model (see Figure 10.1) address multiple social identities from the micro level (Weber, 1998), and, like Weber, incorporate both social identities that are oppressed and those that may be dominant. One's multiple social identities occur within a *context,* which may include aspects such as family background, sociocultural conditions, current experiences, and career decisions and life planning. A *core* identity exists within the center, which includes one's personal attributes, characteristics, and personal identity (Deaux, 1993). Surrounding one's core

FIGURE 10.1. MODELS OF MULTIPLE DIMENSIONS OF IDENTITY.

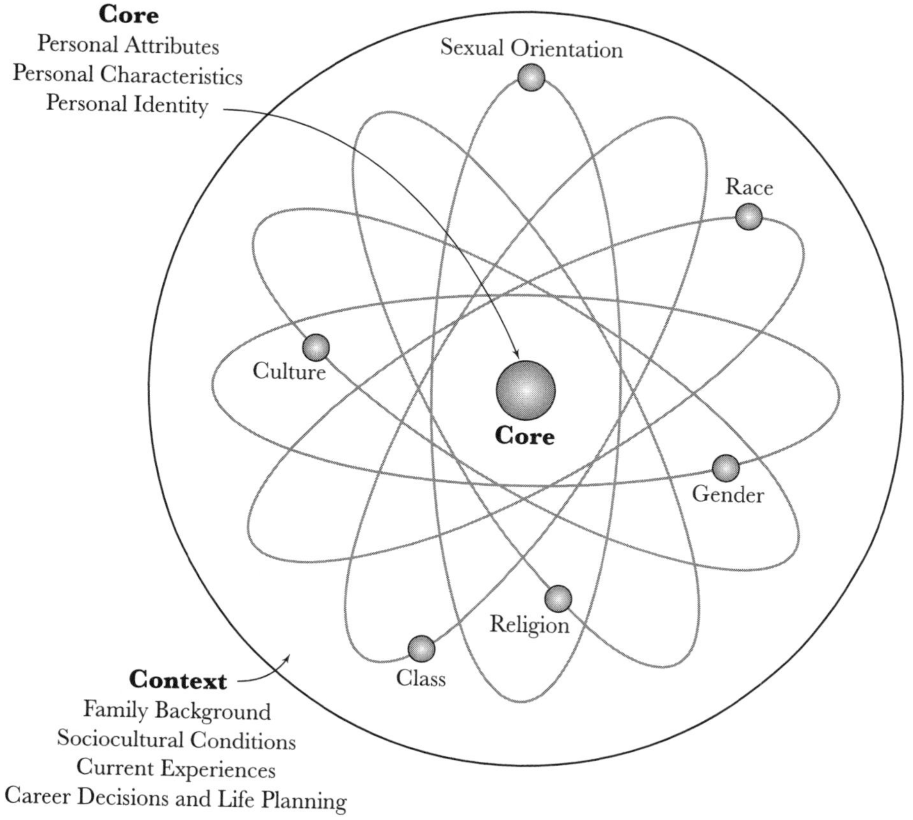

Core
Personal Attributes
Personal Characteristics
Personal Identity

Sexual Orientation
Race
Culture
Core
Gender
Religion
Class

Context
Family Background
Sociocultural Conditions
Current Experiences
Career Decisions and Life Planning

Source: James and McEwen (2000). Reprinted with permission.

identity are multiple intersecting circles (not limited to six as portrayed in Figure 10.1) that represent particular social identities, such as race, class, and sexual orientation. The dots on the circles represent the relative salience to the individual and the degree of connectedness to the core at any one point in time. The intersection of the circles suggests that individuals at times simultaneously experience their social identities. The intersection also implies, as with Weber (1998, 2001), that an individual's social identities must be understood collectively rather than singularly.

Concerning oneself with the multiple dimensions of one's identity is a highly fluid and dynamic process. Sampson (1985) suggests that identity as described by Erikson (1959/1980), as a more or less coherent whole, may be misrepresented. Rather, Sampson encourages a somewhat more "decentralized, nonequilibrium conception of personhood that allows our multiplicity and interconnectedness a time to live" (p. 1210). The social constructions of these identity dimensions in our society challenges each of us to examine them for ourselves and for students and determine how they are a part of one's evolving and developing sense of self.

Multiple identity dimensions can be considered for all six students. For Tiffany, a White woman from Atlanta, we can hypothesize that her gender identity and sexual identity may be developing perhaps to the exclusion of her racial and class identities. Kawezia and Noel seem to be focused on their racial identities; other identity dimensions may or may not be salient for them during this time in college. From the brief vignettes, Josh may be focused on the intersections of his racial, social class, and cultural identities, but perhaps not on his gender or sexual identities.

Maria's gender identity development seems integrally connected with her culture and ethnicity. How concerned she is with her ethnic or racial identity or her identity as an apparently heterosexual woman is not clear. Maria's regional identity may be closely interwoven with her culture and ethnicity, but again we have no information about the salience of locale or place to her identity development.

None of the students except for Drew appears to be addressing identity involved with ability and disability. Drew apparently has considered his identity related to his psychological disability and perhaps his religious identity. We have no evidence of Drew's racial, gender, sexual orientation, or social class identities as a biracial man.

Conclusion

Identity development is complex and suggests many questions, such as the following, for those working with college students.

1. Which identity dimensions are salient for any given individual? Which are "on hold" or not yet addressed? Which have yet to appear? How do you know?
2. In what situations or life statuses are certain dimensions salient, and when are they not? When and how do they emerge, and when do they fade or seemingly disappear?
3. What other dimensions of identity exist for students, and what role do they play?
4. How are the dimensions of an individual's identity socially constructed?
5. How does Helms's (1994) shift from "stages" in identity development to "ego statuses" help us conceptualize and understand the complexities of human development?
6. How is "developmental recycling" represented in students' development?
7. How do our own lenses, experiences, and identities filter what we see and how we understand identity development?
8. How do an individual's identity dimensions interact with one another? How do they interact with other kinds of development? What is the role of environment in identity development, especially in relation to the dimensions of social identity discussed in this chapter? How do the various social identity dimensions interact together and with one's overall development and sense of self?
9. What are some of the critical points in various developmental processes, and how do programming and interventions with students facilitate (or hinder) their development at those critical points?

10. How do student affairs professionals address the holistic development of the student and yet also consider these specific dimensions of development? How do we help students to have a whole and complete experience in terms of their development? How can we learn to use theories to think about and understand the whole student?

There may not be complete answers to these questions, but it is imperative for us to struggle with them. It is difficult work to understand students and to apply theory to their development. We need to struggle regularly and consistently with these questions through continued reading, discussion with colleagues, and reflection. Social identity development theory can help us to understand, not in an absolute sense but with greater complexity and with more integrated meanings.

In conclusion, an objective of this chapter has been to demonstrate that identity and its development in college students are very complex. Identity in its most comprehensive sense encompasses not only the traditional Eriksonian notions of identity but also identity dimensions viewed through important social constructions such as race, gender, sexual orientation, social class, and ability and disability.

Individuals, including college students, who live in the United States must contend with the dominant society and its constructions of race, gender, sexual orientation, and other dimensions of difference. People can never be free from the external pressures of these social constructions to develop themselves without incorporating these dimensions. Thus, as student affairs professionals, we must examine how an individual looks at and incorporates these dimensions of identity within one's sense of self. Such considerations must include racial, sexual, and gender identity development, as well as aspects of ability and disability, social class, religion, and geographic region.

The developmental models of racial, sexual, and gender identity suggest that as an individual develops in each of these areas, the individual's perspectives evolve from an acceptance of and adherence to the views of the relevant dominant group to an increasing acceptance and appreciation of oneself as different from the dominant-group perspectives. One who is part of an oppressed group develops understanding, affirmation, and pride in being part of one's own group, such as being Black, gay, or a woman. For an individual who is part of a dominant group, rather than an unexamined acceptance of and adherence to such group membership, development involves the individual examining the privileges garnered from membership in that group, the group's oppression of others, and the positive values of being a member of that group.

Other dimensions, including ability and disability, social class, religion, and geographic region, although they may not be developmental in nature, are also important components of identity. In the simplest description, an individual either incorporates the society's dominant views of these dimensions or develops a more self-defined identity.

Not only may the dimensions described in this chapter be important components of an individual's identity, but how these dimensions intersect and how they collectively fit into an individual's identity may be even more important. Theory and research are beginning to address how various dimensions may interact with one another and whether or not they are salient to an individual and under what conditions (see Jones, 1997; Jones & McEwen, 2000; Reynolds & Pope, 1991). Along with the privilege of working with college students go our responsibilities as student affairs professionals to understand the complexities of college students' social identities and how these identities are differentially meaningful to students and in what contexts.

References

Alvarez, A. N. (1997). Asian American racial identity: An examination of world views and racial adjustment (Doctoral dissertation, University of Maryland, College Park, 1996). *Dissertation Abstracts International, 57B,* 6554.

Alvarez, A. N. (2002). Racial identity and Asian Americans: Supports and challenges. In M. K. McEwen, C. M. Kodama, A. N. Alvarez, S. Lee, & C.T.H. Liang (Eds.), *Working with Asian American college students* (New Directions for Student Services No. 97, pp. 33–43). San Francisco: Jossey-Bass.

Alvarez, A. N., & Yeh, T. L. (1999). Asian Americans in college: A racial identity perspective. In D. Sandhu (Ed.), *Asian and Pacific Islander Americans: Issues and concerns for counseling and psychotherapy* (pp. 105–119). Huntington, NY: Nova Science.

Asch, A., & Fine, M. (1988). Introduction: Beyond pedestals. In M. Fine & A. Asch (Eds.), *Women with disabilities: Essays in psychology, culture, and politics* (pp. 1–37). Philadelphia: Temple University Press.

Atkinson, D. R., & Hackett, G. (1998). *Counseling diverse populations* (2nd ed). Boston: McGraw-Hill.

Atkinson, D. R., Morten, G., & Sue, D. W. (1998). *Counseling American minorities: A cross-cultural perspective* (5th ed.). Dubuque, IA: McGraw Hill.

Bernal, M. E., & Knight, G. P. (1993). *Ethnic identity: Formation and transmission among Hispanics and other minorities.* Albany: State University of New York Press.

Broido, E. M. (2000). Constructing identity: The nature and meaning of lesbian, gay, and bisexual identities. In R. M. Perez, K. A. DeBord, & K. J. Bieschke (Eds.), *Handbook of counseling and psychotherapy with lesbian, gay, and bisexual clients* (pp. 13–33). Washington, DC: American Psychological Association.

Brown, D. (1970). *Bury my heart at wounded knee: An Indian history of the American west.* New York: Henry Holt.

Brown, L. S. (1989). New voices, new visions: Toward a lesbian/gay paradigm for psychology. *Psychology of Women Quarterly, 13,* 445–458.

Bryan, W. V. (2000). The disability rights movement. In M. Adams, W. J. Blumenfeld, R. Castañeda, H. W. Hackman, M. L. Peters, & X. Zúñiga (Eds.), *Readings for diversity and social justice* (pp. 324–329). New York: Routledge.

Canabal, I. (1996). Latino group identities, collective and personal self-esteem (Doctoral dissertation, University of Maryland, College Park, 1995). *Dissertation Abstracts International, 56B,* 4574.

Cannon, K. G. (1988). *Black womanist ethics.* Atlanta, GA: Scholars Press.

Carter, K. A. (2000). Transgenderism and college students: Issues of gender identity and its role on our campuses. In V. A. Wall & N. J. Evans (Eds.), *Toward acceptance: Sexual orientation issues on campus* (pp. 261–282). Lanham, MD: University Press of America.

Casas, J. M., & Pytluk, S. D. (1995). Hispanic identity development: Implications for research and practice. In J. G. Ponterotto, J. M. Casas, L. A. Suzuki, & C. M. Alexander (Eds.), *Handbook of multicultural counseling* (pp. 155–180). Thousand Oaks, CA: Sage.

Cass, V. C. (1979). Homosexual identity formation: A theoretical model. *Journal of Homosexuality, 4,* 219–235.

Chan, S. (1991). *Asian Americans: An interpretive history.* New York: Twayne.
Chickering, A. W. (1969). *Education and identity.* San Francisco: Jossey-Bass.
Chickering, A. W., & Reisser, L. (1993). *Education and identity* (2nd ed.). San Francisco: Jossey-Bass.
Corbett, M. M. (1995). The relationships between White racial identity and narcissism (Doctoral dissertation, University of Maryland, College Park, 1994). *Dissertation Abstracts International, 56B,* 2318.
Cross, W. E., Jr. (1971). The Negro-to-Black conversion experience: Toward a psychology of Black liberation. *Black World, 20* (9), 13–27.
Cross, W. E., Jr. (1978). The Thomas and Cross models of psychological Nigrescence: A review. *Journal of Black Psychology, 5,* 13–31.
Cross, W. E., Jr. (1991). *Shades of Black: Diversity in African-American identity.* Philadelphia: Temple University Press.
Cross, W. E., Jr. (1995). The psychology of Nigrescence: Revising the Cross model. In J. G. Ponterotto, J. M. Casas, L. A. Suzuki, & C. M. Alexander (Eds.), *Handbook of multicultural counseling* (pp. 93–122). Thousand Oaks, CA: Sage.
Cross, W. E., Jr., & Fhagen-Smith, P. (2001). Patterns of African American identity development: A life span perspective. In C. L. Wijeyesinghe & B. W. Jackson III (Eds.), *New perspectives on racial identity development: A theoretical and practical anthology* (pp. 243–270). New York: New York University Press.
D'Augelli, A. R. (1994). Identity development and sexual orientation: Toward a model of lesbian, gay, and bisexual development. In E. J. Trickett, R. J. Watts, & D. Birman (Eds.), *Human diversity: Perspectives on people in context* (pp. 312–333). San Francisco: Jossey-Bass.
Deaux, K. (1993). Reconstructing social identity. *Personality and Social Psychology Bulletin, 19,* 4–12.
Dill, B. T. (1994). Race, class, and gender: Prospects for an all-inclusive sisterhood. In L. Stone (Ed.), *The education feminism reader* (pp. 42–56). New York: Routledge.
Downing, N. E., & Roush, K. L. (1985). From passive acceptance to active commitment: A model of feminist identity development for women. *Counseling Psychologist, 13,* 695–709.
Eliason, M. J. (1995). Accounts of sexual identity formation in heterosexual students. *Sex Roles, 32,* 821–834.
Erikson, E. H. (1980). *Identity and the life cycle.* New York: Norton. (Original work published 1959).
Fassinger, R. E. (1991). The hidden minority: Issues and challenges in working with lesbian women and gay men. *Counseling Psychologist, 19,* 157–176.
Fassinger, R. E., & Miller, B. A. (1997). Validation of an inclusive model of homosexual identity formation in a sample of gay men. *Journal of Homosexuality, 32* (2), 53–78.
Ferdman, B. M., & Gallegos, P. I. (2001). Racial identity development and Latinos in the United States. In C. L. Wijeyesinghe & B. W. Jackson III (Eds.), *New perspectives on racial identity development: A theoretical and practical anthology* (pp. 32–66). New York: New York University Press.
Fine, M., & Asch, A. (2000). Disability beyond stigma: Social interaction, discrimination, and activism. In M. Adams, W. J. Blumenfeld, R. Castañeda, H. W. Hackman, M. L. Peters, & X. Zúñiga (Eds.), *Readings for diversity and social justice* (pp. 330–339). New York: Routledge.
Fowler, J. (1981). *Stages of faith: The psychology of human development and the quest for meaning.* New York: Harper & Row.
Fox, R. C. (1996). Bisexuality in perspective: A review of theory and research. In B. A. Firestein (Ed.), *Bisexuality: The psychology and politics of an invisible minority* (pp. 3–50). Thousand Oaks, CA: Sage.
Garreau, J. (1981). *The nine nations of North America.* Boston: Houghton Mifflin.
Gordon, M. M. (1964). *Assimilation in American life: The role of race, religion, and national origins.* New York: Oxford University Press.
Harris, A., & Wideman, D. (1988). The construction of gender and disability in early attachment. In M. Fine & A. Asch (Eds.), *Women with disabilities: Essays in psychology, culture, and politics* (pp. 115–138). Philadelphia: Temple University Press.

Helms, J. E. (1990a). An overview of Black racial identity theory. In J. E. Helms (Ed.), *Black and White racial identity: Theory, research, and practice* (pp. 9–32). New York: Greenwood Press.

Helms, J. E. (1990b). Applying the interaction model to social dyads. In J. E. Helms (Ed.), *Black and White racial identity: Theory, research, and practice* (pp. 177–185). New York: Greenwood Press.

Helms, J. E. (1990c). Counseling attitudinal and behavioral predispositions: The Black/White interaction model. In J. E. Helms (Ed.), *Black and White racial identity: Theory, research, and practice* (pp. 135–143). New York: Greenwood Press.

Helms, J. E. (1990d). Generalizing racial identity interaction theory to groups. In J. E. Helms (Ed.), *Black and White racial identity: Theory, research, and practice* (pp. 187–204). New York: Greenwood Press.

Helms, J. E. (1990e). Introduction: Review of racial identity terminology. In J. E. Helms (Ed.), *Black and White racial identity: Theory, research, and practice* (pp. 3–8). New York: Greenwood Press.

Helms, J. E. (1990f). Toward a model of White racial identity development. In J. E. Helms (Ed.), *Black and White racial identity: Theory, research, and practice* (pp. 49–66). New York: Greenwood Press.

Helms, J. E. (1992). *A race is a nice thing to have: A guide to being a White person, or understanding the White persons in your life.* Topeka, KS: Content Communications.

Helms, J. E. (1994). The conceptualization of racial identity and other "racial" constructs. In E. J. Trickett, R. J. Watts, & D. Birman (Eds.), *Human diversity: Perspectives on people in context* (pp. 285–311). San Francisco: Jossey-Bass.

Helms, J. E. (1995). An update of Helms's White and People of Color racial identity models. In J. G. Ponterotto, J. M. Casas, L. A. Suzuki, & C. M. Alexander (Eds.), *Handbook of multicultural counseling* (pp. 181–198). Thousand Oaks, CA: Sage.

Helms, J. E., & Cook, D. A. (1999). *Using race and culture in counseling and psychotherapy: Theory and process.* Boston: Allyn & Bacon.

Helms, J. E., & Piper, R. E. (1994). Implications of racial identity theory for vocational psychology. *Journal of Vocational Behavior, 44,* 124–136.

Herek, G. M. (1986). On heterosexual masculinity: Some psychical consequences of the social construction of gender and sexuality. *American Behavioral Scientist, 29,* 563–577.

Heyck, D.L.D. (1994). *Barrios and borderlands: Cultures of Latinos and Latinas in the United States.* New York: Routledge.

hooks, b. (2000). *where we stand: CLASS MATTERS.* New York: Routledge.

Horse, P. G. (2001). Reflections on American Indian identity. In C. L. Wijeyesinghe & B. W. Jackson III (Eds.), *New perspectives on racial identity development: A theoretical and practical anthology* (pp. 91–107). New York: New York University Press.

Isasi-Díaz, A. M. (1996). *Mujerista theology: A theology for the twenty-first century.* Maryknoll, NY: Orbis.

Jones, S. R. (1996). Toward inclusive theory: Disability as social construction. *NASPA Journal, 33,* 347–354.

Jones, S. R. (1997). Voices of identity and difference: A qualitative exploration of the multiple dimensions of identity development in women college students. *Journal of College Student Development, 38,* 376–386.

Jones, S. R., & McEwen, M. K. (2000). A conceptual model of multiple dimensions of identity. *Journal of College Student Development, 41,* 405–414.

Keppel, B., & Hamilton, A. (1992). *Using the Klein scale to teach about sexual orientation* [Brochure]. Cambridge, MA: East Coast Bisexual Network.

Kerwin, C., & Ponterotto, J. G. (1995). Biracial identity development: Theory and research. In J. G. Ponterotto, J. M. Casas, L. A. Suzuki, & C. M. Alexander (Eds.), *Handbook of multicultural counseling* (pp. 199–217). Thousand Oaks, CA: Sage.

Kich, G. K. (1992). The developmental process of asserting a biracial, bicultural identity. In M.P.P. Root (Ed.), *Racially mixed people in America* (pp. 304–317). Newbury Park, CA: Sage.

Kim, J. (2001). Asian American identity development theory. In C. L. Wijeyesinghe & B. W. Jackson III (Eds.), *New perspectives on racial identity development: A theoretical and practical anthology* (pp. 67–90). New York: New York University Press.

Kinsey, A. C., Pomeroy, W. B., & Martin, C. E. (1948). *Sexual behavior in the human male.* Philadelphia: Saunders.

Kinsey, A. C., et al. (1953). *Sexual behavior in the human female.* Philadelphia: Saunders.

Klein, F., Sepekoff, B., & Wolf, T. J. (1990). Sexual orientation: A multi-variable dynamic process. In T. Geller (Ed.), *Bisexuality: A reader and sourcebook* (pp. 64–81). Ojai, CA: Times Change Press.

Klein, J. W. (1980). *Jewish identity and self-esteem: Healing wounds through ethnotherapy.* New York: Institute on Pluralism and Group Identity, American Jewish Committee.

Kohatsu, E. L. (1993). The effects of racial identity and acculturation on anxiety, assertiveness, and ascribed identity among Asian American college students (Doctoral dissertation, University of Maryland, College Park, 1992). *Dissertation Abstracts International, 54B,* 1102.

Langston, D. (2001). Tired of playing monopoly? In M. L. Andersen & P. Hill Collins (Eds.), *Race, class, and gender: An anthology* (4th ed., pp. 125–134). Belmont, CA: Wadsworth/Thomson Learning.

Levine, H., & Evans, N. J. (1991). The development of gay, lesbian, and bisexual identities. In N. J. Evans & V. A. Wall (Eds.), *Beyond tolerance: Gays, lesbians, and bisexuals on campus* (pp. 1–24). Alexandria, VA: American College Personnel Association.

Love, P. G. (2002). Comparing spiritual development and cognitive development. *Journal of College Student Development, 43,* 357–373.

McCarn, S. R., & Fassinger, R. E. (1996). Revisioning sexual minority identity formation: A new model of lesbian identity and its implications for counseling and research. *The Counseling Psychologist, 24,* 508–534.

McIntosh, P. (2001). White privilege and male privilege: A personal account of coming to see correspondences through work in women's studies. In M. L. Andersen & P. Hill Collins (Eds.), *Race, class, and gender: An anthology* (4th ed., pp. 95–105). Belmont, CA: Wadsworth/Thomson Learning.

Miville, M. L. (1997). An exploratory investigation of the interrelationships of cultural, gender, and personal identity of Latinos and Latinas (Doctoral dissertation, University of Maryland, College Park, 1996). *Dissertation Abstracts International, 58B,* 0458.

Moradi, B., Subich, L. M., & Phillips, J. C. (2002). Revisiting feminist identity development theory, research, and practice. *The Counseling Psychologist, 30,* 6–43.

Mueller, J. (2002, March). *In pursuit of understanding: A model of heterosexual consciousness formation.* Paper presented at the American College Personnel Association conference, Long Beach, CA.

Murphy, R. F. (1987). *The body silent.* New York: Holt.

O'Neil, J. M. (1981). Patterns of gender role conflict and strain: Sexism and fear of femininity in men's lives. *Personnel and Guidance Journal, 60,* 203–210.

O'Neil, J. M. (1990). Assessing men's gender role conflict. In D. Moore & F. Leafgren (Eds.), *Problem solving strategies and interventions for men in conflict* (pp. 23–38). Alexandria, VA: American Association for Counseling and Development.

O'Neil, J. M., Egan, J., Owen, S. V., & Murry, V. M. (1993). The Gender Role Journey Measure: Scale development and psychometric evaluation. *Sex Roles, 28,* 167–185.

O'Neil, J. M., & Fishman, D. M. (1992). Adult men's career transitions and gender-role themes. In H. D. Lea & Z. B. Leibowitz (Eds.), *Adult career development: Concepts, issues, and practices* (pp. 161–191). Alexandria, VA: National Career Development Association.

O'Neil, J. M., Helms, B. J., Gable, R. K., David, L., & Wrightsman, L. S. (1986). Gender-role conflict scale: College men's fear of femininity. *Sex Roles, 14,* 335–350.

Ossana, S. M., Helms, J. E., & Leonard, M. M. (1992). Do "womanist" identity attitudes influence college women's self-esteem and perceptions of environmental bias? *Journal of Counseling and Development, 70,* 402–408.

Parham, T. A. (1989). Cycles of psychological Nigrescence. *Counseling Psychologist, 17,* 187–226.

Parham, T. A., & Helms, J. E. (1985). Attitudes of racial identity and self-esteem in Black students: An exploratory investigation. *Journal of College Student Personnel, 26,* 143–147.

Parks, S. D. (1986). *The critical years: The young adult search for a faith to live by.* New York: Harper & Row.

Parks, S. D. (2000). *Big questions, worthy dreams: Mentoring young adults in their search for meaning, purpose, and faith.* San Francisco: Jossey-Bass.

Phinney, J. S. (1990). Ethnic identity in adolescents and adults: Review of research. *Psychological Bulletin, 108,* 499–514.

Phinney, J. S. (1992). The Multigroup Ethnic Identity Measure: A new scale for use with diverse groups. *Journal of Adolescent Research, 7,* 156–176.

Poston, W.S.C. (1990). The biracial identity development model: A needed addition. *Journal of Counseling and Development, 69,* 152–155.

President's Commission on Disability Issues. (1990). *Reasonable accommodations: Teaching college students with disabilities.* College Park: University of Maryland.

Reichler, R. (1991). A question of invisibility. In L. Hutchins & L. Kaahumanu (Eds.), *Bi any other name: Bisexual people speak out* (pp. 78–79). Boston: Alyson.

Reynolds, A. L., & Hanjorgiris, W. F. (2000). Coming out: Lesbian, gay, and bisexual identity development. In R. M. Perez, K. A. DeBord, & K. J. Bieschke (Eds.), *Handbook of counseling and psychotherapy with lesbian, gay, and bisexual clients* (pp. 35–55). Washington, DC: American Psychological Association.

Reynolds, A. L., & Pope, R. L. (1991). The complexities of diversity: Exploring multiple oppressions. *Journal of Counseling and Development, 70,* 174–180.

Robin, L., & Hamner, K. (2000). Bisexuality: Identities and community. In V. A. Wall & N. J. Evans (Eds.), *Toward acceptance: Sexual orientation issues on campus* (pp. 245–259). Lanham, MD: University Press of America.

Root, M.P.P. (1990). Resolving "other" status: Identity development of biracial individuals. In L. S. Brown & M.P.P. Root (Eds.), *Complexity and diversity in feminist theory and therapy* (pp. 185–205). New York: Haworth.

Root, M.P.P. (Ed.). (1992). *Racially mixed people in America.* Newbury Park, CA: Sage.

Root, M.P.P. (1996a). The multiracial experience: Racial borders as a significant frontier in race relations. In M.P.P. Root (Ed.), *The multiracial experience: Racial borders as the new frontier* (pp. xiii–xxviii). Thousand Oaks, CA: Sage.

Root, M.P.P. (Ed.). (1996b). *The multiracial experience: Racial borders as the new frontier.* Thousand Oaks, CA: Sage.

Ruiz, A. S. (1990). Ethnic identity: Crisis and resolution. *Journal of Multicultural Counseling and Development, 18,* 29–40.

Rust, P. C. (1996). Managing multiple identities: Diversity among bisexual women and men. In B. A. Firestein (Ed.), *Bisexuality: The psychology and politics of an invisible minority* (pp. 53–83). Thousand Oaks, CA: Sage.

Sampson, E. E. (1985). The decentralization of identity: Toward a revised concept of personal and social order. *American Psychologist, 40,* 1203–1211.

Sanford, N. (1962). *The American college.* New York: Wiley.

Sanford, N. (1967). *Where colleges fail: A study of the student as a person.* San Francisco: Jossey-Bass.

Scheer, J. (1994). Culture and disability: An anthropological point of view. In E. J. Trickett, R. J. Watts, & D. Birman (Eds.), *Human diversity: Perspectives on people in context* (pp. 244–260). San Francisco: Jossey-Bass.

Sodowsky, G. R., Kwan, K-L. K., & Pannu, R. (1995). Ethnic identity of Asians in the United States. In J. G. Ponterotto, J. M. Casas, L. A. Suzuki, & C. M. Alexander (Eds.), *Handbook of multicultural counseling* (pp. 123–154). Thousand Oaks, CA: Sage.

Sullivan, P. (1998). Sexual identity development: The importance of target or dominant group membership. In R. L. Sanlo (Ed.), *Working with lesbian, gay, bisexual, and transgender college students* (pp. 3–12). Westport, CT: Greenwood.

Takaki, R. (1993). *A different mirror: A history of multicultural America.* Boston: Little, Brown.

Tatum, B. D. (1997). *"Why are all the Black kids sitting together in the cafeteria?" and other conversations about race.* New York: Basic.

Torres, V. (1999). Validation of a bicultural orientation model for Hispanic college students. *Journal of College Student Development, 40,* 285–298.

Walker, A. (1983). *In search of our mothers' gardens: Womanist prose.* San Diego, CA: Harcourt Brace.

Weber, L. (1998). A conceptual framework for understanding race, class, gender, and sexuality. *Psychology of Women Quarterly, 22,* 13–32.

Weber, L. (2001). *Understanding race, class, gender, and sexuality: A conceptual framework.* New York: McGraw-Hill.

Widick, C., Parker, C. A., & Knefelkamp, L. (1978). Erik Erikson and psychosocial development. In L. Knefelkamp, C. Widick, & C. A. Parker (Eds.), *Applying new developmental findings* (New Directions for Student Services No. 4, pp. 1–17). San Francisco: Jossey-Bass.

Wijeyesinghe, C. L. (2001). Racial identity in multiracial people: An alternative paradigm. In C. L. Wijeyesinghe & B. W. Jackson III (Eds.), *New perspectives on racial identity development: A theoretical and practical anthology* (pp. 129–152). New York: New York University Press.

Wise-Mohr, C. (1992, March 1). MS, the world and me: Who says I'm disabled? *Washington Post,* p. C5.

Worthington, R. L., Savoy, H. B., Dillon, F. R., & Vernaglia, E. R. (2002). Heterosexual identity development: A multidimensional model of individual and social identity. *The Counseling Psychologist, 30,* 496–531.

Zinik, G. (1985). Identity conflict or adaptive flexibility? Bisexuality reconsidered. In F. Klein & T. J. Wolf (Eds.), *Bisexualities: Theory and research* (pp. 7–19). New York: Haworth.

Zinn, H. (1995). *A people's history of the United States: 1492 to present* (rev. and updated ed.). New York: HarperPerennial.

CHAPTER ELEVEN

STUDENT LEARNING IN HIGHER EDUCATION

Patricia M. King

The central mission of higher education is to enhance learning. Both faculty and student affairs staff should be able to articulate their educational purposes and to offer a rationale for the strategies they design to accomplish these ends. Being knowledgeable about student learning concepts and theories provides educators with an important set of tools to use when working with students and colleagues around topics related to learning. Student affairs practitioners not only enhance student learning directly but often indirectly by serving as a resource to faculty, campus administrators, and parents. Today, assisting with the learning process continues to carry special significance and urgency given the need to prepare students for employment, civic, and leadership roles. Doing so remains an unfulfilled challenge that requires a complex understanding of student learning and of the conditions that enhance the achievement of desired educational outcomes.

This chapter begins with a brief discussion of two fundamental questions: what is learning, and what should college students learn? The answers to these questions lay a foundation for the major topic of this chapter, student characteristics affecting learning. This topic is divided into two major sections: theories of learning that focus on students' assumptions about knowledge and the learning process, and those that focus on students' stylistic attributes. The chapter concludes with a review of practices that encourage student learning.

Note: I wish to acknowledge the able assistance of Nancy A. Birk in the preparation of this chapter.

What Is Learning?

There are many common phrases used to describe learning, such as an "a-ha!" experience or "learning is finding out what you don't know you don't know." Learning is sometimes regarded as synonymous with education ("to be a learned person") and knowledge ("book learning"). Learning is also associated with acquired wisdom, which involves showing good judgment, being able to discern what is true, right, or lasting, and being prudent and informed. Learning thus defined—as an *outcome*—includes the knowledge, skills, and attitudes that serve as a foundation for wisdom. Learning defined as a *process*, on the other hand, focuses on the kinds of strategies people use to solve new problems, how they listen to and learn from others, how they respond to feedback and new information, how they gather and interpret data, how they determine its relevance, and how strong the evidence needs to be before they are satisfied that they can make a decision or solve a problem. *Learning* is both a noun and a verb, representing both an outcome and a process of education. How learning is defined may have surprising importance: how college students define learning has been found to be related to how they study (van Rossum & Schenk, 1984; Schommer, Crouse, & Rhodes, 1992).

Learning obviously occurs in a context; educational contexts typically involve four interrelated factors: the educational goals or content, the characteristics and activities of the educator, the characteristics of the learner, and the interactions among learners in the context (Cohen, Raudenbush, & Ball, 2002). When these are mutually reinforcing (or "in alignment"), the potential for students to achieve the educational goals is greatly enhanced. Thus, although the focus of this chapter is on the learner, it is important to acknowledge that other major factors are also very influential in helping students achieve their learning goals.

The question "What is learning?" is one that many people who work on college campuses should be able and willing to discuss with students, parents, and other constituent groups. Educators should be able to both explain and create meaningful learning experiences. Students should be encouraged to identify their own definition of learning and examine how their approach to learning and their prior learning experiences affect their learning goals and strategies. These would be excellent topics of discussion for an orientation program or as part of a college's senior outcomes assessment. Discussion of such issues provides an excellent point of contact between student affairs staff and faculty members.

What Should College Students Learn?

Institutional expectations for student learning influence the kind of learning that takes place. Educators should be able to identify what they intend students to learn from their educational programs and the attributes they hope their graduates will have. Student learning goals are typically described in terms of the knowledge, skills, and attitudes or values students are expected to demonstrate by the time they graduate. While these three sets of attributes are separated for clarity as goals, they are interrelated in the developing person. For example, gaining global awareness requires students to be knowledgeable about such topics as world history, current events, and cultural, economic, and social influences on these events. Students also need to be able to discern others' values and understand the sources and implications of their own value systems. Students should be aware of the interdependence of knowledge, skills, and attitudes so they can more intentionally target their educational efforts and more effectively respond to the problems they confront.

Students' attitudes and values play an important role in what and how they learn. Do students have the disposition to apply critical thinking skills to everyday problems? Do they seek out different perspectives on controversial problems? Do they demonstrate a fundamental respect for other persons in their daily interactions? Do they strive to act ethically in support of the common good? Students should be aware that what and how they learn will influence the kind of people they become. They should actively consider the questions, "What kind of person (citizen, parent, worker, friend) do I want to be?" "What do I need to learn (about myself, about others, about the world around me) to become this kind of person?" and "What do I want to learn while I am a student here?" Faculty and staff should be available and ready to help students develop answers to these questions of personal and professional identity and to support them in recognizing this as a difficult and important part of the process of becoming educated and gaining wisdom.

Another way of answering the question, "What should students learn?" is to consider this educational goal from a different vantage point, what students should learn to *do,* not in the narrow sense of skill development, but in the broader sense of the attributes of a mature person. That is, students should learn the complex array of attributes in cognitive, interpersonal, and intrapersonal domains (Kegan, 1994) that are required to *apply* their knowledge and skills to a variety of problems in many adult roles, whether as employees, as consumers, as community citizens, voters, or family members. Using this approach, students should learn the competencies necessary to apply their knowledge and skills in life contexts.

Proposing a list of the knowledge, skills, and attitudes that students should learn by the time they graduate from college is beyond the scope of this chapter. However, several excellent resources are available for this purpose (Alverno College, 1992; Association of American Colleges, 1985, 1991; Bok, 1986; Bowen, 1980; Donald, 1999; Hirsch, 1987; Mentkowski & Associates, 2000; Rosovsky, 1990).

Student Characteristics Affecting Learning

A dizzying array of approaches to describing and promoting student learning exists in the professional literature, each emphasizing a different aspect of the teaching-learning process. An important common theme of these approaches is that the key to understanding student learning is to understand student differences.

This section opens with a discussion of learning and epistemology; it examines several models that focus on the assumptions underlying students' ways of making meaning and how these are related to their ways of learning. The next section examines stylistic attributes that affect learning, including established models that focus on a range of learning styles and strategies to more recent research on cognition and scientific reasoning.

Learning and Epistemology: Students' Assumptions About Knowledge and Learning

Kolb (1984) made the following provocative assertion: "to understand knowledge, we must understand the psychology of the learning process, and to understand learning, we must understand epistemology—the origins, nature, methods, and limits of knowledge" (p. 37). What is the relationship between understanding knowledge and learning? The models summarized in this section describe students' epistemological assumptions as a way to understand how they define, approach, and interpret learning. These models focus on a very fundamental level of thinking, the underlying assumptions that appear to guide the process of knowing. From this perspective, strategies for learning reflect more than preferred study techniques or procedures for gathering information; they reflect the individual's way of organizing his or her experiences in ways that "make sense," that is, in ways that provide meaningful interpretations of experiences. Constructing one's own knowledge instead of relying on knowledge received from others reflects a major shift in what Kegan (1994) refers to as "self-authorship." (This model is described by Evans in Chapter Nine.)

A common theme among the issues raised by these researchers in this field is that learning is seen in such attributes as becoming able to reconcile contradictions, weigh conflicting or contradictory perspectives, construct a well-reasoned point of view, understand why others might hold different views, and take responsibility for one's behaviors, including one's learning strategies. Learning involves an individual actively attempting to "make sense" of his or her experiences, resulting in a conceptual reorganization of thinking that is in some way more adaptive or that enables the individual to function more effectively.

Perry's Scheme. Perry's seminal study of Harvard and Radcliffe students in the 1950s and 1960s provided the initial impetus for provocative and informative scholarly dialogue about the nature of late adolescent and adult development and the role of higher education in fostering intellectual and ethical development. He conducted open-ended interviews with students at the end of each academic year and identified nine positions to describe their intellectual and ethical development (Perry, 1968/1970, 1981). The early positions are simplistic in form, where students interpret the world in "unqualified polar terms of absolute right-wrong, good-bad" (p. 3), while the latter positions are more complex. Here, students affirm personal commitments "in a world of contingent knowledge and relative values" (p. 3). These nine positions are usually divided into four levels as detailed in Exhibit 11.1.

EXHIBIT 11.1. PERRY'S SCHEME.

1. *Dualism* (positions 1 and 2). The student believes that right answers exist to all questions and that authorities have these answers. The world is viewed in absolute, right-wrong terms. In position 2 some uncertainty is recognized, but it is viewed as a challenge set by authorities for students to learn to find the answers on their own.
2. *Multiplicity* (positions 3 and 4). Uncertainty is now viewed as temporary in areas in which authorities have yet to find the answers. In position 4 uncertainty is seen as so extensive that all opinions are equally valid, and students begin to rely less on authorities.
3. *Relativism* (positions 5 and 6). A major shift in thinking occurs at position 5 as the student comes to view knowledge as contextual and relative and is able to make judgments based on evidence and the merits of an argument.
4. *Commitment in Relativism* (positions 7 to 9). Students test out and evaluate various commitments leading to the development of a personalized set of values, lifestyle, and identity.

Source: Evans (1996). Reprinted with permission.

Perry's work inspired several other researchers (Basseches, 1984; Baxter Magolda, 1992, 2001; Belenky, Clinchy, Goldberger, & Tarule, 1986; Broughton, 1978; King & Kitchener, 1994; Kramer, 1989; Perry, 1968/1970; Schommer, 1994; Sinnott, 1989); their work has refined the constructs, expanded the applications to new groups of students, and applied contemporary sensibilities and new theoretical developments to the ideas that Perry and his team of researchers so eloquently introduced. Each of the several constructivist developmental models of intellectual development that are now available describes age- and/or education-related changes in the process of constructing knowledge, and each has attempted to show how the ways learners construct knowledge (or how they "make sense" of what they learn) has dramatic effects on what and how they learn. (For a comprehensive review of epistemological models, see Hofer & Pintrich, 1997, 2002.) Three that have strong research bases and a clear connection to college students' learning are discussed next.

The Reflective Judgment Model. The reflective judgment model (King & Kitchener, 1994, 2002; Kitchener, in press; Kitchener & King, 1981, 1990) describes a developmental progression in people's assumptions about knowledge (what can be known, how knowledge is gained, certainty of knowledge claims) and how these assumptions are related to how people justify their beliefs. This progression may be observed in the ways people use evidence in making decisions about ill-structured problems, or those that cannot be defined and resolved with completeness and certainty; these include current events where evidence is incomplete or contradictory and historical events where evidence has been lost over time. Using evidence intentionally and honestly reflects the difference "between developing and justifying a position and merely asserting one" (Association of American Colleges, 1991, p. 14). Research on the reflective judgment model has shown that people's assumptions about knowledge correspond closely to the ways they evaluate knowledge claims (including their own beliefs). For example, those who believe judgments can only be made with a measure of certainty (and not absolutely) tend to be skeptical when faced with dogmatic assertions made by others.

The progression of thinking described by the reflective judgment model is summarized in Exhibit 11.2. In this model it is not assumed that individuals are "in" one stage at a time, rather, that they work within a developmental range of stages (Lamborn & Fischer, 1988; see King & Kitchener, 1994, for a discussion of their use of the stage construct), and that their performance varies depending on such factors as support and feedback (Kitchener, Lynch, Fischer, & Wood, 1993).

This model is distinguished by its extensive research base. King and Kitchener (1994) report the responses of over 1700 participants who were interviewed using the Reflective Judgment Interview (RJI) and the results of a ten-year longitudinal study of three different cohorts. Since the publication of that volume, Wood (1997) has completed a comprehensive secondary analysis of all available RJI data, King and Kitchener (2002) have updated their summary of research, and results on the new measure of reflective thinking is reported by Wood, Kitchener, and Jensen (2002).

Teaching for reflective thinking requires that educators create and sustain learning environments conducive to the thoughtful consideration of controversial topics, that they help students learn to evaluate others' evidence-based interpretations, and that they provide supportive opportunities for students to practice making and explaining their own judgments about important and complicated problems. (For examples of specific strategies for promoting reflective thinking, see King, 1992, 2000; King & Kitchener, 1994; Kitchener & King, 1990; and Kroll, 1992.)

The Epistemological Reflection Model. Baxter Magolda (1992) reported the results of a longitudinal study of a cohort of 101 college students in which she mapped their intellectual development across their college years. She described four "qualitatively different ways of knowing, each characterized by a core set of epistemic assumptions" (p. 29). These four approaches (absolute, transitional, independent, and contextual) are associated with different expectations of the learner and his or her peers and instructors about how learning should be evaluated and how educational decisions should be made. In addition to the structural differences between the ways of knowing, Baxter Magolda also described gender-related patterns within each of the first three ways of knowing, patterns that were more often used by either men or women (but not exclusively by either gender). She has emphasized that relational modes of knowing are essential to intellectual development and are often learned in cocurricular settings.

This initial study of college students included an in-depth look at the kinds of courses they believe promoted their intellectual development (Baxter Magolda, 1999) and set the stage for a continuing longitudinal study of their experiences after graduation (Baxter Magolda, 1994, 2001). Continuing to interview thirty-nine of the original participants annually for ten years after graduation, Baxter Magolda (2001) has recently reported on their continuing journeys toward maturity, tracing experiences in many adult contexts, from their jobs, to families and communities, and noting the kinds

EXHIBIT 11.2. SUMMARY OF REFLECTIVE JUDGMENT STAGES.

Prereflective Thinking

Stage 1 *View of Knowledge:* Knowledge is assumed to exist absolutely and concretely; it is not understood as an abstraction. It can be obtained with certainty through direct observation.

Concept of Justification: Beliefs need no justification since there is assumed to be an absolute correspondence between what is believed and what is true. Alternative beliefs are not recognized.

"I know what I have seen."

Stage 2 *View of Knowledge:* Knowledge is assumed to be absolutely certain but not immediately available. Knowledge can be obtained directly through the senses (such as direct observation) or via authority figures.

Concept of Justification: Beliefs are unexamined and unjustified, or justified by their correspondence with the beliefs of an authority figure (such as a teacher or parent). Most issues are assumed to have a right answer, so there is little or no conflict in making decisions about disputed issues.

"If it is on the news, it has to be true."

Stage 3 *View of knowledge:* Knowledge is assumed to be absolutely certain or temporarily uncertain. In areas of temporary uncertainty, only personal beliefs can be known until absolute knowledge is obtained. In areas of absolute certainty, knowledge is obtained from authorities.

Concept of Justification: In areas in which certain answers exist, beliefs are justified by reference to authorities' views. In areas in which answers do not exist, beliefs are defended as personal opinion, since the link between evidence and beliefs is unclear.

"When there is evidence that people can give to convince everybody one way or another, then it will be acknowledged; until then, it's just a guess."

Quasi-Reflective Thinking

Stage 4 *View of Knowledge:* Knowledge is uncertain, and knowledge claims are idiosyncratic to the individual, since situational variables (such as incorrect reporting of data, data lost over time, or disparities in access to information) dictate that knowing always involves an element of ambiguity.

Concept of Justification: Beliefs are justified by giving reasons and using evidence, but the arguments and choice of evidence are idiosyncratic (for example, choosing evidence that fits an established belief).

"I'd be more inclined to believe in evolution if they had proof. It's just like the pyramids: I don't think we'll ever know. Who are you going to ask? No one was there."

Stage 5 *View of Knowledge:* Knowledge is contextual and subjective since it is filtered through a person's perceptions and criteria for judgment. Only interpretations of evidence, events, or issues may be known.

Concept of Justification: Beliefs are justified within a particular context, using the rules of inquiry for that context and by context-specific interpretations of evidence. Specific beliefs are assumed to be context-specific or are balanced against other interpretations, which complicates (and sometimes delays) conclusions.

"People think differently, and so they attack the problem differently. Other theories could be as true as my own, but based on different evidence."

EXHIBIT 11.2. SUMMARY OF REFLECTIVE JUDGMENT STAGES. (*CONTINUED*)

Reflective Thinking

Stage 6 *View of Knowledge:* Knowledge is constructed into individual conclusions about ill-structured problems based on information from a variety of sources. Interpretations that are based on evaluations of evidence across contexts and on the evaluated opinions of reputable others can be known.

Concept of Justification: Beliefs are justified by comparing evidence and opinions on different sides of an issue or across contexts and by constructing solutions that are evaluated by criteria such as the weight of the evidence, the utility of the solution, or the pragmatic need for action.

"It's very difficult in this life to be sure. There are degrees of sureness. You come to a point at which you are sure enough to take a personal stance on an issue."

Stage 7 *View of Knowledge:* Knowledge is the outcome of a process of reasonable inquiry, in which solutions to ill-structured problems are constructed. The adequacy of those solutions is evaluated in terms of what is more reasonable or probable based on the current evidence, and it is reevaluated when relevant new evidence, perspectives, or tools of inquiry become available.

Concept of Justification: Beliefs are justified probabilistically, based on a variety of interpretive considerations such as the weight of the evidence, the explanatory value of the interpretations, the risk of erroneous conclusions, consequences of alternative judgments, and the interrelationships of these factors. Conclusions are defended as representing the most complete, plausible, or compelling understanding of an issue, based on the available evidence.

"One can judge an argument by how well thought out the positions are, what kinds of reasoning and evidence are used to support it, and how consistent the way one argues on this topic is as compared with other topics."

Source: King and Kitchener (1994). Reprinted with permission.

of experiences that enhanced and enabled their ability to handle the demands of adult life that they faced. She mapped four phases in their journeys: following external formulas, the crossroads (signified by the need to look inward for self-definition), becoming the author of one's own life, and the development of an internal foundation to ground their choices. These rich descriptions of their lives as they unfolded yielded a remarkable set of narratives filled with the delight and agony of development in very personal, even raw, terms. One of the most striking elements of these interviews is how vividly they illustrated the connections among various dimensions of development (cognitive, identity, social) that educators and researchers alike seem more inclined to treat separately. Baxter Magolda uses Kegan's (1994) model to capture these interrelationships, as it describes development in cognitive (how we come to know and decide what to believe), intrapersonal (how we view ourselves), and interpersonal domains (how we construct relationships with others). These phases are mapped by these three dimensions in Exhibit 11.3.

EXHIBIT 11.3. FOUR PHASES OF THE JOURNEY TOWARD SELF-AUTHORSHIP.

	Following Formulas	Crossroads	Becoming the Author of One's Life	Internal Foundation
Epistemological dimension: How do I know?	Believe authority's plans: how "you" know	Question plans; see need for own vision	Choose own beliefs; how "I" know in context of external knowledge claims	Grounded in internal belief system
Intrapersonal dimension: Who am I?	Define self through external others	Realize dilemma of external definition; see need for internal identity	Choose own values, identity in context of external forces	Grounded in internal coherent sense of self
Interpersonal dimension: What relationships do I want with others?	Act in relationships to acquire approval	Realize dilemma of focusing on external approval; see need to bring self to relationship	Act in relationships to be true to self, mutually negotiating how needs are met	Grounded in mutuality

Source: Baxter Magolda (2001). Reprinted with permission.

Baxter Magolda has examined a variety of educational issues in light of these four ways of knowing. She suggests that three principles be used to support student learning: validating the student as a knower, situating learning in the students' own experience, and defining learning as mutually constructing meaning. Examples of ways educators can assist students to learn in both classroom and out-of-class experiences (leadership, academic advising, career services, diversity programming, etc.) are explored in depth in Baxter Magolda (2001).

Women's Ways of Knowing. This book (Belenky, Clinchy, Goldberger & Tarule, 1986) was written to explore how women made meaning in their lives and how social institutions (including but not limited to higher education) could better serve the needs of women. This work is grounded in in-depth interviews with 135 women from a wide range of backgrounds that differed by class, ethnicity, education, and geography. In the course of the interviews on topics that ranged from self-concept, moral judgment, relationships, and schooling experiences, they discovered that "the women's epistemological assumptions were central to their perceptions of themselves and their worlds" (p. xviii). So although this work was not originally framed as a study of college student intellectual development, it has made a major contribution to our understanding of how collegiate environments affect women's approaches to meaning-making in college and other settings. (For a compilation of essays inspired by the original publication, see Goldberger, Tarule, Clinchy, & Belenky, 1996.) The authors of *Womens' Ways of Knowing* identified five perspectives "from which women view the world of truth, knowledge and authority" (Clinchy, 2002, p. 64), and their conception of themselves as knowers. Goldberger et al. (1996) offered the following summary of these perspectives:

1. *Silence*—a position of not knowing in which the person feels voiceless, powerless, and mindless.
2. *Received knowing*—a position at which knowledge and authority are constructed as outside the self and invested in powerful and knowing others from whom one is expected to learn.
3. *Subjective knowing*—in which knowing is personal, private, and based on intuition and/or feeling states rather than on thought and articulated ideas that are defended with evidence.
4. *Procedural knowing*—the position at which techniques and procedures for acquiring, validating, and evaluating knowledge claims are developed and honored. We also described two modes of knowing that we first noticed as we described different procedures for knowing that women adopt: *separate knowing,* which is characterized by a distanced, skeptical, and impartial stance toward that which one is trying to know (a reasoning against) and *connected knowing,* which is characterized by a stance of belief and an entering into the place of the other person or the idea that one is trying to know (a reasoning with).
5. *Constructed knowing*—the position at which truth is understood to be contextual; knowledge is recognized as tentative, not absolute; and it is understood that the knower is part of (constructs) the known . . . Constructed knowers valued multiple

approaches to knowing (subjective and objective, connected and separate) and insist on bringing the self and personal commitment into the center of the knowing process" [italics in original] (pp. 4–5).

The work of these authors on separate and connected knowing has particularly sparked a great deal of interest, as it seemed to "ring true" to so many women and to explain their discomfort with traditional "separate" models of instruction in higher education. Clinchy (1996, 2002) has summarized the contrasting features of these two approaches in greater detail; these appear in Exhibit 11.4. She also pointed out that connected knowing is not offered as an approach that is "better" than separate knowing, rather that the effectiveness of each approach depends on the context. She suggested that "all students need to develop skill in both modes so that they can deploy whichever is appropriate on a given occasion" (Clinchy, 2000, p. 32), and noted that those who use a constructed knowing approach "achieve a way of knowing that integrates the two procedures into one" (p. 33), thus increasing their ability to adapt to situational demands.

EXHIBIT 11.4. CHARACTERISTICS OF CONNECTED AND SEPARATE KNOWING.

Aspect	Connected Knowing	Separate Knowing
The name of the game:	The "Believing Game": looking for what is right; accepting	The "Doubting Game": looking for what is wrong; critical
Goals:	Emphasis on meaning: to understand and be understood	Emphasis on validity to justify, test, refine, convince, and be convinced
The relationship between the knowers:	Supportive: reasoning *with* the other	Adversarial, challenging: reasoning *against* the other
The knower's relation to the known:	Personal. Attachment & intimacy: "stepping in"	Impersonal. Detachment and distance: "stepping back"
The nature of agency:	Active surrender	Mastery and control
The nature of discourse:	Narrative	Argument
The role of emotion:	Feelings illuminate thought	Feelings cloud thought
Procedure for achieving (approximating) "objectivity":	Adopting the perspective of the particular other; empathy	Adopting a neutral perspective, "from no position in particular": adhering to rules for avoiding bias
Basis of authority:	Personal experience (own or vicarious)	Mastery of relevant knowledge and methodology
Strengths:	Holistic, inclusive	Narrowing, discriminating
Vulnerabilities:	Absence of conviction; loss of identity, autonomy, and power. Danger of always being the listener	Absence of conviction; alienation and absence of care and intimacy. Danger of never listening

Source: Clinchy (2002). Reprinted with permission.

Summary. Many would point out that claims of the success of a "cognitive revolution" (Brown, 1994) in reforming educational practices in higher education are premature since many college classes and programs are still designed in ways that appear to view learners as "empty vessels" to be filled with knowledge by the teacher. However, the idea that knowledge or understanding is constructed by the knower has greatly enriched the theoretical base for describing and researching cognitive development. Further, the availability of research-based theoretical models showing that the ways in which people construct knowledge evolves in predicable patterns over time have provided frameworks that educators can use in designing developmentally appropriate educational strategies.

Stylistic Attributes That Affect Learning: Students' Assumptions About How to Learn

There are many ways to organize the large body of theory and research on student learning. For this chapter, the term *stylistic attributes* is used to capture the range of student characteristics that reflect students' learning preferences and approaches. In contrast to the assumptions about knowing and learning discussed above in the section on learning and epistemology, these characteristics are typically assumed to be fairly stable over time.

The term *learning style* has become quite familiar to educators seeking to respond helpfully to individual differences among the students with whom they work. Several researchers have argued for the importance of distinguishing between learning styles and strategies and that an understanding of learning strategies is essential for understanding learning styles. Schmeck (1988) defined a learning strategy as "a sequence of procedures for accomplishing learning" (p. 5). A strategy must be intentionally invoked, and it requires a conscious decision to follow a specified plan of action.

Effective learners draw from a broad repertoire of strategies, such as clarifying the author's purpose, outlining the chapter to identify the main points and supporting evidence, making evaluative judgments about the strength of the arguments presented, making predictions, identifying implications, or exchanging sample test questions with friends. Failure to solve a problem may reflect not only a poor choice of strategy but a variety of other factors, such as a lack of necessary skills to implement the strategy, a misunderstanding of the purposes of the activity, or an unwillingness to take the time to use the preferred strategy.

By contrast, a learning style is "a predisposition to adopt a particular learning strategy" (Das, 1988, p. 101), or the habitual use of similar strategies (Kirby, 1988) across situations or contexts, or a preference for processing information (Jonassen & Grabowski, 1993). For example, a student might typically study a text by reviewing the chapter outline, main headings, and summaries, comparing these to his or her class notes, looking up unfamiliar words or concepts, and periodically reviewing memorized information. Establishing this as a student's style requires multiple observations of that student in similar circumstances, not just one observation of a single event (Schmeck, 1988). For a study that examined both preferred styles and used strategies, see Shuford (2000). Although the authors of the work discussed below often do not distinguish between styles and strategies, readers are encouraged to keep this in mind as they read about the approaches described below.

The next section of this chapter summarizes several models that describe different learning styles and strategies. Following these summaries is a discussion that attempts to integrate the major features of the various models, noting their implications for working with college students.

Field Dependence and Independence. Witkin's (1976) work on cognitive style has received a great deal of attention in educational circles. Witkin focused on the dimension of field dependence or independence, measuring the degree to which individuals are heavily influenced by (dependent upon) or relatively uninfluenced by (independent of) their surrounding context. Whereas a field-dependent person tends to see a situation globally (seeing the whole instead of its parts), the field-independent person tends to see a situation more analytically (separating the parts from the whole).

Witkin's model has an extensive (but dated) research base (Bertini, Pizzamiglio, & Wapner, 1986; Witkin & Goodenough, 1981; Witkin, Moore, Goodenough, & Cox, 1977). In 1989, a Herman A. Witkin Memorial Conference was held; in their collection of selected papers prepared for that conference, Wapner and Demick, (1991) noted that a computerized literature search over the last fifteen years had yielded more than 800 published papers. Witkin (1976) reported that field-dependent students tended to be involved in majors and careers that have a strong interpersonal dimension, such as teaching, counseling, and sales. Field-independent students tended to be involved in majors and careers that focus on analytic skills, such as mathematics, engineering, and science. In a comprehensive literature review of studies conducted between 1976 and 1988, Davis (1991) concluded that the construct of field dependence has components consistent with both an ability and a style, but that ability differences seem to be operating to a much greater degree than stylistic differences. Field-independent learners are more efficient than field dependent learners in implementing appropriate strategies and in efficiently using a variety of cognitive processes. Consequently, they do better on many learning and achievement tasks (p. 165).

Some differences by gender and ethnic group have been observed, with White women, Native Americans, African Americans, and Hispanics tending to fall toward the field-dependent end of the continuum, with White and Asian men tending to score at the field-independent end of the continuum (Anderson & Adams, 1992; Shade, 1982). However, there is a great deal of variability in these findings and their interpretations (see, for example, Berry, 1991; Demick, 1991; Santostefano, 1991). Although the volume of research on this construct has slowed significantly in recent years, it continues to inform practice in higher education (Cano, 1999; Ford & Chen, 2001; Garton, Dyer, & King, 2000). For example, some researchers have asked whether learning style affects the strategies students use for searching data bases (Ford, 2000) or for learning in technology-based courses (Grasha & Yangarber-Hicks, 2000); to date, these studies have yielded mixed results.

Psychological Type and Learning Styles. The Myers-Briggs Type Indicator (MBTI) (Myers, 1980) has been used extensively to document differences based on the ways individuals tend to take in information (the perception function) and make judgments (the judgment function). Since the Myers-Briggs model is described by Nancy Evans in Chapter Nine, only its relevance to student learning is noted here.

Although literature reviews report mixed results in terms of validating the model's theoretical claims (for example, see Murray, 1990, and Pittenger, 1993), it has been widely applied in both business and higher education settings (Provost & Anchors, 1987). Jensen (1987) summarized the preferred learning styles by type; these are reprinted here as Exhibit 11.5.

EXHIBIT 11.5. TYPE AND LEARNING STYLES.

Extraversion (E)

Es learn best in situations filled with movement, action, and talk. They prefer to learn theories or facts that connect with their experience, and they will usually come to a more thorough understanding of these theories or facts during group discussions or when working on cooperative projects. Es tend to leap into assignments with little "forethought," relying on trial-and-error rather than anticipation to solve problems.

Introversion (I)

Since Is may be more quiet and less active in the classroom, teachers may feel the need to press them into taking part in group discussions. Such pressure, however, will often only increase their withdrawal. Teachers need to respect their need to think in relative solitude, for that is how they think best. Is will be more willing to share their ideas when given advance notice. This will allow them time to think about how they will become active in the classroom.

Sensory Perception (S)

Ss learn best when they move from the concrete to the abstract in a step-by-step progression. They are thus at home with programmed, modular, or computer-assisted learning. They value knowledge that is practical and want to be precise and accurate in their own work. They tend to excel at memorizing facts.

Intuitive Perception (N)

Ns tend to leap to a conceptual understanding of material and may daydream or act-out during drill work or predominantly factual lectures. They value quick flashes of insight but are often careless about details. They tend to excel at imaginative tasks and theoretical topics.

Thinking Judgment (T)

Ts are most motivated when provided with a logical rationale for each project and when teachers acknowledge and respect their competence. They prefer topics that help them to understand systems or cause-and-effect relationships. Their thought is syllogistic and analytic.

Feeling Judgment (F)

Fs are most motivated when given personal encouragement and when shown the human angle of a topic. Fs think to clarify their values and to establish networks of values. Even when their expressions seem syllogistic, they usually evolve from some personally held belief or value.

Judgment (J)

Js tend to gauge their learning by the completion of tasks: reading "x" amount of books, writing "x" amount of papers, or making "x" amount of reports. They thus prefer more structured learning environments that establish goals for them to meet.

Perception (P)

Ps tend to view learning as a free-wheeling, flexible quest. They care less about deadlines and the completion of tasks. They prefer open and spontaneous learning environments and feel "imprisoned" in a highly structured classroom.

Source: Jensen (1987). Reprinted with permission.

Educators who are aware of these phenomena approaches can help students understand and evaluate their preferred learning strategies and the experiences on which their preferences might be based. They can also help students discern how different learning contexts call for different strategies (for example, strategies for gathering background information for a concert series differ from strategies for identifying solutions to an interpersonal conflict), and encourage students to vary their strategies according to the specific characteristics of the problem at hand. (For a discussion of the importance of fostering personal development concurrently with learning, see King & Baxter Magolda, 1996.)

Surface and Deep Approaches. Marton and Säljö (1976a, 1976b) investigated two distinct strategies students use when reading academic texts. Students who use a surface approach focus on verbatim recall of facts or ideas as if they were self-standing and self-explanatory. They "may well fail to distinguish between essential points and incidental facts or between principles and examples. They are unlikely to relate evidence and conclusions or examine the argument in a critical way" (Entwistle, 1988, p. 25). As a result, they risk missing the main point of the reading. By contrast, students who use a deep approach to learning intentionally try to establish connections between their prior learning and new information or ideas in the text. They have a personally meaningful purpose for learning, and their role as learner includes evaluating and reconstructing knowledge. (This assumption is discussed more fully above in the section on learning and epistemology.) These students use "an active process of learning in which the student challenges the ideas, evidence, and arguments presented by the author, tries to see interrelationships among the ideas presented, and seeks links with personal experience and the outside world" (Entwistle, 1988, p. 24).

A similar pair of contrasting learning styles are Schmeck's (1981) "shallow-reiterative" and "deep-elaborative" information processing approaches. In the first style, students "prefer to assimilate information as given rather than rewording, restating, or rethinking it" (p. 385); in the second, they "classify, contrast, analyze, and synthesize information from different sources" (p. 385). The success of the deep approach was documented by Gadzella, Ginter, and Bryant (1997) in a study of classroom performance, and by Miller, Alway, and McKinley (1987), who found that students who used the deep approach had higher GPAs. Holschuh (2000) found that unlike their low performing classmates, high performing students in introductory biology used more deep learning and domain-specific strategies (that is, those that were pertinent to the demands of this course) and could explain the reasons for choice of strategies. She recommended that instructors as well as staff in learning assistance centers directly teach students about the selection of study strategies for particular types of courses (such as introductory science courses), and the drawbacks of relying heavily on surface strategies such as memorizing terms.

These learning styles reflect not only differences in approaches to learning but also differences in students' conceptions of learning itself. Van Rossum and Schenk (1984) found that virtually all those who used a surface approach defined learning according to one of the two simplest categories, an increase in knowledge or memorization.

By contrast, virtually all those who used a deep approach to learning defined learning as the abstraction of meaning or as an interpretive process aimed at understanding the world.

The deep approach to learning is clearly more consistent with the aim of colleges to teach students to think more critically. Educators should encourage students to read and listen actively, to use a more complex frame of reference than the immediate text or speaker, and to establish connections that link the ideas to each other in context, and that link their prior knowledge to the new ideas presented.

Are there differences by race in students' learning styles? Many authors have raised this question (Anderson, 1988; Bell, 1994; Gadzella, Masten, & Huang, 1999; Hale-Benson, 1988; Shade, 1989), and those who have conducted studies have tended to focus on learning style differences among children of different racial and cultural backgrounds. Shuford (2000) addressed this question in a study of the preferred learning styles, used strategies, and active learning practices of first-year African American and White college students. Her findings point to the importance of differentiating between styles and strategies when considering students' approaches to the learning process and of the need to better understand why students' preferred style was not related to their used strategies. (For a related discussion of cultural factors affecting learning, see Silverman & Casazza, 2000.)

Kolb's Experiential Learning Theory. Kolb (1984) defined learning as "the process whereby knowledge is created through the transformation of experience" (p. 38). He described four adaptive modes of learning, based on how individuals perceive information (through concrete experience or abstract conceptualization) and how they process it (through reflective observation or active experimentation). From these two dimensions, Kolb identified four distinct types of learners (divergers, assimilators, convergers, and accommodators), each characterized by specific competencies.

Divergers take in information through concrete experience and transform it through reflective observation. This style "is associated with *valuing skills:* being sensitive to people's feelings and to values, listening with an open mind, gathering information, and imagining implications of ambiguous situations" (pp. 93–94).

Assimilators take in information through abstract conceptualization and transform it through reflective observation. This style "is related to *thinking competencies:* organizing information, building conceptual models, testing theories and ideas, designing experiments, and analyzing quantitative data" (p. 94).

Convergers take in information through abstract conceptualization and transform it through active experimentation. This style "is associated with *decision skills:* creating new ways of thinking and doing, experimenting with new ideas, choosing the best solution to problems, setting goals, and making decisions" (pp. 94–95).

Accommodators take in information through concrete experience and transform it through active experimentation. This style "encompasses a set of competencies that can best be termed *acting skills:* committing oneself to objectives, seeking and exploiting opportunities, influencing and leading others, being personally involved, and dealing with people" (p. 93).

The explanatory power of Kolb's model is greatly increased by his attention to learning environments that complement each learning style. Applying the model to diversity education, Rainey and Kolb (1995) identified six aspects of learning environments that correspond to each learning mode. In Exhibit 11.6, the four types of learning environments (affectively, perceptually, cognitively, and behaviorally oriented) correspond to the four learning modes (concrete experience, reflective observation, abstract conceptualization, and active experimentation, respectively). Another distinctive feature of Kolb's work is that he discussed developmental implications within dimensions of his model, suggesting that development "is marked by increasing complexity and relativism in dealing with the world and one's experience and by higher-level integrations of the dialectic conflicts among the four primary learning modes" (p. 140).

Multiple Intelligences. Gardner's (1987, 1993) theory of multiple intelligences describes seven distinctive ways people process information. It helps explain what people can and cannot do well and how they become different kinds of problem solvers and problem finders. He defines intelligence as "an ability to solve a problem or to fashion a product which is valued in one or more cultural settings" (Gardner, 1987, p. 25). His theory includes seven domains of intelligence (see Exhibit 11.7), which are assumed to be largely independent. For example, a person who can readily remember names and faces often cannot as readily remember math formulas or words in a poem; linguistic ability does not predict spatial ability. Further, each intelligence is assumed to have its own developmental trajectory, so development across intelligences is assumed to proceed at different paces. He argues that the purpose of education should be to develop diverse intelligences, to help individuals become intelligent in more than one domain.

Different roles or occupations are associated with each type of intelligence, as well as with combinations of the different types. For example, spatial intelligence is required for navigators and sculptors, and interpersonal intelligence is required for counselors and salespeople. Surgeons require both spatial and bodily-kinesthetic intelligence to manipulate scalpels with accuracy and dexterity.

Educators can use Gardner's concept of the seven intelligences to clarify both the content of what they teach (for example, interpersonal or linguistic skills) and the means for students to respond to it (for example, through language, music, or space). Such an approach gives educators a new tool for analyzing and selecting appropriate responses to students who possess intelligences that have not traditionally been stressed in academic environments. For example, it offers more support for the idea that some people prefer to learn using their sight (visual learners), others learn better using their ears (auditory learners), and still others learn better using their tactile or kinesthetic senses (see Sarasin, 1999, for an extended discussion of these three approaches). For examples of instructional techniques in the sciences grounded in multiple intelligences, see Manner (2001).

Self-Regulated Learning. The literature on self-regulated learning is only one slice of a much larger body of literature on teaching and learning and student approaches

EXHIBIT 11.6. LEARNING ENVIRONMENTS AND THEIR DISTINCT VARIABLES.

	Learning Environment			
	Affectively Oriented	**Perceptionally Oriented**	**Cognitively Oriented**	**Behaviorally Oriented**
Purpose	Develop personal awareness and insight	Appreciate and understand how and why things relate	Acquire and master knowledge and skills	Actively apply learning to real life situations
Information source	"Here and now" concrete experience	Multiple data sources viewed in different ways	"There and then" abstract concepts and facts	Activities directed toward requirements of task completion
Rules of behavior	Free expression of feelings, values, and opinions	Emphasis on process and inquiry	Adherence to prescribed objective criteria	Minimal rules in support of learner autonomy
Nature of feedback	Personalized and immediate from teachers and peers	Nonevaluative suggestions rather than critiques	Evaluation of correct or incorrect learner output	Learner judges own performance based on established standards
Teacher role	Role model and colleague	Process facilitator	Interpreter of a field of knowledge	Coach and advisor
Activities	Check-in, guided imagery to create experience, or debate	Causal mapping, maintaining a diary, or brainstorming	Presenting concepts, developing personal theories, or traditional testing	Developing action plans, a simulation, or leaderless work teams

Source: Rainey and Kolb (1995). Reprinted with permission.

EXHIBIT 11.7. GARDNER'S MULTIPLE INTELLIGENCES.

Intelligence	Associated Abilities
Linguistic	Sensitivity to the sounds, rhythms, and meanings of words; sensitivity to the different functions of language
Logical-Mathematical	Sensitivity to and capacity to discern logical or numerical patterns; ability to handle long chains of reasoning
Musical	Abilities to produce and appreciate rhythm, pitch, and timbre; appreciation of the forms of musical expressiveness
Spatial	Capacities to perceive the visual-spatial world accurately and to perform transformations on one's initial perceptions
Bodily-Kinesthetic	Abilities to control one's body movements and to handle objects skillfully
Interpersonal	Capacities to discern and respond appropriately to the moods, temperaments, motivations, and desires of other people
Intrapersonal	Access to one's own feelings and the ability to discriminate among them and draw upon them to guide behavior; knowledge of one's own strengths, weaknesses, desires, and intelligences

Source: Gardner and Hatch (1989) as cited in King (1996). Copyright 1989 by American Educational Research Association. Reprinted with permission.

to studying (for example, Entwistle & Tait, 1995; Feldman & Paulsen, 1994). Pintrich (1995) defined three characteristics of self-regulated learners. First, they actively attempt to control their behavior, motivation, affect, and cognition; this allows them to make adjustments based on the characteristics of the learning environment. Second, these learners are attempting to accomplish a goal; this provides a standard against which they can monitor and adjust their own performance (Hadwin, Winn, Stockley, Nesbit, & Woszczyna, 2001). And third, self-regulated learners are in control of their actions; their behavior is internally motivated rather than being determined by someone else (for example, behaviors done only because the instructor was in the room or required the strategy).

Although the language and underlying theoretical assumptions about development are different, this approach has elements that are similar to Kegan's (1994) concept of self-authorship (for a comparison, see McEvoy, 2002). In both models, students are encouraged to take responsibility for their own learning, for making their own choices about how to respond to the demands of the environments in which they must function (such as where, when, and how to study), and how to make these choices reflect and complement their learning goals. Both also acknowledge that encouraging students to be self-regulated or self-authored may require teachers to adapt to a new role (Schunk & Zimmerman, 1994), that of a guide on the student's educational journey.

The Science of Learning. In the late 1990s, the National Research Council, in cooperation with the National Academy of Sciences, the National Academy of Engineering, and the Institute of Medicine completed a two-year study of student learning.

Their follow-up report by Bransford, Brown, and Cocking (2000), *How People Learn,* is widely regarded as a significant contribution to the field, in part because it is specifically designed to link research on the science of learning to educational practices. This volume is grounded in three key research findings that have a substantive research base and strong implications for teaching.

First, "students come to the classroom with preconceptions about how the world works. If their initial understanding is not engaged, they may fail to grasp the new concepts and information that are taught, or they may learn them for purposes of a test but revert to their preconceptions outside the classroom" (pp. 14–15). This finding is similar to the constructivist epistemological approach introduced above; using it to guide practice requires educators to identify and work with preexisting understandings. In language familiar in student affairs, educators must "accept students where they are."

Second, "to develop competence in an area of inquiry, students must: (a) have a deep foundation of factual knowledge, (b) understand facts and ideas in the context of a conceptual framework, and (c) organize knowledge in ways that facilitate retrieval and application" (p. 16). These observations are grounded in research comparing the problem-solving of experts and novices, where experts show a much more complex understanding of concepts, and which shapes the way they learn about and interpret new information. Accordingly, educators are encouraged to teach their subjects in depth, using many examples from which students can see connections and then extrapolate to new situations.

Third, "a 'metacognitive' approach to instruction can help students learn to take control of their own learning by defining learning goals and monitoring their progress in achieving them" (p. 18). This finding is similar to the earlier discussion of self-regulated learning, including their study strategies. This approach provides a new language and rationale for educators who intentionally foster goal setting and who encourage and expect students to take responsibility for their own choices.

Although the research on which this approach has been based has been done predominantly with students in K–12 educational settings and in science classes, researchers and teachers are beginning to apply these principles to their work with college students. For example, Weigel (2002) used the concept of cognitive apprenticeships (modeling, coaching, scaffolding, and so on) to design technology-assisted instruction. Others (such as Gruber, Law, Mandl, & Renkl, 1996; Holyoak & Koh, 1987; Phye, 2001) have noted the limited evidence of college students' ability to transfer learning to new situations. Bransford and Schwartz (1999) critiqued many transfer studies and proposed an alternative view of transfer, preparation for future learning.

Cognitive science has some conceptual similarities with other approaches to learning but is distinctive in its emphasis on science learning and on neuroscience. Although the connections to educational practices with adults are not yet established, this is an area that has clear potential for higher education, and as such, merits the attention of college educators. As Bransford et al (2000) noted, "One of the hallmarks of the new science of learning is its emphasis on learning with understanding" (p. 8), a goal that directly applies across traditional educational level boundaries.

Summary: Integrating Models of Learning Styles and Strategies. Several of these models of learning styles and strategies include similar sets of elements. Several researchers use contrasting pairs of strategies to describe observed differences. Different combinations of strategies are characterized by a preferred strategy for approaching a problem or situation—for example, a "big picture" approach (seeing the forest) versus a detailed approach (seeing the trees). Some readers may think the prevalent use of dichotomies in strategies conveys an unduly bifurcated view of the world. However, this degree of consistency between theories led Schmeck (1988) to speculate that these dichotomies are collectively describing an underlying construct, which he refers to as *global-holistic* and *focused-detailed* approaches. For example, compare the preferred learning "styles" or reasoning strategies of Witkin's field independents, Kolb's assimilators, those who prefer Myers-Briggs's sensing and thinking approaches, and those with what Gardner would call high logical-mathematical intelligence. Students who prefer these approaches might need more encouragement and practice in seeing the big picture and the main points, undertaking independent projects, seeing implications, considering "What if?" questions, and solving problems that require understanding of conceptual distinctions or theories.

By contrast, consider Witkin's field dependents, Kolb's divergers, those who prefer Myers-Briggs's intuitive and feeling approaches, and those with what Gardner would call high interpersonal intelligence. Students who prefer these approaches might need more encouragement and practice keeping track of relevant details, being accurate and precise, developing logical arguments, solving deductive problems that require step-by-step procedures, and thinking analytically and deductively.

Most learning style models present such contrasting approaches as two equally effective means of addressing and resolving problems. (In fact, only two of the models summarized above designated educationally preferable strategies—the deep versus the surface approach to learning and the scientific reasoning studies, which are developmentally based.) This stance has the advantages of affirming individuals "where they are" and showing respect for individual differences. This focus on appreciating differences and making nonevaluative judgments is appealing to faculty and staff alike, in part because giving feedback to students about their approach is correspondingly descriptive rather than judgmental, which helps create a more inviting and affirming type of contact with students.

The nonjudgmental approach creates difficulties, however, when the student faces problems for which his or her preferred approach is not effective. At such times the student needs to strengthen skills associated with his or her "auxiliary" (nonpreferred) approach; the role of the educator then changes to someone who can help the student overcome whatever obstacles impede his or her success, including acknowledging the weaknesses of the preferred approach.

While this group of learning models uses contrasting styles to point out differences, it is important for educators to note that these styles are frequently the extreme endpoints of a continuum, with many students falling between them. In other words, most people do not rely exclusively on the skills associated with one approach to learning or one end of a given continuum of learning styles. This is an encouraging observation, as the most advanced or adaptive styles and the most effective learning strategies often require integration of elements from both extremes. Educators should be cautioned against the temptation to label a student as though he or she possesses only one set of talents, skills, or sensitivities—as a "visual learner," or a "feeling type," for example—instead of acknowledging the student's attributes as points on a continuum.

When a student is encouraged to learn about his or her learning style, it erroneously implies that the student has just one style. This in turn suggests rigidity rather than flexibility or development as the educational goal. The same concerns apply to a student's "leadership style," which suggests inflexibility or resistance to different styles and an inability to adapt to different needs. Instead students should be encouraged to learn about and evaluate their own preferences for learning, since approaches, styles, and strategies are typically defined in terms of both strengths and weaknesses. They should also be encouraged to develop new strategies for learning that are appropriate to the situation at hand and to practice thinking through their own selection of strategies.

Should educators select their strategies based on culture and race? There appears to be a widespread assumption that learning styles differ for students of different ethnic minority groups. This conclusion may be premature, however: "Although the current research base does not demonstrate definitive links between learning style and race, culture, or gender, consistent cultural and educational findings across such disciplines as psychology, sociology, anthropology and linguistics suggest some correlations" (Anderson & Adams, 1992, p. 20). Most studies of cultural differences in learning styles and strategies have been conducted using school-age children; comparable research using college students has been rather limited (Shuford, 2000). The assertion that significant cultural differences in learning styles can be observed—for example, that African American students and women are field-dependent learners and White males are field-independent learners—is at this point a sweeping generalization unsubstantiated by the research (Frisby, 1993). Students of all cultural and racial backgrounds should be encouraged to develop learning strategies that are flexible and suited for the specific demands and constraints of the problem at hand. In this regard, many ethnic minority college students may have an advantage in that they move between two cultures, the dominant culture and their own, adapting their learning style, language, and dress to the two cultures as needed. Many college students are bicultural (Cortez, 2000), and many students of color live bicultural lives, especially those at predominantly White institutions. Having learned to adapt their strategies to meet cultural demands, they may be more able to adapt to situational demands of different learning environments, such as adopting strategies needed to succeed in analytical, field-independent classrooms (Shuford, 1995). Whether a bicultural background contributes to the paucity of learning style differences among minorities documented in the literature is a topic worthy of additional research.

Taking students' learning strategies into account, educators can help students effectively adapt their methods of learning to the specific tasks and contexts at hand. As Weinstein and Meyer (1991) note, "to be successful in selecting and using a strategy, students must understand under what circumstances a given strategy is or is not appropriate" (p. 17). This task arguably requires both self-authorship and self-regulated learning.

Practices That Encourage Student Learning

How then can educators encourage student learning? This section includes a discussion of the ways in which technology can be used to promote learning and of the conditions that promote learning.

Using Technology to Promote Learning

The rapid increase in the development of technology in the latter decades of the twentieth century has been used both to bridge geographical distances that served as barriers to access for many students and to support instruction and student services. When William Raney Harper established a correspondence program at the University of Chicago in 1890, these efforts were dismissed by many educators as "simply poor excuses for the real thing" (McIsaac & Gunawardena, 2001, p. 1), a criticism still heard regarding some uses of technology in education.

Today, colleges and universities have made major investments in technology and are still exploring and creating ways of applying its potential to improve learning outcomes. While there is a tremendous amount of interest in the design and delivery of technology-based education, little research has been conducted on student learning outcomes (Grasha & Yangarber-Hicks, 2000; McIsaac & Gunawardena, 2001).

Several authors have noted how technology affects relationships, including those between instructors and students and among students. McIsaac and Gunawardena (2001) use the notion of *transactional distance* in educational relationships to describe an important aspect of the instructor-student relationship. Transactional distance is determined by the structure of the course and the nature of the instructor-student dialogue: the more structured and limited the dialogue, the greater the distance experienced by the learner. Thus, "distance is not determined by geography but by the relationship between dialogue and structure" (p. 2).

Because it seems to utilize principles of active learning, many researchers have called for enhanced interactivity in technology-based education (Canada, 2000; McIsaac & Gunawardena, 2001; McLellan, 1999; Rose, 1999; Schwitzer, Ancis, & Brown, 2001), which Liaw and Huang (2000) defined as communication between individuals with the intention of explaining and challenging viewpoints, using either a task or social orientation. Studies have shown that interactivity in online courses actively engaged learners in knowledge construction (for example, Muirhead, 2001; Northrup, 2001; Petraglia, 1998). Enhanced interactivity appears to be correlated with higher academic achievement (Jiang & Ting, 1998) and the perception by students that courses are more meaningful, thus motivating them to perform at higher levels (Parry & Dunn, 2000).

Knowlton (2000) focused on another aspect of online relationships, arguing that technology-based courses should be student centered and that the professor's role in an online classroom is "*to frame* the course and supplement student interactions by providing resources and opportunities" (p. 11; italics in original), as sketched by the outside line in Figure 11.1. He also pointed out that the professor's focus should "on managing the learning experience, not on managing the technology" (p. 11). This figure shows the kinds of resources the instructor can use to frame these opportunities. Knowlton's (2000) model emphasizes the importance of making online courses student-centered and humanizing the online experience through collaboration with the instructor and with peers in a community of learners. This notion is consistent with Baxter Magolda's (1999) call to situate learning in the student's experience and to emphasize the mutual construction of meaning.

Educators and administrators should also be aware that many aspects of technology and technology usage are value-laden, not value-neutral. For example, Knupfer (1998) identified gender stereotypes in Internet advertising and web pages, noting that women were portrayed in decorative, subordinate, or seductive roles while men held positions of activity and authority—even on government web sites. Educators are advised to be sensitive to explicit and implicit values being portrayed in software, advising, and so on, and to sensitize their students to the value dimensions of this medium.

A further concern is teaching students to evaluate the credibility of web sites to make judgments about the inclusion of information found there when preparing one's academic work (Canada, 2000). Many universities offer web pages to assist students in determining whether a source is credible, using criteria such as the intention of the author, the relevance and currency of the material, and the reliability of the content; one such example from the University of Michigan is http://www.lib.umich.edu/ugl/research/evaluation/. Given the evaluative demands involved in

FIGURE 11.1. THE ONLINE CLASSROOM.

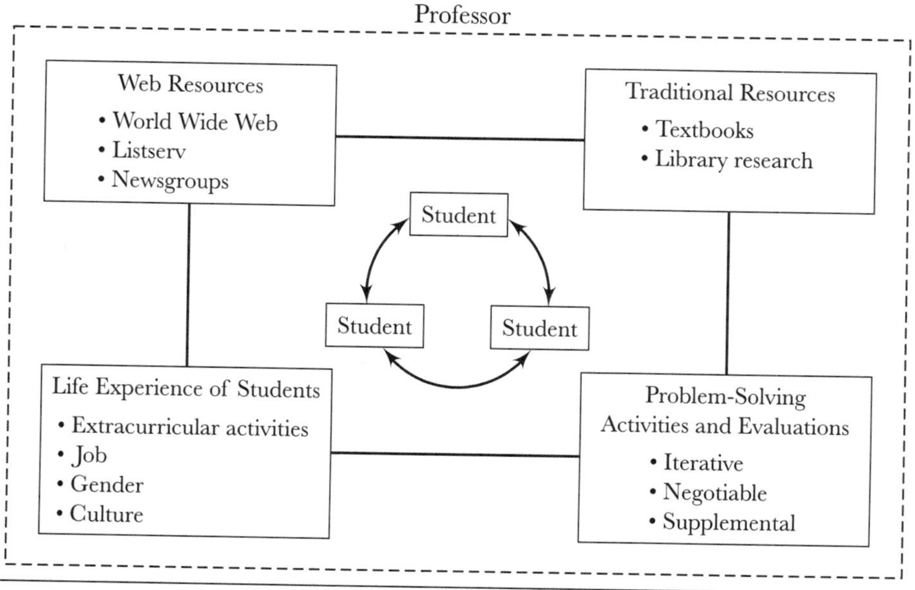

Professor

Web Resources
- World Wide Web
- Listserv
- Newsgroups

Traditional Resources
- Textbooks
- Library research

Student

Student

Student

Life Experience of Students
- Extracurricular activities
- Job
- Gender
- Culture

Problem-Solving Activities and Evaluations
- Iterative
- Negotiable
- Supplemental

Source: Knowlton (2000), p. 12.

making such interpretations, educators are also encouraged to recognize that those functioning at early levels of cognitive development will find such tasks difficult, and perhaps overwhelming, and may need additional assistance learning how to make these kinds of judgments.

Those wishing to learn more about technology-based education are encouraged to consult publications that focus on technology as well as those that focus on education. Suggested web sites to begin learning about education and technology include the following: http://www.ed.gov/Technology/distance.html from the U.S. Department of Education, Office of Educational Technology, and http://www.educause.edu. EDUCAUSE is a nonprofit organization designed to enhance higher education through technology, offering many links to related pages.

Student affairs professionals can play a vital role in supporting positive student learning outcomes in technology-based education (Schwitzer, Ancis, & Brown, 2001) by consulting with faculty about ways to develop a sense of community for students in online courses and providing information on students who use technology, and on strategies to promote interaction (Schwitzer et al., 2001). However, without conceptual models guiding its use (see Weigel, 2002) and research evaluating the effectiveness of technology to promote student learning and development, it will be difficult to address skeptics' concerns that these approaches are, in McIsaac and Gunawardena's (2001) words, "poor excuses for the real thing" (p. 1), and to realize the potential of these new tools to promote student learning and the achievement of desired educational outcomes.

Conditions That Promote Learning

Many excellent resources are now available that identify educational practices that enhance learning (Baxter Magolda, 1992, 1999, 2000, 2001; Brown, 1994; Brown & Campione, 1990; Chickering & Gamson, 1987; Chickering & Reisser, 1993; Claxton & Murrell, 1987; Davis, 1993; Davis & Murrell, 1993; Johnson, Johnson, & Smith, 1991; Love & Guthrie, 1999; Menges & Svinicki, 1991; Silverman & Casazza, 2000; Vasquez & Wainstein, 1990). In addition, several recent national reports have acknowledged the importance of learning principles in creating learning contexts and have called for educators and administrators to apply these when planning educational programs and services. For example, three major professional associations, AAHE, ACPA, and NASPA, created a joint task force to produce a major report on promoting student learning in higher education called "Powerful Partnerships: A Shared Responsibility," which was published in 1998. The title itself reflects one of the main messages of the report, that learning is enhanced when it is seen as a responsibility to be shared by many across the campus. This report is built on ten principles of learning; a full copy of this report is available on the website of each sponsoring organization. Engelkemeyer and Brown (1998) offered examples of campus actions for each learning principle; these are listed with in Exhibit 11.8. This report shows how good practices are tied to principles of learning, and offers a powerful rationale for their implementation.

EXHIBIT 11.8. LEARNING PRINCIPLES AND COLLABORATIVE ACTION.

Learning Principle	Campus Action
1. Learning is fundamentally about *making and maintaining connections:* biologically through neural networks; mentally among concepts, ideas, and meanings; and experientially through interaction between the mind and the environment, self and other, generality and context, deliberation and action.	• Expose students to alternative world views and culturally diverse perspectives. • Give students responsibility for solving problems and resolving conflicts. • Make explicit the relationships among parts of the curriculum and between the curriculum and other aspects of the collegiate experience. • Deliberately personalize interventions appropriate to individual circumstances and needs.
2. Learning is enhanced by *taking place in the context of a compelling situation* that balances challenge and opportunity, stimulating and utilizing the brain's ability to conceptualize quickly and its capacity and need for contemplation and reflection upon experiences.	• Articulate and enforce high standards of student behavior inside and outside the classroom. • Give students increasing responsibility for leadership. • Create environments and schedules that encourage intensive activity as well as opportunities for quiet deliberation. • Establish internships, externships, service-learning, study abroad, and workplace-based learning experiences.
3. Learning is an *active search for meaning* by the learner—constructing knowledge rather than passively receiving it, shaping as well as being shaped by experiences.	• Expect and demand student participation in activities in and beyond the classroom. • Design projects and endeavors through which students apply their knowledge and skills. • Build programs that feature extended and increasingly challenging opportunities for growth and development.
4. Learning is *developmental,* a cumulative process *involving the whole person,* relating past and present, integrating the new with the old, starting from but transcending personal concerns and interests.	• Design educational programs to build progressively on each experience. • Track student development through portfolios that document levels of competence achieved and intentional activities leading to personal development. • Establish arenas for student-faculty interaction in social and community settings. • Present opportunities for discussion and reflection on the meaning of all collegiate experiences.
5. Learning is done by *individuals* who are intrinsically *tied to others as social beings,* interacting as competitors or collaborators, constraining or supporting the learning process, and able to enhance learning through cooperation and sharing.	• Strive to develop a campus culture where students learn to help each other. • Establish peer tutoring and student and faculty mentorship programs. • Sponsor residence hall and commuting programs that cultivate student and faculty interaction for social and educational purposes. • Support activities that enable students from different cultural backgrounds to experience each other's traditions.

(*Continued*)

EXHIBIT 11.8. LEARNING PRINCIPLES AND COLLABORATIVE ACTION. (*CONTINUED*)

Learning Principle	Campus Action
6. Learning is *strongly affected by the educational climate* in which it takes place; the settings and surroundings, the influences of others, and the values accorded to the life of the mind and to learning achievements.	• Build a strong sense of community among all institutional constituencies. • Organize ceremonies to honor and highlight contributions to community life and educational values. • Publicly celebrate institutional values. • Articulate how each administrative and academic unit serves the institution's mission. • Share and use information on how units are performing in relation to this mission.
7. Learning requires *frequent feedback* if it is to be sustained, *practice* if it is to be nourished, and *opportunities to use* what has been learned.	• Recruit students with relevant academic interests as active participants and leaders in related campus life programs and activities. • Organize work opportunities to take advantage of students' developing skills and knowledge. • Collaborate with businesses and community organizations to match students to internship and externship experiences that fit their evolving educational profiles. • Develop student research and design projects based on actual problems or cases presented by external organizations to be resolved.
8. Much learning *takes place informally and incidentally,* beyond explicit teaching or the classroom, in casual contacts with faculty and staff, peers, campus life, active social and community involvements, and unplanned but fertile and complex situations.	• Sponsor programs for students, faculty, and staff that serve both social and educational purposes. • Organize community service and service-learning activities performed by faculty, staff, and students together. • Design campus life programs that relate directly to specific courses. • Link students with peers and with faculty, staff, and community mentors. • Build common gathering places for students, faculty, and staff.
9. Learning is *grounded in particular contexts and individual experiences,* requiring effort to transfer specific knowledge and skills to other circumstances or to more general understandings and to unlearn personal views and approaches when confronted by new information.	• Sponsor events that involve students with new people and situations. • Champion occasions for interdisciplinary discourse on salient issues. • Foster dialogues between people with disparate perspectives and backgrounds. • Expand study abroad and cultural exchange programs.
10. Learning involves the *ability of individuals to monitor their own learning,* to understand how knowledge is acquired, to develop strategies for learning based on discerning their capacities and limitations, and to be aware of their own ways of knowing in approaching new bodies of knowledge and disciplinary frameworks.	• Help students delineate and articulate their learning interests, strengths, and deficiencies. • Reduce the risk to students of acknowledging their own limitations. • Help students select curricular and other educational experiences covering a broad range of learning approaches and performance evaluations. • Create faculty and staff development activities to learn about advances in learning theory and practice.

Source: Engelkemeyer and Brown (October 1998). Reprinted with permission.

In an attempt to summarize the major suggestions from theories and research on learning among college students and national reports on reforming undergraduate education, I offer the following summary. Student learning is enhanced when:

1. Students can *learn with and from each other* and when educational practices take advantage of the social contexts in which learning occurs.
2. Students devote sufficient quantity of time and quality of effort to educationally purposeful activities.
3. Students are *actively engaged* in the learning process.
4. Students can *build on what they already know,* showing how learning is cumulative.
5. The topic is *personally meaningful,* when they see the connections to their lives.
6. *The curriculum and cocurriculum are structured to achieve common learning goals,* both broadly defined (such as develop verbal communication skills) and specifically defined (such as adapt the delivery of a message to different audiences).
7. *Educators in different campus settings reinforce each other's efforts.* They can do so through their shared emphasis on the development of targeted skills, through the use of publicly known frameworks and terms for discussing intended educational outcomes.
8. Students *frequently practice targeted skills* (such as critical thinking and conflict resolution), do so in different settings (such as philosophy class and a judicial board hearing), and receive helpful feedback on their performance.
9. There is *coherence to their learning,* that is, when they learn how various areas of knowledge and skills are related to each other. Interdisciplinary and cluster courses do this, for example, by addressing broad themes such as ecology or leadership from several perspectives.
10. Educators *acknowledge the emotional dimensions* of learning and learn how to integrate such reactions into their frames of reference for learning and understanding. Emotionally charged issues (such as ethical dilemmas, gender roles, and race relations) provide excellent topics to explore these connections, and how emotional reactions can enhance or inhibit learning.
11. Both challenge and support are present.
12. Educators make explicit reference to the process of learning and to students' preferred learning strategies (not styles), and when they encourage students to vary their strategies according to the problem at hand.
13. Educators should encourage students to think how they interact with classmates, how they prepare for class, and how they apply skills learned in one context to another.
14. There is a *reciprocal, trusting relationship* with the educators from whom and with whom they are learning. Educators must respect students as persons (at whatever developmental level they may be exhibiting); students should be willing to try to build on who they are, knowing that building a new self means changing aspects of oneself.
15. There is a *strong institutional commitment to creating a pervasive culture for learning.* For example, Stephen Brookfield suggests that when making decisions, administrators should ask, "How does this decision help institutional members *learn*?"

16. *Student learning is viewed holistically* to include many domains of development. Thus, aspects of learning include at least three dimensions: (a) *cognitive* (evaluating and constructing one's own views in light of available evidence), (b) *interpersonal* (taking others' perspectives into account rather than being consumed or defined by them), and (c) *identity* (possessing an internally generated belief system to guide one's choices).

Because of their proximity to students and the unique vantage points they often enjoy as observers of students' experiences, student affairs staff are in excellent positions to create and collaborate with faculty on initiatives that reflect these conditions. Further, by merit of having studied student learning and development, they have a set of conceptual and informational resources they can use to interpret their observations and to share with other campus colleagues.

Conclusion

Learning takes place both intentionally and serendipitously, through both formal and informal interactions, and in both curricular and cocurricular contexts. Cocurricular learning is powerful because it helps students make connections between ideas, events, learning strategies, and skills, etc., that would otherwise be seen as unconnected, and it gives them opportunities to practice using what they know. How educators choose to encourage learning varies as they respond to many different factors, including student characteristics, institutional purposes and priorities, and distinctive aspects of a given educational or social context. Educators select strategies for encouraging student learning based on their assumptions about students and about the process of learning, as well as on their own preferred styles of teaching (Davis, 1993). Students' selection of learning strategies also depends on their assumptions about the teacher and about the process of learning, as well as on their awareness of themselves as learners (e.g., their strengths, weaknesses, and preferences).

Kegan (1994) used the metaphor of crossing bridges to describe the process of learning and development, noting that "a bridge must be well anchored on both sides, with as much respect for where it begins as for where it ends" (p. 62). Accordingly, this metaphor and the literature discussed in this chapter suggest that educators should be able to determine where the bridge begins (students' current epistemic assumptions, preferred learning strategies, and so on), clarify which journey the student is taking (toward what goals at the other end of the bridge the journey is directed), and help the student navigate the terrain of the bridge—all the while showing respect for the student as a unique human being who is capable of learning to cross new bridges. Educators not only have the opportunity but the responsibility to extend the invitation to learn, to help the student envision the rewards at the next shoreline, and to provide the essential equipment for the journey. Educators who understand the many bridges of learning will be better prepared for this significant role in students' lives.

References

Alverno College. (1992). *Liberal learning at Alverno College.* Milwaukee, WI: Author.

American College Personnel Association (ACPA), American Association for Higher Education (AAHE), National Association of Student Personnel Administrators (NASPA). (1998). *Powerful partnerships.* Washington, DC: Author.

Anderson, J. A. (1988). Cognitive styles and multicultural populations. *Journal of Teacher Education, 39* (1), 2–9.

Anderson, J., & Adams, M. (1992). Acknowledging the learning styles of diverse student populations: Implications for instructional design. In L.L.B. Borders & N.V.N. Chism (Eds.), *Teaching for diversity* (New Directions for Teaching and Learning No. 49, pp. 19–33). San Francisco: Jossey-Bass.

Association of American Colleges. (1985). *Integrity in the college curriculum: A report to the academic community.* Washington, DC: Author.

Association of American Colleges. (1991). *The challenge of connecting learning.* Washington, DC: Author.

Basseches, M. (1984). *Dialectical thinking and adult development.* Norwood, NJ: Ablex.

Baxter Magolda, M. B. (1992). *Knowing and reasoning in college: Gender-related patterns in students' intellectual development.* San Francisco: Jossey-Bass.

Baxter Magolda, M. B. (1994). Post-college experience and epistemology. *Review of Higher Education, 18,* 25–44.

Baxter Magolda, M. B. (1999). *Creating contexts for learning and self-authorship: Constructive-developmental pedagogy.* Nashville, TN: Vanderbilt University Press.

Baxter Magolda, M. B. (Ed.). (2000). *Teaching to promote intellectual and personal maturity: Incorporating students' worldviews and identities into the learning process* (New Directions for Teaching and Learning No. 82). San Francisco: Jossey-Bass.

Baxter Magolda, M. B. (2001). *Making their own way: Narratives for transforming higher education to promote self-development.* Sterling, VA: Stylus.

Belenky, M. F., Clinchy, B. M., Goldberger, N. R., & Tarule, J. M. (1986). *Women's ways of knowing: The development of self, voice, and mind.* New York: Basic Books.

Bell, Y. R. (1994). A culturally sensitive analysis of Black learning styles. *Journal of Black Psychology, 20* (1), 47–61.

Berry, J. W. (1991). Cultural variations in field dependence-independence. In S. Wapner & J. Demick (Eds.), *Field dependence-independence: Cognitive style across the life span* (pp. 289–308). Hillsdale, NJ: Erlbaum.

Bertini, M., Pizzamiglio, L., & Wapner, S. (Eds.). (1986). *Field dependence in psychological theory, research, and application: Two symposia in memory of Herman A. Witkin.* Hillsdale, NJ: Erlbaum.

Bok, D. C. (1986). *Higher learning.* Cambridge, MA: Harvard University Press.

Bowen, H. (1980). *Investment in learning.* San Francisco: Jossey-Bass.

Bransford, J. D., Brown, A. L., & Cocking, R. R. (Eds.). (2000). *How people learn: Brain, mind, experience, and school.* Washington, DC: National Academy Press.

Bransford, J. D., & Schwartz, D. (1999). Rethinking transfer: A simple proposal with multiple implications. *Review of Research in Education, 24,* 61–100.

Broughton, J. (1978). Development of concepts of self, mind, reality, and knowledge. In W. Damon (Ed.), *Social cognition* (New Directions for Child Development No. 1, pp. 75–100). San Francisco: Jossey-Bass.

Brown, A. L. (1994). 1994 AERA presidential address: The advancement of learning. *Educational Researcher, 23* (8), 4–12.

Brown, A. L., & Campione, J. C. (1990). Communities of learning and thinking, or a context by any other name. In D. Kuhn (Ed.), *Developmental perspectives on teaching and learning thinking skills.* Contributions to Human Development, Vol. 21 (pp. 108–125). Basel, Switzerland: Karger.

Canada, M. (2000). Students as seekers in online courses. In R. E. Weiss, D. S. Knowlton, & B. W. Speck (Eds.), *Principles of effective teaching in the online classroom* (New Directions for Teaching and Learning No. 84, pp. 35–40). San Francisco: Jossey-Bass.

Cano, J. (1999). The relationship between learning style, academic major, and academic performance of college students. *Journal of Agricultural Education, 40* (1), 30–37.

Chickering, A. W., & Gamson, Z. (1987). *Seven principles for good practice in undergraduate education.* Winona, MN: Winona State University, Seven Principles Resource Center.

Chickering, A. W., & Reisser, L. (1993). *Education and identity* (2nd ed.). San Francisco: Jossey-Bass.

Claxton, C. S., & Murrell, P. H. (1987). *Learning styles: Implications for improving education practices* (ASHE-ERIC Higher Education Report No. 4). Washington, DC: Association for the Study of Higher Education.

Clinchy, B. M. (1996). Connected and separate knowing: Toward a marriage of two minds. In N. R. Goldberger, J. M. Tarule, B. M. Clinchy, & M. F. Belenky (Eds.), *Knowledge, difference, and power: Essays inspired by Women's Ways of Knowing* (pp. 205–247). New York: Basic Books.

Clinchy, B. M. (2000). Toward a more connected vision of higher education. In M. B. Baxter Magolda (Ed.), *Teaching to promote intellectual and personal maturity: Incorporating students' worldviews and identities into the learning process* (New Directions for Teaching and Learning No. 82, pp. 27–35). San Francisco: Jossey-Bass.

Clinchy, B. M. (2002). Revisiting Women's Ways of Knowing. In B. K. Hofer & P. R. Pintrich (Eds.), *Personal epistemology: The psychology of beliefs about knowledge and knowing* (pp. 63–88). Washington, DC: American Psychological Association.

Cohen, D. K., Raudenbush, S., & Ball, D. (2002). Resources, instruction, and research. In R. Boruch & F. Mosteller (Eds.), *Evidence matters: Randomized trials in education research* (pp. 80–119). Washington, DC: Brookings Institution Press.

Cortez, C. E. (2000). The diversity within: Intermarriage, identity, and campus community. *About Campus, 5* (1), 5–10.

Das, J. P. (1988). Simultaneous-successive processing and planning: Implications for student learning. In R. R. Schmeck (Ed.), *Learning strategies and learning styles* (pp. 101–129). New York: Plenum Press.

Davis, J. K. (1991). Educational implications of field dependence-independence. In S. Wapner & J. Demick, (Eds.), *Field dependence-independence: Cognitive style across the life span.* Hillsdale, NJ: Erlbaum.

Davis, J. R. (1993). *Better teaching, more learning: Strategies for success in postsecondary settings* (pp. 149–175). Phoenix, AZ: Oryx Press.

Davis, T. M., & Murrell, P. H. (1993). *Turning teaching into learning: The role of student responsibility in the collegiate experience* (ASHE-ERIC Higher Education Report No. 8). Washington, DC: George Washington University, School of Education and Human Development.

Demick, J. (1991). Organismic factors in field dependence-independence: Gender, personality, psychopathology. In S. Wapner & J. Demick, (Eds.), *Field dependence-independence: Cognitive style across the life span* (pp. 209–243). Hillsdale, NJ: Erlbaum.

Donald, J. G. (1999). Motivation for higher-order learning. In M. Theall (Ed.), *Motivation from within: Approaches for encouraging faculty and students to excel* (New Directions for Teaching and Learning No. 78, pp. 27–35). San Francisco: Jossey-Bass.

EDUCAUSE home page (n.d.). Retrieved May 6, 2002, from http://www.educause.edu

Engelkemeyer, S. W., & Brown, S. C. (1998, October). Powerful partnerships: A shared responsibility for learning. *AAHE Bulletin, 51,* 10–12.

Entwistle, N. (1988). Motivational factors in students' approaches to learning. In R. R. Schmeck (Ed.), *Learning strategies and learning styles* (pp. 21–51). New York: Plenum Press.

Entwistle, N., & Tait, H. (1995). Approaches to studying and perceptions of the learning environment across disciplines. In N. Hativa & M. Marincovich (Eds.), *Disciplinary differences in teaching and learning: Implications for practice* (New Directions for Teaching and Learning No. 64, pp. 93–103). San Francisco: Jossey-Bass.

Evans, N. J. (1996). Theories of student development. In S. R. Komives & D. B. Woodard, Jr. (Eds.), *Student services: A handbook for the profession* (3rd ed., pp. 164–187). San Francisco: Jossey-Bass.

Feldman, K. A., & Paulsen, M. B. (1994). Teaching and learning in the college classroom. *ASHE Reader Series.* Needham Heights, MA: Ginn Press.

Ford, N. (2000). Cognitive styles and virtual environments. *Journal of the American Society for Information Science, 51,* 543–557.

Ford, N., & Chen, S. Y. (2001), Matching/mismatching revisited: An empirical study of learning and teaching styles. *British Journal of Educational Technology, 32* (1), 5–22.

Frisby, C. L. (1993). One giant step backward: Myths of Black cultural learning styles. *School Psychology Review, 22,* 535–557.

Gadzella, B. M., Ginter, D. W., & Bryant, G. W. (1997). Prediction of performance in an academic course by scores on measures of learning style and critical thinking. *Psychological Reports, 81,* 595–602.

Gadzella, B. M., Masten, W. G., & Huang, J. (1999). Differences between African American and Caucasian students on critical thinking and learning style. *College Student Journal, 33,* 538–542.

Gardner, H. (1987). The theory of multiple intelligences. *Annals of Dyslexia, 37,* 19–35.

Gardner, H. (1993). *Multiple intelligences: The theory in practice.* New York: Basic Books.

Garton, B. L., Dyer, J. E., & King, B. (2000). The use of learning styles and admissions criteria in predicting academic performance and retention of college freshmen. *Journal of Agricultural Education, 41* (2), 46–53.

Goldberger, N. R., Tarule, J. M., Clinchy, B. M., & Belenky, M. F. (Eds.). (1996). *Knowledge, difference, and power: Essays inspired by Women's Ways of Knowing.* New York: Basic Books.

Grasha, A. F., & Yangarber-Hicks, N. (2000). Integrating teaching styles and learning styles with instructional technology. *College Teaching, 48* (1), 2–10.

Gruber, H., Law, L-C., Mandl, H., & Renkl, A. (1996). Situated learning and transfer. In P. Reimann & H. Spada (Eds.), *Learning in humans and machines: Towards an interdisciplinary learning science* (pp. 168–188). New York: Elsevier.

Hadwin, A. F., Winn, P. H., Stockley, D. B., Nesbit, J. C., & Woszczyna, C. (2001). Context moderates student' self-reports about how they study. *Journal of Educational Psychology, 93,* 477–487.

Hale-Benson, J. E. (1988). *Black children: Their roots, culture, and learning styles* (3rd ed.). Baltimore: The Johns Hopkins University Press.

Hirsch, E. D., Jr. (1987). *Cultural literacy: What every American needs to know.* Boston: Houghton Mifflin.

Hofer, B. K., & Pintrich, P. R. (1997). The development of epistemological theories: Beliefs about knowledge and knowing and their relation to learning. *Review of Educational Research, 67,* 88–140.

Hofer, B. K., & Pintrich, P. R. (Eds.). (2002). *Personal epistemology: The psychology of beliefs about knowledge and knowing.* Mahwah, NJ: Erlbaum.

Holschuh, J. P. (2000). Do as I say, not as I do: Higher, average, and low-performing students' strategy use in biology. *Journal of College Reading and Learning, 31* (1), 94–108.

Holyoak, K. J., & Koh, K. (1987). Surface and structural similarity in analogical transfer. *Memory and Cognition, 15,* 332–340.

Jensen, G. H. (1987). Learning styles. In J. Provost & S. Anchors (Eds.), *Applications of the Myers-Briggs Type Indicator in higher education* (pp. 181–206). Palo Alto, CA: Consulting Psychologists Press.

Jiang, M., & Ting, E. (1998). *A study of students' perceived learning in a web-based online environment.* Paper presented at the WebNet99 World Conference on the WWW and Internet Proceedings, Honolulu, HI.

Johnson, D. W., Johnson, R. T., & Smith, K. A. (1991). *Cooperative learning: Increasing college faculty instructional productivity* (ASHE-ERIC Higher Education Report No. 4). Washington, DC: George Washington University, School of Education and Human Development.

Jonassen, D. H., & Grabowski, B. L. (1993). *Handbook of individual differences, learning, and instruction.* Hillsdale, NJ: Erlbaum.

Kegan, R. (1994). *In over our heads: The mental demands of modern life.* Cambridge, MA: Harvard University Press.

King, P. M. (Ed.). (1992). [Special issue on reflective judgment.] *Liberal Education, 78* (1).

King, P. M. (1996). Student cognition and learning. In S. R. Komives & D. B. Woodward, Jr., (Eds.), *Student services: A handbook for the profession* (3rd ed., pp. 218–243). San Francisco: Jossey-Bass.

King, P. M. (2000). Learning to make reflective judgments. In M. B. Baxter Magolda (Ed.), *Linking student development, learning, and teaching* (New Directions for Teaching and Learning No. 82, pp. 15–26). San Francisco: Jossey-Bass.

King, P. M., & Baxter Magolda, M. B. (1996). A developmental perspective on learning. *Journal of College Student Development, 37*, 163–173. Reprinted in the 40th Anniversary Issue of the *Journal of College Student Development, 40*, 599–609.

King, P. M., & Kitchener, K. S. (1994). *Developing reflective judgment: Understanding and promoting intellectual growth and critical thinking in adolescents and adults.* San Francisco: Jossey-Bass.

King, P. M., & Kitchener, K. S. (2002). The reflective judgment model: Twenty years of research on epistemic cognition. In B. K. Hofer & P. R. Pintrich (Eds.), *Personal epistemology: The psychology of beliefs about knowledge and knowing* (pp. 37–62). Mahwah, NJ: Erlbaum.

Kirby, J. R. (1988). Style, strategy and skill in reading. In R. R. Schmeck (Ed.), *Learning strategies and learning styles* (pp. 229–274). New York: Plenum Press.

Kitchener, K. S. (in press). Skills, tasks, and definitions: Discrepancies in the understanding and data on the development of folk epistemology. *New Ideas in Psychology.*

Kitchener, K. S., & King, P. M. (1981). Reflective judgment: Concepts of justification and their relationship to age and education. *Journal of Applied Developmental Psychology, 2*, 89–116.

Kitchener, K. S., & King, P. M. (1990). The reflective judgment model: Transforming assumptions about knowing. In J. Mezirow & Associates (Eds.), *Fostering critical reflection in adulthood: A guide to transformative and emancipatory learning* (pp. 159–176). San Francisco: Jossey-Bass.

Kitchener, K. S., Lynch, C. L., Fischer, K. W., & Wood, P. K. (1993). Developmental range of reflective judgment: The effect of contextual support and practice on developmental stage. *Developmental Psychology, 29*, 893–906.

Knowlton, D. S. (2000). A theoretical framework for the online classroom: A defense and delineation of a student-centered pedagogy. In R. E. Weiss, D. S. Knowlton, & B. W. Speck, *Principles of effective teaching in the online classroom* (New Directions for Teaching and Learning No. 84, pp. 5–14). San Francisco: Jossey-Bass.

Knupfer, N. N. (1998). Gender divisions across technology advertisements and the WWW: Implications for educational equity. *Theory into Practice, 37* (1), 54–63.

Kolb, D. A. (1984). *Experiential learning: Experience as the source of learning and development.* Englewood Cliffs, NJ: Prentice Hall.

Kramer, D. A. (1989). The development of an awareness of contradiction across the life span and the question of postformal operations. In M. L. Commons, J. D. Sinnott, F. A. Richards, & C. Armon (Eds.), *Adult development. Vol. 1: Comparisons and applications of developmental models* (pp. 133–159). New York: Praeger.

Kroll, B. (1992). *Teaching hearts and minds: College students reflect on the Vietnam War in literature.* Carbondale, IL: Southern Illinois University Press.

Lamborn, S. D., & Fischer, K. W. (1988). Optimal and functional levels in cognitive development: The individual's developmental range. *Newsletter of the International Society for the Study of Behavioral Development, 14* (2), 1–4.

Liaw, S. S., & Huang, H. M. (2000). Enhancing interactivity in web-based instruction: A review of the literature. *Educational Technology Magazine,* 41–45.

Love, P. G., & Guthrie, V. L. (1999). (Eds.). *Understanding and applying cognitive development theory* (New Directions for Student Services No. 88). San Francisco: Jossey-Bass.

Manner, B. M. (2001). Learning styles and multiple intelligences in students: Getting the most out of your students' learning. *Journal of College Science Teaching, 30*, 390–394.

Marton, F., & Säljö, R. (1976a). On qualitative difference in learning: I. Outcome and process. *British Journal of Educational Psychology, 46,* 4–11.

Marton, F., & Säljö, R. (1976b). On qualitative difference in learning: II. Outcome as a function of the learner's conception of the task. *British Journal of Educational Psychology, 46,* 115–127.

McEvoy, A. P. (2002). *Self-authorship and self-regulation.* Unpublished paper, University of Michigan.

McIsaac, M. S., & Gunawardena, C. N. (2001). Distance education. In D. H. Jonassen (Ed.), *Handbook of research for educational communications and technology.* Retrieved May 7, 2002, from the Association for Educational Communications and Technology Web site: http://www.aect.org/Intranet/Publications/edtech/13/index.html.

McLellan, H. (1999). Online education as interactive experience: Some guiding models. *Educational Technology Magazine,* 36–42.

Menges, R. J., & Svinicki, M. D. (Eds.). (1991). *College teaching: From theory to practice* (New Directions for Teaching and Learning No. 45). San Francisco: Jossey-Bass.

Mentkowski, M., & Associates. (2000). *Learning that lasts: Integrating learning, development, and performance in college and beyond.* San Francisco: Jossey-Bass.

Miller, C. D., Alway, M., & McKinley, D. (1987). Effects of learning styles and strategies on academic success. *Journal of College Student Personnel, 28,* 399–404.

Muirhead, B. (2001). Interactivity research studies. *Educational Technology and Society, 4* (3), 108–112.

Murray, J. B. (1990). Review of research on the Myers-Briggs Type Indicator. *Perceptual and Motor Skills, 70,* 1187–1202.

Myers, I. B. (1980). *Gifts differing.* Palo Alto, CA: Consulting Psychologists Press.

Northrup, P. (2001). A framework for designing interactivity into web-based instruction. *Educational Technology, 41,* 31–39.

Office of Educational Technology (2001, April 30). Distance learning. Retrieved May 6, 2002, from http://www.ed/gov/Technology/distance.html

Parry, S., & Dunn, L. (2000). Benchmarking as a meaning approach to learning in online settings. *Studies in Continuing Education, 22,* 219–234.

Perry, W. G., Jr. (1968/1970). *Forms of intellectual and ethical development in the college years: A scheme.* New York: Holt, Rinehart and Winston.

Perry, W. G., Jr. (1981). Cognitive and ethical growth: The making of meaning. In A. W. Chickering & Associates (Eds.), *The modern American college: Responding to the new realities of diverse students and a changing society* (pp. 76–116). San Francisco: Jossey-Bass.

Petraglia, J. (1998). *Reality by design: The rhetoric and technology of authenticity in education.* Mahwah, NJ: Erlbaum.

Phye, G. D. (2001). Problem-solving instruction and problem-solving transfer: The correspondence issue. *Journal of Educational Psychology, 93,* 571–578.

Pintrich, P. R. (1995).Understanding self-regulated learning. In P. R. Pintrich (Ed.), *Understanding self-regulated learning* (New Directions for Teaching and Learning No. 63, pp. 3–12). San Francisco: Jossey-Bass.

Pittenger, D. J. (1993). The utility of the Myers-Briggs Type Indicator. *Review of Educational Research, 63,* 467–488.

Provost, J. A., & Anchors, C. (1987). *Applications of the Myers-Briggs Type Indicator in higher education.* Palo Alto, CA: Consulting Psychologists Press.

Rainey, M. A., & Kolb, D. A. (1995). Using experiential learning theory and learning styles in diversity education. In R. R. Sims & S. J. Sims (Eds.), *The importance of learning styles: Understanding the implications for learning, course design, and education* (pp. 129–146). Westport, CT: Greenwood Press.

Rose, A. D. (1999). New educational technologies: Connection or autonomy? *Adult Learning, 10* (4), 3–4.

Rosovsky, H. (1990). *The university: An owner's manual.* New York: Norton.

Santostefano, S. (1991). Cognitive style as a process coordinating outer space with inner self: lessons from the past. In S. Wapner & J. Demick (Eds.), *Field dependence-independence: Cognitive style across the life span* (pp. 269–286). Hillsdale, NJ: Erlbaum.

Sarasin, L. C. (1999). *Learning style perspectives: Impact in the classroom.* Madison, WI: Atwood.

Schmeck, R. R. (1981, February). Improving learning by improving thinking. *Educational Leadership, 38,* 384–385.

Schmeck, R. R. (1988). An introduction to strategies and styles of learning. In R. R. Schmeck (Ed.), *Learning strategies and learning styles* (pp. 3–19). New York: Plenum Press.

Schommer, M. (1994). Synthesizing epistemological belief research: Tentative understandings and provocative confusions. *Educational Psychology Review, 6*, 293–319.

Schommer, M., Crouse, A., & Rhodes, N. (1992). Epistemological beliefs and mathematical text comprehension: Believing it is simple does not make it so. *Journal of Educational Psychology, 84* (4), 435–443.

Schunk, D. H., & Zimmerman, B. J. (1994). (Eds.). *Self-regulation of learning and performance: Issues and educational applications.* Hillsdale, NJ: Erlbaum.

Schwitzer, A. M., Ancis, J. R., & Brown, N. (2001). *Promoting student learning and student development at a distance.* Lanham, MD: American College Personnel Association/University Press of America.

Shade, B.J.R. (1982). Afro-American cognitive style: A variable in school success? *Review of Educational Research, 53*, 219–244.

Shade, B.J.B. (1989). The influence of perceptual development on cognitive style: Cross ethnic comparisons. *Early Child Development and Care, 51,* 137–155.

Shuford, B. (1995). *Learning styles of African American college students.* Unpublished manuscript, Bowling Green State University, Bowling Green, OH.

Shuford, B. (2000). *Learning styles and strategies of first-year college students.* Unpublished doctoral dissertation, Bowling Green State University, Bowling Green, Ohio.

Silverman, S. L., & Casazza, M. E. (2000). *Learning and development: Making connections to enhance teaching.* San Francisco: Jossey-Bass.

Sinnott, J. D. (1989). Life-span relativistic post-formal thought: Methodology and data from everyday problem-solving studies. In M. L. Commons, J. D. Sinnott, F. A. Richards, & C. Armon (Eds.), *Adult development: Vol. 1. Comparisons and applications of developmental models* (pp. 239–278). New York: Praeger.

The University of Michigan Shapiro Undergraduate Library. (2002, April 3). Criteria for web site evaluation. Retrieved May 6, 2002, from http://www.lib.umich.edu/ugl/research/evaluation/

van Rossum, E. J., & Schenk, S. M. (1984). The relationship between learning conception, study strategy and learning outcome. *British Journal of Educational Psychology, 54,* 73–83.

Vasquez, J. A., & Wainstein, N. (1990). Instructional responsibilities of college faculty to minority students. *Journal of Negro Education, 59,* 599–610.

Wapner, S., & Demick, J. (Eds.). (1991). *Field dependence-independence: Cognitive style across the life span.* Hillsdale, NJ: Erlbaum.

Weigel, V. B. (2002). *Deep learning for a digital age: Technology's untapped potential to enrich higher education.* San Francisco: Jossey-Bass.

Weinstein, C. E., & Meyer, D. K. (1991). Cognitive learning strategies and college teaching. In R. F. Menges & M. D. Svinicki (Eds.), *College teaching: From theory to practice* (New Directions for Teaching and Learning No. 45, pp. 15–26). San Francisco: Jossey-Bass.

Witkin, H. A. (1976). Cognitive style in academic performance and in teacher-student relations. In S. Messick & Associates (Eds.), *Individuality in learning* (pp. 38–72). San Francisco: Jossey-Bass.

Witkin, H. A., & Goodenough, D. R. (1981). *Cognitive styles: Essence and origins* (Psychological Issues Monograph 51). New York: International Universities Press.

Witkin, H. A., Moore, C. A., Goodenough, D. R., & Cox, P. W. (1977). Field-dependent and field-independent cognitive styles and their educational implications. *Review of Educational Research, 47,* 1–64.

Wood, P. K. (1997). A secondary analysis of claims regarding the Reflective Judgment Interview: Internal consistency, sequentiality, and intra-individual differences in ill-structured problem solving. In J. C. Smart (Ed.), *Higher education: Handbook of theory and research,* Volume XII (pp. 243–312). Edison, NY: Agathon Press.

Wood, P. K., Kitchener, K. S., & Jensen, L. (2002). Considerations in the design and evaluation of a paper and pencil measure of reflective thinking. In B. K. Hofer & P. R. Pintrich (Eds.), *Personal epistemology: The psychology of beliefs about knowledge and knowing* (pp. 277–294). Mahwah, NJ: Erlbaum.

CHAPTER TWELVE

ORGANIZATIONAL THEORY

George D. Kuh

Constant change is a fact of life. As a result, every college or university must monitor its core functions—including student affairs—to make certain they are effectively meeting the needs of increasingly diverse students and the expectations of an expanding number of stakeholders (The third imperative, 1999; Woodard, Love, & Komives, 2000). More than ever, student affairs professionals must understand how people, organizational structures, and governance processes influence one another. To describe and understand these phenomena, theories about organizational behavior have been developed.

The term *organizational behavior* represents a personification, an attempt to give human characteristics to inanimate entities such as colleges and universities (Weick, 1979). A student affairs office does not perform; it is the people in the office that are responsible for what is accomplished. In this chapter, *organizational behavior* refers to the interactions among organizational actors; organizational events are the outcomes of their attitudes, beliefs, and actions. Identifying the actors, the actors' roles, and the relationships between the actors and organizational actions is difficult, as institutions of higher education are increasingly vulnerable to such external influences as changing economic conditions and the agendas of legislators, corporate and philanthropic foundations, accrediting bodies, and state education commissions. These influences, coupled with an increase in the number of students, faculty, and administrators from historically underrepresented groups, add another measure of complexity to an environment already characterized by competing values and preferences among faculty, professional staff, administrators, and students.

Organizational theory is an eclectic field, drawing from sociology, social psychology, anthropology, philosophy (Morgan, 1986; Pfeffer, 1982), cybernetics (Birnbaum, 1988), and the study of sense-making (Weick, 1995), chaos, and complexity (Peters, 1987;

Waldrop, 1992; Wheatley, 1992) to explain such processes as resource allocation, policy making, personnel management, leadership, restructuring, and reengineering. Just as different student development theories account for some aspects of growth and behavior but not others, so it is with organizational theories. In this sense, an organizational theory is a window through which to view the behavior of individuals and groups (students, faculty members, student affairs professionals) in the context of a complex organization interacting with and being shaped by external exigencies and special interest groups. What one sees depends on which window one looks through (Birnbaum, 1988; Bolman & Deal, 1991). That is, by looking at behavior through one window, certain events, actions, and relationships appear coordinated and purposeful; however, viewed through another window the same interactions may look chaotic or dysfunctional.

In a practitioner's mind, concepts from various organizational views are mixed with experience, becoming theories-in-use (Argyris & Schön, 1978)—highly personal, individualized patterns of understanding. Being familiar with multiple theoretical windows increases the possibility that one's theories-in-use will generate more accurate interpretations of events and actions than are possible using any single view (Kuh, 1984). In this chapter, three conventional and three postconventional views of organizational behavior are discussed, including their implications for student affairs professionals and institutional change and improvement. (Exhibit 12.1 summarizes the differences between the conventional and postconventional views.)

EXHIBIT 12.1. CONVENTIONAL AND POSTCONVENTIONAL ASSUMPTIONS ABOUT ORGANIZATIONS.

Conventional Views	*Postconventional Views*
Hierarchical structures are normal, necessary, functional, and desirable.	Heterarchical or cross functional interactions are uninhibited by structures and facilitate organizational learning and effective management; organizational processes and structures evolve over time.
Organizations are independent from one another and insulated from the external environment.	Organizations are interdependent and influenced by changes in the external environment.
Communication channels are clearly delineated and consistently used.	Information is available from many sources inside and beyond the institution and flows in many directions.
Expertise, control, and authority are commensurate with position and exercised by supervisors.	Any person at any level has the potential to influence organizational behavior in an effective, positive, creative manner.
Goals are shared direct behavior and are tied directly to outcomes.	Relationships among events, individual behavior, technologies, and outcomes are unpredictable, frequently ambiguous, and constantly changing.
Reliability and predictability of organizational processes are hampered only by factors such as knowledge and technology.	Qualities of indeterminacy, morphogenesis, action learning, and self-organizing compromise expectations for reliability and predictability but are necessary for organizational adaptation and change.

Source: Adapted from Kuh, Whitt, and Shedd (1987).

Conventional Views of Organizations

Conventional views of organizational behavior developed during an era (1900 to 1960) when the closed-system approach to understanding organizations was dominant. That is, complex organizations, including institutions of higher education, were generally portrayed as impermeable to external influences. A key assumption of conventional views was that a competent administrator could manipulate factors that affected institutional performance. A closed-systems approach to alcohol abuse in residence halls would focus exclusively on a student's behavior (and, perhaps, differences in hall environments) but would ignore societal drinking habits, campus norms common to affinity and fraternal groups, family histories of alcohol use, and so on (Kuh, 1994).

Conventional approaches emphasize three properties: (1) hierarchical structures and controls; (2) clear communication channels; and (3) stability, reliability, and predictability (Clark, 1984; Kuh, Whitt, & Shedd, 1987). Three views of organizations emphasize these characteristics, to varying degrees: rational-bureaucratic, collegial, and political. The collegial and political views were developed specifically to understand behavior in colleges and universities.

Rational-Bureaucratic View

The objective of the rational-bureaucratic organization is to routinize tasks, functions, and processes, much like an assembly line routinizes production (Weber, 1947). The guiding premise is that routinization leads to improved organizational effectiveness and efficiency. No wonder "an efficient, well-oiled, smooth-running machine" was once a popular metaphor for organizations!

Viewed through the rational-bureaucratic window, institutions of higher education have seven characteristics:

1. *Hierarchical authority or a clear chain of command.* Every individual is responsible to someone in a higher office (for example, the senior student affairs officer, or SSAO, has more authority and responsibility than associate deans or entry-level staff).
2. *Limits on authority.* Specific people are responsible for specific, clearly defined areas of organizational performance.
3. *Division of labor.* Efficiency is maximized and assigning responsibility for specific functions to certain persons and groups minimizes duplication of effort.
4. *Technical competence.* Workers have the requisite training.
5. *Standard operating procedures.* The tasks that must be performed to attain the organization's objectives are carefully prescribed.
6. *Rules for work.* Requirements and competence levels for various positions are specified.
7. *Differential rewards.* Salary and perquisites are tied directly to seniority and position in the hierarchy (Hage, 1980; Morgan, 1986).

To impose order, exert control, and produce desired outcomes, the rational-bureaucratic manager must

- Clarify values
- Set goals
- Determine the tasks needed to attain the goals
- Standardize tasks so anyone can perform them
- Designate responsibility for various functions to specific groups and individuals
- Delineate standard operating procedures in policy and procedure manuals
- Establish contingency plans, including who is to take what actions when (Allison, 1971; Chaffee, 1983; Pfeffer, 1982).

Policy decisions are centralized; that is, a handful of senior staff makes decisions to ensure high-quality performance and progress toward organizational goals. The organizational structure indicates who is responsible for sharing what kind of information with whom. Certain people evaluate information for accuracy and disseminate it as necessary to appropriate individuals and groups. For example, resident assistants (RAs) convey information about residence hall policies and practices to students and report problems to supervisors. The director of residence life reports the most important information from RAs to the SSAO on a need-to-know basis. In turn, the SSAO informs the campus senior executive officer about events in the residence halls and usually represents student life to external audiences, such as parents and community leaders. Effectiveness depends on accurate information and appropriate "technology" (that is, the means by which the organization does its work). Inadequate information or flawed technology creates problems. For example, tardy financial aid awards may be explained by obsolete or poorly designed software that does not accommodate recent changes in federal aid guidelines. Flawed technology could also include cumbersome communication networks, such as decision-making processes that exclude legitimate stakeholders, or human error, such as failure to consult with student government officers with regard to tuition and technology-related fee increases.

Rational-bureaucratic principles coupled with scientific management concepts (Fayol, 1949; Gulick & Urwick, 1937; Taylor, 1911) spawned such management techniques as management by objectives (MBO), planned programming and budgeting systems (PPBS), and other hyperrational planning and control mechanisms (Clark, 1985). The human relations management approach (Argyris, 1964; Likert, 1967; Mayo, 1945; McGregor, 1960) subsequently emphasized the importance of such factors as motivation and morale to organizational performance.

As with all organizational views, the rational-bureaucratic window has limitations, particularly when applied to an institution of higher education. For example, people can assimilate only so much information at any one time (see Exhibit 12.2). Because of this "bounded rationality" (Simon, 1957), no one can be aware of everything that takes place in a complex organization. People must "satisfice"—that is, they must act on incomplete knowledge (Simon, 1957; Weick, 1979). Specialization, standardization, routinization,

EXHIBIT 12.2. ADVANTAGES AND CHALLENGES OF CONVENTIONAL ORGANIZATIONAL VIEWS.

View	*Advantages*	*Challenges*
Rational-Bureaucratic	Appeals to reason and logic. Clearly defined roles, functions, responsibilities, scope of authority, and relationships. Performance is standardized. Prospective approach. Emphasizes productivity.	Incompatible with certain values of the academy (such as autonomy, equity, multiple areas of expertise, decisions by peers). Expectations for goal consensus and control often are not met. Oversimplifies complex problems. Constrained by information-processing limits. Measures of productivity not well suited to purposes of higher education.
Collegial	Consistent with traditions of academy. Responsive to persuasive argument of colleagues. Based on democratic principles. Ensures representation.	Inefficient (labor-intensive and time-consuming). Insensitive to power differentials, resource availability, and policy implementation issues.
Political	Acknowledges importance of power and conflict resolution. Emphasizes policy making as a process for issue management. Encourages collaboration among disparate stakeholder groups.	Incongruent with certain values of the academy (such as openness, fairness, self-governance). Reinforces status quo. Exchanges achievement and merit or influence in decision making.

and repetition inhibit organizational flexibility (Hage & Aiken, 1970; Strange, 1983) and blunt change efforts (Morgan, 1986), and they discourage individual initiative, innovation, and risk taking (Peters & Waterman, 1982; Vaill, 1984). In addition, faculty and professional staff expect autonomy, not close supervision. Standardization is difficult when activities are not similar across jobs. Although some functions are more effective when routinized (for example, registration and financial aid), others may not be (such as career planning and student activities). For these reasons, a hybrid organizational form—the professional bureaucracy—evolved in institutions of higher education and other organizations with large numbers of highly educated personnel to take advantage of the unusual amount of expertise they possess (Mintzberg, 1979).

These limitations do not mean that expert judgment and logical analysis are unimportant or that reason never prevails. In fact, most actions in a college or university are rational—to someone. The fatal flaw of the rational-bureaucratic view is the assumption that managers can and should anticipate, account for, and attempt to control all the possible contingencies that may bear on a decision (see Exhibit 12.2), an expectation that cannot be met by any individual or organization. Equally important, such traditions as academic freedom and collegial governance are incompatible with certain rational-bureaucratic principles, as explained below.

Collegial View

The collegial view is based on two enduring values of the academy: professional autonomy and a normative compliance system (Austin & Gamson, 1983). Faculty and staff are highly trained in their respective fields, and therefore they expect to determine the conditions under which they perform. Compliance is normative in that faculty and professional staff are motivated more by the belief that their work is significant than by fear of sanctions from superiors (Etzioni, 1961). As a result of its allegiance to these two values, faculty and student affairs professionals almost universally endorse the collegial view of organizations as the preferred way to organize and govern an institution of higher education.

Collegial processes foster commitment, satisfaction, and productivity by allowing people to shape their destiny through participating in governance structures such as personnel committees and faculty senates. Through these structures faculty members determine priorities, work conditions, and standards of quality as well as select new colleagues and evaluate the performance of peers (Baldridge, Curtis, Ecker, & Riley, 1977; Birnbaum, 1988; Chaffee, 1983; Kanter, 1983). The structures are reproduced at various levels (for example, the entire institution, academic departments, student organizations, and residences).

For collegial processes to be effective, people must be open to new ideas. They must share and clarify their positions through discussion, and they must change their position when presented with compelling reasons to do so. While some roles and processes are delineated, such as the role of the president pro tempore of the faculty senate and the use of Robert's Rules of Order, specific procedures are not prescribed for universal use but emerge through reasoned discourse among peers at each individual campus.

However, the collegial view tends to oversimplify life in institutions of higher education. In addition, collegial decision making and policy formulation are time-consuming. The increasing influence of external agencies and factors, such as the economy, sunshine laws, threats of litigation, and parental wishes, have eroded the integrity of collegial processes. For these reasons and others, faculty members have less time and are less willing to devote their energy to institutional governance. Taken together, these factors have reduced the utility of the collegial view for making certain types of decisions, such as resource allocations and decisions concerning physical plant expansion. Finally, the collegial view does not explicitly address conflict resolution or the role of power in decision making, two realities of life in colleges and universities that are featured in the political view of organizations.

Political View

When powerful stakeholders compete for limited resources or differ on important issues, conflict is inevitable. Policy alternatives may be proposed to address differences in views or to respond to the interests of various groups. People with similar interests often form coalitions to advocate a particular alternative. Lobbying and debating take place both in public forums and in private. Sometimes these negotiations result in new or changed policies (Baldridge et al., 1977). Some form of ratification, such as voting or formal acknowledgment by institutional leaders, usually determines the preferred policy option (Baldridge, 1971).

Although the political view implies that many faculty and staff will be involved in decision and policy making, this is not necessarily the case. In part this is because few issues are of sufficient importance to stimulate active involvement by large numbers of stakeholders (March & Olsen, 1976). Unless an issue is of high salience to members of one or more groups, people are not likely to invest limited energy and time in the deliberations.

The political view acknowledges the uneven distribution of power within an institution of higher education, which challenges the "myth of organizational rationality" (Morgan, 1986, p. 195), including expectations for rational decision making and goal-directed, functionally interdependent units. For example, sometimes a decision is made without the knowledge of those individuals who will be affected by it, leading to feelings of alienation and problems in implementing decisions or policies (see Exhibit 12.2). And when implemented, a policy or practice may look very different from what was adopted (Lipsky, 1980). Also, the debates and lobbying associated with decisions may exacerbate, rather than ameliorate, differences between groups, thus creating more tension.

Faculty and student affairs staff who expect their institution to be a community of equals may reject or feel threatened by the political view. Conflict and competition are perceived as antithetical to the traditions of collegial decision making and governance. Some people associate institutional politics with Machiavellian behavior and ruthless self-interest, considering conflict to be a dysfunctional condition triggered by lamentable circumstances such as personality problems, rivalry, and role dissonance. Conflict associated with self-interest cannot be avoided, however. For example, when faculty and students learn that funds have been allocated for additional scholarships for students with certain talents, such as athletes and musicians who do not have financial need, one or more groups will likely challenge the wisdom of such decisions. Staff may disagree on how to allocate funds for professional development or programming, who remains on duty during spring break, which student groups get offices in the union, or the institution's policies on student activism or hate speech. As resources become scarcer and the number of special interest groups increases, colleges and universities will experience more, not less, competition. The political view is particularly useful for identifying those who are most likely to be influential in the process and for maximizing the potential benefits of conflict management and collaborative policy making.

Implications of Conventional Views

In conventional views of organizations, goals are presumed to be clear and uniformly validated; people either decide together (as in the collegial and political views) or are told by a superior (as in the rational-bureaucratic view) how to attain the organization's goals. Logic and reason are instrumental in problem solving, planning, and policy making. Control and responsibility are exercised from the top down. Confusion, poor performance, and differences of opinion are addressed by following the rules of engagement specific to the preferred view. In the collegial approach, for example, disagreements are ameliorated via the appropriate governance committee; in the rational-bureaucratic approach, managers use the chain of command to fix the "part" of the organizational machine that is not functioning properly. Occasionally the preferences of some persons or coalitions may supersede the goals of others, creating conflict and, perhaps, confusion (the political view—see Exhibit 12.1). Change is brought about by decisive leaders who rearrange resources and personnel to respond to threats and opportunities in the external environment (Di Maggio & Powell, 1983; Lawrence & Lorsch, 1967; Pfeffer & Salancik, 1978; Thompson, 1967; Zucker, 1987). Success is measured by accuracy of predictions, comprehensiveness of plans, and the degree to which organizational goals and objectives are attained. That is, if staff serve students well and the student affairs division runs smoothly and meets the expectations of the president and governing board, student affairs is considered effective.

For more than half a century, conventional views shaped expectations of how people should behave in institutions of higher education. These views assumed colleges and universities were closed systems, for the most part independent of external forces. But circumstances have changed. Institutions of higher education are increasingly vulnerable to market and other forces in an increasingly unpredictable world. In addition, people from more diverse backgrounds are working and studying in postsecondary institutions.

As Heydinger (1994) asserts, "Twenty-first century higher education must become mission-driven, customer-sensitive, enterprise-organized, and results-oriented. . . . We need a new organizational paradigm: one that will focus us on those we serve; allocate resources based on demonstrable success; provide flexibility that will permit timely responses to changing student and research needs; eliminate unnecessary layers of oversight by placing more responsibility with those we serve" (p. 1). Therefore, student affairs staff need different windows to look through in order to make sense of the complicated and rapidly changing institutions in which they work.

Postconventional Views of Organizations

Postconventional views hold that colleges and universities are complex open systems, influenced by external events and changing conditions on and off the campus. Instead of being orderly, linear, and goal-directed, the postconventional organization encourages sharing information simultaneously in various directions and interactions within, across, and beyond organizational boundaries to respond to developing circumstances (see Exhibit 12.1). Moreover, colleges have the capacity to evolve into qualitatively different forms as they adapt to changes in their external environment and internal conditions. Indeed, they must change and adapt to survive (Allen & Cherrey, 2000; Heydinger, 1994; Tierney, 1999)! This perspective on organizations shares many of the qualities characteristic of paradigm shifts in other fields, such as history, law, economics, psychology, and physics (Gleick, 1987; Kuhn, 1970; Lincoln, 1985; Schwartz & Ogilvy, 1979; Wheatley, 1992).

To stimulate creative thinking about how organizations function under conditions of instability and uncertainty, imaginative metaphors for organizations have been invoked by various authors (Morgan, 1986), including "flying seesaws" (Hedberg, Nystrom, & Starbuck, 1976), "garbage cans" (Cohen, March, & Olsen, 1972), "psychic prisons" (Morgan, 1986), and "rain-forest tribes" (Schroeder, Nicholls, & Kuh, 1983). In this section, three postconventional views are described: organized anarchy, culture, and the learning organization. Although we have less experience looking through the newer, postconventional windows, they more accurately describe many of the rapidly changing external and internal conditions student affairs professionals must contend with.

Organized Anarchy

The organized anarchy view (Cohen & March, 1974) is the most familiar of the postconventional windows. It was developed specifically to describe six characteristics peculiar to colleges and universities: ambiguous, conflicting goals; unclear technologies; loose coupling; fluid participation; a highly educated professional work force; and clients who participate in institutional governance (Baldridge et al., 1977; Birnbaum, 1988; Cohen & March, 1974; Weick, 1976, 1979).

Colleges and universities have multiple goals that occasionally conflict (Gross & Grambusch, 1968). For example, many faculty members say they get mixed messages regarding the relative value of teaching and research. Administrators receive many more legitimate requests for funding than they can accommodate (for salary increases, new equipment, and student aid, to name a few). A student activities director wants to create additional leadership opportunities for students of color; a career counselor is charged with increasing the number of employers recruiting on campus; the director of commuter affairs wants to increase security in the parking lots—all of these goals are worthwhile, but some of them cannot be realized because of limited resources (Association of Governing Boards, 1999; Zusman, 1999).

Unclear technology (Cohen & March, 1974) refers to an inability to consistently describe and replicate important processes, such as the use of relationship therapy in the campus mental health center or in theory-based residence hall programs. In almost every field, professionals rely on tacit information, their experience, and enlightened judgment when working with clients (Schön, 1987). For example, an estimated 80 percent of the vision problems encountered by optometrists do not fit the correction categories taught in professional school (Schön, 1983). When many different individuals exercise professional judgment in an organization, numerous approaches to performing tasks typically develop. The complexity of tasks such as student development programming and the absence of reliable, comparative data about the efficacy of various approaches contribute to unclear technology in student affairs.

Coupling refers to the strength of the relationships between or among elements in an organization (Weick, 1976). For example, residence life may be affected by the performance of admissions and financial aid staff—rooms might be left vacant if enough students do not apply or if financial aid awards are not made promptly. Conventional views expect such organizational units as the admissions office, residence halls, and student activities offices to be tightly coupled, meaning that communication is direct and immediate and responses are immediate and predictable. For various reasons, however, tight coupling is the exception, not the rule, in most educational institutions (Weick, 1985) (see Exhibit 12.3).

EXHIBIT 12.3. ADVANTAGES AND CHALLENGES OF POSTCONVENTIONAL ORGANIZATIONAL VIEWS.

View	*Advantages*	*Challenges*
Organized Anarchy	Richly descriptive of life in institutions of higher education. Images are intuitively appealing and evocative. Compatible with academy values (such as autonomy, minimal supervision). Acknowledges retrospective understanding rather than prescriptive models.	Information not always available to those who need it. Legitimates and encourages divided loyalties. Hinders coordinated response to issues and crises. Does not suggest implications for staff and leader behavior. Challenges basic assumptions about effective organizing.
Culture	Acknowledges context as important variable in understanding behavior. Explains unusual and routine behavior. Accommodates different behaviors (subcultures) within institution or student affairs units. Acknowledges validity of subjective views. Emphasizes importance of mutual shaping.	Lacks conceptual specificity. Insights gleaned from one experience or institution not transferable to others. Organizational properties cannot be manipulated or controlled. Requires different expectations for leader behavior. May exclude or undervalue contributions of historically underrepresented groups.
Learning Organization	Compatible with cybernetic, action learning principles (such as mutual shaping, evolutionary change). Acknowledges importance of all members of organization. Deemphasizes formal structures and procedures, which encourages innovation, creativity, and organizational change. Encourages continuous learning of staff through role expansion, involvement in problem solving, and systemic change.	Some concepts are counterintuitive about organizations. Requires collaboration and networking. Emphasizes complexity, paradox, and continuous change over simplicity and search for correct solutions. Challenges traditional cultural values and norms.

In part this is due to the complexity and range of specialized functions performed in institutions of higher education (admissions, student development programming, legal services, career planning, psychological and health services, financial aid, food services, recreation, entertainment, and so on). Although responsible for all division employees, the SSAO is in contact with relatively few on a daily or weekly basis. Further, information (or a lack thereof) about what takes place in the career planning office rarely affects what recreational sports, student activities, or judicial affairs staff do, particularly in larger institutions. Information does not always get to those individuals who are in the best position to act. If counseling center staff members are not aware of a student's conflict with a roommate, the student may perceive that the institution is uncaring and unresponsive. At the same time, loose coupling can be advantageous. In loosely coupled organizations, staff operate with minimal supervision and interference and assume greater responsibility for their work (Weick, 1976, 1979, 1985). For example, poor attendance at the student union's film series does not, fortunately, affect the financial aid or health services offices. Because mistakes in one area are isolated from other parts of the system, staff may be more likely to seek their own solutions to problems or to respond to opportunities independently; greater risk taking and innovation are encouraged.

Fluid participation, common in institutions of higher education, describes situations in which people who might ordinarily participate in decision making are absent when decisions are made (which may affect the quality of the decision) or in which people may not be available to implement a decision they made (which may affect the quality of the implementation) (Cohen & March, 1974). Because the student activities director is attending a professional meeting, a decision about raising the activity fee may be delayed another year. Or those present may decide to raise the fee without the input of the student activities office, which could have a deleterious effect on future relations between students and administrators. Fluid participation is also illustrated by the high turnover of both students and staff. At most colleges and universities more than a quarter of students are new to the institution every year. Students spend only about eight months a year on campus. Some institutions expect entry-level student affairs staff to leave after two or three years for financial reasons. As a consequence, considerable effort is required to teach newcomers how to advise student government or what to expect during orientation activities.

Anarchistic qualities of colleges and universities are accentuated by the presence of highly autonomous professionals who expect to determine the character of their work environment, such as program development and availability to students. Many faculty members, particularly those at prestigious institutions, have a stronger allegiance to their discipline and national network of peers than to their employing institution (Clark, 1985). Obligations to professional associations sometimes conflict with institutional expectations, creating tensions (Baldridge et al., 1977).

At many institutions, such as the University of Kansas and Earlham College, student participation in institutional governance committees is widespread. Though this practice can have numerous benefits such as giving students opportunities to practice enlightened citizenship, student involvement in campus governance can prolong decision making, as student representatives must be oriented to governance structures and processes once or twice a year, and meetings must be scheduled when students are available. In the past few decades, the number of stakeholders expecting to participate in institutional decisions has expanded to include alumni, corporate and philanthropic sponsors, local and federal government officials, and parents (Birnbaum, 1988). As the number of stakeholders seeking a voice increases, decision-making processes become more complicated and time-consuming.

The organized anarchy view is unsettling to those who expect their institution to act rationally in predictable ways. The playful terms used to describe decision making seem incongruent with serious social science and decisive, visionary institutional leadership. Nevertheless, the organized anarchy perspective is descriptively rich and intuitively appealing because it accurately portrays the special qualities of life in colleges and universities that are overlooked by conventional views. For example, perhaps new procedures must be developed to allocate student activity fees because the people involved did not participate in the process the previous year or do not remember the decision-making rules (unclear technology). Or the assistant dean who conceptualized the recent reorganization of student government is on leave pursuing a doctorate at another institution (fluid participation), and someone unfamiliar with the new structure becomes the student government advisor. Such experiences are not necessarily random or without meaning, as is suggested by the term *anarchy.* Certain patterns and themes emerge out of annual events and daily interactions; some are even predictable. For example, students arrive in early September, the spring term class schedule must be prepared the preceding fall, and the annual spring fling weekend irritates the faculty, tests the patience of student affairs staff, and brings great pleasure to students and local merchants. Therefore, student affairs staff should not forget the first word of the phrase *organized anarchy.*

A Cultural Phenomenon

Another way to view college or university life is to think of it as a cultural phenomenon. An institution's culture represents a complex, elusive web of assumptions, beliefs, and values (Kuh & Whitt, 1988; Schein, 1992; Tierney, 1988) that encourage, support, and reward certain behaviors over others. It imposes order and brings coherence to daily life by determining what people consider important and what they will and will not do (Louis, 1983). And because people have their own constructions of institutional life, multiple interpretations are legitimate. That is, the interpretations of events depend on the context in which the events occur and the meaning given to the events by the actors, or "culture-bearers" (Allaire & Firsirotu, 1984). This explains in part why members of historically underrepresented groups may feel alienated by what their institution values and the way it does things (Kuh & Love, 2000), why debates occur annually about the best way to conduct performance reviews, and why student affairs staff rarely modify their behavior following the arrival of a new dean or president.

Culture is not a static entity, however; it is continually evolving. An institution's culture is shaped in part by its external environment—economic and social conditions, the background and values of the people who live near the college, and so on. Also, while the institution's culture may influence how an individual thinks and behaves, new faculty, staff, and students from historically underrepresented groups bring with them different attitudes and perspectives that have a shaping influence on the institution's culture (Rhoads & Valadez, 1996; Tierney, 1999). New staff members committed to using student development theory can influence certain features of the culture, such as the language used to communicate ideas. All these influences and more must be taken into account when trying to understand and appreciate an institution's culture.

Levels of Culture. Cultural properties can be divided into four levels (Schein, 1992): artifacts, perspectives, strategic values, and assumptions (Kuh & Hall, 1993; Lundberg, 1990). Artifacts, the most visible level, include such physical, verbal, and behavioral properties as language, stories, and sagas (Clark, 1972/1984), images, daily and periodic rituals, ceremonies, signs, and symbols (Morgan, 1986; Van Maanen, 1984)—"the physical layout, the dress code, the manner in which people address each other, the smell and feel of the place." (Schein, 1990, p. 111). Perspectives are patterns of behavior that have become widely shared; they define the way things should be and how things are done. An organization's strategic values are reflected in the sense of "what should be" compared with "what is." Many values are conscious, explicitly articulated, and guide group members in dealing with new or key situations. Espoused values are reflected in what people say but not necessarily in what they do (Argyris & Schön, 1978). Taken together, assumptions constitute a worldview (Lundberg, 1990) and define the nature of relations between people in their environment—how we treat each other, what constitutes "truth," and the relative importance of various tasks and activities. Assumptions essentially define the organization's "reality" (Morgan, 1986), determining how its members perceive, think about, and feel about things (Schein, 1993).

Subcultures. Most colleges and universities have several clearly differentiated subgroups among their students, faculty, and administrators; these groups tend to differ from one another in their values and beliefs (Clark, 1989; Clark & Trow, 1966; Kuh, Siegel, & Thomas, 2001; Martin, 1992). For example, student affairs staff often perceives events and activities differently from some of their faculty colleagues. This is due, in part, to their being socialized in different "cultures of orientation" (Van Maanen, 1984, p. 215). Subcultures are positive forces when they engender a sense of identity, cohesiveness, and loyalty to the institution or when they make success possible for persons in an alienating environment, such as African American students at a predominantly White campus (Kuh & Love, 2000; Watson et al., in press). But when a subculture's values and norms deviate significantly from the institution's expectations of appropriate behavior, such as when a fraternity tolerates hazardous use of alcohol by its members (Kuh & Arnold, 1993), the group can have a deleterious influence. On the other hand, the presence of such groups can stimulate productive disagreements about institutional goals and values. Such disagreements are inevitable, in fact, and they can provoke appropriate institutional change if the institution is forced to examine culturally embedded practices that inhibit certain individuals and groups from realizing their learning and personal development goals.

The culture window is best used as an interpretive lens for understanding and appreciating the nuances of a particular group's behavior (Kuh, 1993). For example, culture may explain why the goals of student affairs professionals are sometimes perceived as being inconsistent with the expectations of faculty and students, or why newcomers perceive certain aspects of institutional life differently from people who have been there some time. By examining values and beliefs, events can be understood that otherwise might seem mysterious, out of place, debilitating, or irrational. Looking through the culture window also provides a constant reminder that while institutions may be similar in many ways, they also differ in ways that affect how their members interpret and respond to what seem to be the same phenomena.

However, the culture window does not reveal everything that one needs to know about what takes place in a college or university. Culture concepts lack semantic precision, which can dampen their analytical power. Because meaning is context-bound, insights from one setting are not necessarily applicable to other settings; thus those who hope to develop a set of generalizable guiding principles will not be satisfied with the contextual restrictions imposed by a cultural perspective (Kuh, 1993) (see Exhibit 12.3). Some observers suggest that culture is not controllable and is therefore difficult—if not impossible—to change, at least in the short term (Kuh & Whitt, 1988). Others see culture as just another set of organizational properties that must adapt to changing external forces and internal circumstances (Tierney, 1999). These conflicting interpretations point to a potential limitation of the value of the cultural view for administrators coping with a rapidly changing external environment. As Pritchett and Pound (1993) put it, "We've entered an era where the organization must adopt a 'do what works' mentality. . . . In times past it was acceptable to settle for gradually evolving culture change. . . . [Today,] if the culture doesn't adapt—rapidly—everybody loses" (p. 8). It's incumbent on those who use a cultural view to find ways to modify dysfunctional elements of their institutional culture.

Learning Organizations

The learning organization view is the newest of the three postconventional windows. This view draws on three metaphors—the hologram, the brain, and the thermostat—that provide insight into how colleges and universities cope with the turbulent, sometime chaotic environmental forces that demand continuously changing institutional functions, processes, and structures.

A hologram is a photographic record of a dynamic process of interaction, integration, and differentiation. If a hologram breaks, any of its parts can be used to re-create the entire image (Morgan & Ramirez, 1983); that is, everything is encoded into everything else (Morgan, 1986). The institution-as-hologram metaphor suggests that each student affairs staff member is critical to the success of the operation and reflects both the character of the student affairs division and the institution's mission and values.

The brain combines features found nowhere else in nature: it acquires, stores, organizes, retrieves, and manipulates disparate pieces of information in a resilient, flexible, inventive, and integrative way; moreover, it has an elastic capacity to improve these functions (Morgan, 1986). Given the dynamic, rapidly changing circumstances facing institutions of higher education, it is highly desirable for a college or university to develop brainlike, continuous learning qualities.

A thermostat triggers a furnace or air conditioner in response to temperature changes (Birnbaum, 1988; Morgan, 1986). Similarly, a learning organization continually senses, monitors, and scans its internal and external environments and determines what the organization needs to adequately respond. When significant gaps exist between environmental demands and institutional processes, structures and resources, the institution must adapt in order to survive. As the scope and magnitude of changes reach a certain point, a qualitatively different organizational form may emerge. This morphogenetic change process is called self-organizing (Bertalanffy, 1968; Caple, 1985; Prigogine & Stengers, 1984) and requires four conditions: redundancy, requisite variety, minimum critical specification, and action learning (Morgan, 1986).

Redundancy means that staff members can perform a range of functions and can do the jobs of others; thus, generalists are valued over specialists. Through networking and information sharing, people learn how their work affects others, fostering teamwork and improved productivity (Allen & Cherrey, 2000; Wheatley, 1992). Both self-knowledge and organizational knowledge increase as staff learn more about student affairs and how their work influences others and the institution as a whole (Senge, 1990, 1999). Total Quality Management approaches emphasize this approach (Seymour, 1992).

Requisite variety means that the "internal diversity of any self-regulating system must match the variety and complexity of its environment" (Morgan, 1986, p. 100). For example, as increasing numbers of students of color matriculate, student affairs divisions need to reflect the characteristics of the diverse student body by hiring more people of color. In this way the values and attitudes of the student affairs staff may become more compatible with important characteristics of the external and internal environments. The personal values of staff must also be in harmony with institutional values. This does not imply unyielding, dogmatic adherence to institutional norms or policies, but rather respect for evolving collective purposes and goals.

Minimal critical specification refers to having the fewest number of people needed to perform essential functions and adapt to changing circumstances—whatever it takes to get the job done. Thus, to increase organizational flexibility and responsiveness to emerging issues, staff members and students should not be unduly constrained by rules and time-honored customs or organizational structures and processes that block institutional improvement.

Organizations typically respond to problems using a form of single-loop learning—the process of detecting and correcting errors assumed to have brought about the "problem" (Argyris & Schön, 1978). That is, when problems arise the usual reaction is to try to return the system to "normal" functioning. Action learning, on the other hand, is a form of double loop learning (Morgan, 1986; Senge, 1990), which is the reflective practice of "learning to learn"—an acquired ability to question normative behavior and evaluate guiding principles in the context of the changing demands the organization is facing. Double-loop learning requires a measure of risk taking because cautious, routine behavior often prevents one from being creative, responsive, and taking initiative (Peters, 1995).

For a student affairs unit to become a learning organization, its practitioners must cultivate five skills or "disciplines" as Senge (1990) described them:

1. *Systems thinking*—the ability to see that individual events and actions are interrelated and are part of a bigger pattern that is often difficult to discern.
2. *Personal mastery*—a commitment to lifelong learning, manifested by continually clarifying and deepening one's understanding or "vision" of the organization, focusing on important, core issues, and practicing patience in the face of sometimes paradoxical circumstances and demands to produce immediate improvement.
3. *Mental models*—an ability to discover and modify the assumptions, generalizations, and visual images that shape the way faculty, staff, students, and others perceive the world and affect how they behave.
4. *Shared vision*—an ability to unite people around a common sense of purpose and commitment.
5. *Team learning*—an ability to contribute to collaborative problem solving with coworkers and students, producing accelerated results.

Holograms, cybernetics, minimum critical specifications, and double-loop learning may be at first puzzling and even nonsensical to student affairs staff expecting (or hoping for) stability, order, and control (see Exhibit 12.3). These ideas are essential, however, for understanding and experimenting with ways to respond to changing circumstances. Indeed, sensing direction through variety, action, and involvement of many persons throughout the student affairs division is quite compatible, humane, and even sensible in the ambiguous, loosely coupled, occasionally chaotic world of student affairs.

Implications of Postconventional Views of Organizations

Postconventional views of organizations share five qualities. First, they assume that colleges and universities are open systems shaped by rapidly changing and unpredictable external forces and internal circumstances. Change occurs morphogenetically via the seemingly spontaneous adaptation and differentiation of structures and processes in response to interactions between the external environment and intentional (or unintentional) acts by institutional leaders and others (Schwartz & Ogilvy, 1979).

Second, because each institution is unique, policies and practices that work in one setting may not work in another (see Exhibit 12.3). Moreover, there are no single right answers in most situations, but rather a range of potentially productive responses.

Third, people mutually construct and context reality; that is, they make sense of ambivalent and sometimes conflicting goals, messages, and activities. This runs counter to conventional views' assumption of a single shared reality. As with a hologram, multiple constructions of reality reflect the whole of the institution, but from different perspectives. Through mutually shaping interactions, faculty, staff, and students develop a "collective unconscious" or culture—a set of beliefs, assumptions, norms, and practices that is continually evolving. Though institutions have hierarchical structures, the relationships between subsystems, such as the student activities office or a particular student organization, and higher-order systems, such as the division of student affairs or the institution, must be allowed to evolve into new forms through experience (Morgan, 1986; Senge, 1990, 1999). Reflection, flexibility, and adaptability are indispensable.

Fourth, postconventional views embrace a systemic perspective on organizational performance. Thus, they discourage people from concentrating on isolated problems (such as low voter turnout for student government elections or poor class attendance in lower-division courses) and emphasize understanding big-picture issues (such as inadequate levels of student engagement in the institution's social and academic subsystems) (Garvin, 1993; Senge, 1999). For example, to understand why students cannot make tuition payments requires knowledge about their background and cultural orientation to incurring debt, the local cost of living, the current availability of loans, and so on. Thus, student affairs staff need to look beneath the surface and discover the motivations and desires grounded in people's mental models or "tacit assumptions (unquestioned beliefs behind all decisions and actions) and hidden cultures (shared but unwritten rules for each member's behavior)" (Kilmann, 1985, p. 8).

Finally, postconventional views suggest that "change can be triggered from anywhere" (Allen & Cherrey, 2000, p. 106), acknowledging that chaotic elements in contemporary organizations can make any member of the organization a valuable source of information and influence for improving the organization. Contrary to conventional views, in which those near the top of the hierarchy are seen as having more expertise and power, postconventional views suggest that those persons closest to the effective point of action are best positioned to immediately identify and solve problems and to help develop policy (Kuh, 1985). Many entry-level staff members, for example, are competent—perhaps uniquely qualified—to help students deal with problems and to revise institutional policies. Moreover, the increasingly multicultural nature of colleges and universities demands that change initiatives insure the workplace is welcoming to members of historically underrepresented groups. The biggest challenge, then, is to find ways to involve people at all levels of the organization in meaningful, sustainable institutional change (Allen & Cherrey, 2000; Hollyman & Howie, 1994).

Guiding Principles for Organizational Redesign

No detailed road map to successful organizational change exists, though many have offered suggestions in this regard (Brown, 1997; Fried & Associates, 1995; Frost, 1996;

Levin, 1998; Peterson et al., 1997; Pope, 1995; Vaill, 1996). However, there are a handful of organizational change principles that, taken together, summarize the key concepts. The principles for organizational change that follow are presented with student affairs divisions in mind and encompass the types of activities that have promise for modifying institutional policies, practices, and cultural moorings with an eye toward promoting student learning and institutional effectiveness. The principles are grounded in the literature on organizational design (Argyris, 1990; Birnbaum, 1988; Bolman & Deal, 1991; Hannan & Freeman, 1989; Hedberg et al., 1976; Kanter, 1983; Keidel, 1995; Morgan, 1988; Pritchett & Pound, 1993; Senge, 1990, 1999; Vaill, 1989; Weick, 1979) and improvement of postsecondary institutions (for example, Ewell, 1997; Heydinger, 1994; Kuh, 1996; Peterson et al., 1997; Tierney, 1999). A balanced approach to implementing the principles fuses intentional change efforts through leadership and management interventions as legitimated in the traditional rational adaptation view of organizational change (for example, Creamer & Creamer, 1986; Lawrence & Lorsch, 1967; Thompson, 1967) and the unpredictable organizational adaptations that sometimes occur represented by views from random transformation (Hannan & Freeman, 1984) and chaos theory (Waldrop,1992).

Enacting the principles is more complicated and time-consuming than the following discussion implies. Systemic change efforts almost always encounter resistance. For a more thorough treatment of managing organizational change in colleges and universities consult Eckel, Hill, Green, and Mallon (1999), Kezar and Eckel (2002), Peterson et al. (1997), and Tierney (1999). Also, Talbot in Chapter Nineteen offers some excellent guidance for shaping change in multicultural organizations.

Generate Enthusiasm for Institutional Renewal

Although institutions and divisions are constantly changing, the consequences of change may be more or less desirable (Woodard et al., 2000). Thus, something in addition to serendipity is needed to insure a future consistent with our best aspirations and to get people to work together to create the institution we desire.

Any efforts to change the direction of the student affairs division must be clearly linked to a perceived or felt organizational need. Moreover, a clear, compelling case for change must be made—why things must be done differently (Eckel et al., 1999). For this reason it's imperative that senior student affairs professionals and the president encourage and periodically state their commitment to the change process and provide incentives and rewards for such efforts. Even so, it's not sufficient to assert that change is important, or that rational argument will win over colleagues.

It's also important that the change agenda invite and take into account input from many different groups and does not assign blame for the way things are but articulates the preferred future. One approach is to ask a series of questions to collectively craft a vision of what the student affairs division wants to be in the near future. By asking questions like "What are we doing?" and "Why are we doing it this way?" staff members can determine whether current routine practices are still relevant to the changing needs and interests of students and evolving institutional conditions.

Some institutions have found that establishing a fixed-term "think force" or other specially constituted group of administrators, key faculty members, students, and governing board members is effective in launching the effort. Such a high-profile group adds legitimacy to the initiative and can engender commitment from others. This group might also be charged with connecting different initiatives and individuals to create support and synergy for the change agenda. One or more champions of change from inside the student affairs division are needed to create a sense of anticipation and to establish the momentum for change (Pritchett & Pound, 1993). These people may be current staff, or they may need to be imported (for example, a new academic or student affairs dean). In any case, these change agents must exhibit confidence, enthusiasm and commitment; devote enormous energy to the endeavor; be flexible in adapting to unpredictable external and internal pressures; and understand the conditions that foster learning and institutional effectiveness described in the research.

Establish a Shared Vision and Common Language

Whether the change initiative is division-wide or localized to a specific functional area such as residential programs or career services, it's critical to articulate a shared vision of what the student affairs division is trying to accomplish. Such a mindscape is needed so that people can see how their work contributes to attaining the organization's goals as they perform their daily tasks. Maintaining a clear focus on the objectives to be accomplished must be viewed as an ongoing process that requires people to continually reflect on what they are trying to achieve (Garvin, 1993; Kezar & Eckel, 2002; Senge, 1999).

To communicate the vision and what is to be accomplished a common language is needed. The words and concepts that undergird student affairs work and the change agenda must be crafted in a way that insures clear communication both within and beyond the student affairs division. This is essential in order to discover how the work of the student affairs division contributes to the "big picture" of institutional effectiveness and changes that can enhance the productivity of student affairs and the larger institution.

Focus on Aligning Systems, Processes, and Products

Virtually all organizational change experts say that a systems approach is needed to bring about the desired results, not simply tinkering with administrative structures. A reorganization of office names, reporting lines, and administrative structures may provide the illusion of change, but such moves typically do not result in doing things differently, doing different things, or enhanced learning for students and overall improved effectiveness of the division.

Systemic change implies a realignment of core functions and the processes by which they are enacted in order to realize the desired complementarity among programs and services within and beyond the student affairs division (Woodard et al., 2000). As Tierney (1999, p. 164) says, "Paint the whole picture. Think big." That is, organization-wide thinking and action are needed to take into account, and perhaps modify, such institutional elements as educational mission, institutional values, curriculum, resources, student experiences outside the classroom, and so on.

That said, most interventions are best implemented by "working small" (Tierney, 1999, p. 166)—focusing on changes of a scale that are manageable and some of which can be accomplished within a reasonable period of time to demonstrate progress. Electronic technology offers much promise in this regard. Whatever the functions and processes to be changed, student affairs professionals should turn to what the research shows to be effective practices.

Another key to successfully aligning core division and institutional functions and processes for systemic change is having leaders with skills and proficiencies consistent with the tasks at hand at all levels of the institution (Birnbaum, 1988). This means that student affairs professionals throughout the student affairs division must cultivate the ability to discern larger patterns of change from what seem to be isolated, unconnected incidents. Both small and large scale events (Brigham, 1996) can be used to help student affairs professionals discover the relationships between their actions, institutional events, and consequences, some of which may have obvious short-term effects and others that may have subtle, long-term consequences for students and the institution. Such periodic gatherings can help keep the division from getting distracted by other issues that will surely arise and provide much-needed opportunities for networking with other key players within and beyond the student affairs division and institution which is essential to generate and sustain momentum and institutionalize changes.

Time and Timing

Aligning student experiences outside the classroom with the institution's educational mission and curricular experiences requires time, focus, and considerable energy. Selecting the right time to initiate the change strategy is also important (Bolman & Deal, 1991). A change effort might be introduced to coincide with the arrival of a new president, academic dean, or senior student affairs officer to capitalize on the uncertainty and expectations for change that often accompany the arrival of a new leader. Champions of the change must stay long enough for changes to take root (Kezar & Eckel, 2002).

Data-Driven Reflection

Student affairs professionals must become proficient at action learning in order to discover novel and increasingly progressive solutions to the complex problems facing their students and institution (Argyris & Schön, 1978). This means we must become comfortable with testing assumptions; reflecting on and questioning how the division of student affairs is operating; and—if appropriate—working toward changing the institution's norms, policies, and processes (Garvin, 1993).

This cannot be done effectively in an ad hominem fashion or by relying on anecdotes or personal experience. Rather, systematically collected information about the performance of the division and student experiences is needed to draw data-based conclusions about the efficacy of such efforts. Both results-oriented performance and the processes by which these results are produced must be considered. The latter is a good indicator of the degree to which the institution's values are being enacted.

Systemic Change Means Cultural Change

According to Tierney (1999) institutions of higher education must pay less attention to structure and much more to culture. This does not suggest that organizational structures do not matter; they do. Indeed, the way in which student affairs offices and reporting lines are arranged may very well be an obstacle to change. But most of what gets in the way of systemic change and improving organizational performance is not structure-dependent, but rather is cultural in nature (Kezar & Eckel, 2002). This is because people themselves determine the social contexts in which they work, "the entire spectrum of roles, responsibilities, expectations, and interactions" (Tiberius & Billson, 1991, p. 68).

As explained earlier, the culture that people develop over time has a powerful shaping influence on virtually all aspects of organizational life, including who and what kinds of activities are valued. Two aspects of institutional culture are especially pertinent with regard to improving educational effectiveness and enhancing the learning climate on campus for all students: (1) promoting cooperation and collaboration between academic and student affairs and (2) embracing multiculturalism.

Collaboration: A Key to Organizational Improvement

Most of the programs and policies that have the potential to foster student learning require collaboration among faculty, administrators, student affairs professionals, and others (Kuh, Schuh, Whitt, & Associates, 1991; Schroeder, 1999; Terenzini & Pascarella, 1994) so that functions, processes, and structures can be adapted appropriately throughout the organization (Garvin, 1993; Senge, 1990). When a "we-they" mentality exists, system thinking and action are impossible. Perceived power and status differences between faculty and student affairs staff can exacerbate misunderstandings. Trust and good will are important; their absence can undercut even the most elegant, well-funded change strategy. This can be ameliorated somewhat by intentionally creating partnerships and cross-functional collaboration that reflect the simultaneous "loose-tight" cybernetic properties of high-performing organizations (Birnbaum, 1988; Peters & Waterman, 1982; Senge, 1990; Vaill, 1989).

One nontrivial challenge is for faculty and student affairs professionals to become aware of and understand how their mental models influence their behavior (Arnold & Kuh, 1999; Kuh, 1996). Faculty members, student affairs professionals, and students have different views about the world, the institution, and their contributions to learning and institutional performance. Mental models are "deeply ingrained assumptions, generalizations, or even pictures or images that influence how we understand the world and how we take action" (Senge, 1990, p. 8). Most people are unaware of their mental models and how those shape behavior, including how they reinforce routine practices. Therefore, discovering the assumptions about important goals, values, and activities at the core of student affairs work is necessary for changing the institutional culture from one that is bifurcated into two independent spheres (academic and student affairs) to one where collaboration is the norm. It's also important to reconstitute reward systems that favor independent performance (such as individual faculty or staff member productivity) over collaboration, as this aspect of institutional culture will make it difficult to focus on common concerns.

One way to expand in short order the number of people who are primed for collaboration is to send a cross-functional team to visit "model" programs at other institutions (Kuh & Hinkle, 2002). Such ventures are particularly powerful if the activities to be examined elsewhere have immediate direct implications for work back on campus. For example, Indiana University Bloomington took a core group of more than a dozen academic administrators, faculty members, and student affairs professionals to the University of Missouri-Columbia to see and hear first hand from people like them about the promising educational practices being implemented at the sister school. This was a key step toward understanding the practical applications of the research and theory that support a number of interrelated undergraduate improvement efforts. Moreover, the trip introduced the participants to the vision and language of student success in a way that convinced key people that adopting promising practices was not only doable but preferable to the way the campus was currently operating (Hossler, Kuh, & Olsen, 2001).

Another way to build in collaboration is to hire informed, skilled, committed professionals who are predisposed to collaboration and who know how to put into action what they know from the higher education literature to represent best practice. The goal is not to produce institutional hegemony; in fact, as the next point indicates it is quite the opposite. Rather, it is to intentionally seek out, select, and socialize colleagues with needed pockets of expertise who share the vision of promoting student success by building an effective educational institution through collaboration (Collins & Porras, 1997). Collaboration beyond the campus, such as cooperative ventures with colleagues at other institutions, can also be productive as such support is invaluable for fostering change and innovation (Eckel et al., 1999; Tierney, 1999).

Cultivating A Multicultural Organization

Infusing multiculturalism throughout the student affairs division is no longer simply a desirable goal, it is essential. Diverse work environments are often more productive than less diverse settings (Hurtado & Dey, 1997), and students who interact frequently with peers from diverse backgrounds report gaining more from their college experience (Milem & Hakuta, 2000; Smith & Associates, 1997). For these reasons it's essential that colleges and universities be re-designed so they are sensitive to the many forms of diversity that now characterize our world and our campuses. There are some things that student affairs divisions are uniquely well situated to do on campus in terms of promoting, establishing, and sustaining organizational multiculturalism.

One key is making certain well-trained role models from historically underrepresented groups hold responsible positions throughout the division. Another is providing training and programming that address issues that all organizations face when dealing with the inevitable challenges multiculturalism presents (Katz, 1989).

Excellent recommendations in this regard are provided by Grieger (1996), Jackson and Holvino (1988), Manning and Coleman-Boatwright (1991), Pope (1993, 1995), and Tierney (1993), along with Talbot (See Chapter Nineteen).

Conclusion

No single view of organizations can account for everything that takes place in an institution of higher education or its division of student affairs. The six organizational windows described in this chapter are grounded in different assumptions about power, control, causality, relationships, and change. Although the different views produce conflicting descriptions and interpretations, taken together they can help student affairs staff understand why institutions and student affairs units in the future be flexible, responsive, and forward-looking. For this reason, every one of these windows can be instructive, depending on the events and behaviors one wishes to understand.

Conventional views, for example, adequately describe some of the more predictable institutional functions (such as registration, record keeping, and payroll). At the same time, however, they often impose unnecessary and undesirable psychological limits on the actions of leaders and followers alike, obfuscating action learning and evolutionary change processes. Whereas stability, reliability, predictability, and control are valued in conventional views, ambiguity, surprise, and change are featured in postconventional views.

Working on a college campus today is like white-water rafting. To negotiate the rapids, one must use a variety of psychological and behavioral skills to change direction. One also must take into account as many variables as possible: the current, eddies, rocks, the laws of physics, other rafts and paddlers, and so forth. Moment by moment, student affairs professionals must decide when to let the river have its way and when to use their professional knowledge, judgment, and skill to change its direction. To survive in the white water of the coming decades, student affairs staff must embrace ambiguity, risk taking, team-building, and continuous learning. Collaboration and networking—with faculty, students, and others—is essential (Allen & Cherrey, 2000; American College Personnel Association, 1994; Kuh, 1996; National Association of Student Personnel Administrators, 1995). The key challenge is to prepare oneself intellectually and emotionally to be a master of change (Kanter, 1983), dedicated to radically redesigning student affairs work and institutions of higher education on a continuing basis. Such masters of change are institutional treasures. Seek them out. Support them. Better yet, become one of them. Your life will be more interesting, and your institution will be more productive!

References

Allaire, Y., & Firsirotu, M. E. (1984). Theories of organizational culture. *Organization Studies, 5,* 193–226.

Allen, K. E., & Cherrey, C. (2000). *Systemic leadership: Enriching the meaning of our work.* Lanham, MD: University Press of America.

Allison, G. T. (1971). *Essence of decision: Explaining the Cuban missile crisis.* Boston: Little, Brown.

American College Personnel Association. (1994). *Student learning imperative: Implications for student affairs.* Alexandria, VA: American College Personnel Association.

Argyris, C. (1964). *Integrating the individual and the organization.* New York: Wiley.

Argyris, C. (1990). *Overcoming organizational defenses: Facilitating organizational learning.* Wellesley, MA: Allyn & Bacon.

Argyris, C., & Schön, D. A. (1978). *Organizational learning: A theory of action perspective.* Reading, MA: Addison-Wesley.

Arnold, K., & Kuh, G. D. (1999). What matters in undergraduate education? Mental models, student learning, and student affairs. In E. J. Whitt (Ed.), *Student learning as student affairs work: Responding to our imperative* (pp. 11–34). Washington, DC: National Association of Student Personnel Administrators.

Association of Governing Boards of Universities and Colleges (1999). *Ten public policy issues for higher education in 1999 and 2000,* AGB Public Policy Paper Series, No. 99–1. Washington, DC: Association of Governing Boards of Universities and Colleges.

Austin, A. E., & Gamson, Z. F. (1983). *Academic workplace: New demands, heightened tensions* (ASHE-ERIC Higher Education Research Report No. 10). Washington, DC: Association for the Study of Higher Education.

Baldridge, J. V. (1971). *Power and conflict in the university: Research in the sociology of complex organizations.* New York: Wiley.

Baldridge, J. V., Curtis, D. V., Ecker, G. P., & Riley, G. L. (1977). *Alternative models of governance in higher education.* In J. V. Baldridge & T. E. Deal (Eds.), *Governing academic organizations* (pp. 2–25). Berkeley, CA: McCutchan.

Bertalanffy, L. von. (1968). *General system theory* (2nd ed.). New York: Braziller.

Birnbaum, R. (1988). *How colleges work: The cybernetics of academic organization and leadership.* San Francisco: Jossey-Bass.

Bolman, L. G., & Deal, T. E. (1991). *Reframing organizations: Artistry, choice, and leadership.* San Francisco: Jossey-Bass.

Brigham, S. E. (1996, November/December). Large-scale events: New ways of working across the organization. *Change,* 28–37.

Brown, J. S. (1997). On becoming a learning organization. *About Campus, 1* (6), 5–13.

Caple, R. B. (1985). Counseling and the self-organization paradigm. *Journal of Counseling and Development, 64,* 173–178.

Chaffee, E. E. (1983). *Rational decision-making in higher education.* Boulder, CO: National Center for Higher Education Management Systems.

Clark, B. R. (1984). The organizational saga in higher education. In R. Birnbaum (Ed.), *ASHE reader in organization and governance in higher education* (pp. 36–41). Washington, DC: Association for the Study of Higher Education. (Reprinted from *Administrative Science Quarterly, 17,* 178–184, 1972.)

Clark, B. R. (1989). The academic life: Small worlds, different worlds. *Educational Researcher, 18* (5), 4–8.

Clark, B. R., & Trow, M. (1966). The organizational context. In T. Newcomb & E. Wilson (Eds.), *College peer groups: Problems and prospects for research* (pp. 17–70). Chicago: Aldine.

Clark, D. L. (1985). Emerging paradigms in organizational theory and research. In Y. S. Lincoln (Ed.), *Organizational theory and inquiry: The paradigm revolution* (pp. 43–78). Newbury Park, CA: Sage.

Cohen, M. D., & March, J. G. (1974). *Leadership and ambiguity: The American college president.* New York: McGraw-Hill.

Cohen, M. D., March, J. G., & Olsen, J. P. (1972). A garbage can model of organizational choice. *Administrative Science Quarterly, 17* (1), 1–25.

Collins, J. C., & Porras, J. I. (1997). *Built to last: Successful habits of visionary companies.* New York: Harper-Collins.

Creamer, D. G., & Creamer, E. G. (1986). Applying a model of planned change to program innovation in student affairs. *Journal of College Student Personnel, 27,* 19–26.

Di Maggio, P. J., & Powell, W. W. (1983). *Power and the structure of society.* New York: Norton.
Eckel, P., Hill, B., Green, M., & Mallon, D. (1999). *Reports from the road: Insights on institutional change.* Washington, DC: American Council on Education.
Etzioni, A. (1961). *A comparative analysis of complex organizations: On power, involvement, and their correlates* (2nd ed.). New York: Free Press.
Ewell, P. T. (1997). Organizing for learning: A new imperative. *American Association for Higher Education Bulletin, 50* (4), 3–6.
Fayol, H. (1949). *General and industrial management.* London: Pitman.
Fried, J., & Associates (Eds.). (1995). *Shifting paradigms in student affairs: Culture, context, teaching and learning.* Lanham, MD: American College Personal Association/University Press of America.
Frost, C. F. (1996). *Changing forever: The well-kept secret of America's leading companies.* East Lansing: The Michigan State University Press.
Garvin, D. A. (1993, July–August). Building a learning organization. *Harvard Business Review,* pp. 78–91.
Gleick, J. (1987). *Chaos: Making a new science.* New York: Viking.
Grieger, I. (1996). A multicultural organizational checklist for student affairs. *Journal of College Student Development, 37,* 561–573.
Gross, E., & Grambusch, P. (1968). *University goals and academic power.* Washington, DC: American Council on Education.
Gulick, L., & Urwick, L. (1937). *Papers on the science of administration.* New York: Columbia University Institute of Public Administration.
Hage, J. (1980). *Theories of organization: Form, process, and transformation.* New York: Wiley.
Hage, J., & Aiken, M. (1970). *Social change in complex organizations.* New York: Random House.
Hannan, M. T., & Freeman, J. (1984). Structural inertia and organizational change. *American Sociological Review, 49,* 149–164.
Hannan, M. T., & Freeman, J. (1989). *Organizational ecology.* Cambridge, MA: Harvard University Press.
Hedberg, B., Nystrom, P., & Starbuck, W. (1976). Camping on seesaws: Prescriptions for self-designing organization. *Administrative Science Quarterly, 21,* 41–65.
Heydinger, R. B. (1994). A reinvented model for higher education. *On the Horizon: The Environmental Scanning Newsletter for Leaders in Education, 3* (1), 1–2, 4–5.
Hollyman, B. P., & Howie, R. L., Jr. (1994, December 19). Mastering change: Information technology integration in successful enterprises. *Business Week* (Special Advertising Section), pp. 1–12.
Hossler, D., Kuh, G. D., & Olsen, D. (2001). Finding (more) fruit on the vines: Using higher education research and institutional research to guide institutional policies and strategies. (Part II) *Research in Higher Education, 42,* 223–235.
Hurtado, S., & Dey, E. L. (1997). Achieving the goals of multiculturalism and diversity. In M. D. Peterson, D. A. Dill, L. A. Mets & Associates (Eds.), *Planning and management for a changing environment* (pp. 405–431). San Francisco: Jossey-Bass.
Jackson, B. W., & Holvino, E. (1988). Developing multicultural organizations. *Journal of Religion and the Applied Behavioral Sciences, 9* (2), 14–19.
Kanter, R. M. (1983). *The change masters.* New York: Simon & Schuster.
Katz, J. (1989). The challenge of diversity. In C. Woolbright (Ed.), *Valuing diversity on campus: A multicultural approach* (pp. 1–21). Bloomington, IN: Association of College Unions–International.
Keidel, R. W. (1995). *Seeing organizational patterns: A new theory and language of organizational design.* San Francisco: Berrett-Koehler.
Kezar, A., & Eckel, P. (2002). Examining the institutional transformation process: The importance of sensemaking, interpretive strategies, and balance. *Research in Higher Education, 43,* 295–328.
Killman, R. H. (1985). *Beyond the quick fix: Managing five tracks to organizational success.* San Francisco: Jossey-Bass.

Kuh, G. D. (1984). A framework for understanding student affairs work. *Journal of College Student Personnel, 25,* 25–31.

Kuh, G. D. (1985). What is extraordinary about ordinary student affairs organizations. *NASPA Journal, 23,* 31–43.

Kuh, G. D. (1993). Appraising the character of a college. *Journal of Counseling and Development, 71,* 661–668.

Kuh, G. D. (1994). Creating campus climates that foster student learning. In P. Mable & C. Schroeder (Eds.), *Realizing the educational potential of residence halls* (pp. 109–132). San Francisco: Jossey-Bass.

Kuh, G. D. (1996). Guiding principles for designing seamless learning environments for undergraduates. *Journal of College Student Development, 37,* 135–148.

Kuh, G. D., & Arnold, J. A. (1993). Liquid bonding: A cultural analysis of the role of alcohol in fraternity pledgeship. *Journal of College Student Development, 34,* 327–334.

Kuh, G. D., & Hall, J. (1993). Using cultural perspectives in student affairs. In G. D. Kuh (Ed.), *Using cultural perspectives in student affairs work* (pp. 1–20). Alexandria, VA: American College Personnel Association.

Kuh, G. D., & Hinkle, S. E. (2002). Enhancing student learning through collaboration between academic affairs and student affairs. In. R. M. Diamond (Ed.), *Field guide to academic leadership* (pp. 311–327). San Francisco: Jossey-Bass.

Kuh, G. D., & Love, P. G. (2000). A cultural perspective on student departure. In J. Braxton (Ed.), *Rethinking the departure puzzle: New theory and research on college student retention* (pp.196–212). Nashville, TN: Vanderbilt University Press.

Kuh, G. D., Schuh. K. H., Whitt, E. J., & Associates. (1991). *Involving colleges: Successful approaches to fostering student learning and development outside the classroom.* San Francisco: Jossey-Bass.

Kuh, G. D., Siegel, M. J., & Thomas, A. (2001). Higher education: Values and culture. In D. Creamer, R. Winston, and T. Miller (Eds.), *The professional student affairs administrator: Educator, leader, and manager* (pp. 3–38). Muncie, IN: Accelerated Development.

Kuh, G. D., & Whitt, E. J. (1988). *The invisible tapestry: Culture in American colleges and universities* (ASHE-ERIC Higher Education Report No. 1). Washington, DC: Association for the Study of Higher Education.

Kuh, G. D., Whitt, E. J., & Shedd, J. D. (1987). *Student affairs, 2001: A paradigmatic odyssey* (ACPA Media Publication No. 42). Alexandria, VA: American College Personnel Association.

Kuhn, T. S. (1970). *The structure of scientific revolutions* (2nd ed.). Chicago: University of Chicago Press.

Lawrence, P., & Lorsch, J. (1967). *Organization and environment.* Cambridge, MA: Harvard University Press.

Levin, J. S. (Ed.). (1998). *Organizational change in the community college: A ripple or a sea change?* (New Directions for Community Colleges No. 102). San Francisco: Jossey-Bass.

Likert, R. (1967). *The human organization.* New York: McGraw-Hill.

Lincoln, Y. S. (1985). [Introduction]. In Y. S. Lincoln (Ed.), *Organizational theory and inquiry: The paradigm revolution* (pp. 29–40). Newbury Park, CA: Sage.

Lipsky, M. (1980). *Street-level bureaucracy: Dilemmas of the individual in public services.* New York: Russell Sage Foundation.

Louis, M. R. (1983). Organizations as culture-bearing milieux. In L. Pondy, P. Frost, G. Morgan, & T. Dandridge (Eds.), *Organizational symbolism* (pp. 39–54). Greenwich, CT: JAI.

Lundberg, C. C. (1990). Surfacing organizational culture. *Journal of Managerial Psychology, 5* (4), 19–26.

Manning, K., & Coleman-Boatwright, P. (1991). Student affairs initiatives toward a multicultural university. *Journal of College Student Development, 32,* 367–374.

March, J. G., & Olsen, J. P. (1976). *Ambiguity and choice in organizations.* Bergen, Norway: Universitetsførlaget.

Martin, J. (1992). *Cultures in organizations: Three perspectives.* New York: Oxford University Press.

Mayo, E. (1945). *The social problems of an industrial civilization.* Boston: Harvard University Graduate School of Business.

McGregor, D. (1960). *The human side of enterprise.* New York: McGraw-Hill.
Milem, J. F., & Hakuta, K. (2000). The benefits of racial and ethnic diversity in higher education. In D. Wilds (Ed.), *Minorities in higher education: Seventeenth annual status report* (pp. 39–67). Washington, DC: American Council on Education.
Mintzberg, H. (1979). *The structuring of organizations.* Englewood Cliffs, NJ: Prentice Hall.
Morgan, G. (1986). *Images of organization.* Newbury Park, CA: Sage.
Morgan, G. (1988). *Riding the waves of change: Developing managerial competencies for a turbulent world.* San Francisco: Jossey-Bass.
Morgan, G., & Ramirez, R. (1983). Action learning: A holographic metaphor for guiding social change. *Human Relations, 37,* 1–28.
National Association of Student Personnel Administrators. (1995). *Reasonable expectations.* Washington, DC: Author.
Peters, T. J. (1987). *Thriving on chaos: Handbook for a management revolution.* New York: Harper & Row.
Peters, T. J. (1995). *Pursuit of wow.* New York: Random House.
Peters, T. J., & Waterman, R. H., Jr. (1982). *In search of excellence: Lessons from America's best run companies.* New York: Harper & Row.
Peterson, M. W., Dill, D. A., Mets, L. A., & Associates (1997). *Planning and management for a changing environment.* San Francisco: Jossey-Bass.
Pfeffer, J. (1982). *Organizations and organizational theory.* Boston: Pitman.
Pfeffer, J., & Salancik, G. (1978). *The external control of organizations: A resource dependence perspective.* New York: Harper & Row.
Pope, R. L. (1993). Multicultural organizational development in student affairs: An introduction. *Journal of College Student Development, 34,* 201–205.
Pope, R. L. (1995). Multicultural organizational development: Implications and applications for student affairs. In J. Fried & Associates (Eds.), *Shifting paradigms in student affairs: Culture, context, teaching and learning* (pp. 233–249). Lanham, MD: University Press of America.
Prigogine, I., & Stengers, I. (1984). *Order out of chaos.* New York: Bantam Books.
Pritchett, P., & Pound, R. (1993). *High-velocity culture change: A handbook for managers.* Dallas, TX: Pritchett.
Rhoads, R., & Valadez, J. (1996). *Democracy, multiculturalism and the community college: A critical perspective.* New York: Garland.
Schein, E. H. (1990). Organizational culture. *American Psychologist, 45* (2), 109–119.
Schein, E. H. (1992). *Organizational culture and leadership* (2nd ed.). San Francisco: Jossey-Bass.
Schein, E. H. (1993, Winter). How can organizations learn faster? The challenge of entering the green room. *Sloan Management Review,* 61–68.
Schön, D. A. (1983). *The reflective practitioner: How professionals think in action.* New York: Basic Books.
Schön, D. A. (1987). *Educating the reflective practitioner: Toward a new design for teaching and learning in the professions.* San Francisco: Jossey-Bass.
Schroeder, C. C. (1999). Forging educational partnerships that advance student learning. In G. S. Blimling & E. J. Whitt (Eds.), *Good practices in student affairs: Principles to foster student learning* (pp. 133–156). San Francisco: Jossey-Bass.
Schroeder, C. C., Nicholls, G. E., & Kuh, G. D. (1983). Exploring the rain forest: Testing assumptions and taking risks. In G. D. Kuh (Ed.), *Understanding student affairs organizations* (New Directions for Student Services No. 23, pp. 51–65). San Francisco: Jossey-Bass.
Schwartz, P., & Ogilvy, J. (1979). *The emergent paradigm: Changing patterns of thought and belief* (SRI International Analytical Report No. 7). Menlo Park, CA: Values and Lifestyles Program.
Senge, P. M. (1990). *The fifth discipline: The art and practice of the learning organization.* New York: Doubleday/Currency.
Senge, P. M. (1999). *The dance of change: The challenges of sustaining momentum in learning organizations.* New York: Currency/Doubleday.
Seymour, D. T. (1992). *On Q: Causing quality in higher education.* New York: Macmillan.

Simon, H. A. (1957). *Administrative behavior.* New York: Free Press.

Smith D. G., & Associates (1997). *Diversity works: The emerging picture of how students benefit.* Washington, DC: Association of American Colleges and Universities.

Strange, C. C. (1983). Traditional perspectives on student affairs organizations. In G. D. Kuh (Ed.), *Understanding student affairs organizations* (New Directions for Student Services No. 23, pp. 5–13). San Francisco: Jossey-Bass.

Taylor, F. W. (1911). *The principles of scientific management.* New York: Harper.

Terenzini, P. T., & Pascarella, E. T. (1994). Living with myths: Undergraduate education in America. *Change, 26* (1), 28–32.

The Third Imperative. (1999). *Policy Perspectives, 9* (1), 1–9.

Thompson, J. D. (1967). *Organizations in action.* New York: McGraw-Hill.

Tiberius, R. G., & Billson, J. N. (1991). The social context of teaching. In R. J. Menges & M. D. Svinicki (Eds.), *College teaching: From theory to practice* (New Directions for Teaching and Learning No. 45, pp. 67–86). San Francisco: Jossey-Bass.

Tierney, W. G. (1988). Organizational culture in higher education: Defining the essentials. *Journal of Higher Education, 59,* 2–21.

Tierney, W. G. (1993). *Building communities of difference: Higher education in the twenty-first century.* Westport, CT: Bergin & Garvey.

Tierney, W. G. (1999). *Building the responsive campus: Creating high performance colleges and universities.* Thousand Oaks, CA: Sage.

Vaill, P. B. (1984). The purposing of high-performing systems. In T. J. Sergiovanni & J. Corbally (Eds.), *Leadership and organizational culture: New perspectives on administrative theory and practice* (pp. 85–104). Urbana: University of Illinois Press.

Vaill, P. B. (1989). *Managing as a performing art: New ideas for a world of chaotic change.* San Francisco: Jossey-Bass.

Vaill, P. B. (1996). *Learning as a way of being: Strategies for survival in a world of permanent white water.* San Francisco: Jossey-Bass.

Van Maanen, J. (1984). Doing old things in new ways: The chains of socialization. In J. Bess (Ed.), *College and university organization: Insights from the behavioral sciences* (pp. 211–247). New York: New York University Press.

Waldrop, M. M. (1992). *Complexity: The emerging science at the edge of order and chaos.* New York: Simon & Schuster.

Watson, L., Wright, D., Terrell, M., & Associates (in press). *How minority students experience college: Implications for policy and practice.* Sterling, VA: Stylus.

Weber, M. (1947). *The theory of social and economic organization.* London: Oxford University Press.

Weick, K. E. (1976). Educational organizations as loosely coupled systems. *Administrative Science Quarterly, 21,* 1–19.

Weick, K. E. (1979). *The social psychology of organizing* (2nd ed.). Reading, MA: Addison-Wesley.

Weick, K. E. (1985). Sources of order in underorganized systems: Themes in recent organizational theory. In Y. S. Lincoln (Ed.), *Organizational theory and inquiry: The paradigm revolution* (pp. 106–136). Newbury Park, CA: Sage.

Weick, K. E. (1995). *Sensemaking in organizations.* Thousand Oaks, CA: Sage.

Wheatley, M. J. (1992). *Leadership and the new science: Learning about organization from an orderly universe.* San Francisco: Berrett-Koehler.

Woodard, D. B., Love, P., & Komives, S. R. (2000). *Leadership and management issues for a new century* (New Directions for Student Services No. 92). San Francisco: Jossey-Bass.

Zucker, L. G. (1987). Institutional theories of organization. *Annual Review of Sociology, 13,* 443–464.

Zusman, A. (1999). Issues facing higher education in the twenty-first century. In P. Altbach, R. Berdahl, & P. Gumport (Eds.), *American higher education in the twenty-first century: Social, political, and economic challenges* (pp. 109–148). Baltimore: The Johns Hopkins University Press.

CHAPTER THIRTEEN

DYNAMICS OF CAMPUS ENVIRONMENTS

C. Carney Strange

Much has changed in American higher education since the late nineteenth century U.S. President James Garfield once claimed, "The ideal college is Mark Hopkins at one end of a log and a student at the other" (Rudolph, 1962, p. 243). Hopkins, a renowned Williams College educator, served as the institution's leader from 1836 to 1872 and stood as the consummate gentleman scholar of his day. Since his time, though, postsecondary education has clearly transformed itself. From the simple "log" has grown an enormous enterprise of stone, brick, concrete, and steel, offering a gallery of architectural designs, functions, and purposes. From one end of the log, the singular gentleman scholar has evolved into a host of new faculty roles and responsibilities; from the other end, the lone, awestruck student has changed as well, replaced now by a chorus of new learners, voicing an increasingly rich score of liberal, technical, and vocational educational interests and goals. Higher education in America has indeed changed, giving rise to a maze of state, private, and community-based institutions that are as difficult to comprehend for the faculty and administrators who serve them as it is for the students who must choose among them.

As confusing as it may be, going off to college is at once exciting, challenging, and rewarding for many; for some, however, it may be intimidating and even terrifying. From the first turn into a campus parking lot of the local community college, the adjustment to new living quarters in a distant residential campus, or entry into the first classroom on the schedule, most institutional environments offer numerous and complex choices, with consequences good or bad for the learning, growth, and development of students. How those choices are understood and negotiated ultimately determines the success of this goal. An essential challenge facing postsecondary educators today is the creation and maintenance of campus environments that attract, satisfy, and sustain students in their efforts to achieve their educational goals.

Student affairs practitioners play a major role in supporting this effort. As campus enrollment managers and orientation directors, they recruit and acclimate new students to the college environment. As residence hall directors, they assist students in meeting the challenges of communal living and learning. As directors of adult and commuter education programs, they enhance students' sense of belonging and their belief that they matter to their institution (Schlossberg, Lassalle, & Golec, 1988). As student activities and organizations advisors, they engage students in the opportunities of campus involvement and leadership. As personal counselors, they aid students in understanding the adjustments required of life transitions; and as academic, career, and vocational advisors, they assist students in choosing a personally fulfilling academic and occupational goal. What is needed to guide these functions and practices is a comprehensive model of campus environments that describes their various features and how they can encourage student growth and development (Strange, 1983; Strange & King, 1990). According to this "ecological perspective," incorporating "the influence of environments on persons and persons on environments" (Banning & Kaiser, 1974, p. 371), institutions themselves bear responsibility for the design and creation of campus environments, arranged appropriately for meeting educational purposes.

Over the past two decades a number of conceptual reviews have highlighted various models for understanding the interaction between students and their campus environments (for example, see Baird, 1988; Huebner & Lawson, 1990; Moos, 1979; Pascarella, 1985; and Strange, 1991, 1993, 1994). However, more recently a comprehensive framework has emerged that synthesizes this material and orients it towards a scheme of educational purposes and designs (Strange & Banning, 2001). This chapter presents an overview of this framework, focusing first on four dimensions of campus environments: (1) the design and quality of physical features; (2) the collective characteristics of human aggregates, or groups of people; (3) the dynamics of campus organizational structures and designs; and (4) the collective meanings members construct around these dimensions and attribute to them. This analysis is completed with a model of environmental purposes related to the success of student learning, moving first from an examination of those components that include and secure students in various campus settings, second to those that engage students in significant forms of involvement, and third to those that invite them into full membership in the learning community. (See Exhibit 13.1.)

Concepts Related to Campus Environments

A thirty-minute tour of any campus can reveal much about its essential environmental characteristics and dynamics. From the size, layout, condition, and design of its buildings, facilities, spaces, and landscapes; the collective appearance and style of its students, faculty, and staff; the structure and organization of its administrative systems and practices; and from the nature of its principal academic and social presses, traditions, customs, and symbols, immediate and powerful impressions emerge of whether "this is a good place to be." (See Exhibit 13.2.) The sidewalk that encourages

EXHIBIT 13.1. DESIGNING FOR EDUCATIONAL PURPOSES.

- *Promoting inclusion and safety*
  Physical (such as wayfinding)
  Human Aggregate (such as differentiated groupings)
  Organizational (such as human scale design)
  Constructed (such as relational social climate)
- *Encouraging involvement*
  Physical (such as accessibility)
  Human Aggregate (such as heterogeneous groupings)
  Organizational (such as complexity and innovation)
  Constructed (such as cultures of involvement)
- *Building community*
  Physical (such as territory and space)
  Human Aggregate (such as congruence and differentiation)
  Organizational (such as dynamic structures)
  Constructed (such as traditions and artifacts)

Source: Strange and Banning (2001).

EXHIBIT 13.2. COMPONENTS OF CAMPUS ENVIRONMENTS.

Physical—natural and synthetic features and designs (such as landscaping, terrain, placement of buildings, internal lighting)

Human Aggregate—collective characteristics of participants (such as arrangements of people in relation to common traits)

Organizational—organized structures that serve specific goals (such as decision making, rules, rewards, complexity)

Constructed—collective perceptions of people in a setting (such as attributions of campus press, climate, culture)

Source: Strange and Banning (2001).

us to walk around a building rather than across the rain-soaked muddy pathway; the characteristic styles, conversations, and actions of students and staff; the expectations and procedures we follow (or ignore) in the execution of our responsibilities; and finally, the distinctive values and impressions we intuit from the very air we breathe in the setting all help us understand and communicate to others "what it's like to be here." These four sets of components—physical, human aggregate, organizational, and constructed—comprise the various sources of environmental influence on human behavior on any campus. Recognizing them, as well as their dynamics, is an important first step in understanding how they may be shaped to achieve educational purposes.

Physical Components

All campuses contain physical features, both natural and synthetic; natural features might include geographic location, terrain, climate, and weather; synthetic features entail architectural design, spatial arrangements, amenities, and layouts. Both kinds of features contribute to various conditions of light, density, noise, temperature, air quality, and aesthetics to create a powerful influence on individuals' attraction to and satisfaction within any environment.

The physical features of a campus are often among the most important factors in creating a visitor's critical first impression of an institution (Sturner, 1973; Thelin & Yankovich, 1987). In a firsthand study of campus life at twenty-nine different colleges, Boyer (1987) concluded, "it was the buildings, the trees, the walkways, the well-kept lawns—that overwhelmingly won out. The appearance of the campus is, by far, the most influential characteristic during campus visits, and . . . when it comes to recruiting students, the director of buildings and grounds may be more important than the academic dean" (p. 17). Admissions offices have begun more recently to capitalize on the power of these images, using web pages and virtual tours to provide potential students with a quick, economical, manicured survey of campus life in the privacy of their home.

Concepts of campus physical environments draw from a variety of fields, such as art and architecture (for example, Dober, 1992; Gaines, 1991; Sommer, 1969), ecological psychology (for example, Barker, 1968), and cultural anthropology (for example, Moffatt, 1989). All of these disciplines contribute to an understanding of the college campus as a "place apart" (Stern, 1986, p. 41) whose physical features interact with and influence a range of behaviors, attitudes, and outcomes relative to its educational mission. Physical features also set broad limits on the phenomena that can occur, a dynamic of "intersystems congruence" (Michelson, 1970, p. 25), making some behaviors more likely than others. For example, a large theater-style classroom with immovable seating may set limits on the extent to which group discussions can occur, regardless of the types of students involved or the best efforts of the instructor. On the other hand, some phenomena are encouraged because of physical limitations, as is often evident on commuter campuses where bare paths are quickly worn through green lawns to find the shortest distance between parking lots and the classroom buildings. Although components of the physical environment may not directly cause specific attitudes or behaviors, its features present challenges, through nonverbal messages, functional and symbolic limitations, and various artifacts (Strange & Banning, 2001) that must be negotiated in order to achieve intended purposes.

For some students, the features of an institution's on-campus residence halls shape their first impressions of campus life. The number of floors, the location of stairwells and elevators, the design of inner spaces, and the use of amenities all play an important role in the quality of their campus experience (Heilweil, 1973). For many others, pathways from parking garages to commuter centers do the same. Distances to communal facilities, the location of maintenance and disposal equipment, and the marking and lighting of walkways can all create quick impressions of comfort or risk. Further, opportunities for the development and expression of personal identity often lie in the flexibility students enjoy in shaping and arranging the spaces they use. Where students are encouraged to individualize the design of their own spaces, a sense of territoriality (Schroeder, 1979), personal space (Anchors, Schroeder, & Jackson, 1978), wayfinding (Arthur & Passini, 1992), and community (Ender, Kane, Mable, & Strohm, 1980) develops.

All aspects of the campus physical environment are important to the quality of students' campus experiences and can serve as prohibitive or positive forces for the learning, growth, and development in students' lives (Strange, 1983). As Dober (1992) concluded, "Each campus deserves to be a special place and to have a distinctive image that communicates, at the least, the institution's purpose, presence, domain, and values" (p. 280).

Human Aggregates

A key focus of this perspective is that the dominant features of any particular environment reflect the dominant characteristics of the people within it (Astin, 1962, 1968; Astin & Holland, 1961). Therefore, in order to understand the likely impact of an environment, knowledge of its inhabitants' collective characteristics is essential. Thus, many of the same models and theories used to understand interpersonal styles and other differences among students (see Chapters Nine and Ten) are used to understand the dynamics of human aggregate features of any environment.

Subcultures, Typologies, and Styles. Various models describe patterned differences among groups of students, in the form of subcultures, types, and styles. Clark and Trow (1966) first explored the implications of campus subcultures with their identification of academic, nonconformist, collegiate, and vocational students. Subsequently, the work of Holland (1973) on vocational interests, the psychological types of Myers (1980), and the learning orientations of Kolb (1983) have also received the attention of researchers and educators seeking to understand the dynamics of campus aggregates.

Astin (1993) constructed an empirically derived typology of college students from self-reported student responses to the Cooperative Institutional Research Program's (CIRP) national freshman survey. According to Astin, each of seven types (Scholars, Social Activists, Artists, Hedonists, Leaders, Status Strivers, and Uncommitted Students) is characterized by select values, background characteristics, institutional characteristics, and academic major preferences. For example, Scholars come from well educated families, enroll in private colleges and universities, hold high expectations for academic success, and tend to major in the sciences. In contrast, Status Strivers come from less educated parents, have poorer high school academic records, place a premium on materialistic values, spend more time on the social experiences of college, and gravitate toward careers in business. Interestingly, Status Strivers are also overrepresented among African American and Chicano students. The effects of the dominant characteristics and attributes of various campus aggregates can be seen from these descriptors; whole institutional cultures and images have emerged from the distinctions attributed to these types. For example, where would a Williams College be without its Scholars, creating an institutional milieu supportive of academic and intellectual pursuits? Where would an Indiana University be without Status Strivers and their rich traditions of involvement in residence hall life, campus activities, Greek-letter organizations, and intercollegiate athletics? Would a Morehouse or Spelman be the same without its Leaders?

Human aggregate models reduce environmental differences to the collective effects of members' characteristics, personalities, and types. Thus, assessments of the collective characteristics of an environment's inhabitants, whether demographic (by gender, age, or racial-ethnic composition, for example) or psychological (by personality types or learning styles), provide a descriptive measure of the environment's dominant features.

Person-Environment Interactions. Human aggregate models are instructive of the dynamics of person-environment interactions, as a function of environmental differentiation and consistency (Holland, 1973). A highly differentiated, or focused, aggregate is dominated by one single type or characteristic (all women, all African Americans, all commuters, and so on); an undifferentiated aggregate is more diffuse and characterized by the presence of many different types. Differentiated aggregates are readily distinguished both by participants and observers, precisely because they encourage select behaviors, values, attitudes, and expectations and discourage those dissimilar. Undifferentiated aggregates are more flexible and open to a variety of influences and are consequently more difficult to understand due to their lack of any clear focus.

Consistency of types in any human aggregate also affects its dynamics. Highly consistent aggregates contain individuals of similar types and "provide similar rewards and demands"; inconsistent aggregates "provide divergent rewards and demands" (Holland, 1973, p. 34). Thus, interest types adjacent in Holland's hexagonal model (for example, Social and Enterprising types) are presumed to share greater similarity than those that are opposite (such as Artistic and Conventional types). Furthermore, a person is said to be congruent with a given environment if his or her type is the same or nearly the same as the dominant type within that environment. This observation is critical for understanding the extent to which a person is likely to be attracted to, satisfied with, and stable within that environment. Individuals who share much in common with an environment are predicted to be most attracted to that setting. Once inside, they are likely to be encouraged for exactly those behaviors, values, attitudes, and expectations that attracted them to that particular environment in the first place, thus reinforcing the similarities between them. Congruent person-to-environment matches allow individuals to exercise their strengths and to avoid their dislikes or weaknesses. Consequently, the likelihood of any given person's remaining in a congruent environment is quite high.

Degrees of environmental differentiation and consistency, and person-to-environment congruence, are important for understanding how individuals will function within any human environment and whether they are likely to adapt to it, leave it, or try to change it. These dynamics lie at the heart of any retention effort, and they illuminate the "chilly climate" experience on some campuses for women (Hall & Sandler, 1982, 1984), students of color, and lesbian, bisexual, gay, and transgendered students, implicating that such groups, among others, have been historically disadvantaged by a Caucasian, male-dominated, and heterosexist culture.

Organized Environments

Most any environment exhibits characteristics of an organized system, with varying degrees of formal structure (Blau, 1973), as certain goals or outcomes shape decisions about the use of various resources and strategies. It is common practice to "get organized" to facilitate such decisions, by establishing plans, rules, and guidelines for group functioning; by allocating resources; and by identifying those who will share authority and responsibility for making substantive and procedural choices (Etzioni, 1964). Thus faculty construct syllabi to outline course goals and assignments; departments define procedural guidelines and degree requirements; student groups plan for programs; residence life staff create structures for encouraging student participation; and campus administrators establish rules for efficient use of limited resources.

Organizational Structures. It is the presence of specific goals in an environment (whether implicit or explicit) that gives rise to its organizational structures (Hage & Aiken, 1970; Hage, 1980) that, in turn, influence certain behaviors and sustain certain organizational milieus, from the dynamic to the static. Dynamic environments are flexible in design and respond more readily to change; static environments resist change. The extent to which organized environments are likely to exhibit these characteristics can be understood in reference to their degrees of complexity, centralization, formalization, stratification, production, and efficiency (Hage & Aiken, 1970).

Organizational complexity refers to the occupational subunits and specialties in a particular setting, as well as the extent and intensity of knowledge and expertise required of each. Colleges and universities are typically characterized by a high degree of complexity, with a variety of highly credentialed professionals. Many different departmental subunits require a variety of specialties dedicated to meeting the needs of campus constituents. Departments of natural sciences, for example, require advanced training and preparation of appropriate personnel in order to meet the goals of teaching chemistry and biology courses. Career planning and placement offices require the services of professionally prepared counselors who can effectively assist students in sorting through the maze of their occupational interests, skills, and choices. In the context of various campus subenvironments, for example, complexity might be reflected in the number of classroom discussion groups or specialized student organization task groups. Colleges and universities are, by nature, professional organizations that generally place a concerted emphasis on staff development and continuing education, another dimension of complexity.

Centralization refers to the way in which power is distributed in an organization. Thus, for purposes of allocation and coordination, academic administrators must decide what courses will be offered and when they will be scheduled; faculty determine the number, type, and due dates of assignments for individual classes; and staff implement plans for the expenditure and accounting of various budgets. Where few individuals share such power for decision making, organizations are said to be highly centralized; organizations where many or all share decision-making power equally are said to be decentralized. A highly centralized classroom, for example, is apparent when an instructor makes all the decisions about the course syllabus, assigned readings, and papers and relies principally on lectures. In contrast, a seminar format, where the students and instructor work collaboratively to create the syllabus around student interests and learning styles, grading practices are negotiated, and an open discussion format is preferred, might be described as a decentralized learning environment.

Organizational formalization attends to the importance of rules (whether written or customarily understood) in a given setting, their number, their specificity, and their enforcement. Highly formalized units enforce many explicit rules, which are thought to provide guidelines for efficient functioning and lend a degree of predictability to organizational efforts. Degrees of formalization in various campus environments might be reflected in student codes, administrative manuals and job descriptions, college catalogs, course syllabi, organizational constitutions and bylaws, and customary understandings of "how things are done." High degrees of formalization are associated generally with organizational rigidity and resistance to change.

Stratification reflects the differential distribution of rewards in a system. Highly stratified systems have many different levels of status, distinguished by differential rewards (such as income, esteem, and prestige), with those higher in the organization receiving greater recognition and rewards. Highly stratified systems tend to preserve status distinctions and restrict members' mobility. Higher stratification, for example, might be apparent in a classroom where the distance between the students and the instructor is maintained by formal titles and formal academic authority; in a student organization where rewards (such as access to office space and equipment, titles, and campus recognition) are differentially distributed to group leaders; and in a residence hall where the head resident and assistants are distinguished significantly from other residents by higher status and appreciably better living arrangements. Other relevant distinctions might include class levels (for example, seniors have greater claim on campus facilities than first-year students), majors (students in the "hard sciences" may be attributed greater intellectual value than other students), or status (sports teams may have access to preferential course schedules and special campus living arrangements). While power and rules exert a conforming influence, stratification tends to be more divisive, since reward structures are cast into a competitive framework, and those who share disproportionately in the rewards are vested in maintaining the status quo.

Production refers to the relative emphasis on quantity or quality of an organization's products or services. All organizations need to produce in order to justify their existence and create a sense of accomplishment among participants. When quantity of production is high, a well-functioning system is assumed. A drop in quantity of production often signals a need for reexamination and evaluation of practices and procedures. Colleges are often driven by production mandates, for example, with students requesting certain classes more frequently or trustees inquiring about the number of graduates placed, as indicators of mission effectiveness. Credit hours completed, retention rates, number of minorities enrolled, advisee contacts, research grants received, and articles published, to name a few, are all familiar indices of production in an academic environment. Annual reports teem with such data, and measures like these are frequently invoked for purposes of resource reallocation.

However, increased production often involves a trade-off with quality. For example, while student credit hours are stimulated by economies of scale, increasing both enrollments and class sizes, the quality of the learning experience may be attenuated with fewer opportunities for the kinds of intellectual exchanges and assignments that promote the development of critical reasoning. This may have implications for the ability of an institution to meet educational goals.

Organizational efficiency emphasizes the cost reduction of products or services; maximum efficiency, like high productivity, is assumed to reflect a smooth, well-functioning unit. Like other complex organizations, colleges and universities pursue efficient use of resources by means of a variety of institutional strategies. For example, restricting access to copying machines, raising minimum enrollment levels, and assigning lower-salaried graduate teaching assistants to large introductory sections all have the effect of lowering the cost of production. Ensuring high occupancy rates in residence halls and keeping classrooms full also reduce the cost of physical plant investments. However, cost reduction is particularly difficult to monitor and evaluate in the context of an academic setting. What is an efficient number of resources to produce a graduate of a program, a student leader, a publication in a professional journal, or a grade of A in a particular course? What is the cost of a new idea? Answers to such questions are inherently value-laden and invariably contested, further complicating any discussion about efficiency. Perhaps too often, though, the most important outcomes of a college experience (for example, development of tolerance for ambiguity) are reduced to available metrics that may not capture the essence of such goals.

Organizational Designs. The distinction between dynamic and static organizational designs is important for understanding environments most often associated with successful educational experiences. Dynamic environments combine higher degrees of complexity with lower centralization, formalization, stratification, and efficiency, and they place a relatively high emphasis on the quality of products or services (Hage & Aiken, 1970). For example, in a classroom higher complexity might be reflected in the employment of multiple perspectives and a variety of learning tasks assigned. Degrees of centralization and formalization may be lowered by engaging students actively in the planning and implementation of course goals and offering creative options (such as cooperative projects, independent assignments, and multiple-format exams). This, of course, demands a more labor-intensive process for instructors and students alike, lowering degrees of efficiency. But dynamic educational environments encourage substantive involvement, responsibility, and creativity on the part of members—the essence of developmentally powerful systems (Astin, 1985; Strange, 1981, 1983).

Static environments, with opposite characteristics, tend to discourage change and innovation. For example, a course syllabus without input requires little investment from students and may reflect few of their learning interests and goals; rigidly formatted class assignments are less likely to respond to their individual learning styles and needs; insistence on formal titles and status may diminish the kind of personal interaction that supports the risk taking needed to explore new ideas; and an overemphasis on efficiency ("We just don't have time to explore that") and quantity of readings or assignments may invoke a "just get it done" attitude among students as the term unfolds. A key point in this analysis is that developmental environments exhibit characteristics of dynamic organizations, wherein individual differences are appreciated, participation is expected, interactions are personal, and risk taking is encouraged (Strange, 1983).

Organizational designs can also affect participant morale. A static classroom environment, for example, might prove comforting to students at one level of development (such as Dualism), but discouraging and boring to students at other levels (such as Relativism) (Perry, 1970). Varying personalities may respond differently to the same environment as well. Sensing and Judging types (Myers, 1980), or Conventional and Realistic types (Holland, 1973), might enjoy the routine and standardization of a predictable, static class arrangement, but such designs may ultimately frustrate Intuitive Perceivers and Artistic or Social types. Likewise, student organizations structured around a hierarchical model of charter-based roles and powers may be less attractive to students socialized in a relational ethic or who prefer a less legalistic arrangement (Forrest, Hotelling, & Kuk, 1986; Gilligan, 1982). The overall structure reflected in an organized environment may or may not be compatible with participant characteristics. For example, students who are inexperienced in leadership and involvement may be unprepared to assume the responsibilities of membership in a self-directed group. In such cases, a more highly structured and fixed organizational design may be most appropriate. On the other hand, a more advanced student group may become disinterested in a highly structured system that allows for little student input. Thus a general understanding of students' developmental characteristics (see Chapter Nine) is a critical source of information for constructing appropriate organizational environments.

Constructed Environments

Models of constructed environments assume that a consensus of how participants subjectively perceive and characterize their environment offers a measure of environmental press, social climate, or culture. These perceptions, in turn, exert a directional influence (Moos, 1986) and affect how individuals are likely to react to particular environments. Thus whether people are attracted to, remain satisfied with, or stable within an environment is a function of how they perceive, construct, and evaluate the environment. In essence, as these models imply, perceptions of an environment constitute its reality.

Environmental Press. Pace and Stern (1958) were among the first to apply a systematic, perceptual approach to the study of college campuses in developing an interactive model of individual needs and environmental presses. Environmental press is inferred from self-reports of perceived activities in an environment. For example, if 80 percent of a representative sample of students on a particular community college campus report that students frequently spend time in cooperative work assignments, a significant "press toward vocational achievement" might be inferred. Through various empirical analyses, Pace and Stern (1958) and Saunders (1969) identified a factorial structure of eleven potentially distinctive environmental presses on various campuses: aspiration level, intellectual climate, student dignity, academic climate, academic achievement, self-expression, group life, academic organization, social form, play-work, and vocational climate. Accordingly, a small, selective residential college might exhibit a greater press toward aspiration level, intellectual climate, and academic achievement, while a public regional institution might lend itself to greater presses toward work and vocational climate.

Social Climate. Sharing a similar set of assumptions about the social construction of human environments, Moos (1986, 1979) authored a model of social climate, describing the nature and effects of various "environmental personalities." Social climate is composed of three sets of dimensions: (1) relationship dimensions, reflecting participants' involvement, mutual support, and expressiveness in the setting; (2) personal growth and development dimensions, identifying areas of personal achievement related to the setting's underlying purpose; and (3) system maintenance and change dimensions, reflecting the setting's clarity, control, and responsiveness to change. These three domains guide the assessment and understanding of the key aspects of any social environment and manifest themselves in specific ways, depending upon the context of the environment being examined. For example, in classrooms, relationship dimensions focus on the degrees of student involvement, affiliation, and teacher support; personal growth and development dimensions assess task orientation and competition; and system maintenance and system change dimensions include order and organization, rule clarity, teacher control, and innovation (Moos & Trickett, 1974). In residence halls, relationship dimensions focus on students' involvement and the emotional support they offer one another; personal growth dimensions reflect degrees of student independence, traditional social orientation, and emphasis on competition, academic achievement, and intellectuality; and system maintenance dimensions are expressed in the amount of order, student influence, and innovation present (Moos, 1979).

To complete a picture of the various interactive social climates that affect students' lives, Moos (1981) also described task-focused group environments, helpful for understanding students' experiences as participants in campus groups and organizations; work environments (Moos & Insel, 1974), important for examining the experiences of students who hold jobs (either on or off campus); and family environments (Moos, 1974), helpful in understanding the basic set of relationships that students, traditional and nontraditional alike, bring with them to college and that may form a foundation for their experiences there. Each of these social climate dimensions may vary along a continuum, from low to high, and may create a special focus or orientation for it. For example, with the University Residence Environment Scale, Moos (1979) and Moos and Gerst (1974) identified six characteristic environments or "personalities" he attributed to various living groups: relationship-oriented, traditionally socially oriented, supportive achievement-oriented, competition-oriented, independence-oriented, and intellectually-oriented environments. Likewise, varying emphases on certain dimensions in classrooms, task groups, work settings, and family environments may create distinctive orientations of one sort or another. For example, one work environment might be very competitive and another one very supportive; one family environment may express a strong achievement orientation while another might emphasize independence.

These various environmental orientations have been found to be related as well to differing physical and human aggregate configurations, at least in the context of on-campus living environments. For example, Moos (1979) found that units composed of a greater proportion of single rooms are more oriented toward competition and less toward supportive achievement, independence, intellectuality, and relationships. Further, all-male residence halls tend to be more competition-oriented, all-female units tend to be more traditionally socially oriented, and coed units tend to be independence-oriented and intellectually oriented. Finally, supportive, achievement-oriented and relationship-oriented residence halls tend to be almost exclusively female or coed.

Campus Culture. Another set of ideas sharing this focus on constructed environments comes from a growing literature applying concepts of organizational culture to college and university environments (Chaffee & Tierney, 1988; Horowitz, 1987; Kuh, 1993; Kuh & Whitt, 1988; Moffatt, 1989). Schein (1992) referred to culture as "a pattern of shared basic assumptions that the group learned as it solved its problems of external adaptation and internal integration that has worked well enough to be considered valid and, therefore, to be taught to new members as the correct way to perceive, think, and feel in relation to those problems" (p. 12). Problems of *external adaptation* include establishing a core mission, specific goals derived from that mission, a means to attain the goals, criteria for measuring success, and strategies for remediation when goals are not being met. *Internal integration* includes establishing and maintaining a common language and set of concepts, determining criteria for membership, deciding how power is used, delimiting relationships, discerning the nature of rewards and punishments, and defining an ideology that helps the group face inexplicable events (Schein, 1985). Culture, then, is essentially "a social construction" (Chaffee & Tierney, 1988, p. 10), reflected in traditions, stories, ceremonies, histories, myths, heroines and heroes, interactions among members, policies and practices, symbols, and missions and philosophies.

There are essentially four levels of campus culture—artifacts, perspectives, values, and assumptions (Dyer, 1986; Kuh & Hall, 1993; Lundberg, 1985; Schein, 1985). Most campuses have some distinctive physical artifacts—usually buildings, landscape features, or various other physical attributes—that mark points of interest on a typical admissions tour. A founders' hall, a majestic library, a multicultural center, or a technologically advanced classroom building can each serve to convey some of the core values that shape an institution's culture and the historical roots from which it came. Verbal artifacts incorporate language, stories, and myths, including "terms of endearment" (Kuh, Schuh, Whitt, & Associates, 1991, p. 84) associated with specific institutions. Stories about significant campus leaders, personalities, and even mythical figures convey key moments of institutional history and construct personal models of emulation consistent with institutional values. Behavioral artifacts might include key celebratory activities and events that connect members to the institution (such as orientation and convocation), acknowledge their participation in institutional subcultures and groups (such as Gospel choir), or send them on their way following completion of their educational experience (such as commencement). Various campus rituals also serve to connect the past to the present (Masland, 1985), as happens regularly, for example, when anniversary classes are remembered at homecoming or during alumni week.

Perspectives, or "socially shared rules and norms," constitute a second level of institutional culture, and define the "way things are done" and "determine what is 'acceptable behavior' for students, faculty, staff, and others in various institutional settings" (Kuh & Hall, 1993, p. 6). Thus students become quickly aware of appropriate campus customs, attire, and ideologies and are able to recognize certain perspectives as "typical" of those that constitute and reflect institutional culture.

Values, a third level of institutional culture, convey the "espoused as well as the enacted ideals of an institution or group . . . and serve as the basis on which members of a culture or subculture judge situations, acts, objects and people" (Kuh & Hall, 1993, p. 6). College catalogs, convocation speeches, campus mission statements, and significant planning documents are important sources for understanding institutional values in their espoused form.

Finally, the fourth and deepest level of institutional culture includes assumptions, or "tacit beliefs that members use to define their role, their relationship to others, and the nature of the organization in which they live" (Kuh & Hall, 1993, p. 7). Schein (1992) suggested that all the various other artifacts of organizational culture reflect these fundamental assumptions and define and shape the core elements of institutional culture.

In summary, these models and theories suggest that the various environmental components of colleges and universities can positively influence students through physical features that are facilitative, human aggregate characteristics that are reinforcing, and organizational structures that are dynamic. They also suggest that the effects of such features, characteristics, and structures are mediated through meanings constructed and attributed to them by participants. How such components come together to effect educational purposes and enhance student learning is the focus of the next section in the context of specific environmental conditions—inclusion, safety, involvement, and community (Strange & Banning, 2001).

Designing for Educational Success

Learning entails engagement with new experiences and opportunities that challenge an individual's present ways of viewing, understanding, and responding to the world. At the core of any significant learning process is the element of risk. Acquiring new methods of meaning making and responding to the world involve steps that are uncertain. Old familiar ways of functioning offer a sense of comfort and are not easily abandoned as new situations arise. From this perspective, learning may be seen as a progression of steps in meaning making and understanding toward increasingly complex and advanced ways of viewing and interacting with the world. This requires both the acquisition of new information as well as access to opportunities for the exercise of new skills, competencies, and ways of understanding and acting. This stepwise understanding of learning implies a corresponding hierarchy of educational environment purposes and designs, beginning with the need for conditions that promote inclusion and safety, followed by the need for environments that encourage involvement and community (Strange & Banning, 2001). (See Figure 13.1.)

An educational institution must present first an inclusive and safe environment for students. Without a basic sense of belonging to the institution, free from threat, fear, and anxiety, attempts at other more advanced learning goals will likely fail. The first step for campus leaders, then, is to assure that the physical, human aggregate, organizational, and constructed aspects of campus environments create such conditions and serve such purposes.

Inasmuch as education engages students in risk taking, educationally purposeful environments must also involve them in experiences that require taking on meaningful roles and responsibilities. Without their participation and involvement, students remain detached from the kinds of opportunities that call for their investment and responsibility for their own learning.

Finally, while conditions of inclusion, safety, and involvement are important, they alone are insufficient to assure an integrated, whole learning experience for students; this requires conditions of community, where environmental goals, structures, values, people, and resources come together in a seamless experience for purposes of self-actualization and fulfillment. It is within a community, whether in the form of a class, a student organization, a commuter center, a peer training program, or a residence hall floor, to cite a few examples, that participants experience a complete sense of membership in a setting.

Each of the four components of campus environments discussed above (physical, human aggregate, organizational, and constructed) has the potential, whether in real

FIGURE 13.1. A HIERARCHY OF LEARNING ENVIRONMENT PURPOSES.

Source: Strange and Banning (2001).

or virtual form, for contributing to the inclusion, safety, involvement, and communal experience of students. For example, attending to "wayfinding" (Arthur & Passini, 1992; Hunt, 1984) is important for effecting a feeling of belonging and security in a setting, arguably a worthwhile goal for any campus admissions or orientation program. Offering a sufficient variety of differentiated aggregate groupings of human scale design (for example, clubs and organizations) gives participants a chance to connect to something familiar, thereby encouraging involvement. Finally, differentiation of territorial spaces (such as a multicultural student center), along with dynamic and facilitative organizational structures, make possible the emergence and maintenance of strong learning communities, affirmed over time in traditions and other artifacts of culture.

As campuses move further towards the use of computer-mediated systems to support human communications (Santoro, 1995) and instruction (Berge & Collins, 1995), it remains to be seen as to whether such technologies will be able to deliver these same conditions in virtual form. Some have extolled the possibilities of "virtual communities" (Rheingold, 1993) for bringing people together and fostering learning (Palloff & Pratt, 1999). Others, however, have cautioned of overdependence on computer technologies and the potential dangers of human "cocooning" (Popcorn, 1991), or self-isolation, in such systems. Both the promises and perils of computer mediation are legitimate perspectives (Michalski, 1995). Regardless, the features associated with traditional, sensual communities must be applicable to virtual communities on campus if they are to be successful in supporting student learning. A key may be found in the connectivity generated by these virtual forms as the glue that holds learners and teachers together rather than geographic proximity. Certainly virtual and face-to-face communities could enrich each other.

Assessment for Environmental Impact

Drawing from materials presented above, Figure 13.2 integrates these environmental concepts into a three-dimensional matrix of campus design for purposes of assessment and action. Three essential questions are addressed in this matrix:

- What principal components are involved in this particular environmental assessment or action?
- What is the impact of the current design of these components?
- What is the intended focus or purpose of this design?

Answers to these three questions can alert educators to current conditions of campus environments as well as the intended design of environments to be created.

In regard to the first question, any campus assessment or action must identify the environmental components of concern. Are the physical dimensions of the campus environment involved? Is the focus primarily on natural (such as landscape) or synthetic (such as building layout) aspects? Or both? Are the compositions of particular aggregates (for example, campus affinity groups) at issue? Are there concerns related

FIGURE 13.2. CAMPUS DESIGN MATRIX.

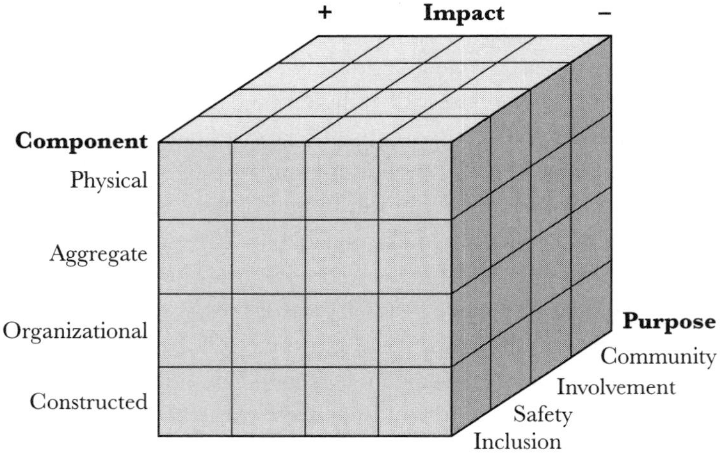

+ Impact –

Component
Physical
Aggregate
Organizational
Constructed

Purpose
Community
Involvement
Safety
Inclusion

Source: Strange & Banning (2001).

to the organizational dimensions of the setting (such as decision-making structures)? How do participants construct this condition or phenomenon of interest (such as social climate or press)?

With respect to the impact of current designs, the second dimension of this matrix, it is helpful to consider a continuum of possible effects (see Exhibit 13.3). At one end of the continuum, environments can be seen as essentially negative, including those that are actively stressful or limiting, resisting, and inhibiting. At the other end are environments seen as essentially positive, that is, those that release capacities, allowing behaviors to occur, and those that actively stimulate and challenge individuals toward growth. In the middle are those environments that neither enhance nor inhibit individuals but rather select favored characteristics (Moos, 1986). Of course, the nature of the impact depends on the characteristics of the individuals experiencing the environmental condition, a tenet thought to be central to understanding human behavior, as a function of the interaction of persons and environments: $B = f(P \times E)$ (Lewin, 1936). For example, a highly differentiated affinity group, such as a student

EXHIBIT 13.3. FIVE CONCEPTIONS OF ENVIRONMENTAL IMPACT.

\+ Environments are active and *positive* forces

- Stimulate and challenge individuals toward growth
- Release capacities, allow behaviors to occur
- Select favored characteristics
- Limit, resist, or inhibit behaviors
- Actively engender stress

– Environments are essentially *negative* and stressful

Source: Strange and Banning (2001).

organization or club, may be a very positive force for individuals who share much in common with the group but may be actively stressful for those who don't. Also, it makes sense that environmental selection of certain characteristics depends on what is favored by the environment. Again, those who exhibit certain characteristics (for example, high academic test scores on an honors program application) are most favored in the selection process of such an environment.

Third, this campus design matrix identifies the intended purpose(s) of the environmental condition. Is the concern one of inclusion or exclusion of certain students in campus life? Is the question of safety at stake, physical or psychological? Are the current environmental components and impacts related in some way to dimensions of involvement? To what extent, if any, does the environmental assessment or planned action relate to the establishment and maintenance of campus community?

Identification and evaluation of environmental components, impacts, and purposes are important first steps in campus assessment and design. The value of this matrix is that it requires consideration of the larger campus ecology, with reference to current impacts and intended purposes. As an evaluative tool, use of this matrix can alert educational planners to conditions that warrant particular attention. For example, a campus retention committee may focus on the role of small, differentiated orientation groups (an aggregate component) in having a powerful positive impact toward purposes of safety and inclusion in the campus environment. For another example, the lack of participatory structures in a particular department (an organizational component) might signal the limiting, resisting, and inhibiting impact on students who wish to become involved.

Institutional leaders can also use this matrix to systematically plan the design of new or renovated campus environments, considering their impact and purpose. For example, if plans for a new or renovated student center invoke images of a facility for building campus community, then the impact of its current location and proposed design changes must be considered carefully in light of its capacity for including, securing, and involving as many students as possible. Do the plans suggest a facility that is accessible to all (a physical component)? What student groups might be located in the building, for purposes of increasing campus-wide involvement (an aggregate component)? What rules will govern the use of this facility (an organizational component)? What images of the facility are conveyed to students as they consider the facility's space and layout (constructed component)? At each point, campus planners can consider whether the intended designs will add to the stress of some students (such as students with disabilities), and ultimately, whether it will serve as a powerful positive force in campus life. This kind of analysis can assist institutions in anticipating environmental challenges and conditions that, if impervious to alteration or redesign, can at least be responded to in supportive ways.

Conclusion

Campus educators and policy makers would do well to review how their practices and policies reflect the principles highlighted in this literature on campus environments. The potency of any educational environment, whether a classroom, a residence hall, a student organization, or an entire campus, is a function of its design (planned or not), what it encourages and expects students to do, and what ends it serves. Effective educational settings take advantage of their physical, human aggregate, organizational, and constructed features to offer inclusive, safe, involving, and communal environments to sustain and challenge students to learn, develop, and grow.

References

Anchors, S., Schroeder, C., & Jackson, S. (1978). *Making yourself at home: A practical guide to restructuring and personalizing your residence hall environment.* Washington, DC: ACPA Media Publications.

Arthur, P., & Passini, R. (1992). *Wayfinding.* New York: McGraw-Hill.

Astin, A. W. (1962). An empirical characterization of higher educational institutions. *Journal of Educational Psychology, 53,* 224–235.

Astin, A. W. (1968). *The college environment.* Washington, DC: American Council on Education.

Astin, A. W. (1985). *Achieving educational excellence: A critical assessment of priorities and practices in higher education.* San Francisco: Jossey-Bass.

Astin, A. W. (1993). An empirical typology of college students. *Journal of College Student Development, 34,* 36–46.

Astin, A. W., & Holland, J. L. (1961). The environmental assessment technique: A way to measure college environments. *Journal of Educational Psychology, 52,* 308–316.

Baird, L. L. (1988). The college environment revisited: A review of research and theory. In J. C. Smart (Ed.), *Higher education: Vol. 4. Handbook of theory and research* (pp. 1–52). New York: Agathon Press.

Banning, J. H., & Kaiser, L. (1974). An ecological perspective and model for campus design. *Personnel and Guidance Journal, 52,* 370–375.

Barker, R. G. (1968). *Ecological psychology: Concepts and methods for studying the environment of human behavior.* Stanford, CA: Stanford University Press.

Berge, Z., & Collins, M. (1995). Computer-mediated communication and the online classroom: Overview and perspectives. In Z. L. Berge & M. P. Collins (Eds.), *Computer mediated communication and the online classroom, Vol. 1.* (pp. 1–27). Cresskill, NJ: Hampton Press.

Blau, P. M. (1973). *The organization of academic work.* New York: Wiley.

Boyer, E. L. (1987). *College: The undergraduate experience in America.* New York: Harper & Row.

Chaffee, E. E., & Tierney, W. G. (1988). *Collegiate culture and leadership strategies.* New York: American Council on Education/Macmillan.

Clark, B. R., & Trow, M. (1966). The organizational context. In T. M. Newcomb & E. K. Wilson (Eds.), *College peer groups: Problems and prospects for research* (pp. 17–70). Chicago: Aldine.

Dober, R. P. (1992). *Campus design.* New York: Wiley.

Dyer, W. G., Jr. (1986). The cycle of cultural evolution in organizations. In R. H. Kilman, M. J. Saxton, R. Serpa, & Associates (Eds.), *Gaining control of the corporate culture* (pp. 200–229). San Francisco: Jossey-Bass.

Ender, K., Kane, N., Mable, P., & Strohm, M. (1980). *Creating community in residence halls.* Washington, DC: ACPA Media Publications.

Etzioni, A. (1964). *Modern organizations.* Englewood Cliffs, NJ: Prentice Hall.

Forrest, L., Hotelling, K., & Kuk, L. (1986). *The elimination of sexism in the university environment* (ERIC Document Reproduction Service No. ED 267348). Paper presented at the second annual Student Development Through Campus Ecology symposium, Pingree Park, CO.

Gaines, T. A. (1991). *The campus as a work of art.* New York: Praeger.

Gilligan, C. (1982). *In a different voice: Psychological theory and women's development.* Cambridge, MA: Harvard University Press.

Hage, J. (1980). *Theories of organizations: Form, process, and transformation.* New York: Wiley.

Hage, J., & Aiken, M. (1970). *Social change in complex organizations.* New York: Random House.
Hall, R. M., & Sandler, B. R. (1982). *The classroom climate: A chilly one for women?* Washington, DC: Project on the Status and Education of Women, Association of American Colleges.
Hall, R. M., & Sandler, B. R. (1984). *Out of the classroom: A chilly campus climate for women?* Washington, DC: Project on the Status and Education of Women, Association of American Colleges.
Heilweil, M. (1973). The influence of dormitory architecture on resident behavior. *Environment and Behavior, 5,* 377–412.
Holland, J. L. (1973). *Making vocational choices: A theory of careers.* Englewood Cliffs, NJ: Prentice Hall.
Horowitz, H. L. (1987). *Campus life: Undergraduate cultures from the end of the eighteenth century to the present.* New York: Knopf.
Huebner, L. A., & Lawson, J. M. (1990). Understanding and assessing college environments. In D. Creamer & Associates, *College student development: Theory and practice for the 1990s* (American College Personnel Association Media Publication No. 49, pp. 127–151). Alexandria, VA: American College Personnel Association.
Hunt, M. (1984). Environmental learning without being there. *Environment and Behavior, 16,* 307–334.
Kolb, D. (1983). *Experiential learning: Experience as the source of learning and development.* Englewood Cliffs, NJ: Prentice Hall.
Kuh, G. D. (Ed.). (1993). *Cultural perspectives in student affairs work.* Lanham, MD: American College Personnel Association.
Kuh, G. D., & Hall, J. E. (1993). Using cultural perspectives in student affairs. In G. D. Kuh (Ed.), *Cultural perspectives in student affairs work* (pp. 1–20). Lanham, MD: American College Personnel Association.
Kuh, G. D., Schuh, J. H., Whitt, E. J., & Associates. (1991). *Involving colleges: Encouraging student learning and personal development through out-of-class experiences.* San Francisco: Jossey-Bass.
Kuh, G. D., & Whitt, E. J. (1988). *The invisible tapestry: Cultures in American colleges and universities* (ASHE-ERIC Higher Education Report Series No. 1). Washington, DC: Association for the Study of Higher Education.
Lewin, K. (1936). *Principles of topological psychology.* New York: McGraw-Hill.
Lundberg, C. C. (1985). On the feasibility of cultural intervention in organizations. In P. J. Frost, L. F. Moore, M. R. Louis, C. C. Lundberg, & J. Martin (Eds.), *Organizational culture* (pp. 169–186). Beverly Hills, CA: Sage.
Masland, A. T. (1985). Organizational culture in the study of higher education. *Review of Higher Education, 8,* 157–168.
Michalski, J. (1995). The role of technology. In K. Gozdz (Ed.), *Community building: Renewing spirit and learning in business* (pp. 259–269). San Francisco: New Leaders Press.
Michelson, W. (1970). *Man and his urban environment: A sociological approach.* Reading, MA: Addison-Wesley.
Moffatt, M. (1989). *Coming of age in New Jersey: College and American culture.* New Brunswick, NJ: Rutgers University Press.
Moos, R. H. (1974). *Family environment scale—Form R.* Palo Alto, CA: Consulting Psychologists Press.
Moos, R. H. (1979). *Evaluating educational environments.* San Francisco: Jossey-Bass.
Moos, R. H. (1981). *Group environment scale manual.* Palo Alto, CA: Consulting Psychologists Press.
Moos, R. H. (1986). *The human context: Environmental determinants of behavior.* Malabar, FL: Krieger.
Moos, R. H., & Gerst, M. (1974). *The university residence environment scale manual.* Palo Alto, CA: Consulting Psychologists Press.
Moos, R. H., & Insel, P. (1974). *Work environment scale technical report.* Palo Alto, CA: Stanford University, Department of Psychiatry, Social Ecology Laboratory.
Moos, R. H., & Trickett, E. J. (1974). *Classroom environment scale manual.* Palo Alto, CA: Consulting Psychologists Press.
Myers, I. B. (1980). *Gifts differing.* Palo Alto, CA: Consulting Psychologists Press.

Pace, C. R., & Stern, G. G. (1958). An approach to the measurement of psychological characteristics of college environments. *Journal of Educational Psychology, 49,* 269–277.
Palloff, R. M., & Pratt, K. (1999). *Building learning communities in cyberspace: Effective strategies for the online classroom.* San Francisco: Jossey-Bass.
Pascarella, E. T. (1985). College environmental influences on learning and cognitive development: A critical review and synthesis. In J. C. Smart (Ed.), *Higher education: Vol. 1. Handbook of theory and research* (pp. 1–61). New York: Agathon Press.
Perry, W. G. (1970). *Forms of intellectual and ethical development in the college years: A scheme.* New York: Holt, Rinehart and Winston.
Popcorn, F. (1991). *The Popcorn report.* New York: Doubleday.
Rheingold, H. (1993). *The virtual community: Homesteading on the electronic frontier.* Reading, MA: Addison-Wesley.
Rudolph, F. (1962). *The American college and university: A history.* New York: Knopf.
Santoro, G. (1995). What is computer-mediated communication? In Z. L. Berge & M. P. Collins (Eds.), *Computer mediated communication and the online classroom, Vol. 1.* (pp. 11–27). Cresskill, NJ: Hampton Press.
Saunders, D. R. (1969). A factor analytic study of the AI and CCI. *Multivariate Behavioral Research, 4,* 329–346.
Schein, E. H. (1985). *Organizational culture and leadership.* San Francisco: Jossey-Bass.
Schein, E. H. (1992). *Organizational culture and leadership* (2nd ed.). San Francisco: Jossey-Bass.
Schlossberg, N. K., Lassalle, A., & Golec, R. (1988). *The mattering scale for adults in higher education* (6th ed.). College Park, MD: University of Maryland.
Schroeder, C. C. (1979). Territoriality: Conceptual and methodological issues for residence educators. *Journal of College and University Housing, 8,* 9–15.
Sommer, R. (1969). *Personal space.* Englewood Cliffs, NJ: Prentice Hall.
Stern, R. A. (1986). *Pride of place: Building the American dream.* Boston: Houghton Mifflin.
Strange, C. C. (1981). Organizational barriers to student development. *National Association of Student Personnel Administrators Journal, 19,* 12–20.
Strange, C. C. (1983). Human development theory and administrative practice in student affairs: Ships passing in the daylight? *National Association of Student Personnel Administrators Journal, 21,* 2–8.
Strange, C. C. (1991). Managing college environments: Theory and practice. In T. K. Miller, R. B. Winston, Jr., & Associates (Eds.), *Administration and leadership in student affairs: Actualizing student development in student affairs* (2nd ed., pp. 159–199). Muncie, IN: Accelerated Development.
Strange, C. C. (1993). Developmental impacts of campus living environments. In R. B. Winston, Jr., S. Anchors, & Associates, *Student housing and residential life: A handbook for professionals committed to student development goals* (pp. 134–166). San Francisco: Jossey-Bass.
Strange, C. C. (1994). Student development: The evolution and status of an essential idea. *Journal of College Student Development, 35,* 399–412.
Strange, C. C., & Banning, J. (2001). *Educating by design: Creating campus learning environments that work.* San Francisco: Jossey-Bass.
Strange, C. C., & King, P. (1990). The professional practice of student development. In D. Creamer & Associates (Eds.), *College student development: Theory and practice for the 1990s* (ACPA Media Publication No. 49, pp. 9–24). Alexandria, VA: American College Personnel Association.
Sturner, W. F. (1973). The college environment. In D. W. Vermilye (Ed.), *The future in the making* (pp. 71–86). San Francisco: Jossey-Bass.
Thelin, J. R., & Yankovich, J. (1987). Bricks and mortar: Architecture and the study of higher education. In J. C. Smart (Ed.), *Higher education: Vol. 3. Handbook of theory and research* (pp. 57–83). New York: Agathon Press.

CHAPTER FOURTEEN

STUDENT SUCCESS

John M. Braxton

What is student success? Who defines it? Both individual students and institutions define success in relation to the extent to which they achieve their goals. As such, success is a "value laden term" (Floyd, 1988, p. 6). The definition of student success hinges on what achievements the student and/or the institution value. This chapter will explore related concepts of departure, persistence, and retention and the important role of social integration for student success. Further it will present guideposts to foster student integration into the social communities of a college or university.

Because students enroll with varied backgrounds and intentions, an individual student's goals may differ from those of his or her peers. Three general types of student goals are enrollment goals, academic experience goals, and social experience goals. An enrollment goal is the reason(s) that the student is at the institution. Motivations can range from a student's intent to complete just a single course to the aim of earning a degree. Other enrollment goals can be to gain credentials to be promoted at work; to achieve the required academic preparation, course credits, and grades to be eligible to transfer to another institution; or to gain experience and exposure in the hope of getting signed to play a professional sport. Examples of academic experience goals are gaining subject knowledge, developing critical thinking skills, earning passing grades, earning high grades to be competitive for graduate school admission, or studying abroad. Students' social experience goals may be to develop lifelong

---

Note: I would like to acknowledge the important contribution of Amy Hirschy to this chapter. She played a critical role in the development of the section on student success. Ms. Hirschy serves as my graduate research assistant in the Department of Leadership and Organizations, Peabody College, Vanderbilt University. She is a candidate for the Ph.D. in Higher Education Administration.

friendships, acquire and practice leadership skills, or maintain a balance among family, work, and school commitments. Each individual student is likely to simultaneously have several goals, some of which overlap amongst these three types.

Similarly, institutional goals for student success will vary among colleges and universities, depending in part on their missions and student populations. Two-year colleges and universities, for example, tend to enroll a larger percentage of older students who are more likely to be married and work while attending school part-time (National Center for Education Statistics, 1998). The goals of these nontraditional students reflect their different life stages, and their ambitions may not match the educational intentions of an eighteen-year-old residential college student (Martens, Lara, Cordova, & Harris, 1995). Hence, campus leaders must consider the needs of their students when they assess student success.

Moreover, colleges and universities have their own agendas for what growth students should experience while in attendance. General goals are often embedded in the institution's mission statement, such as developing an educated citizenry, transmitting culture, and providing liberal learning. Pascarella and Terenzini (1991) provide evidence of specific effects of college on students in a variety of areas, including acquisition of attitudes and values, communication skills, critical thinking, cognitive development, and moral development.

Because of the diversity of student populations (and their goals), the definition of "student success" remains broad. What remains central, however, is that leaders in college and university settings need to understand what their students' intentions are so they can then evaluate how the institution supports or inhibits students' goal achievement. Acknowledging that students may not be fully aware of their goals upon enrollment, institutional leaders should create methods to help students clarify their values, identify their goals, and develop plans to achieve them (Floyd, 1988). Further, institutional leaders who are committed to student success should intentionally design methods to gather self-reported goals (Gratton & Walleri, 1989; Tinto, 1993) and evaluate programs and services to determine how effectively they are supporting their students' ambitions.

Student Success and Retention

Based on the discussion above, student success does not equate with degree attainment for all students. It is important to recognize that withdrawal from an institution may advance a student's goals, not inhibit them. Temporary enrollment intentions such as job retraining and institutional transfers are common and not bound by a particular institutional type (Tinto, 1993). Also, students withdraw from colleges and universities for a plethora of reasons that are individually (such as health or family reasons) and institutionally influenced (such as tuition increases or program elimination). A student may perceive a better fit at another institution, which ultimately contributes to that student's success. As such, the goal of a college or university is not to have zero student departure prior to degree attainment, as persisting at the institution (or at any other institution) may not be the best idea for all students. Therefore, one should note that individual institutional persistence rates should not be confused with system persistence rates, which include other educational venues.

Student persistence and departure can now be viewed in the larger context of enrollment decisions. While there are several circumstances where a student's enrollment goal is not to leave with a diploma, most students do intend to earn a degree. Therefore, much of the literature on student retention assumes that most students enroll in colleges and universities with graduation as their primary goal.

Thus, student persistence looms as a significant and essential gateway for student success, success for both the individual student and the institution. Student departure from higher education occurs at such a rate that student success is problematic. Tinto (1993) reports that the first year departure rate in two-year colleges is 44 percent and is 26.8 percent in four-year institutions. First-year departure rates also vary dramatically across colleges and universities of different levels of undergraduate admissions selectivity. Institutions practicing open admissions register a departure rate of 45.5 percent in contrast to the 8 percent rate of highly selective colleges and universities. Tinto also notes that the majority of student departures take place during the first year of college. Moreover, the vast proportion of student departure is voluntary, as Tinto states that less than 25 percent of student departure is due to academic dismissal (p. 49). Given that a significant proportion of student departure is voluntary, understanding such departure requires a consideration of various theoretical perspectives that seek to account for this phenomena. Understanding voluntary departure is essential to student success.

By design, student affairs professionals have multiple, on-going opportunities to interact with students, and as such, they can intentionally influence a student's college experience. Research indicates that student involvement in and outside the classroom promotes greater social and academic integration, which can then lead to persistence (Astin, 1996; Kuh, Schuh, Whitt, & Associates, 1991; Pascarella & Terenzini, 1983; Tinto, 1993). Thus, student affairs staff members play an important role in student retention. Charged with managing student-related crises; counseling students regarding personal, academic, and career issues; fostering student leadership opportunities; providing a safe, clean environment conducive to student development; and often coordinating the student withdrawal and reentry enrollment process, student affairs programs address many of the factors that research has shown to be critical in student satisfaction and retention.

Given such a configuration of roles for student affairs professionals in the process of student retention, an understanding of multiple theoretical perspectives on college student retention is necessary for effective role performance. Accordingly, such theoretical orientations are described in the next section of this chapter.

Theoretical Perspectives on College Student Departure

College student departure presents an ill-structured problem to scholars and practitioners who want to assure student success in college (Braxton & Mundy, 2001). Ill-structured problems require the identification of a number of solutions that might not alleviate the problem rather than a single solution (Kitchener, 1986; Wood, 1983). As an ill-structured problem, college student departure requires the consideration of multiple theoretical perspectives derived from different academic disciplines (Braxton & Mundy, 2001).

Tinto (1986) identifies four theoretical perspectives on college student departure: economic, organizational, psychological, and sociological. These four perspectives offer a way to view the phenomena of college student departure, each with a different set of forces worthy of consideration. The underlying assumptions of each of these theoretical orientations are described and constructs from each theoretical perspective that might account for student departure decisions are identified.

The choice of quantitative or qualitative methodological approaches depends on the topic pursued by research. Although the thrust of these theoretical perspectives suggests that quantitative research methods might be used to test them, qualitative methods may also be used when this approach best fits a study's purpose and design.

The Economic Perspective

The weighing of the costs and benefits of continued attendance at a particular college or university constitutes the focus of the economic perspective on college student departure (Tinto, 1986). Such economic reasoning also applies to student departure from higher education as a social system. This perspective represents a special case of human capital theory advanced by Becker (1964). At base, human capital theory postulates that education, training, or other types of learning represent personal investments that result in returns on this investment such as financial earnings. If the return on the investment in education outweighs the costs of the investment, then an individual is motivated to expend the necessary effort to acquire education.

By extension, students will depart a particular college or university if they perceive that the costs of continued attendance outweigh the benefits of continued attendance. Such perceived costs include tuition and foregone earnings, whereas benefits include future earnings and prestige accrued from earning a degree from a particular college or university. These costs and benefits also apply to decision to depart from higher education. Financial aid represents one consideration in the calculation of costs and benefits. Financial aid reduces the costs of attendance at a particular college or university as well as higher education as a social system. St. John, Cabrera, Nora, and Asker (2000) provide an extensive discussion of the role of financial aid and other economic factors in the departure process.

Tinto (1986) points out the limitations of the economic perspective in accounting for student departure decisions. He asserts that the economic perspective neglects social and nonmonetary factors internal and external to the individual student and to the focal college or university. The economic perspective also ignores student psychological characteristics as well as organizational forces that influence student decisions to persist. Thus, the economic perspective offers limited explanatory power to account for college student departure decisions. It does, however, account for the role of economic forces, forces generally neglected by psychological, organizational, and sociological perspectives.

Organizational Perspectives

No single organizational theory exists to account for student departure decisions. Nevertheless, the underlying assumptions of this perspective offer another way to view student departure decisions. The organizational perspective concentrates on the role of organizational structure and organizational behavior in influencing student departure (Berger & Braxton, 1998; Braxton, 2000). Some dimensions of organizational structure that may influence student departure decisions include institutional size, institutional admissions selectivity, institutional resources and goals, faculty-student ratios, and the bureaucratic structure of colleges and universities (Tinto, 1986). Because conceptual linkages between these aspects of organizational structure and student departure decisions have not been made, these structural characteristics lack explanatory power in accounting for student departure (Tinto, 1986). Nevertheless, they may wield various influences on student departure.

Organizational behavior, or the behavior of individuals in institutional leadership roles in colleges and universities, may also affect the college withdrawal decisions of students. Such individuals include the president, the senior academic affairs officer, senior student affairs officers, and academic deans. The prevailing mode of organizational functioning may impact student departure decisions (Braxton, 2000). These forms of organizational functioning include the rational-bureaucratic, the collegial, the political, and the anarchical (Birnbaum, 1988). (See Chapter Twelve for descriptions of the forms of organizational functioning.) Different goals, values, and methods of decision making define each of these forms of organizational functioning. Berger (2000a) calls these forms organizational dimensions that define the environment of an organization. Research by Berger indicates that these organizational dimensions wield influences on student outcomes. By extension, the influence of organizational functioning on student departure decisions may vary across the four modes of organizational functioning or organizational dimensions.

Institutional communication, fairness in the administration of institutional rules and regulations, and students' ability to participate in decision making are additional forms of organizational behavior posited to have a positive impact on student departure decisions (Bean, 1983; Berger & Braxton, 1998; Braxton & Brier, 1989). Presidential styles and the administrative styles of senior academic and senior student affairs officers are also forms of organizational behavior that may affect student adjustment and satisfaction with college (Astin & Scherrei, 1980; Berger & Braxton, 1998) and in turn, student departure decisions.

A strength of the organizational perspective on college student departure is that it focuses attention on the influence organizational structure and organizational behavior may exert on student departure decisions (Tinto, 1986). However, the organizational perspective is limited as it ignores economic, psychological, and social forces that may also affect student departure. Chapters Twelve and Thirteen in this book discuss additional dimensions of the organized environment.

Psychological Perspectives

The psychological perspective centers attention on the role of student psychological characteristics and processes in the student departure process (Tinto, 1986). Tinto points out that the psychological perspective enjoyed a predominant status in studies of retention in the time period following World War II. Such psychological characteristics and processes transpire at the level of the individual student and at the level of the college environment.

Individual Level. Bean and Eaton (2000) advance a psychological model of college student departure. Their model uses constructs derived from attitude-behavior theory, coping behavioral theory, self-efficacy theory, and attribution (locus of control) theory as foundation. This model assumes that behavior is a choice. Student entry characteristics (such as past behavior, initial self-efficacy, initial locus of control, and initial coping strategies) influence student interactions with the institutional environment. Self-efficacy pertains to an individuals' perceptions of their ability to engage in activities necessary to achieve a particular outcome (Bandura, 1986, 1997). Bean and Eaton assert that a strong sense of self-efficacy builds confidence in a student to adapt to a particular college or university. Locus of control refers to whether an individual attributes experiences and outcomes to causes internal or external to themselves (Rotter, 1966). People with an internal locus of control attribute outcomes they have experienced to their own skill or abilities. In contrast, people with an external locus of control believe outcomes are outside their control and due to luck or fate (Weiner, 1986). Self-efficacy and locus of control shape students' reactions to their interactions with institutional bureaucracy, the academic system, the social system, and the external environment. These reactions require students to make new psychological assessments pertaining to their level of self-efficacy, locus of control, and ways of coping with stress. These assessments are based, in part, on past behaviors and choices. However, a revised view of their status on these psychological characteristics may result. If positive self-efficacy, reduced stress, and an internal locus of control result as an outcome of such personal assessments, then academic and social integration results, which in turn, leads to institutional fit and loyalty to the focal institution. Institutional fits and institutional loyalty result in an intent to persist, which in turn, results in the decision to remain at the focal institution.

Bean and Eaton advise individuals interested in a greater understanding of how the various psychological processes involved in this model function to read the psychological theory literature. Bean and Eaton do not offer explanations for the proposed linkages in this model.

Although Bean and Eaton's model is a psychological theory advanced to account for student departure, other psychological characteristics and processes that may influence student departure have been derived from psychological theories which seek to explain other phenomena. Such psychological characteristics and processes occur at the level of the individual student and at the level of the environment of the college or university (Braxton, 2000).

College student development theories constitute a set of psychological characteristics that may be extended to account for student departure decisions. Braxton (2000) suggests such student development theories as Chickering and Reisser's (1993) vectors of development, Perry's theory of cognitive and ethical development (1970, 1981), King and Kitchener's Reflective Judgment Model (1994), and Baxter Magolda's (1992) patterns of knowing might be extended to explain student withdrawal decisions. Schlossberg, Waters, and Goodman (1995) posit a model of how adults, such as college students, navigate life changes. This model is also included. Chapters Nine, Ten, and Eleven discuss additional individual dimensions of development. These student development theories might be extended to explain student withdrawal decisions. These theories delineate student entry characteristics that may influence how students interpret their experiences with the college environment. The identification of such student entry characteristics resonates with Tinto's (1986) assertion that one view inherent in the psychological perspective on college student departure assumes that student psychological characteristics influence the way students respond to their experiences at the college or university of attendance. Responses to such experiences influence student departure decisions.

The type of student entry characteristic delineated by each theory as well as rudimentary formulations regarding their linkage with student departure are described for Perry and King and Kitchener. Readers are referred to Chapter Nine for a discussion of Chickering and Reisser's vectors of development. Readers are also directed to Chapter Eleven for a discussion of Baxter Magolda's patterns of knowing. Both vectors of development and ways of knowing function as entry characteristics that relate to student departure decisions.

From Perry's (1970) theory of cognitive and ethical development, nine positions that structure the way students view the world in general and the nature and origin of knowledge in particular emerge. Students enter college on one of these positions. Because these positions on Perry's continuum of student cognitive and ethical development vary in their complexity, student reactions to their experiences in college may also vary because of their position on this continuum.

King and Kitchener's (1994) Reflective Judgment Model delineates seven stages of human knowing and beliefs and the rationales that individuals use to warrant their knowledge claims and beliefs. These stages vary in their complexity. College students also enter college at one of these stages of "reflective judgment." Students' interpretations of their college experiences vary as a consequence of their stage in King and Kitchener's model.

Schlossberg et al. (1995) offer a transition model of how adults manage change in their lives. The three parts of the model are approaching transitions, taking stock of coping resources, and taking charge. Transitions can be events that are anticipated (such as marriage) or unanticipated (such as divorce or significant illness), and non-events.

Non-events are situations that an individual expected which did not occur, such as not having a significant romantic relationship or a child.

Life events and how individuals cope with them affect college students' persistence and departure decisions. Mattering and marginality are two constructs, in particular, delineated by Schlossberg that influence how students cope with life events associated with attending college. Mattering facilitates persistence in college, because when students feel that someone in the institution cares about them, takes an interest in them, and pays attention to their experience, they feel they matter. As a result, students feel connected and that they belong (Schlossberg, Lynch, & Chickering, 1989). In contrast, the perception of marginality may lead to departure. After a transition from a familiar environment (such as family, high school friends) to a new environment (such as the college environment), students experience a shift from a sense of belonging to a feeling of marginality. Where once the roles and expectations were clear, the new environment brings uncertainty. Students unable to resolve uncertainty may depart (Schlossberg, 1984). See Chapter Twenty-Five for a more detailed discussion of these two important concepts.

In addition to psychological characteristics derived from student development theories, biculturalism is another psychological characteristic that may be relevant to accounting for the college departure of minority students (Braxton, 2000; Rendon, Jalomo, & Nora, 2000). Biculturalism pertains to the ability of minority students to learn and function in both the predominately White culture and in the culture of their racial or ethnic group at the same time (Polgar, 1960; Valentine, 1971). Minority students enter college with varying degrees of biculturalism. The greater the degree of biculturalism exhibited, the greater the adjustment of minority students to the culture of a predominately White college or university. See Chapter Ten to explore the complexities of bicultural identity development.

Environmental Level. Environments at the level of the residence hall and at the level of the college or university are psychological entities that are predicted to influence various student outcomes and may also influence college student retention. Moos (1979) demonstrates the effects of the environments of residence halls on such student outcomes as involvement in the student body, academic orientation, and academic achievement. He identifies ten domains that comprise the environments of residence halls. These domains of social climate array themselves into three broad categories: relationships, personal growth, and systems maintenance and change. If these domains influence student outcomes, then these domains may also affect the interpretations students make of their college experiences. Such interpretations may, in turn, impact the departure decisions of college students.

Environments or climates at the level of the college or university may also impact student departure. Baird (2000) and Strange in Chapter Thirteen postulate that the behavior of college students is influenced by their perceptions of the climates of their college or university. Such behaviors influence their judgments of their collegiate experiences, and such judgments affect departure decisions. Baird points to the dimensions of the psychological climate identified by Pace (1984) as important in departure decisions because these dimensions affect student satisfaction: friendliness, supportiveness, helpfulness, and intellectual satisfaction.

Conceptual explanations for the basic linkages between the above psychological characteristics and processes and the interpretations students make of the college experience because of these psychological factors have not been developed. Readers wishing to use these theories to account for student departure should read the literature pertinent to each theory to develop such conceptual explanations. However, Bean and Eaton's psychological model might be extended to include the various psychological characteristics derived from the theories of student development outlined above.

The identification of psychological characteristics that students hold at entrance to college and the delineation of psychological environmental dimensions represent a clear strength of the psychological theoretical orientation to college student departure. Student entry characteristics represent an important element in the college student departure process. Nevertheless, the neglect of economic factors, organizational structure and behavior, and social forces diminish the explanatory power of the psychological perspective to account for college student departure decisions.

Sociological Perspectives

The influence of social structure and social forces on the departure decisions of college students characterizes the sociological perspective on college student departure (Braxton, 2000; Tinto, 1986). Three sets of theoretical formulations that are, at base, sociological in their orientation are described in this section of the chapter: cultural capital and retention, student culture, and Tinto's interactionalist theory of college student departure.

Cultural Capital. Berger (2000b) extends the formulations of Bourdieu's (1973, 1977) theory of social reproduction to account for student departure. The notion of cultural capital is a central construct in Bourdieu's theory. Cultural capital is a symbolic form of capital and is the type of knowledge valued by the elite members of society (McDonough, 1997). Such knowledge, which is not taught in schools, takes the form of habits, manners, styles of speech, educational credentials, and lifestyle preferences (Bourdieu, 1973). For example, cultural capital manifests itself in social interactions among peers in the form of conversations about travel abroad and attending such cultural events as the symphony, the ballet, or a Broadway play.

Cultural capital plays an important role in the college student departure process. Berger (2000b) asserts that both individual students and individual colleges and universities possess varying degrees of cultural capital. As a consequence, Berger postulates that students are more likely to persist in a given college or university if their level of cultural capital matches the level of cultural capital embedded in the social and organizational systems of a given college or university. A likelihood of student departure results from wide discrepancies in such levels of cultural capital.

Student Culture. The culture of a student peer group is a defining characteristic of that group. Student peer groups play a pivotal role in the social communities of colleges and universities (Braxton, 2000). The culture of a student peer group influences the development of the group as well as the attitudes, values, norms, and behaviors endorsed by the group (Kuh & Whitt, 1988; Kuh, 1995).

Kuh and Love (2000) advance eight propositions that relate student culture to the process of college student departure. The first proposition states: "the college experience, including a decision to leave college, is mediated through a student's cultural meaning-making system" (p. 201). The student's culture of origin, which may be composed of the immediate family, friends, school, and community, shapes one's meaning-making system.

Kuh and Love's second proposition holds that "one's culture of origin mediates the importance attached to attending college and earning a college degree" (p. 202). The probability of persistence increases if one's culture of origin values attending and completing college (Bean & Vesper, 1992; Roth, 1985).

Kuh and Love's third proposition is that understanding a student's ability to successfully navigate the institution's culture depends on knowledge of the student's culture of origin and the culture of the college or university. This proposition assists institutional policy makers and developers of programs to reduce departure.

The fourth proposition advanced by Kuh and Love (2000) takes this form: "the probability of persistence is inversely related to the cultural distance between a student's culture of origin and the cultures of immersion" (p. 204). Put differently, the greater the degree of correspondence between a student's culture of origin and the cultures of the college or university of attendance, the greater the likelihood of student persistence.

However, Kuh and Love acknowledge that students who evince great cultural distance may persist under certain conditions. Their fifth proposition stipulates such a condition: "students who traverse a long culture distance must become acclimated to dominant cultures of immersion or join one or more enclaves" (p. 204). Such students may find "cultural enclaves" or groups that espouse values, attitudes, and beliefs similar to their own. If such students are unable to acclimate themselves to the dominant culture or are unable to join a cultural enclave group, then departure is likely.

Moreover, if students continue to spend time in their culture of origin after matriculating in a given college or university, cultural stress may result and departure is more likely. Such is the form of Kuh and Love's sixth proposition.

Kuh and Love also recognize the importance of the cultural connections students make with the academic and social systems of a given college or university. Their seventh proposition stipulates, "the likelihood that a student will persist is related to the extensity and intensity of one's sociocultural connections to the academic program and to affinity groups" (p. 205). Similarly, Kuh and Love's eighth proposition states "students who belong to one or more enclaves in the cultures of immersion are more likely to persist, especially if group members value achievement and persistence" (p. 207).

Tinto's Interactionalist Theory. Tinto's Interactionalist Theory of college student departure enjoys paradigmatic status among theoretical perspectives on college student departure (Braxton, Sullivan, & Johnson, 1997). Paradigmatic status signifies that considerable consensus around the potential validity of Tinto's theory exists and is indexed in the large number of citations (n = 400+) to Tinto's theory by late 1994 and the number of doctoral dissertations (n = 170) addressing Tinto's theory by early 1995 (Braxton et al., 1997).

Tinto's Interactionalist Theory regards student departure as a consequence of the individual student's interaction with the college or university as an organization. The meanings the individual student ascribes to such interactions with the formal and informal dimensions of the college or university at the level of the institution play an important role in student departure decisions (Braxton et al., 1997; Tinto, 1986, 1993). The process of student retention is viewed as longitudinal or unfolding over time as a student interacts with the college or university as an institution.

Tinto (1975) posits that students enter college with various individual characteristics (family background, individual attributes, and precollege schooling experiences). Socioeconomic status, parental educational level, and parental expectations are family background characteristics identified by Tinto. He delineates academic ability, race, and gender as individual student attributes. According to Tinto, precollege schooling experiences include the characteristics of the student's secondary school, the student's high school academic achievement, and social attainments of the student. These clusters of individual entry characteristics are presumed to directly influence student departure decisions, as well as students' initial commitments to the institution and to the goal of college graduation. Initial commitment to the institution and initial commitment to the goal of graduation influence the level of a student's integration into the academic and social systems of the college or university.

Academic integration consists of structural and normative dimensions. Structural integration entails the meeting of explicit standards of the college or university, whereas normative integration pertains to an individual's identification with the normative structure of the academic system.

Tinto suggests student academic performance as an index of a student's degree of structural integration into the academic system of a college or university, as grades signify the degree to which a student has met the values and objectives for student academic achievement set by a given college or university. He contends that the intellectual development of a student indicates the level of a student's normative integration because intellectual development reflects the student's appraisal of the institution's academic system. Tinto also asserts that normative integration takes the form of congruency between the individual's intellectual development and the intellectual environment of the college or university.

Social integration refers to the extent of congruency between the individual student and the social system of a college or university. Tinto posits that informal peer group associations, extracurricular activities, and interactions with faculty and administrators are mechanisms of social integration (1975). Braxton (2000) calls such mechanisms antecedents of social integration. Moreover, Tinto carefully points out that social integration occurs both at the level of the college or university and at the level of a subculture of the institution.

Academic and social integration affect the subsequent commitments of students. Specifically, the greater the student's level of academic integration, the greater the level of subsequent commitment to the goal of college graduation. In addition, the greater the student's level of social integration, the greater the level of subsequent commitment to the focal college or university (Tinto, 1975). The student's initial level of commitments—institutional and graduation goal—also influence their level of subsequent commitments. In turn, the greater the levels of both subsequent institutional commitment and commitment to the goal of college graduation, the greater the likelihood the individual will persist in college.

Tinto offers two additional propositions. First, high levels of commitment to the goal of graduation from college can compensate for low levels of institutional commitment. Second, high levels of social integration may compensate for low levels of academic integration and vice versa.

The sociological perspective focuses attention on the influence of social structure and social forces on student departure decisions. However, this perspective generally neglects the importance of economic, psychological, and organizational influences on such decisions. However, the formulations of Tinto's Interactionalist Theory permit the incorporation of constructs from economic, psychological, and organizational theoretical orientations into the structure of its argument (Braxton, 2000; Braxton et al., 1997; Tinto, 1986, 1993). Put differently, economic factors, psychological characteristics and processes, organizational structure and organizational behavior, and social structure and social forces serve as "helper" theories to increasing understanding of Tinto's core constructs of academic and social integration.

The theoretical perspectives described in this chapter seek explanations for voluntary undergraduate student departure. Student departure from graduate education also requires explanation. In Appendix B of his book *Leaving College: Rethinking the Causes and Cures of Student Attrition* (1993), Tinto advances a longitudinal theory of doctoral student persistence. Student affairs professionals interested in graduate student departure are referred to this Appendix.

Applying Theory to Practice

The application of theory to practice constitutes an essential requirement for the day-to-day work of student affairs practitioners. The selection of theory to guide practice poses a daunting task given the number of theoretical perspectives available for selection by student affairs practitioners. Evans, Forney, and Guido-DiBrito (1998) assert that theories vary in their usefulness. Walsh (1973) offers qualities that a theory must exhibit: comprehensiveness, clarity and explicitness, consistency, parsimony, and heurism. As McEwen reprises in Chapter Eight, questions to assess the utility of a theory to practice include (Knefelkamp, 1978): On what population is the theory based? How was the theory developed? Is the theory descriptive? Is the theory explanatory? Is the theory prescriptive? Does the theory produce ideas for research? Finally, is the theory useful to practice?

Although these criteria and questions are important to assessing a theory, adequate research-based support for a theory represents an indispensable criterion for the selection of a theory to guide practice. If research fails to support a theory, then unreliable and ineffective practice based on such a theory will likely result. Put differently, practice based on an unsupported theory rests on a bed of quick sand.

Woodard, Mallory, and De Luca (2001) advance a framework for use by student affairs practitioners to organize findings from research on college student retention which examine institutional policies, programs, and procedures designed to reduce college student departure. The dimensions of this framework include student characteristics, institution-wide characteristics, academic good practices, and student affairs good practices. This framework provides a useful vehicle for the application of theory and research designed to reduce student departure.

The delineation of guideposts for day-to-day professional practice also provides the basis for the development of institutional policies, programs, and practices designed to reduce student departure. The development of these guideposts also constitutes an example of the application of theory and research to practice. Research identifying sources of influence on social integration provide the foundation for the development of such guideposts.

Of the various theoretical perspectives presented in this chapter, Tinto's Interactionalist Theory has been the object of extensive research. An appraisal of empirical support for the propositions of Tinto's theory identifies four strongly supported, logically connected propositions (Braxton et al., 1997). A narrative statement of these robustly supported propositions assumes the following form. Students enter college with various characteristics that influence their initial level of commitment to the college or university that they chose to attend. This initial level of institutional commitment also affects their subsequent commitment to the institution. Social integration also affects subsequent institutional commitment. The greater a student's degree of social integration, the greater their subsequent commitment to the institution. The greater the degree of a student's subsequent commitment to the institution, the greater their likelihood of persisting in college. The role played by social integration and subsequent institutional commitment varies between residential and commuter institutions (Braxton et al., 1997). These later two propositions are strongly supported in residential colleges and universities but are modestly backed by research in commuter institutions. Social integration also plays an important role in the persistence of racial and ethnic minority students (Nora & Cabrera, 1996; Pascarella, 1985; Stoecker, Pascarella, & Wolfle, 1988).

Despite its compelling nature, academic integration is noticeably absent from this discussion of reliable sources of influence in student departure decisions. Empirical support for the influence of academic integration on subsequent commitment to the goal of college graduation (Braxton et al., 1997), subsequent institutional commitment (Braxton & Lien, 2000), and persistence (Braxton & Lien) is modest at best. Consequently, academic integration is not judged to be a reliable source of influence on the departure decisions of college students. Thus, fostering social integration constitutes an important role for student affairs practitioners to assume.

Guideposts for Fostering Social Integration

Braxton (2000) asserts that reliable knowledge that partially explains college student departure results from these strongly supported relationships. The relationships between social integration and subsequent institutional commitment and subsequent institutional commitment and student persistence are of critical importance to the application of Tinto's theory to practice. Tinto (1993) recognizes the centrality of social integration through the articulation of his third principle of effective retention. This principle holds that effective retention programs concentrate on the integration of all students into the social communities of a college or university. The realization of this principle depends on the development of institutional policies and programs that foster social integration. In addition to policies and programs, the achievement of this principle of effective retention also depends on the day-to-day practice of student affairs practitioners. Accordingly, there are four guideposts for student affairs practitioners to follow in the day-to-day performance of their professional responsibilities. These guideposts spring from research findings that identify factors that foster or impede student social integration. If applied, these "guideposts" foster student integration into the social communities of a college or university. Put differently, these guideposts constitute instruments for the achievement of Tinto's second principle of effective retention.

Know the students you serve in the performance of your day-to-day professional responsibilities. This guidepost requires the assessment of the psychological characteristics of the students. Student affairs professionals should know the developmental status as measured using various theories of college student development of the students they serve. The family backgrounds of students should also be known.

The stress coping strategies used and degree of career self-efficacy that characterize students are more specific psychological characteristics that student affairs professionals should know about the students with whom they have frequent contact. Stress coping strategies and career self-efficacy emanate from research findings that identify these two student psychological characteristics as wielding an influence on social integration. The stress coping strategy of positive reinterpretation and growth exercises a positive effect on social integration (Bray, Braxton, & Sullivan, 1999). Positive reinterpretation and growth refers to an individual's efforts to view a source of stress in a positive light (Carver, Scheier, & Weintraub, 1989). In contrast, the coping strategy of denial negatively affects social integration (Bray et al., 1999). Denial as a coping strategy entails the refusal of an individual to accept the reality of the existence of the source of stress (Carver et al., 1989). Career self-efficacy is the extent of self-confidence a student has in his or her ability to engage in information gathering about careers and educational requirements. Research indicates that the higher a students' degree of career self-efficacy, the greater his or her degree of social integration (Peterson, 1993).

The financial needs of students should also be known. Research conducted by Cabrera, Nora, and Castaneda (1992) suggests that students who receive financial aid in contrast to those students who do not receive aid exhibit greater degrees of social integration. Consequently, the financial aid and financial need requests of all students should receive serious consideration. Student affairs practitioners should assist students who talk with them about their financial aid needs in attaining needed funds from the institution or from other sources. Students who demonstrate a need for small amounts of financial aid should not be ignored. At a minimum, the student affairs practitioner should make referrals to other campus offices charged with financial aid.

Communicate academic and social rules and regulations important to students in an effective manner to all students. This guidepost requires that student affairs practitioners develop methods of communication that reach all students. Effective communication should be an abiding concern of student affairs practitioners in their day-to-day professional activities. Research finds that keeping students well informed of rules and regulations positively affects social integration and student persistence (Berger & Braxton, 1998; Braxton & Brier, 1989).

Enforce rules and regulations pertaining to student life in a fair manner. Put differently, students must perceive that student affairs practitioners enforce rules and regulations in a consistent way across all students and all circumstances. The basis for this guidepost is the research finding that the perception held by students that rules and regulations are fairly enforced facilitates social integration (Berger & Braxton, 1998).

Encourage and create opportunities for social interaction among students. Peer social interactions constitute a daily occurrence for most college students. Student affairs practitioners should encourage such informal interactions among students, especially those students that appear socially isolated. Opportunities for social interactions among students also embed themselves in a vast array of policies and programs under the administration of student affairs practitioners. This guidepost also emphasizes the need for the structuring of opportunities for student social interactions in such policies and programs. Examples of such policies and programs include orientation programs for first-year students, residence halls, and social activities for commuting students. For example, Braxton and McClendon (2001) recommend that orientation programs should develop numerous opportunities for students to socially interact with their peers. They also recommend that multiple opportunities for residents of residence halls to participate in face-to-face interactions with other students should be developed. Braxton and McClendon also urge the development of social environments for students in commuter colleges and universities. Student affairs professionals should consider the development of such environments. Residential colleges and universities should also develop such social environments for their commuting students.

Research findings suggest peer social support (Napoli & Wortman, 1998) and peer involvement (Berger & Milem, 1999; Milem & Berger, 1997) both exert a positive influence on social integration. Peer involvement take place through studying with other students, socializing with friends, and talking with classmates out of class (Berger & Milem; Milem & Berger). Research also demonstrates that living on campus facilitates the social integration of first-year students (Pascarella & Chapman, 1983; Christie & Dinham, 1991).

Closing Thoughts

This chapter concentrates on undergraduate student success with student persistence functioning as an important and essential gateway to success. Success at the graduate student level in general and graduate student retention in particular has not received attention in this chapter. Graduate student retention and research using economic, organizational, psychological, and sociological concepts constitute important topics for serious inquiry. With the exception of Tinto's Interactionalist Theory, a sociological theoretical perspective, research using the various theoretical perspectives presented has not been reviewed in this chapter. Student affairs scholars may choose to conduct studies on these important topics.

The topic of college student departure has been the focus of empirical research for over seventy years (Braxton, 2000). In the last thirty years, our knowledge and understanding of this process has increased substantially. Some sources of influence on departure are known and are described in this chapter. Nevertheless, four significant challenges lie ahead. First, research testing the various theoretical perspectives outlined in this chapter is needed to further understanding of this ill-structured problem. Although extensive, current knowledge is incomplete and belies the ill-structured nature of the problem of student departure. Second, student affairs practitioners must keep pace with research on college student departure. The application of theory and research to practice constitutes a challenge to student affairs professionals whose heavy load of daily responsibilities frequently prevent the reading of the literature on college student retention. The third challenge resides in the need to continually examine current practices to assure that such practices resonate with the findings of research. Current practice may require adjustment or even abandonment. The actual transformation of research findings into ways useful to practice constitutes a fourth challenge. The guideposts presented in this chapter and the framework for organizing research findings described by Woodard, Mallory, and De Luca (2001) serve as models for such transformations.

The meeting of these four challenges assures that institutional policies, programs, and procedures designed to prevent unnecessary student departure and increase the probability of student success rest on a sturdy groundwork of theory and research. The steadfast efforts of student affairs practitioners and scholars of student departure to meet these challenges are needed to assure college student success.

References

Astin, A., & Scherrei, R. (1980). *Maximizing leadership effectiveness.* San Francisco: Jossey-Bass.

Astin, A. W. (1996). Involvement in learning revisited: Lessons we have learned. *Journal of College Student Development, 37,* 123–134.

Baird, L. L. (2000). College climate and the Tinto model. In J. M. Braxton (Ed.), *Reworking the student departure puzzle* (pp. 62–80). Nashville, TN: Vanderbilt University Press.

Bandura, A. (1997). *Self-efficacy: The exercise of control.* New York: W. H. Freeman & Co.

Bandura, A. (1986). *Social foundations of thought and action: A cognitive theory.* Englewood Cliffs, NJ: Prentice Hall.

Baxter Magolda, M. (1992). *Knowing and reasoning in college: Gender-related patterns in students' intellectual development.* San Francisco: Jossey-Bass.

Bean, J. P. (1983). The application of a model of turnover in work organizations to the student attrition process. *The Review of Higher Education, 6,* 129–148.

Bean, J. P., & Eaton, S. B. (2000). A psychological model of college student retention. In J. M. Braxton (Ed.), *Reworking the student departure puzzle* (pp. 48–61). Nashville, TN: Vanderbilt University Press.

Bean, J. P., & Vesper, N. (1992). Student dependency theory: An explanation of student retention in college. Paper presented at the annual meeting of the Association for the Study of Higher Education, Minneapolis, October.

Becker, G. S. (1964). *Human capital.* New York: National Bureau of Economic Research.

Berger, J. B. (2000a). Organizational behavior at colleges and student outcomes: A new perspective on college impact. *The Review of Higher Education, 23,* 177–198.

Berger, J. B. (2000b). Optimizing capital, social reproduction, and undergraduate persistence: A sociological perspective. In J. M. Braxton (Ed.), *Reworking the student departure puzzle* (pp. 95–124). Nashville, TN: Vanderbilt University Press.

Berger, J. B., & Braxton, J. M. (1998). Revising Tinto's interactionalist theory of student departure through theory elaboration: Examining the role of organizational attributes in the persistence process. *Research in Higher Education, 39,* 103–119.

Berger, J. B., & Milem, J. F. (1999). The role of student involvement and perceptions of integration in a causal model of student persistence. *Research in Higher Education, 40,* 641–664.

Birnbaum, R. (1988). *How colleges work.* San Francisco: Jossey-Bass.

Bourdieu, P. (1973). Cultural reproduction and social reproduction. In R. Brown (Ed.), *Knowledge, education, and cultural change* (pp. 189–207). London: Collier Macmillan.

Bourdieu, P. (1977). *Outline of a theory of practice.* Translated by R. Nice. Cambridge, UK: University Press.

Braxton, J. M. (Ed.). (2000). *Reworking the departure puzzle.* Nashville, TN: Vanderbilt University Press.

Braxton, J. M., & Brier, E. M. (1989). Melding organizational and interactional theories of student attrition: A path analytic study. *Review of Higher Education, 13,* 47–61.

Braxton, J. M., & Lien, L. (2000). The viability of academic integration as a central construct in Tinto's interactionalist theory of college student departure. In J. M. Braxton (Ed.), *Reworking the student departure puzzle* (pp. 11–28). Nashville, TN: Vanderbilt University Press.

Braxton, J. M., & McClendon, S. A. (2001). The fostering of social integration through institutional practice. *The Journal of College Student Retention: Research, Theory and Practice, 3,* 57–71.

Braxton, J. M., & Mundy, M. E. (2001). Powerful institutional levers to reduce college student departure. *The Journal of College Student Retention: Research, Theory and Practice, 3,* 91–118.

Braxton, J. M., Sullivan, A. S., & Johnson, R. M. (1997). Appraising Tinto's theory of college student departure. In J. C. Smart (Ed.), *Higher education: Handbook of theory and research, 12,* 107–164. New York: Agathon Press.

Bray, N. J., Braxton, J. M., & Sullivan, A. S. (1999). The influence of stress-related coping strategies on college student departure decisions. *Journal of College Student Development, 40,* 645–657.

Cabrera, A. F., Nora, A., & Castaneda, M. B. (1992). The role of finances in the persistence process: A structural model. *Research in Higher Education, 33,* 571–593.

Carver, C. S., Scheier, M. F., & Weintraub, J. K. (1989). Assessing coping strategies: A theoretically based approach. *Journal of Personality and Social Psychology, 56,* 367–383.

Chickering, A. W., & Reisser, L. (1993). *Education and identity.* San Francisco: Jossey-Bass.

Christie, N. G., & Dinham, S. M. (1991). Institutional and external influences on social integration in the freshman year. *Journal of Higher Education, 62,* 413–435.

Evans, N. J., Forney, D. S., & Guido-DiBrito, F. (1998). *Student development in college: Theory, research and practice.* San Francisco: Jossey-Bass.

Floyd, D. L. (1988). *Toward mastery leadership: Strategies for student success. Summary report of a colloquium.* Columbia, MD: American College Testing Program.

Gratton, M., & Walleri, R. D. (1989, June 25–27). *Connections for student college success and institutional effectiveness.* Paper presented at Effectiveness and Student Success: Transforming Community Colleges for the 1990s, Chicago.

King, P. M., & Kitchener, K. S. (1994). *Developing reflective judgment: Understanding and promoting intellectual growth and critical thinking in adolescents and adults.* San Francisco: Jossey-Bass.

Kitchener, K. (1986). The reflective judgment model: Characteristics, evidence, and measurement. In R. Mines & K. Kitchener (Eds.), *Adult cognitive development.* New York: Praeger.

Knefelkamp, L. (1978). A reader's guide to student development theory: A framework for understanding, a framework for design. Unpublished manuscript.

Kuh, G. D. (1995). Cultivating high stakes student culture research. *Research in Higher Education, 36,* 563–576.

Kuh, G. D., & Love, P. G. (2000). A cultural perspective on student departure. In J. M. Braxton (Ed.), *Reworking the student departure puzzle* (pp. 196–212). Nashville, TN: Vanderbilt University Press.

Kuh, G. D., Schuh, J. H., & Whitt, E. J., & Associates. (1991). *Involving colleges: Successful approaches to fostering student learning and development outside the classroom.* San Francisco: Jossey-Bass.

Kuh, G. D., & Whitt, E. J. (1988). *The invisible tapestry: Culture in American colleges and universities* (ASHE-ERIC Higher Education Report No. 1). Washington, DC: Association for the Study of Higher Education.

Martens, K., Lara, E., Cordova, J., & Harris, H. (1995). Community college students: Ever changing, ever new. In S. R. Helfgot & M. M. Culp (Eds.), *Promoting student success in the community college* (New Directions for Student Services No. 69, pp. 5–15). San Francisco: Jossey-Bass.

McDonough, P. (1997). *Choosing colleges: How social class and schools structure opportunity.* Albany, NY: SUNY Press.

Milem, J. F., & Berger, J. B. (1997). A modified model of college student persistence: Exploring the relationship between Astin's theory of involvement and Tinto's theory of student departure. *Journal of College Student Development, 38,* 387–400.

Moos, R. H. (1979). *Evaluating educational environments.* San Francisco: Jossey-Bass.

Napoli, A. R., & Wortman, P. M. (1998). Psychosocial factors related to retention and early departure of two-year community college students. *Research in Higher Education, 39,* 419–455.

National Center for Education Statistics. (1998). *Profile of undergraduates in U.S. postsecondary education institutions: 1995–96, with an essay on undergraduates who work* (NCES 98–084, by L. J. Horn & J. Berktold. Project Officer: A. G. Malizio.). Washington, DC: U.S. Department of Education.

Nora, A., & Cabrera, A. (1996). The role of perceptions of prejudice and discrimination on the adjustment of minority students to college. *Journal of Higher Education, 67,* 119–148.

Pace, C. R. (1984). *College and university environment scales: Technical manual.* (2nd ed.) Princeton, NJ: Educational Testing Service.

Pascarella, E. T. (1985). Racial differences in factors associated with bachelor's degree completion: A nine-year follow-up. *Research in Higher Education, 23,* 351–373.

Pascarella, E. T., & Chapman, D. W. (1983). A multi-institutional path analytic validation of Tinto's model of college student withdrawal. *American Education Research Journal, 20* (1), 87–102.

Pascarella, E. T., & Terenzini, P. T. (1983). Predicting voluntary freshman year persistence/withdrawal behavior in a residential university: A path analytic validation of Tinto's model. *Journal of Educational Psychology, 75,* 215–226.

Pascarella, E. T., & Terenzini, P. T. (1991). *How college affects students: Findings and insights from twenty years of research.* San Francisco: Jossey-Bass.

Perry, W. G. (1970). *Forms of intellectual and ethical development in the college years: A scheme.* Troy, MO: Holt, Rinehart and Winston.

Perry, W. G. (1981). Cognitive and ethical growth: The making of meaning. In A. W. Chickering & Associates (Eds.), *The modern American college: Responding to the realities of diverse students and a challenging society* (pp. 70–116), San Francisco: Jossey-Bass.

Peterson, S. L. (1993). Career decision-making self-efficacy and institutional integration of underprepared college students. *Research in Higher Education, 34,* 659–685.

Polgar, S. (1960). Biculturalism of Mesquakie teenage boys. *American Anthropologist, 62,* 217–235.

Rendon, L. I., Jalomo, R. E., & Nora, A. (2000). Theoretical considerations in the study of minority student retention in higher education. In J. M. Braxton (Ed.), *Reworking the student departure puzzle* (pp. 127–156). Nashville, TN: Vanderbilt University Press.

Roth, M. (1985). Immigrant students in an urban commuter college: Persisters and dropouts. Ph.D. dissertation. Adelphi University, Garden City, NY.

Rotter, J. B. (1966). Generalized expectancies for internal versus external control of reinforcement. *Psychological Monographs 80* (1, whole No. 609).

St. John, E. P., Cabrera, A. F., Nora, A., & Asker, E. H. (2000). Economic influences on persistence reconsidered: How can finance research inform the reconceptualization of persistence models? In J. M. Braxton (Ed.), *Reworking the student departure puzzle* (pp. 29–47). Nashville, TN: Vanderbilt University Press.

Schlossberg, N. K. (1984). *Counseling adults in transition: Linking practice with theory.* New York: Springer.

Schlossberg, N. K., Lynch, A. Q., & Chickering, A. W. (1989). *Improving higher education environments for adults.* San Francisco: Jossey-Bass.

Schlossberg, N. K., Waters, E. B., & Goodman, J. (1995). *Counseling adults in transition: Linking practice with theory* (2nd ed.). New York: Springer.

Stoecker, J. E., Pascarella, E. T., & Wolfle, L. M. (1988). Persistence in higher education: A 9-year test of a theoretical model. *Journal of College Student Development, 29,* 196–209.

Tinto, V. (1975). Dropouts from higher education: A theoretical synthesis of recent research. *Review of Educational Research, 45,* 89–125.

Tinto, V. (1986). Theories of college student departure revisited. In J. C. Smart (Ed.), *Higher education: Handbook of theory and research, Vol. 2,* (pp. 359–384). New York: Agathon Press.

Tinto, V. (1993). *Leaving college: Rethinking the causes and cures of student attrition* (2nd ed.). Chicago: University of Chicago Press.

Valentine, C. A. (1971). Deficit, difference, and bi-cultural models of Afro-American behavior. *Harvard Educational Review, 19,* 137–157.

Walsh, W. B. (1973). *Theories of person-environment interaction: Implications for the college student.* Iowa City: American College Testing Program.

Weiner, B. (1986). *An attributional theory of motivation and emotion.* New York: Springer-Verlag.

Wood, P. (1983). Inquiring systems and problem structure: Implications for cognitive development. *Human Development, 26,* 249–265.

Woodard, D. B., Mallory, S. L., & De Luca, A. M. (2001). Retention and institutional effort: A self-study framework. *NASPA Journal, 39,* 53–83.

PART FOUR

ORGANIZING AND MANAGING PROGRAMS AND SERVICES

Since the last edition of this text, the stewardship of our universities and colleges has continued to come under close, if not intense, scrutiny by the public, legislative bodies, and governing boards. The public has challenged our institutions of higher education to improve the quality of the undergraduate experience and assess and evaluate espoused outcomes. Continuing financial stress and demands for measurable outcomes have sparked major restructuring efforts at most colleges and universities. The rethinking, restructuring movement is not simply the result of an imperative to become more "efficient" or "leaner and meaner"; rather, the push has been to fundamentally rethink and reorganize our institutions to focus them on student learning and on serving an expanding and increasingly diverse population of students. How student affairs professionals organize activities and functions to meet these objectives, and how they acquire the requisite knowledge base to do so, is the topic of this section.

Chapter Fifteen, by Gwen Dungy, provides an overview of management trends and models with an emphasis on decision making and communication within an academic context. The various functions of student affairs are briefly described, organizational options are presented, and trends and issues related to educational organizations are discussed.

Planning and budgeting activities are powerful forces in the current restructuring environment. Most institutions have moved away from conventional models of planning to inclusive participatory approaches that are more responsive to the contextual needs of the organization and more realistic concerning future financial resources. In Chapter Sixteen, John Schuh describes strategic planning and defines various approaches to the budgeting process. He concludes with a discussion of trends in financing and budgeting.

Nothing has changed so dramatically since the last edition of this book as the use of technology in higher education. The pace of technological change is so rapid that by the time this edition is printed, there will be new advances in software and hardware that were not in existence when Will Barratt penned his discussion of technology. In Chapter Seventeen, Barratt discusses the paradox of technology and offers a brief history of information technology. He then describes the nexus of student affairs practice and technology followed by a detailed section on technological competencies in student affairs. He concludes with three fundamental questions for the practitioner on the use of technolgy in student affairs.

Probably the area that challenges the student affairs practitioner the most is human resources. Chapter Eighteen, by Jon Dalton, is a primer on selecting, hiring, developing, supervising, and evaluating professional, clerical, and student staff. He begins the chapter by establishing a framework of goals for human resource management and examining the core values that support such goals. He then discusses the importance of developing core competencies and individual talents and concludes with a discussion of the practical tasks of human resource management and advice to the practitioner.

The concepts, strategies, and advice provided in these chapters serve as a helpful framework for practitioners to reflect upon and examine their approach to the administration of programs and services. There are no fixed formulas but rather a blend of models and experiences that can be used depending on the setting. We are slowly coming to understand that success in addressing change and new challenges is built on refining our roles and developing new strategies and structures while remaining faithful to the core principles and values that have served our profession so well during the last century.

CHAPTER FIFTEEN

ORGANIZATION AND FUNCTIONS OF STUDENT AFFAIRS

Gwendolyn Jordan Dungy

This chapter is based in part on Arthur Sandeen's chapter on the same subject in the third edition of this book. In the years since then, demographics, economics, technology, and other variables have changed higher education. This has presented both opportunities and challenges. The challenge is to consistently provide quality programs and educational services. Thus professionals must understand a variety of structures and functions of student affairs in all types of colleges and universities. So we begin with an overview of recent organizational change in student affairs and continue with brief descriptions of traditional and emerging functional areas.

For each functional area, major professional organizations and primary publications are listed. Many professionals belong to larger and more comprehensive organizations such as the National Association of Student Personnel Administrators (NASPA) or the American College Personnel Association (ACPA), so these are not listed as primary associations for functional areas. Instead, there is an alphabetical list of professional associations with their web addresses. Concluding sections project future trends and why they may be the impetus for organizational change in student affairs.

Note: I am grateful to Arthur Sandeen for the model on which this chapter is based. Also, many thanks and much appreciation to those who assisted in the research for this chapter, without whom it would be incomplete: Rhondie Voorhees, doctoral student, College Student Personnel Administration, University of Maryland, College Park; Sherry Mallory, Assistant to the Vice Chancellor for Student Affairs, University of Arkansas, Fayetteville; Jenny Michael and Leah Ewing Ross, NASPA staff; NASPA leaders; and kind editors.

Structure and Change

In the last decade of the twentieth century, there was a flurry of organizational change in higher education. Why? Because, historically, education has tended to look to business to initiate change in its own structure and management. Birnbaum (2000) acknowledges that "although the similarities between businesses and universities are superficial, the more we appear to be business enterprises, the more that business solutions are likely to be prescribed for our problems." So, more often than not, "The answer is restructuring and reinvention" (p. 217).

Change and restructuring in some institutions, colleges, and universities may be needed, but they, unlike businesses, are "loosely coupled systems in which managers with limited authority provide support for relatively autonomous specialists performing complex tasks with relatively stable structures" (Birnbaum, 2000, p. 150).

To get a national perspective on the extent and nature of the change in student services that has occurred, the National Association of Student Personnel Administrators (NASPA) surveyed its membership in December 1996 and again in 1998. Data from the surveys indicate that most traditional student services remain; nevertheless, significant changes have been made.

Overall, 69 percent of those responding to the NASPA survey reported some organizational changes in student affairs at their institutions. Respondents at doctoral, research, and liberal arts institutions were the most likely to report change. The most common areas of change had to do with enrollment management and its placement within the institution.

Traditionally, student affairs has been a stand-alone division with the senior student affairs administrator reporting to the president, whether the organizational structure was centralized or decentralized. There are significant differences in the decision-making authority and budget autonomy of individual departments, depending on whether traditional hierarchy is in place.

It is common, particularly in large student affairs units, for core functions such as budget management, personnel decisions, and day-to-day management tasks to occur in a decentralized environment where each unit head, in effect, serves as the senior student affairs administrator. The complexity of most student affairs units demands autonomy on departmental levels. On smaller campuses, decentralization is less common. In larger and more complex organizations the climate is changing.

This is because parents, legislators, and the community in which the college or university presides have demanded greater centralization of decision making. In addition, the interdependency of many departments within student affairs and across the institution calls for a centralized model to ensure that the best balance is struck between student and institutional interests. Each new class of students affects a wide range of offices such as admissions, financial aid, on- and off-campus housing, and dining services. Housing and Residence Life departments, for instance, need to anticipate and manage available beds for incoming and continuing students. Housing officials cannot do this well unless there is close and frequent communication with all offices and departments that influence the incoming class of students, so it calls for some centralization of information and decision making.

Some institutions have combined academic affairs and student affairs into one reporting unit with the provost or academic vice president as the senior administrator. The strength of this model is twofold: it enables student affairs personnel to become more familiar with the priorities of the academic division, and it allows them to develop closer relationships with faculty in order to more effectively help students to learn in a holistic and coordinated manner.

Familiarity with the academic area is imperative when the intensity and acceleration of change can affect the climate for effective student learning. Not only is attention to academics and the pace of change increasingly important, "Change will occur from examining basic underlying assumptions and from changing these assumptions to align with institutional and societal values and principles" (Woodard, Love, & Komives, 2000, p. 9). In other words, student affairs, regardless of organizational alignment, should be poised to initiate change in all functional areas based on investigation, flexibility, and adaptability to the environment.

During the most recent period of extensive organizational change, some student affairs operations that had been reporting to the provost or academic vice president have reverted to a direct line reporting to the president. One strength of this model is that it allows the senior student affairs administrator to sit at the "small table" on the president's cabinet or executive council to insure that decisions are made with the best understanding of how they will affect the learning, development, welfare, and rights of students.

Dickeson (1999) developed a matrix of twenty-three student affairs programs and suggested that the programs could be administratively located in academic affairs, student life, administration, or university advancement (p. 50).

Whichever model is used, student affairs cannot be isolated and risk becoming ineffective because it is disconnected from any part of the university. Institutions of higher education can no longer function as "closed systems" (Kuh, 1996, p. 277). Kuh suggests a new organizational paradigm, in which "student affairs staff need different windows to look through in order to make sense of the complicated and rapidly changing institutions in which they work" (p. 278).

Functional Areas in Student Affairs

Student affairs professionals work in a wide range of functional areas within many types of institutions. These include, but are not limited to, four-year colleges and universities; two-year and community colleges; historically Black colleges and universities; Hispanic-serving institutions; tribal colleges and universities; religiously affiliated schools; women's institutions; and for-profit institutions. All these vary greatly by size, reputation, resources, geographic region, and academic specialization; and each institution has its own mission, history, traditions, and culture. Due to this extraordinary diversity of institutions, student affairs divisions have evolved uniquely within each institution.

The importance of such contexts cannot be overemphasized. There are many similarities among them, but often there are major differences in expectations. The unique needs of different students should influence how student affairs and educational programs are provided.

In the United States, for example, tribal colleges and universities often focus on preserving the language and culture of the students' heritage. Hispanic and historically Black institutions may pay greater attention to the relationship between the institution and the community. Similarly, religiously affiliated and gender-specific colleges and universities may have unique missions that dictate student affairs priorities. Community colleges pride themselves on being particularly sensitive to the needs of returning students and students who might be pursuing a degree by attending multiple institutions because of convenience, so community colleges might focus more on academic advising and articulation with transfer institutions.

Of course, the size and resources of the college or university will influence all this. At larger institutions, each functional area may have a separate office with a specialized staff. Smaller, less well-funded schools may have a small staff that is responsible for a wider range of programs and services.

Some of the functional areas described in this section could be called "traditional"—that is, they have stood the test of time and are relatively uniform across institutions. Among these are admissions, records, financial aid, and counseling. The main problem with that is it often roots the "organization in higher education's history, culture, traditions, and structures and transcends the particular issues at hand or the characteristics of any single institution or even national context" (Eckel, Green, Hill, & Mallon, 1999, p. 3). Underlying assumptions may not be questioned when demographics and environmental contexts change.

Other student services functions could be labeled as "emerging," meaning that they are being adopted by more institutions each year but not yet by the majority of schools. Yet it is likely that they will contribute to comprehensive change in the future that links functions with outcomes. In every organizational structure, student affairs professionals should try to organize themselves so that they can use both old and new techniques to help students succeed in their academic life.

Academic Advising

The academic advisor's job is to help the student create a plan of study that has a good chance to allow him or her reach a goal. This must be supportive but also academically and developmentally appropriate for a given student.

Academic advising offices may be situated within academic affairs or student affairs and may be centralized within the institution or decentralized throughout various colleges and departments. They may also be integrated or linked with offices such as orientation programs and the counseling center.

The major professional organization of academic advisors is the National Academic Advising Association; the primary publication is the *NACADA Journal*.

Admissions

The basic job of admissions personnel is to tell prospective students about the institution and its programs, as well as to recruit, screen, and accept applicants. This is a complex and sophisticated operation that includes identifying, engaging, and attracting the right mix of students for a particular institution.

Some admissions offices are part of student affairs; others are in enrollment management (often with the registrar and financial aid offices). Usually they are part of an enrollment management model and report to the provost, executive vice president, or president.

The major professional organization of admissions officers is the National Association of College Admissions Counselors; the primary publications are the *Journal of College Admissions* and the *College Board Review.*

Assessment, Research, and Program Evaluation

Colleges and universities often gather information about their students, including, but not limited to, grades, test scores, and demographics. Some also gather information about student attitudes and opinions through large-scale national projects, such as the National Survey of Student Engagement or the Cooperative Institutional Research Program, as well as through locally designed instruments.

Demographic data gathering and reporting and related research activities are sometimes undertaken by the institutional research office of a given university. In larger institutions, an additional office focused solely on student affairs research may exist. These offices have a plethora of titles and can be based either within student affairs or within academic affairs; the titles of these offices often include words such as student affairs research, assessment, or evaluation (Malaney, 1999).

The major professional organizations of student affairs researchers include the American Educational Research Association and the Association for Institutional Research; the primary publications are the *Review of Research in Education, Research in Higher Education,* and *Standards for Educational and Psychological Testing.*

Athletics

In some institutions, particularly small liberal arts colleges and community colleges, student affairs divisions have responsibility for intercollegiate athletics. These programs provide opportunities for students to formally compete with students at other institutions in a variety of sports. Their portfolio also includes gender equity, financial support, and institutional position within the athletic conferences (Sandeen, 1996).

The major professional organizations for those who work in college athletics are the National Collegiate Athletic Association, the National Association of Intercollegiate Athletics, and the National Junior College Athletic Association; the primary publications are the *NCAA Manual,* the *NCAA News,* and the *JUCO Review.*

Campus Safety

Depending on the philosophy and traditions of the school, safety or law enforcement officials will usually report to either the office of business affairs or student affairs. When they report to business affairs, most likely the orientation is toward protecting the buildings and physical assets of the campus. When they report to student affairs, they probably focus more on student development and community safety by involving students in the process of taking responsibility for their own safety and the welfare of the campus community.

The major professional organization of campus safety officers is the International Association of Campus Law Enforcement Administrators; the primary publication is the *Campus Law Enforcement Journal.*

Career Development

Over the years, the scope of career development services has broadened considerably. In addition to helping students find satisfying and rewarding employment, career development specialists also help students with career exploration, planning their job search, and other skills such as resume writing, interviewing, and making effective presentations. Career development specialists may also help students locate opportunities for internships and cooperative education experiences.

Although career centers are most often situated within student affairs, on some campuses they may be housed in academic affairs or in the institution's development office. On larger campuses, career services may be decentralized into academic units or departments, especially within professional schools.

The major professional organizations of career development specialists are the National Career Development Association and the National Association of Colleges and Employers; the primary publications include the *Journal of Career Planning and Employment, Career Development Quarterly,* and *Spotlight on Career Services, Recruitment, and HR/Staffing.*

College or Student Unions

A college or student union is often the "heart" of the campus; at many institutions, it functions as a service center and gathering place for students, faculty, staff, and alumni. Services may include a bookstore, coffee shop, food court, computer center, travel service, and other amenities that support community and the lives of students.

The major professional organizations of student union staff members are the Association of College Unions International and the National Association of Campus Activities; the primary publications are The *ACUI Bulletin* and *Programming.*

Community Service and Service Learning Programs

Community service is usually a volunteer program not connected to a for-credit academic program. Often these programs are housed in student affairs where staff, through community contacts, help students find a volunteer site.

Service learning has evolved into an academic program with a large experiential and reflection component. Many programs have their origin in student affairs; over the years, however, they have migrated to the academic area because of the credit tied to an academic department.

The primary professional organizations of staff members who work in this area include the National Campus Compact, the National Society for Experiential Education, and the Association for Experiential Education; the primary publications include *The Compact News,* the *NSEE Quarterly,* and the *Journal of Experiential Education.*

Commuter Services and Off-Campus Housing

Commuter students may be defined as "all students who do not live in institution-owned housing on campus" (Jacoby, 2000, p. 4). The needs of commuter students are important for most campuses to address. Staff in commuter services advocate on behalf of commuter students and ensure that commuters have adequate access to campus facilities, services, recreational opportunities, and dining options. Their job is to make sure commuter students are able to participate fully in the academic and social life of the campus.

Often, assistance in finding off-campus housing is one of the most important services needed by commuter students, so many commuter services offices try to help. In addition, staff often provide students with information about the market value of rental units in the area, rental agreements, landlord-tenant relationships, and how to be a responsible neighbor.

An emerging trend in this area is to fully integrate commuter students into living-learning communities connecting classroom and out-of-class experiences, a benefit traditionally enjoyed by residential students (Stevens, 2000).

The major professional organization of staff members in commuter services and off-campus housing offices is the National Clearinghouse for Commuter Programs; the primary publication is *Commuter.*

Counseling and Psychological Services

Administrators and staff in most American colleges and universities believe strongly in the importance of helping students work through psychological and emotional issues that may affect their academic success and personal development. The counseling services office, usually known as the counseling center, plays a primary role. Usually these are staffed by professionals who are trained and, in most cases, licensed; these professionals provide counseling and psychological services to students. In addition, they often provide crisis response counseling to the entire campus community.

Counseling center staff not only react and respond to campus crises but frequently engage in outreach activities with other campus units and departments, as well as with agencies from the community. The counseling center may be housed within student health services, operate as an independent office within student affairs, or be attached to a medical center (Sandeen, 1996).

The major professional organizations in this specialty include the Division of Counseling Psychology of the American Psychological Association, the American Counseling Association, and the Association of University and College Counseling Center Directors; the primary publications include the *Counseling Psychologist,* the *Division 17 Newsletter* (published by the American Psychological Association), and the *Journal of Counseling and Development.*

Dean of Students Office

Many of the functions described in this chapter are part of the dean of students office, which typically responds to students, faculty, staff, parents, community members, and others concerned with student-related issues or concerns that arise on campus. Often this office carries the burden of helping students while establishing and enforcing both community standards and institutional standards at the same time. It also may be responsible for organizing and directing the institution's response to student crises.

The major professional organizations of dean of students office staff include the National Association of Student Personnel Administrators and the American College Personnel Association; the primary publications are *Net Results* (NASPA's online magazine), the *NASPA Journal,* the *Journal of College Student Development,* and *About Campus.*

Dining and Food Services

Food service programs vary greatly from one institution to the next; services range from vending machines to full-service food courts that rival commercial establishments outside the campus. Dining services staff may also provide a wide array of programs and information for students on such topics as nutrition, food labels, and wellness. Some institutions have extensive catering operations for formal and special events; others contract for these services with private companies. Dining services operations often report to student affairs divisions, although sometimes the responsibility for managing food services is shared with another administrative unit in the institution, such as the business office.

The major professional organization of dining and food services employees is the National Association of College and University Food Services (NACUFS); the primary publication is *Newswave,* which is published by NACUFS.

Disability Support Services

Colleges and universities are required to provide support services for students with disabilities. The emphases and extent of these services depend on the nature of the institution. Staff in disability support services provide academic services such as note takers and interpreters; they also work to improve physical access on campus for students with mobility challenges, advise students about their rights and responsibilities, and provide outreach and consultation to other campus offices and academic units.

Disability support services staff often assume the role of advocate for students with disabilities; in this role, they work on behalf of students and the institution to ensure that legal obligations are met and that students are given appropriate support and accommodation by the campus community. Staff also work to educate members of the campus community about the needs and experiences of students with disabilities.

The major professional organization of staff in disability support services is the Association on Higher Education and Disability; the primary publication is the *Journal of Postsecondary Education and Disability.*

Enrollment Management

In a competitive environment in higher education, colleges and universities have made recruitment and retention of students a priority. Many campuses have combined previously independent operating units related to recruitment and retention into formal units called enrollment management. The goal is to insure that critical areas for recruitment and retention such as admissions, records, financial aid, student research, and marketing are working together to create a comprehensive plan to enroll more students, to shape the composition of the class, to reduce attrition rates, and to develop appropriate publications, services, and electronic alternatives for interacting with the college or university.

Enrollment management can report to student affairs, but more often than not, the reporting line will be to the provost, executive vice president, or the president.

The major professional organizations of enrollment management professionals include the National Association for College Admission Counseling and the American Association of Collegiate Registrars and Admissions Officers; the primary publications are the *Journal of College Admissions* and *College & University.*

Financial Aid

The role of the financial aid office is to help students create a plan to finance their education. Although the primary duty of financial aid officers is to assess student financial needs and make decisions about student aid packages, staff may also assist students with their personal financial planning while in college. In addition to working with student aid recipients, financial aid staff work closely with government agencies, banks, loan guarantee agencies, and corporate and individual donors.

The major professional organization of financial aid officers is the National Association of Student Financial Aid Administrators; the primary publications are the *NASFAA Newsletter* and the *Journal of Student Financial Aid.*

Fundraising and Fund Development

In recent years, a number of student affairs divisions have added fundraising and fund development to their portfolios. Student affairs offices involved in fund development generally concentrate on annual giving and on attaining special gifts for a particular project or program in student affairs.

A significant operational aspect of student affairs units who have fund development as a function is close communication and cooperation with the institution's advancement or development office. It is particularly important that a coordinated effort between the office of advancement and the fundraising function in student affairs is in place.

The major professional organization of fund development officers is the Council for the Advancement and Support of Education; the primary publications are *Currents* and the *Chronicle of Philanthropy*.

Graduate and Professional Student Services

An emerging function within student affairs is in the area of graduate and professional education. This function also can be found within traditional student affairs organizational structures but is more likely to be housed in a graduate or professional school or college. As such, student affairs professionals work very closely with faculty and academic administrators to deliver support services. They must also work to bridge the gap between postbaccalaureate students and services designed for undergraduate students.

This office may be responsible for a multitude of functions that include admissions, alumni relations, judicial affairs, orientation, student organizations, leadership programs, and academic functions such as fellowships and assistantships. In addition, the office serves to connect students with academic and nonacademic resources, assists families and international students in transition, and advocates on behalf of students to insure staffs in various institutionwide offices meet their needs. Emerging trends include orienting students to graduate and professional education, developing graduate student centers to house resources for graduate students, addressing the unionization of graduate and teaching assistants, and building professional development programs.

Because of the nature of graduate and professional education, there is not a single professional organization for professionals in this area. In addition to generalist organizations such as ACPA and NASPA, these professionals tend to affiliate with organizations such as the Council of Graduate Schools, the Association of American Medical Colleges, the Association of American Law Schools, and the American Assembly of Collegiate Schools of Business.

Greek Affairs

Greek affairs offices for fraternities and sororities typically emphasize community building, socialization, and adherence to the values of scholarship, leadership, and community services. Special emphases are on educating for an understanding of differences and the elimination of alcohol abuse, drug use, and hazing. Some Greek organizations have houses, and Greek affairs professionals often are involved in the management of these houses. Staff for Greek affairs place a major emphasis on working with students to determine their own level of accountability and responsibility for their actions. Staff work in Greek affairs is particularly complex because of the dual role of educator and monitor who advocates for the interest of students while protecting the institution from charges of liability.

The major professional organization of Greek life professionals is the Association of Fraternity Advisors; the primary publication is *Perspectives.*

Health Services

Health services for students and, sometimes, for faculty and staff can be provided through on-campus facilities or through partnerships with off-campus agencies or hospitals. When the campus has a medical center, the student health service may be linked administratively to the medical school or affiliated hospital.

The primary purpose of student health services is to provide immediate medical assistance to students who are ill or injured; student health services also encourage individual good health and provide leadership in promoting the concept of a healthy campus.

Senior health educators are responsible for ensuring the assessment, planning, implementation, and evaluation of health and wellness programming. This may involve recruiting and training student peer educators, writing grant proposals, serving on committees, coordinating community contacts, and managing program staff. Less senior health educators are program coordinators and are responsible for program implementation such as HIV test counseling and health-related workshops and events. Depending on the school, health educators may also assume a faculty role.

The major professional organization for staff working in campus health services is the American College Health Association; the primary publication is the *ACHA Journal.*

International Student Services

Many campuses welcome large numbers of international students to their communities and have established offices and services to meet their unique needs. The primary goal of these offices is to insure that students' goals are compatible with the institutions' mission and resources.

Staff in these offices assist students with visa and passport issues and provide many of the functions that student affairs, as a whole, provides for all students.

The major professional organization of international student service staff is NAFSA: Association of International Educations; the primary publications are the *NAFSA Newsletter* and *International Educator Magazine.*

Judicial Affairs

To ensure that the academic integrity, ethics, and behavioral standards of the institution are maintained, many colleges and universities have established a student judicial affairs office to develop, disseminate, interpret, and enforce campus rules and regulations. While these duties are assumed on some campuses by the dean of students office, other campuses have created an entirely separate office to emphasize the importance of this function and to respond effectively to large numbers of cases.

The major professional organization of campus judicial affairs officers is the Association of Student Judicial Affairs; the primary publications are *Synthesis*, the *ASJA Newsletter*, the *Journal of College and University Law*, and *The College Student and the Courts*.

Leadership Programs

Leadership programs are increasing at a significant rate in colleges and universities. The Council for the Advancement of Standards in Higher Education (CAS) noted that over 600 campuses were teaching leadership courses by the end of the 1980s (Miller, 1997). Two years later in a publication by the Kellogg Foundation, the estimate for the number of leadership programs was at 800 (Zimmerman-Oster & Burkhardt, 1999). In an article on outstanding leadership programs, Boatman (1999) stated, "Most colleges and universities also offer credit-bearing and cocurricular programs to help students develop their leadership abilities" (p. 325).

Most programs function as a partnership between academic and student affairs for integrated training of undergraduate students. Programs vary in that some are for credit, some offer noncredit workshops for student leaders, and some are attached to academic programs in an integral way and are required for graduation. These programs aim to help students acquire self-awareness and communication skills, among other skills, for better interaction in their daily lives and in their professional career. Key in these programs is their emphases on critical thinking and skill building.

The major professional organization of leadership programs staff is the National Clearinghouse for Leadership Programs; the primary publications are *Concepts and Connections* and the *Leadership Studies Journal.*

Lesbian, Gay, Bisexual, and Transgender (LGBT) Student Services

The primary purpose of LGBT services is to provide resources and services that encourage a welcoming and safe environment for lesbian, gay, bisexual, and transgender students, faculty, and staff. These services also provide educational opportunities and programming for members of the campus community.

Every institution implements LGBT services according to its mission, culture, and leadership. The strength of the student affairs division in which an LGBT services office is housed has a tremendous influence on the funding and overall effectiveness of the services and programming.

The major professional organization of LGBT services staff is the National Consortium of Directors of LGBT Resources in Higher Education; there is no primary publication.

Multicultural Student Services

Traditionally housed in student affairs, the mission of multicultural student services is to welcome, support, empower, and integrate all students into the life of the campus. Staff work with individual students, groups of students, and with the campus as a whole to foster a climate that values and seeks to understand the impact and implications of diversity in a democratic society. A major thrust of the multicultural affairs office is to retain and graduate students of color at a rate that is the same or better than the majority student body. Looking at students holistically, an emphasis is placed on the educational, cultural, personal, and social goals of each student.

The major professional organizations of multicultural student affairs staff include the National Coalition Building Institute, the National Conference on Race and Ethnicity in American Higher Education, the Hispanic Association of Colleges and Universities, and Asian-Pacific Americans in Higher Education; the primary publications include *Black Issues in Higher Education, Hispanic Outlook,* the *Journal of American Indian Education,* and the *Journal of Asian American Studies.*

Orientation and New Student Programs

Student affairs staff in orientation and new student programs are responsible for welcoming new students to the campus, as well as for introducing them to the history, traditions, educational programs, academic requirements, and student life of the institution.

Orientation programs may last one or two days, or they may extend throughout the entire first year. In the past, these programs focused almost exclusively on practical matters such as registration, finances, and housing. In recent years, however, new student programs have become much more extensive and have grown to involve parents, student leaders, faculty, and community leaders.

The major professional organization of staff in orientation and new student programs is the National Orientation Directors Association; the primary publications are the *Journal of the Freshman Year Experience* and the *Journal of College Orientation and Transition.*

Recreation and Fitness Programs

The primary purpose of most campus recreation and fitness programs is to promote good health and wellness, to teach physical skills, and to encourage positive social interaction among students.

Facilities and services offered by these programs may include weight rooms, swimming pools, aerobics and yoga classes, climbing walls, ropes courses, and a variety of courts for activities such as basketball, racquetball, and tennis. On some campuses, as many as 90 percent of all students participate in recreation and fitness programs.

The major professional organization of campus recreation staff is the National Intramural Recreational Sports Association; the primary publication is the *NIRSA Journal.*

Religious Programs and Services

Colleges and universities sponsor programming and support for a variety of religious faiths through campus chaplains. With the increase in student-initiated religious groups and spiritual collectives, the challenge for campus religious programs and services is to minister to a group with a broad spectrum of beliefs and faiths that might be unfamiliar to students and staff.

Public colleges often rely on off-campus support for religious services while private colleges (especially those that are religiously affiliated) often hire full-time staff to plan and develop programs and activities for the campus community. The primary professional organizations for staff in this area include the National Association of College and University Chaplains, the Association of College and University Religious Affairs, and the National Campus Ministry Association; the primary publications are *Dialogue,* the *NACUC News,* and the *Realm of Higher Education.*

Registration Services

More often than not, registration is managed by the office of the registrar and is part of the enrollment management function. As such, it is often linked structurally with the offices of admissions and financial aid. These offices typically have responsibility for all of the processes associated with enrollment and registration for classes. In addition, the registrar's office is responsible for keeping the official academic records of all current and former students. The office usually works closely with the bursar's office, which is responsible for managing all student accounts.

The primary professional organization of registrar's office staff is the American Association of Collegiate Registrars and Admissions Officers; the primary publication is *College and University.*

Residence Life and Housing

With respect to campus living options, some colleges and universities are exclusively residential while others are exclusively commuter; most fall somewhere in between. For campuses that do offer on-campus living for students, the office responsible for this service is usually called residence life, residential life, or the campus housing office.

The primary responsibility of residence life is to provide healthy, clean, safe, and educationally supportive living environments that complement the academic mission of the institution. Areas of responsibility may include the selection, training, and supervision of the student and professional staff members who live and work in campus residence halls. Other responsibilities may include room assignments, facilities management, and educational programming and services.

In recent years, a number of housing offices have partnered with academic affairs to create living-learning centers for students. Some institutions provide specialized wings or halls for students with common interests or class schedules; others provide faculty-in-residence programs.

The major professional organization of staff members in residence life is the Association of College and University Housing Officers International; the primary publications are the *Journal of College and University Student Housing* and the *ACUHO-I Talking Stick.*

Student Activities

Student activities is responsible for providing a range of programs and services, including cultural programs, leadership programs, campus entertainment, and off-campus trips, as well as for advising student clubs and organizations (including student government).

Student activities supports the learning process by offering a variety of ways for students to become involved and engaged in the life of the campus outside the classroom. The role of student activities staff can be challenging in some settings (such as community colleges and commuter schools) because students' time demands and other commitments prevent them from taking advantage of the enrichment programs offered through student activities.

The primary professional organization of student activities staff is the National Association for Campus Activities; the primary publication is *Campus Activity Programming*.

Women's Centers

The function of Women's Centers varies according to the type and culture of the institution and the population served. Through counseling and educational materials, the centers focus on issues such as equity, leadership, money management, safety, health, strategies to combine family and work, and relationship violence.

Institutional missions and cultures may differ, but staff of the various women's centers agree that the overarching goal of a women's center is to promote equity on campus and to make the climate more accepting and encouraging for women. Some centers serve students primarily and others are open to and serve all women in the campus and surrounding community.

The major professional organization of Women's Center staff is the National Women's Studies Association; the primary publication is the *NWSA Journal*.

Trends and Influences Related to Organization and Functions

Most trends in higher education are preceded by external influences that become the proverbial "mothers of invention." See, for example, Birnbaum's (2000) discussion of management fads in higher education. Some trends and influences that will affect student affairs will be transformative; others less noticeable.

Transformation will be necessary, in some cases, for colleges and universities to remain relevant and central in preparing citizens for the next generation. As Kuh (1996) asserts, "when significant gaps exist between environmental demands and institutional processes and structures, the institution must adapt in order to survive" (p. 285).

Whereas the education, development, and welfare needs of students currently addressed by the organization and functions of student affairs will remain, other programs may be needed to address new needs, as well as the delivery of traditional programs and services.

External forces will compel student affairs to alter, evolve, and transform roles and functions to keep pace, and often lead in establishing trends that will have a positive and powerful impact on student learning and development.

Technology, globalization, online learning, students as consumers, and other demands of a new generation of students are among the influences that will drive trends in the organization and functions of student affairs in the not-too-distant future.

Into the Next Century

Future organizational structures of functions in student affairs will have impetus from students and external forces. By listening closely to students, student affairs will be able to help shape the inevitable transformation of colleges and universities.

With the competition from within traditional higher education and from for-profit and corporate institutions of higher education, institutions will want to find ways to distinguish themselves to students. How a college or university organizes its student affairs functions may be the most promising way to demonstrate quality above and beyond basic academic expectations.

Effective organization of student affairs functions in the future will include strategic alliances within and across institutions. Duplication of some services will be eliminated, and institutions will share services in order to reallocate resources to new functions, services, and programs. These strategic alliances will have economic advantages for the institution as well as education and service value for students.

Technology will drive organizational structures, functions, and cross-institutional partnerships. As students, both on and off campus, request web-based courses and services, more institutions will collaborate in order to increase the quality and affordability of services for students who expect easy access to all services all the time. Programs and services generally offered by student affairs are being categorized into "suites" that cooperating institutions can agree on as common functions of student affairs for all students at every type of institution.

In one program, the administrative core includes functions in enrollment services such as admissions, records, and financial aid; the communications suite includes communications between students, between faculty and students, between faculty and staff, and between students and the institution; the academic suite includes academic advising, academic counseling, assessment and testing, and all academic support services, as well as the library and bookstore; the personal services suite includes personal and career counseling, wellness services, orientation, and budgeting and banking; and the student communities suite includes student activities and all cocurricular programs such as special programs for population segments such as international students and students who are currently served by the office of multicultural affairs (Shea & Blakely, 2002).

Roles and functions of staff will require increased levels of sophistication in anticipating how students will navigate through a web-based array of services.

Anticipating that technology will have a powerful impact on the organization of student affairs, student affairs professionals will need to be diligent in helping to shape and interpret the institutional priorities that affect student learning and development. Sandeen (1996) wrote that "student affairs does not become effective on a campus as a result of the power arrangements described on an organizational chart; it earns its role by successfully accomplishing tasks deemed important to the institution" (p. 436).

Student affairs professionals will have to keep in mind that organizational structures are less important than a common understanding of the purpose of student affairs at a particular college or university. Although each institution will shape distinctive aspects of student affairs based on institutional mission and priorities, defining common and consistent characteristics of effectiveness must be measured against standards of the profession.

The Council for the Advancement of Standards in Higher Education (CAS) prepares and publishes specific standards and guidelines for most functional areas in student affairs. These functional areas may be defined differently across institutions. Accordingly, each set of standards and guidelines is translated into useful self-assessment guides designed for heuristic value in establishing programs, conducting self-studies, and evaluating programs. The CAS approach to quality assurance in student affairs practice is through self-regulation and self-assessment.

As discussions continue regarding the purpose of student affairs, Hartley (2001) explored the predominance of student learning as the emphasis for student affairs since the 1994 ACPA statement *The Student Learning Imperative: Implications for Student Affairs* was published. Student affairs staff have used the statement to help faculty and the institution understand the nature of teaching and learning outside the classroom. This framework will continue to be used, and student affairs' contributions to learning will continue to be valued goals. However, Hartley's conclusion may be both profound and prophetic in predicting significant change in the organization and functions of student affairs as staff respond to trends and influences: "[S]tudent affairs divisions will do students and their institutions a disservice if, in an effort to promote student learning, they distance themselves from the difficult work of developing the whole student. Both student learning and student development are the work of student affairs" (p. 236).

For example, a prominent issue at the beginning of the first decade of the twenty-first century is how students adopt and integrate their spiritual development into the content of their academic learning and into the collegiate context of their lives. This learning and development task involves the whole student and requires collaboration among faculty and student affairs staff regardless of organizational structure.

Relationships among educators, faculty, and student affairs transcend the boundaries and hierarchies of organizational structure. As these groups work together, effective student affairs professionals in all colleges and universities will continue to ask themselves: What is the relationship between our work—what we do—and successful education outcomes for students?

Professional Associations

American Assembly of Collegiate Schools of Business: www.aacsb.edu/
American Association of Collegiate Registrars and Admissions Officers: www.aacrao.org/
American Association of Community Colleges: www.aacc.nche.edu/
American Association of Higher Education: www.aahe.org/
American College Health Association: www.acha.org/
American College Personnel Association: www.acpa.nche.edu/
American Council on Education: www.acenet.edu/
American Counseling Association: www.counseling.org/
American Educational Research Association: www.aera.net/
American Psychological Association: www.apa.org/about/division/div17.html
Asian Pacific Americans in Higher Education:
socrates.berkeley.edu/~ethnics+/apahe/main.html
Association of American Colleges and Universities: www.aacu-edu.org/
Association of American Law Schools: www.aals.org
Association of American Medical Colleges: www.aamc.org/
Association of College Unions International: acuiweb.org/
Association of College and University Housing Officers International: www.acuho.ohio-state.edu/
Association of College and University Religious Affairs: www.upenn/edu/chaplain/acura/
Association for Experiential Education: www.aee.org
Association of Fraternity Advisors: www.fraternityadvisors.org/
Association on Higher Education and Disability: www.ahead.org/
Association for Institutional Research: www.airweb.org
Association of Student Judicial Affairs: asja.tamu.edu/
Association of University and College Counseling Center Directors: www.aucccd.org/
Council for the Advancement and Support of Education: www.case.org
Council of Graduate Schools: www.cgsnet.org/
Hispanic Association of Colleges and Universities: www.hacu.net
Historically Black College and Universities: www.collegeview.com/college/niche/hbcu
International Association of Campus Law Enforcement Administrators: www.iaclea.org/
NAFSA: Association of International Educators: www.nafsa.org
National Academic Advising Association: www.nacada.ksu.edu/
National Association of Campus Activities: www.naca.org
National Association of College Admissions Counselors: www.nacac.com/index.html
National Association of College and University Chaplains: www.nacuc.net
National Association of College and University Food Services: www.nacufs.org/
National Association of Colleges and Employers: www.naceweb.org/
National Association of Intercollegiate Athletics: www.naia.org/
National Association of Student Affairs Professionals: www.naspa.org
National Association of Student Financial Aid Administrators: www.nasfaa.org/
National Association of Student Personnel Administrators: www.naspa.org/
National Campus Compact: www.compact.org/
National Campus Ministry Association: www.campusministry.net
National Career Development Association: www.ncda.org/
National Clearinghouse for Commuter Programs: www.inform.umd.edu/CampusInfo/
Departments/commute/NCCP/
National Clearinghouse for Leadership Programs: www.inform.umd.edu/CampusInfo/
Departments/OCP/NCLP/
National Coalition Building Institute: www.ncbi.org/
National Collegiate Athletic Association: www.ncaa.org/

National Conference on Race & Ethnicity in American Higher Education: www.occe.ou.edu/NCORE
National Consortium of Directors of LGBT Resources in Higher Education: www.lgbtcampus.org/
National Intramural-Recreational Sports Association: www.nirsa.org/
National Junior College Athletic Association: www.njcaa.org
National Orientation Directors Association: noda.tamu.edu/
National Society for Experiential Education: www.nsee.org/
National Women's Studies Association: www.nwsa.org

References

Birnbaum, R. (2000). *Management fads in higher education: Where they come from, what they do, why they fail.* San Francisco: Jossey-Bass.

Boatman, S. A. (1999). The leadership audit: A process to enhance the development of student leadership. *NASPA Journal, 37*, 325–336.

Dickeson, R. C. (1999). *Prioritizing academic programs and services and reallocating resources to achieve strategic balance.* San Francisco: Jossey-Bass.

Eckel, P., Green, M., Hill, B., & Mallon, W. (1999). *On change III, taking charge of change: A primer for colleges and universities.* Washington, DC: American Council on Education.

Hartley, M. (2001). Student learning as a framework for student affairs—rhetoric or reality? *NASPA Journal, 38*, 224–236.

Jacoby, B. (2000). Why involve commuter student in learning? In B. Jacoby (Ed.), *Involving commuter students in learning.* (New Directions for Higher Education No. 109, pp. 3–12). San Francisco: Jossey-Bass.

Kuh, G. D. (1996). Organizational theory. In S. R. Komives & D. B. Woodard, Jr. (Eds.), *Student services: A handbook for the profession* (3rd ed., pp. 269–296). San Francisco: Jossey-Bass.

Malaney, G. D. (Ed.). (1999). *Student affairs research, evaluation, and assessment: Structure and practice in an era of change* (New Directions for Student Affairs no. 85). San Francisco: Jossey-Bass.

Miller, T. K. (1997). CAS standards contextual statement. In *Council for standards in higher education* (pp. 111–112), Washington, DC: Council for the Advancement of Standards in Higher Education.

Sandeen, A. (1996). Organization, functions, and standards of practice. In S. R. Komives & D. B. Woodard, Jr. (Eds.), *Student services: a handbook for the profession* (3rd ed., pp. 435–457). San Francisco: Jossey-Bass.

Shea, P., & Blakely, B. (2002). Designing web-based student services collaboration style. In D. J. Burnett & D. G. Oblinger (Eds.), *Innovation in student services: Planning for models blending high touch/high tech* (pp. 161–173). Ann Arbor, MI: Society for College and University Planning.

Stevens, R. A. Jr. (2000). Welcoming commuter students into living-learning programs. In B. Jacoby (Ed.), *Involving commuter students in learning* (New Directions for Higher Education No. 109, pp. 71–79). San Francisco: Jossey-Bass.

Woodard, D. B., Love, P., & Komives, S. R. (2000). The changing landscape of higher education. In D. B. Woodard, P. Love, & S. R. Komives (Eds.), *Leadership and management issues for a new century* (New Directions for Student Services No. 92). San Francisco: Jossey-Bass.

Zimmerman-Oster, K., & Burkhardt, J. C. (1999). *Leadership in the making: Impact and insights from leadership development programs in U.S. colleges and universities.* Battle Creek, MI: W. K. Kellogg Foundation.

CHAPTER SIXTEEN

STRATEGIC PLANNING AND FINANCE

John H. Schuh

The fiscal environment in which higher education operates continues to experience stress according to a variety of observers. For over five decades, budgets have risen faster than the gross domestic product (Balderston, 1995). Woodard and von Destinon (2000) say that "the Higher Education Price Index has risen more than five-fold since 1961 and the Consumer Price Index has risen four-fold" (p. 328). Costs have escalated (Clodfelter, 1996; The College Board, 2001), state support for higher education has diminished (Leslie & Fretwell, 1996), and doubts about the affordability of college have persisted (NACUBO, 2002). Even after discounting for grant aid, net prices continue to rise faster than inflation (National Center for Education Statistics, 2001; Wellman, 2001). In part because of increasing costs, higher education is suffering from an erosion of public confidence: "The withdrawal of public support for higher education can only accelerate as students, parents, and taxpayers come to understand that they paid for an expensive education without receiving fair value in return" (Wingspread Group, 1993, p. 2).

Bowen (1996) has identified certain "laws" that govern higher education costs. Among these are that institutions of higher education have virtually no limit on the amount of money they can spend on "seemingly fruitful education ends" (p. 123); each raises all the money it can; and each spends all it raises. As a consequence, these systemic laws, which illustrate the fiscal environment in which higher education operates, begin to explain why higher education has financial problems.

Leslie and Fretwell (1996) developed an excellent taxonomy of reasons that describe why higher education is facing fiscal stress. External reasons include periodic economic recessions, changing student demographics, more complex and problematic budgeting as a consequence of increasing sources of support, macropolitical tax limitation politics, micromanagement by state governments, political disaffection by voters, and increased legal requirements. Institutions also are suffering from internal sources of stress, according to these authors, including deferred maintenance, tuition discounting (Redd, 2000), lack of incentives to change, and management problems.

While some assert that student affairs has experienced disproportionate budget reductions over the past decade (Woodard, Love, & Komives, 2000), the data suggest that, as a percentage of institutional expenditures, student affairs expenditures have remained stable (National Center for Education Statistics, 2001). Nevertheless, student affairs practitioners need to be able to anticipate and proactively address resource-related concerns (Woodard et al., 2000). This chapter addresses selected issues in strategic planning and defines various approaches to the budgeting process. Specifically, it addresses the following questions:

1. What is strategic planning, and what are the elements in the strategic planning process?
2. What are common approaches to budgeting in higher education, and what are the advantages and disadvantages of these approaches?
3. What are the differences between cash accounting and accrual accounting, and how are these approaches utilized in higher education?
4. How does one prepare a unit budget?
5. What are some current budgeting issues facing student affairs officers?

Strategic Planning Approaches

Over the past several decades, various approaches to planning that were initiated and developed by business and government have been adapted and adopted by institutions of higher education (see Birnbaum, 2001). Many notable models have catchy acronyms: PPBS (Planning, Programming, and Budgeting Systems), MBO (Management by Objectives), PERT (Program Evaluation Review Technique), and MIS (Management Information Systems) (Baldridge & Okimi, 1982), as well as TQM (Total Quality Management) and CQI (Continuous Quality Improvement). These represent both theory and practice approaches, but no single one predominates among the nearly 4,000 institutions of higher education in the United States. Nevertheless, institutions of higher education take planning seriously. For example, El-Khawas (1994) indicated that a wide variety of significant actions have been taken by institutions of higher education to reorganize and restructure their programs and administrative activities.

Developing partnerships with other units on campus also can be an important strategy in the delivery of programs, services, and learning experiences (see, for example, Lenning & Ebbers, 1999, on developing learning communities). Other chapters in this book address the situation; see especially those by Upcraft on assessment and evaluation and Schroeder on establishing and sustaining partnerships.

Strategic planning is defined by Rowley, Lujan, and Dolence (1997) as "a formal process designed to help an organization identify and maintain an optimal alignment with the most important elements of its environment" (p. 15). For higher education, these authors identify the following key questions institutions must answer:

- Who will our students be?
- What should we teach?
- How should we teach it?
- How will students learn?
- What are society's needs?
- How does society expect us to meet its needs?
- What role will learning play?
- How will we pay for it?

Obviously student affairs units will have to help answer many of these questions, especially in the context of the contemporary emphasis on the role of student affairs in student learning (American College Personnel Association, 1996). Moreover, the development of collaboration between academic and student affairs (see Schroeder, 1999) suggests that these key elements of higher education will have to work together to identify ways of advancing institutions of higher education.

Peterson (1999) described the primary purpose of strategic planning as fostering "institutional adaptation by assuring congruence between an institution and its relevant and often changing environment, by developing a viable design for the future of the institution, by modifying it as needed, and by devising strategies that facilitate its accomplishment" (p. 32). Elements of a strategic plan in his view include environmental assessment (assessing the broad environment in which the institution functions), institutional assessment (clarifying strengths and weaknesses), values assessment (considering values, aspirations, and ideals), and master plan creation (devising a strategic plan based on the first three elements) (Peterson). To apply this approach to a division of student affairs, suppose that the bonded indebtedness of a residence hall system had just been retired but that all of the residence facilities were more than twenty-five years old. At this time the vice president wants to determine if renovating the residence halls or building new ones makes the most sense. A place to start is to examine broad, regional demographic and economic trends to understand the kind of facilities that might be needed in the future. An assessment of current strengths and weaknesses of the physical assets would be conducted, followed by an analysis of the role of residence halls in the education of students, and finally a master plan could be developed.

Keller (1997) suggests elements for the strategic planning process. The most important, in his view, is that a senior campus leader be the "champion of strategic change" (p. 163); Meyerson and Johnson (1993) agree. Besides a strong senior leader, Keller also indicates that other important institutional leaders need to be committed to planning and that campus leaders who refuse to go along with new strategic initiatives or who try to sabotage them be disciplined or separated. Another important element in linking leadership to the strategic planning process is for senior leaders in student affairs to develop their vision for success and their strategic priorities based on institutional priorities. "Acceptance of and support for the institutional mission, then, seems a prerequisite to success in the student affairs profession" according to

Lyons (1993, p. 14), and as a consequence, strategic planning in a student affairs division must be congruent and consistent with broader institutional priorities.

Keller (1997) emphasizes that good communication is indispensable in strategic planning, as do Meyerson and Johnson (1993). Keller claims "a major necessity . . . is to capture their attention and hold it despite the unrelenting barrage of other claims" (p. 165). In this case "their" refers to other members of the campus community. He identified four other ingredients of success in planning: developing a proposal of what should be accomplished that is designed to encourage discussion and debate; trimming deeply enough and capturing new money so that innovations can occur; paying close attention to finances; and achieving "small wins" (Weick, 1984), meaning that small but significant changes are an excellent strategy for creating change in a complex social system such as a college or university. Small but sure successes will lead to additional changes.

The success or failure of planning in student affairs depends in part on perceptions and attitudes about the nature of the planning process. Moreover, the attitudes and behavior of the senior student affairs officer (SSAO) and other top-level staff play a key role in the successful execution of planning. Bean (1983) suggests, "many chief student affairs officers believe that they can plan rationally, despite evidence to the contrary" (p. 41). He indicates that plans are influenced more by subjective than objective knowledge. If the SSAO and other staff assume that planning will follow a logical, rational process, a likely consequence is disillusionment and disappointment. Accordingly, student affairs administrators need to better understand and appreciate subjective aspects of planning.

Strategic planning has been described cogently by Neufield (1999). She believes that attention can be placed on a small number of problem and opportunity areas. To accomplish strategic planning, she has identified several aspects of the process. First, she believes that strategic planning should concentrate on key operating decisions facing the institution in the intermediate future, such as in the next three years. Then she emphasizes that strategic planning employs a participatory planning process, as was suggested above. Next Neufield indicates that attention to process as well as products is critical. Recall Keller's assertion that communication is crucial in the process. Then, Neufield points out that long and medium time frames are employed but are recast from time to time. What this means is that periodic reviews of the planning process are conducted, and plans are adjusted as circumstances dictate. Finally, she indicates that strategic planning "employs a long-run perspective but focuses on specific tactics and issues" (p. 53).

Again, this is consistent with Keller's perspective that a number of "small wins" can lead to substantial institutional change in the aggregate, over time. In student affairs this might mean beginning with modest collaborative activities with colleagues in academic affairs, but over time major change might occur. For example, faculty who may not have played a formal role in new student orientation are invited to conduct a session for students on academic adjustments, or a learning community or two may have been inaugurated in the residence halls. Over time, faculty may play an increasing role by doing a number of orientation sessions related to academic adjustments for new students. In the learning community example, other residence halls may follow the success of the lead residence hall, and ultimately other learning communities will be developed.

The Planning Process

Various authors have identified the elements of the strategic planning process over the years (Clugston, 1986; Cope, 1981; Keller, 1983; Kotler & Murphy, 1981; Pillinger & Kraack, 1980). These elements include examining critical trends in the environment and assessing threats and opportunities, assessing institutional strengths and weaknesses, determining strategic directions based on the institutional mission and assessments of opportunities and strengths, establishing program priorities, and reallocating resources from low-priority to high-priority programs. Following is an example of a strategic planning process based on the elements listed above and adapted from the models developed by Ern (1993) and Meyerson and Johnson (1993).

1. *Initiate the planning process.* This first step involves assembling a planning team, identifying work assignments, and developing a timetable. As is the case with any activity of this sort, identifying the various constituencies affected by the plan is crucial. Moreover, making sure team members have the necessary skills, commitment, and time to devote to the process is essential to its success. Recall the comments of Keller (1997) who asserted that strong leadership is an essential aspect of the planning process.

2. *Review the institution's mission statement.* Dill (1997) observes that a mission statement could play a crucial role in the planning process. He concludes that "when mission is conceived as a set of strategic decisions governing the relationship of a college or university to its environment, and as a consensually developed set of strategic criteria grounded in the culture and traditions of a particular institution, then mission is central to the implementation of a successful planning and resource allocation process" (p. 188). Lyons (1993) adds, "The most important factor that determines the shape and substance of student affairs is the mission of the institution" (p. 14). In the course of developing a strategic plan for student affairs, reviewing the mission statement will serve as a useful reminder of what the institution is about and what it aspires to achieve.

3. *Assess the environment.* During this step both the external and internal environments are reviewed, and assumptions about each are identified. External environmental factors might include the priorities of the governing board or state legislature, and internal factors could include the strengths and weaknesses of staff.

The information gleaned from environmental scanning provides snapshots of the threats to and opportunities for the student affairs division and the institution as a whole. Institutional and student affairs officers continuously assessing external environments are like air traffic controllers observing blips on a radar screen. Student affairs professionals should keep track of social, economic, political, and technological trends in their environment. The threats and opportunities represented by changing environmental conditions create challenges that require a vigorous response.

Assessing the internal environment includes analyzing the strengths and weaknesses of the student affairs division. One strategy for conducting this assessment is to perform a SWOT (strengths, weaknesses, opportunities, and threats) analysis. Rowley et al. (1997) describe strengths and weaknesses as applying to the internal environment and opportunities and threats as pertaining to the external environment. Examples of strengths in a particular student affairs division might include strong senior leadership and excellent computing capability; weaknesses could include lack of space and dependence on sales of services for income. Opportunities could include potential federal grants for disadvantaged students; threats could include a stagnant state economy and a declining population of traditional-aged students.

Assessment of academic departments typically involves comparisons of research productivity and other measures with peer departments at other institutions. Although student affairs departments need to identify exemplary programs at peer institutions, their primary focus should be on responding to the threats and opportunities that affect their own institution's mission. Campuswide issues that transcend departmental boundaries, such as the quality of student life or enrollment management, will increasingly be priority concerns for student affairs administrators. The process of determining strengths and weaknesses inevitably involves asking questions about what is done, why it is done, and how well it is done, as well as investigating how services are organized and funded. Moreover, who asks the questions will largely determine the credibility and impact of the assessment. Involving students and faculty in the process may require that more time is spent on the process, but this involvement provides valuable perspectives from individuals other than just student affairs professionals.

4. *Develop a vision and goals for success.* If the student affairs division were working at maximum capacity, what would it look like? What would its activities be? How would students be served? What kind of impact on students would the division have? Asking questions like these contributes to developing a hypothetical view of what the division might become. Rowley et al. (1997) recommend that those involved in the process "must think of ways to reduce the impacts (sic) of threats and weaknesses and ways to seize opportunities and enhance strengths" (p. 125). The division probably will not realize its vision to its full potential, but this step is nevertheless a useful exercise in providing focus for what might be undertaken to improve the current operating status of student affairs.

5. *Develop preliminary plans for each unit.* Each unit within the division of student affairs should have a set of plans that support and complement the goals of the overall division. For example, the division might have the goal of improving access to the institution for members of historically disadvantaged groups. Supporting this goal would include aggressive recruitment of such students by the admissions staff, special financial aid packages from the financial aid office, and ongoing mentoring programs for the students. The division's goals ought to be prioritized and each unit's plans developed accordingly.

6. *Review preliminary plans.* This review should be conducted in the context of the student affairs vision and the assessments of the internal and external environments. Individual unit plans should be reviewed, as well as the overall plan for the division.

Remember that the unit plans and the overall divisional plan will be developed simultaneously but separately. The relationship between the plans should be symbiotic and complementary; that is, they should support one another, and success for one will help ensure success for the others.

In the review of preliminary plans, an element that ought to be considered is how to measure the impact of any changes contemplated on the targets of change. Some, such as Dolence and Norris (1999), would argue that strategic decision making should be driven by data in the form of key performance indicators. For example, an institution's graduation rate might be a key performance indicator. Another approach is to deal with problems more conceptually and bring in potential measures after the conceptual work has been completed. Either way, information must be developed that can serve as a measure of success. A variety of examples of strategic indicators exist in the higher education literature (Ewell, 1999; Rowley et al., 1997; Taylor & Massy, 1996) that can be used in the development of indicators of success. Whether a planning team chooses to identify its indicators at this point in the process, earlier, or even later, it is important to remember that data will be needed to demonstrate the impact of the changes that are implemented.

In student affairs, examples of strategic indicators include residence hall retention rates from one academic year to the next, the debt load of students who use loans to help them pay for their education, placement rates of graduates, and participation rates of students in various actuates. By themselves these indicators may not definitively demonstrate success or failure, but over time they can indicate trends and provide a point of departure for further analysis and study.

7. *Identify alternatives and determine a final plan.* A variety of potential plans may emerge based on different environmental assessments and different aspects of the student affairs vision. At this time, selecting the plan that will work best given the mission of the institution and the vision for student affairs is important. For example, if one goal for the division is to improve the institution's retention rate, one approach might be to enroll more students of higher academic ability. That approach has certain implications for admissions and financial aid. Another approach might be to improve tutoring and other support programs. If both approaches cannot be implemented, a choice has to be made. Consequently, resources available to implement each aspect of the plan need to be identified. Rarely will enough resources be available to do everything that is desired.

Determining Program Viability

At times, decisions may have to be made about redefining and redeploying certain programs, or even which programs should be continued, eliminated, or scaled back. Pillinger and Kraack (1980) identified the following criteria for use in making such decisions:

- *Essentiality.* Is the function essential or peripheral to the university's or the student affairs division's mission (see Lyons, 1993)? The institution's mission statement shapes student affairs. Accordingly, the functions of student affairs should at least complement and support the institution's mission statement.

- *Quality.* Does the program or service consistently maintain a high standard of excellence? This standard may be measured by peer ratings, faculty recognition, student evaluation, program contributions to knowledge or practice, and so on.
- *Availability.* To what degree is the function available outside the student affairs unit or the university? Increasingly, when services are provided outside student affairs or the institution, they will not be duplicated inside the student affairs division. Among targets for this kind of questioning are food services, bookstores, housing, and health services.
- *Need or demand.* What is the student, institutional, and societal demand for this function? Need or demand may be measured by the number of students or staff served by a program or service, the number of student visits to a particular office, the work load of program staff, and so on. To what degree does the function meet current and future projections of need or demand? Is there a legal or public mandate for the function?
- *Efficiency.* How effective is the program at providing the most service for the least money? Could the function be performed appropriately with fewer resources? This analysis may involve comparing units of services produced to resources used.
- *Outcomes.* One other criterion needs to be added to Pillinger and Kraack's list—student learning. The effect of a program or activity on students is best measured through a process called outcomes assessment. As Schuh and Upcraft (2001) assert, "Perhaps the most critical question asked of student affairs focuses on the impact of student services, programs, and facilities" (p. 153). Those that have a demonstrable, positive influence on students should be continued; those that do not benefit students are candidates for restructuring or removal.

Several excellent resources are available for those who wish to explore program review and resource reallocation in greater detail. The reader is referred to the work of Mets (1997) and Dickeson (1999) for additional ideas concerning the program review process.

Developing Action Steps and Implementing the Plan

After the strategic plan has been finalized, it is time to put it into action. Action steps for implementing the plan are determined at this point. A timetable is developed to ensure the work is completed on a timely basis. No matter how widespread consultations with other institutional actors have been, the plan will generate resistance. Some of the people affected will feel they have not been involved in the planning process, or they may not like the plan. Getting people to accept the plan and begin work toward implementing it will require deliberate, ongoing effort. Simply assuming people will accept the plan because you say they should is an exercise in wishful thinking.

Evaluating the Plan

The final step is to review the plan and its effect on institutional personnel and programs. Is the vision for student affairs emerging as a result of the plan's implementation? Are student affairs services and programs successfully supporting the vision? What midcourse changes need to be made? For example, if one goal was to improve retention and the strategy chosen for achieving it was an enhanced tutoring program, are students who participated earning better grades and being retained at a higher rate? If not, why not? Is the training program for the tutors adequate? What adjustments should be made in recruiting tutors? These questions and others would have to be addressed if the program were not successful.

Planning Problems

The reader should not leave this discussion of strategic planning with the notion that this process is easy or can be accomplished without tremendous commitment and effort. Bean and Kuh (1999) have developed a typology of planning problems. On their list are such sets of problems as disagreement about goals, uneven participation, poor information and communication, and the interdependence of units and inadequate resources. The words of Keller (1997) also are worthy of heeding: "Lastly there has been a flurry of opinion that strategic planning doesn't work" (p. 158). Meyerson and Johnson (1993) have identified a variety of impediments to planning, including the autonomous nature of departmental operations, the political environment in which decisions are made, the loose organization of institutions of higher education, and their systemic resistance to change. They conclude, "strategic planning is not a panacea. . . . Strategic planning may help an organization avoid major mistakes or make incremental changes that benefit it over the long term" (p. 89). More importantly, they identify three factors critical to the success of strategic decision making in higher education: "consensus, leadership, and the management of the process of change" (p. 89).

Linking planning to budgeting is one way to ensure long-term success. Brinkman and Morgan (1997) characterize the situation this way: "Today, most analysts of planning and budgeting, at least in the nonprofit sector, assume or advocate a comprehensive, sequential, and rational linking between these two managerial activities" (p. 288). Vandament (1989) adds, "A crucial element in strategic planning is a strong, formal link between planning and budgeting to overcome the natural tendency of long-range plans to lie unused on the shelf" (p. 30). The next section describes a variety of approaches to budgeting and suggests several strategies for improving the budgeting process.

Budgeting

Budgeting is the process by which resources are allocated to support programs, services, activities, and learning opportunities. Operational (meaning year-to-year) budgeting has as its focus "on the next year, but at most institutions where the budgeting process runs smoothly, it incorporates objectives for three to five years in the future" (Dickmeyer,

1996, p. 539). "While expressed in dollars and cents, the annual operating budget represents the identification of the types and extent of personnel, equipment, and other resources deemed necessary to carry out the academic programs or other activities authorized by the plan and a projection of where the funds to support these resources are expected to come from" (Tellefsen, 1990, p. 83). Budgeting is an absolutely essential activity in higher education, and it is crucial to the success of student affairs units.

Budgeting Approaches

This section begins with a brief discussion of line items, a common way of depicting revenue sources and expenditures. Several budgeting approaches are then introduced, including incremental, program, and responsibility-centered budgeting. Most institutions of higher education utilize one or a combination of these approaches. Two other budgeting approaches, formula and zero-base budgeting, are not discussed since they appear to be employed less commonly than in previous years. Readers seeking more information about these approaches should consult Woodard and von Destinon (2000). The reader also is referred to Dickmeyer (1996) for information about other forms of budgeting, including alternate level, quota, investment, incentive budgeting or intramural funding, and capital budgeting.

Line Items. Line items are used to depict revenue sources and expenditures categories in budgets and can be found in a wide variety of budgets. Often, line items are divided into personnel and nonpersonnel categories. Personnel categories can be as detailed as having a line for every salaried position funded by a budget, along with fringe benefits, and wages for hourly employees. Nonpersonnel items may include office supplies, telecommunications, equipment rental, utilities, and other items depending on the nature of the department or program funded by the budget.

Why, then, are line items used? For one thing, they are easy to understand. It does not take much of an accounting background to understand the concepts underlying line-item budgets. Second, they are easy to construct. New resources are added to a department's budget whenever possible, perhaps without serious questions being raised about the efficacy of the programs and activities the department provides. Third, they provide for good budgetary controls, in that the budget manager can determine literally on a line-by-line basis the extent to which revenues are meeting projections and expenditures are in line with expectations.

Incremental Budgeting. Incremental budgeting "is based on the previous year's allocation, and the budget is adjusted based on guidelines provided by the budget office" (Woodard & von Destinon, 2000, p. 332). It is the most widely used approach to budgeting in higher education (Vandament, 1989). This type of budget is often depicted by line items. Put simply, this approach takes the previous year's budget and makes a percentage or incremental change in it. For example, the total amount of money allocated to salaries is increased by three percent, or funding for supplies is cut by two percent. In the end, budget managers adjust their budgets accordingly, and the work of budgeting is accomplished. Douglas (1991) observes that this approach works well in institutions that have similar budgets throughout their divisions and departments.

Incremental budgeting has some disadvantages. Perhaps foremost among them is that it "does not force the institution to examine priorities in a way that encourages annual reallocation, reductions, and elimination of programs" (Woodard & von Destinon, 2000, p. 333). Dickmeyer (1996) adds, "Responsibility for setting assumptions and priorities may be shirked with incremental budgeting" (p. 544). Moreover, it makes the assumption that all aspects of a budget category can be increased or decreased at the same rate, which may not be the case. For example, annual increases in the cost of employee health insurance premiums may be much greater than annual increases in employee life insurance programs. Remember that strategic planning challenges an institution to develop a vision of what it might become, and thus it may require dramatic changes in organization and programs. Incremental budgeting does not lend itself well to making major changes in an institution's educational program and services.

Program Budgeting. Program budgeting is not a new concept (Muston, 1980). "Program budgeting emphasizes the idea that budgets flow from ideas" (Dickmeyer, 1996, p. 545). According to Steiss (1972), a program is a "group of interdependent, closely related services or activities which possess or contribute to a common objective or set of allied objectives" (p. 157). Program budgeting consists of five tasks: identifying goals, analyzing current programs, developing a multiyear plan, analyzing and selecting alternative programs, and evaluating the programs.

Douglas's (1991) appraisal of program budgeting is that it allows the overall cost associated with a program to be examined. Novick (1973) suggests that program budgeting provides for a formal, systematic method of improving decisions concerning resource allocation. Finally, program budgeting provides clear, basic information for planners and managers who must choose between various alternatives. Once the choices are made between alternatives, detailed planning can begin. Program budgeting provides a big-picture approach to budgeting and planning and identifies the path and direction of programming for the next several budget cycles.

Responsibility Centered Budgeting. The final budgeting approach discussed here is responsibility center (or cost center) (Balderston, 1995) budgeting. This form of budgeting also has been referred to as Responsibility Centre Management, Value Centered Management, Revenue Centre Management, and other, similar titles (Lang, 2001). Finney (1994) defines a cost center as "a unit of an organization for which costs are budgeted and collected, implying measurable characteristics of performance and responsibility" (p. 174). "Responsibility-centered budgeting has evolved, more recently, as a way to extend centralized planning and decision-making and to make each instructional unit financially responsible for its activities" (Woodard & von Destinon, 2000, p. 335). Units are expected to generate enough revenue (including charges to other departments) to cover their expenses. Lee and Van Horn (1983) point out that this approach works best with self-contained units, such as a hospital or athletic department. It is more difficult for units that support the activities of the entire campus, such as the registrar's office. It also may engender competition among units for students. For example, students may not be encouraged to change majors if such an action has revenue implications.

According to Stocum and Rooney (1997), an advantage of this form of budgeting is "it allows deans to shift funds from one spending category to another, depending on need, with accountability only for the total" (p. 51). On the other hand, they point out that this responsibility center budgeting can mean "academic programs can become driven entirely by financial entrepreneurship" (p. 51). Adams (1997) asserts that this form of budgeting results in "pressure to reduce the number of professors, for professors to teach more courses, to recognize only funded research and contracted service, and to eliminate majors and graduate programs with small enrollments, regardless of their importance for the culture" (p. 61). At UCLA, this form of budgeting was implemented with misgivings on the part of some. The authors of one description of what resulted indicated that it was too early to determine the success of this approach at UCLA (Wilms, Teruya, & Walpole, 1997). About this form of budgeting, Strauss, Curry, and Whalen (2001) observe, "Can responsibility center budgeting work at a public institution of higher education? Of course, it can. What is required is leadership and the ability of an institution to earn income and retain unspent balances. And of the two, leadership is by far the most important" (p. 607).

Accounting Methods

Depending on the kinds of accounts a student affairs office manages, at least two different forms of accounting—cash or accrual—may be used.

Cash accounting is defined as a form of bookkeeping in which "revenue, expense, and balance sheet items are recorded when cash is paid or received" (Finney, 1994, p. 174). Accrual accounting is a system in which "revenue is recorded when earned and balance sheet account charges are recorded when commitments are made" (p. 173), regardless of when funds are actually received or disbursed. "In other words, the accrual basis attempts to determine the real economic impact of what has occurred during a given period of time rather than simply determining how much cash was received or disbursed" (Meisinger & Dubeck, 1996, p. 469).

What are the implications of different accounting approaches for student affairs budget managers? Cash accounting may be used for accounts supported by the institution's general fund (supplied by tuition and state revenues for a state-assisted institution). The accounting process may include encumbrances (commitments for expenditures), but it is not, for the most part, dramatically different from balancing a checkbook. Funds are deposited in various accounts on a routine basis at the beginning of the fiscal year or, at some schools, more often. Expenses are deducted on a monthly basis, and the account manager must make sure that expenditures do not exceed budgeted amounts. When cash accounting is coupled with line item budgeting, the purpose becomes obvious. Budgets are protected and overdrafts avoided. The quality of spending is not an important issue in this approach; the real concern is to make sure the budget is balanced at the end of the fiscal year.

On the other hand, when accrual accounting is used—as it frequently is for programs and services funded without state revenues or tuition dollars (such as student housing, the bookstore, or the student union)—the manager has to make sure revenue projections are realistic and expenditures are kept within the revenue level realized. This form of accounting is more complicated than cash accounting—just because revenues appear on a budget statement, it does not follow that 100 percent of that amount will actually be collected. In fact, accrual accounting forces the budget manager to approach the budgeting cycle more like a manager of a for-profit business. Delving into the subtleties and nuances of accounting practices is beyond the scope of this chapter; however, budget managers in institutions of higher education must understand the distinctions between cash and accrual accounting and realize that the accrual basis, while it provides a more accurate financial picture, also has additional risks.

Preparing Budgets

Budgeting in higher education can be very accommodating. Fincher (1986) observes "the budgeting process in institutions of higher education is successful because it has many accommodating features. Within hours after the arrival of a new fiscal year, budgeting-in-amendment begins" (p. 76). That is, changes to the adopted budget for the fiscal year begin almost as soon as the budget goes into effect. Regardless of how accommodating budgeting procedures may be, student affairs staff need to pay close attention to the budgeting process. They need to avoid the behavior Woodard, Love, and Komives (2000) have described: "*student affairs professionals do not place a premium on understanding the financial and budgeting structure and processes of their institutions*" (authors' italics) (pp. 71–72). Remember this as we discuss the process of preparing a budget for a discrete department within a student affairs division. Much of what is described hereafter is based on Robins' (1986) excellent discussion on unit budgeting and reflects a combination of the features of incremental budgeting.

Budget forms are distributed by the institution's budget office to department heads, usually during the spring. These forms, along with guidelines concerning percentage adjustments to salaries and operating expenditures, provide the basis for the department head's work. The guidelines often provide an acceptable range for salary increases and guidance on how supply budgets may be amended for the next year. Salary guidelines also might indicate whether salary adjustments should include awards for meritorious service. In some instances merit must be recognized. In other cases, merit awards may be added to the basic cost-of-living increase.

The materials provided by the budget office address many of the following expense categories: personnel costs, which includes salaries and wages; operating expenses, which could include office supplies, telecommunications, postage, and perhaps utilities; capital, which includes equipment purchases; fringe benefits, which includes such items as retirement, insurance, and Social Security costs; and travel expenses. Different institutions organize these categories in different ways, but all these items are typically found in the budget preparation material. The information supplied for personnel costs tends to be quite detailed; such information as position number, rank, or grade, percentage of time worked, and length of appointment, along with current salary information, may be provided for every position. The unit head's job is to apply the budgetary guidelines to the various categories of the budget.

Guidance is usually provided for this task. The budget office prepares estimates for the next fiscal year for the cost of such items as postage, telephone rental, office supplies, and the like. The unit head must merely apply the necessary adjustments to the budget items within these categories. In the area of salaries, as mentioned earlier, cost-of-living and merit increases may be recommended for each salary grade. Merit increases should be linked to performance reviews; if they are not, the unit head will have a difficult time explaining to the unit's employees why some of them received larger increases than others. Merit increases should not be awarded unless unequal increases can be validly justified.

After completing the unit budget, the unit head forwards the budget material to the division head for review. This review examines such factors as compliance with the guidelines prepared by the budget office, internal consistency, and compatibility with budgetary plans prepared by other unit heads. The division head has to be concerned with all of the same issues as the unit heads, but he or she also needs to make sure that the budget plans fit nicely with one another. If one department consistently receives larger increases (or smaller decreases) than other units, the division head will have to explain why, not only to his or her supervisor but also to disgruntled employees. When the division head completes work on the budget, it is forwarded through normal channels for review by appropriate campus offices.

Pembroke (1985) points out that student affairs professionals are often perceived to have limited expertise in their ability to prepare and manage a budget. He suggests five budget preparation principles designed to assist the student affairs officer: knowing the budget guidelines, knowing what is possible, observing deadlines, helping to forecast potential problems, and reexamining the division's mission. These five principles provide a good basis for developing unit budgets. They will keep the budget officer in good standing with the campus budget office.

Woodard and von Destinon (2000) offer some additional budgeting recommendations, including determining the contribution of the unit to the divisional and institutional mission, measuring the workload of staff in individual units, trying to provide measurable outcomes for a unit, determining if most activities help students do things for themselves, protecting services designed to maintain ethical, health, and safety standards, and identifying new sources of revenue. To this list, The Pew Higher Education Research Program (1996) recommends that across the board cuts be resisted. Pew concludes, "Democratic [budget] cutting represents not just a failure of will, but, more significantly, a failure to understand that maintaining quality in some areas will require a reduction or elimination of others" (p. 515). For example, if an institution downsizes one unit and assigns a number of its activities to another unit that does not have adequate staff or expertise to take on the additional responsibilities, the institution is only fooling itself. Funds might be saved, but students will be poorly served. Little good will result. The reader is referred to Woodard (1993, 1995) and Woodard and von Destinon (2000) for additional discussions of the budget development process.

Budgeting for Auxiliary Services

Auxiliary services, according to Ambler (2000) can represent "as much as eight percent or more of a chief student affairs officer's fiscal responsibility" (p. 131) and can include such units as student housing, student unions, health services, food services, and bookstores. Building a budget for an auxiliary service incorporates some of the principles described above but includes several additional features. Auxiliaries must review such additional factors as changes in debt service, utilities, and institutional overhead charges in the development of their budgets. Auxiliary budgets are segregated from other institutional budgets and are designed to be operated without institutional subsidy, meaning that they are to generate the revenue necessary to fund their operations. In fact, Lennington (1996), asserts that auxiliary enterprises "provide an opportunity to generate revenues that can be used to subsidize" (p. 87) the institution's academic mission.

Once an auxiliary service budget is developed, consultation should be arranged with appropriate constituent groups. In fact, the auxiliaries may even have budget committees that include students, faculty, or graduates. The role of these committees can range from being advisory to actually having to approve changes in fee charges before the changes are submitted for governing board approval. In some states, such as Indiana, Iowa, and Kansas, approval of room and board rates by the state's governing board is scheduled much earlier in the academic calendar than changes in other fees or tuition. As a consequence, the budget manager may have to forecast costs for as long as eighteen months or more. This requires great skill and good luck, because an intervening external variable, such as an oil embargo or crop failure, can have a major negative impact on the auxiliary service's budget.

Auxiliary unit heads should heed the same advice given for other unit heads regarding personnel expenditures. The director of the student union typically cannot award employees 6 percent raises, even if the money is available, if the average increase for all staff at the institution is 4 percent. Nor can fringe benefits be adjusted differently, such as providing a better retirement package for auxiliary unit staff or more vacation days. Auxiliaries generally function within the budgeting framework of their institution, even if they must generate virtually all of their operating revenue.

Trends in Finance and Budgeting

There are a number of trends in finance and budgeting of which student affairs professionals should take notice. Several of those trends are identified and discussed in this section.

Downsizing and Reallocation

One unpleasant aspect of budgeting in the past few years has been dealing with institutional mandates to downsize many operations. Downsizing refers to eliminating positions or, in some cases, entire units. Downsizing results from institutions simply not having a sufficient revenue stream to support all the activities and services they would like to provide. When funding sources are insufficient, hard choices have to be made. Determining which essential programs and services need to be provided and which can be eliminated is an exercise that senior leaders and department heads are forced to undertake. Downsizing will likely result in fundamental changes in programs and services and many unhappy staff, faculty, and students. Involving students and faculty in the process is crucial. In many ways the process, if time permits, will resemble the strategic planning process described earlier in this chapter. One approach to downsizing is outsourcing, described next.

Outsourcing or Privatization

One strategy related to downsizing—outsourcing or privatization—involves entering into contracts with enterprises outside the institution to provide services that have become quite expensive for the institution to offer itself. Food service operations, for example, have been outsourced for years. One institution went from losing about $100,000 per year when the college operated its own food service to an annual rebate from a contractor of $168,000 (Angrisani, 1994). Although such savings are not always the case, outsourcing represents one attractive scenario for senior administrators looking for ways to cut expenditures.

Moneta and Dillon (2002) point out that "The prospect of turning over a college or university administrative service to a private provider continues to generate anxiety, resistance and fear among many of us who have directly managed one or more of those services" (p. 31). They believe, however, that outsourcing can be wise if circumstances so indicate. "Nonetheless, it is likely and in many cases desirable, to convey management responsibility for some campus service to a private partner where the benefits derived from those relationships outweigh risks of continued self operation or are likely to enhance service quality or economics" (p. 31).

Rush, Kempner, and Goldstein (1995) have developed six categories of decisions that need to be made in determining whether or not to outsource a service or operation. Included in this six are financial, human resources, mission and cultural factors, management control and efficiency, the quality of services, and legal and ethical considerations. They add the following about outsourcing: "Regardless of the size, location or affiliation of the institution, and no matter what functional area is under consideration, campus decision makers need to use a structured methodology that supports efficient and effective decision making" that can withstand the scrutiny of various campus constituencies (p. 6).

As an example of the kinds of activities that have been privatized, the University of Delaware outsourced the following activities in the past several years: food service, laundry facilities, computer networking, personal computer maintenance, mainframe computer maintenance, the university pharmacy, and energy conservation efforts (Roselle, 1994). While not all institutions choose to move in the direction of privatizing services, this option may be considered as a way of decreasing expenditures and eliminating the headaches associated with some aspects of institutional management.

One should not assume that outsourcing is a panacea, however. When a unit such as a bookstore is outsourced, employees can be affected. Private companies may not have similar pay scales or fringe benefit packages as institutions of higher education. Even if the employees do not lose their jobs in an outsourcing arrangement, there is an excellent chance that their total compensation will be reduced. This presents quite an ethical dilemma for the student affairs officer faced with solving a budgetary problem.

Another issue that may be influential in an outsourcing decision is the contemporary interest of many students in issues related to the environment and worker rights. Levine and Cureton (1998) have described a resurgence in student activism; if outsourcing is conducted without sensitivity to the environment and worker rights, student dissent may result. Consequently, it is important to remember that even when outsourcing appears to be the only solution to a problem, it may not come without cost.

Increasing Revenues

While outsourcing and downsizing are used to reduce costs, two recent trends have emerged in higher education to help raise additional revenues. One is to apply substantial overhead charges to auxiliary units for services provided by general administrative units on campus, such as purchasing, accounting, security, and the like. Auxiliaries at public institutions typically are expected to pay their way without subsidies from the campus general fund and at some private institutions are designed to subsidize the institution's general fund. At some institutions, contributions from auxiliaries actually exceed the value of the services provided by the institution. Situations exist where some units, such as health services, are charged rent for the space they occupy in a campus building. In other circumstances, charges are assessed for custodial and maintenance services without the auxiliary being given the option of hiring its own staff or contracting with a private firm. The consequence of levying overhead charges is that additional funds are provided for other needs on campus, such as faculty salaries, library support, and other activities charged to an institution's general fund.

Another option is to charge students dedicated fees or activity fees for student affairs units. These might include a special fee to pay the debt on student affairs buildings (such as the student union) or a dedicated health services or counseling fee. These fees reduce the pressure on the general fund and allow the institution to take the political position that tuition increases have been slowed. Quite obviously, dedicated, mandatory fees represent additional costs to students. Whether the trend of charging additional fees to students will continue or even accelerate in the future is unknown. Given the lack of fiscal health in higher education over the past decade, more fees quite possibly will be charged to students.

Fundraising

One other fairly recent development in the area of generating additional revenue is that of fundraising. Jackson (2000) asserts that student affairs has been encouraged to seek external funds for programs in recent years. As a relative newcomer to the fundraising table, student affairs has to overcome some barriers in developing fundraising efforts. Among these is dealing with the history and tradition of fundraising on various campuses where student affairs did not have an active role in fundraising. Another is cultivating prospective donors who may have regularly targeted their gifts at other aspects of the institution. The third is convincing staff that fundraising is a worthy use of their time.

Nevertheless, some aspects of student affairs have excellent potential for fundraising. Among these are facilities for students, such as recreation facilities, student unions, and residence halls. Another is programming for students, which can include leadership development activities, travel to student conferences, and support for speakers to come to campus. Finally, there are some aspects of fundraising in student affairs that have a long history of success. Student scholarship support is a primary example. Most campuses are actively engaged in scholarship development, and if financial aid is part of the student affairs portfolio, this record of activity should not be overlooked. Jackson (2000) is optimistic about fundraising in student affairs: "Student affairs programs now have the opportunity to help their institutions finance projects that may not have been funded by external sources a decade ago" (p. 610). He urges student affairs staff to "gain support for programs in a manner similar to deans, faculty and staff in academic departments" (pp. 610–611).

Conclusion

Student affairs officers must possess strong planning and budgeting skills. Financial pressure on student affairs units will continue to rise in the future. States are running short of funds, and the federal government cannot be looked to as a dependable source of revenue. Student fees will likely increase at a faster rate than tuition, and the use of downsizing and outsourcing will increase in frequency. Given this unpleasant scenario, student affairs managers and leaders have no choice but to develop strong planning and budgeting skills or face dire consequences.

This chapter examined some of the more salient issues related to these topics. Planning and budgeting are central activities in the contemporary financial environment of higher education. A high level of expertise will serve all student affairs officers well, helping them develop programs that provide learning opportunities for students while simultaneously meeting the administrative and organizational needs of their institution.

References

Adams, E. M. (1997, September/October). Rationality in the academy: Why responsibility center budgeting is a wrong step down the wrong road. *Change, 29* (5), 59–61.

Ambler, D. A. (2000). Organizational and administrative models. In M. J. Barr, M. K. Desler, & Associates, *The handbook of student affairs administration* (2nd ed., pp. 121–134). San Francisco: Jossey-Bass.

American College Personnel Association. (1996). The student learning imperative: Implications for student affairs. *Journal of College Student Development, 37,* 118–122.
Angrisani, C. (1994). Students' needs dictate contract decision. *On-Campus Hospitality, 16* (4), 22–26.
Balderston, F. E. (1995). *Managing today's university: Strategies for viability, change, and excellence.* San Francisco: Jossey-Bass.
Baldridge, J. V., & Okimi, H. P. (1982). Strategic planning in higher education. *American Association for Higher Education Bulletin, 35* (6), 15–18.
Bean, J. P. (1983). Planning as a self-fulfilling prophecy. In G. D. Kuh (Ed.), *Understanding student affairs organizations* (New Directions for Student Services Sourcebook Series No. 23, pp. 39–50). San Francisco: Jossey-Bass.
Bean, J. P., & Kuh, G. D. (1999). A typology of planning problems. In M. W. Peterson (Ed.), *ASHE reader on planning and institutional research* (pp. 120–132). Needham Heights, MA: Simon & Schuster.
Birnbaum, R. (2001). *Management fads in higher education.* San Francisco: Jossey-Bass.
Bowen, H. R. (1996). What determines the cost of higher education? In D. W. Breneman, L. L. Leslie, & R. E. Anderson (Eds.), *ASHE reader on finance in higher education* (pp. 113–127). Needham Heights, MA: Simon & Schuster.
Brinkman, P. T., & Morgan, A. W. (1997). Changing fiscal strategies for planning. In M. W. Peterson, D. D. Dill, L. A. Mets, & Associates, *Planning and management for a changing environment* (pp. 288–306). San Francisco: Jossey-Bass.
Clodfelter, C. T. (1996). *Buying the best: Cost escalation in elite higher education.* Princeton, NJ: Princeton University Press.
Clugston, R. M. (1986, February). *Strategic planning in an organized anarchy: The emperor's new clothes.* Paper presented at the annual meeting of Association for the Study of Higher Education, San Antonio, TX.
Cope, R. (1981). Environmental assessments for strategic planning. In N. Poulton (Ed.), *Evaluation of management and planning systems* (New Directions for Institutional Research Sourcebook Series No. 31, pp. 5–15). San Francisco: Jossey-Bass.
Dickeson, R. C. (1999). *Prioritizing academic programs and services: Reallocating resources to achieve strategic balance.* San Francisco: Jossey-Bass.
Dickmeyer, N. (1996). Budgeting. In D. W. Breneman, L. L. Leslie, & R. Anderson (Eds.), *ASHE reader on finance in higher education* (pp. 539–561). Needham Heights, MA: Simon & Schuster.
Dill, D. D. (1997). Focusing institutional mission to provide coherence and integration. In M. W. Peterson, D. D. Dill, L. A. Mets, & Associates, *Planning and management for a changing environment* (pp. 171–190). San Francisco: Jossey-Bass.
Dolence, M. G., & Norris, D. M. (1999). Using key performance indicators to drive strategic decision making. In M. W. Peterson (Ed.), *ASHE reader on planning and institutional research* (pp. 526–538). Needham Heights, MA: Simon & Schuster.
Douglas, D. O. (1991). Fiscal resource management: Background and relevance for student affairs. In T. K. Miller, R. B. Winston, Jr., & Associates, *Administration and leadership in student affairs* (pp. 615–641). Muncie, IN: Accelerated Development.
El-Khawas, E. (1994). *Restructuring initiatives in public higher education: Institutional response to financial constraints* (ACE Research Brief No. 8). Washington, DC: American Council on Education.
Ern, E. H. (1993). Managing resources strategically. In M. J. Barr, M. K. Desler, & Associates, *The handbook of student affairs administration* (pp. 439–454). San Francisco: Jossey-Bass.
Ewell, P. T. (1999). Identifying indicators of curricular quality. In M. W. Peterson (Ed.), *ASHE reader on planning and institutional research* (pp. 539–551). Needham Heights, MA: Simon & Schuster.
Fincher, C. (1986). Budgeting myths and fictions. In L. L. Leslie & R. E. Anderson (Eds.), *ASHE reader on finance in higher education* (pp. 73–86). Lexington, MA: Ginn.
Finney, R. G. (1994). *Basics of budgeting.* New York: AMACOM.
Jackson, M. L. (2000). Fundraising and development. In M. J. Barr, M. K. Desler, & Associates, *The handbook of student affairs administration* (2nd ed., pp. 597–611). San Francisco: Jossey-Bass.

Keller, G. (1983). *Academic strategy: The management revolution in American higher education.* Baltimore: Johns Hopkins University Press.

Keller, G. (1997). Examining what works in strategic planning. In M. W. Peterson, D. D. Dill, L. A. Mets, & Associates, *Planning and management for a changing environment* (pp. 158–170). San Francisco: Jossey-Bass.

Kotler, P., & Murphy, P. (1981). Strategic planning for higher education. *Journal of Higher Education, 52,* 470–489.

Lang, D. W. (2001). A primer on responsibility centre budgeting and responsibility centre management. In J. L. Yeager, G. M. Nelson, E. A. Potter, J. C. Weidman, & T. G. Zullo (Eds.), *ASHE reader on finance in higher education* (2nd ed., pp. 568–590). Boston, MA: Pearson.

Lee, S. M., & Van Horn, J. C. (1983). *Academic administration.* Lincoln: University of Nebraska Press.

Lenning, O. T., & Ebbers, L. H. (1999). *The powerful potential of learning communities: Improving education for the future.* (ASHE-ERIC Higher Education Report Vol. 26, No. 6). Washington, DC: The George Washington University, Graduate School of Education and Human Development.

Lennington, R. L. (1996). *Managing higher education as a business.* Phoenix, AZ: ACE/Oryx.

Leslie, D. W., & Fretwell, E. K., Jr. (1996). *Wise moves in hard times: Crafting and managing resilient colleges and universities.* San Francisco: Jossey-Bass.

Levine, A., & Cureton, J. S. (1998). *When hope and fear collide.* San Francisco: Jossey-Bass.

Lyons, J. W. (1993). The importance of institutional mission. In M. J. Barr, M. K. Desler, & Associates, *The handbook of student affairs administration* (pp. 3–15). San Francisco: Jossey-Bass.

Meisinger, R. J., Jr., & Dubeck, L. W. (1996). Fund accounting. In D. W. Breneman, L. L. Leslie, & R. E. Anderson (Eds.), *ASHE reader on finance in higher education* (pp. 465–491). Needham Heights, MA: Simon & Schuster.

Mets, L. A. (1997). Planning change through program review. In M. W. Peterson, D. D. Dill, L. A. Mets, & Associates, *Planning and management for a changing environment* (pp. 340–359). San Francisco: Jossey-Bass.

Meyerson, J. W., & Johnson, S. L. (1993). Planning for strategic decision making. In R. T. Ingram & Associates, *Governing public colleges and universities: A handbook for trustees, chief executives, and other campus leaders* (pp. 77–90). San Francisco: Jossey-Bass.

Moneta, L., & Dillon, W. L. (2002). Strategies for effective outsourcing. In L. Dietz & E. Enchelmayer (Eds.), *Developing external partnerships.* (New Directions for Student Services No. 96, pp. 31–49). San Francisco: Jossey-Bass.

Muston, R. A. (1980). Resource allocation and program budgeting. In C. H. Foxley (Ed.), *Applying management techniques* (New Directions for Student Services No. 9, pp. 79–92). San Francisco: Jossey-Bass.

NACUBO. (2002). *Explaining college costs.* Washington, DC: Author.

National Center for Education Statistics. (2001). *Digest of education statistics, 2000.* Washington, DC: U.S. Department of Education.

Neufield, B. (1999). Conceptual distinctions in university planning. In M. W. Peterson (Ed.), *ASHE reader on planning and institutional research* (pp. 50–59). Needham Heights, MA: Simon & Schuster.

Novick, D. (1973). *Current practice in program budgeting.* London: Heinemann.

Pembroke, W. J. (1985). Fiscal constraints on program development. In M. J. Barr, L. A. Keating, & Associates, *Developing effective student services programs: Systematic approaches for practitioners* (pp. 83–107). San Francisco: Jossey-Bass.

Peterson, M. W. (1999). Analyzing alternative approaches to planning. In Author (Ed.), *ASHE reader on planning and institutional research* (pp. 11–49). Needham Heights, MA: Simon & Schuster.

The Pew Higher Education Research Program. (1996). The other side of the mountain. In D. W. Breneman, L. L. Leslie, & R. E. Anderson (Eds.), *ASHE reader on finance in higher education* (pp. 511–518). Needham Heights, MA: Simon & Schuster.

Pillinger, B. B., & Kraack, T. A. (1980). Long range planning: A key to effective management. *NASPA Journal, 18,* 2–7.

Redd, K. E. (2000). *Discounting toward disaster: Tuition discounting, college finance, and enrollments of low-income undergraduates.* USA Group Foundation New Agenda Series, *3* (2). Indianapolis: USA Group Foundation.

Robins, G. B. (1986). Understanding the college budget. In L. L. Leslie & R. E. Anderson (Eds.), *ASHE reader on finance in higher education* (pp. 28–56). Lexington, MA: Ginn.

Roselle, D. P. (1994). *A retrospective view: Management of the University of Delaware since 1990.* Unpublished manuscript, University of Delaware, Newark.

Rowley, D. J., Lujan, H. D., & Dolence, M. G. (1997). *Strategic change in colleges and universities: Planning to survive and prosper.* San Francisco: Jossey-Bass.

Rush, S. C., Kempner, D. E., & Goldstein, P. J. (1995). Contract management: A process approach to making the decision. In *Peterson's contract services for higher education* (pp. 5–9). Princeton, NJ: Peterson's.

Schroeder, C. C. (1999). Forging educational partnerships that advance student learning. In G. S. Blimling & E. J. Whitt (Eds.), *Good practice in student affairs* (pp. 133–156). San Francisco: Jossey-Bass.

Schuh, J. H., & Upcraft, M. L. (2001). *Assessment practice in student affairs.* San Francisco: Jossey-Bass.

Steiss, A. W. (1972). *Public budgeting and management.* Lexington, MA: Heath.

Stocum, D. L., & Rooney, P. M. (1997, September/October). Responding to resource constraints: A departmentally based system of responsibility center management. *Change, 29* (5), 51–57.

Strauss, J., Curry, J., & Whalen, E. (2001). Revenue responsibility budgeting. In J. L. Yeager, G. M. Nelson, E. A. Potter, J. C. Weidman, & T. G. Zullo (Eds.), *ASHE reader on finance in higher education* (2nd ed., pp. 591–607). Boston, MA: Pearson.

Taylor, B. E., & Massy, W. F. (1996). *Strategic indicators for higher education.* Princeton, NJ: Peterson's.

Tellefsen, T. E. (1990). *Improving college management: An integrated systems approach.* San Francisco: Jossey-Bass.

The College Board. (2001). *Trends in college pricing.* Washington, DC: Author.

Vandament, W. E. (1989). *Managing money in higher education.* San Francisco: Jossey-Bass.

Weick, K. E. (1984). Small wins: Redefining the scale of social problems. *American Psychologist, 39* (1), 40–49.

Wellman, J. V. (2001). *Looking back, going forward: The Carnegie Commission tuition policy.* Washington, DC: The Institute for Higher Education Policy, The Ford Foundation, and The Education Resources Institute.

Wilms, W. W., Teruya, C., & Walpole, M., (1997, September/October). Fiscal reform at UCLA: The class of accountability and academic freedom. *Change, 29* (5), 41–49.

Wingspread Group on Higher Education. (1993). *An American imperative: Higher expectations for higher education.* Racine, WI: Johnson Foundation.

Woodard, D. B., Jr. (1993). Budgeting and fiscal management. In M. J. Barr, M. K. Desler, & Associates, *The handbook of student affairs administration* (pp. 242–259). San Francisco: Jossey-Bass.

Woodard, D. B., Jr. (Ed.). (1995). *Budgeting as a tool for policy in student affairs.* (New Directions for Student Services No. 70). San Francisco: Jossey-Bass.

Woodard, D. B., Jr., Love, P., & Komives, S. R. (2000). *Leadership and management issues for a new century.* (New Directions for Student Services No. 92). San Francisco: Jossey-Bass.

Woodard, D. B., Jr., & von Destinon, M. (2000). Budgeting and fiscal management. In M. J. Barr, M. K. Desler, & Associates, *The handbook of student affairs administration* (2nd ed., pp. 327–346). San Francisco: Jossey-Bass.

CHAPTER SEVENTEEN

INFORMATION TECHNOLOGY IN STUDENT AFFAIRS

William Barratt

Information technology (IT) changes quickly. New software and hardware are being introduced at a dizzying pace, and before this chapter can be revised and reprinted even more will change in IT. Writing about IT is like taking a snapshot of a marathon that has no clear rules, no clear route, and new competitors being added at odd times. This chapter presents a brief history of IT and an introduction to how IT is being used in student affairs. Most of this chapter is dedicated to describing IT competencies appropriate for student affairs professionals. These competencies are based on current practice and current software, but any such list should be seen as constantly changing. A list of IT resources is included at the end of the chapter as a starting point for learning more about IT and student affairs.

The Paradox of Information Technology

The interpersonal relationships between students and student affairs professionals create and reinforce the face-to-face paradigm that drives our knowledge base and our skill set. While not as immiscible as oil and water, student affairs and IT do take some effort to mix. Student affairs is a face-to-face, direct service, social environment with social norms and social values (Holland 1966; Strange & Banning, 2001). Working with things, like computers, does not appeal to our hearts in student affairs. Morrill, Oetting, and Hurst (1974) described three methods of intervention: direct service, consultation, and media. Direct service and consultation are interpersonal, appealing to the social norm in student affairs. Media, in this case IT, does not require social interactions with students and may not be perceived as mainstream to the social environment in student affairs.

Standards for professional preparation in student affairs reinforce this face-to-face paradigm by specifying studies and training in working directly with students (Council for Accreditation of Counseling and Related Educational Programs, 2001; Council for the Advancement of Standards in Higher Education, 2001). Computer-mediated interactions are becoming commonplace, and you need to acquire and enhance the IT knowledge and skills needed to use IT when interacting with students.

New developments in IT can increase the efficiency of current practice, confirming and strengthening our current practices and paradigms. They can also lead us to gain new capabilities that will shift our practices and paradigms.

A Brief History of Information Technology

The records of old civilizations all use some kind of information technology, whether stone, paper, or petroglyph. Prehistoric times are literally pre-IT times; they are the epochs of unrecorded history.

Old Information Technology: Paper and Ink

The development of papyri in Egypt around 3000 BC and the invention of paper in China in 105 AD (Institute of Paper Science and Technology, 2002) facilitated increased recording of information. Paper did not completely replace older IT (we still produce stone monuments) but was used for appropriate organizational, social, and personal ends.

The printing press, invented in the 1400s, made printing more efficient, and the later invention of movable type made it even more so, because a unique printing plate for each page of text was no longer required. Once printing became more efficient, more material could be printed, widening the world's available knowledge base; more people had access to more information. The wider availability of printed material was an important feature of the European Renaissance and Reformation (Green, 1964).

Thomas Edison's development of the spirit duplication or mimeograph process in 1876 and Chester Carlson's development of the copy machine process in the mid-twentieth century greatly increased individual access to information. These developments made it even easier for people in an industrialized nation to create printed media, again widening the available knowledge base.

Old IT created an image on paper ever cheaper, ever better, and ever faster. The image may have been text or graphics, but the process of putting ink onto paper is now a very efficient version of what the Egyptian and Chinese scribes did millennia ago.

New Information Technology: Digital Media

Storing and retrieving information electronically in a digital format is relatively new. The digital computer was invented by John Atanasoff and Clifford Beery at Iowa State University (Department of Computer Science, Iowa State University, 2002) between

1937 and 1942 to solve difficult mathematical problems. The development of computers and programming gave rise to the development of digital word processing, digital process control, digital music, digital movies, and the countless digital computing tasks we take for granted today.

Once it became easy and inexpensive to capture and manipulate digital data, there was a press to digitize all manner of sound, graphics, and video information; the transformation is still under way. New IT may or may not transform higher education (Cohen, 1998; Cuban, 1986), but it has already changed student affairs practice.

Dynamic Information Technology

New IT is dynamic; new competencies and practices generated by it are more fluid than those generated by older models. The knowledge and skills needed to use new hardware and software change with every new release, but the rate of change is not constant. Word processing software, for instance, hasn't changed significantly or often, but high-performance desktop videoconferencing software and hardware will change often and dramatically for the next few years.

Some people find this dynamic new IT an unparalleled opportunity, and others dread the disorder it brings. Waiting for the opportunity to select a stable combination of software and hardware is untenable; change is the only constant.

Student Affairs Practice and Information Technology

This section outlines how IT is used in student affairs on campus and explores some of the challenges IT has presented and will present in the future. Information technology is a fact of life on the modern campus, seen everywhere from vending machines using student IDs as cash cards to campuswide information systems controlling payroll and enrollment. IT on campus enables student affairs professionals to more efficiently use old methods of interacting with students and to develop new methods of interacting with students to achieve their development and learning goals.

IT in student affairs is an accidental success (Barratt, 2001). People are working hard to achieve good results without an integrated plan. There are at least two problems preventing generalizations about IT practices in student affairs. First, different offices have different needs. Second, different campuses have different needs. The IT needs in residence life for scheduling and plant management are quite different from the IT needs of a student life office. Considering just word processing, for example, one office may produce letters and formal text documents, while another may produce brochures and flyers.

Differences between campuses are equally dramatic. IT issues on a campus with 1,500 students are quite different from those on a campus with 36,000 students. Larger campuses can take advantage of economies of scale but may not be able to respond quickly to student needs. Small campuses may not have the staff to provide sophisticated applications and a dynamic web presence, but IT challenges may create interesting and new partnerships between student affairs offices and other campus offices when student affairs staff sit on committees with the staff from purchasing, business affairs, human resources, and other areas to solve campuswide IT-oriented problems.

Efficiency

While the differences are important, so is the need for everyone to use IT to increase office efficiency and take advantage of it to interact with students. Increases in efficiency using IT can be dramatic or subtle. In some financial aid offices, IT has created a two-part system where one office section is dedicated to data management and another works directly with students. This frees staff to work on financial advising, planning, and other developmental interactions with students.

Web Sites

One primary media for computer-mediated interactions is the web. Some student affairs web sites are great, others poor. Some web sites simply take all the old paper and transfer it to the web; this is referred to as "brochure ware" because it takes no advantage of the capabilities of web-based documents and web sites. It takes time and effort to learn how to create appropriate web sites, but current software makes it much easier.

Information Technology Staff

The student affairs information technologist probably knows more about IT and may be the one who educates and mentors others. Alternatively, he or she may simply manage the servers and write software applications for the office. The advantages of having a designated IT staff member are obvious, but the disadvantage is that these individuals may be perceived as being solely responsible for individually solving problems that are everyone's problems. Problems involving IT are generally referred to the IT person. Unfortunately, many of these problems are not technical problems but reflect student affairs practices and policies. Appropriate IT planning and practice require informed input from all organizational levels, and delegating this task to one individual may not result in inclusive and effective IT practices.

One advantage of having someone designated as the student affairs IT staff member is the opportunity to create new partnerships on campus. Coordinating IT efforts across the campus occupies many committee hours, and having a student affairs professional representative on these committees is important.

Student Expectations

Students today expect campuswide access to IT. The title of "most wired campus" has taken on a status similar to the "best colleges" list. Residence halls need an Internet "port per pillow," two phone lines in every residence hall room, and a cable TV connection. The campus must have convenient computer labs with multiple platforms including Mac, Windows, UNIX, Linux, and specialty platforms for specific academic programs. EDUCAUSE (2002b), whose mission "is to advance higher education by promoting the intelligent use of information technology," has developed a consumer guide to evaluate campus IT resources (EDUCAUSE, 2002a).

Students also want access to faculty and staff. If students have an e-mail and chat-preferred style of communication and student affairs professionals have a face-to-face, phone, and paper-preferred style of communication, the result may be missed communication.

Student Misconduct

Student misconduct issues range from sending harassing e-mails to hacking into university systems. Codes of student conduct and campus IT policies should be used to manage this. Judicious additions to older policies, as outlined by Barr (Chapter Seven), can cover most instances of student misconduct.

The ready availability of the Internet leads directly to new problems on campus: Internet addiction, Internet gambling, the availability of prescription medication from abroad over the Internet without a physician's prescription, and other totally new problems. The Internet may even lead to interpersonal problems such as the breakdown of community and social isolation and to political and economic issues related to the inequality of access.

"Internet abuse" and "Internet addiction" are terms used more often in the popular media than in scholarly journals. Stories are written about dependent Internet users who have become more attached to their online friends than to their "real" friends (Parks & Floyd, 1996; Sandberg, 1997; Shellenbarger, 1996). Many of these stories have no published research to back them up. It is difficult to distinguish between "normal" Internet use and "abnormal" or overuse. True Internet addiction, like all addictions, results in personal, family, academic, and occupational problems (DeAngelis, 2000).

More people use the net every year, but to date only a few individuals have been diagnosed as addicted to the Internet (Greenfield, 1999) because few fit the profile of an addict based on the current *Diagnostic and Statistical Manual of Mental Disorders.* If social pathologies exist involving the Internet, then there is a need for further research related to these pathologies (Griffiths, 1997). Major depression has also been related to addictive Internet use. Young (1996) stated that maladaptive cognitions such as low self-esteem, low self-worth, and clinical depression triggered pathological Internet use.

The breakdown of interpersonal communities and social isolation has been studied with varied results (Kraut et al., 2002). Sheperd and Edelmann (2001) suggest positive social benefits to Internet use but note that a great deal of research has yet to be done. Online communities have appeared in staggering numbers. An Internet search using the words "online" and "community" produced references to over one million web pages. While online communities must, of necessity, be different from interpersonal communities, these virtual communities are a fact of Internet life.

The variability in student access to computers has created the "digital divide" (U.S. Department of Commerce, 1999; U.S. Department of Education, Office of Information Technology, 2002). Some students come to campus having used IT at home and in school, and others come to campus with little or no experience. Relying on IT as a primary way to interact with students will place some students at an automatic disadvantage. There is also evidence of a growing digital divide between elite and minority-serving institutions (Young, 2002). Whether at the individual or institutional level, the digital divide is one of the functions of privilege that must be the subject of concern, reflection, and action on the part of student affairs professionals.

Distance Education Student Services

Distance education students need to have access to the same services, educational programming, and interaction with student affairs staff as on-campus students, but the traditional idea of office hours does not apply at a distance. Student services have been built around on-campus students. Consensus on best practices for distance education and especially for distance education student services has not emerged because the area is so new. The development of best practices in services for distance education students will need to build on current statements about best practice in student services like the "Good Practice in Student Affairs" material (Blimling & Whitt, 1999).

Telephone, e-mail, and web-based interactions have become important methods of communicating with distance education students, and some offices have instituted "chat" hours when someone is available to conduct an Internet chat with an off-campus student. Accommodating distance-education students will be a challenge.

Information Technology Competencies in Student Affairs

Assertions about IT competencies are statements about what should be true about the desired level of staff members' IT knowledge base and skill set. In IT, with software and hardware in a dynamic state, statements about competencies need to avoid the specific as much as possible and focus on the ability to use IT to further the student affairs mission and learning goals.

Competencies need to be articulated both for individuals and for departments. Not all staff members need to know how to do all things. Some IT staff members' competencies might be minimal, reflecting their work. Other staff may need a higher level of competence to ensure that the student affairs mission can be achieved. Individual competencies reflect what an individual does working alone, and department-level competencies include competencies about integrating IT applications with other staff, about integrating IT into the daily work processes, and about using IT in new and creative ways to further our work as student affairs professionals.

It is tempting to list a complete set of competencies in each IT area and create a checklist to determine if staff members and staffs have necessary competencies. Unfortunately the dynamic nature of IT precludes any list from completeness and accuracy. Competencies will be described here in general terms and will only cover what seems appropriate as of this writing. Emerging applications and IT will change, and defining and achieving competence is an ongoing process.

General Knowledge Base

The appropriate knowledge base for student affairs professionals should encompass most available features of common types of software, the problem being that "common types of software" is an ever-expanding list. To gain an appropriate knowledge base requires an investment in learning. Knowing what is possible is a prerequisite for IT to develop solutions to contemporary problems to meet the student affairs mission.

General Skill Set

Once a knowledge base has been established, the skills to use software must be mastered and expanded. Sensitivity to learning styles is required when enhancing staff skill competencies. Ideally, staff member skill sets are enhanced in their daily work through using ever more sophisticated features. Enhancing skills takes time dedicated to learning; that time should be seen as an investment in both the staff member and the department.

Managing Information Technology

When considering IT competencies it is tempting to focus only on the technical skills for each application. IT has become integrated into student affairs and like other specialties requires appropriate management. Planning, staffing, budgeting, and evaluating IT requires a substantial knowledge base but does not require extensive IT skills. Managers must be able to plan appropriately and to take advantage of new and emerging IT practices to further the student affairs student development and learning mission on campus. They must be able to determine appropriate areas and levels of competence for staff members, and they must know the work processes in their area and must be able to apply IT practices to existing work to increase efficiencies.

IT is expensive. Money and time spent on IT means money and time that cannot be spent elsewhere, and it is an ongoing expense. Hardware needs to be regularly replaced, and staff need to be regularly trained (Oberlin, 1996). Staff time commitments are expanding as new campus committees and work groups are formed which need representation from someone in student affairs.

Selecting Software

Knowing which software to use is complicated. Most people have a preferred word processor, but a campus or a student affairs division could possibly want to use some other nonpreferred application. Alternatively, a campus may support certain software and proscribe other software. It is important to learn the current campus IT climate on a specific campus before making any kind of decision.

Most decisions about which application software to use are not need-based. Brands of software for word processing, spread sheet manipulation, database management, presentations, web-page editing, e-mail, and chat are remarkably similar to each other in features but slightly different in look and feel. As a general rule, knowledge and skills about multiple applications are important in being able to develop criteria to select software. Learning two similar applications, for example two word processing programs, is an excellent way to develop a knowledge base about word processing software.

Operating Systems

Perhaps the most important competence is the ability to use at least one operating system (OS). While there are many excellent operating systems for desktop computers, the most common are MAC OS and Windows—both of which come in many versions. Having the knowledge base and skills necessary to take advantage of an operating system are crucial. Key competencies are the ability to install software, modify the desktop, move information among multiple applications, manage folders and files on a disk, and back up data files.

While local area network (LAN) operating systems are generally transparent to the user, some basic knowledge of the campus LAN OS is also essential for using software applications appropriately. Being able to share files among computers without e-mail attachments or physically exchanging disks is one important LAN OS feature.

General Applications

The most important general competence in using any software is knowing how to learn to use the software. The menu bar and help menus have replaced software manuals, but learning this way does not appeal to everyone. It is also important to know how to enter and format text or data. Contemporary software uses similar menus and strategies to format fonts, format pages, and prepare documents for printing. Knowing how to use these should be a basic professional competence.

Word Processing and Desktop Publishing

Many people feel competent to operate word processing software, but their ability to do so may be limited to using basic features they may have learned some time ago. Today an appropriate level of competence should reflect both the capabilities of newer software and the ways in which it can be used in a student affairs office. Student affairs professionals should have a strong knowledge of at least one of the market-leading software programs and gain familiarity with at least one more, because students and other professionals use a wide array of word processing software.

Distinctions between word processing software and desktop publishing software are blurring. Creating a text-only word-processed document is a very limited aspect of what occurs in a student affairs office. Desktop publishing software can facilitate student learning and development media.

Basic word processing competencies for everyone in student affairs, in addition to general software competencies, include creating documents, manipulating fonts, formatting text, using headings and lists, creating basic tables, and saving and importing files in common formats such as .rtf (rich text format), .txt (text), or .html (hypertext markup language). The ability to create a letter that is merged with a name and address list is also important.

Advanced competencies include knowing how to create headings, create a table of contents or index, link documents, create .pdf files, work with master and subdocuments, and link documents with spreadsheets and other applications.

Spreadsheet and Data Analysis

Spreadsheets are used for a variety of tasks from financial modeling to statistical analysis to organizing lists and data sets. A basic knowledge of at least one and preferably two programs is important. Popular spreadsheets should meet anyone's basic needs, but advanced statistical analysis may require a more advanced program. Basic competencies include data entry and data definition, cutting, copying, and pasting within cells and across multiple cells, and formatting a spreadsheet for viewing or printing. Basic data analysis competencies are the ability to calculate descriptive statistics. Basic file skills are saving and importing files using alternate formats such as .csv (comma delimited format), .dif (data interchange format), or .html (hypertext markup language). These are crucial when working with other offices.

Advanced competencies might include the ability to integrate the spreadsheet with other applications such as word processors, databases, presentation software, and web pages.

Database Management

The ability to create, maintain, and use databases is integral to student affairs. Lists of organizations, officers, and rooms, are examples of databases. Current database software allows for sophisticated data management and retrieval. Database systems can enhance program evaluations by providing accurate and timely reports.

One of the more recent developments in database management can be seen on campus portals. The material presented on the campus portal page may consist of segments of information, news, weather, campus events, and other relevant information. The web page itself is a shell completed by individually updated segments of database information that is maintained separately from the web page, often in a database.

Basic competencies in using database software are creating and modifying a database, retrieving the data to create appropriate reports, and importing and exporting data. Advanced competencies are creating linked databases and linking the database with other application software.

Presentation Software

Presentation software is a tool to enhance the effectiveness of learning, and presentations can be effective with multiple learning styles. On first examination, computer-generated presentations are digitally driven slides and overheads, but advanced features of presentation software permit things never before possible using overheads. Basic competencies include the ability to create and save presentations; modify font colors and formats; appropriately use slide transitions; include computer-generated graphs, graphics, sound, animations, and video; incorporate hyperlinks into the presentation; and generate handouts and notes. Advanced competencies are the ability to launch other programs, browsers, videos, and applications from within a presentation, saving a presentation as a web page or site, and creating special themes and graphics.

Communication

Text-only e-mail (no graphics, no attachments, no .html) was one of the first developments of what became the Internet (Media Trails, 2001). Modern e-mail software, like modern word processing software, has a wide array of features to enable the user to effectively communicate with others. Basic competencies are managing fonts, creating and managing distribution lists, managing folders for retaining messages, creating signatures, attaching files to messages, subscribing and unsubscribing from e-mail lists, and forwarding mail to other users. Advanced competencies include using .html-based messages, managing discussion lists, and getting messages from other e-mail accounts using POP or IMAP.

Chat technology is emerging as an everyday application. Because of competition and advances in technology, chat software is dynamic. The addition of voice and video to chat applications is an emerging commercial battle, as is the addition of whiteboards, desktop sharing, file sharing, and file attachments. Basic competencies include the ability to create a chat session, create and use a chat room, and create an appropriate user profile. Like chat technology, bulletin boards or discussion boards are becoming increasingly common; the ability to access bulletin boards, retrieve and post messages, and follow message threads is important.

Desktop videoconferencing has changed dramatically in the past few years and will continue to change. Inexpensive webcams now come bundled with an array of software enabling users to connect directly with each other in point-to-point conferences or to create video broadcasts. The revolution in IT development in this area has tremendous implications for distance, adult, and professional continuing education.

Videoconferencing beyond the desktop is becoming less expensive, easier to use, and higher in quality, but it still requires a significant investment in equipment and software. Connections for high quality videoconferencing are a significant cost issue, but the technology is very dynamic.

Audio-Video and Graphics Software

Digital audio, video, and graphics software are rapidly becoming easier to use. Digital still images, digital video, and digital sound, as well as the software to manipulate them, are readily available and relatively inexpensive. With the ready availability of digital multimedia students have an expectation of multimedia learning resources in their classes and on campus.

Basic skills are the ability to use software to produce appropriate graphics and video. The level of skill should certainly reflect the level of need in an office or division. Advanced skills might be those required to create an audio and video CD.

Information Retrieval

There are two important competencies in information retrieval—finding information and evaluating the quality of the information. Finding material on the Internet or a local area network (LAN) is like locating something in a warehouse: you need to know where things are stored. Fortunately, search engines provide some indexing for the Internet, but search engines are limited in the amount of the Internet indexed and indexing criteria. Using multiple search engines appropriately to locate material on the Internet is a basic skill. Having the skill to search within specific sites, such as ERIC, is important for all student affairs professionals. Most LANs have no directory or index, and finding material on one's own campus LAN may be more difficult than finding obscure references on the Internet.

Using a browser is a basic skill, and the ability to use at least two browsers is essential because of their different operations. Basic browsing skills go beyond the ability to enter a universal resource locator (url) and find a specific web page. Other important skills include adding entries to a list of favorites or bookmarks, accessing ftp sites (the url begins with ftp://), telnet sites (telnet://), and even files on the desktop (file://). Using a browser to access and subscribe to news groups on Usenet is also an important basic skill.

Campus Software Systems

Each campus has software to perform basic business functions and to keep records of student academic performance, bills paid, bills due, class schedules, and the myriad business functions of the campus. Much of campus software is dedicated to solving the business and record keeping problems on campus, but applications for student affairs problems are available in some areas and are becoming available in other areas.

Knowing what information is stored on the campus system and having the skill to retrieve the appropriate information is important. On campuses with a minimum GPA requirement for students joining organizations, the ability to access appropriate student records is necessary. Being able to use the campuswide system to further the student affairs mission is certainly a basic skill.

Partnerships have emerged between software vendors to create a large-scale integrated IT presence, extending to courseware and instructional applications, campus portals, e-mail, career and job placement web sites, and even to student organization web space. These partnerships provide unprecedented opportunities and challenges on the campus but have generally not included student affairs in development and implementation.

Groupware

Software to share files, schedules, and digital information among individuals on a LAN is emerging as a new area of IT applications. Rather than sharing schedules on paper and sharing files on disks or as e-mail attachments, groupware allows multiple people to work with a shared set of files. Basic competencies are the ability to create and use shared files and calendars among a group of users. Advanced competencies include the ability to create user groups, search schedules electronically for free meeting times, and cocreate and track document editing within a work group. Some groupware even includes project management features, an essential tool for anyone working with multiple people on a project.

Web Site Design and Maintenance

The knowledge base and skill set needed for information retrieval is related to the knowledge and skills used in creating web sites. By understanding the information architecture and features of a successful web site, student affairs professionals become more capable of creating appropriate web sites to promote student development and learning. Information architecture is the overall design of a web site that enables, or inhibits, access to information.

Creating web pages and web sites is as easy as creating documents, but creating effective web pages and web sites is as difficult as creating effective documents. In designing and maintaining web sites the knowledge base is more important than the skill set. Current software makes creating web sites more a matter of content and format and less a matter of learning .html (hypertext markup language).

Web site information architecture and design competencies include understanding the purpose of the site, the intended audience, how the site can be scaled up or down depending on future needs, and how to make it easy for users to locate information within three mouse clicks. Even mundane things like the look and feel of pages can make web sites more or less effective as student development and learning tools. Advanced skills are the ability to create active server pages and use advanced formatting features such as style sheets, or to create and embed scripts into a page.

Web sites are no longer used only on the Internet. Many campuses are encouraging students to create portfolios of their learning experiences, much like Brown and Citrin's student development transcript (1977). Using a web page as a user interface and table of contents, students can collect material in a variety of digital formats and save them onto a single large-volume disk or CD.

Instructional Software

Courseware is designed to support the teaching mission of the university and can be used to meet many student development and learning needs. Educational programming, whether for student leadership classes or a resident assistant training program, can benefit from using courseware.

Basic skills in using courseware are the ability to enter text and documents, modify text and documents, and use the tools available for courseware, such as e-mail, chat technology, discussion boards, and share files.

Confidentiality and Data Security

The lock-and-key practices used to keep confidential material secure should act as a metaphor for keeping digital information secure. Stored data in a file cabinet can be kept under lock and key, restricting access to individuals who have the key. In the digital world, access to data can be locked with a password. Unfortunately, just as many filing cabinets are easy to open, many simple password programs are easy to break.

Level of risk is important when deciding about security. File security is not an everyday issue for most student affairs professionals, but confidentiality is a part of the daily activity for staff in student conduct or in counseling. Students in practicum and internship classes are aware of the need for confidentiality of client and office records but need to know how keep their class case notes secure on disks or laptops. If computer-stored information must be kept confidential, then something must be done to protect it beyond a machine password (easily foiled) or a word processing password (easily hacked).

Password protection denies access to files on a disk, and encryption software creates a section of a disk that is encrypted requiring a passphrase (a multiword password) for access. Software featuring strong encryption will provide a level of security that may require a supercomputer and several years of work to compromise (Network Associates, 2000). Basic skills should be the ability to protect data files appropriately.

Secure e-mail communication over the Internet uses similar encryption software, but it requires both sender and receiver to have the same software to allow them to encrypt and decrypt messages. Appropriately encrypted e-mail can be considered secure even if it goes over the Internet (Network Associates, 2000).

While few campuses issue digital IDs to students, it may soon become commonplace. Knowledge of emerging issues and technology covering digital signatures will become important as communication increasingly relies on digital technologies and digital signatures.

Virus Protection

Virus protection should be a fact of life for anyone using a computer. Virus makers regularly find new ways to exploit software and operating systems. Increasingly, documents and e-mail messages have embedded files that can be infected by a virus, and opening e-mail in some applications, or the attached document with the appropriate program, will trigger the virus. Basic skills should cover the ability to use and update virus protection.

PDA and Hand-Helds

The array of small hand-held digital devices seems to increase weekly. One of the most common features of personal data assistants (PDAs) is their connectivity with a larger computer. This connection synchronizes the data in both computers, allowing files to be uploaded and downloaded, appointments to be synchronized, and addresses and documents to be updated. Some of the more advanced PDAs can accomplish this synchronization and even access the Internet using wireless technology.

Many PDAs can be connected to the Internet though a desktop computer. In this way e-mail, web pages, and other material designed especially for the PDA can be loaded into a portable device. Most major media outlets provide material for anyone's PDA. Surprisingly, few campuses provide daily information to be downloaded into a PDA on events of interest. Such material would assist with student development and learning, providing an additional publicity vehicle. Using available software to create a campus information web site for PDAs is a simple venture.

With slightly more skill, the PDA user can download myriad other applications and material. A popular download is a city guide, available for most major metropolitan areas. These typically list locations of interest, hours, restaurant guides, and other tourist information. Only a few campuses provide campus guides for students' PDAs or an electronic version of the campus viewbook.

The basic knowledge base for PDAs is an overall picture of their capabilities and of the full range of commercial hardware and software. Taking advantage of the technology will require familiarity with what is being used by students and staff on a campus. Basic skill competencies will depend on the specific PDA and on the operating system being used. The ability to use standard PDA features to download and install new software and download material from the Internet are important.

Assistive Technologies

IT has provided technologies that enable people with physical challenges to more easily function on the campus. From large format computer displays to text readers for the visually impaired, IT helps in the student development and learning process. A basic familiarity with the built-in features of the Windows and Mac operating systems is an excellent starting point, and the skill to use these features is essential.

The full range of assistive technologies is a specialty area in itself, but creating web site designs that meet the needs of the visually impaired is a key skill. The entire campus collection of pages must be accessible, and student affairs professionals have always advocated for equal access. Standards and guidelines have been established by the Center for Applied Special Technology (CAST) for accessibility, and familiarity with these is essential. A basic skill would be the ability to use "Bobby" from CAST (2001) to review web pages for accessibility.

Using Information Technology to Enhance Work Processes

Perhaps the most important knowledge base and skill set of all is the ability to make all parts of IT in a student affairs division work together. IT should be used to help student affairs professionals achieve their goals and missions. Increasing the efficiency of work processes may free staff to interact with students. Integrating work processes within IT may free even more staff time, reducing routine work.

Achieving Information Technology Competence

Learning is the acquisition of knowledge, and skill is the result of experience. Learning IT is an ongoing process occurring in workshops and at desks. Once the knowledge base and skill set competencies needed in a student affairs office have been articulated, individual educational plans can be developed for staff. Workshops helping staff to learn about specific IT applications are common on many campuses. Individual tutoring by student affairs IT staff members is widely used to help upgrade staff skills, and desktop learning works well for the self-motivated.

Conclusion

Interpersonal interactions in student affairs are becoming augmented with media and computer-mediated interactions. To appropriately use media and IT requires mastery of a knowledge base and skill set. The knowledge and skill set required change regularly, but the changes also bring new opportunities to interact with students. IT will play a role in furthering our goals of student development and learning. How big a role remains uncharted territory and will be a matter of choice for the student affairs profession.

Three questions should guide the appropriate use of IT in student affairs. How can we use IT to increase efficiencies of current practices? How can we use IT to redesign our practices to be more effective? How can we use IT to facilitate student development and learning in new ways?

Increasing efficiency using IT, or fitting current practices to current IT, is a paradigm-confirming solution. In most offices redundant activities (such as data entry, correspondence, communication, and office filing practices) can immediately be made more efficient with IT. Further examination of work, by individuals or by a committee, can identify ways to make repetitive and labor-intensive work processes more efficient using IT. It is important to note that not every work practice can be made more efficient using IT, but its appropriate use should save costs.

Redesigning work processes is another paradigm-affirming solution. Work processes reflect our mental models of what needs to be done and how we should do it. By changing work processes, our mental models shift. For example, keeping an official list of recognized student organizations is done easily on paper. That official list can also be saved as a web page and made available on the Student Life web pages, increasing the efficiency of distribution and lowering costs.

Discovering innovative ways to use IT to facilitate student development and learning is a paradigm-shifting solution. An example of new ways to use IT is the development of student organization online communities using web pages, chat technologies, and discussion boards. Another example would be the use of online interactive tutorials involving students in playing out various leadership or conflict resolution scenarios and offering pre- and postscenario reflective self-diagnostic exercises.

Discovering *new* ways to use IT to facilitate student development and learning is a paradigm-cracking solution. Some point to the lack of examples to date of paradigm-cracking applications of IT as evidence that IT is simply the latest iteration of technological innovation to be used in student affairs work; others argue that the chance to use IT to do things never before possible is an exercise in working outside of the box, an enterprise in which student affairs professionals have yet to fully engage.

Knowledge and skills in IT are foundation competencies that change often. The uses of technology are moving ahead faster than the study of the effects of technology. This chapter is bereft of references based on structured inquiry because there is so little in the published literature in general and very little in the student affairs literature specifically. This situation is changing as research into how technology affects students grows. In the meantime, IT will continue to change. Today's solutions may appear quaint next year, and today's competencies may be outdated.

The extent to which IT may enhance student development and learning has yet to be evaluated. Identifying solutions in the form of new technologies might, or might not, solve old problems in new ways. Students will undoubtedly be using IT more tomorrow than today. Students will be inventing and exploring new technologies in their daily lives, and this presents an ever-changing landscape for student affairs professionals.

References

Barratt, W. (2001). *Managing information technology in student affairs.* Paper presented at National Association of Student Personnel Administrators, Seattle, WA.

Blimling, G., & Whitt, E. (1999). *Good practice in student affairs.* San Francisco: Jossey-Bass.

Brown, R., & Citrin, R. (1977). A student development transcript: Assumptions, uses and formats. *Journal of College Student Personnel, 18,* 163–168.

Center for Applied Special Technology. (2001). *Welcome to Bobby 3.2.* Peabody, MA: Author. Retrieved on November 15, 2001, from http://www.cast.org/bobby/

Cohen, M. (1998). *The shaping of American higher education: Emergence and growth of the contemporary system.* San Francisco: Jossey-Bass.

Council for Accreditation of Counseling and Related Educational Programs. (2001). *CACREP Accreditation Manual.* Alexandria, VA: Author.

Council for the Advancement of Standards in Higher Education. (2001). Preparation standards and guidelines at the master's degree level for student affairs professionals in higher education. Washington, DC: Author.

Cuban, L. (1986). *Teachers and machines: The classroom use of technology since 1920.* New York: Teachers College Press.

DeAngelis, T. (2000). Is Internet addiction real? More research is being conducted to explore the way people use—and misuse—the Internet. *APA Monitor, 31* (4). Retrieved from http://www.apa.org/monitor/apr00/addiction.html

Department of Computer Science, Iowa State University. (2002). *John Vincent Atanasoff and the birth of the digital computer.* Ames, IA: Author. Retrieved from http://www.cs.iastate.edu/jva/jva-archive.shtml

EDUCAUSE. (2002a). *EDUCAUSE guide to evaluating information technology on campus.* Washington, DC: Author. Retrieved from http://www.educause.edu/consumerguide/

EDUCAUSE. (2002b). *Mission statement.* Washington, DC: Author. Retrieved from http://www.educause.edu/about.html

Green, V.H.H. (1964). *Renaissance and reformation; survey of European history between 1450 and 1660.* New York: St. Martin's Press.

Greenfield, D. (1999). Gambling on the internet: A brief note. *Journal of Gambling Studies, 12,* 471–473.

Griffiths, M. (1997). Psychology of computer use: XLIII. Some comments on "Addictive use of the Internet" by Young. *Psychological Reports, 80,* 81–82.

Holland, J. (1966). *The psychology of vocational choice: a theory of personality types and model environments.* Waltham, MA: Blaisdell.

Institute of Paper Science and Technology. (2002). *The invention of paper.* Atlanta, GA: Author. Retrieved from http://www.ipst.edu/amp/museum_invention_paper.htm

Kraut, R., Kiesler, S., Boneva, B., Cummings, J. N., Helgeson, V., & Crawford, A. M. (2002). Internet paradox revisited. *Journal of Social Issues, 58,* 49–74.

Media Trails (2001). *Invention of E-mail.* Retrieved from http://www.mediatrails.com/internetfacts2.html

Morrill, W., Oetting, E., & Hurst, J. (1974). Dimensions of counselor functioning. *Personnel and Guidance Journal, 52,* 354–359.

Network Associates. (2000). *An introduction to cryptography.* Santa Clara, CA: Author.

Oberlin, J. L. (1996). The financial mythology of information technology: Developing a new game plan. *Cause/Effect, 19,* 21–29.

Parks, M. R., & Floyd, K. (1996). Making friends in cyberspace. *Journal of Communication, 46,* 80–97.

Sandberg, J. (1997, June 16). Talk is cheap. *The Wall Street Journal,* p. R20.

Shellenbarger, S. (1996, Nov. 20). Growing web use alters the dynamics of life at home. *Wall Street Journal,* p. B1.

Sheperd, R.-M., & Edelmann, R. J. (2001). Caught in the web. *Psychologist, 14,* 520–521.

Strange, C., & Banning, J. (2001). *Educating by design: Creating campus learning environments that work.* San Francisco: Jossey-Bass.

United States Department of Commerce. (1999). *Falling through the net: Defining the digital divide.* Retrieved from http://www.ntia.doc.gov/ntiahome/fttn99/contents.html

United States Department of Education, Office of Information Technology. (2002). *ED programs that help bridge the digital divide.* Retrieved from http://www.ed.gov/Technology/digdiv.html

Young, J. R. (2002, June 21). Experts say technology gap among colleges perpetuates "digital divide" in society. *The Chronicle of Higher Education.*

Young, K. S. (1996). Psychology of computer use: XL. Addictive use of the Internet: A case that breaks the stereotype. *Psychological Reports, 79,* 899–902.

Organizations and On-Line Resources

Academic360.com (http://academic360.com/). A metacollection of Internet resources that have been gathered for the academic job hunter.

American Association for Higher Education (http://www.aahe.org); material on portfolios (http://aahe.ital.utexas.edu/electronicportfolios/index.html)
American College Personnel Association (http://www.acpa.nche.edu)
Association for Counselor Education and Supervision, Technology Interest Network, Technical competencies for counselor education students: Recommended guidelines for program development. Retrieved 2002 from http://filebox.vt.edu/users/thohen/competencies.htm
The Center for Internet Studies (http://www.virtual-addiction.com/)
The Chronicle of Higher Education (http://chronicle.com/)
Digital Signatures (http://www.softwareindustry.org/issues/1digsig.html)
EDUCAUSE (http://www.educause.edu/)
InterNIC (http://www.internic.net/). Internet domain name registration services.
National Association of Student Personnel Administrators (http://www.naspa.org/)
Network Associates *Introduction to Cryptography* (2000) ftp://ftp.pgpi.org/pub/pgp/6.5/docs/english/IntroToCrypto.pdf.
StudentAffairs On-Line (http://www.studentaffairs.com/ejournal/).
StudentAffairs.com (http://www.studentaffairs.com)
United States Department of Education, Office of Educational Technology (http://www.ed.gov/Technology/digdiv.html)
US Internet Council (http://www.usic.org/)

Software

Videoconferencing: NetMeeting (http://www.microsoft.com/windows/netmeeting/), Yahoo Messenger (http://messenger.yahoo.com/)
SCT–Banner (http://www.sct.com)
PeopleSoft (http://www.peoplesoft.com)
Security and encryption: Pretty Good Privacy (PGP) (http://web.mit.edu/network/pgp.html), Drivecrypt (http://www.drivecrypt.com/)

Magazines

Converge (http://www.convergemag.com/)
OnlineLearning (http://www.onlinelearningmag.com/)
Syllabus (http://www.syllabus.com/)

Books

Bates, A. W. (2000). *Managing technological change.* San Francisco: Jossey-Bass.
Hawke, C. S. (2001). *Computer and internet use on campus.* San Francisco: Jossey-Bass.
Katz, R., & Associates. (1999). *Dancing with the devil.* San Francisco: Jossey-Bass.
Katz, R., & Oblinger, D. (Eds.) (2000). *The "E" is for everything.* San Francisco: Jossey-Bass.
Luker, M. (Ed.) (2000). *Preparing your campus for a networked future.* San Francisco: Jossey-Bass.
Rodrigues, D., & Rodrigues, R. (2000). *The research paper and the world wide web* (2nd ed.) NY: Prentice Hall (http://cw.prenhall.com/bookbind/pubbooks/rodrigues2/)

CHAPTER EIGHTEEN

MANAGING HUMAN RESOURCES

Jon C. Dalton

One of the most challenging and rewarding aspects of student affairs administration is the leadership and management of staff. While few individuals enter the student affairs profession to become managers, almost every advancement in leadership requires greater skills in human resource management. To be successful as a leader in the profession, one must understand the nature of student affairs organizations as well as how to effectively manage their staff and resources. This is especially important in times of institutional restructuring and downsizing in which great emphasis is placed on efficiency and productivity.

This chapter begins with a framework of goals for human resource management and examines the core values that support those goals. Building upon this conceptual framework, the chapter then examines the importance of developing core competencies and individual talents. The second half of the chapter focuses on the practical tasks of human resource management: recruitment, supervision, staff development, and several specific problem issues.

Human Resource Management Today

So many changes have occurred in the field of human resource management that a quick overview of recent developments may be useful. Until late in the twentieth century, many of our beliefs about organizations and human resource management were shaped by the effort to apply science and rational thinking to human organizations

---

Note: The author would like to acknowledge Ashley Tull, doctoral student in higher education administration at Florida State University, for contributions made to the chapter.

(see Chapter Twelve). Such thinking led to bureaucratic models of organization that emphasized division of labor, specialization of roles, hierarchies of authority, and an elaborate system of rules and laws that governed relationships and processes.

This approach to organizational structure stressed chains of command, delegation of authority, and unity of command. It was believed that such an approach would maximize efficiency and enable leaders to order and predict outcomes. For much of the twentieth century, this bureaucratic model was the dominant approach in organizational and management theory.

The bureaucratic model has several problems, however. These became increasingly apparent during the 1970s and 1980s with the rise of a new global marketplace and various alternative management approaches. Employees did not always act in predictable ways; rules did not cover every situation; innovation could be stifled by rigid, ingrained regulations and procedures; and bureaucracies were often too cumbersome to respond to rapidly changing environments. As Seymour (1994) asserts, a paradigm shift became necessary in management philosophy and practice.

Student affairs administration has experienced a shift in management and leadership approaches over the past several decades. Student affairs leaders no longer manage their organizations in any single fashion but, instead, borrow from a variety of management and leadership styles, suited for their organization and institution. Sandeen (2001), in his book *Making a Difference: Profiles of Successful Student Affairs Leaders,* stated, "there is no single formula for successful leadership in student affairs administration" (p. 4). Taylorism or Scientific Management, a system thought to standardize tasks for efficiency (Mogensen, 1996), has since given way to alternative forms including benchmarking, value added, six-sigma quality improvement, and others (Donkin, 2001). Standardization of tasks is no longer the norm in student affairs work. While thought by some to be management fads of the nineties, several trends emerged at the end of the twentieth-century—including benchmarking, reengineering (Rinehart, 2001), and the accountability movement—which are still active today.

Consequently, new approaches to organizational and management theory developed that stressed a more decentralized, collaborative, and change-oriented approach. Concepts such as cross-training, boundary spanning, participatory decision making, and quality circles reflect a new emphasis on interactive processes and less organizational rigidity and hierarchy. The new theories also recognize modern pluralism, in which social relationships are much more complex and diverse and in which there is great concern for the creation and maintenance of communities. These changes helped form the current style of human resource management in student affairs, and they can help explain some of the new directions explored in this chapter.

A Conceptual Framework for Human Resource Management

Four essential tasks provide a broad conceptual framework for human resource management in student affairs:

1. *Helping employees fulfill the responsibilities for which they were hired.* Managers represent the employing organization and have a primary responsibility to ensure that those who

are hired to perform essential student affairs tasks do so in an efficient and effective manner. Human resource management in student affairs must be grounded in the recognition that colleges and universities create student affairs positions in order to fulfill essential organizational goals and purposes. Managers must provide the necessary leadership to insure accountability for the tasks for which employees are hired to perform.

2. *Helping employees master the specific competencies necessary for success in assigned duties.* An important role of student affairs human resource managers is to provide the means for every employee to be successful in performing his or her assigned duties. While some employees can "hit the ground running," most need some time and assistance to adjust to the specific requirements of their position. This is especially true for new professionals. Harned and Murphy (1998) argue that the guidance received in the early stages of professional work is especially critical to long-term success. Staff also need opportunities to enhance their skills and knowledge in order to perform their duties with greater expertise. Thus a primary goal of human resource management is to ensure that employees are given the necessary support and resources to be successful in their job.

3. *Helping employees understand and cope—professionally and personally—with the culture and requirements of their work environment.* Student affairs work occurs within the context of a variety of higher education and community settings and thus requires some understanding of the broader work environment. Colleges and universities are unique settings with special traditions, practices, customs, values, and organizational structures and procedures. Moreover, the many departments and offices within a college or university have their own organizational culture and practices. Employees should understand both the larger institutional culture and the specific local cultures that constitute their own work environment.

4. *Helping employees engage in continual learning, professional development, and personal renewal.* Richmond (1986) claims that the supervisor is responsible for performance and growth and ultimately the continued employment of staff with the institution. Richmond's advice may overstate the responsibility of the supervisor, but his emphasis upon the critical influence of supervision on employee performance and development is well taken. Cone (1968) argues that organizational obsolescence occurs when staff lose the technical, interpersonal, and political skills necessary to perform their jobs. Student affairs positions are so demanding in terms of time and pressure that burnout and obsolescence are ever-present dangers. Individuals need opportunities for development and renewal to adapt to the changing circumstances of their lives and work environment. Employees who increase their knowledge and skills and grow professionally are much more likely to be effective in their work and relationships.

Lindquist (1981) points out that there is usually an important personal dimension to professional development, which cannot be overlooked. Personal concerns have a way of intruding into all domains. For example, staff members struggling with financial problems, children leaving home, or personal health problems will likely bring these concerns to their job, whether they intend to or not. The student affairs leader must recognize these hidden concerns and how such problems affect employee performance and relationships.

Productivity is ultimately a function of the vitality and energy employees bring to their work. Most of us can remember the enthusiasm we felt about our first job and the energy we poured into it. Such high energy and enthusiasm can be maintained if employees are given opportunities for personal renewal and development (Kay, 1974). Later in this chapter we will examine in more detail how to organize a comprehensive staff development program.

In summary, the goals of human resource management relate to four essential objectives:

- *The organization:* helping employees fulfill the responsibilities for which they were hired
- *The task:* helping employees master necessary job skills
- *The situation:* helping employees thrive in the work culture and environment
- *The person:* helping employees achieve personal and professional development and renewal

This conceptual framework is useful in developing a practical and effective program for human resource management that is faithful to the purposes of student affairs work. Moreover, the four objectives outlined above are applicable to all employees—professionals, support staff, and student employees. (The best method for applying them depends, of course, on different groups of employees and different institutional settings.)

The Place of Values in Human Resource Management

Every model of human resource management has explicit and implicit values. High-performing organizations function within a context of particular values (Kuh, 1983). Effective organizations communicate their values clearly and help employees identify with and support those values. Young (1993; also see Chapter Five) identifies four philosophical schools of thought that have informed the values of the student affairs profession: rationalism, empiricism, pragmatism, and postmodernism. Values are important in organizations because they help define how and why certain things should be done. Values are what bind organizations together and create a sense of common purpose (Pastin, 1991). So it is important to identify and briefly discuss the values essential to effective human resource management and development. These values are summed up in the following five statements:

1. *Employees are individuals with unique abilities and needs that transcend group characteristics.* One should not lose sight of employees' individuality, no matter how many employees one supervises nor how routine or common their duties. Every person brings something special and different to his or her job. Recognizing individuals' needs and valuing their personal contributions are very important to successful supervision and in building effective teams and organizations.

2. *Excellence in organizations requires a high level of regard for and utilization of the talents of organizational members.* Personnel costs are typically the greatest single budget item in

student affairs organizations. Thus, a student affairs organization's personnel represent its greatest financial investment. Unfortunately, employees are too often viewed merely as workers who provide specific and often narrowly defined service roles rather than as a rich source of talent that can serve the organization in many ways. (The concept of talent development will be examined more fully later in the chapter.)

3. *Fairness and equal consideration in relationships with employees is the bedrock of human resource management.* This is one of those rules learned in kindergarten: be fair! Like most simple truths in life, it is easy to comprehend but very difficult to practice. Because employees are so different from one another (and some are more agreeable than others), leaders are often inclined to treat them differently. But the perception that a leader favors or gives preferential treatment to some employees on matters relating to job performance can be very damaging to the leader's effectiveness and to organizational excellence. Conversely, leaders who are perceived as fair can command great loyalty and even sacrifice from employees.

4. *The most powerful motivator of human development is personal challenge.* This is created by high performance standards, feedback, and a clear reward structure. As with student development, challenge is the key to employee growth and development. Individuals respond to expectations of high performance when they are challenged to do so and given consistent support and recognition by leaders.

5. *Effective organizations have identifiable shared values and beliefs that provide a common framework of purpose and meaning for employees.* The importance of a clear sense of organizational values has been repeatedly stressed in research on organizational development (Adams, 1984; Albanese, 1978; Kuh, 1983; Schein, 1988). Individuals' efforts are energized and focused when there is widespread agreement on organizational goals (Du Brin, 1978). For example, promoting the welfare of students is a central goal of student affairs organizations. Highly visible, shared goals such as this help integrate organizations by giving employees a clear sense of organizational values, clear objectives, and a sense of common purpose. An organization's core values should be clearly articulated by leaders and integrated into all aspects of the organization's activities.

Talent Development: Maximizing Human Potential

One of the most important changes in human resource management in recent years has been the recognition of the employee as a dynamic organizational participant whose talent and potential for productivity and innovation are often untapped. Jacoby, Astin, and Ayala (1987) describe talent development as a process of focusing on changes and improvement in employees' performance, starting when they are first hired. When a new staff member is hired, the organization is gaining an individual who can not only perform certain tasks but also potentially do many other things to further the organization's goals. When an individual's potential talents are ignored, both the individual and the organization lose. But when employees are viewed as individuals with diverse talents that can be tapped and developed, the benefits can be enormous.

Few job roles in higher education remain static. Rather, job responsibilities are constantly undergoing alterations to respond to changing circumstances and changing student populations. Employees are constantly changing in their knowledge and capabilities. Consequently, human resources must be viewed as dynamic and full of potential. Thus a primary task of the leader is to identify, develop, and channel the resource of employee talent in the midst of ever-changing circumstances. This task is particularly challenging today because of increasing diversity in the student affairs work force. More men and women from a variety of racial, ethnic, and cultural backgrounds are represented in student affairs work than in the past, and this trend will continue in the future. Increasing human diversity provides a richer array of talent and resources; leaders must see the potential of such diversity and provide opportunities to tap the advantages it offers.

Since human development is a lifelong process, it is important to provide for and facilitate employees' continuing development. Student affairs organizations should be concerned with providing staff not only with the necessary skills for their current jobs but also skills required for their future development. A distinction should be made between training and development. According to Anthony, Kacmar, and Perrewe (2002), training provides staff necessary skills they can use on the job immediately, while development provides employees knowledge that can be used on the job immediately or in the future. Most individuals regard their career as a major focal point of their personal growth and development. Employees want to succeed in their jobs and welcome opportunities that will both enhance their development and benefit their organization. Effective student affairs leaders look for ways to promote talent development so that employees have the opportunity to continue to grow and thereby achieve sustained excellence in their work.

Many student affairs organizations have now employed human resource development specialists to identify staff training needs and coordinate training and development initiatives. Human resource development specialists may work as full-time staff or be employed on a contractual basis. The use of staff development committees made up of departmental staff from across the organization is another useful training and development strategy. Staff development committees are recommended for large student affairs organizations, where training needs may not be apparent to upper levels of administration. Staff development committees can also provide professional development opportunities for those members who are appointed or selected to serve. Information on training and development trends in student affairs, higher education, and human resource management can be obtained from the National Association of Student Personnel Administrators (NASPA), American College Personnel Association (ACPA), College and University Professional Association for Human Resources (CUPA-HR), American Society for Training and Development (ASTD), and the Society for Human Resource Management (SHRM).

Some of the most important management strategies for promoting talent development include the following:

1. *Assess employees' basic skills and knowledge.* To utilize employees' talents, one must know what they are. Some information about employees' skills and talents is gained

from resumes and interviews, but unfortunately many employee skills, interests, and abilities go unrecognized. A basic assessment of employee skills and knowledge should be conducted at the time of hiring and then updated on a regular basis as part of the annual evaluation process. This assessment should also gather information on employees' attitudes, interests, and self-knowledge. Such information will help leaders understand the personality and personal perspectives of each employee—often very important factors in an employee's success or failure.

2. *Design specific learning and performance objectives.* Supervisors can encourage talent development by working with employees to design learning and performance objectives and then, as Clement and Rickard (1992) stress, providing regular informal feedback to employees on their accomplishments. For example, young staff members typically have limited experience in budget management and planning. A good supervisor can work with new professionals to design practical training in budget management that enhances their basic knowledge and skills and, at the same time, provides them with some important personal mentoring and feedback. Such an approach helps identify promising areas for professional growth and achievement and serves as a powerful personal motivator.

3. *Focus on changes and improvement in employees' performance.* Too often, the focus in evaluations of employee performance is solely on correcting problems. The most effective way to correct failures is to help employees understand as clearly as possible what is expected of them and to provide specific directions on how to achieve the required level of performance. This is the mentoring role of supervision, and it can be one of the most useful and rewarding roles of leadership.

4. *Recognize and reward achievement.* Recognizing and rewarding achievement are the most powerful motivators for developing employees' talents and performance (Sandeen, 1991). There are many ways to reward achievement in job performance, including salary increases, glowing performance evaluations, special assignments, expanded job responsibilities, verbal praise, and personal complimentary notes. All of these means of recognition and reward can be especially effective when combined within a consistent pattern of supervision. Bringing out the best in employees is directly related to the support and recognition they receive for their talents. Salary increases are certainly appreciated, but they are often less important than other forms of recognition for a job well done.

5. *Train employees for leadership.* One of the basic principles of talent development is to help employees maximize their skills and abilities for leadership. Leadership is more than excellent job performance. Leadership involves an understanding of problems and issues that go beyond one's own job description and a willingness to take responsibility for solving those problems even when there is no requirement or expectation to do so. Training employees for leadership is a powerful means of developing individual talent and strengthening organizations.

6. *Measure learning and development outcomes.* Supervisors are often unable to systematically document improvements in employee performance. Assessing development is a difficult task in any area of human development, and it is especially difficult in the workplace. The most effective supervisors work with employees to establish specific

performance goals, identify the means for achieving those goals, and then evaluate whether employees actually achieve them.

Staff Development: Common Knowledge and Core Competencies

As Terkel (1974) eloquently put it, "Most people have work that is too small for their spirits" (p. 175). Human development is an inescapable aspect of effective personnel management. It provides opportunities for training, motivating staff, developing teamwork, and enhancing organizational effectiveness. Deegan, Steele, and Thielen (1990) claim that staff development is the pillar of any system of management. Moreover, student affairs staff trained in human development theory are more likely to recognize the importance of ongoing personal development and to expect it from their leaders. Development activities provide an essential bridge from employees' graduate education to their professional practice. Staff development programs help employees make the necessary personal transition from studying a profession to becoming a professional. Furthermore, staff development provides a baseline of content and skills training that ensures those employees without a degree in student affairs possess the necessary competencies to fulfill their job roles and responsibilities.

The dramatic impact of computer technology on our society is mirrored in the student affairs profession (see Chapter Seventeen). Hardly any area of student affairs has been unaffected by the computer revolution. Moreover, the pace of change, both in hardware and software, has been swift and dramatic, requiring staff to almost constantly upgrade their computer skills. Familiarity with general computer technology is important for all student affairs staff, as is competence in specific applications used by particular student affairs professionals. Thus, staff development programs should include opportunities for employees to develop knowledge and skills in computer technologies used in student affairs settings.

An important contemporary staff development strategy is the promotion of team building and collaboration. Many new management theories stress the importance of employee involvement in quality circles or other small teams that promote an exchange of ideas and shared problem solving. (Some of the new constructs emerging in postconventional organizations are discussed by George Kuh in Chapter Twelve.)

As Baier (1985) points out, the work of student affairs requires a wide variety of skills, including counseling, teaching, supervising, managing budgets, knowing group dynamics, and managing computer technology. Student affairs organizations are composed of individuals with very different professional training, experience, and job responsibilities. This great diversity of roles and specializations often makes it difficult to achieve a sense of common purpose and shared objectives within a student affairs organization.

Consequently, all staff should possess certain basic knowledge and competencies geared toward achieving the goals of the organization. Canon (1985) describes this as a remediation process, in which employees are provided a common ground of knowledge and core skills. Following are some of the most important aspects of this common ground:

1. *The nature and history of the institution.* Every employee should be familiar with the origin, traditions, and historic mission of the institution where they work. Such information helps staff understand and appreciate why the institution has its present form and practices and how their role fits into the institutional culture.

2. *The goals, policies, and procedures of the student affairs organization.* Every student affairs organization has certain policies and procedures that guide the organization and define its boundaries and standards of professional practice. Not only should employees be familiar with these organizational policies and procedures, they should also understand the rationale behind them. Some practices are required by law, some by state governing boards, some by institutions, and some by student affairs organizations themselves.

3. *A profile of the characteristics of students served.* Institutions of higher education differ widely in part because they serve very different student bodies. For example, students who attend predominantly undergraduate residential colleges generally have quite different characteristics from students who attend urban commuter institutions or community colleges. It is important to recognize that the work of student affairs is shaped by the unique characteristics and needs of different student populations (see Chapter Three).

Not only do student characteristics differ by institutional type, they also change over time. Consequently, student affairs staff should be familiar with the profile of the student body they serve, including such information as basic demographics, educational aspirations, academic achievement, personal goals and values, prior activities and experiences, and current needs. Much information is usually available about students from the admission, testing, and matriculation processes. Freshmen data generated by UCLA's Higher Education Research Institute each spring provide a comprehensive national report on entering freshmen, both nationally and by institution. *The Chronicle of Higher Education* and other higher education publications are also good sources of information about today's college student body. Levine and Cureton's *When Hope and Fear Collide: A Portrait of Today's College Student* is a qualitative account of college student's activities that is very useful in understanding student characteristics. Sadly, student affairs staff do not always take full advantage of such information.

4. *Ethical standards of practice.* Every profession within higher education needs clear standards of right and wrong to guide its members in their work. Knowing the standards of one's profession and institution is an important prerequisite for ethical practice. It is particularly important for student affairs staff, since they are often the most visible role models on campus. As Canon (1989) suggested, student affairs staff serve as the conscience of the campus.

"Right" and "wrong" in professional practice are defined by the ethical standards established by professional organizations and individual colleges and universities. In addition, law and social mores define many areas of ethical conduct. Student affairs practice includes some special ethical standards and obligations. One such standard in many student affairs organizations is that staff members do not have consenting sexual relationships with students. Student affairs staff need to understand and observe such standards in their work, and they must have the opportunity to examine them as a regular part of their professional preparation and practice.

5. *Basic communication skills.* While it may seem unnecessary to provide training in communication skills, student affairs staff do need ongoing opportunities for learning how to communicate effectively. There are two reasons for this. First, as has been discussed above, student affairs staff come from many disciplines and backgrounds. Consequently, they often have difficulty understanding one another's perspective and communication style.

Second, student affairs work is very often done in teams or small work groups, in which collaboration and interpersonal communication are essential. In such situations, being effective in one's job depends upon good listening skills, knowing how to give constructive feedback, and being able to interact effectively with colleagues and students. This is particularly important in highly diverse institutions.

6. *Leadership skills.* In every student affairs position, success depends to some degree on specific leadership competencies such as decision-making skills, the ability to organize and plan, a capacity to work effectively with others, and an ability to take the initiative. As mentioned previously, some individuals have a special talent for leadership that can be enhanced through training and practice. But every staff member can be taught certain basic leadership skills and given opportunities to develop them. Encouraging leadership skills and helping staff to see themselves as leaders are powerful tools for staff development and effective performance. (See Chapter Twenty for a detailed discussion of leadership.)

7. *Time management skills.* A common dilemma for student affairs staff is how to manage all the demands of their jobs and live up to the numerous expectations placed upon them. When student affairs staff are unable to manage the heavy demands of their job, they burn out, lose interest, become resentful, or simply look for another place to work. Sometimes they do all three. Student affairs work is by nature time-consuming, demanding, and sometimes hectic, because of the energy and needs of students and the busy pace of university life. Staff need to develop basic coping and time management skills so they can work effectively in such settings.

Finally, two highly individualized staff development activities should be mentioned. Mentoring and self-directed training can be effective techniques for staff development in some situations. In a mentoring relationship, a more experienced professional serves as a personal advisor and resource guide for a less experienced staff member. Mentor relationships can be beneficial for the mentor as they can gain a sense of renewal and redefined purpose serendipitously through the process of mentoring staff members (Zachary, 2000). Self-directed training permits staff members to learn independently and focus on particular skills or knowledge that may be of special interest or relevance. Self-directed activities also enable individuals to study at their own pace while still participating in an organized educational program.

Staff development programs come in all shapes and sizes. Although there is not space in this chapter to describe each type in detail, the following list includes the most popular types:

- New staff orientation
- Workshops and seminars
- Newsletters and in-house communications
- Self-directed study
- Leaves of absence for formal academic course work
- Temporary staff assignments
- Interdepartmental staff exchanges
- Mentoring
- Team projects and group activities
- Staff development committees
- Coaching
- Combinations of the above (a "cafeteria approach")

Recruiting Staff: Tips on Finding the Best Employees

Any organization can only be as good as the individuals it employs. Hiring talented and capable employees for every job role in the organization is one of the most important functions of student affairs leaders. Although even the most effective search process cannot guarantee that the best candidate will always be hired, it will enhance the odds of generating the best possible pool of candidates.

Unfortunately, many excellent candidates are lost in job searches because of problems such as delays, miscommunication, the appearance of disorganization, lack of attention or enthusiasm, or a need for information. When competing for top candidates who may also be considering other job offers, any one of these problems can result in the loss of a good candidate. Consequently, staff recruitment must be organized and administered in a very efficient manner. An effective search consists of the following steps:

1. *Orient the search committee.* Every search committee member needs to be clear about the demands of the position and the kind of candidate being sought to fill it. Failure to orient the search committee is the single most common reason why search committees wind up disagreeing over final candidates. The supervisor responsible for the position to be filled should normally provide this orientation. He or she should be as specific as possible about the necessary qualifications and the most important responsibilities of the position. The committee should also clearly understand its role and authority in the search process.

2. *Draw up an accurate job description.* To conduct an effective search, a current and accurate job description must be available. Investing sufficient time and effort in clearly defining job duties and required qualifications will save the search committee and interviewers from wasted time and effort as they sort through the candidates for the job. Trying to hire the right candidate for a position with an ill-defined job description is like trying to find an unfamiliar destination without a road map. When writing the job

description, time should be taken to conduct a task analysis. Task analysis is described by Desimone, Werner, and Harris (2002) as "a systematic collection of data about a specific job or group of jobs to determine what an employee should be taught to achieve optimal performance" (p. 137). The task analysis is usually conducted by the hiring supervisor and provides an opportunity to update the knowledge, skills, and abilities portion of the job description. Task analysis also identifies learning opportunities for newly hired staff. Staff responsibilities are ever changing in student affairs administration and supervisors need to take the opportunity to review current expectations and bring the job description more in line with the actual job being performed by the individual in the position. You are never quite sure where you are going, and you often don't realize when you have arrived. The job description is the road map to hiring the best candidate. Without it there is sure to be confusion and disagreement.

3. *Follow job-posting guidelines.* Posting is the process of publicly advertising a vacant position and formally announcing that candidates are being sought. The public announcement is generally made only after the job description has been clearly defined and the search committee has been formed and oriented. Requirements and customs differ with respect to how posting is conducted; thus it is important to be clear about what your institution expects. Many institutions are required to follow specific guidelines in listing positions to comply with affirmative action and other state and federal regulations. The basic principle behind such guidelines is to ensure that a wide and diverse pool of qualified individuals are informed of the job vacancy and have an equal opportunity to compete for the position.

4. *Screen all job applicants.* All applicants' written credentials and supporting materials are reviewed to narrow the field of candidates down to a group of finalists. Those candidates who are not qualified for the position are eliminated, and the candidates with the strongest credentials and experience are identified.

5. *Interview the finalists.* The next step is to conduct personal interviews with the finalists to determine which are the most qualified. This is usually accomplished through campus visits, telephone calls, or other personal contacts designed to learn as much as possible about the candidates. Interviewing is in many respects the most crucial stage in the search process. Most candidates who advance to the interview stage are capable individuals who have demonstrated, at least on paper, that they can provide the leadership needed for the position. The purpose of the interview process is to determine which individual, if any, provides the best fit for the position. The interview process is also an important opportunity for candidates to assess whether the job is a good fit for themselves. Many things about a candidate cannot be determined solely through written credentials. A person's personality, communication skills, interpersonal skills, and leadership skills can best be determined through personal interaction in a series of structured interviews in which a variety of individuals can observe and evaluate the candidate.

6. *Check of the applicant's references.* Reference checks are important in the hiring process of any new staff member. This is often an overlooked and underemphasized step in the process. We may think we know a candidate well based on interviews, but can we can learn much more from those who have supervised or worked with the

candidate in the past. The chair or members of the search committee or the hiring supervisor can conduct reference checks. The use of a standard list of questions, used with all candidates, is best for collecting an equal amount and type of data on each candidate.

7. *Make the hiring decision.* If the search process works well, the best choice is usually apparent. When there is clear agreement and enthusiasm about a single candidate who is judged to clearly excel, the hiring decision is a happy task. But when there is no clearly superior candidate, the hiring decision is a difficult one indeed. At this point the hiring official has the responsibility to weigh all the information and recommendations and determine who should be offered the job.

Before any job offer is officially made, it is very important to verify that final hiring authority has been secured. Some institutions, for example, require clearance from the affirmative action office before a job offer is extended. Job offers are generally not official until all necessary paperwork is complete and the institution's final hiring authority has given its written approval. It is important to recognize the distinction between authorization to search and authorization to hire.

Ultimately, unit supervisors are responsible for the candidate who is hired; consequently, they should make the final determination of which candidate provides the best fit for the position. In the event that the supervisor's decision differs substantially from the recommendations of the screening committee, the committee should be provided with an explanation of the decision.

8. *Orientation of the new staff member.* The recruitment and selection of new staff should not end with the job offer. The organizational entry and orientation of the new employee should be coordinated by staff within the organization and may include members of the search committee, where appropriate. Desimone et al. (2002) stated, "Orientation programs are designed to introduce new employees to the job, their supervisor and co-workers, and the organization" (p. 300). The orientation process is also important for the new staff member for learning about job expectations, organizational culture, and their role within the organization. A well-conducted orientation can ensure a smooth transition and contribute significantly to the job satisfaction and retention of the new staff member.

Supervision: The Art of Getting the Best Out of Employees

Almost every employee wants to succeed and looks for ways to continue to grow and be successful. Often what employees need and look for in terms of supervision does not cost a great deal of money nor require a large investment of time. Most staff want simply to know that their work matters and that it makes a difference.

There are some effective ways to let staff know that what they do matters and makes a valuable contribution to the organization. The following strategies are especially effective in motivating employees to enhance their performance:

1. *Notice good work.* Nothing encourages good performance like noticing good work. Noticing good work can be as simple as a comment or complimentary note or as formal

as pinning a medal on an employee. Good work should never go unnoticed. Noticing quality work is one of the most important roles of managers and one of the most powerful stimulants for promoting excellence.

2. *Maintain a personal touch.* Nothing kills incentive like the perception that one is simply a faceless member of an organization. Much of life is filled with the impersonal experiences of waiting in lines, fighting traffic, dealing with crowds and strangers, and so on. Supervisors who focus on individual employees, get to know them personally, and touch base with them occasionally on a personal level can develop strong loyalty and commitment from employees. These small efforts yield large performance dividends. Boyett and Conn (1992) claim that the heart of the new management style is to treat people as individuals so that they are motivated to be creative and make significant contributions.

3. *Interpret the meaning of employees' work.* Often employees perform roles or tasks that are so specialized or isolated that they have difficulty seeing how their efforts affect overall outcomes. Leaders can play a very important role in helping employees see the larger context of their work and understand how it contributes to organizational outcomes.

4. *Communicate shared values.* As noted above, it is very important for employees to understand their work in the context of the organization's shared goals and values. Adams (1984) claims that effective organizations, like effective people, operate best as integrated wholes. Understanding the shared values of the organization helps individual staff members see their work in the context of a broader purpose and meaning. Leaders help motivate staff when they talk about the shared values of the organization and communicate their personal commitment to and support for those values.

5. *Communicate personal values.* Unfortunately, too many supervisors assume that they must keep their own personal values and beliefs private, since values are often subjective and contentious. It is impossible to mask them, however, since what a person values and believes always finds a way into his or her conduct and communications. Moreover, employees expect leaders to have convictions about the most important aspects of their work and human relationships, to articulate personal values, and to model them in their behavior.

6. *Practice synergistic leadership.* A synergistic style of supervision places strong emphasis on joint effort, two-way communication, and a cooperative, mutual investment in achieving organizational goals (Winston & Creamer, 1997). One of the strengths of this style of supervision is its emphasis on actively involving employees in defining organizational goals and helping them to feel a personal sense of loyalty and pride in the achievement of the goals.

It is true that supervisors relinquish a certain amount of power in this approach to supervision, but they gain a more highly motivated employee who has a much deeper personal stake in the success of the enterprise. The synergistic approach can take more time because a supervisor must provide opportunities for dialogue, feedback, and a certain amount of disagreement that can develop as part of the two-way communication. A supervisor cannot expect loyalty and pride to develop in staff if they do not support genuine opportunities for staff to make meaningful contributions to defining and achieving organizational goals.

One of the temptations of leaders is to utilize their power to expedite organizational processes. When the pressure is on it becomes tempting to resort to an authoritative style both for convenience and for sake of time. However, when supervision adopts an authoritative style it results in something being done to staff rather than a cooperative activity (Winston & Creamer, 1997).

The best supervisors seem to be those who have developed a collegial relationship with staff, who respected staff competency and participation but actively led and guided, usually through collaborative leadership styles, but sometimes through specific direction and control. A supervisor must not be hesitant to use authority in their leadership role because there will be inevitable circumstances that require immediate and direct action. It has been my experience that a synergistic supervisory style makes it much easier to take directed action when it is needed because there usually exists a high level of trust and loyalty among employees.

7. *Recognize and handle burnout and stress.* Ward (1995) stated, "The student affairs field currently faces many pressures—budget reductions, downsizing, growing student activism, facility decay, racial tensions and rapid advances in technology, to name a few" (p. 35). These pressures can lead to burnout and stress among student affairs professionals. Burnout has negative physical consequences and can also lead to the loss of sustaining interest and commitment over time. The ability to sustain professional work at a high level of productivity and commitment depends upon a lifestyle that renews and regenerates. Renewal is not only a matter of reducing physical stress through exercise and good health habits; it is also a matter of rekindling one's spirit through creative diversions and outlets of relaxation. Student affairs roles can be notoriously demanding on one's time and energies. While it is possible to burn the candle at both ends when one is young, such a lifestyle has a long-time corrosive effect on enthusiasm, energy, and spirit.

The ability to sustain high energy and commitment to work over time requires a discipline of renewal that is a regular part of one's personal and professional lifestyle. Different things are renewing for different people but some of the ways in which many find regeneration include physical exercise, study and reflection, meditation, travel, hobbies, time with family and friends, or writing. While many things may qualify as "renewing" for different individuals, the effects they share in common include the reduction of stress, diversion from the primary tasks and responsibilities of work, the opportunity for reflection and new perspectives on self and work, and the opportunity for feedback and reflection on the meaning and purpose of one's work and contributions. Activities for renewal may include temporary job assignments, interdepartmental job exchanges, teamwork or group projects, conference attendance, and participation in mentoring relationships, as mentioned earlier.

Good supervisors provide structured opportunities for renewal of their staff through staff development activities and personal mentoring and feedback. Preventing burnout, however, is ultimately a responsibility of every professional and a function of their ability to develop a sustaining and renewing lifestyle.

Supervising Different Types and Levels of Positions

Supervision is one of the most difficult tasks of student affairs leadership. At one end of the continuum of student affairs staff are highly trained professional staff who, like faculty, feel they should not be supervised by anyone. At the other end of the continuum are the new and inexperienced employees who often need extensive supervision in order to perform their assigned tasks. Student affairs professionals may be surprised at the different types of positions they are expected to supervise in the higher education setting. What is often unexpected is the wide range of other types of positions a student affairs professional may supervise including paraprofessionals, part-time staff, hourly labor positions, graduate assistants, student employees, contract employees, temporary staff, and sometimes even faculty.

The management of teams within the organization can be challenging. Wagner and Hollenbeck (2001) defined teams as "a type of group characterized by tight interdependence, cross-functional expertise, and differential information among members" (p. 574). Student affairs organizations are notorious for assembling teams to address issues affecting students or solve complex problems. Teams are used for advisory and planning purposes, appellate decisions, assessment and accreditation, and selection committees to name a few. The greatest strengths of teams can also be their greatest downfall. Team members bring with them expertise and leadership experience from within their department or specific field, but the team's task may require a combination of staff attributes for a solution or team action, causing conflict among team members when disagreement occurs. The purpose for appointment of staff members to serve as a team must be clearly defined, and a leader should be appointed or selected by the membership. Effective teams require good followers, as well as good leaders.

There are several reasons for such diversity of job roles in student affairs. First, the diversity and complexity of contemporary student services in higher education requires staff with a wide range of skills and training. Second, student affairs organizations typically include large physical plant operations such as residence halls, student unions, recreation centers, and health centers. These types of operations require support personnel in the skilled trades, maintenance, custodial, security, and clerical. Third, student services operations are affected by the seasonal changes of the academic calendar so that a diverse mix of full-time, part-time, and temporary employees are needed to operate programs and facilities efficiently.

Supervising such a diverse work force requires an understanding of the policies, rules, and procedures that apply to different classes of employees and an understanding of the needs and expectations of individuals who work in such diverse job roles. The work schedules of hourly workers must, for example, be documented and managed in a much more formal and detailed fashion than professional staff whose work schedules are much more flexible and open. Student affairs organizations are one of the largest employers of students on campus. Supervision of students involves not only the knowledge of particular employment guidelines and procedures, but also a special trust and responsibility for their welfare and development.

Such a wide range of skill levels and responsibilities on the part of staff requires highly refined supervisory skills. Moreover, the greater the level of supervisory responsibility the wider the range of types of employees there are to supervise. Normally, as one progresses in their career there are expanding levels of supervisory responsibility. Experience is a great teacher and one develops the knowledge and competency to supervise an increasingly wider range of employees through practice and reflection.

While it is important to understand the special needs and circumstances of different types of employees, good supervision also requires consistency and uniformity of leadership style and values. Employees need to feel, regardless of their differences, that their supervisor is fair, consistent, and concerned about them. Good supervision does not require expert knowledge about every employee's work, but it does require good human relations skills and high ethical standards.

Good supervisors provide an appropriate level of direction and feedback to help employees to achieve greater levels of self-direction. Excellence in supervision provides the right levels of support and direction at times when they are needed. Too much supervision is ineffective, and perhaps more so, than too little supervision. The effective supervisor does not get in the way of a good employee and seeks to encourage their autonomy. In this regard it is important to note how critical supervision is for new professionals and student employees. More directed supervision is usually needed for these employees and requires considerable time and individuation.

Where Managers Fail

Some areas of human resource management are especially difficult trouble spots that merit special discussion. Failure to recognize the following mistakes and handle them appropriately can result in serious personnel problems:

1. *Underestimating personnel issues.* Personnel issues can be highly deceiving. What appears to be a minor problem can mask a torment of feelings and complexity. Never underestimate an employee's problem. Treat every issue seriously until the nature of it is more fully known.

2. *Rewarding the wrong behavior.* It is a common failing of managers to "grease the squeaky wheel," to give in to persistent pressure or give the greatest attention to those who make the greatest noise. Pressure tactics used by some employees can make it difficult for leaders not to compromise, but rewarding the wrong behavior weakens a leader's credibility with all employees and sets him or her up for repeated failures.

3. *Pursuing the task without a vision.* Every employee needs to have a well-defined set of tasks; nothing is quite as frustrating on the job as an ill-defined assignment. Yet every employee must also be able to see how their specific responsibilities fit into the mission and goals of the department and division. Seeing only the trees, without a guiding perspective on the forest, makes one's work seem ultimately unsatisfying and unimportant. But a task imbued with a vision is powerful and energizing for the employee.

4. *Pursuing the vision without a task.* Hickman (1992) notes that charismatic leaders motivate organizations to action, but managers are necessary to run them. Some leaders set powerful visions for their organization but are ineffective at translating those visions into practical tasks for their staff. Consequently, when the emotion and energy of the vision wanes, there is little accomplished on an ongoing basis to sustain the vision. Managers fail when they create lofty goals but do not help employees translate those goals into practical and achievable tasks.

5. *Failing to see leadership as service.* Every leader is tempted by the power and influence of leadership. No matter how great or small the leadership role, there is a constant threat of self-importance. It is especially important in student affairs to maintain a service-oriented leadership style. When leaders keep a clear perspective on their role as enablers of others they seem better able to keep their personal needs in balance with the needs of others. Much of new management theory stresses the facilitating role of effective leaders.

6. *Ignoring your own advice.* One of the quickest and easiest ways to fail as a manager is to ignore your own advice. Leaders who consistently do themselves what they expect others to do provide a very powerful example for employees. No exceptions go unnoticed by employees, and repeated exceptions completely undermine a leader's moral authority. No leader should expect others to respect what they are not prepared to honor themselves.

Things That Go Bump in the Night

Some contemporary human resource problems in student affairs are so complex and intense that they are the source of many sleepless nights for student affairs leaders. Recognizing the following issues and preparing for them can help student affairs leaders negotiate this difficult terrain when the going gets really rough:

1. *Economic and organizational downsizing.* At some point every organization faces changes that threaten the status quo. In recent years, much of higher education has been going through a process of restructuring. (See Chapter Fifteen for a thorough examination of organizational restructuring in higher education.) Such times are very threatening to employees and create special challenges for leaders. Employees need to understand what changes are taking place and why. The worst enemy of leadership in such situations is rumor. The perception that changes are occurring in an orderly and just manner is critical to employee morale and productivity. The most important tool of leadership in such tough times is a well-thought-out plan of action that incorporates the input of many staff and utilizes an effective process of communication. Bad news is bad news, but it can be minimized through responsible and humane administration. Also, as increasing numbers of colleges and universities choose to hire private firms to provide a variety of support services, leaders must adapt to working with contract employees.

2. *Sexual harassment.* Complaints about sexual harassment have become much more frequent in higher education since the 1990s. New laws prohibiting such conduct have

been enacted, and existing laws are more strongly enforced than in the past. Education and awareness regarding problems of sexual harassment have helped change social attitudes and empower individuals to take action against such mistreatment. Student affairs organizations must clearly prohibit such conduct, educate employees regarding procedures for redressing sexual harassment, and strongly administer sanctions when such behavior occurs.

3. *Discrimination and equal treatment.* Unlawful discrimination against individuals is not only illegal, it tears at the fabric of any organization. Discrimination dehumanizes individuals based on human characteristics over which they have no ultimate control. Student affairs leaders must be constantly vigilant, committed, and result-oriented with respect to this issue. As college students and the higher education work force become increasingly diverse, the incidence of illegal discrimination and unequal treatment is likely to increase. As with sexual harassment, the key management responsibilities are to clearly prohibit such conduct, to educate employees regarding procedures for redressing it when it does occur, and to administer strong sanctions for all violations. An important prevention strategy is to institute an active education and awareness program that fosters appreciation of differences and socializes employees to embrace pluralism in the workplace.

For some issues related to discrimination, a clear legal or moral consensus is lacking—both in the workplace and in society at large—concerning how employers should proceed. One such issue pertains to domestic partner relationships. Some colleges and universities provide housing, insurance, and other benefits to domestic partners of gay, lesbian, and bisexual employees; other institutions do not. If there are neither institutional guidelines to follow nor a clear consensus on the proper course of action, student affairs leaders must determine the appropriate actions through a consideration of pertinent legal, ethical, and political variables. Such issues are often the most difficult test of leadership.

4. *When things fall apart: leadership and organizational change.* One of the eventualities of professional work is that sooner or later leaders and organizations change—often at the same time. Familiar patterns and practices are disrupted, and employees experience uncertainty about their roles and livelihood. While such changes are often viewed with anxiety and fear, they almost always present an opening for new opportunities and directions. Staff are more likely to succeed during times of significant change if they maintain a positive outlook. Employees can help shape the direction of change by offering creative ideas and solutions to problems. Learning to adjust to change and effectively utilize the change process are very important professional survival skills.

5. *When good people do bad things: dealing with individual failures.* All of us fail at some point in our career. When failure is the result of sheer negligence, ineptitude, or deception, it may be difficult to execute the necessary disciplinary action, but it is usually not difficult to determine that some corrective action is needed. Dealing with the failures of good employees is another situation. When a good employee fails, the task of responding to the failure is more complex. One temptation is to ignore the failure, because the employee so seldom fails; another is to overreact to the failure, because it

is simply out of character for the employee. Both responses can hurt the employee's development and relationship with you, the supervisor. It is very important to openly acknowledge the failures of good employees but to do so in a way that also affirms their overall strengths and contributions.

6. *Terminating employees:* Student affairs administrators have a plethora of euphemisms for the term "firing." We "terminate" employees, "let them go," "non-renew" their contracts, and "give them notice," but seldom do we "fire" them. The truth is that higher education administrators and student affairs administrators in particular have great difficulty in firing employees. Except for grievous causes, terminating an employee usually involves a lengthy process in which the employee is given time to exhaust any grievance appeals and find other employment. Student affairs supervisors have special difficulty in terminating employees because of their training as helping professionals, their collegial culture, or their deeply rooted beliefs in the developmental potential of all individuals. For those who practice a synergistic style of supervision, having to terminate an employee also involves at least some recognition that the supervisor has failed as well as the employee.

In these situations, student affairs supervisors are prone to agonize too much about an employee's termination. When a supervisor fails to act judiciously in terminating an employee the result can be a protracted process that takes an inevitable toll on the student affairs organization as well as the particular individuals involved. Much poor supervision is condoned by a too benevolent, too indecisive leadership style that shies from the difficult task of removing the incompetent or poorly performing employee in a caring but professional manner.

The termination of an employee should be the final stage of a process of performance evaluation, guidance, and probationary review. Every employee needs to have regular evaluation of his or her performance and reasonable opportunities to take corrective action. Everyone fails at some time and good employees are no exception. Everyone needs a reasonable opportunity to learn from mistakes and to correct problems in performance. When employees clearly know what is expected of them and receive direct and timely feedback they usually always improve their performance.

Good supervision does not, however, always work. Some employees lack and cannot gain the necessary skills to perform their jobs. Some seek to obfuscate and deny any responsibility for failure. Worse, some engage in personal diatribe and denial in which they adopt a vitriolic attitude toward the supervisor and the organization. When termination of employment is warranted the student affairs supervisor must act decisively and in a proactive manner to implement the separation process. Supervisors fail when, in their efforts to be benevolent and considerate or to assuage their own feelings of guilt, they fail to act promptly and firmly.

Supervisors must also recognize that job failure is not the end for employees and often is a powerful motivator for positive change and growth. Most people respond to termination with greater resourcefulness than we are inclined to think, especially if the termination process is handled in a professional, respectful, and transparent manner.

7. *Collective bargaining.* This is a topic often ignored in student affairs literature. Collective bargaining in postsecondary education occurred mostly in the 1960s and

1970s and slowed notably in the 1980s (Cohen & Brawer, 1996). Most collective bargaining in higher education has occurred with community colleges and statewide higher education systems and more specifically with faculty and support staff (Winston & Creamer, 1997). While many student affairs administrators may not be covered under a union contract, their work may be affected by those on their campuses who are covered under contract (such as for faculty, support staff, and service workers). "The advent of collective bargaining has made student affairs involvement in faculty roles in governance more complicated" (Miller, 2000, p. 46). Many student affairs administrators rely on faculty involvement, either formally through committees, or informally for advisory purposes. Miller says, "Even the casual influence of faculty opinion can be difficult because the ways in which faculty members use their time is often a matter of contract" (p. 46). Resident assistants at the University of Massachusetts at Amherst recently voted to unionize (Bellis, 2002; Hoover, 2002; Williams, 2002), making them the first union of undergraduate students. This may be a first, but it will not likely be the last effort by student affairs staff to unionize. Collective bargaining will likely be a topic of interest for student affairs administrators in the future. Information on the topic can be obtained from several sources including the American Association of University Professors (AAUP), National Educational Association (NEA) Higher Education Research Center, and the National Center for the Study of Collective Bargaining in Higher Education and the Professions at Baruch College.

Conclusion

In *Workplace 2000* (Boyett & Conn, 1992), the authors forecast a future in which technology, global competition, and consumer demands will increasingly require more flexible, creative, and team-oriented workplaces. These changes are already well under way in American business and industry, and they are increasingly common in American colleges and universities. It seems clear that the traditional, hierarchical student affairs organization, with its highly specialized service units and independent specialists, will move toward a flatter organizational structure characterized by much greater integration of roles and employee participation. Student affairs staff of the future will make greater use of technology to manage services, be more directly involved in a wider array of problem solving, and give greater priority to continual improvement in the quality of programs and services for students. These changes will require student affairs staff who are good communicators, who are flexible and innovative, who can work effectively in teams, and who are committed to continual learning.

Those who aspire to supervise student affairs staff in the future must be visionary leaders as well as practical managers. They must be able to articulate goals and motivate their staff to commit to them. They must model the values they espouse and be able to inspire their employees to actively participate in all aspects of the student affairs mission. Because of this orientation toward flexibility and change, there will be less certainty and stability in student affairs jobs in the future; the profession will be even more challenging and fulfilling, however, because of the greater involvement and commitment of staff.

In many respects, student affairs professionals are likely to respond quite readily to these developments. The boundary-spanning nature of their work and their historic emphasis on service, shared values, and participation will make it easier for them to thrive in this new environment. Hopefully this chapter has provided some practical strategies for increasing managers' effectiveness in working with those with whom they share a common mission—students.

References

Adams, J. D. (1984). *Transforming work.* Alexandria, VA: Miles Reeve Press.

Albanese, R. (1978). *Managing toward accountability for performance.* Homewood, IL: Irwin.

Anthony, W. P., Kacmar, K. M., & Perrewe, P. L. (2002). *Human resource management: A strategic approach* (4th ed.). Orlando, FL: Harcourt.

Baier, J. L. (1985). Recruiting and training competent staff. In M. J. Barr, L. A. Keating, & Associates (Eds.), *Developing effective student service programs: Systematic approaches for practitioners.* San Francisco: Jossey-Bass.

Bellis, D. (2002, April 23). Students morph into crisis managers. *USA Today,* p. D10.

Boyett, J. H., & Conn, H. P. (1992). *Workplace 2000: The revolution reshaping American business.* New York: Penguin.

Canon, H. J. (1985). Developing staff potential. In U. Delworth, G. R. Hanson, & Associates (Eds.), *Student services: A handbook for the profession* (pp. 439–455). San Francisco: Jossey-Bass.

Canon, H. J. (1989). Guiding standards and principles. In U. Delworth, G. R. Hanson, & Associates (Eds.), *Student services: A handbook for the profession* (2nd ed., pp. 57–79). San Francisco: Jossey-Bass.

Clement, L. M., & Rickard, S. T. (1992). *Effective leadership in student services: Voices from the field.* San Francisco: Jossey-Bass.

Cohen, A. M., & Brawer, F. B. (1996). *The American community college* (3rd ed.). San Francisco: Jossey-Bass.

Cone, L. M., Jr. (1968). Toward a management theory of managerial obsolescence: An empirical and theoretical study. Unpublished doctoral dissertation, New York University.

Deegan, W. L., Steele, B. H., & Thielen, T. B. (1990). *Translating theory into practice: Implications of Japanese management theory for student personnel administrators* (NASPA Monograph Series No. 3). Washington, DC: National Association of Student Personnel Administrators.

Desimone, R. L., Werner, J. M., & Harris, D. M. (2002). *Human Resource Development* (3rd ed.). Orlando, FL: Harcourt.

Donkin, R. (2001). *Blood, sweat and tears: The evolution of work.* New York: Texere.

Du Brin, A. J. (1978). *Fundamentals of organizational behavior.* New York: Pegasus Press.

Harned, P. J., & Murphy, M. C. (1998). *Creating a culture of development for the new professional.* (New Directions for Student Services No. 84, pp. 43–53). San Francisco: Jossey-Bass.

Hickman, C. R. (1992). *Mind of a manager, soul of a leader.* New York: Wiley.

Hoover, E. (2002, March 6). Resident assistants at U. of Massachusetts at Amherst vote to unionize [Electronic version]. *The Chronicle of Higher Education.*

Jacoby, M. A., Astin, A. W., & Ayala, F. (1987). *College student outcomes assessment* (ASHE-ERIC Higher Education Report No. 7). Washington, DC: Association for the Study of Higher Education.

Kay, E. (1974). *The crisis in middle management.* New York: American Management Associates.

Kuh, G. D. (Ed.). (1983). *Understanding student affairs organizations* (New Directions for Student Services No. 23). San Francisco: Jossey-Bass.

Levine, A., & Cureton, J. S. (1998). *When hope and fear collide: A portrait of today's college student.* San Francisco: Jossey-Bass.

Lindquist, J. (1981). Professional development. In A. W. Chickering & Associates, *The modern American college: Responding to the new realities of diverse students and a changing society* (pp. 730–747). San Francisco: Jossey-Bass.

Miller, T. E. (2000). Institutional governance and the role of student affairs. In M. J. Barr, M. K. Desler, & Associates. *The handbook of student affairs administration* (2nd ed., pp. 37–49). San Francisco: Jossey-Bass.

Mogensen, V. (1996). The future is already here: Deskilling of work in the "office of the future." In C. Bina, L. Clements, & C. Davis (Eds.), *Beyond survival: Wage labor in the late twentieth century* (pp. 177–197). Armonk, NY: M. E. Sharpe.

Pastin, M. (1991). *The hard problems of management: Gaining the ethics edge.* San Francisco: Jossey-Bass.

Richmond, D. R. (1986). The young professional at the small college: Tips for professional success and personal survival. *NASPA Journal, 24,* 32–37.

Rinehart, J. (2001). Transcending Taylorism and Fordism? Three decades of work restructuring. In R. Baldoz, C. Koeber, & P. Kraft (Eds.), *The critical study of work: Labor, technology and global production.* (pp. 179–195). Philadelphia, PA: Temple University Press.

Sandeen, A. (1991). *The chief student affairs officer: Leader, manager, mediator, educator.* San Francisco: Jossey-Bass.

Sandeen, A. (2001). *Making a difference: Profiles of successful student affairs leaders.* Washington, DC: National Association of Student Personnel Administrators.

Schein, E. H. (1988). *Organizational culture and leadership.* San Francisco: Jossey-Bass.

Seymour, D. (1994). *Total quality management on campus: Is it worth the effort?* (New Directions for Student Services No. 86). San Francisco: Jossey-Bass.

Terkel, S. (1974). *Working.* New York: Pantheon Books.

Wagner, J. A., & Hollenbeck, J. R. (2001). *Organizational behavior: Securing competitive advantage* (4th ed.). Orlando, FL: Harcourt.

Ward, L. (1995). Role stress and propensity to leave among new student affairs professionals. *NASPA Journal, 33,* 35–43.

Williams, M. G. (2002, April 26). Why a union for RA's makes no sense [Electronic version]. *The Chronicle of Higher Education.*

Winston, R. B., & Creamer, D. G. (1997). *Improving staffing practices in student affairs.* San Francisco: Jossey-Bass.

Young, R. B. (1993). *Identifying and implementing the essential values of the profession* (New Directions for Student Services No. 61). San Francisco: Jossey-Bass.

Zachary, L. J. (2000). *The mentor's guide: Facilitating effective learning relationships.* San Francisco: Jossey-Bass.

PART FIVE

ESSENTIAL COMPETENCIES AND TECHNIQUES

Developing professional competence is an ongoing, experiential process of knowing, being, and doing. Grounded in appropriate philosophies and values, research, theory, and good judgment, competence supports effective implementation of good practice. Formal graduate preparation in any field is often focused on expanding knowledge, with limited time devoted to how to apply that knowledge. Thus new professionals must seek mentors and practical learning experiences; they must also solicit feedback from trusted colleagues as they add to their competencies. Moreover, the student affairs professional must remain current in the literature, pursue essential new skills, and access innovative resources to benefit both the institution and its students.

Competencies are an embedded component of professional roles. Previous editions of *Student Services* included a section on the primary roles of student affairs professionals: administrators, counselors, student development educators, and ecology managers. Since we expanded other sections, we had to make the difficult decision to remove the former, very valuable section on roles and models for practice. We encourage the reader to read that section in the second edition.

An overview of these key roles provides the context for practice. As Delworth and Hanson note in the second edition, student affairs professionals were in the past regarded as surrogate parents and disciplinarians, administrators, and counselors. Legal and societal changes have diminished the surrogate parent role. Professional developments outlined in the previous chapters have signaled the emergence of the student development educator and ecology manager roles. As student development educators, student affairs staff apply theoretical frames to help students achieve a positive educational experience and to learn about themselves and others. As ecology managers, student affairs staff seek to shape the educational environment to enhance student experiences and build and nurture the educational community. Each student affairs professional's role likely includes some combination of these roles and models. Practitioners need to assess their personal and professional interests to determine which combination of roles matches their interests, personal philosophy, skills, career goals, and convictions concerning how they can best impact the student experience.

Each student affairs role requires a specialized set of competencies, and many competencies are shared among several roles. While there are dozens of specialized competencies that could be addressed for each role, the nine chapters in Part Five identify and describe key competencies used by many student affairs professionals for all roles.

The part begins in Chapter Nineteen with Donna Talbot's exploration of multiculturalism and diversity, important competencies in all roles. In Chapter Twenty, Judy Rogers describes why leadership is so essential for administrative roles, particularly in effecting campus change. Larry Roper, in Chapter Twenty-One, presents teaching and training—the key competencies required for student development educators. In Chapter Twenty-Two, Roger Winston presents an overview of counseling, with an emphasis on helping skills for different settings. In a new chapter, Chapter Twenty-Three, Patrick Love describes the roles of academic advising and consultation. Saunie Taylor writes in Chapter Twenty-Four on using resolution and mediation skills as a way to solve conflicts and reach informed decisions. In Chapter Twenty-Five, Denny Roberts challenges the reader to think about the role of and skills necessary for community building and programming. Lee Upcraft introduces the reader to some of the basic definitions surrounding the issue of assessment and offers a comprehensive assessment model for student affairs in Chapter Twenty-Six. The section on competencies concludes with Chapter Twenty-Seven, a new chapter, in which Stan Carpenter discusses professionalism.

Many of these competency domains have become very specialized areas requiring extensive education and experience. Each chapter might be explored to determine if advanced education in that area would benefit your individual practice. For example, no professional should claim to be a counselor without proper preparation. Those interested in counseling might study Chapter Twenty-Two to determine its place in student affairs practice and to make decisions concerning their need for further training in order to help students in a caring, responsive manner.

The competencies presented in this part are applicable to many functional areas beyond student affairs as well. Also, other competencies could have been addressed, and we encourage readers to explore such needed competencies as futures forecasting, facilities management, fundraising, and developmental supervision. Student affairs professionals must continually scan the developing needs of the profession and the changing needs of students and institutions to stay helpful and timely.

We encourage each student affairs professional to approach his or her professional development as if recertification were required on a regular basis. If that were the case, what new competencies, skills, awareness, and knowledge bases would you need to develop? This part provides basic information and referrals for additional information on many important competencies.

CHAPTER NINETEEN

MULTICULTURALISM

Donna M. Talbot

At this point in the history of higher education, there can no longer be any doubt that our campuses will continue to host more and more diverse student populations (Murdock & Hoque, 1999). The growth (or increase in visibility) of students who are United States ethnic minorities, bilingual with English as their second language, international, lesbian/gay/bisexual/transgendered, women, adult learners, individuals with psychological or physical disabilities, and persons who hold a variety of religious affiliations cannot be ignored. Though the changes in today's campus diversity are addressed more fully in Chapter Three, a few relevant demographics are cited here to highlight the need for multicultural competency in student affairs.

As a nation, as well as within our institutions of higher education, we have met and often exceeded numerical projections for particular populations (international students, students of color, women, adult students, and so on). Because of the increased rate of immigration during the 1990s and the higher birth rates of U.S. ethnic minority populations, approximately 66.8 percent of the 18.9 million population increase was attributable to minority populations (Murdock & Hoque, 1999). If future projections continue to be accurate, "the proportion of the total U.S. population composed of members of minority groups would be 47.2 percent in 2050 compared to 24.3 percent in 1990" (p. 8). Extrapolating from this data, Murdock and Hoque suggest that by 2050 the percentage of Anglo students will drop to 57.6 percent while the percentage of students who are Hispanic will increase to 17.4 percent. Similarly, the percentage of students who are African American will increase to 13.0 percent, and other minority groups will increase to 12.0 percent of the student population. In some states and educational institutions, these shifts are already a reality. Along with the internal shifting demographics affecting higher education, the increased enrollment of international students is remarkable. Between 1990 and 1999, international student enrollment increased by approximately 22.4 percent (Institute of International Education, 1999), growing from over 407,000 students to over 490,000 students. What used to be the typical "traditional college student" (White, middle-class, male, able-bodied, Christian, heterosexual, eighteen to twenty-two years old) is merely an image that exists in the minority (at least numerically) on college campuses.

While these statistics capture some of the general shifts occurring in all institutions of higher education, it is important to remember that these numerical changes are not yet occurring evenly throughout all types of institutions in all geographic areas. There is still a great deal of stratification within the educational system, with the greatest changes being felt by community colleges and public institutions, usually in border states and states considered to be ports to other nations (such as Florida, New York, California, etc.).

Because of the changing demographics and, more importantly, the differing needs of these populations, what used to be the "traditional college experience" (attending a four-year institution) has given way to a growth in the popularity of community colleges, institutions specializing in distance education, corporate colleges (educational entities created by businesses to educate or retool employees specifically for their business), religious institutions, and more. It seems that as more traditional institutions of higher education are unable or unwilling to respond to the changing demographics, other entities develop or reemerge in popularity to capture this market. For many institutions, the continued enrollment of diverse students will depend largely on their ability to address the needs of these populations.

As institutions of higher education face the challenges and conflicts associated with many varied perspectives, cultures, values, and ways of thinking that are inherent in these diverse populations, the student affairs profession can play a pivotal role in helping institutions to negotiate these challenges effectively. This will require student affairs professionals to act as guides for the journey toward multiculturalism. Being able to serve as a guide will require each professional to have the awareness, knowledge, and skills for working with diverse constituents.

A recent editorial in the *Journal of College Student Development* (Blimling, 2001) briefly outlined higher education's rationale for pursuing diversity. This discourse moved from a deficit model (the need to reduce social injustices and the effects of historical discrimination) to a need to respond to the workforce realities. None of these arguments were able to convince all stakeholders in higher education that embracing diversity and reforming our institutions to meet the needs of diverse populations are positive and necessary moves. Finally, Blimling suggests that the last twenty years of research has demonstrated that "diversity makes you smarter" (p. 518). "Students who attend institutions with a diverse population of students, faculty, and staff report greater learning, increases in various measures of interpersonal competencies, develop greater self-confidence, are less likely to hold irrational prejudices, make greater gains in critical thinking, and have greater involvement in civic and community service behaviors (Beckham, 2000; Gudeman, 2000; Gurin, 1999; Pascarella, Palmer, Moye, & Pierson, 2001; Pettigrew & Tropp, 2000; Milem, 1999; Smith, Gerbick, Figueroa, Watkins, Levitan, et al., 1997; Sedlacek, 1987)" (p. 518). Given the preponderance of evidence suggesting that diverse college environments are associated with increases in student learning, the charge for all higher education faculty and staff seems evident. We need to be creating programs, curricula, and environments that support diversity, multicultural education, and diverse populations.

Though this charge seems simple, perhaps even oversimplistic to some, the challenges and conflict inherent in diverse communities are complex and thorny. Colleges and universities will need informed and skilled professionals to help them create positive learning environments that capitalize on the opportunities presented by a multicultural community.

Three models for individual and organizational multicultural development are presented in this chapter. Applications and implications of the models are explored using examples from college campuses. The effect of privilege and oppression on higher education is discussed. Finally, resources and references are shared for use in further personal and professional multicultural development.

The Journey Toward Multiculturalism

One of the greatest obstacles to discussing diversity and multiculturalism is the lack of common definitions to clarify the concepts involved. Perhaps this is grounded in people's fear of looking ignorant, insensitive, or exclusionary. Yet, how can we know where we are trying to go if we do not know where the journey can take us? With the analogy of a journey in mind, this chapter outlines the maps, landmarks, detours, and hazards along the road to multiculturalism. The maps are the theoretical and practice models developed for achieving multiculturalism. The landmarks are the developmental phases and tasks presented by the theoretical models and the techniques and tools that promote multicultural development. The detours are represented by short breaks or plateaus in growth, retreats from uncomfortable or unfamiliar situations, and smoke screens that stop individuals and organizations from clearly seeing the necessary steps for moving toward multiculturalism. Finally, the hazards are represented by overt and covert challenges to diversity and the costs associated with greater sensitivity to oppression and diversity. The journey toward multiculturalism is fraught with detours and hazards; however, having a well-drawn and usable map and recognizing the landmarks along the way will help make the journey a successful one.

At this point, it is important to make a cautionary note about using these or any other models or theories. Models and theories are useful because they attempt to aggregate and simplify human behaviors and attributes so that students, practitioners, and educators can digest them easily and then use them in developing goals and educational programs. Yet, it is exactly because they aggregate and simplify that models or theories can be misleading—because they can obscure individual differences. Any model or theory must be used with a healthy dose of caution. Consider them maps or guides for understanding people, not templates to be applied like cookie cutters.

Beliefs, Assumptions, and Definitions

Certain beliefs and assumptions serve as the foundation for the concepts presented in this chapter. First, learning not only to tolerate but also to accept and appreciate diverse populations is not an optional activity for student affairs professionals. There are many reasons for this assumption, not the least of which is our professional codes of ethics (see Resources for NASPA's Standards of Professional Practice and ACPA's Statement of Ethical Principles and Standards). Additionally, in our global communities in higher education, as well as in the workforce, individuals who cannot accept and appreciate diverse populations are, more often than not, considered a liability. Given the fact that diversity is a growing reality on our campuses, and that interactions with diverse populations and perspectives contribute to individual's ability to think more complexly, we can no longer risk hiring individuals who will not or cannot contribute to a positive, global, learning community. A second assumption is that the multicultural journey described below begins with individual self-assessment and self-work, especially for those who have memberships in social groups that ascribe them privilege. Therefore, for most professionals in student affairs (Whites), the multicultural journey must begin by examining White identity development and White privilege (see Chapter Ten). For those professionals who identify as heterosexual, the journey may begin with an exploration of their development as a heterosexual ally (Broido, 2000). Finally, for student affairs professionals who are members of various social groups that typically experience oppression or marginalization in the U.S., there are also a variety of identity development models that will enhance self-awareness (again, see Chapter Ten).

Definitions

In this chapter, the terms *diversity* and *multiculturalism* are considered related, but not completely interchangeable. *Diversity* is a structure that includes the tangible presence of individuals representing a variety of different attributes and characteristics, including culture, ethnicity, sexual orientation, and other physical and social variables. According to Pusch and Hoopes (as cited in Pusch, 1979), *multiculturalism* is a state of being in which an individual feels comfortable and communicates effectively with people from any culture, in any situation, because she or he has developed the necessary knowledge and skills to do so. In other words, the multicultural person has mastered the process of continually learning about culture, quickly and effectively, so that he or she can adapt to a variety of different cultural settings with minimal discomfort. An assumption embedded in this definition should not be overlooked nor taken for granted—it assumes that the journey toward multiculturalism is an ongoing, developmental process that can be learned. This process involves self-awareness, knowledge, and the development of skills. Multiculturalism is not an inherent characteristic of any individual, no matter his or her race, ethnicity, sexual orientation, or gender; rather, it is based on an individual's ability and openness to learn. It is also understood, however, that while an individual's ethnicity or culture does not determine his or her ability to strive for multiculturalism, it does impact the individual's worldview, which shapes how that person perceives differences in cultures.

Ethnicity refers to racial or national characteristics determined by birth; *culture,* on the other hand, is much broader and more inclusive. Hoopes and Pusch (1979) define it as follows: "Culture . . . includes values, beliefs, linguistic expression, patterns of thinking, behavioral norms, and styles of communication which a group of people has developed to assure its survival in a particular physical and human environment. . . . Culture is the response of a group of human beings to the valid and particular needs of its members" (p. 3). Using this definition, the vast array of populations filling campus communities can be incorporated into the concept of culture: Asian Americans, Jews, men, Latinos, Gays, Muslims, women, various international populations, nontraditional students, Whites, and so on. While it is important to recognize all cultures that influence the campus environment and the work of student affairs professionals, it is also important to recognize that not all cultures have been incorporated into higher education equally; some are still struggling to be recognized and heard in institutions today.

For ease of discussing culture, we often group people into very large categories (race, sexual orientation, gender, etc.), as if individuals who share some single characteristic are all alike. The danger in doing this is that it becomes too easy to disallow for individual differences within groups and even easier to stereotype based on group membership. However, there are also benefits to recognizing large groups of people who share some common characteristic, such as the ability to conduct research that predicts the needs and differences among groups of people.

Race has become a particularly controversial and elusive term to define. Historically race was considered a biological or scientific term to classify the human species. More recently, it has become obvious that race is a socially constructed concept that has changing boundaries that are influenced by laws, history, emotions, and politics (Root, 1992). A clear example of this is that race has been classified differently four times since 1870 by the U.S. Census Bureau. A historic review of the construct of race reveals that there has been an ongoing debate since the nineteenth century about whether any "pure races" actually exist (Wehrly, Kenney, & Kenney, 1999).

Organizations may make a similar journey to the multicultural journey for individuals. Jackson and Holvino (1988) synthesized some key attributes of a multicultural organization from the earlier work of Jackson and Hardiman (1981). These attributes, which are discussed more fully later in this chapter, describe and define an organization that is striving toward multiculturalism. This definition not only acknowledges an organization's efforts to transform itself (in that it includes members of diverse groups and reflects the interests of diverse cultural and social groups) but also its responsibilities beyond its own interests (in that it acts to eradicate social injustice within the organization and on a broader social context). A factor that cannot be overlooked is that organizational change occurs only when there are committed and skilled individuals who are willing to instigate that change.

The definitions and the models shared in this chapter recognize that in U.S. society, both historically and to a large degree today, there is a "dominant, powerful" group or culture that has privileges others do not. Typically and historically, that powerful group has been ascribed the following attributes: White, male, heterosexual, middle- to upper-class socioeconomic status, and able-bodied. For the discussions in this chapter, any individuals or groups of people who are not described by these characteristics are considered potentially marginalized or disempowered in U.S. society, as well as on our college campuses.

Models of Multicultural Development

There are several models that outline the changes an individual or organization must make in order to move toward a more inclusive or multicultural framework. These models are the maps an individual or organization follows on their journey toward multiculturalism. As with any model or roadmap, use caution in adhering to it so strictly that you don't recognize the changes and individual differences that exist. Presented here are just three of those different models, varied in complexity and scope. These particular models, though originally developed to address specifically racial and ethnic issues, are rigorous and adaptable enough to include the many cultures that are addressed in this chapter.

Development of Intercultural Sensitivity

Bennett (1986) describes a model he calls the Development of Intercultural Sensitivity. The focus of this model is the individual's ability to achieve sensitivity to differences by passing through a continuum from lack of experience and low tolerance to increased experience and appreciation for diversity. The six stages in this continuum are as follows:

1. *Denial* occurs when there is physical and/or social isolation that prohibits any contact with significant cultural differences. The individual remains in complete ethnocentrism, where his or her own worldview is unchallenged and is central to all reality.
2. *Defense* involves the recognition of differences. This recognition represents a threat to the individual's view of the world. Typical responses in this stage include denigration of difference and assumption of cultural superiority.
3. *Minimization* is characterized by the attitude that "basically, all humans are alike." This is an attempt to trivialize any differences that exist, stressing only cultural similarities.
4. *Acceptance* is divided into two phases. In the first phase there is recognition and acceptance of behavioral differences; in the second phase there is recognition and acceptance of differences in fundamental cultural values. This stage marks the shift from ethnocentrism to ethnorelativism.

5. *Adaptation* is based on the acceptance of difference as a relative process. The individual develops the ability to empathize with a person of a different culture in a particular, immediate situation.
6. *Integration* involves the evaluation of events and situations in a cultural context. Adler describes an individual in this stage as "a person who is always in the process of becoming a part of and apart from a given cultural context" (Adler, 1977, quoted in Bennett, 1986, p. 186).

Pedersen's Multicultural Development Model

Pedersen's Multicultural Development model (1988), which comes out of the counseling literature, is an educational model rather than a medical model (that is, it is based on the assumption that the audience is healthy and normal and has an interest in becoming more multiculturally aware). The three stages of Pedersen's model are awareness, knowledge, and skill. Unlike other multicultural theorists, Pedersen focuses on three broad areas that need to be developed in an individual. Awareness represents the affective domain; knowledge represents the cognitive domain; and skill represents the behavioral domain. Fundamental to this model is the belief that by teaching multicultural development an individual will increase his or her repertoire of beliefs, knowledge, and behaviors for use in a variety of situations. The stages in Pedersen's model can be summarized as follows:

1. *Awareness.* In this stage an individual must learn accurate and appropriate attitudes, opinions, and assumptions about cultures. This includes awareness of oneself as a cultural being and one's own culture in relation to others. This is especially important for White people because they often see themselves as "having no culture." The White culture is usually used as the yardstick to which other cultures are compared; however, it is rarely ever defined or examined.
2. *Knowledge.* At this stage an individual acquires information or comprehension of different cultures and cultural beliefs. This represents the integration of cognition and beliefs.
3. *Skill.* At this stage the individual learns to translate beliefs and knowledge into action. The individual learns how to interact appropriately and effectively with persons from other cultures. Individuals in this stage learn to identify appropriate actions that will allow them to be accepted by persons from different cultures.

Multicultural Organizational Change

In 1993, Pope introduced and expanded the concept of multicultural organizational development for the work of student affairs professionals. Multicultural organizational development (MCOD) is a term coined by Jackson and Holvino (1988). This work was an outgrowth of the organizational development (OD) literature that recognized that changes in any organization must be planned and systemic; however, it also acknowledged that traditional OD efforts had not changed the oppressive nature of the workplace environment for historically marginalized groups. According to Jackson and Holvino (1988), a multicultural organization has the following attributes:

- Reflects the contribution and interests of diverse cultural and social groups in its mission, operations, and product or service delivery
- Acts on a commitment to eradicate social oppression in all forms within the organization
- Includes the members of diverse cultural and social groups as full participants, especially in decisions that shape the organization
- Follows through on broader external social responsibilities, including support of efforts to eliminate all forms of social oppression and to educate others in multicultural perspectives (p. 83)

Though the definition of MCOD fits well with higher education, the model is clearly designed for the business world. Valverde (1998, pp. 22–23) developed a schema (see Exhibit 19.1) for visualizing the "stages of multiculturing a campus" which seems to parallel the models developed for transforming the curriculum (Schuster & Van Dyne, 1985). In this schema, a campus moves sequentially through five phases beginning with *monocultural* (devoid of any minority traits) and ending with *transformed* (multicultural in all aspects). This schema was paired with a two-dimensional axis that depicts different campus populations' "capacity to transform a campus": one axis represents the level of influence one has on the environment based on involvement or participation, and the other axis represents the amount of time one spends on campus resulting in the ability to create change (see Figure 19.1). Valverde postulates that since students are such a transient population, they spend only a small amount of time on campus and, therefore, have little influence on transforming the campus. According to this model, elected officials have the highest level of influence and the greatest amount of time to transform the campus. Between students and elected officials are staff, faculty, administrators, and regents (moving from lowest to highest influence and time). Clearly, this model was developed focusing specifically on integrating racial and ethnic minorities into higher education.

EXHIBIT 19.1. STAGES OF MULTICULTURING A CAMPUS.

Stages	One	Two	Three	Four	Five
Type	Monocultural Campus	Ethnocentric Campus	Accommodating Campus	Transitional Campus	Transformed Campus
Characteristic	Devoid of minority traits	Dominant White culture, which admits minorities	Personnel and policies modified to accommodate People of Color	Limited pluralism	Multicultural in all aspects

Source: Valverde and Castenell (1998), p. 22.

FIGURE 19.1. GROUP CAPACITY TO TRANSFORM CAMPUS.

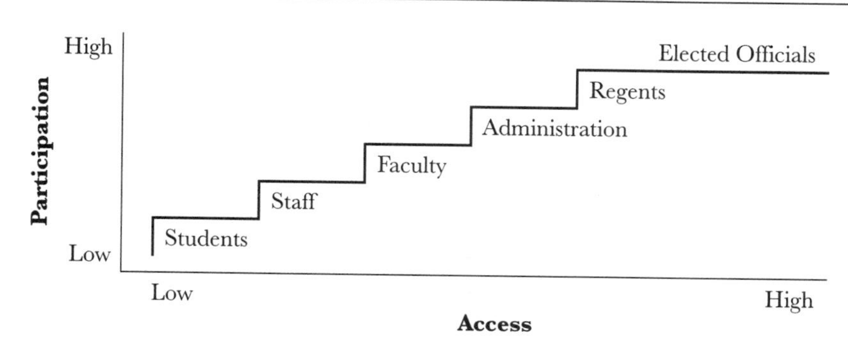

Source: Valverde and Castenell (1998), p. 23.

Then, in 1996, Grieger attempted to "translate the theoretical model of Multicultural Organizational Development into the specifics of everyday pragmatic professional practice, while building ongoing diagnosis and evaluation into its methodology" (p. 564). She did this by developing a fifty-eight-item Multicultural Organizational Development Checklist for Student Affairs (MODC) (see Exhibit 19.2). This checklist is intended to provide a holistic assessment of a division of student affairs's journey towards becoming a multicultural organization.

While each of these models moves us closer to understanding how institutions of higher education achieve multicultural organizational change, none are sufficient. However, when combined, they have the potential of providing a fairly comprehensive, systemic approach to MCOD in higher education (see Exhibit 19.3).

EXHIBIT 19.2. SELECTED ITEMS FROM THE MULTICULTURAL ORGANIZATIONAL DEVELOPMENT (MOD) CHECKLIST FOR STUDENT AFFAIRS.

LEADERSHIP AND ADVOCACY

The chief student affairs officer is a vocal advocate for diversity and multiculturalism within the division and on an institutional level.

POLICIES

The student code of conduct clearly prohibits engaging in racist, sexist, biased, sexually harassing, or sexually or physically assaultive behavior.

EXPECTATIONS FOR MULTICULTURAL COMPETENCY

The division [of student affairs] provides systematic and ongoing training regarding the development of multicultural competencies (i.e., attitudes, knowledge, and skills).

SCHOLARLY ACTIVITIES

Student affairs professionals engage in research, writing, and professional presentations on multicultural issues.

STUDENT ACTIVITIES AND SERVICES

Programs offered in residence halls regularly address issues of diversity and multiculturalism.

Source: Grieger (1996), pp. 569–572.

EXHIBIT 19.3. STAGES OF MULTICULTURAL ORGANIZATIONAL DEVELOPMENT IN HIGHER EDUCATION.

Stages	One	Two	Three	Four	Five
Type	Monocultural Campus	Ethnocentric Campus	Accommodating Campus	Transitional Campus	Transformed Campus
Characteristic	Devoid of "non-dominant group" traits	Dominant White, male, hetero culture, which admits select "others"	Personnel and policies modified to accommodate diverse populations	Limited pluralism	Multicultural in all aspects
Major Behavioral Markers	**Mission** of the institution does not address any commitment to any type of diversity.	**Mission** may not address commitment to diversity.	**Mission** reflects commitment to diversity but may not be integrated into life of the institution.	**Mission** reflects commitment to diversity and is followed fairly consistently.	**Mission** reflects commitment to diversity and is followed consistently.
	Institutional leadership is not representative of diversity.	**Institutional leadership** is not representative of diversity.	**Institutional leadership** may begin to include representatives of some diverse populations in certain areas, such as student affairs.	**Institutional leadership** is representative of diverse populations (usually those represented on campus or in certain areas).	**Institutional leadership** is representative of many diverse populations in all facets of leadership.
	Advocacy for diversity does not exist.	**Advocacy** for diversity probably does not exist.	**Advocacy** for some areas of diversity exists but may not include a call for action.	**Advocacy** for a campus climate which embraces diversity may exist.	**Advocacy** for a campus climate which embraces diversity is evident and active.
	Policies do not address diversity.	**Policies** do not address diversity except for admissions requirements.	**Policies** begin to address accommodation of diverse populations.	**Policies** clearly articulate a commitment to diverse populations and may address multiculturalism.	**Policies** are widely distributed and clearly communicate a commitment to diverse populations and multiculturalism.
	Recruitment efforts do not address diversity.	**Recruitment** of staff does not necessarily address diversity.	**Recruitment and retention** addresses the need for increases in diverse staff.	Staffing patterns and **recruitment** efforts reflect a growing commitment to diversity.	Staffing patterns and efforts to **recruit and retain** diverse staff reflect a commitment to diversity.

Multicultural competency training does not exist.	**Multicultural competency training** does not exist.	**Multicultural competency training** may occur sporadically.	**Multicultural competency training** exists consistently in certain areas and for certain groups on campus.	**Multicultural competency training** is provided for all levels of campus community regarding a variety of diverse populations (whether visible or not).
There are no **expectations** for **multicultural competency**.	There are no expectations for **multicultural competency**.	There may be **expectations** for **multicultural competency** in some areas, regarding select populations.	Expectations for **multicultural competency** exist in most areas and address many diverse populations.	Expectations for **multicultural competency** exist for all staff.
Scholarly activities do not address diversity.	**Scholarly activities** do not address diversity.	**Scholarly activities** may focus on multicultural issues.	**Scholarly activities** focus on multicultural issues and may be supported by the institution.	**Scholarly activities** on multicultural issues are supported financially and administratively.
Campus services and organizations do not address diversity.	**Campus services and organizations** do not address diversity.	**Campus services and organizations** may address diversity.	**Campus services and organizations** address the importance of meeting the needs of diverse persons.	**Campus services and organizations** emphasize the need to include and address diverse populations.
The **curriculum** does not address diversity.	The **curriculum** does not address diversity.	The **curriculum** may address some areas of diversity.	The **curriculum** addresses multiculturalism.	The **curriculum** is infused with multicultural issues and addresses all facets of diversity.
The **physical environment** is not designed for diversity.	The **physical environment** is not designed for diversity.	The **physical environment** may be inviting to some diverse populations.	The **physical environment** reflects an appreciation for some diverse populations.	The **physical environment** reflects an awareness of and appreciation for all diverse populations.
Diagnosis and evaluation do not take multiculturalism into account.	**Diagnosis and evaluation** do not take multiculturalism into account.	**Diagnosis and evaluation** may address some areas of multiculturalism.	**Diagnosis and evaluation** are conducted to assess the barriers to creating a multicultural organization.	**Diagnosis and evaluation** are conducted regularly to assess the effectiveness of multicultural change.

The "tentative model" presented in Exhibit 19.3 attempts to integrate and modify the significant work in the organizational models summarized above. Some of the changes to these models were influenced by the following assumptions:

1. MCOD must occur in the entire institution, not just the Division of Student Affairs, for it to be holistic and systemic.
2. Addressing only issues of diversity that obviously exist on campus is self-serving and may not represent true multicultural organizational change.
3. Inclusion of some areas of diversity, but not others, does not result in true multicultural organizational change (such as embracing issues of race but not addressing homophobia or sexism).
4. All members of the community (students, faculty, staff, and trustees) have a vested interest in and ability to contribute to the multicultural development of the institution.
5. For an institution to experience MCOD, it must also be committed to eliminating all forms of oppression and providing multicultural education to the broader community in which it exists.

Commonalities Across Models

Some commonalties exist across the models presented. Each assumes that the individual or organization has a desire to move toward multiculturalism; there must be a willingness to learn and to begin the journey. The models also assume that there is a dominant culture with dominant norms. All emphasize that some level of self-awareness and awareness of others must be achieved and monitored. In the organizational development model, professionals must be aware of the behavioral markers that constitute multicultural development for the institution. For each of these models, there is an initial introduction of difference that begins the developmental process. This contact with difference can be accidental, or it can be planned.

The stages, components, or phases of these models are not meant to be seen as having distinct, rigid boundaries. As is true for most student development theories, individuals may revisit, retreat, or stagnate as they progress through the stages. Stages or phases may overlap as an individual moves from one to another. Also, individuals usually do not journey toward multiculturalism by embracing all cultural groups at once; they may need to take several journeys, adding new cultural groups each time. For example, under Pedersen's Multicultural Development model, it is possible that an individual could still be in the awareness stage (struggling with himself or herself as a cultural being) while transitioning into the knowledge stage (beginning to gather information about White identity development). Another alternative is that an individual may have reached the action or skill stage in the journey with regard to African Americans but may still be at the beginning of the awareness stage with regard to persons who are LGBT. Some of this will depend on many external factors, not the least of which is contact with particular populations.

Other similar developmental models that can be used are the Intercultural Learning Process (Hoopes, 1979; Jefferson, 1986), the Cultural Broker model (Stage &

Manning, 1993), or the Cultural Environment Transitions model (Manning & Coleman-Boatwright, 1991). Before beginning a long journey, it is important to feel comfortable and confident with the map that will guide it. Therefore, in the journey toward multiculturalism it is important to find a strong model that can be understood and that seems to fit. While each model seems to have an endpoint or final stage, in reality the journey toward multiculturalism is never-ending. Cultures evolve and change constantly; therefore, the need to learn and adapt to the new and changing populations on campuses is continuous.

Applications of the Models

Consider the following students and hypothetical situations at Anywhere University:

Thomas is an RA at Anywhere University. He is White, twenty years old, and from a rural, homogeneous community. He attended his local community college before transferring to Anywhere University, which has a moderately sized, growing multicultural population.

Jenny is a first-generation Korean American student in her junior year at Anywhere University. She and her parents are sure that Jenny will be a doctor. Although Jenny is a naturalized citizen, she speaks with an accent; at home, she and her parents always converse in their native tongue.

Carlos is a graduate student from Costa Rica at Anywhere University. He came to the U.S. to study engineering. His family is very proud that he will develop career skills that will help their country when he returns. Since coming to the U.S., Carlos has started to question some of his traditional Latino upbringing and has begun to enjoy many American freedoms and beliefs.

Kelby is a sophomore at Anywhere University. He is African American and has recently self-identified as gay. Kelby is a psychology major; he plays several intramural sports; and he loves to dance. This year, for the first time since going to college, Kelby has become involved in a number of activist student organizations, including the Gay, Lesbian, and Bisexual Alliance and the Pan-African Power student group.

Jenny, Kelby, Carlos, and Thomas could easily be students on any campus in the United States. However, how such students are perceived (and consequently how they are treated) may vary greatly, depending on the level of multiculturalism attained by the student affairs professionals who work with them and the level of commitment to diversity exhibited by the university they attend. How they interact with each other may also depend on their level of development toward multiculturalism and their level of minority or White identity development (see Chapter Ten) (Atkinson, Morten, & Sue, 1993; Helms, 1990). Examples of this and particular situations involving Jenny, Kelby, Carlos, and Thomas are explored below.

As noted, applying the multicultural development models can be complex. Consider each of our four students, using the multicultural development models as a guide or map for understanding their behavior.

Having achieved the status of RA, it would be hard to imagine that Thomas would be in the denial stage of the Intercultural Sensitivity model (Bennett, 1986), at least with respect to ethnic minorities. At this point in his college career, Thomas has probably been exposed to students from different ethnic backgrounds; thus his worldview has been challenged, and he has been forced to begin his journey with the acknowledgment that cultural differences exist. However, if his local community college was representative of his rural, homogeneous community, his interaction with any persons different from himself could be limited. Clearly, due to the nature of the "invisible minority" (Fassinger, 1991), Thomas may not knowingly have come into contact with gay men, lesbians, or bisexuals; thus his journey regarding this population may not yet have begun.

If he were in the minimization stage of development, Thomas might look at Kelby and Jenny as if they were just "two other human beings," claiming he is "color-blind" and "gender-blind." He would trivialize the cultural differences that separate him from Jenny and Kelby, eliminating any chance of intercultural understanding in the process. While he would probably acknowledge that Carlos and he were different since they come from different countries, Thomas probably would not have any knowledge or understanding of Carlos' culture. In this stage, Thomas would not be able to see that his behaviors could be interpreted as racist. Simple interactions or discussions with Jenny and Kelby that emphasize the cultural differences that exist around topics like holidays or religious beliefs might begin to push Thomas out of the minimization stage. Visiting and celebrating Kwanza with Kelby's family or dining with Jenny's traditional Korean family would challenge Thomas's basic beliefs that people are all alike despite their different cultural and ethnic backgrounds.

If Thomas continues to move along the continuum, he will begin to see Kelby and Jenny as cultural beings different from himself. In the acceptance stage, these differences are perceived as necessary and fundamental, but they are not evaluated. That is to say, at this stage, Thomas would not label some differences as good and others as bad. He will not begin the process of sorting through and selecting cultural beliefs, practices, and values from a variety of cultures until later in the journey. At this stage, Thomas would also start to recognize the importance of talking with Carlos about his traditional Latino culture, as well as Carlos' questions about his own culture. However, Thomas will probably not be able to understand the struggles that Carlos is experiencing.

If Thomas reaches the integration stage, he will begin to see his interactions with Jenny and Kelby in a cultural context. He will attempt to evaluate his own behaviors from Jenny's and Kelby's cultural perspective as well as his own; decisions about his behavior will be made incorporating all of these viewpoints. At this stage, Thomas will realize that Carlos is at a "cultural crossroad" and probably needs help that he cannot offer; if trained properly, Thomas will refer Carlos to an appropriate source on his campus (such as international student services or counseling).

Under Pedersen's Multicultural Development model, Thomas would be encouraged to explore his own culture (White culture) and its impact on how he works with individuals who are different from himself; he would probably begin to read about White racial identity development (Helms, 1990) as he moves toward the knowledge stage. Meanwhile, Thomas would watch how other White people behave and begin to notice similarities, as well as differences, in other ethnic groups. In the knowledge stage, Thomas would seek out information to help him understand the different cultures he comes into contact with. He would probably study the Minority Identity Development model (Atkinson et al., 1993) and the Sexual Orientation Identity Formation model (Cass, 1996), as well as study specific historical and cultural information about African Americans, Asian Americans, and gays, lesbians, and bisexuals. Thomas might even begin to attend programs developed by International Student Services to help Americans understand various international populations. This would be Thomas's attempt to acquire knowledge about his residents' potential developmental issues and experiences on campus and in society.

Finally, in the skill stage of Pedersen's model, Thomas would apply his new awareness and knowledge. This might include attending gay rights meetings or discussions of African American or Asian American history. Thomas might plan and facilitate a program for his hall that addresses racial tensions on campus. Depending on his relationship with Jenny or Kelby, he might engage in discussions with them about their experiences as ethnic minorities on campus. (Given the characteristics of Kelby and Jenny described above and taking into account minority identity development, it is more likely that Kelby would be able to engage in these discussions than Jenny.)

Now, considering the stages of multicultural organizational change of Anywhere University using the model in Exhibit 19.3, imagine Thomas attends an institution that is considered to be a Monocultural campus. In such an institution he would not be expected to plan culturally sensitive programming; in fact, he would likely receive subtle messages to stay away from such "difficult topics." If Anywhere University was an Accommodating campus, Thomas might be expected to demonstrate multicultural competency and provide diversity education for his hall; this would probably be dependent on his supervisor, the level of commitment in the Division of Student Affairs, and the importance of recruitment and retention of diverse populations. In a Transformed campus, the mission, as well as all the symbols, policies and procedures, curricula, and activities, would reflect a commitment to diversity. Not only would Thomas be expected to demonstrate multicultural competency, he would also receive ongoing training in this area. Thomas would also have a diverse group of colleagues (other RAs and supervisors) with whom he could work to produce multicultural programs. All students would have a voice in framing the organizational structure, and diversity would be embedded in all programming. For example, a simple and very visual example is that posters for a couples' communication workshop would portray gay, heterosexual, and lesbian couples, and the faces would reflect a variety of ethnic populations.

These snapshots of Thomas, Jenny, Carlos, and Kelby at Anywhere University are helpful, but they do not answer several important questions: What tools or techniques are used to move an individual or organization along these models of multicultural development? What are some available resources to use during the journey? What prevents an individual or organization from developing multiculturally?

Developing Competencies

Once an individual or organization has decided to take the journey toward multiculturalism, the initial focus must be on awareness of self and others. Sue and Sue (1999) emphasize the importance of self-awareness: an individual who is unaware of his or her own cultural values is like a cup with a hole. Without knowledge of the hole, the liquid inside leaks out onto the owner, the floor, and anything else it touches. This is also true of the unaware student affairs professional whose own cultural values will leak out and spill over everyone they contact.

For many individuals, especially those in higher education, the natural tendency is to make learning multiculturalism a cognitive process, because this is familiar and relatively nonthreatening (Sue et al., 1982). Naturally, the cognitive or academic component of the journey must be addressed. There are many resources available that relate to student affairs and various diverse populations. For example, there are publications (Atkinson & Hackett, 1995; Belch, 2000; Gilligan, 1982) that address issues and needs of nonethnic American minority populations (women, people with disabilities, the elderly); these materials define the populations and discuss their inclusion in the term *minority.* There has been a steady increase in understanding of lesbian, gay, and bisexual issues by student affairs professionals (Croteau & Lark, 1995; Croteau & von Destinon, 1994; Croteau & Talbot, 2000) as well as students (D'Augelli, 1991; Evans & Broido, 1999; Fassinger, 1991; Wall & Evans, 2000). Similarly, there has been a growth in student affairs and related publications that address the development, needs, and experiences of ethnic minorities and international students (Brown & Robinson Kurpius, 1997; Cuyjet, 1997; Hernandez, 2000; Kodama, McEwen, Liang, & Lee, 2001; McEwen, Roper, Bryant, & Langa, 1990; Reynolds & Pope, 1991; Rodriguez, Guido-DiBrito, Torres, & Talbot, 2000). Finally, publications have addressed the training, skills, knowledge, and experience needed for helping professionals to understand themselves as cultural beings and to work effectively with diverse populations (Helms, 1992; McEwen & Roper, 1994; Ortiz & Rhoads, 2000; Parker, 1998; Sue & Sue, 1999; Talbot, 1996; Wall & Evans, 2000). These are just a few of the key resources readily available to student affairs professionals in their journey to understand multiculturalism. Still, each of the models outlined earlier indicate a need for development beyond the cognitive arena if true multiculturalism is to be obtained.

Once individuals have become self-aware, become aware of cultures different from their own, and acquired knowledge about those cultures, it is time for them to experience difference. The goal is to provide stimulation on affective and behavioral levels, as well as the cognitive level. Individuals should explore their openness, comfort, and discomfort with difference. Recognizing that there will be some discomfort, learning to understand and manage that discomfort is an important component of multicultural development.

Tools and Techniques

As mentioned above and in the models presented earlier in this chapter, tapping into the affective aspects of multicultural development and developing skills to be more effective with diverse populations is critical. This can be especially difficult in an academic setting like a classroom. However, the following are some tools and techniques that have been designed to address the noncognitive arena.

Parker's Multicultural Action Plan (1998). This is a three-level plan that parallels the multicultural development process. This plan should be self-designed by the individual implementing the plan, after engaging in a process of self-reflection and evaluation. The first level is observation, in which the individual (the "armchair observer") is exposed to cultural differences from a "safe distance." The second level is investigation, in which the individual (the "objective detective") gathers information about himself or herself and others from a closer distance. The information is processed, evaluated, and incorporated into the individual's way of perceiving the world. Finally, the third level is transformation, in which the individual (the "transforming participant") is prepared for immersion by awareness and knowledge gained from the earlier stages. The contact at the third level is expected to be close and intense, preferably having the individual experience what it is like to be the "minority" in a different culture. Along with experiencing the three levels of the action plan, there needs to be a forum or mechanism for the individual to process his or her experiences. This is an excellent tool for the classroom or for staff development.

Power and Privilege Exercise (Stanton & Grande, 1998). In this exercise, participants are asked to line up, shoulder to shoulder, holding hands. They are instructed that as the facilitator reads statements, they should take a small step forward if they could respond yes to the statement; conversely, if they would normally respond no, or the statement does not apply to their life experience, they should take a small step backwards. As the facilitator continues to read statements about privilege (see Exhibit 19.4 or McIntosh's article for examples), the participants begin to struggle to stay connected to fellow participants (with whom they are holding hands) as some move forward and some move backwards. This experience parallels real life. After reading as many statements as possible (given the space used), the facilitator draws an imaginary line in front of the participants. If that imaginary line represented "success in life," given where participants are now positioned, if asked to run to the line, what is the likelihood that everyone could get there at the same time?

Some simple training techniques that have been very effective in helping individuals move along the multicultural continuum include the following: bringing in panels of culturally diverse individuals, attending events in which the individual is in the minority (perhaps for the first time), simulation exercises such as *BaFa BaFa* (Shirts, 1977) and *Star Power* (1993), role playing, and being asked to represent a different voice (Belenky, Clinchy, Goldberger, & Tarule, 1986).

During a semester-long introductory student affairs course, students were asked to take on the voice of a population other than their own (such as gay, lesbian, or

EXHIBIT 19.4. EXAMPLES OF STATEMENTS TO USE FOR THE PRIVILEGE EXERCISE.

- I can shop alone at a store and not be followed or harassed by store employees.
- I can go into a music shop and count on finding the music of my race represented, into a supermarket and find the staple foods that fit with my cultural traditions, into a hairdresser's shop and find someone who can deal with my hair.
- I can walk down the street holding hands with my partner without fear of personal harm.
- I can hang pictures of my partner on my wall at work without fear that I may lose my job.
- I can easily buy posters, postcards, picture books, greeting cards, dolls, toys, and children's magazines featuring people of my race.
- In a group I am not asked to speak for my race.
- I can dress in an outfit with the assurance that it will not be considered by others as an invitation for sexual advances.
- I do not have to worry when choosing a neighborhood to live that my neighbors may mistreat me due to my romantic relationship.
- I can be assured that professors will not overlook my raised hand or my classroom comments.

bisexual; people of color; persons with disabilities; or international students). This experience assumes that as student affairs professionals, we "sit at the table" where decisions are made around policies, programs, and resources in higher education. Another factor embedded in this simulation is that there are populations who are typically not "sitting at the table" or given a voice in higher education. After getting over their initial fear of representing the issues for this voice inaccurately (especially with students from the represented groups in class), students reported feeling challenged, angry, and frustrated with the absence of their voice in the literature and the lack of services on campus that sensitively addressed their needs. Students reported feeling alienated, at times, by the profession they intended to enter. This led to some constructive discussions about how they might be more inclusive in their practices as student affairs professionals, as well as how they might struggle to have underrepresented populations in higher education given voice in their institutions. This is just one example of the benefits of experiential activities in the classroom.

Language

For the most part this chapter has focused on the "big picture." It has discussed societal and educational dilemmas, institutional interventions, multicultural models and their applications, and scholarly resources for understanding culture and cultural differences. These concepts and issues can all seem somewhat distant and larger than any one individual. It must be remembered that continuing the journey toward multiculturalism and maintaining ground already gained in this struggle is a day-to-day activity.

Each day, every one of us carries one of the most powerful weapons available to human kind in the struggle for multiculturalism—and we utilize this weapon without even knowing it. That weapon is the language we use. Language plays a pivotal role in our effectiveness as change agents on our campuses. Language can be used to maintain power differentials and the status quo, or it can be used to challenge others to think. When college-age males are referred to as "young men" and college-age females are referred to as "girls," a power differential is maintained: men have higher status than girls. When race becomes a discussion about "us" and "them," segregated thinking is perpetuated. When the only legitimate coupling acknowledged in language and written documents is husband and wife, the status quo of heterosexist thinking is maintained. When terminology such as "wheelchair bound" is used to describe a person with a mobility impairment, images of dependency and forced physical oppression are projected onto individuals who use assistive technologies. Finally, when outdated and inappropriate terms like *Oriental* are used to refer to all peoples of Asian descent, the wholeness and development of entire ethnic groups are denied. These are just a few examples of the power of misused language. It takes vigilance to constantly monitor one's daily language. Like culture and fashion, language is dynamic. Terms that were appropriate yesterday are not necessarily appropriate today; language that is correct today may not be acceptable tomorrow. Effective student affairs professionals cannot use outdated, inappropriate language regarding diversity and multiculturalism. Oftentimes, populations who have experienced oppression and marginalization in the educational system listen very carefully for verbal cues as to whether or not other individuals (usually those in positions of power) are allies or potential oppressors. Sensitivity to language issues in written materials is addressed thoroughly in numerous publications, including the *Publication Manual of the American Psychological Association* (American Psychological Association, 2001, pp. 61–76). Given the importance of language, it is critical that student affairs professionals use the necessary resources to educate themselves.

Walking Our Talk

In the early 1990s, as part of a national study evaluating the level of diversity training in student affairs master's degree programs (Talbot, 1996), students interviewed mentioned "walking our talk" as a recurring theme. Though faculty told students that diversity and multiculturalism were very important, they did not always feel as if these words were matched with deeds. Students watched faculty to see if diversity played an important role in faculty members' and administrators' personal and professional lives outside the classroom; generally this did not seem to be the case. This inconsistency disturbed most graduate students. They wanted faculty and student affairs practitioners to "walk their talk" regarding their commitment to multiculturalism and diversity. Though the original study took place in the early 1990s, I have continued to discuss the concept of "walking our talk" with students and staff. Currently, our students and staff are more sophisticated around issues of diversity and multiculturalism than they were ten or twenty years ago. Yet, there is still a need and spoken desire to have good role models to demonstrate how to negotiate what seem like sensitive and potentially explosive cultural issues. Many equate "walking our talk" with role modeling multicultural competence.

Maintaining a consistent and vigilant commitment to diversity is challenging; the roadblocks and hazards are many. It is not uncommon to hear a strong advocate for diversity being labeled "politically correct." At one time, "politically correct" was a positive phrase in the multicultural movement, used to describe individuals making an effort to use appropriate language, challenging closed-mindedness, and learning new behaviors, knowledge, and skills. Along the way this expression was coopted by opponents of diversity, and its meaning seemed to shift. Now "politically correct" is used to shut people down—suggesting that someone is overzealous about diversity but does not necessarily really believe in it. This backlash against multiculturalism and outspokenness on the issues, manifested by this turnaround in the use of the expression "politically correct," indicates that the challenge is being heard. People often put up smoke screens to cloud the issues when they fear that change is in the air and they are not ready for change. As long as individuals are clear about their motivation for advocating for multiculturalism and diverse populations, being labeled "politically correct," however it is used, is preferable to being seen as ignorant and insensitive to diversity.

Other roadblocks that keep individuals from completing their journey toward multiculturalism are the fear of saying the wrong thing, the fear of not being sufficiently knowledgeable about the topic, and the fear of looking foolish. These fears must be addressed; they will not disappear on their own. In fact, they may occasionally be well founded. If you choose to take this journey, it is impossible not to make mistakes. You will step on toes, and you will reveal a lack of knowledge. This is to be expected. But if handled genuinely and respectfully, most people will overlook these shortcomings and recognize your efforts more than your mistakes.

As a master's student in a counseling program, I remember feeling paralyzed during our practice counseling sessions. I was terrified that I would have a negative impact on my client by saying the wrong thing. Finally, my instructor said something to me that I often share with my students as I teach multicultural issues in counseling and development. "There are no bad responses, only bad recoveries." When he said this, I realized that if I was sincere, genuinely interested in trying to learn and help, and attentive to cues that I had made a mistake, I could address these errors and "my recovery" would be interpreted positively. Over the years, this has almost always been my experience.

The Role of Privilege and Oppression in Education

It would be difficult to address multiculturalism and training without touching upon the topic of oppression. Oppression is an interesting phenomenon: one person or group of people maintains overwhelming power over another person or group of people. One of the goals of oppression is to maintain the status quo, to allow one person or group to stay in power. Some educators (Freire, 1970/2000; Manning, 1994) believe that the pedagogical base of the American educational system is oppressive in nature. Outside of experiential education and Montessori training, the traditional educational system in the United States is designed to make individuals conform. Children are taught not to speak unless spoken to; the teacher talks and the student listens; the teacher chooses and forces his or her choices upon the students; the students are empty vessels waiting to be filled with knowledge by their teachers (Freire, 1970/2000). This type of educational system is hierarchical and does not foster creative, critical thinking. It assumes that students have no knowledge to share and the teacher has no knowledge to gain. In this type of system, the responsibility for educating rests with the teacher; communication is one-way.

"Pedagogy for liberation" emphasizes the need for all participants to be active and responsible both for educating and being educated. To benefit from this model, all participants must be aware, informed, and open to others' ideas. This is achieved through honest dialogue and exchange of ideas from a variety of perspectives (Manning, 1994). This redefinition of education as dialogical rather than hierarchical helps diminish the oppressor-oppressed relationship between teacher and student. The new roles created are that of teacher-student and student-teacher (Freire, 1970/2000). This ideology fits nicely with the models for multicultural development.

Many experts in cross-cultural and intercultural training (Corvin & Wiggins, 1989; Sabnani, Ponterotto, & Borodovsky, 1991; Sue & Sue, 1999) believe that individuals (especially Whites) must engage in self-exploration as cultural beings (Ortiz & Rhoads, 2000) and antiracism training. This training must expose individuals to the racist, sexist, heterosexist system that exists in the United States and the privileges that are associated with being a member of the dominant group. Accepting these privileges, whether or not one actively protects them, helps to maintain the system. This is an uncomfortable thought for most well-meaning individuals who do not see themselves as privileged. McIntosh (1989, 1992) writes about the ordinary, everyday ways in which Whites experience privileges denied people of color. These include, but are not limited to, being able to rent an apartment anywhere one can afford it without fear of being turned away for unknown reasons; being able to go shopping without being followed or harassed by the store detective or manager; being able to easily purchase cards, posters, greeting cards, dolls, and other toys featuring people of one's own race; and never being asked to speak for one's entire culture or race. While any one such incident does not by itself define the balance of power in society, the totality of such events repeated on a daily basis reinforces the belief or perception that one group is preferable to others.

Conclusion

The complexity of the issues involved in striving for multiculturalism is evident. Equally evident is the need to gain competency in this area in order to be an effective and ethical student affairs professional. Though the journey toward multiculturalism is fraught with roadblocks and hazards, maps (multicultural development models) and landmarks (tools and techniques, stages of development) exist to guide the trip. The biggest step, which must start with each individual and organization, is the decision to begin the journey in the first place.

References

American Psychological Association. (2001). *Publication manual of the American Psychological Association* (5th ed.). Washington, DC: Author.

Atkinson, D. R., & Hackett, G. (Eds.). (1995). *Counseling diverse populations.* Dubuque, IA: Brown.

Atkinson, D. R., Morten, G., & Sue, D. (1993). *Counseling American minorities: A cross-cultural perspective* (4th ed.). Dubuque, IA: Brown.

Belch, H. A. (2000). *Serving students with disabilities* (New Directions for Student Services No. 91). San Francisco: Jossey-Bass.

Belenky, M. F., Clinchy, B. M., Goldberger, N. R., & Tarule, J. M. (1986). *Women's ways of knowing: The development of self, voice, and mind.* New York: Basic Books.

Bennett, M. J. (1986). A developmental approach to training for intercultural sensitivity. *International Journal of Intercultural Relations, 10,* 179–196.

Blimling, G. S. (2001). Diversity makes you smarter. *Journal of College Student Development, 42,* 517–519.

Broido, E. M. (2000). Ways of being an ally to lesbian, gay, and bisexual students. In V. A. Wall & N. J. Evans (Eds.), *Toward acceptance: Sexual orientation issues on campus* (pp. 345–369). Lanham, MD: University Press of America.

Brown, L. L., & Robinson Kurpius, S. E. (1997). Psychosocial factors influencing academic persistence of American Indian college students. *Journal of College Student Development, 38,* 3–12.

Cass, V. C. (1996). Sexual orientation identity formation: A Western phenomenon. In R. P. Cabaj & T. S. Stein (Eds.), *Textbook of homosexuality and mental health* (pp. 227–251). Washington, DC: American Psychiatric Press.

Corvin, S. A., & Wiggins, F. (1989). An antiracism model for White professionals. *Journal of Multicultural Counseling and Development, 17,* 105–114.

Croteau, J. M., & Lark, J. S. (1995). On being lesbian, gay, or bisexual in student affairs: A national survey of experiences on the job. *NASPA Journal, 32,* 189–197.

Croteau, J. M., & Talbot, D. M. (2000). Understanding the landscape: An empirical view of lesbian, gay, and bisexual issues in the student affairs profession. In V. A. Wall & N. J. Evans (Eds.), *Toward acceptance: Sexual orientation and today's college campus.* Washington, DC: ACPA Media Board.

Croteau, J. M., & von Destinon, M. (1994). A national survey of job search experiences of lesbian, gay, and bisexual student affairs professionals. *Journal of College Student Development, 35,* 40–45.

Cuyjet, M. J. (Ed.). (1997). *Helping African American men succeed in college* (New Directions for Student Services No. 80). San Francisco: Jossey-Bass.

D'Augelli, A. R. (1991). Gay men in college: Identity processes and adaptations. *Journal of College Student Development, 32,* 140–146.

Evans, N. J., & Broido, E. M. (1999). Coming out in residence halls: Negotiation, meaning making, challenges, supports. *Journal of College Student Development, 40,* 658–668.

Fassinger, R. E. (1991). The hidden minority: Issues and challenges in working with lesbian women and gay men. *Counseling Psychologist, 19,* 157–176.

Freire, P. (2000). *Pedagogy of the oppressed.* New York: Continuum. (Original work published 1970)

Gilligan, C. (1982). *In a different voice.* Cambridge, MA: Harvard University Press.

Grieger, I. (1996). A multicultural organizational development checklist for student affairs. *Journal of College Student Development, 37,* 561–573.

Helms, J. E. (1990). Toward a model of White racial identity development. In J. E. Helms (Ed.), *Black and White racial identity: Theory, research, and practice* (pp. 49–66). New York: Greenwood Press.

Helms, J. E. (1992). *A race is a nice thing to have.* Topeka, KS: Content Communications.

Hernandez, J. C. (2000). Understanding the retention of Latino college students. *Journal of College Student Development, 41,* 575–588.

Hoopes, D. S. (1979). Intercultural communication concepts and the psychology of intercultural experience. In M. D. Pusch (Ed.), *Multicultural education: A cross-cultural training approach* (pp. 11–38). La Grange Park, IL: Intercultural Network.

Hoopes, D. S., & Pusch, M. D. (1979). Definitions of terms. In M. D. Pusch (Ed.), *Multicultural education: A cross-cultural training approach* (pp. 2–8). La Grange Park, IL: Intercultural Network.

Institute of International Education. (1999). *Open doors, 1998–99: Report on international educational exchange.* New York: Institute of International Education.

Jackson, B., & Hardiman, R. (1981). *Organizational stages of multicultural awareness.* Amherst, MA: New Perspectives.

Jackson, B. W., & Holvino, E. (1988). Developing multicultural organizations. *Journal of Religion and the Applied Behavioral Sciences, 9,* 83–88.

Jefferson, F. C. (1986). Training develops multicultural awareness. *Bulletin of the Association of College Unions-International, 54,* 12–16.

Kodama, C. M., McEwen, M. K., Liang, C.T.H., & Lee, S. (2001). A theoretical examination of psychosocial issues for Asian Pacific American students. *NASPA Journal, 38,* 411–437.

Manning, K. (1994). Liberation theology and student affairs. *Journal of College Student Development, 35,* 94–97.

Manning, K., & Coleman-Boatwright, P. (1991). Student affairs initiatives toward a multicultural university. *Journal of College Student Development, 32,* 367–374.

McEwen, M. K., & Roper, L. D. (1994). Interracial experiences, knowledge, and skills of master's degree students in graduate programs in student affairs. *Journal of College Student Development, 35,* 81–87.

McEwen, M. K., Roper, L. D., Bryant, D. R., & Langa, M. J. (1990). Incorporating the development of African-American students into psychosocial theories of student development. *Journal of Student Development, 31,* 429–436.

McIntosh, P. M. (1989, July–August). White privilege: Unpacking the invisible knapsack. *Peace and Freedom,* 10–12.

McIntosh, P. M. (1992). White privilege and male privilege: A personal account of coming to correspondences through work in women's studies (Working Paper No. 189). Wellesley, MA: Wellesley College Center for Research on Women.

Murdock, S. H., & Hoque, M. N. (1999). Demographic factors affecting higher education in the United States in the twenty-first century. In G. H. Gaither (Ed.), *Promising practices in recruitment, remediation, and retention* (New Directions for Higher Education No. 108, pp. 5–13). San Francisco: Jossey-Bass.

Ortiz, A. M., & Rhoads, R. A. (2000). Deconstructing Whiteness as part of a multicultural educational framework: From theory to practice. *Journal of College Student Development, 41,* 81–93.

Parker, W. M. (1998). *Consciousness-raising: A primer for multicultural counseling* (2nd ed.). Springfield, IL: Thomas.

Pedersen, P. (1988). *Handbook for developing multicultural awareness.* Alexandria, VA: American Association of Counseling and Development.

Pope, R. L. (1993). Multicultural-organization development in student affairs: An introduction. *Journal of College Student Development, 34,* 201–205.

Pusch, M. D. (Ed.). (1979). *Multicultural education: A cross-cultural training approach.* La Grange Park, IL: Intercultural Network.

Reynolds, A. L., & Pope, R. L. (1991). The complexities of diversity: Exploring multiple oppressions. *Journal of Counseling and Development, 70,* 175–180.

Rodriguez, A. L., Guido-DiBrito, F., Torres, V., & Talbot, D. M. (2000). Latina college students: Issues and challenges for the 21st century. *NASPA Journal, 37,* 511–527.

Root, M. P. (Ed.). (1992). *Racially mixed people in America.* Newbury Park, CA: Sage.
Sabnani, H. B., Ponterotto, J. G., & Borodovsky, L. G. (1991). White racial identity development and cross-cultural counselor training: A stage model. *Counseling Psychologist, 19,* 76–102.
Schuster, M. R., & Van Dyne, S. R. (1985). Placing women in the liberal arts: Stages of curricular transformation. *Harvard Educational Review, 54,* 413–428.
Shirts, G. (1977). *BaFa BaFa: A cross culture simulation* [Simulation exercise]. Del Mar, CA: Simulation Training Systems.
Stage, F., & Manning, K. (1993). *Enhancing the multicultural campus environment: A cultural brokering approach* (New Directions in Student Services No. 60). San Francisco: Jossey-Bass.
Stanton, A. R., & Grande, S. E. (1998, March). *Facing power and privilege: Educating multiculturally competent counselors.* Paper presented at the meeting of the American Counseling Association, Indianapolis, IN.
Star Power [Simulation exercise]. (1993). Del Mar, CA: Simulation Training Systems.
Sue, D., Bernie, J., Doreen, A., Weinberg, L., Pedersen, P. B., Smith, E., & Vasquez-Nuttal, E. (1982). Position paper: Cross-cultural counseling competencies. *Counseling Psychologist, 10,* 45–52.
Sue, D. W., & Sue, D. (1999). *Counseling the culturally different* (3rd ed.). New York: Wiley.
Talbot, D. M. (1996). Master's students' perspectives on their graduate education regarding issues of diversity. *NASPA Journal, 33,* 163–178.
Valverde, L. A. (1998). Future strategies and actions: Creating multicultural higher education campuses. In L. A. Valverde & Castenell, L. A. (Eds.). (1998). *The multicultural campus: Strategies for transforming higher education* (pp. 19–29). Walnut Creek, CA: AltaMira Press.
Valverde, L. A., & Castenell, L. A. (Eds.). (1998). *The multicultural campus: Strategies for transforming higher education.* Walnut Creek, CA: Alta Mira Press.
Wall, V. A., & Evans, N. J. (Eds.). (2000). *Toward acceptance: Sexual orientation issues on campus.* Lanham, MD: University Press of America.
Wehrly, B., Kenney, K. R., & Kenney, M. E. (1999). *Counseling multiracial families.* Thousand Oaks, CA: Sage.

CHAPTER TWENTY

LEADERSHIP

Judy Lawrence Rogers

"May you live in interesting times." This ancient proverb has never been more relevant than today. The interesting times that confront people in the United States at the turn of the twenty-first century demand new ways of thinking, new ways of learning, new ways of relating, new ways of organizing, and new ways of leading (Allen & Cherrey, 2000). The emerging sciences of chaos theory, complexity, and quantum physics prompt people in Western culture to reexamine their Newtonian science beliefs that the universe is marked by separateness and individualism. Rather, from a quantum lens, the universe is comprised of relationships—everything is connected to everything else in a pattern of unbroken wholeness (Bohm, 1980; Wheatley, 1999).

A striking example of this newly recognized wholeness is the ecology movement, which over the last forty years has demonstrated that nothing in nature exists in isolation. Every living thing is bound together in a vast web of connection (Capra, 1996). People's daily lives are shaped by the reality of interconnectedness, from their involvement with and reliance on the Internet, to the influence of globalization on almost every culture in the world. The rapid and constant dissemination of information shows that the Newtonian belief in control is an illusion—information can no longer easily be hoarded and used as a source of power and control over others. Today, the world is marked by the quantum qualities of change, ambiguity, synchronicity, turbulence, surprise, and order emerging from the chaos.

What is the role of leadership in making meaning in a quantum world? If people are to let go of the notion that they can control events and create change by implementing mechanistic processes, then how do they solve problems, transform outdated systems and structures, and create a better society? These are the questions facing those who would take leadership in higher education institutions. What are the skills. perspectives, attitudes, and approaches needed to lead in a world of flux, change, and paradox? If the Newtonian images of leadership are no longer adequate, what are more useful metaphors for twenty-first century leadership?

Any exploration of new forms of leadership would best begin by placing it in a historical context. How has leadership been viewed up to this point? That in itself is a challenging question, as defining leadership has proved to be a difficult task. As Bennis (1959) observed, "Always, it seems, the concept of leadership eludes us or turns up in another form to taunt us again with its slipperiness and complexity. So we have invented an endless proliferation of terms to deal with it. . . . and still the concept is not sufficiently defined" (p. 259). Burns (1978) agreed: "Leadership is one of the most observed and least understood phenomena on earth" (p. 2). Without a commonly accepted definition of leadership, it is even more difficult to discuss the competencies, behaviors, and beliefs needed to develop it. Different perspectives of leadership call for a different set of skills and attitudes. This chapter presents an overview of the dominant theories of leadership that have shaped our understanding of the concept in Western culture over the past one hundred years. Then, given this theoretical foundation, it explores the competencies, behaviors, and beliefs that one will need to successfully practice leadership in colleges and universities today. In order to put the "messiness" of the leadership literature in perspective, the chapter begins with a brief discussion of how theories are created and how they gain credibility.

In his celebrated work entitled *The Structure of Scientific Revolutions,* Kuhn (1970) describes the rise and fall of dominant paradigms in scientific thought. He defines a paradigm as a set of assumptions that guides our thinking and behavior, shaping our view of the world and how it operates. A paradigm gains favor when it does a better job than its competitors in describing reality. The value of a paradigm is that it allows researchers to operate from an accepted conceptual foundation, a common baseline, rather than having to continually explain and argue for the assumptions that guide their research. Thus a paradigm shapes what we "see," and consequently it shapes what we study and how we study it.

But as Kuhn explains, no paradigm can explain all the facts that confront it. While a paradigmatic lens allows us to see certain things about the world, it can blur or hide other aspects. Anomalies arise in the research that cannot be explained by the prevailing paradigm, prompting us to question the paradigm's basic assumptions. Research begins to either address the anomalies within the parameters of the existing paradigm (if it can) or to present a new paradigm altogether, one that can better explain and respond to the anomalies. Thus a new paradigm is born, which after a period of debate and validation becomes a new set of common assumptions that guides a community's thinking and behavior. It is by this process of establishing new paradigms, researching their parameters, applying them to practice, dealing with their anomalies, and debating their value for explaining reality that we create new knowledge. Kuhn says this process forms the structure of scientific revolutions.

The idea that paradigms come and go attests to the fact that our understanding of nature is only partial at best; at any given time, depending on the lens used, there are aspects of the world that we see and aspects that we do not see. In order to compensate for what is obscured by strongly held assumptions and paradigms, it has been suggested that we use multiple perspectives to more fully understand the world around us and to better guide our practice as professionals (Morgan, 1997). In Chapter Twelve, Kuh takes a multiperspective approach to organizational theory, presenting both conventional and emergent views. Each theory explains some aspects of organizational functioning, but we must view organizations through all of these lenses together in order to come closer to understanding the realities of organizational life. This chapter takes the same approach.

Since the industrial revolution, when it first became a popular subject of study, there have been several prevailing paradigms about the nature of leadership. Each has contributed to our understanding of the concept, but none can stand alone as a definitive set of assumptions about what leadership is. This fact demonstrates one other significant parameter of the study of leadership: the ideas about what constitutes leadership are socially constructed (see McEwen's discussion of theory as social construction in Chapter Eight). The images, definitions and stories that we in Western culture have selected to define leadership arise from our own experiences, contexts, and values. In collectively deciding on images and on language that capture what leadership is, we participate in creating its reality. Leadership is not something that exists outside of us; rather it is what we as a community and as a culture decide it is. Given that, this chapter provides several lenses for examining the concept of leadership; you can then draw conclusions about the behavior of both leaders and their collaborators based on the assumptions you choose to operate from. It is hoped that the ideas in this chapter will prompt you to examine your own "theories in use" (Argyris & Schön, 1974) about leadership. The perspectives offered here, based on emerging conceptions of leadership for the twenty-first century, can help you uncover your assumptions about leadership, examine them, and decide which to keep or modify and which to discard. Let us begin the journey by examining conventional definitions of leadership.

Conventional Views of Leadership

One of the most comprehensive reviews of the literature on leadership was conducted by Stogdill (1974), who found that "there are almost as many definitions of leadership as there are persons who have attempted to define the concept" (p. 259). A few representative definitions illustrate how leadership was conceptualized in the twentieth century:

- Leadership is "the ability to impress the will of the leader on those led and induce obedience, respect, loyalty, and cooperation" (Moore, 1927, p. 124).
- "Leadership can be conceptualized as an interaction between a person and the members of a group. . . . One person, the leader, influences, while the other person responds" (Gordon, 1955, p. 10).
- Leadership is "the process of influencing human behavior so as to accomplish the goals prescribed by the organizationally appointed leader" (Prince & Associates, 1985, p. 7).
- "Managers do things right. Leaders do the right thing" (Bennis & Nanus, 1985, p. 21).

In examining these definitions for their underlying assumptions, several themes emerge that characterize conventional notions of leadership. These themes emanate from the dominant theories of leadership which shaped our understanding of the concept for most of the twentieth century, including, trait theory, behavioral theories, and contingency theories (Bowditch & Buono, 1990; Yukl, 1994). The first theme is that leadership is the property of an individual. One person—a leader—provides leadership. A leader interacts with followers primarily to get them to do what he or she wants them to do. A leader may influence either through persuasion or power, but the point is to get the followers to accomplish the goals the leader sets (Rost, 1991).

The second theme is that leadership pertains primarily to formal groups or organizations. Leaders are those who hold authority within organizations and have a complement of subordinates reporting to them. The role of the leader is to monitor, control, and direct subordinates to ensure maximum effectiveness in completing organizational tasks. Subordinates—persons who hold positions lower in the organizational hierarchy—are not usually considered leaders. Leadership is reserved for those who have been given a certain rank within the organization.

A third theme or assumption about leadership stems directly from the previous one; throughout the twentieth century, the concepts of leadership and management have been integrally intertwined. The words *leadership* and *management* are often used interchangeably (Rost, 1991; Yukl, 1994). When a distinction *is* drawn, as in the above quote from Bennis and Nanus, leadership is simply considered to be *good* management: "Hence there is no such thing as bad leadership because when leadership is bad, it is characterized as management" (Rost, 1994, p. 3). The confusion of leadership with management points to a deeply embedded assumption in the conventional perspective on leadership, an assumption that has shaped studies of what constitutes a good leader.

Implications of the Conventional View of Leadership

These assumptions about leadership have shaped the dominant image of effective leadership in American society. An effective leader is a hero, a masterful planner who sits atop a pyramid of power, controlling the people and processes of an organization. A leader is decisive, tough-minded, unemotional, analytical, and skilled at wielding power. A leader is an expert who creates a vision for his or her organization and through a process of exchange with followers motivates them to buy into it. Leadership is the domain of individuals—powerful, all-knowing individuals. This view of leadership, which resonates with the values of the rational-bureaucratic model of organizations (see Chapter Twelve), has been labeled the industrial paradigm of leadership (Rost, 1991).

Think for a moment about your own perspective on leadership. How many of the concepts embodied in the industrial paradigm of leadership are embraced by your image of a leader? How do those concepts influence your ideas about who can play a leadership role in the groups or organizations you participate in? How do they shape your assessment of your own ability to be a leader? How do they shape your behavior when you are placed into a position of leadership? How do they shape the way you design leadership development programs for the students you work with? It is important that you recognize the assumptions that guide your thinking and behavior related to leadership. The industrial paradigm of leadership presents *one* way to conceptualize leadership; although it has been the dominant perspective for most of the twentieth century in the United States, it is not the only perspective. Let us now examine some other perspectives.

Alternative Views of Leadership

A number of scholars broke with mainstream thinking about leadership in the latter part of the twentieth century. The work of three of these authors—Greenleaf (1970), Burns (1978), and Foster (1986)—is highlighted here. Each represents a shift away from the assumptions of the industrial paradigm of leadership and provides us with additional insights about the nature and definition of leadership. (Exhibit 20.1 contrasts the characteristics and images of industrial and postindustrial leadership.)

Servant Leadership

In his 1970 book *The Servant as Leader*, Greenleaf made a radical departure from the industrial paradigm's conception of leaders as all-knowing, all-powerful heroes. He proposed instead that "the great leader is seen as servant first" (p. 2). Greenleaf based this conclusion on changes he saw emerging in American society. The concepts of

EXHIBIT 20.1. CHARACTERISTICS AND IMAGES OF INDUSTRIAL AND POSTINDUSTRIAL LEADERSHIP.

Industrial Paradigm: Conventional Leadership	Postindustrial Paradigm: Collaborative Leadership
Individual focus	Relational
Command and control	Noncoercive persuasion
Rational, unemotional, analytical	Intellectual, emotional, spiritual
Power over	Power with
Hero	Servant
Competitive	Collaborative
A leader is a leader all the time	Leadership is "episodic"
Transactional	Transforming
Leadership is equated with position in the hierarchy	Leadership roves among group members based on expertise and commitment
Grounded in Western perspectives	Grounded in Western and Eastern perspectives
Social responsibility is minimized	Social responsibility is a central value

Source: Rogers and Ballard (1995), Rost (1994), Senge (1990).

power and authority were being critically examined, and cooperation and support were emerging as more productive ways for people to relate to one another.

Greenleaf stressed that a servant leader is not only *seen* as a servant, he or she *is* first and foremost a servant. The servant leader takes care to ensure that other people's greatest needs are met and that they therefore "become healthier, wiser, freer, more autonomous, more likely themselves to become servants" (p. 7). The qualities, abilities, and beliefs of servant leaders include: listening before acting (in order to better understand a situation); exhibiting empathy for and acceptance of those who follow their lead; developing their intuition and an ability to "foresee the unforeseeable" (p. 14); leading by persuasion; forging change by "convincement rather than coercion" (p. 21); being able to conceptualize reforms and make others see the same possibilities; and empowering those they serve by creating opportunities and alternatives for them. The servant leader recognizes that the first step to changing the world is to change oneself. A well-known example of servant leadership is Mother Theresa. Through her work serving and advocating for the poor, leadership accrued to her.

Transforming Leadership

In 1978, Burns further extended the debate about what leadership comprises by describing two forms of leadership, transactional and transforming. According to Burns, transactional leadership is comprised of organizational bartering—exchanging wants and needs between leaders and followers. People follow a transactional leader because he or she will help them achieve their goals; thus it is obvious to followers that it is in their own best interest to do what the leader asks in order to get their needs met (Kellerman, 1984). The transactional image of leadership closely parallels the industrial paradigm.

Transforming leadership goes beyond the notion of exchange. Burns asserted that transforming leadership demonstrates two essential qualities—it is relational, and it is about producing real change. Burns explains that "transforming leadership occurs when one or more persons engage with others in such a way that leaders and followers raise one another to higher levels of motivation and morality" (p. 20). Thus transforming leadership inspires a commingling of needs, aspirations, and goals in a common enterprise. The purpose of this engagement between leaders and followers is to bring about change. In fact, in Burns' view, the ultimate test of practical leadership is the realization of intended, necessary change. Transforming leadership has a moral dimension as well, because those engaged in it "can be lifted *into* their better selves" (p. 462). This moral purpose of transforming leadership was particularly evidenced by Burns' argument that both the processes used to bring about change and the intended change itself must be ethical. Burns cites Mohandas Gandhi as an example of a transforming leader.

Burns' seminal work enlightened people to the fact that leadership is really about transformation. Transforming leadership forges a relationship between leaders and followers in which both are elevated to more principled levels of judgment. It is about leaders and followers engaging one another in a change process. It is about power "to" rather than power "over." And, in the manner described by Kuhn (1970), Burns' and Greenleaf's ideas began to transform notions of leadership over the past several decades.

Critical Leadership

Foster (1986) and other critical theorists (such as Smyth, 1989) homed in on the idea of transformational leadership by examining the content of the change leadership can bring about. They believed leadership should focus on restructuring society: "Leadership is and must be socially critical, it does not reside in an individual but in the relationship between individuals, and it is oriented towards social vision and change, not simply, or only, organizational goals" (Foster, 1986, p. 46). Transforming leaders and their followers can pursue a vision of greatness together, but the critical question is, Whose vision is it? According to the critical perspective, for transforming leadership to actually transform, it must prompt those engaged in the process to question the assumptions their vision is based upon. Thus, critical transforming leadership requires reflection and analysis. It causes us to ask on whose behalf we use our power. It makes a place for all voices and arguments, regardless of race, class, or gender (Quantz, Rogers, & Dantley, 1991). Since the critical model of leadership is about changing the human condition, leadership can spring from anywhere; it is not confined to an organizational hierarchy. In this view, leadership is a courageous political act aimed at creating conditions that empower followers to become leaders themselves.

And, finally, Foster (1989) offers that critical transforming leadership is not "a special or unique occurrence, one that is found only in certain grand moments of human history. Rather, it happens in everyday events, when commonplace leaders exert some effect on their situations" (p. 52). A good example of critical transforming leadership is the work of the Brazilian educator Paulo Freire, who through his teaching methods enlightened the peasants in his country about the power they possessed to change the conditions that oppressed them (Freire, 1970).

Implications of Alternative Views of Leadership

There are several common themes that emerge in analyzing these three alternative perspectives on leadership. First, leadership is a relationship; it is not the "property" of any individual. Leadership tasks are accomplished with both leaders and followers—followers are an essential part of the equation. The role of the leader is to serve followers and to create conditions that encourage them to become leaders themselves. Second, leadership is about change. For both leaders and followers, change begins within and then emanates outward into the community. Leadership requires critical reflection and analysis in order to determine if the vision of change being pursued is inclusive or if it excludes or diminishes some members of the community. Third, leadership can be done by anyone, not just by people who are designated leaders.

Again, reflect on your current image of leaders and leadership. Do you see leaders as servants, change agents, and people who share power with others? Have you considered that leadership can come from anyone, whether or not they are a designated leader? Have you considered leadership as a relationship between leaders and followers rather than as something a leader practices independently? Have these perspectives shaped the way you practice leadership with colleagues and students? These alternative perspectives on leadership gained credence because they captured some aspects of our experience with leadership better than the conventional view. These perspectives involve aspects of leadership that are not addressed by the industrial paradigm, and thus they prompted a search for a new paradigm of leadership for the twenty-first century.

The Postindustrial Paradigm of Leadership

In his book *Leadership for the Twenty-First Century,* Rost (1991) proposed a new paradigm of leadership. As Kuhn (1970) has made clear, one does not pronounce a new paradigm without substantial evidence of its need. And so it was with Rost. He argued convincingly that the industrial paradigm was not adequate to explain the realities of leadership today or to define the type of leadership needed in the twenty-first century. What are the realities that prompted Rost to promote a new leadership paradigm?

The Argument for a New Paradigm of Leadership

As previously described, the new sciences have opened our eyes to aspects of the universe and human existence that we did not see clearly before. Newtonian science taught us all about our "particle-like" existence, that is, who we are separate from others. Quantum theory explores our "wave-like" dimensions, that is, who we are in relationship with others (Zohar, 1997). Allen and Cherrey (2000) have labeled this shift in perspective the "dawning of the networked, knowledge era" (p. 1).

In a network versus a hierarchical system, boundaries are blurred. Networks are in constant flux and they behave in nonlinear ways. Change occurs through influencing the network at various places in the system rather than through the controlled, step-by step processes that are engaged in hierarchical organizations. Networks are extremely complex and require that people be comfortable with ambiguity to function well in them (Allen & Cherrey, 2000).

A networked world poses new significance for the role of knowledge in our lives and also for the way we learn. Thus Allen and Cherrey (2000) also propose that American society is moving from the industrial era to a knowledge era. In a knowledge-based world, continual learning is paramount as people constantly respond to change and turbulence in the environment. In a knowledge era it becomes clear that it is impossible for one person, the leader, to know everything. Rather, cooperation with others allows one to expand his or her knowledge base and creativity is fostered through collaboration.

In this new world view, where we recognize the primacy of relationships, there is a need for new metaphors for leadership. The hierarchical, command and control image of the industrial culture no longer works in most situations. It is in the context of a networked, knowledge era that Rost (1994), expanding on the works of Greenleaf, Burns, and Foster, offered his postindustrial definition of leadership for our consideration.

Defining Postindustrial Leadership

Rost's (1994) definition of leadership is this: "Leadership is an influence relationship among leaders and their collaborators who intend real changes that reflect their mutual purposes" (p. 7). There are several essential elements in this definition of leadership, and each responds to the context of a networked, knowledge era. First, leadership is a relationship—a collaboration among people who have a shared purpose. They pool their knowledge, their resources, and their commitment to bring about a particular change. Second, this leadership group attempts to nudge the system into change through their collective action. They attempt to influence each other and influence the system where they can. They do not operate under the illusion that they can change the system through mechanisms of control but rather through noncoercive persuasion. Finally, just as boundaries are blurred in a networked era, so too is the role of leader. In leadership relationships in the postindustrial paradigm, leadership is "episodic." One is not a leader all of the time; rather one is "the leader" when one chooses to exert the greatest influence on the change process. Thus the boundary between "leaders" and "collaborators" is blurred, roles are in flux in response to the demands from the environment. (Again, review Exhibit 20.1 to compare and contrast the values and characteristics of industrial and postindustrial leadership.)

Implications of the Postindustrial Paradigm of Leadership

The postindustrial, collaborative view of leadership is rapidly gaining credence at this time in history (Zohar, 1997). Numerous authors, building on the perspectives of Greenleaf, Burns, and Foster and using Rost's definition as a base line, have fleshed out new images and understandings of leadership for a networked, knowledge era. Most notably Wheatley (1999), drawing on the quantum perspective that "relationship is the key determiner of everything" (p. 11), eloquently elaborates on the relational nature of leadership. Bensimon and Neumann (1993) urge us to see leadership in its collective form "occurring among and through a group of people who think and act together" (p. 2). Heifetz (1994) proposes that leadership is about adaptive work, where leaders and collaborators engage in reality testing and in "respecting conflict, negotiation and a diversity of viewpoints" (p. 26) in accomplishing shared community goals. Lipman-Blumen (1996) defines "connective leaders" as those who can effectively deal with the highly charged tensions of diversity and interdependence in a global context. Komives, Lucas, and McMahon (1998) offer a relational leadership model comprised of five interacting elements, specifically, leadership is inclusive, empowering, purposeful, ethical, and process oriented.

Collaborative Leadership

A particularly relevant exposition of postindustrial, collaborative leadership for the student affairs and higher education arena is provided in *Leadership Reconsidered* (Astin & Astin, 2000). These authors view leadership as "a group process whereby people work together in order to foster change and transformation" (p. 11). They depict the purposes of this collaborative form of leadership as encompassing the following values:

- To create a supportive environment where people can grow, thrive, and live in peace with one another
- To promote harmony with nature and thereby provide sustainability for future generations
- To create communities of reciprocal care and shared responsibility where every person matters and each person's welfare and dignity is respected and supported (p. 11)

This articulation of the intended outcomes of collaborative leadership clearly demonstrates links to the moral purpose of leadership of which Burns (1978) wrote and also responds to Foster's (1986) critical leadership theory ideals of social justice, equity, respect for difference and diversity, and social responsibility. Collaborative leadership models are grounded in democratic assumptions, that is, the belief that in a complex world, "answers are to be found in community"—in group-centered organizations where everyone participates and learns continually (Senge, 1990). Martinez-Coslo (1996) contends that the elements of postindustrial, collaborative leadership "foster pluralism which occurs when minority group members participate fully in the dominant society, yet maintain their cultural differences" (p. 55). In the same vein, Selsky and Smith (1994) have developed a model for leadership practices in diverse communities that incorporates the principles and values of postindustrial leadership. Thus, collaborative leadership models resonate fully with higher education's push to create democratic campus cultures based in an ethic of care (Boyer, 1990; Rhoads & Black, 1995; Tierney, 1993).

There is an additional, emerging theme in the literature exploring postindustrial, collaborative leadership models. The spiritual dimension of leadership is being recognized as a critical component of leading in a networked, knowledge era (Bolman & Deal, 1995; Briskin, 1998; Hagberg, 1994; Palmer, 1992; Secretan, 1997; Zohar, 1997). The constant flux, ambiguity, and paradox that mark life in twenty-first century organizations require organization members to embrace constant change. Collaborative leaders have to step outside of their traditionally defined roles; they have to suffer risks as they influence organizational transformation. To bring about deep change in others, collaborative leaders also have to reinvent themselves (Quinn, 1996). This kind of profound personal change occurs on the spiritual level (Zohar, 1997).

The argument is persuasive that a networked, knowledge era requires collaborative leaders who operate from their souls, from their inner power, not leaders who operate out of fear or ego gratification (Hagberg, 1994). The key to successful collaborative leadership is continuous personal change and ongoing critical reflection about one's relationship to diverse others. It involves a rebirth, a journey from which the leader emerges empowered and empowering. But this journey is demanding; it involves facing one's own demons (Palmer, 1992). It means becoming familiar with and embracing one's shadow side (one's fears, prejudices, insecurities, etc.). Hagberg (1994) agrees and adds, "To transform organizations we need to transform ourselves. We need to become whole. And that is a profound spiritual journey requiring courage" (p. 230).

The collaborative leadership paradigm responds to the demands of a networked, knowledge era. It also carries out the expressed values of higher education to create vibrant, democratic communities based in justice and equity. Finally, collaborative leadership has the potential to engage the spiritual dimension as people work together to enact change.

Application of the Collaborative Leadership Model

Is collaborative leadership practiced in higher education? Yes, we have some examples of this new leadership paradigm in action. For instance, some student groups likely demonstrate collaborative leadership. Consider the example of the peer education drama troupes that are prevalent on college campuses across the country. The students in these troupes come together because of their mutual dedication to educating their peers about important social issues. Their goal is social justice—to change society, to free it from drug abuse, sexual assault, racism, homophobia, sexual harassment, and so on through education in the form of skits and role plays. While these groups typically have a designated leader (sometimes a student affairs professional who serves as coordinator), leadership does not rest solely with this person. Leadership roves among the members of the troupe, depending on the task to be performed, the issue to be addressed, and the expertise of the members. For example, the most skilled writer in the troupe takes a leadership role when new scripts must be conceptualized and written. The most experienced actors or actresses take the leadership position when skits are rehearsed and new members trained. The most visionary or articulate member of the group may have the most influence on defining the troupe's values, setting its policies, deciding on new projects, and so on. It is important to understand that while the designated "leader"—the coordinator—may take a leadership role at times, he or she is not the real leader all the time. In fact, in an empowered group the coordinator may play a primarily collaborative role, with short periods of being a leader. The student members are also collaborators as well as leaders, depending on the context and the task. The influence such leaders and collaborators exert is in the form of noncoercive persuasion; it comes from all directions, not just from the coordinator (from the top down). The leaders and collaborators are engaged in a give-and-take relationship because they desire to bring about real change. The changes they intend reflect their mutual purposes. And engaging in this kind of transforming work surely taps into deep questions of meaning and purpose for the troupe members. Thus their spiritual selves are expressed as they interact with others about these critical social issues.

Examples of postindustrial, collaborative leadership can also be found among other constituents of a university community, including student affairs staff, academic administrators, support staff, and faculty. For instance, the learning organization movement is beginning to reshape the way educational institutions think about how they are structured (Senge, Kleiner, Roberts, Ross, & Smith, 1994). In learning organizations, cross-functional task forces and committees are often created. The author recently participated in a change process that exhibited the elements of collaborative leadership and can serve as an example. The situation involved changing a particular campus policy, and it required the buy-in of several student affairs offices, faculty from one department, academic administrators, and students. The steering committee that took the initiative to change the policy (it was not mandated from above) included members of the groups listed. There was not a hierarchical leader on the steering committee, rather, as different issues arose, various members took leadership based on their experience with the issue. Decisions were made as the process unfolded, and they emerged from the collective thinking of the group rather than being made by a "designated leader." Members of the committee readily shared information and ideas, and thus we continually learned from each other. Differences in perspective were valued as they helped us to analyze the policy change from many different angles. The roles of facilitator and task monitor also roved among the group from meeting to meeting.

My observation is that two important factors played into the success of this collaborative leadership process. First, members of the committee viewed each other as equals. No matter what someone's title and position in the institutional hierarchy, in this particular process everyone was valued equally for the knowledge they could bring to the problem. Second, each member of the committee had a very clear sense of shared purposes and goals, and this "vision" guided us through the ambiguity, uncertainty, and conflict that is endemic to any change process.

Any staff group in student affairs (such as residence life, student activities, or admissions) can adopt principles of collaborative leadership and operate primarily in the way described above. It simply requires individuals who have the commitment and the competencies necessary to let go of bureaucratic roles and rules and who can create the conditions in which collaborative leadership relationships can form. Together, such a community of believers can pursue a transformational cause.

The Central Role of Ethics in Collaborative Leadership

Burns (1978) and the critical theorists (Foster, 1986; Smyth, 1989) challenged people to consider the content of the change transforming leaders seek to make. In their eyes, change should have a moral purpose. Rost (1993) and Astin and Astin (2000) continued this emphasis on the moral and ethical dimension of leadership in their exposition of postindustrial, collaborative leadership. Ethics is at the heart of collaborative leadership (Ciulla, 1995). There are two general ethical issues to consider if one operates from the premise that leadership is a relationship. The first question to ask is whether the *process* of how leadership is practiced is ethical. The second question is whether the *change* that leaders and collaborators intend is morally acceptable (Rost, 1993).

How do we as leaders and collaborators evaluate whether the process of change and the intended change itself are ethical? First, we each have to critically reflect on our own values. What are my core values? How do they influence my thinking and behavior? How do my values influence an evaluation of ethical situations? Second, we have to realize when circumstances have led us into ethical dilemmas. Have I developed a keen sense of when the process or intended outcomes of leadership are raising ethical questions? Third, we have to call on a set of guidelines to help us weigh ethical dilemmas. Have I identified a set of ethical principles that can help me when faced with thorny ethical issues? (See Chapter Six for a discussion of ethical principles and frameworks.) Fourth, at times we need others' perspectives to help us sort through the decisions before us. Have I cultivated trusted, wise mentors who can help me weigh the issues when I get stuck?

Assessing the process and intended outcomes of collaborative leadership calls on everyone in the leadership relationship to be cognizant of their decisions and actions at all times. Ethical reflection is a central component of collaborative leadership and a critical element in leadership development.

Competencies, Behaviors, and Beliefs

The next question for consideration is this: what are the competencies, behaviors, and beliefs that will enhance one's ability to successfully participate in leadership relationships in the twenty-first century? The conventional "leader as hero" approach focused leadership development efforts almost exclusively on teaching *individuals* to be leaders (Drath & Palus, 1994). A quick review of the literature, including student affairs publications, demonstrates how deeply leadership development programs are invested in the belief that developing individuals is the primary objective of leadership education. In the postindustrial view of leadership, the focus of education shifts from developing a leader to enhancing everyone's ability to participate in the process of leadership (Drath & Palus).

The following list of competencies is suggested as a foundation for student affairs professionals seeking to successfully engage in collaborative leadership. This is not meant to be a recipe for how to engage in leadership, since it is clear that each leadership relationship is unique and takes on the characteristics of those who have chosen to participate in a particular change effort. But the following competencies will surely enhance the effectiveness of any leadership relationship.

Ongoing Self-Development and Change

Greenleaf (1970) eloquently taught that change begins with us: "If a flaw in the world is to be remedied, to the servant, the process of change starts in here, in the servant, not out there" (p. 33). Mohandas Gandhi helped free his country from the British by spinning his own cloth and collecting his own salt from the sea rather than continuing to support British monopolies that kept his country in servitude. His example prompted a revolution. Rosa Parks decided she would no longer be discriminated against and humiliated by segregation and so refused to move to the back of a bus. Her act of individual courage set an example that mobilized the civil rights movement. Candy Lightner, out of her grief and a fierce determination that the death of her child would have a greater purpose, founded Mothers Against Drunk Driving, the grassroots movement that changed American social consciousness about drinking and driving. The point here is that people who engage in collaborative leadership need to identify what they believe in deeply and demonstrate by example and personal courage their commitment to change. Their example will influence others and initiate the process of building a community of believers.

Collaborative leaders such as those described above both develop and tap into their emotional and spiritual dimensions in their leadership work. Emotional intelligence consists of the ability to know one's feelings, to manage one's feelings, to motivate oneself, to recognize emotions in others, and to handle relationships (Goleman, 1998; Mayer & Salovey, 1997). Spiritual intelligence represents "a dynamic wholeness of the self in which the self is at one with itself and with the whole of creation" (Zohar & Marshall, 2000, p. 124). Spiritual intelligence takes people beyond their current reality, beyond their ego needs, joys, problems, and plans and puts them in a broader context. It is the source of thinking that moves beyond current paradigms and transforms patterns of thought (Zohar & Marshall, 2000). Collaborative leaders fully engage the emotional and spiritual levels of the self, in addition to the intellectual dimension, in pursuing the changes they seek to make in the world.

Developing oneself, committing to a core set of values, employing all dimensions of the self in leadership work is enhanced through continual critical reflection and evaluation, such as engaging in deep thought about the meaning of one's actions and experiences. What did I just do? Why did I do it? What did I learn from this? What would I do differently to become more effective in the future (Lappé & Du Bois, 1994)? These questions, pondered on a regular basis, will lead to continual self-development and change.

Building Authentic Relationships with Diverse Others

People who engage in collaborative leadership value individual differences. They seek to understand the world from others' perspectives. They genuinely want to learn from the unique insights that each person brings to the change effort. Collaborative leaders practice highly developed listening skills in which they silence their own "inner chatter" in order to be truly present with another. Collaborative leaders also engage in dialogue, a powerful form of communication that expands our awareness, enriching it to develop more complex meaning. Dialogue is the conduit through which community members learn from difference (Zohar, 1997). (A more extensive description of the dialogue process is provided in Chapter Twenty-Four.) When each participant in the leadership relationship is valued and included, they are freed to contribute their full selves, their ideas, hopes, dreams, and commitment to the group's purpose. Martinez-Coslo (1996) agrees and states that when participants' histories are shared and issues of injustice addressed, then trust is established and a truly collaborative process occurs. Postindustrial leadership is grounded in the assumption that all voices must be welcomed and heard for the leadership process to have integrity and for the intended change to be reflective of the relevant larger context.

Structuring a Collaborative Learning Environment

Postindustrial leadership is a process by which leaders and collaborators come together around mutual purposes and influence each other in their intention to bring about real change. This requires a fundamental belief in the power of group process and team learning. Clearly, one must develop group process skills to engage in collaborative leadership, for example, understanding the roles group members play, knowing how to influence the group's process, and providing feedback to group members.

Collaborative leadership in a networked, knowledge era also requires a learning focus. According to Senge (1990) this means that a group must function in a mode of inquiry, recognizing that everybody can learn continually. As the group practices learning together, shared meaning and a sense of mutual ownership emerge. People take risks and learn from failure. Senge refers to this as "commitment to the whole" (p. 171) where people are continually learning how to learn together.

Bensimon and Neumann (1993) examined successful leadership teams in colleges and universities. Their research discovered that successful leadership groups were "thinking" teams. They engaged and fully included the multiple perspectives each team member brought to the process. They examined issues from many angles, valuing criticism as well as support of suggested courses of action. Bensimon and Neumann's study provides an example of "communities of commitment" where learning is a continual and collective process.

Sharing Power

Collaborative leaders share power. They do "with" group members not "for" or "to" them. All participants in the leadership relationship have a voice in decision making, in influencing the agenda of the group, and in building mutual purposes. Thus postindustrial leaders let go of control and instead create opportunities and alternatives so that group members can choose autonomy (Greenleaf, 1970).

In a networked, knowledge world people must get comfortable with ambiguity. Collaborative leaders recognize that they do not have all the answers and in fact, are highly dependent on their group members to interpret new information from the environment and to make meaning of it. Rather than the all-knowing, all-powerful image of the conventional leader, collaborative leaders project an image of being "confident but uncertain" (Langer, 1989, p. 143). They are confident of the shared purposes that the group has established and believe in the power of the collective learning process, but are uncertain about exactly how those purposes will be accomplished.

They hold no pretenses that they can control outcomes or guarantee the future. Thus, collaborative leaders keep the focus on the core purposes of the organization and allow the group members to discover the best methods for actualizing those purposes. Collaborative leaders share power in ways that generate more power for all.

Engaging in Creative Conflict Conducted with Civility

People who engage in collaborative leadership must work through and understand the inevitable conflict that will result from engaging so many diverse perspectives as the group forges mutual purposes. Palmer (1987) observed that there is no learning without conflict. Conflict is not to be avoided but rather valued for what it can teach us. However, differences must be expressed in a context of respect, openness, and trust. Members critique each other's views with the intent of developing new creative insights, not for the purpose of diminishing or degrading another's perspectives. The collaborative leader is vigilant in assessing the tone of conflict situations and in mediating expressions of anger so that the environment remains "safe" for difference (Lappé & Du Bois, 1994). (Also see Chapter Twenty-Four for a further discussion of conflict mediation.)

Forging Shared Purposes

If the process of creating shared values, vision, and purposes is an inclusive one, then members of the leadership relationship come to share congruent images of what the group is trying to accomplish. These shared purposes become an internal control for members' behavior and guide their decision making. The vision is invoked continually as the process of change unfolds, fueling the members' commitment to change. Drath and Palus (1994) refer to this aspect of leadership as "meaning making in a community of practice" (p. 4). The ability to engage persons in forging mutual purposes, to help them make meaning of their involvement in the community and its values, to articulate those purposes as a means to prompt change, is at the heart of postindustrial, collaborative leadership.

Asking Critical Questions

Collaborative leaders engage in critique of the status quo. Is our process ethical? Are the changes we intend beneficial or harmful to others? Are the assumptions that guide our work grounded in democratic and emancipatory principles, or do they marginalize some members of the community? Do the values of equity, justice, and community truly shape our actions, or do we just give these ideals lip service? How do we remain vigilant in critiquing what we do so that we do not drift from our commitment to socially responsible purposes? People who engage in collaborative leadership are not lulled into complacency with the way things are, but rather constantly assess what they do, why they do it, and who their work serves.

Developing a Systemic View

Finally, leaders and collaborators must be able to take a step back and see the bigger picture, the context within which they wish to initiate change. They need to take a holistic, systemic view. For student affairs professionals this means understanding higher education organizations and how they function, as well as understanding the societal milieu in which they exist. The use of multiple perspectives to make sense of how organizations operate provides a much richer analysis than the use of only one view. Using the different "logics" that emanate from different organizational models (see Chapter Twelve) provides leaders and collaborators with a variety of strategies to employ in making the changes they intend. Also, recognizing that the internal and external environments in which student affairs professionals operate are becoming more uncertain, turbulent, and interconnected helps us frame the processes of change in systemic terms instead of relying solely on the language and images of the linear, rational perspective of the conventional paradigm. Using multiple frames to interpret the experiences of the leadership group and to more fully understand the context in which change is to be initiated will enhance the work of student affairs professionals as postindustrial leaders and collaborators.

Conclusion

The fact that "there are almost as many definitions of leadership as there are persons who have attempted to define it" (Stogdill, 1974, p. 259) is even more reason for student affairs professionals to engage in rigorous intellectual analysis and personal self-assessment concerning what it means to be a leader. The purpose of this chapter has been to introduce you to the debate about what leadership comprises and to challenge you to examine your currently held assumptions about leadership. Your assumptions shape how you think about and practice leadership and also how you approach leadership development activities with the students you work with. It is important that you recognize which paradigms of leadership have the greatest influence on you. It is also important to critically examine your assumptions throughout your professional career so that they remain relevant in a rapidly changing world.

Fitzgerald (1936) observed that the mark of a first-rate intellect is the ability to hold two opposing views in the mind at the same time and still be able to function. That is the challenge for those who would take leadership today. The quantum view has not replaced the Newtonian perspective. Rather, quantum physics contains the values of Newtonian science enfolded within itself. What we now know however, given the new quantum perspective, is that Newtonian physics is valid over a much narrower range of experience (Zohar, 1997). The implication for leadership practice is that we need not completely dismiss the conventional and industrial paradigm of leadership. Sometimes it is appropriate for a leader to exercise control, to define goals, to impose structure, and to be the expert. It is just that the conventional paradigm is no longer relevant in *every* situation, which was once the belief. Instead, collaborative leadership is a better fit in a wider array of circumstances in the context of a networked, knowledge world (Zohar). Our choice as leaders then is not one paradigm over another, (i.e., either-or), but rather both. Twenty-first century leadership comprises "leadership that is aware of different paradigms, leadership that can assess the worth of a given paradigm for a given context and choose between options" (Zohar, p. 91).

These are the consequences, for better or worse, of living in a time when our culture is undergoing a transition to a new paradigm.

Understanding the assumptions and language of both the postindustrial and industrial perspectives on leadership will help you make better sense of a world in transition. Also, being clear about your own theoretical framework and understanding the frameworks of the people you work with will increase your ability to understand others, lead with them, and thus bring about real and positive change.

References

Allen, K. E., & Cherrey, C. (2000). *Systemic leadership.* Lanham, MD: University Press of America.

Argyris, C., & Schön, D. A. (1974). *Theory in practice: Increasing professional effectiveness.* San Francisco: Jossey-Bass.

Astin, A., & Astin, H. (2000). *Leadership reconsidered: Engaging higher education in social change.* Battle Creek, MI: W. K. Kellogg Foundation.

Bennis, W. G. (1959). Leadership theory and administrative behavior: The problem of authority. *Administrative Science Quarterly, 4,* 259–260.

Bennis, W. G., & Nanus, B. (1985). *Leaders: The strategies for taking charge.* New York: Harper & Row.

Bensimon, E. M., & Neumann, A. (1993). *Redesigning collegiate leadership.* Baltimore: Johns Hopkins University Press.

Bohm, D. (1980). *Wholeness and the implicate order.* London: Routledge & Kegan.

Bolman, L. G., & Deal, T. E. (1995). *Leading with soul.* San Francisco: Jossey-Bass.

Bowditch, J. L., & Buono, A. F. (1990). *A primer on organizational behavior* (2nd ed.). New York: Wiley.

Boyer, E. L. (1990). *Campus life: In search of community.* Princeton, NJ: The Carnegie Foundation for the Advancement of Teaching.

Briskin, A. (1998). *The stirring of soul in the workplace.* San Francisco: Berrett-Koehler.

Burns, J. M. (1978). *Leadership.* New York: Harper & Row.

Capra, F. (1996). *The web of life.* New York: Anchor Books.

Ciulla, J. (1995). Leadership ethics: Mapping the territory. *Business Ethics Quarterly, 5,* 5–28.

Drath, W. H., & Palus, C. J. (1994). *Making common sense: Leadership as meaning making in a community of practice.* Greensboro, NC: Center for Creative Leadership.

Fitzgerald, F. S. (1936). *The crack-up.* New York: New Directions.

Foster, W. (1986). *Paradigms and promises.* Buffalo, NY: Prometheus Books.

Foster, W. (1989). Toward a critical practice of leadership. In J. Smyth (Ed.), *Critical perspectives on educational leadership* (pp. 39–62). London: Falmer.

Freire, P. (1970). *Pedagogy of the oppressed.* New York: Continuum.

Goleman, D. (1998). What makes a leader? *Harvard Business Review, 76* (6), 93–102.

Gordon, T. (1955). *Group-centered leadership.* Boston: Houghton Mifflin.

Greenleaf, R. K. (1970). *The servant as leader.* Newton Center, MA: Robert K. Greenleaf Center.

Hagberg, J. O. (1994). *Real power.* Salem, WI: Sheffield.

Heifetz, R. A. (1994). *Leadership without easy answers.* Cambridge, MA: Harvard University Press.

Kellerman, B. (1984). Leadership as a political act. In B. Kellerman (Ed.), *Leadership: Multidisciplinary perspectives* (pp. 63–89). Englewood Cliffs, NJ: Prentice Hall.

Komives, S. R., Lucas, N., & McMahon, T. (1998). *Exploring leadership.* San Francisco: Jossey-Bass.

Kuhn, T. S. (1970). *The structure of scientific revolutions* (2nd ed.). Chicago: University of Chicago Press.

Langer, E. (1989). *Mindfulness.* Reading, MA: Addison-Wesley.

Lappé, F. M., & Du Bois, P. M. (1994). *The quickening of America: Rebuilding our nation, remaking our lives.* San Francisco: Jossey-Bass.

Lipman-Blumen, J. (1996). *The connective edge: Leading in an interdependent world.* San Francisco: Jossey-Bass.

Martinez-Coslo, M. (1996). Leadership in communities of color: Elements and sensitivities of a universal model. *The Journal of Leadership Studies, 3* (1), 55–75.

Mayer, J., & Salovey, P. (1997). What is emotional intelligence? In P. Salovey & D. Sluyter (Eds.), *Emotional development and emotional intelligence* (pp. 3–31). New York: Basic Books.

Moore, B. V. (1927). The May conference on leadership. *Personnel Journal, 6,* 124–128.

Morgan, G. (1997). *Images of organization* (2nd ed.). Newbury Park, CA: Sage.

Palmer, P. J. (1987). Community, conflict and ways of knowing. *Change,* September-October, pp. 20–25.

Palmer, P. J. (1992). *Leading from within: Reflections on spirituality and leadership.* Washington, DC: Servant Leadership Press.

Prince, H. T., & Associates (Eds.). (1985). *Leadership in organizations* (3rd ed.). West Point, NY: United States Military Academy.

Quantz, R. A., Rogers, J. L., & Dantley, M. E. (1991). Rethinking transformative leadership: Toward the democratic reform of schools. *Journal of Education, 173* (3), 96–118.

Quinn, R. (1996). *Deep change.* San Francisco: Jossey-Bass.

Rhoads, R., & Black, M. (1995). Student affairs educators as transformative educators: Advancing a critical cultural perspective. *Journal of College Student Development, 36,* 413–420.

Rogers, J. L., & Ballard, S. C. (1995). Aspirational management: Building effective organizations through shared values. *NASPA Journal 32,*162–178.

Rost, J. C. (1991). *Leadership for the twenty-first century.* New York: Praeger.

Rost, J. C. (1993). *Leadership: A discussion about ethics.* Unpublished manuscript, University of San Diego.

Rost, J. C. (1994). *Moving from individual to relationship: A postindustrial paradigm of leadership.* Paper presented at the meeting of the American Educational Research Association, New Orleans.

Secretan, L. H. (1997). *Reclaiming higher ground.* New York: McGraw-Hill.

Selsky, J., & Smith, A. (1994). Community entrepreneurship: A framework for social change leadership. *Leadership Quarterly,* 5, 277–296.

Senge, P. M. (1990). *The fifth discipline.* New York: Doubleday/Currency.

Senge, P. M., Kleiner, A., Roberts, C., Ross, R. B., & Smith, B. J. (1994). *The fifth discipline fieldbook.* New York: Currency.

Smyth, J. (1989). *Critical perspectives on educational leadership.* London: Falmer.

Stogdill, R. M. (1974). *Handbook of leadership: A survey of the literature.* New York: Free Press.

Tierney, W. (1993). *Building communities of difference.* Westport, CT: Bergin & Garvey.

Wheatley, M. J. (1999). *Leadership and the new science: Learning about organization from an orderly universe* (2nd ed). San Francisco: Berrett-Koehler.

Yukl, G. (1994). *Leadership in organizations* (3rd ed.). Englewood Cliffs, NJ: Prentice Hall.

Zohar, D. (1997). *Rewiring the corporate brain.* San Francisco: Berrett-Koehler.

Zohar, D., & Marshall, I. (2000). *SQ: Connecting with our spiritual intelligence.* New York: Bloomsbury.

CHAPTER TWENTY-ONE

TEACHING

Larry D. Roper

Among the most important roles student affairs professionals perform are facilitating student learning and development and supporting the educational mission of their institution. No other activities can immerse them so intimately in the life and success of their institutions as involvement as educators and student learning specialists. By virtue of their educational role they have many opportunities to create and respond to learning needs. Student affairs professionals provide orientation, training, and education for professional and student employees. They may teach credit-bearing courses such as orientation or leadership, on some campuses they may have faculty status, and as supervisors they offer workshops and organize other development and training experiences. Student affairs leaders are in a position to actively support their academic colleagues and enhance the effectiveness of the teaching they provide; others educate directly and formally through their own roles as teachers and trainers. The degree to which professionals are effective in these educational roles will determine how well they are linked to the primary mission of their institution—educating students. The purpose of this chapter is to provide an introduction to the teaching and educator roles of the student affairs professional. The chapter will also include information on essential skills professionals should possess if they are to be effective as educators and support the teaching mission of higher education.

Educator roles, which include teaching and training, vary widely from campus to campus, but certain criteria for effectiveness are common. These criteria are based on extensive research on effective teaching and student learning. While this chapter will focus specifically on teaching, other chapters in this book provide insight into subject matter important for student affairs professionals to teach.

This chapter is aimed at all student affairs professionals, given that the core value of student affairs is to serve as educators. The research cited here should be especially helpful for developing a rationale for student affairs professionals' teaching roles and for identifying specific strategies to achieve desired outcomes. The emphasis in this chapter is on information related to effective teaching; active, cooperative, and collaborative learning; facilitating groups; leading discussions; team building; teaching multicultural populations; and training other trainers. These topics are highlighted because they represent the core activities in the daily lives of student affairs professionals and are vital to faculty members' success as teachers.

Research on Teaching

Teaching and learning are the core activities of the collegiate culture. As such, they are a major focus of those seeking to evaluate the success of colleges and universities. Informed critics of higher education have raised questions about the relationship between teaching and learning and the appropriateness of dominant pedagogical approaches for contemporary college students (Bess & Associates, 2000). There has been growing public concern about the relevance of the subject matter being taught and the approaches used to engage students in learning activities. Among the criticism levied against college teachers are claims that they are afflicted with such maladies as "narration sickness" (Freire, 1970, p. 57) and that they enact rituals of control in the classroom (hooks, 1994). A growing body of research points to the limitations of lecture, the most traditional form of teaching (Bess & Associates, 2000; Finkel, 2000; Taylor, Marienau, & Fiddler, 2000). Further, the growing presence and assertiveness of a diverse population of adult learners has raised new challenges to traditional teaching styles (Barnes, Christensen, & Hansen, 1994; Christensen, Garvin, & Sweet, 1991; Meyers & Jones, 1993).

Traditional Teaching

Traditional instruction consists of teachers performing as lecturer and students assuming the role of listener. This "teaching as telling" approach (Christensen et al., 1991, p. 3) constructs the classroom as a teacher-centered environment (Bruffee, 1993). When a classroom is teacher-centered it provides little space for student-to-student interaction and seriously limits teacher-student interaction. In the traditional classroom, students learn as isolated, independent individuals; they have little, if any, opportunity for meaningful connection with their co-learners (hooks, 1994). Research strongly supports the position that teaching methods that isolate learners do not maximize learning outcomes (for example, see Barnes et al., 1994; Bruffee, 1993; Meyers & Jones, 1993; Palmer, 1998). Colleges and universities are now challenged to reacculturate educators and encourage their adoption of methods that are appropriate for the educational outcomes defined for students (Bruffee, 1993).

While it is documented that good teaching does not necessarily consist of lecturing, the dominant practice in higher education is influenced by the assumption that the core activities of teachers are rooted in talking, telling, explaining, instructing, and professing (Finkel, 2000). This assumption remains in place despite research that shows students' evaluations of teachers reveal greater learning, deeper understanding, and higher appreciation of subject matter in learning situations where lecture is not the dominant teaching technique. The paradox that teachers face is reconciling the expectation that they should speak and impart knowledge, while others expect them to construct interactive learning environments. Educators are pressed to reconcile a range of expectations and adopt practices that meet the needs of learners and others to whom they are accountable.

Good Teaching

Educators should ground themselves in sound practices of "good teaching" that maximize student learning. What is good teaching? Passmore (1970) describes teaching as an activity aimed at *achieving* learning, a process that includes respecting the intellectual integrity of the student and the student's capacity for independent judgment. Menges (1981) asserts that teaching is "the intentional arrangement of situations in which appropriate learning will occur" (p. 556). Teaching is a relationship that promotes student engagement in the construction of knowledge (Christensen et al., 1991). Good teachers possess such qualities as "enthusiasm; knowledge of the subject area; organization; clarity; concern and caring for students; use of higher cognitive level skills in discussions and examinations; use of visual aids; encouragement of student learning and student discussion; provision of feedback; and avoidance of harsh criticism" (Goodwin & Stevens, 1993, p. 166).

The dimensions of good teaching, as described in *Seven Principles for Good Practice in Undergraduate Education* (Chickering & Gamson, 1991), include the following: encouraging student-faculty interaction; encouraging cooperation among students; encouraging active learning; providing prompt feedback; emphasizing time on task; communicating high expectations; and respecting diverse talents and ways of knowing. Good teachers view teaching as a transformational activity in which the teacher is a guide, coach, and facilitator of student learning (McLaughlin & Talbert, 1993). Good teaching can engender qualitative shifts in students that transform the students, their views of themselves, their knowledge, and the world (Taylor et al., 2000). At the same time, teaching is much more than an activity. Teaching is embedded in relationships and involves connectedness among the teacher, the subject, and students (Palmer, 1998). Teaching is also a process of engagement, one that resembles a "performative act" (hooks, 1994, p. 11). At the same time teaching can be viewed in a sterile way, as nothing more than a role that is apart from a relationship with learners—one can be called a teacher even if students do not learn (Bennett, 1995).

Bruffee (1993) suggests that a teacher's most important responsibilities are to build "knowledge communities" and to represent these communities in such a way as to "reacculturate" potential members (p. 3). According to Finkel (2000), "good teaching is the creating of those circumstances that lead to significant learning in others" (p. 8). Finkel concludes that "teaching through telling" is an approach that is hazardous to promoting effective learning. The challenge is to adapt to a model of "teaching with your mouth shut"—one where the teacher is a guide, consultant, and facilitator, among other roles.

Silverman and Casazza (2000) identified seven principles that grew out of their attempts to link theory, teaching, and research in ways that can inform practice. These principles, if adopted, are expected to produce positive learning environments and successful educational experiences:

- Teachers who use concrete examples and suggest practical applications help learners connect prior knowledge to new information.
- Social integration and sense of community are linked to persistence in college.
- Environments characterized by critical dialogue, integrative learning, and risk taking promote student learning and development.
- Peer teaching promotes active learning, academic achievement, and retention in college.
- Adult learners prosper in learning environments that allow for autonomy and self-direction.
- Students with disabilities benefit when necessary accommodations are provided.
- Students learn better when their cultural identities are incorporated into their academic lives (p. 132)

Research on teaching draws a powerful connection among attributes of the teacher, student, learning environment, and subject matter. Successful teachers are able to construct situations that will maximize the influence of each in such a way that students experience optimal learning. Teachers do not work as solo performers; they work within the context of learning communities. As such, successful teachers will display capability as community builders, facilitators, processors of learning experiences, and guides in the learning process.

Student Learning: Desired Outcomes

Every institution establishes its own goals for what it hopes to impart to students, which means there are no universal outcomes towards which all colleges and universities aspire. At the same time, research reveals that no matter the institution, successful students complete their college experience with general and specialized skills, knowledge, and values acquired as a result of their participation in higher education (National Center for Postsecondary Teaching, Learning, and Assessment, 1995). It is also known that students leave our institutions prior to completing academic degrees without having benefited fully from what a relevant and responsive educational experience can give them (Tinto, 1993). Student affairs is a knowledge community, yet its educators do not always have a clear understanding of and direction for their roles as educators.

As a knowledge community, student affairs has its own curriculum and methodologies appropriate to the profession's subject matter. Student affairs educators are challenged to find ways to embed teaching as a central theme in student affairs work. Student affairs professionals should assertively manifest a commitment to promote learning that advances their institution's mission, their profession's values, and their students' growth, development, and learning. Those who work in student affairs are keenly aware that teaching is not merely a role, but an activity and process that involves relationships and community building. Student affairs professionals should possess clear standards of what constitutes good teaching within the profession; energy should be focused on constructing and answering important questions about the roles and responsibilities of individual educators and their performance in teaching and learning activities. Among the questions that might be posed individually and collectively are: What is good teaching within the context of student affairs work? How will I know if I am a good teacher? How do I know that I am the kind of teacher that professional standards suggest I should be? What is my relationship with learners? How do I engage learners? Who do learners experience me as? How do I go beyond my *role* as a teacher to act on my *responsibilities* as a teacher?

As educators student affairs professionals play a key role in preparing students to lead socially and professionally meaningful lives in a changing and challenging world. When students are successfully educated they will be prepared not only to respond effectively to the issues that arise in their own lives but to confront and respond appropriately and creatively to social and institutional dilemmas they encounter.

Educators define their roles, frame their teaching sphere (their sphere of educational influence), organize their curriculum (subject matter), identify potential learning audiences, and choose appropriate teaching methods. As Mines, King, Hood, and Wood (1990) suggest, student affairs practitioners have abundant opportunities to create learning environments in which they can effectively link their work to the major goals of their institution. As they create teaching situations, they can use them to impart whatever knowledge and skills they believe are important for learners to acquire. The obligation of student affairs educators is to identify the skills and knowledge needed by students and to create learning situations that will foster their development.

The goals associated with teaching relate to enhancing students' knowledge, awareness, or skills—student learning outcomes. In the context of colleges and universities, student learning is typically defined in terms of "the learning of basic knowledge in science, mathematics, and the social sciences; cognitive abilities, such as oral and written communication skills, critical thinking, and problem solving; as well as the development of students' values and attitudes toward learning" (National Center for Postsecondary Teaching, Learning, and Assessment, 1995, p. 4).

Among the goals generally ascribed for good college teaching are enhancing students' problem solving, critical analysis, and higher-order thinking (McLaughlin & Talbert, 1993); fostering student identity resolution (Widick & Simpson, 1978); challenging students to think critically and reflect on the assumptions underlying their ideas and actions; helping students understand different forms of knowledge, our current social condition, the meaning of past events, and possibilities for the future; helping students place themselves in the world (Shor, 1992); and helping students uncover their own and others' realities and re-create knowledge (Freire, 1970). These goals are consistent with the developmental goals drawn upon for student affairs work (see Chapters Eight through Ten). The outcome goals associated with the college experience leave no doubt that good student affairs work is synonymous with good teaching—if student affairs educators achieve the learning outcomes identified for effective teaching, they will honor the core values of the profession.

Teaching is a transformative activity. Effective teaching has the ability to create remarkable shifts in students' knowledge, awareness, skills, and ways of being. The challenge presented to educators is to identify the appropriate approach to a particular course or subject matter in order to produce the most positive outcomes for students. Classrooms and other learning environments (such as retreats, workshops, and paraprofessional training sessions) can and do vary widely in terms of atmosphere, depending on the view the educator has of his or her role and the nature of learning to occur. Some educators may see themselves as merely imparting knowledge, while others envision themselves as collaboratively acquiring knowledge along with students (McLaughlin & Talbert, 1993). Some educators disconnect their roles from ideas about student learning and others make student learning the focus of their approach to teaching (Christensen et al., 1991).

While there has been a great deal of criticism of the lecture format as the dominant method of teaching, it is also known that lecture has been found to be as effective as any other method when recall of information is tested (Erickson & Strommer, 1991). However, lecture is not effective in situations where deeper understanding is the desired outcome. Therefore, mere lecture falls short of helping educators to fulfill all of the roles needed from them in teaching situations. Finkel (2000) suggests there are five major responsibilities that teachers have: to organize the inquiry of students; to help students understand the texts, without imposing the teacher's understanding; to help students acquire the skills needed to pursue inquiry; to evaluate students' work; and to participate in the inquiry. The teacher is challenged to distinguish between *understanding* and *skills.* For example, one must distinguish between the skill of analysis and understanding of concepts (Finkel).

Proponents of transformative learning see learning as more than the accumulation of knowledge. One view is that learning can be seen as *reproductive learning, preparatory-to-action learning,* and *reconstructive learning* (Taylor et al., 2000). These types of learning are on a continuum ranging from acquiring and storing knowledge, to taking in procedures and facts so that they can be used in a practical way, to the abstraction of meaning. Reconstructive learning is seen as the transformative stage because that is the level at which the learner experiences deep change and focuses on changing as a person (Taylor et al., 2000).

Transformative learning also offers educators descriptions of particular domains of learning that can be helpful in identifying the teaching approach that may best support their desired outcomes. According to Cranton (1994), learning can take the form of *instrumental learning,* gaining technical knowledge; *communicative learning,* gaining practical knowledge; and *emancipatory learning,* gaining knowledge that transforms the learner. Instrumental learning environments will focus on empirical inquiry, reading from books, interviewing practitioners, and developing an approach based on information gained. Communicative learning involves gaining insight into others' perspectives and the students making their own perspectives known. Emancipatory learning involves critical self-reflection that focuses on the instrumental and communicative learning domains but also includes the integration of self-knowledge (Cranton, 1994).

Effective educators will recognize the continuum along which learning can happen. With this recognition, the goals of teaching may range from the teaching of facts and concepts to fostering a deep understanding of subject matter that causes students to explore who they are, what their relationship is to knowledge, and how they need to change in order to be in alignment with their view of the world. The goal and role of teaching is not confined to imparting content knowledge; it also includes responsibility to cultivate in students the ability to think. A key dimension in promoting deep thinking and transformation of learners is the opportunity for reflection.

The educational continuum along which student affairs educators will teach might range from orientation to developmental instruction, with training assuming the midpoint on the continuum. The primary outcomes of the education provided by student affairs educators relate to enhancing students' knowledge, awareness, or skills.

Reflection and Processing

Students and educators should be provided the opportunity to engage in critical reflection with colleagues (Silverman & Casazza, 2000; Taylor et al., 2000). In this case, reflection refers to the opportunity to think about how one is learning and what one is learning (Taylor et al., 2000) and exploring experiences in order to lead to new understanding and appreciation (Cranton, 1994). According to Palmer (1998) students need to be presented with space in which they can have solitude. Solitude and silence provide the opportunity for students to gain a deep sense of their inner selves and also to reflect on what they have heard and what they have said. Skillful teachers are able to find a successful balance between action and reflection in the classroom or other educational contexts (Brookfield, 1990). They also model for students respect for the positive meaning of silence.

Time allotted to reflection allows students to delve into the deepest meaning of the learning experience; it permits learners to reach within themselves and connect to learning in a way that constant immersion in content cannot. Regardless of the teaching context, students need to have reflective experience. For example, in online or distance learning situations students should be asked to reflect on their own learning process, how using technology influenced that process, and what they have learned about technology during the process (Palloff & Pratt, 2001). Through the cocreation of meaning and knowledge students are able to achieve transformative learning experiences.

Ongoing reflection experiences are an essential component of identity development; it is through reflection that the learner is able to connect their humanity to the knowledge they have acquired. Glazer (1999) reminds educators that: "Our sense of identity can be established in two different ways: either from outside in or from inside out. What comes from outside in is understood as imposition or indoctrination. What emerges from inside out—arises out of our experience—we understand as expression" (p. 79). Reflective moments allow students to make connections among details, to apply abstraction or theory, and to assume active responsibility for understanding themselves and material (Finkel, 2000).

One example of how student affairs educators might apply reflection is to ask a student enrolled in a first-year experience to consider the questions Who am I? and How do I know that I am who I think that I am? Through this exercise students will be required to think of themselves in the abstract (beliefs, values, aspirations, and commitments) and in the concrete (actual behaviors). The teacher can help students to draw connections among the congruent and incongruent aspects of their conceptions of themselves and the realities of their daily behaviors.

In the context of learning the teacher can use the outcomes of students' reflections as the focus of their efforts to process the teaching and learning activity. Through processing the teacher can assist students in drawing connections between the learning activities and their behaviors, capabilities, beliefs, purpose, and the environment (Taylor et al., 2000).

Educators themselves may engage in two types of reflection, reflection-in-action or reflection-on-action. Reflection-in-action is often described as "thinking on your feet," when one pauses during teaching activities to determine the next best step to take. Reflection-on-action normally occurs after teaching or training when one reflects on the experience and determines what should come next in the learning sequence. Naturally, reflection-on-action is more in-depth because the teacher has significantly more time than when one reflects in the midst of the teaching experience. Cranton (1994) offers examples of three types of reflection that teachers can facilitate with learners: *content reflection,* when the content of a problem is investigated or examined; *process reflection,* when the learner stops to think and considers the problem-solving strategies to be used; and *premise reflection,* when the problem itself is questioned and the basic premise underlying the posing of the problem is questioned.

When reflection is effectively fused into a teaching or training experience for teachers or students it can provide a solid foundation for future growth and development (Taylor et al., 2000). Reflection is a crucial phase of the learning process for which the teacher should consciously plan.

Training as a Form of Teaching

Because student affairs professionals serve as employers, supervisors, and administrators, they are presented with numerous teaching opportunities. The various roles provide student affairs educators with responsibility for the orientation, growth, and development of students and staff. These responsibilities include teaching others the knowledge, skills, and awareness needed to function inside and outside our institutions. In some instances the efforts to help others learn is viewed as teaching; at other times these efforts are described as training. Clearly there are times when the terms can be used interchangeably. What the efforts are called may not be as important as understanding the processes involved in performing them effectively.

Historically student affairs has had to assume responsibility for staff training. The inclination to use paraprofessionals in helping and advising roles necessitates the creation of training programs that can impart the necessary skills and knowledge. Employing students in roles such as AIDS educators, peer counselors, resident advisors, and conflict mediators dictates that they receive adequate and appropriate training to fulfill those roles (Carns, Carns, & Wright, 1993). Additionally, when new staff members come to an institution, processes are needed for helping them become familiar with the people, culture, and structures. Training programs provide such grounding for professional success (Merriam & Caffarella, 1991). Training comes in the form of pre-service and in-service activities, credit courses, collaborative programs with other campuses, teleconferences, consultants, and off-campus workshops and conferences. Offering appropriate training programs influences success in student affairs roles and increases the effectiveness of staffs and institutions (Creamer & Shelton, 1988).

Training can be conducted on either an individual or a group basis. Training allows organizational members to respond effectively to changing political, technological, and social influences (Gallessich, 1982). Student affairs training serves many functions: it is a form of continuous professional development (Creamer & Shelton, 1988); it provides a means of teaching needed skills and reducing stress (Winston & Buckner, 1984; Woodard & Komives, 1990); it is used to educate staff to teach others (Fulton, 1978); and it provides a way for us to prepare staff to perform specific tasks (Delworth & Yarris, 1978).

The goal of training is to enhance individuals' knowledge, skills, and attitudes. In general, training serves organizations by preparing those who have been charged with managing organizational processes to respond to particular situations, manage change, and support organizational effectiveness (Stewart, 1991). Sometimes training is approached as a means of improving performance or compensating for performance deficiencies (Gallessich, 1982). In other situations training is used as a means to prepare people for new roles within an organization. Margolis and Bell (1989) describe four types of training:

1. *Administrative training* provides information on policies, procedures, and rules. This type of training usually covers such things as organizational paperwork, requisition procedures, and other information needed to get work done.
2. *Professional-technical training* emphasizes skills needed to complete one's job responsibilities. In student affairs this might include such things as counseling skills, teaching skills, and confrontation skills. This type of training is directed at enhancing the skills of analysis and judgment.
3. *Mechanical-technical training* focuses on such things as how to operate and maintain office equipment, how to access electronic mail, how to use computers and voice mail, and how to transfer telephone calls.
4. *Interpersonal training* teaches staff how to work with others and resolve work-related issues. Training in this area may focus on such skills as interviewing, conflict resolution, and communication skills.

Student affairs professionals will find themselves involved in each of these four types of training. Housing professionals will teach resident assistants to complete incident reports and room inventories; peer advisors will need to be taught basic helping skills; new employees will need to be guided through how to complete travel vouchers and operate a copy machine; and frontline staff will be taught how to handle upset, demanding, or distressed students. Training is necessary in order to ensure that staff can meet the basic demands of their jobs. Because of the irregularity with which people join and leave organizations, training may occur either in planned or impromptu situations. No matter the conditions under which training is provided, the goal is to help people master knowledge, skills, and awareness (Nilson, 1990).

Simply stated, effective training is achieved when the learners master the information conveyed and are able to translate it into appropriate behavior (Warshauer, 1988). There are certain required steps to be followed if formal training programs are to be effective. Among those steps are the following: accurately identifying the needed skills and knowledge; articulating the needed affective, cognitive, and skill requirements in behavioral terms; assessing trainees' knowledge and skill levels; developing a format and sequence for training (moving from simple to complex skills); determining training techniques; planning for ongoing supervision and monitoring; evaluating the procedures; developing a process to train cotrainers, if needed; implementing and evaluating the training program; and redesigning the program based on feedback (Delworth & Yarris, 1978).

In any learning situation, the educator is responsible for planning, implementing, and evaluating the learning experience. Teaching and training are most effective when the teacher-trainer forges a partnership with the learners and involves them in diagnosing their learning needs, formulating their learning goals, designing their learning activities, and evaluating their learning outcomes. Such partnerships make the learning program more learner-centered and potentially more effective than programs in which the learner is not actively involved (Merriam & Caffarella, 1991). Teaching and training techniques should be respectful of learners and acknowledge their diversity. (In Chapter Eleven King describes diversity in learning styles and issues affecting learning readiness.) Our challenge is to create mechanisms to facilitate the professional effectiveness of individuals; provide them with the knowledge, skills, and awareness necessary to function in their role; and achieve some level of uniformity in carrying out our institution's policies and procedures. This should be done in a way that contributes positively to the achievement of the institution's mission. By increasing staff competence and enhancing their knowledge, we are able to increase their value as organizational assets. The development of innovative, nontraditional learning options can dramatically enhance the talent and human capital within our organizations (Stewart, 1997).

Finally, trainers may need to distinguish the immediacy of the learners' need for information. Students will likely react differently if they know they will have an immediate need to apply the information they are being taught. Just-in-time training (JITT) is based on the belief that people are most highly motivated to learn when they know that they will need to soon apply the learning (Rippey, 1993). Just-in-time training has been effectively applied in classroom and training situations; it is an efficient way to provide learning during times of rapid change or crisis.

Essential Knowledge and Skills

The essential skills and knowledge necessary to be effective teachers include the following: knowledge of active, cooperative, and collaborative learning and the ability to promote them; understanding group dynamics and the ability to facilitate groups; understanding discussion and dialogue and the ability to lead them and promote reflection; knowledge of the use of teams in organizations and the ability to promote team building; understanding multicultural populations and the ability to teach diverse learners; and the ability to train other trainers. Effective student affairs professionals are able to translate these skills and knowledge into professional behaviors in their roles as teachers.

Active, Cooperative, and Collaborative Learning

Research is clear that actively involving learners increases learning, enhances relationships with peers and with the teacher, and leads to greater learner satisfaction with the learning experience. The approaches used to achieve maximum learning outcomes include such methods as active learning, cooperative learning, collaborative learning, and the case study method (Barnes et al., 1994; Bruffee, 1993; Erickson & Strommer, 1991; Garibaldi, 1992; Johnson, Johnson, & Smith, 1991; Tiberius & Billson, 1991). These approaches are all learner-centered, and they all focus on creating a participatory learning environment. Effective educators possess knowledge of each of these approaches and can readily determine appropriate situations in which to utilize them.

Active learning techniques display the following basic characteristics: student tasks involve more than sitting and listening; emphasis is placed on skill development rather than on transmitting information; learners are involved in higher-order cognitive activities such as analysis, synthesis, and evaluation; involvement includes experiential activities; and emphasis is placed on exploring learners' attitudes and values (Bonwell & Eison, 1991). The use of active learning strategies is viewed as one of the major commitments educators can make to acknowledging the diversity of learners on our campuses. Because women and culturally diverse students bring unique ideas and needs to campus, traditional teaching styles are not viewed as being responsive to them (Meyers & Jones, 1993). Active learning techniques are promoted for cognitive, philosophic, and pragmatic reasons. Students retain less information when they learn passively. Critical thinking and artistic sensibilities cannot be cultivated through lectures, and students are generally dissatisfied with passive learning (Christensen et al., 1991).

Active learning strategies include role plays, simulations, computer-based instruction, debates, peer teaching, in-class writing, and cooperative learning (Bonwell & Eison, 1991). Student affairs professionals must make use of the resources available to them to create active learning situations when they teach.

Cooperative learning involves the use of small groups to maximize learning by fostering positive interdependence, requiring face-to-face interaction, exacting individual accountability, and offering opportunities for group processing (Johnson et al., 1991).

Collaborative learning involves a partnership between the teacher and students. In this model, the students and teacher jointly construct knowledge on a particular subject or issue. Generally the goal of collaborative learning is to encourage critical thinking,

In collaborative learning situations, the teacher provides instructions, organizes groups (including assigning roles), provides stimulus questions, facilitates processing of group work, and brings closure to the discussion (Bruffee, 1993). Student affairs professionals might employ collaborative learning techniques by giving a copy of their institution's mission statement to a group of new employees. The trainer may want to identify key words in that statement and ask the group to reach a consensus on what those words mean for their roles and responsibilities. In subsequent sessions the trainer might help the learners grapple with the challenges inherent in attempting to translate a confusing document into appropriate professional practice and organizational alignment.

Facilitating Groups

There are distinct differences between teaching and facilitating learning. "Facilitation of learning is often more informal and multidirectional than traditional instruction" (Brooks-Harris & Stock-Ward, 1998, p. 8). Teaching usually takes the form of teachers transferring knowledge they have acquired to the learners; facilitation involves acknowledging the different ways people learn and creating environments to nurture and support their learning (Warshauer, 1988). Teachers can be categorized as facilitators of learning groups—groups whose purpose is to ensure that members acquire certain knowledge, skills, information, or procedures (Johnson & Johnson, 2000). The primary role of facilitators is to create an environment that allows group members to learn easily (Stewart, 1991). Facilitators need knowledge and skills that will actively engage learners; assist learners in acquiring new information and conceptualizing their understanding; allow learners to actively experiment with new knowledge and skills; and support learners in personalizing the learning by developing plans to apply it to their own lives (Brooks-Harris & Stock-Ward). Facilitators must possess the intervention skills to solve problems that arise in groups and the ability to turn those situations into learning experiences for participants (Warshauer). Effective facilitators are good communicators. Facilitators are able to show that they value individual group members and are willing to share power and leadership. They are flexible and open to new ideas, and they are honest with participants concerning their observations (Stewart). Regardless of the teaching situation, good facilitation skills are essential. A skillful facilitator will increase the value of the learning experience for group members and increase the possibility of engagement by learners in learning activities (Brookfield, 1990).

Facilitators will bring to bear skills that may not surface in traditional teaching situations; among those skills are: setting ground rules and norms; clarifying goals for the learning experience; reflecting; paraphrasing; reinforcing; probing; encouraging brainstorming; and encouraging self-disclosure (Brooks-Harris & Stock-Ward, 1999). Each of the skills used in facilitation constitutes a specific competency and when used in concert increases the effectiveness of the facilitator and learning for the participants.

Leading Discussion and Dialogue

Discussion and dialogue are the core activity in organizational life and active learning situations. Conversations help learners resolve contradictions; they are the primary vehicle through which learners personalize their relationships with their peers, share their reflections, and crystallize their thinking on issues (Johnson et al., 1991). Because both discussion and dialogue are important components of active learning environments, educators need specific skills for maximizing the potential of each. Discussions typically focus on having the learner break issues into parts, justify and defend perspectives, and persuade or sell ideas. The goal of discussion in learning situations is to gain agreement on one meaning. Dialogue focuses on seeing the whole of the parts, drawing connections, learning through inquiry, and exploring assumptions. The goal of dialogue is to create shared meaning among learners (Elinor & Gerard, 1998). The ability to lead discussions and dialogue is a key indicator of one's ability to effectively grasp active learning concepts. The act of encouraging conversation graphically illustrates a fundamental shift from a traditional teaching approach. In conversation-focused learning environments, the balance of power shifts toward a more democratic paradigm than in traditional learning environments; the educator moves away from focusing solely on content, toward considering the learning process and classroom climate as well. In conversation-centered learning situations the teacher shifts from the traditional stance of making declarative explanations to using questioning, listening, and responding to promote learning (Christensen et al., 1991). Discussion and dialogue leaders must be sensitive to the fact that learners may feel threatened. Activities should be designed to provide a safe climate that will allow students to share their thoughts, feelings, and observations. Conversation leaders should be skilled at using questions to inspire involvement and motivate learning (Bonwell & Eison, 1991).

Team Building

Colleges and universities, like many other organizations, have increasingly come to rely on cross-functional and interdepartmental groups to accomplish various tasks. Because of decreases in the size of the work force and increases in educational initiatives on campuses, leaders have had to respond with creative arrangements to further institutional missions. The use of task forces, strategic planning committees, search committees, Total Quality Management techniques, and self-directed work groups have created situations where members of organizations are brought together to work with people with whom they may not be familiar. Campus leaders have an obligation to make sure these groups are equipped with the knowledge and skills to function effectively (Lubin & Eddy, 1987). The various groups that function on campuses are often referred to as "teams" (quality teams, diversity teams, programming teams), but we do not often acknowledge them as such by providing them with the training necessary to function relative to their charge. Teams that receive training are better able to respond to change and are more likely to achieve their stated objectives (Stewart, 1991). Providing members with shared learning experiences is one way to build effective teams and to achieve the necessary alignment (Senge, 1990).

Educators need knowledge of group-building and team-building strategies. Team builders should help group members get to know one another, clarify their goals, establish communication, define and solve problems, and make decisions. The goal of the trainer is to improve the group's effectiveness so that it can achieve the desired results (Dyer, 1995). Leaders of groups require the knowledge and skills to guide groups through the team-development process. Most importantly, teachers and trainers should possess knowledge about team building and utilize the proper resources to facilitate building effective teams. Among the useful techniques in team-building are ice breakers, trust-building activities, consensus-building activities, experience-based activities (such as ropes courses and adventure training), communication enhancement activities, and conflict resolution strategies.

Teaching Multicultural Populations

Supporting diversity is embedded in the missions and strategic goals of most colleges and universities. One of the major challenges related to this effort is creating positive learning environments that support diverse student populations. Teachers are challenged to find appropriate and effective means of teaching on ethnically, racially, and culturally diverse college campuses. As teachers and trainers, among the challenges is to be cognizant of the presence of racism, sexism, classism, and other negative attitudes and behaviors directed at certain groups. Teachers should be aware of the spectrum of diversity that can be represented in classroom or training situations. For example, the increasing number of students with disabilities means that teachers must be prepared to make necessary accommodations. Educational efforts must be truly multicultural in that they should provide information, explore attitudes, and influence behaviors in order to liberate the learner to work and learn across cultures (Roper & Sedlacek, 1988). Teaching diverse populations means addressing similarities and differences, being inclusive of a wide range of issues, and being clear about the aspects of diversity being addressed (Thomas, 1996).

Aspects of cooperative and collaborative learning build positive intergroup relations—specifically contact theory (Allport, 1954). Contact theory suggests that positive relationships are more likely to develop between people of different racial and ethnic backgrounds if they possess equal status, their interaction is institutionally sanctioned and supported, and they work toward a common goal. Contact theory is the basis of cooperative learning techniques (Slavin, 1990). As educators design teaching and training activities, it is necessary to be aware of the role these activities can play in advancing the relationship-building component of the institutional mission statement. There are specific strategies educators can use to facilitate more positive relationships among members of groups (Roper, 1988); these include: creating equal-status environments, using activities that require cooperation, and illustrating to learners that there is institutional support for group interaction. The group investigation method, which requires group inquiry, data gathering, group discussion, interpretation of information, and synthesis of information into a group product, is an effective approach to building positive intergroup relationships.

A successful strategy for building positive relationships in a multicultural group learning experience is to engage the group in a project that requires them to identify, describe, design, and implement an intervention, and report on results of a real community issue. Students, paraprofessionals, and professional staff connect with each other and deepen their shared commitment to issues when they are able to jointly investigate and apply their own creative intervention to social or institutional issues (Roper, 1988). Such educational strategies require the teacher to work with the learning groups to develop relationship guidelines and establish ground rules for managing group conflicts. The design for the project supports the main components of contact theory: equal status relationships, interaction that is institutionally sanctioned and supported, and work that is focused towards a common goal. In addition, the outcomes of work that will likely produce an intervention that will be of value to the educational community.

Training Other Trainers

Organizations have increasingly come to rely upon members of their own work force to act as trainers for other employees. In many organizations, after certain employees have gone through particular learning experiences, they are called upon to train other potential trainers (Fulton, 1978). Through the use of train-the-trainer workshops, staff members are able to pass their knowledge and skills directly to their peers (Leinfuss, 1993). In some organizations the use of peers to train others serves to increase commitment, such as in the area of diversity training (Cox, 1994). In student affairs there are numerous situations where colleagues are called upon to train other trainers. Educators are challenged to understand the difference between how to teach learners purely for their own sake and how to teach learners so that they might in turn teach others. In train-the-trainer workshops, leaders may need to employ more demonstration and simulation activities so that learners can have the opportunity to apply the teaching and training activities they will use when they train others. Trainers need to be aware of learners' feelings, provide them with appropriate and sensitive feedback, and support them as they offer training to others. Train-the-trainer workshops are typically used for training orientation leaders, resident advisors, sexuality educators, peer helpers, teaching assistants, and student coaches, to name a few.

Conclusion

Teachers build relationships with learners while providing them with the knowledge, skills, and awareness necessary to function in their social and professional roles. The roles and responsibilities of teachers can no longer be carried out according to a rigid script. Each learning situation must be constructed as a unique experience, directly in response to the group or individual for whom it is intended—taking their needs, challenges, life situations, and personal characteristics into account. Educators must consciously develop the competencies needed in order to be good teachers and trainers. Content is important, but content loses meaning when it is not presented in a way learners can understand and translate into the desired behavior.

The information in this chapter has been aimed at helping student affairs educators find grounding for their educational roles. The goal is to provide exposure to important concepts in teaching and stimulate thinking about the importance of the concepts to the work of student affairs professionals. Specifically, regardless of whether one is in a teaching or training role, one must utilize techniques that are respectful of the diversity and capabilities of learners. Traditional lecture and presentation formats alone are no longer appropriate or sufficient. A wide range of strategies should be utilized to reach and engage learners. As student affairs educators work with groups of learners, they act as representatives of the professions knowledge community—a knowledge community rooted in a tradition of attending to the needs of individuals, respecting individual dignity, promoting high-level understanding and critical thinking, celebrating diversity while recognizing commonalities, and encouraging openness to new ideas and perspectives. As teachers, student affairs professionals are well positioned to honor that tradition. As they teach, student affairs educators should not lose sight of the fact that they are working to achieve the grand aims of their institutional mission—moving individuals to the highest level of human functioning they can achieve.

References

Allport, G. W. (1954). *The nature of prejudice.* Garden City, NY: Doubleday/Anchor.

Barnes, L. B., Christensen, C. R., & Hansen, A. J. (1994). *Teaching and the case method: Text, cases, and readings* (3rd ed.). Boston: Harvard Business School Press.

Bennett, C. I. (1995). *Comprehensive multicultural education: Theory and practice* (3rd ed.). Boston: Allyn & Bacon.

Bess, J. L., & Associates (2000). *Teaching alone, teaching together: Transforming the structure of teams for teaching.* San Francisco: Jossey-Bass.

Bonwell, C. C., & Eison, J. A. (1991). *Active learning: Creating excitement in the classroom* (ASHE-ERIC Higher Education Report No. 4). Washington, DC: School of Education and Human Development, George Washington University.

Brookfield, S. D. (1990). *The skillful teacher: On technique, trust, and responsiveness in the classroom.* San Francisco: Jossey-Bass.

Brooks-Harris, J. E., & Stock-Ward, S. R. (1999). *Workshops: Designing and facilitating experiential learning.* Thousand Oaks, CA: Sage.

Bruffee, K. A. (1993). *Collaborative learning: Higher education, interdependence, and the authority of knowledge.* Baltimore: Johns Hopkins University Press.

Carns, A. W., Carns, M. R., & Wright, J. (1993). Students as paraprofessionals in four-year colleges and universities: Current practice compared to prior practice. *Journal of College Student Development, 34,* 358–363.

Chickering, A. W., & Gamson, Z. F. (1991). Seven principles for good practice in undergraduate education. In A. W. Chickering & Z. F. Gamson (Eds.), *Applying the seven principles of good practice in undergraduate education* (New Directions for Teaching and Learning No. 47, pp. 63–69). San Francisco: Jossey-Bass.

Christensen, C. R., Garvin, D. A., & Sweet, A. (1991). *Education for judgment: The artistry of discussion leadership.* Boston: Harvard Business School Press.

Cox, T., Jr. (1994). *Cultural diversity in organizations: Theory, research, and practice.* San Francisco: Berrett-Koehler.

Cranton, P. (1994). *Understanding and promoting transformative learning: A guide for educators and adults.* San Francisco: Jossey-Bass.

Creamer, D., & Shelton, M. (1988). Staff development: A literature review of graduate preparation and in-service education of students. *Journal of College Student Development, 29,* 407–414.

Delworth, U., & Yarris, E. (1978). Concepts and processes for the new training role. In U. Delworth (Ed.), *Training competent staff* (New Directions for Student Services No. 2, pp. 1–15). San Francisco: Jossey-Bass.

Dyer, W. G. (1995). *Teambuilding: Current issues and new alternatives* (3rd ed.). Reading, MA: Addison-Wesley.

Elinor, L., & Gerard, G. (1998). *Dialogue: Rediscover the transforming power of conversation.* New York: Wiley.

Erickson, B. L., & Strommer, D. W. (1991). *Teaching college freshmen.* San Francisco: Jossey-Bass.

Finkel, D. L. (2000). *Teaching with your mouth shut.* Portsmouth, NH: Boynton/Cook.

Freire, P. (1970). *Pedagogy of the oppressed* (M. B. Ramos, Trans.). New York: Continuum.

Fulton, D. R. (1978). Teaching staff to be trainers. In U. Delworth (Ed.), *Training competent staff* (New Directions for Student Services No. 2, pp. 75–81). San Francisco: Jossey-Bass.

Gallessich, J. (1982). *The profession and practice of consultation: A handbook for consultants, trainers of consultants, and consumers of consultation services.* San Francisco: Jossey-Bass.

Garibaldi, A. (1992). Preparing teachers for culturally diverse classrooms. In M. E. Dilworth (Ed.), *Diversity in teacher education: New expectations* (pp. 23–39). San Francisco: Jossey-Bass.

Glazer, S. (1999). *The heart of learning: Spirituality in education.* New York: Jeremy P. Tarcher/Putnam.

Goodwin, L. D., & Stevens, E. A. (1993). The influence of gender on university faculty members' perceptions of "good" teaching. *Journal of Higher Education, 64,* 166–185.

hooks, b. (1994). *Teaching to transgress: Education as the practice of freedom.* New York: Routledge.

Johnson, D. W., & Johnson, F. P. (2000). *Joining together: Group theory and group skills* (7th ed.). Boston: Allyn & Bacon.

Johnson, D. W., Johnson, R. T., & Smith, K. A. (1991). *Cooperative learning: Increasing college faculty instructional productivity* (ASHE-ERIC Higher Education Report No. 4). Washington, DC: School of Education and Human Development, George Washington University.

Leinfuss, E. (1993). Training in the age of downsizing [CD-ROM]. *Computerworld, 27.* Abstract obtained from *Expanded Academic Index,* 1993, Abstract No. 13400856.

Lubin, B., & Eddy, W. B. (1987). The development of small group training and small group trainers. In W. B. Eddy & C. C. Henderson, Jr. (Eds.), *Training theory and practice* (pp. 3–15). Alexandria, VA: NTL Institute.

Margolis, F. H., & Bell, C. R. (1989). *Understanding training: Perspectives and practices.* San Diego, CA: University Associates.

McLaughlin, M. W., & Talbert, J. E. (1993). New visions of teaching. In D. K. Cohen, M. W. McLaughlin, & J. E. Talbert (Eds.), *Teaching for understanding: Challenges for policy and practice* (pp. 1–10). San Francisco: Jossey-Bass.

Menges, R. J. (1981). Instructional methods. In A. W. Chickering & Associates, *The modern American college: Responding to the new realities of diverse students and a changing society* (pp. 556–581). San Francisco: Jossey-Bass.

Merriam, S. B., & Caffarella, R. S. (1991). *Learning in adulthood: A comprehensive guide.* San Francisco: Jossey-Bass.

Meyers, C., & Jones, T. B. (1993). *Promoting active learning: Strategies for the college classroom.* San Francisco: Jossey-Bass.

Mines, R. A., King, P. M., Hood, A. B., & Wood, P. K. (1990). Stages of intellectual development and associated critical thinking skills in college students. *Journal of College Student Development, 31*, 538–547.

National Center for Postsecondary Teaching, Learning, and Assessment. (1995). *Realizing the potential: Improving postsecondary teaching, learning and assessment.* (The National Report of The National Center for Postsecondary Teaching, Learning, and Assessment). University Park, PA: Author.

Nilson, C. (1990). *Training for non-trainers: A do-it-yourself guide for managers.* New York: AMACOM.

Palloff, R. M., & Pratt, K. (2001). *Lessons from the cyberspace classroom: The realities of online teaching.* San Francisco: Jossey-Bass.

Palmer, P. J. (1998). *The courage to teach: Exploring the inner landscape of a teacher's life.* San Francisco: Jossey-Bass.

Passmore, J. (1970). *The philosophy of teaching.* Cambridge, MA: Harvard University Press.

Rippey, R. (1993). Learning from corporate education programs. In L. Curry, Jr., J. E. Wergin, & Associates, *Educating professionals: Responding to new expectations for competencies and accountability* (pp. 212–226). San Francisco: Jossey-Bass.

Roper, L. D. (1988). Relationship among levels of social distance, dogmatism, affective reactions, and interracial behaviors in a course on racism (Doctoral dissertation, University of Maryland, 1988). *Dissertation Abstracts International, 49* (10A), 3168.

Roper, L. D., & Sedlacek, W. E. (1988). Student affairs professionals in academic roles: A course on racism. *NASPA Journal, 26*, 27–32.

Senge, P. M. (1990). *The fifth discipline: The art and practice of the learning organization.* New York: Doubleday.

Shor, I. (1992). *Empowering education: Critical teaching for social change.* Chicago: University of Chicago Press.

Silverman, S. L., & Casazza, M. E. (2000). *Learning and development: Making connections to enhance teaching.* San Francisco: Jossey-Bass.

Slavin, R. E. (1990). *Cooperative learning: Theory, research, and practice.* Boston: Allyn & Bacon.

Stewart, J. (1991). *Managing change through training and development.* San Francisco: Jossey-Bass/Pfeiffer.

Stewart, T. A. (1997). *Intellectual capital: The new wealth of organizations.* New York: Doubleday.

Taylor, K., Marienau, C., & Fiddler, M. (2000). *Developing adult learners: Strategies for teachers and trainers.* San Francisco: Jossey-Bass.

Thomas, R. R., Jr. (1996). *Redefining diversity.* New York: AMACOM.

Tiberius, R. G., & Billson, J. M. (1991). The social context of teaching and learning. In R. J. Menges & M. D. Svinicki (Eds.), *College teaching: From theory to practice* (New Directions for Teaching and Learning No. 45, pp. 67–86). San Francisco: Jossey-Bass.

Tinto, V. (1993) *Leaving college: Rethinking the causes and cures of student attrition.* Chicago: The University of Chicago Press.

Warshauer, S. (1988). *Inside training and development: Creating effective programs.* San Diego, CA: University Associates.

Widick, C., & Simpson, D. (1978). Developmental concepts in college instruction. In C. A. Parker (Ed.), *Encouraging development in college students* (pp. 27–59). Minneapolis: University of Minnesota Press.

Winston, R. B., Jr., & Buckner, J. D. (1984). The effects of peer helper training and timing of training on reported stress in resident assistants. *Journal of College Student Personnel, 25*, 430–436.

Woodard, D. B., Jr., & Komives, S. R. (1990). Ensuring staff competence. In M. J. Barr, M. L. Upcraft, & Associates (Eds.), *New futures for student affairs: Building a vision for professional leadership and practice* (pp. 217–238). San Francisco: Jossey-Bass.

CHAPTER TWENTY-TWO

COUNSELING AND HELPING SKILLS

Roger B. Winston, Jr.

As Williamson (1939), one of the pioneers of the student affairs profession, observed over sixty years ago, all students have problems and personal concerns that their college or university can and should help them address. Another pioneer of the student affairs field, Wrenn (1951), argued, "the only justification for student personnel services is that they can be shown to meet the needs of students. . . . These include both the basic psychological needs of all young people and the specific needs that are the direct results of the college experience" (pp. 26–27).

There is probably no student affairs division in the United States that has sufficient counseling center staff to address the plethora of student needs and expectations for assistance. If a student affairs division is to satisfy Wrenn's raison d'être for the profession, then all or most of its staff must possess well-developed helping skills and utilize them in their daily interactions with students. This chapter is based on this simple premise. It focuses on counseling or helping competencies from the perspective of the student affairs professional, who may work in a wide variety of settings, such as student activities, housing, financial aid, international student services, or admissions. This chapter is addressed to student affairs professionals who do not view themselves, either by reason of academic preparation or the responsibilities of their position, as professional counselors or mental health professionals but who work with students with needs that can be adequately addressed by the adroit use of interpersonal helping skills and knowledge.

These individuals are called "allied professional counselors," adopting the terminology of Delworth and Aulepp (1976). Professionals who work in counseling and career services centers are expected to have more advanced counseling knowledge and skills, gained through academic preparation and supervised practice. They can properly be called professional counselors. Even though all competent student affairs professionals should possess carefully cultivated and practiced helping skills, they also must recognize the limits of their expertise and make appropriate referrals to qualified mental health professionals when the interventions needed exceed their level of competence. Most student affairs practitioners are not (and should not be) trained as professional counselors. This chapter provides general information about helping skills; anyone seeking to provide in-depth, ongoing psychological assistance should seek appropriate academic preparation in counseling or counseling psychology and supervised practice from qualified professionals. In states that provide for licensure of professional counselors and psychologists, it is desirable to acquire that credential both as a testament to appropriate professional preparation and minimum knowledge and a safeguard against personal and institutional legal liability.

As student affairs professionals' careers advance, they tend to spend less time in direct contact with students and more time interacting with staff members. Helping skills are still needed, however, in this capacity; only the clientele has changed, from students to staff (Winston & Creamer, 1997). Several well-known leadership theorists—for example, Hersey, Blanchard, and Johnson (1996); Kouzes and Posner (1987); and Blake, Mouton, and Williams (1981)—emphasize the essential skills of communicating care and concern, creating a supportive atmosphere, and sharing decision making as the foundations of effective organizational leadership. A working knowledge of helping skills and interventions greatly increases a work supervisor's capability to create positive relationships and environments.

In the past decade, there have been substantial increases in the number of students who enter college with serious mental health problems and illnesses that require ongoing attention from professional counselors, psychologists, or psychiatrists. In a 2001 survey of counseling center directors, 85 percent reported an increase in the number of enrolled students with severe psychological problems. The directors also reported an increase in cases of sexual assault concerns (over 33 percent), alcohol problems (45 percent), other illicit drug use (49 percent), learning disabilities (71 percent), self-injury (51 percent), and eating disorders (38 percent) (Gallagher, 2001, p. 10).

This chapter addresses the essential components of helping and various models for understanding the helping process and determining appropriate interventions (including making effective referrals). In this chapter, particular attention is focused on helping students deal with common developmental concerns, such as making transitions (for example, when first entering college, returning to college after an extended absence, or transferring from another institution), selecting an academic major, making career decisions, and dealing with interpersonal relationships with peers, parents, and institutional authority figures, because these are among the most frequently encountered concerns of undergraduates (Chickering & Reisser, 1993). Some of the factors that affect the nature of helping relationships, such as gender and ethnicity, are briefly identified. Finally, ethical issues particularly pertinent to allied professional helpers are examined.

Helping People

One should undertake the role of helper to assist the helpee in addressing her or his needs, issues, or concerns—not to meet the helper's needs or to provide the helpee with helper-devised solutions. As Brammer and MacDonald (1999) note: "Helping is . . . a process of encouraging the helpee to learn how to learn. In the helping process helpees learn more effective ways of coping with their present feelings and environmental demands, as well as techniques for solving personal problems, methods of planning, and techniques for discriminating among value choices" (p. 21). Basically, the helping process seeks to create conditions where helpees can learn how to solve their present and future problems using their own resources.

Components of the Helping Relationship

Rogers (1957, 1961) initiated the great debate—which has continued for nearly fifty years—about the necessary and sufficient conditions for helping individuals change their behavior and attitudes. He argued that it is the character and attitudes of the helper that are most crucial to facilitation of constructive change, much more so than his or her knowledge and expertise. He asserted that "if I can provide a certain type of relationship, the other person will discover within himself [sic] the capacity to use that relationship for growth and change, and personal development will occur" (Rogers, 1961, p. 33). He identified three personal characteristics or necessary conditions that he considered to be of supreme importance: genuineness, or congruence; unconditional positive regard, or acceptance; and accurate empathic understanding.

Genuineness is the extent or degree to which the helper is nondefensive and authentic in interacting with the helpee. Genuine helpers do not play roles, do not attempt to change or conceal their values from the helpee, and are "real." To be an effective helper, one must truly want to help. Acting solely on a perceived responsibility to "help students" because of one's position cannot be concealed for long, and it will ultimately be recognized by helpees as fraudulent.

Unconditional positive regard, also known as nonpossessive warmth, refers to the extent that helpers communicate an attitude of nonevaluative caring and respect for the helpee as a person. Rogers (1967) asserted that because helpers often encounter persons who hold contrary values systems, they should be aware of their own values and beliefs and not try to conceal them. To pretend acceptance interferes with the helping relationship and destroys genuineness, and it can seldom be concealed from the helpee for extended periods of time. Helpers must be careful, however, not to attempt to impose their values upon the helpee or communicate disrespect toward or disapproval of the helpee's values.

Empathy refers to the degree to which helpers can successfully communicate their awareness and understanding of another person's frame of reference and feelings in language attuned to that individual. Empathy involves two processes. First, helpers must understand the inner world (values, attitudes, and feelings) of the other person. Then they must communicate that understanding by using the other person's frame of reference in their dialogue. Brammer and Shostrom (1982) maintain that in responding empathetically, a helper tries to "think with, rather than for or about the client. [Empathy] . . . is the capacity to respond to another's feelings and experiences as if they were your own" (p. 160).

Other theorists (Carkhuff, 1969; Egan, 2001; Gazda et al., 1999; Ivey & Authier, 1978) have also described necessary conditions for creating a helping interaction. They depart somewhat from Rogers by maintaining that there are specific, identifiable skills that effective helpers intentionally utilize. These skills can be taught and explained from a basically behavioral frame of reference. Unlike Rogers, who emphasized the primacy of being a certain kind of person rather than of employing certain techniques, these theorists argue that successful helpers need to learn certain skills and to behave in specific ways designed to assist others. These additional skills and techniques include concreteness, self-disclosure, immediacy, and confrontation.

Concreteness refers to the helper's assisting the helpee in identifying the specific feelings associated with the experiences being described. The helper's task is to assist helpees to convert vague statements about themselves and their concerns into concrete expressions. This can prove revelatory for helpees, who are often unaware of the intensity or even the presence of some emotions associated with an event until called upon to verbalize them.

Self-disclosure involves *judicious* revelation of the helper's past or present situation as a means of communicating the helper's understanding of the helpees' concerns and offering reassurance about the helpee's ability to deal with his or her problems. There is often a danger, however, that through self-disclosure the helper may begin to focus on his or her needs rather than those of the helpee. As Gazda and his colleagues (1999) noted, "When helper self-disclosure is premature or irrelevant to the helpee's problem, it tends to confuse the helpee or put the focus on the helper. The helper steals the spotlight" (p. 16). Self-disclosure, if used appropriately and timed sagaciously, can allow the helper to model attitudes and behaviors that helpees may find useful in understanding their feelings and emotions and changing their attitudes and behaviors.

Immediacy is a form of self-disclosure that deals with what is going on between the helper and the helpee at the present moment. Its principal value is to facilitate helpees' becoming more aware of their behaviors in the relationship and to help them bring out into the open unverbalized thoughts and feelings associated with the helper. This is a powerful tool, but only after a trusting relationship has been developed. If inappropriately timed (particularly too early in the relationship), immediacy may frighten helpees and lead to premature termination of the relationship.

Finally, confrontation is viewed as an action tool that invites helpees to examine their behaviors and attitudes more carefully and to become aware of discrepancies between their feelings or words and their behavior. Confrontation assists helpees in coming to grips with the reality of their situation. To be effective, confrontation must be preceded by the establishment of a caring and trusting relationship. Corey (1995) asserts that confrontation is an invitation for helpees to look at the "discrepancies between [their] attitudes, thoughts, or behaviors. Confrontation that is done in a tentative (yet direct and honest) manner can be an extension of caring and respect for clients. It can encourage them to examine certain incongruities and to become aware of . . . ways that they might be blocking their personal strengths" (p. 90). It must be emphasized that confrontation can only be effective after helpers and helpees have established firm relationships committed to solving problems. If used prematurely, it can often be perceived by helpees as either an attack or a personal rejection, and it will usually lead to termination of the relationship without resolution of the problems. Confrontation should be used sparingly and only after the relationship is *firmly* established. As a general rule, avoid confrontation if in doubt.

A Model of the Helping Process

Carkhuff (1969) proposed a four-phase model of the helping process that, although somewhat oversimplified, has proven effective as the basis for the initial training of professional, paraprofessional, and allied professional counselors. (See Figure 22.1.)

In the initial phase, Pre-Helping, the helper attends to the helpee as she or he begins to talk about her or his concerns. The helper assumes a physical posture that reflects concentration on and concern for what the helpee is saying and feeling. The helper observes "the context, appearance, and behavior of the helpee for cues to the helpee's physical, emotional, and intellectual state" and listens for content, feeling, and meaning—the reason behind the helpee's feelings (Anthony & Vitalo, 1982, p. 70). This has the effect of involving helper and helpee in a mutual effort to deal with the helpee's concerns or problems, and it clearly communicates the helper's interest and desire to be of assistance.

Phase I calls for the helper to use responding skills to communicate to the helpee that he or she understands the content, feeling, and meaning of the helpee's message. The Carkhuff training model involves using the now familiar "You feel ______ because ______" type of statement. (For example, "You *feel* rejected *because* she went out with some of her friends in her major without you.") This assists helpees in exploring themselves and their problems more fully. Often helpees develop important insights into themselves when they hear a concerned person orally expressing what they have been feeling but were either unaware of or unwilling to acknowledge.

FIGURE 22.1. CARKHUFF'S BASIC MODEL OF THE HELPING PROCESS.

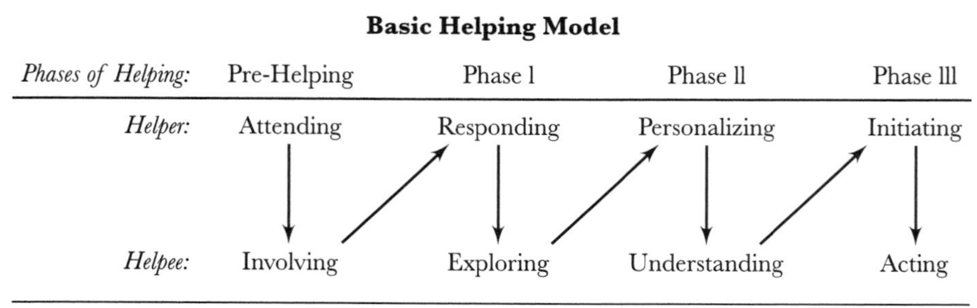

Source: Anthony and Vitalo (1982), p. 70.

Responding can also help a troubled person discover feelings he or she has been attempting to suppress or deny. If a helper makes an honest mistake about how the helpee is feeling, usually the helpee will correct the error and tell the helper how she or he is or was feeling.

Phase II is called personalizing. The helper attempts to hold the helpee directly accountable for her or his current state. Anthony and Vitalo (1982) explain that "personalizing the problem means developing the response deficit or vulnerability that the helpee experiences by making the helpee directly accountable for the problem he or she is having" (p. 72). Typical statements include "You feel ______ because you ______" or "You feel ______ because you cannot ______." For example, "You feel disappointed in yourself because you didn't take preparing for the test seriously enough." This may be expanded to responses such as, "You feel ______ because you cannot ______ and you want to ______." For example, "You feel confused because you asked Henry to go out with you and your friends after he seemed so friendly, and then he not only refused but put you down as well, and you want to know why you misread his interest in you so badly." The latter kind of response can be the transition from the helpee's understanding his or her problem to an action phase in which the helpee begins to establish goals and make plans for accomplishing them. As Anthony and Vitalo (1982) comment, "The ultimate test of the helper's personalizing skills is the level of self-understanding the helpee achieves concerning what he or she wants to achieve" (p. 73).

Initiating, Phase III in the model, involves assisting the helpee to specify goals, make plans for accomplishing them, and move toward action. The helper must remain focused on the helpee's goals, not his or her own goals. The helper must be aware that if the helpee's goals are to be accomplished, the helpee must "own" them and approach accomplishing them in ways that fit his or her typical life pattern. The helper plays somewhat of a teacher's role; the helper must assist the helpee to act in ways he or she feels most comfortable with, even if they are not necessarily the most efficient methods available. The obvious, "easy," answers for the helper may be too anxiety producing or require a greater level of personal maturity or experience to be realistic solutions to a helpee's problem. If the helpee in such a situation is pushed to adopt the helper's advice, there is a high probability that the helpee's problems actually can become worse or at least be perceived as more complicated.

Most effective helpers possess the basic skills identified in this model, whether or not they subscribe to it. Some people are somewhat offended by the use of formulaic techniques such as "You feel _____ because _____" statements. One can appreciate the importance and therapeutic benefits of establishing a relationship between the helper and the helpee, as Rogers advocates, without accepting all the phenomenological baggage Rogers attaches to the process. Substantial research documents the effectiveness of these types of models for teaching basic helping skills (Carkhuff, 1969; Kasdorf & Gustafson, 1978; Lambert, 1982). I contend that basic helping skills are learned (through extensive practice accompanied by critical feedback) and that student affairs practitioners need to master them as part of their repertoire of essential student development and administrative-management skills. In my opinion, a student affairs practitioner, at any level, who is not skillful in helping students deal with their personal concerns is probably too expensive for most student affairs divisions to employ because to some degree they are dead weight.

Application of Helping Skills

One of the essential tasks the allied professional counselor must accomplish when dealing with issues or concerns that students have been unable to satisfactorily resolve is to determine the nature of the problems and whether the allied professional counselor can (or should) offer assistance or whether different or greater expertise is required. In other words, the helper needs to make an assessment of the person, her or his situation or context, and the helper's ability to deal with it.

Central to the process of making an assessment is how students' problems and concerns are conceptualized. As can be seen in Exhibit 22.1, students' concerns

EXHIBIT 22.1. CONCEPTUALIZING STUDENTS' CONCERNS.

Range of Students' Concerns		
Developmental Concerns	**Unclear Concerns**	**Remedial Concerns**
Characteristics or Cues • Behavior or issues are predicted by developmental theory as appropriate to students' age, stage, or level. • Concern is directly or indirectly related to the present environment. • Problem is interpersonal or skill- or knowledge-oriented. • Student is basically coping with the situation, though not to his or her satisfaction. • Student is willing and able to initiate action.	*Characteristics or Cues* • Problem appears to be a mixture of developmental and remedial concerns. • Student is unable to identify source of problem or concern, which may be expressed as general dissatisfaction with life or the institution. • Presenting problem is incongruent with level or intensity of emotion expressed or with nonverbal behavior. • Student is unable to analyze own behavior realistically. • Student is unable to formulate realistic, coherent plans of action. • Student shows lack of motivation to address problems. • Student blames others excessively. • Student pours out confused or rambling monologue.	*Characteristics or Cues* • Behavior is not consistent with developmental theory's projections for student of that stage, age, or educational level. • Student is dysfunctional in meeting daily responsibilities. • Problem is centered in past or basically unrelated to present environment and current experiences. • Concern is intrapersonal. • Persistent pattern of self-defeating or self-destructive behavior is evident. • Student indicates intention to do harm to self or others. • Student reports persistent, chronic depression; anxiety; physical illness; pain; or discomfort; or has experienced trauma. • Student has highly unrealistic self-image or self-assessment.

Source: Adapted from Ender and Winston (1982).

can be conceptualized as falling on a continuum, with one end anchored by "developmental" concerns and the other end by "remedial" concerns (Ender & Winston, 1982).

Developmental Concerns. Developmental concerns are the normal issues and problems encountered by basically effective people. They may be characterized by several of the following clues or characteristics:

1. *The problem is predicted by developmental theory as appropriate or expected for a student of a given age or educational level.* For instance, Shuronda, an entering freshman at a residential college, is homesick the first few days or weeks of the first term. She is experiencing appropriate feelings that are predicted by developmental theory and shared to varying degrees by many of her classmates.

2. *The problem is directly or indirectly related to the present environment.* The student has encountered a situation that requires new responses, and he or she is in the process of analyzing the situation and deciding upon or trying out new ways of coping or reacting. For example, Jacob, a thirty-year-old sophomore who has not yet crystallized a decision about his academic specialization, is facing the college's requirement that he specify a major or academic concentration. The environment has mandated a decision. In addition, he also may feel considerable internal and external pressures to complete his degree as quickly as possible because of family responsibilities and financial pressures.

3. *The problem concerns interpersonal relationships or is caused by a skill or knowledge deficit.* Suppose Jill has difficulty mastering the content of a history course; her problem would be developmental in nature if it could be addressed by acquiring more information, spending more time on assignments, or acquiring new academic skills. Likewise, if the problem involves an interpersonal relationship (such as a marriage), it is not chronic, and it is centered around a particular issue or incident in the immediate or short-term past (perhaps a lack of time for attending to all the wants of one's children since resuming full-time study), then the concern would be classified as developmental.

4. *The student is basically coping with the situation, although not to his or her satisfaction.* Blocher (1987) describes coping as an individual's having control over large segments of his or her long-term transactions with his or her environment, although there may be a lack of satisfactory control over short-term transactions: "Behavior is purposeful and largely goal-oriented. . . . Problems and difficulties tend to be readily identifiable in terms of specific roles or relationships" (p. 155). For example, Juan is considering getting married, but his parents disapprove of his chosen mate and think he is too young. He can listen to his parents' concerns and appreciate their point of view while not allowing it to interfere with his meeting his academic demands or forcing him to terminate the relationship. He is torn between a desire to comply with his parents' wishes and a desire to be autonomous and to make his own decisions and to start a life with his partner. Even though the situation is not comfortable, he is able to cope as he searches for a solution. His concern would be classified as developmental. (Juan's concerns must also be understood within his specific cultural context. Many Hispanic cultures emphasize the importance of maintaining close connections with

one's family, which may mean that resisting parental wishes is more difficult for Juan than for many Anglo students.)

5. *The student is able and willing to initiate action to deal with the problem.* The student recognizes the demands of her or his environment and is willing to face those demands by altering her or his behavior, seeking assistance, or initiating a project on her or his own to deal with the situation. For example, Chang is having difficulty in an English course, even though he has used the same study techniques and routines he found effective in other English courses during the first year of college. He recognizes that he is not doing well and searches the environment for sources of help. A critical element that makes this a developmental concern is that he wants to take action; he is not attempting to deny the problem in the hope that it will disappear or seeking unproductive ways of reducing stress, such as cutting class.

Remedial Concerns. At the opposite end of the continuum from developmental concerns are remedial concerns. Characteristics or cues that help define or identify remedial concerns include the following:

1. *The student's behavior or reported feelings are inconsistent with the predictions of developmental theory for a person of that age or educational experience.* For example, Bob, a graduate student, has been unable to establish a romantic relationship with anyone in either high school or college. Bob is not performing as developmental theory predicts for someone his age. His concerns are remedial in nature. (The same concerns encountered by a high school sophomore would probably be regarded as developmental.)

2. *The student's behavior is basically dysfunctional, preventing her or him from performing daily tasks.* Students who are unable to function well enough to eat regular meals, sleep at night, attend classes, satisfy academic requirements, and maintain personal hygiene are in a condition that requires remedial assistance. Often these dysfunctional behaviors have the obvious accompanying symptom (or cause) of excessive use of alcohol or other drugs. It is generally unwise, however, for an allied professional counselor to attempt a diagnosis of the causes of dysfunctional behavior patterns.

3. *The problem is centered in the past or is basically unrelated to the student's current environment.* Students whose present unproductive behavior is an extension of past dysfunctional behavior are operating in a remedial mode. For instance, Juanita's inability to establish close friendships predated her entry into college and is not a result of her college environment. Her problem is not simply having no close friends on campus this term; her problem establishing interpersonal relationships has a long history and is evidence of a persistent pattern of ineffective or self-defeating behavior. In the case of Jill who was having difficulty with a history course mentioned earlier, if her difficulties stem from a learning disability, then her concerns would fall at the remedial end of the continuum and would require assistance from a professional skilled in diagnosing learning disabilities and designing strategies to overcome them.

4. *The student reports persistent chronic depression, anxiety, illness, pain, or other discomfort that does not seem to have a medical explanation.* Students who hold highly unrealistic self-images or self-assessments often act in an erratic or alienating fashion that may be the result of developmental deficiencies or mental illness. Likewise, students who

are frequently involved in acrimonious or hostile interactions (sometimes even physical assaults) with peers are operating in a remedial mode. Students who are addicted to alcohol or other drugs or who experience eating disorders such as bulimia or anorexia are dealing with remedial concerns that require the assistance of professionals skilled in the treatment of those specific illnesses. Students who have been attacked, sexually molested, or experienced other highly traumatic events generally require professional medical and psychotherapeutic services. These events often cause significant disruption of the developmental pattern typical for most college students.

5. *The student has a problem that is basically intrapersonal in nature.* A problem involving deep-seated internal conflicts that interfere with a student's ability to be purposeful in her or his behavior or to find personal satisfaction in any activity is indicative of a remedial condition. For example, long-standing feelings of inferiority, low self-esteem, and anxiety attacks fall into this category. Treatment of these kinds of problems is generally lengthy and requires intensive therapy by highly skilled professionals.

6. *The student reports an intention to harm others or threatens suicide.* These behaviors fall at the extreme remedial end of the continuum of concerns. Bernard and Bernard (1985) suggest a number of indicators that identify students with an increased likelihood of attempting suicide:

- A member of the student's family has attempted suicide.
- The student has made previous suicide attempts.
- The student has experienced the loss of a parent through death, divorce, or separation. Suicide is more likely if the loss led to destabilization of the family.
- The student reports feelings of being a burden, being useless, or being hopeless.
- The student has given away prized possessions or put her or his personal affairs in order. These behaviors are indicators of a suicidal orientation and are especially important if they occur after the loss of a loved one, a pet, or a job.
- The student has suffered a prolonged state of agitated depression.

Unclear Concerns. Many student concerns do not obviously fall at the extremes of the continuum; that is, they are not easily classified as developmental or remedial. When allied professional helpers listen to students talk about their concerns or problems, they commonly hear a mixture of both remedial and developmental concerns and considerable confusion and ambiguity. Evidence that alerts the helper that a student's concerns are unclear include (but are not limited to) the following:

1. *The student is unable to identify the source of his or her concern.* That is, the student expresses a vague or pervasive dissatisfaction with life or the educational experience, without providing any specifics or identifying causes or circumstances that are the sources of dissatisfaction.

2. *There is a lack of congruence between the presenting problem and the intensity of the student's emotions or nonverbal behavior.* For example, a student may complain about making a poor grade on a minor test while behaving in a highly emotionally disturbed manner—an obvious incongruence exists between the real importance of the concern and the level or intensity of emotion expressed.

3. *The student seems unable to analyze his or her own behavior realistically.* For example, Frank may complain about hallmates' being unfriendly, while he rejects invitations from them to eat in the dining room or to engage in informal bull sessions. He is verbalizing one thing while behaving in a contrary fashion.

4. *The student shows a lack of motivation to address concerns or is unable to formulate realistic plans of action.* The student talks about his or her problems, but when encouraged to try various approaches to dealing with them, he or she seems reluctant to take action or makes excuses to justify inaction.

5. *The student blames others excessively.* That is, whatever the issue, the student finds that the responsibility belongs to someone else; it is never his or her own fault. The student may be fixated on a singular event or individual (perhaps parent, teacher, or love interest), which is seen as the root of all current concerns.

6. *The student cannot seem to get focused.* One of the most frequently encountered clues that a student's concerns are unclear (both to himself or herself and to the helper as well) are seemingly confused and rambling monologues that pour out a mass of issues, concerns, problems, fears, and seemingly irrelevant facts, accompanied by a relatively high level of emotion.

Assessing Students' Concerns

The allied professional counselor needs to assess the nature of students' concerns in order to formulate an appropriate response or plan of action. Blocher (1966) has cautioned, however, that assessment or diagnosis is most effective when it is continuous and tentative. Assessments must be frequently checked, revalidated, and revised as necessary. Blocher warns helpers to always view their assessments as hypothetical and therefore tentative. If the assessment of the student's concerns remains fixed and new observations are shut out, the helper's responses may become increasingly inappropriate and can lead to premature termination of the relationship or inappropriate (unhelpful) action by the helper.

Gazda et al. (1999) suggest that students come to helpers or counselors for four basic reasons: to request information, to request an appropriate action, to request an inappropriate action (or interaction), or for understanding and involvement.

The first, a request for information, is relatively simple. The helper provides the requested information, tells the student where it is available, or joins the student in searching for the information. The second request, for an appropriate action, is also relatively straightforward. The helper does what is requested. These two requests can be presented in less straightforward ways, however. For instance, students are sometimes embarrassed that they do not know something. Rather than simply ask for information, they hint around the subject in the hope that the helper will volunteer the information. The same is true of a request for action; students sometimes describe their needs to the helper rather than simply requesting assistance. For example, Kisha walks into her residence hall's office and begins talking about waiting for her roommate to return with her key to their room. She is describing her need to get into her room, in the hope that the helper will volunteer to unlock her door without her having to ask (and possibly be turned down or called irresponsible).

Sometimes students make a request for an inappropriate action. This may take a number of forms, from requests that the helper excuse them from a college requirement, overlook a rule, or solve their problems for them ("Please tell my mother the college requires me to stay here this weekend"). Helpers must discriminate between appropriate and inappropriate requests. When they encounter inappropriate requests, helpers must tactfully explain why the request is not appropriate while reassuring the student that the helper cares about her or his welfare and understands the problem or concerns from the student's perspective. Refusal to do what is requested should not be equated with rejection of the person making the request. This distinction needs to be communicated clearly to the student, not just implied. Helpers should take care to clearly communicate to helpees the reason that they cannot fulfill their requests and show respect and understanding for the helpees and their circumstances.

Finally, students often seek out allied professional counselors with requests for understanding and involvement. Sometimes this is explicit ("I have a problem that is really bothering me. Will you help me?"). More often, though, students approach their important concerns gradually, testing the helper's receptiveness and skill with "decoy" issues as they move closer to voicing their real concerns. For example, students often bring a "safe" problem to a helper, such as a simple request for information, as a means of establishing contact with the staff member and gauging his or her openness to helping, trustworthiness, and competence as a helper. If they become convinced that the potential helper can handle their real issues, they then reveal their more significant concerns. The helper must first earn the privilege to be of assistance. The helper earns that privilege by communicating a willingness to become involved in the student's problems, by listening carefully to both the content of the student's "safe" issue and the tone or affect of its communication, and by demonstrating an understanding and appreciation of the student's situation and perspectives.

Helping Interventions

Once the helper and the student have explored the student's concerns, the time arrives for action. Exhibit 22.2 summarizes possible actions that may be initiated, depending upon the assessed nature of the student's concerns and the skills and knowledge of the helper.

If the student's concerns are basically developmental in nature, then the helper should be able to offer a variety of interventions. These include further self-exploration or exploration of the problem; identification of possible goals and alternative means of addressing them; identification of resources available on the campus or in the community; provision of information or identification of information sources; referral to agencies that have programs already established to address the student's concerns; providing encouragement, reassurance, and support; and teaching specific skills or strategies, which might range from simple study techniques to time-management strategies, goal-setting procedures, stress-reduction (relaxation) techniques, or social skills. These interventions may be offered informally, one-on-one, or through programs, such as intentionally structured groups (Winston, Bonney, Miller, & Dagley, 1988).

EXHIBIT 22.2. CONCEPTUALIZING ADVISING AND COUNSELING INTERVENTIONS.

Range of Advising and Counseling Interventions		
If Concern Is Developmental	**If Nature of Concern Is Unclear**	**If Concern Is Remedial**
• Assist in self-exploration. • Explore alternatives. • Assist in identifying desired goals. • Assist in devising a plan of action to accomplish goals. • Identify resources and services. • Provide information. • Teach specific strategies or techniques. • Refer to established program especially designed to address issue. • Provide encouragement, reassurance, and support. • Provide positive feedback.	• Act as sounding board as a means of facilitating exploration of the concern. • Respond to student in ways that communicate empathy, respect, genuineness, and concern. • Encourage active problem solving. • Confront student about incongruence between behavior or talk and actions. • Decide whether concerns are basically developmental or remedial in nature and proceed appropriately.	• Show concern and willingness to listen. • Explore alternatives for addressing concern. • Describe available resources for dealing with concern. • Offer information and assistance in initiating contact with appropriate referral source. • Offer encouragement and support. • If there appears to be danger to self or others, take extraordinary measures to assure that student receives assistance from appropriate professionals.

Source: Adapted from Ender and Winston (1982).

If the student's concerns are unclear, the allied professional counselor needs to act as a sounding board as a means of facilitating further exploration. This is done primarily by showing the student empathy, respect, and genuineness and demonstrating a commitment to helping the student clarify his or her situation. Encouraging the student to become active in the problem-solving process, expressing reassurance, and confronting incongruence (but only after a trusting and caring relationship has been established) may be appropriate strategies for helping the student clarify his or her issues and associated feelings. If applied with patience and sincerity, these techniques usually allow both the student and the helper to determine the nature of the concern—whether developmental or remedial.

If the student's concerns are remedial in nature, the helper has the responsibility to assist the student in contacting a campus or community agency or individual who has the necessary resources and expertise. Once an assessment has revealed that a student's concerns are basically remedial in nature, the student should be assisted in getting help, not just told to "go see Dr. X" or "call Office Y for an appointment." In the case of potential suicide or harm to others, the helper should take the steps necessary to assure that the student makes contact with appropriate resources. If the student refuses referral, then the appropriate authorities on the campus should be informed of the potential danger—even without the student's approval or permission.

Dealing with Disturbed and Disturbing Students

Delworth (1989) points out that on most campuses there are occasions that a student's behavior is so personally dysfunctional or disruptive to the living and learning environments that student affairs professionals must take action to constrain the student's behavior. She proposed the Assessment-Intervention of Student Problems (AISP) Model (see Exhibit 22.3), which can be used both to determine whether intervention is required and to identify the kinds of interventions needed.

Student affairs professionals are faced with (a) humanitarian issues related to making sure that students get the medical or psychological services they need, (b) professional obligations to safeguard the academic integrity of the institution and all students' learning environments, and (c) legal and ethical issues related to assuring fair and equitable treatment of students while also respecting their personal autonomy and due process and privacy rights.

Delworth suggests that institutions form a campus intervention team that is skilled in use of the AISP Model and has developed procedures and strategies for dealing with these types of situations. Key personnel from each of the following services should be members of the team: (a) campus mental health services, (b) campus security or police, (c) institution's legal counsel, (d) campus disciplinary or student judiciary unit, and (e) a senior-level student affairs administrator. Other ad hoc members of the team might include a senior residence life administrator, director of student activities, representative from academic affairs or an academic department, and a Greek Life staff member depending on the nature of the problematic situation and the locus of its focus.

Brown and DeCoster (1989) admonish, however, that the intervention team must be cautious in exercising its power to remove students from the campus; there must really be a danger or significant disruption imminent if the team does not initiate action. It must be kept in mind that the Americans with Disabilities Act prohibits exclusion of students solely because they have a mental disorder. It should be the responsibility of the intervention team to weigh both students' rights of self-determination and their constitutional rights of due process as well as the good of the institution and the rights of other students to pursue their education without undue distraction and disorder.

Allied professional counselors should not hesitate to contact appropriate institutional officials when they encounter students who are either a danger to themselves or others or who are disturbing the educational environment severely enough to prevent peers from pursuing their educational endeavors.

EXHIBIT 22.3. ASSESSMENT CATEGORIES OF PROBLEM STUDENTS.

I. *The Disturbing Student* (Lacks skills in establishing close, age-appropriate relationships; very self-centered but wants to establish relationships)

Type A: Immature
- Shows immature reactions to many aspects of college life
- Plays pranks
- Does not respect property of others
- Overreacts to minor problems
- May abuse alcohol
- Gets angry and upset easily
- Has low frustration tolerance
- Engages in illegal activities that tend to be overt (such as disorderly conduct)

Type B: Con Artist
- Wants to manipulate and control
- Tests limits
- Usually can be charming
- Engages in illegal activities that tend to be overt (such as drug dealing)

II. *The Disturbed Student* (Specific behaviors and patterns of behavior are out of sync with other students; often marked patterns of moving away from or against others; may overly fixate on one goal or idea; may evince overall rigid, highly dualistic thinking; may make inappropriate or off-task remarks; seems angry and destructive toward self or others)

Type A: Inward Focus
- Depressed, withdrawn—perhaps to the point of being suicidal
- Little involvement in classes and campus life

Type B: Outward Focus
- Angry at world and particular persons—perhaps to the point of being homicidal
- May be involved, but with less frequency, in "mainstream" groups

A-B 1: Symptoms are recent; following known precipitating cause
A-B 2: Symptoms are recent; no known cause
A-B 3: Symptoms are long-standing; no real change
A-B 4: Symptoms are long-standing; worsening after period of better adjustment
A-B 5: Symptoms are long-standing; worsening steadily

III. *The Disturbed/Disturbing Student* (Any combination of I and II are possible) Some typical combinations include:
- Student is disturbing residence hall and campus security with stories of being attacked in his or her residence hall room every night by an enemy (or any other persistent and illogical complaint), thus evincing *disturbed* behavior.
- Student is depressed and withdrawn (*disturbed*) except when drinking. Student then picks fights, destroys residence hall property, and so on (*disturbing*).
- Student misuses financial aid (*disturbing*) in order to pay for a medical operation on a disorder that physicians cannot verify, thus evincing *disturbed* behavior.
- Student is *disturbing* residence hall floor by threatening to commit suicide, following the death of a close relative (*disturbed*).

Source: Delworth (1989), p. 5.

Assisting Students in Making Life Decisions

Some student affairs professionals, for various reasons, have come to view career counseling as being fundamentally different from personal counseling and the sole province of career services staff. This is an artificial distinction that can lead to unfortunate consequences for students. The same helping skills are required in dealing with career concerns as in addressing other areas of life.

Another misconception sometimes associated with career counseling is the use of assessment instruments. Career counseling is seen primarily as the process of administering inventories to students and interpreting the results. This has led to the conception among some students that all that is required in making a career decision is to "take a test and find out what I'm supposed to be." As a consequence of this misinformed folklore, students often become disillusioned with their institution and its student affairs staff's ability or willingness to provide assistance.

A further danger in trying to separate career and personal counseling is the fact that one of the "safest" (and most socially acceptable among student peers) presenting problems for students is career indecision. If counselors fail to be sensitive to a student's total span of concerns, they may not allow the student to bring up issues that are emotionally more threatening to him or her. To assume that career decisions are in some way inherently different from other life decisions is to misunderstand both the content and the process of career development.

As pointed out in Chapter Nine, students are called upon to achieve several developmental tasks during the "traditional" college years. The most important of these tasks include recognizing and accepting the need to make career decisions, becoming aware of interests and abilities, obtaining information about the world of work and how personal interests and abilities relate to occupations, identifying possible fields and level of work consistent with interests and abilities, and selecting and following through with educational programs that can lead to satisfying careers. For older students who are returning to college, these same developmental issues must be confronted. They generally have more life experiences to draw upon and a greater knowledge of the world of work than their younger classmates, however. On the other hand, older students often feel compelled to complete their academic programs in the shortest period of time, which may preclude them from making careful and accurate assessments of their interests and abilities or from pursuing academic fields that do not seem to lead directly to post-college jobs.

Kinnier and Krumboltz (1984) suggest that there are six major obstacles to career fulfillment, and that the role of career counseling is to assist people in overcoming them.

- People acquire inaccurate information or maladaptive beliefs about themselves and the world. They often operate under presuppositions they have never examined.
- People are uncertain about their own priorities. They feel unclear or conflicted about what they really want to value.
- People are unaware of their own abilities and interests and how their skills and preferences are related to the occupational structure of society.
- Although a wealth of occupational information is available, people find it difficult to ask pertinent questions, to motivate themselves to find answers, to penetrate the overwhelming mass of material, and to distinguish biased information from facts.

- People generally do not have a systematic method for making career-related decisions. They often make decisions haphazardly.
- People find that obtaining a job is a lonely, frustrating task for which they are ill prepared (p. 311)

All of these obstacles fall at the developmental end of the continuum, and therefore they are issues that all student affairs professionals should be able to address. Rayman (1993) asserts, "a reasonable goal for the undergraduate curriculum might be sufficient self-understanding to provide a sense of direction and purpose in life" (p. 14). If this is accepted, then there is no question that all student affairs practitioners should possess the basic knowledge and skills needed to assist students in developing these important aspects of their lives. Almost all students can benefit from assistance in this area; consequently, no career services center can carry the responsibility alone. Much broader institutional involvement is required.

The use of personality, interests, and abilities inventories can help students get a better, more organized picture of themselves. It must be stressed, however, that they are not essential to career exploration. The danger is that students (and in some cases counselors) come to view these inventories as career counseling in and of themselves. These kinds of instruments only provide information—almost always information that the student already knows but may not have placed into a career context. The important task is to help the student integrate the information in a way that is useful for making career decisions and developing plans of action. Computer programs designed to bring together the various kinds of information generally needed in making career decisions are perhaps a step in the right direction, but many, if not most, students will benefit from additional exploration and opportunities to reflect about their decisions with a person who possesses good counseling skills.

If students seem unable to grapple with the decision-making process or resist doing the necessary homework to learn about occupations, educational qualifications, and personal interests, then referral to a counseling or career services center may be in order. Referral, however, should not be a helper's first response to students who express indecision about careers and academic majors.

Minimum Skills and Knowledge Required of Allied Professional Counselors

All allied professional counselors need a minimum core of skills and knowledge to function effectively on today's campus. They need a clear understanding of their institution's philosophy and mission and should be able to articulate it to students. Helpers should educate students about the opportunities available in the collegiate environment and should promote the ideal of an educated person. They have the responsibility to encourage and assist students in making personal meaning of their educational experiences. This is the very core of the idea that student affairs should be about student learning (ACPA, 1996; AAHE, ACPA, & NASPA, 1998).

Student affairs professionals need a working knowledge of college student development and learning theories. They need to understand both themselves and the students they work with as developing persons (Chickering & Reisser, 1993; Evans, Forney, & Guido-DiBrito, 1998; Saunders & Cooper, 2001). They must know what is theoretically expected of a person of a particular age and educational experience. It is especially important that helpers be able to sort behavior patterns within a theoretical framework.

Student affairs practitioners need to understand the student population they work with. As Wright (1987) has pointed out, most theories of student development have not taken adequate notice of the environments many minority students come from and the unique forces that influence their development. Likewise, many theorists—for example, Baxter Magolda (1992), Belenky, Clinchy, Goldberger, and Tarule (1986), Chickering and Reisser (1993), Gilligan (1982), Josselson (1992), Straub (1987), and Straub and Rodgers (1986)—have demonstrated that women have a unique perspective and their development is not identical to that of men. Chickering and Havighurst (1981), Schlossberg (1984, 1989), and Schlossberg, Lynch, and Chickering (1989) have pointed out the importance of understanding the returning adult student as well. These differences need to be understood so that would-be helpers have a theoretical context in which to place what they observe about students' behavior.

Students have a right to expect allied professional counselors to be knowledgeable about the institution's rules, regulations, and policies. From a student's point of view, the only thing worse than not having needed information is being given incorrect information. At most institutions, the campus grapevine is fed by a mixture of accurate information, honest appraisals of programs, services, and professionals, practical survival tactics, as well as campus myths and obsolete information. Even in small institutions, remaining informed and current is a task that requires constant attention. Conscious effort must be directed at seeking out information; it is very easy to assume that nothing outside of one's own department changes.

Allied professional counselors should not be expected to be measurement experts. They, however, do need to have a command of informal assessment techniques, though, to help them make decisions about whether to address a student's concern directly or make a referral. They should also be intelligent users of standardized assessment information. For example, student affairs professionals should understand and be able to interpret for students academic measures such as SAT and ACT scores and scores on any other achievement or placement tests used by their institution. They also should be knowledgeable about and able to use and interpret instruments that have been devised to assess students' intellectual, psychosocial, and moral development.

Student affairs professionals need to understand the basics of creating a helping relationship, as described previously. They cannot predict or choose when they will be called upon to be helpers; opportunities and challenges are presented daily.

Counselors can provide valuable services by helping students identify their needs, offering support in addressing them, and making effective referrals to the appropriate campus or community services or programs. Most institutions have many potentially effective programs to assist students that are underutilized because students are simply unaware of them or are reluctant to contact them due to misconceptions about their services or resources or fear of being stigmatized ("only dumb or screwed up people go there").

Counselors need a repertoire of interventions appropriate to their functions. Student affairs practitioners should be able to assist students who are having non-chronic problems managing their time, choosing a major, investigating a career, or employing effective study techniques, for example. They should be able to help students overcome non-chronic problems related to stress and anxiety and interpersonal relationship problems with peers, parents, and authority figures. They also need to be knowledgeable about the career development process and skilled in helping students initiate activities that can lead to satisfying academic and career decisions.

Ethical Issues and Factors That Affect the Helping Relationship

As Marylu McEwen pointed out in Chapter Eight, many current developmental theories display a White male bias, either from using White males as research participants or from inadvertently incorporating a White male perspective in interpretations of data. As student bodies have become more diverse, the student affairs profession has become more aware of different perspectives on development. McEwen's chapter on new perspectives (Chapter Ten) discusses numerous factors that can significantly influence the course of student development. Of particular importance are the factors of gender, ethnicity, age, and sexual orientation.

Lee (1997) points out that cultural diversity is a characteristic of all helping relationships, and all counseling is multicultural in nature. Seldom do helpers and helpees match perfectly on cultural variables. Both the helper and the helpee bring to their relationship a variety of cultural variables such as age, gender, educational level, religious beliefs and practices, ethnic background, sexual orientation, and socioeconomic or social class—all of which affect how they perceive the world. Even though the new awareness of multicultural issues in helping has made helpers more aware of their own and others' backgrounds and worldviews, there remain potential pitfalls to avoid (Lee).

- There is a danger in assuming that all people of a particular cultural background are the same.
- The focus on cultural dissimilarities may serve to accentuate human differences, which may lead to renewed forms of intolerance.
- Helpers who are unaware of cultural dynamics in their interactions with helpees from diverse backgrounds may inadvertently become engaged in practices that can alienate helpees.

Counselors outside of designated counseling, career, and mental health centers on campus encounter several troubling, practical ethical problems. Particularly important are issues related to confidentiality and determination of competence. The American College Personnel Association's "Statement of Ethical Principles and Standards" (1993, p. 91) specifies that students should be informed about the limits placed on confidentiality. A problem often arises, however, in the way students approach staff for help—they often initially present a problem that does not appear to have confidentiality implications. But as discussed above, once a relationship is established, students sometimes make radical, unanticipated shifts in the content of their concerns, placing the student affairs practitioner in a vulnerable position. For example, the student may acknowledge having violated institutional rules (or even committed a serious criminal act) that the staff member has been charged by the institution to enforce. From a legal perspective, most student affairs practitioners, unless they are clergy or licensed counselors or psychologists, do not have privileged communication, that is, the right to keep confidential (even if called as a witness in court) what a student in the course of a helping relationship discloses.

Another major ethical issue centers round the helper's competence. It is not uncommon for lonely, socially isolated students to "latch on" to a staff member, especially in residence halls, and consume many hours talking about their feelings of alienation, rejection, and isolation. They often resist initiating action to change their situation and refuse referral to other agencies. The allied professional counselor may feel that such a student has a definite remedial concern and that his or her counseling competence is not adequate to address the student's problems. But what is the staff member to do when the student refuses referrals and continues to "hang around" the staff member's office or living quarters? The ACPA Ethical Standards specify that if the student refuses referral, the practitioner does not have an ethical responsibility to continue the relationship. Even though this appears clear cut, in actual practice, it may not be a simple matter to disengage from needy, clinging students.

Because student affairs practitioners may be called upon to be allied professional counselors unexpectedly, there is a danger of becoming involved in a dual relationship. A dual relationship is one in which the counselor is placed in conflicting roles; for example, as the supervisor of a student paraprofessional and as a counselor to the staff member, or as advisor to a student organization and counselor to the president. It is important that allied professional counselors be on guard to avoid such situations or to terminate the helping relationship through referral when anticipated or recognized.

These problems do not have simple answers. Staff members who have frequent and informal daily contact with students (especially in residence halls, student organizations, Greek Life offices, and student unions) should make a point of specifying in group presentations the limits to the confidentiality students can expect and the scope of actions and responsibilities that are relevant to the particular roles they play. Student affairs practitioners should seek consultation with mental health professionals and with their supervisors when they encounter problems. Alerting students to the limits of action and confidentiality inherent in their professional position is an important first step. This ideal is often difficult to realize, however, given the pressures of time and the peripatetic way students often choose to initiate help-seeking relationships.

Conclusion

Despite the fact that the student affairs field requires specialized education, has minimum standards for entry, and is recognized as a specialty in higher education, we will have difficulty defending it as a profession unless we can demonstrate that student affairs practitioners contribute directly to the learning and personal enrichment of students. Well-developed skills and extensive knowledge in interpersonal helping are essential tools in student affairs professionals' repertoire of responses and interventions, no matter what their primary position or responsibilities.

These skills require development and constant attention. Although some people possess "natural helping skills," they are seldom sufficient to adequately meet the myriad legitimate concerns college students face today. Students have a right to expect expert assistance and support in addressing these concerns. Only through extensive formal education and training in helping skills accompanied by supervised practice followed by periodic evaluation and feedback can student affairs professionals hope to maintain effective helping skills.

References

American Association for Higher Education [AAHE], American College Personnel Association [ACPA], & National Association of Student Personnel Administrators [NASPA]. (1998). *Powerful partnerships: A shared responsibility for learning.* Washington, DC: Authors.

American College Personnel Association [ACPA]. (1993). Statement of ethical principles and standards. *Journal of College Student Development, 34,* 89–92.

American College Personnel Association [ACPA]. (1996). *Student learning imperative.* Washington, DC: Author.

Anthony, W. A., & Vitalo, R. L. (1982). Human resource development model. In E. K. Marshall, P. D. Kurtz, & Associates, *Interpersonal helping skills: A guide to training methods, programs, and resources* (pp. 59–92). San Francisco: Jossey-Bass.

Baxter Magolda, M. B. (1992). *Knowing and reasoning in college: Gender-related patterns in students' intellectual development.* San Francisco: Jossey-Bass.

Belenky, M. F., Clinchy, B. M., Goldberger, N. R., & Tarule, J. M. (1986). *Women's ways of knowing: The development of self, voice, and mind.* New York: Basic Books.

Bernard, M. L., & Bernard, J. L. (1985). Suicide on campus: Response to the problem. In E. S. Zinner (Ed.), *Coping with death on campus* (New Directions for Student Services No. 31, pp. 69–83). San Francisco: Jossey-Bass.

Blake, R. R., Mouton, J. S., & Williams, M. S. (1981). *The academic administrator grid: A guide to developing effective management teams.* San Francisco: Jossey-Bass.

Blocher, D. H. (1966). *Developmental counseling.* New York: Ronald Press.

Blocher, D. H. (1987). *The professional counselor.* New York: Macmillan.

Brammer, L. M., & MacDonald, G. (1999). *The helping relationship: Process and skills* (7th ed.). Boston: Allyn and Bacon.

Brammer, L. M., & Shostrom, E. L. (1982). *Therapeutic psychology: Fundamentals of counseling and psychotherapy* (4th ed.). Englewood Cliffs, NJ: Prentice Hall.

Brown, V. L., & DeCoster, D. A. (1989). The disturbed and disturbing student. In U. Delworth (Ed.), *Dealing with the behavioral and psychological problems of students* (New Directions for Student Services No. 45, pp. 43–56). San Francisco: Jossey-Bass.

Carkhuff, R. R. (1969). *Helping and human relations: A primer for lay and professional helpers* (2 vols.). New York: Holt, Rinehart and Winston.

Chickering, A. W., & Havighurst, R. J. (1981). The life cycle. In A. W. Chickering & Associates, *The modern American college: Responding to the new realities of diverse students and a changing society* (pp. 16–50). San Francisco: Jossey-Bass.

Chickering, A. W., & Reisser, L. (1993). *Education and identity* (2nd ed.). San Francisco: Jossey-Bass.

Corey, G. (1995). *Theory and practice in counseling and psychotherapy* (5th ed.). Monterey, CA: Brooks/Cole.

Delworth, U. (1989). The AISP model: Assessment-intervention of student problems. In U. Delworth (Ed.), *Dealing with the behavioral and psychological problems of students* (New Directions for Student Services No. 45). San Francisco: Jossey-Bass.

Delworth, U., & Aulepp, L. (1976). *Training manual for paraprofessionals and allied professionals programs.* Boulder, CO: Western Interstate Commission for Higher Education.

Egan, G. (2001). *The skilled helper: A systematic approach to effective helping* (7th ed.). Monterey, CA: Brooks/Cole.

Ender, S. C., & Winston, R. B., Jr. (1982). Training allied professional academic advisers. In R. B. Winston, Jr., S. C. Ender, & T. K. Miller (Eds.), *Developmental approaches to academic advising* (New Directions for Student Services No. 17, pp. 85–103). San Francisco: Jossey-Bass.

Evans, N. J., Forney, D. S., & Guido-DiBrito, F. (1998). *Student development in college: Theory, research, and practice.* San Francisco: Jossey-Bass.

Gallagher, R. P. (2001). *National survey of counseling center directors.* Alexandria, VA: International Association of Counseling Services.

Gazda, G. M., Asbury, F. R., Balzer, F. J., Childers, W. C., & Phelps, R. E. (1999). *Human relations development: A manual for educators* (6th ed.). Boston: Allyn & Bacon.

Gilligan, C. (1982). *In a different voice: Psychological theory and women's development.* Cambridge, MA: Harvard University Press.

Hersey, P., Blanchard, K. H., & Johnson, D. E. (1996). *Management of organizational behavior: Utilizing human resources* (7th ed.). Englewood Cliffs, NJ: Prentice Hall.

Ivey, A. E., & Authier, J. (Eds.). (1978). *Microcounseling: Innovations in interviewing, counseling, psychotherapy, and psychoeducation* (2nd ed.). Springfield, IL: Thomas.

Josselson, R. (1992). *The space between us: Exploring the dimensions of human relationships.* San Francisco: Jossey-Bass.

Kasdorf, J., & Gustafson, K. (1978). Research related to microtraining. In A. E. Ivey & J. Authier (Eds.), *Microcounseling: Innovations in interviewing, counseling, psychotherapy, and psychoeducation* (2nd ed., pp. 323–376). Springfield, IL: Thomas.

Kinnier, R. T., & Krumboltz, J. D. (1984). Procedures for successful career counseling. In N. C. Gysbers & Associates, *Designing careers: Counseling to enhance education, work, and leisure* (pp. 307–335). San Francisco: Jossey-Bass.

Kouzes, J. M., & Posner, B. Z. (1987). *The leadership challenge: How to keep getting extraordinary things done in organizations* (2nd ed.). San Francisco: Jossey-Bass.

Lambert, M. J. (1982). Relations of helping skills to treatment outcome. In E. K. Marshall, P. D. Kurtz, & Associates, *Interpersonal helping skills: A guide to training methods, programs, and resources* (pp. 26–58). San Francisco: Jossey-Bass.

Lee, C. C. (1997). The promise and pitfalls of multicultural counseling. In C. C. Lee (Ed.), *Multicultural issues in counseling: New approaches to diversity* (2nd ed., pp. 3–13). Alexandria, VA: American Counseling Association.

Rayman, J. R. (1993). Contemporary career services: Theory defines practices. In J. R. Rayman (Ed.), *The changing role of career services* (New Directions for Student Services No. 62, pp. 3–21). San Francisco: Jossey-Bass.

Rogers, C. R. (1957). The necessary and sufficient conditions of therapeutic personality change. *Journal of Consulting Psychology, 21,* 95–103.

Rogers, C. R. (1961). *On becoming a person.* Boston: Houghton Mifflin.

Rogers, C. R. (1967). *Person to person: The problem of being human.* New York: Pocket Books.

Saunders, S. A., & Cooper, D. L. (2001). Programmatic interventions: Translating theory to practice. In R. B. Winston, Jr., D. G. Creamer, T. K. Miller, & Associates, *The professional student affairs administrator: Educator, leader, and manager* (pp. 309–340). New York: Brunner-Routledge.

Schlossberg, N. K. (1984). *Counseling adults in transition.* New York: Springer.

Schlossberg, N. K. (1989). *Overwhelmed: Coping with life's ups and downs.* Lexington, MA: Lexington Books.

Schlossberg, N. K., Lynch, A. Q., & Chickering, A. W. (1989). *Improving higher education environments for adults: Responsive programs and services from entry to departure.* San Francisco: Jossey-Bass.

Straub, C. A. (1987). Women's development of autonomy and Chickering's theory. *Journal of College Student Personnel, 28,* 198–205.

Straub, C. A., & Rodgers, R. F. (1986). An exploration of Chickering's theory and women's development. *Journal of College Student Personnel, 27,* 216–224.

Williamson, E. G. (1939). *How to counsel students: A manual of techniques for clinical counselors.* New York: McGraw-Hill.

Winston, R. B., Jr., Bonney, W. C., Miller, T. K., & Dagley, J. C. (1988). *Promoting student development through intentionally structured groups: Principles, techniques, and applications.* San Francisco: Jossey-Bass.

Winston, R. B., Jr., & Creamer, D. G. (1997). *Improving staffing practices in student affairs.* San Francisco: Jossey-Bass.

Wrenn, C. G. (1951). *Student personnel work in college: With emphasis on counseling and group experiences.* New York: Ronald Press.

Wright, D. J. (1987). Minority students: Developmental beginnings. In D. J. Wright (Ed.), *Responding to the needs of today's minority students* (New Directions for Student Services No. 38, pp. 5–22). San Francisco: Jossey-Bass.

CHAPTER TWENTY-THREE

ADVISING AND CONSULTATION

Patrick Love

Advising may be the universal task in student affairs, because it exists at the foundation of much of the work we do. This is, of course, the case for those positions for which advising is the central task, such as academic, career, and student organization advising. But advising is an important competency for most other positions as well, including those in financial aid, judicial affairs, residence life, commuter affairs, and new student orientation. Advising is the out-of-class activity provided to all students (Frost, 1991) and, therefore, in many cases may be the only opportunity for a student to develop a personal link with the institution (Nutt, 2000). Advising is the practice through which a student's development can be directly encouraged. It is the strategy used most often to increase student retention (Beal & Noel, 1980; Crockett, 1978, 1985). In fact, "good advising may be the single most underestimated characteristic of a successful college experience" (Light, 2001, p. 81). The skills of advising form the foundations of other administrative competencies, such as a staff supervision, evaluation, training, and leadership development, and, although it is related, advising should not be confused with counseling, which is addressed in Chapter Twenty-Two.

Advising is not merely providing advice. Providing advice is a unidirectional relationship in which a person who "knows better" tells another person what to do. Advising is a helping relationship between two people and a dynamic process of mutual discovery and self-determination. An advisor helps individuals identify choices and take responsibility for the choices they make. While the advisor may indeed have more knowledge and experience than the advisee and be aware of the "bigger picture," the goal of advising is to generate learning, growth, and self-determination, in addition to sharing information, opinion, and one's accumulated wisdom. Winston, Miller, Ender, and Grites (1984) describe this type of advising relationship as "a systematic process . . . intended to aid students in achieving educational, career, and personal goals through the utilization of the full range of institutional and community resources. It both stimulates and supports students in their quest for an enriched quality of life. Developmental advising relationships focus on identifying and accomplishing life goals, [and] acquiring skills and attitudes that promote intellectual and personal growth" (p. 19).

Advising goes beyond the one-on-one relationships of such activities as academic and career advising. So, in addition to discussing advising in individual relationships, this chapter also focuses on advising groups. These sections are followed by a discussion of current issues facing individual and group advisors, including challenges facing today's students, technology, and assessment. The chapter concludes with a focus on a different type of advising relationship, the issue of serving as an organizational consultant (an institutional advisor).

Advising Individuals

Most research regarding advising has focused on academic advising, but the information presented in this section applies to any position that involves advising individual students. The topics addressed are the goals of advising, the skills and competencies of advising, including interpersonal skills, problem solving, and understanding, and applying developmental and learning theory.

Goals of Advising

The goals for academic advising (Habley, 2000), as created by a NACADA task force and incorporated into the work of the Council for the Advancement of Standards (CAS) for Academic Advising, are:

- Assisting students in self-understanding and self acceptance
- Assisting students in considering their life goals by relating their interests, skills, abilities, and values to careers, the world of work, and the nature and purpose of higher education
- Assisting students in developing an educational plan consistent with their life goals and objectives
- Assisting students in developing decision-making skills
- Providing accurate information about institutional policies, procedures, resources, and programs
- Referring students to other institutional or community support services
- Assisting students in evaluating or reevaluating progress toward establishing goals and educational plans
- Providing information about students to the institution, college, academic departments, or some combination thereof (pp. 40–41)

While these have been promulgated as goals of academic advising, one also can see where most of these goals fit virtually any individual advising relationship in higher education.

Skills and Competencies of Advising

Advising involves a complex set of skills, competencies, and knowledge bases. An academic advisor must begin an advising relationship with clear knowledge of institutional academic programs and curricular requirements. Other individual advisors need to know the policies and procedures governing their advising relationships with students. Important skills and competencies for individual advisors include interpersonal skills, problem solving, and understanding and applying developmental and learning theory.

Interpersonal Skills. Interpersonal skills are made up of active listening, questioning, and referral skills (Nutt, 2000). Active listening skills are the foundation of any effective interpersonal interaction and include:

- Establishing and maintaining appropriate eye contact
- Not interrupting with solutions before students have fully explained their ideas or problem
- Being aware of body language that indicates lack of attention or discomfort on the part of the advisor and unexpressed feelings on the part of the advisee
- Being wary of emotional involvement or reactions, which can distract and reduce ability to listen
- Focusing on both the content and tone of student words
- Acknowledging what students are saying through verbal and nonverbal feedback
- Reflecting on or paraphrasing what has been said (Burley-Allen, 1995; Nutt)

The key to effective questioning is focusing on the concerns of the student, not the concerns of the advisor (Nutt, 2000). This involves using both open-ended and close-ended questions. Questions also communicate appropriate role expectations. In an effective advising relationship there is mutual responsibility for guiding the discussion. An advisor can communicate both inappropriate and appropriate role expectations through the form of questions, such as "How can I help you?" (less appropriate—communicates that an advisor's role is to solve problems) versus "What issues should we discuss?" (appropriate—communicates that a student role is to shape the meeting agenda and that there is a shared responsibility for problem solving).

Effective referrals depend on an advisor's listening and questioning skills because the first step in referring a student is to determine the student's concerns in order to recognize the need for a referral. The advisor also needs knowledge of appropriate referral services and their availability. The probability of an effective referral is enhanced when the advisor has already taken the time to visit possible referral services and has established relationships with specific individuals to whom students can be referred (Nutt, 2000). The advisor also needs to be able to explain in a clear, open, and sensitive manner why there is a need for a referral to another source of assistance. A referral should involve direct communication with the service to which the student is being referred. There should be a sensitive transfer of the student from the present advising relationship to the new helping relationship. This can involve working with the student to set up an appointment or actually walking the student to the new office. Finally, effective referrals include following up with students about the referral and the assistance they received to ensure that their needs were met (Nutt).

Problem Solving. Effective problem solving requires a partnership between advisor and advisee. Just as advising is not solely providing advice, problem solving is not merely supplying solutions. The role of the advisor is to work with the student in the problem solving process. Obviously, the interpersonal skills described above are prerequisites to effective problem solving. Advisors must also avoid establishing premature boundaries that might restrict the ability to see creative solutions. "This means overcoming our personal predispositions, defenses, and habits so we really do have as many choices as possible. . . . [This involves] looking for ways of becoming "unstuck," of taking a new and different look, or redefining the problem in a manner that may provide a new perspective" (Napier & Gershenfeld, 1987, p. 341).

There are both rational and intuitive elements to problem solving. One typical example of a rational system of problem solving is as follows:

1. *Problem identification.* Working together to define the problem at hand; exploring beneath the surface of the presenting problem (such as choice of major) in order to discover possible root problems (such as fear of disappointing parents).
2. *Diagnosis.* Gathering data about the problem, including the degree of urgency and stress, other underlying factors, the degree to which this problem is affecting others, and the degree to which the student "owns" the problem (as opposed to believing the problem actually lies somewhere else).
3. *Generating alternatives.* Identifying the possible solutions to the problem. Upon doing so, additional data may need to be gathered.
4. *Selecting solutions.* Evaluating alternatives for potential effectiveness and consequences, selecting a solution, creating a plan of action, and discussing obstacles to implementing the plan (such as internal resistance on the part of the student).
5. *Implementation.* Putting the plan into action.
6. *Evaluation and adjustment.* Evaluating the implementation for effectiveness and making necessary adjustments (Napier & Gershenfeld, 1987)

Effective problem solving involves both rational and intuitive elements. As any effective problem solver has discovered, relying only on a rational process is problematic because it implies that all necessary information is available and interpretable, and that is rarely the case. "Many of the most creative decisions . . . result from some unexpected thought, from an aside said in jest, from a moment when defenses were down, or at a point of exhaustion, frustration, or exasperation" (Napier & Gershenfeld, p. 341). Therefore, it is important that intuitive aspects of problem solving are also incorporated into the advising relationship. Advisors need to encourage students to listen to, explore, understand, and trust their instincts and hunches as well. For example, when deciding upon a major or career, a student can utilize interest or personality inventories, interview people in the careers, and list pros and cons of pursuing a particular career. These tend to be rational elements of the problem solving process. Intuitive aspects include reflecting on a visit to a work site related to the career and exploring with one's advisor how it felt to be there or imaging what a future in that career would be like. Both rational and intuitive elements interact and contribute to the effectiveness of the problem-solving process.

Understanding and Applying Developmental and Learning Theory. As indicated in the introduction to this chapter, the advising relationship is a wonderful opportunity to facilitate the development of students. Student development and learning theory can help in explaining many of the complicated issues facing students. Effective advising requires knowledge of a wide array of developmental and learning theories (Creamer, 2000), the ability to discover levels of development through the advising relationship, and the ability to provide appropriate challenges to stimulate reflection and action that may lead to further development. While some scholars (for example, Gordon & Steele, 1995) argue for knowledge of an exhaustive set of developmental and developmentally related theories, Creamer suggests the most important areas of focus should be on identity theory, meaning-making theory (cognitive-structural theories), and typology or personality theories. Many of these theories are reviewed in Chapters Nine and Ten.

Creamer (2000) holds that students' advising needs change as they progress in their development. It is therefore important that advisors be able to assess the developmental status of the students with whom they work. Formal assessment involves the use of validated and reliable structured interviews or paper-and-pencil instruments. While such instruments can be effective for persistent personality type assessment (such as the Myers Briggs Typology Indicator), Love and Guthrie (1999) argue "rarely are the time, opportunity, or resources available to conduct formal assessments" (p. 86). Instead, they suggest that professionals develop the skill of intentional informal assessment which requires: knowledge and understanding of theory and qualitative data techniques (observation, clinical interviewing); identification of one's own biases and assumptions; the ability to look for evidence of developmental levels in the experiences of students; and self-reflection and self-evaluation of one's abilities in this area. Intentional informal assessment requires a mind-set different from typical advising relationships, and it requires practice.

Advising Groups

The types of student groups on campus that use staff as advisors are numerous, and they range widely in size, purpose, and degree of formality and structure. Formal groups include student government, Greek organizations, residence hall associations, academic clubs and organizations, honors societies, on-campus military groups, and advocacy and support organizations, such as those for students of color, or lesbian, gay, bisexual, and transgendered students. Many of the same skills and knowledge sets that underlie effective individual advising apply to group situations; however, additional skills sets and considerations are involved. As in individual advising, it is important to be aware of institution-specific expectations for the function and role of group advisor. The knowledge bases and skills addressed later in this section are group motivation, group dynamics, and group development.

Group Advisor Functions and Roles

Bloland (1967) identified three related functions of the group advisor: maintenance, group growth, and program content. Maintenance functions are those that help to continue and protect the group, such as preserving the history of the group, and guarding against rule, policy, or ethics violations. Group growth functions are described below in the group development section and focus on helping the group improve its performance and work toward its goals. The program content functions are where the advisor appropriately shares her or his expertise in the areas of group focus, such as conducting Robert's Rules of Order workshops for student government leaders.

Dunkel and Schuh (1998) identify a number of essential roles for advisors of student groups: mentor, supervisor, teacher, leader, and follower. They cite DeCoster and Brown's (1982) definition of a mentor as a more experienced person in a relationship with a less experienced person based on modeling behavior and on an extended, shared dialogue. A mentor relationship is also one in which both people choose the relationship; a mentoring relationship cannot be assigned or forced on one individual by the other. The advisor of a student organization, therefore, may have the opportunity to serve as a mentor to the students in the organization. Dunkel and Schuh identify supervision as one of the skills of a group advisor, in that supervision and group advising both involve team building, performance planning, individual and group communication, recognition and documentation of individual and group actions, encouraging self-assessment on the part of group members, and evaluating individual and group performance.

Group advising also involves the role and skills of teacher. As an advisor of a student group the focus and content of the teaching role focuses on such topics as group roles and responsibilities, meeting facilitation, leadership, and group problem solving (Dunkel & Schuh, 1998). While the advisor attempts to encourage the development of effective leadership and followership among the members of the group, the advisor also will serve in the roles of leader and follower. A person attempting to influence others toward the accomplishment of a task or goal is exerting leadership according to Hersey and Blanchard (1988), so the very nature of an advising position includes the notion of leadership. The advisor is attempting to influence the development of leaders within the student group and attempting to influence positive group development and functioning. Dunkel and Schuh caution group advisors to be aware of their bases of influence as they teach students about appropriate and effective uses of power.

In order to be most effective, the group advisor also needs to play the role of follower. That is, the advisor will need to "get out of the way" and allow the group to function, strive, and sometimes fail. Individual and organizational failure can be an important learning tool, if handled in a caring and sensitive way. There are also events that may be too important to allow failure. In these instances, it may be appropriate for the advisor to rescue the group but then use the situation as a teachable moment after the event has been completed.

Group Motivation

According to Dunkel and Schuh (1998), "understanding what motivates students may be [the] single most desirable skill" (p. 77). Motivation exhibited by group members can range from no initiative being exhibited to an obvious innate desire to contribute and participate. Comprehending the range of motivation levels in the group and the factors that influence them is a vital competency for group advisors. This requires being able to identify and assess the needs, wants, and drives (Hersey & Blanchard, 1988) of the students involved in the group. A common mistake of inexperienced advisors is making the assumption that the motivations of the group match their own motivation, match the initial motivation espoused by group members (which may or may not match the enacted motivation), or match the motivation of the most involved students. Assessment of motivation levels needs to be ongoing, especially in the development of a new group. It can be conducted informally and intentionally through conversations with group members or with formal exercises done as a part of ongoing group development.

Group Dynamics

Group dynamics is the study of the interpersonal processes that occur in groups that affect individual group members and overall group functioning. Group dynamics includes such concepts as group cohesion, group conflict, leader emergence and effectiveness, group effectiveness, and the influence of groups on individuals. An understanding of basic concepts of group dynamics contributes to the effectiveness of a group advisor and to the success of the group.

Johnson and Johnson (1991) indicate that an effective group is one that accomplishes its goals, maintains good working relationships among its members, and adapts to shifting conditions in ways that improve its effectiveness. They also provide a nine-point model of group effectiveness:

1. Group goals must be clearly understood, be relevant to the needs of group members, highlight the positive interdependence of members, and evoke from every member a higher level of commitment to their accomplishment.
2. Group members must communicate their ideas and feelings accurately and clearly.
3. Participation and leadership must be distributed among members.
4. Appropriate decision-making procedures must be flexible in order to match them with the needs of the situation.

5. Conflicts should be encouraged and managed constructively.
6. Power and influence need to be approximately equal throughout the group.
7. Group cohesion needs to be high.
8. Problem-solving adequacy should be high.
9. The interpersonal effectiveness of members needs to be high (Dunkel & Schuh, 1998, p. 84)

It is the understanding and effective facilitation of group dynamics that contribute to the process of group development.

Group Development

Group development can be seen as the subset of group dynamics that focuses on the processes related to the growth, development, maturation, transition, and, sometimes, decline of group functioning. Napier and Gershenfeld (1987) proposed five interacting phases of group development: (1) the beginning; (2) movement toward confrontation; (3) compromise and harmony; (4) reassessment; and (5) resolution and recycling. The beginning is the formative phase of group development: the time period when group members come together, establish goals and expectations for the group, share and learn about similarities and differences among group members, experience the discomfort and optimism of a new group, and establish some basic ground rules of group functioning. The advisor can assist in helping the group work through this phase by conducting appropriate ice breakers, facilitating training in group functioning, and assisting the group with goal identification and planning. In the "movement toward confrontation" phase, initial feelings of discomfort continue to be worked through, the optimism of starting something new begins to wane, leadership and power relationships emerge and unfold, subgroups may form around distinctions and divisions in the group, and conflict among members may emerge. The advisor can best help groups in this phase by surfacing areas of difference and suggesting clarification, conducting training in conflict identification and resolution, and facilitating leadership development activities.

Most groups then tend to enter a "compromise and harmony" phase where differences are resolved, and working relationships grow in effectiveness. It is possible that excessive harmony can actually reduce the efficiency of the group if any lingering or new conflict is repressed, potentially resulting in passive resistance or passive-aggressive behavior. As an advisor, identifying possible instances of repressed conflict can help the group continue to develop. This is also the phase where groups can be strongly encouraged and pushed in their work, given increased levels of strength and resilience. Then as groups continue their work and experience some accomplishments, they enter the "reassessment" phase of functioning. Goals, expectations, and plans are revisited and revised. This may also be the time when the group is amenable to greater self-assessment of their performance, which the advisor can help to facilitate. Finally, Napier and Gershenfeld (1987) identify a "resolution and recycling" phase of group development. If the group is at a high level of maturity and functioning, conflict tends to be more open, constructive, and accepted as an important element of creative group performance. Depending on the group, the advisor can assist with appropriate concluding activities if the group will cease to function or with issues of leadership transition for groups that experience cyclical turnover.

Issues in Individual and Group Advising

Whether someone is involved in the process of individual advising or group advising, advisors will face a number of similar issues. This section provides information on the needs of today's students, the impact of technology on advising, and the role of assessment in advising.

The Needs of Today's Students

Every advisor has the same challenge when working with students, that is, treating them as unique individuals while using knowledge about subgroups to inform the advising relationship. During the past several decades research on a variety of student subgroups has been conducted. Examples of such groups include adult students, first-generation college students, students with learning disabilities, lesbian, gay, bisexual, and transgendered students, students of color, international students, student athletes, and graduate and professional students. In addition to published resources, the NACADA website (http://www.nacada.ksu.edu/) provides up-to-date information on advising various student subpopulations.

Beyond the variety of subpopulations that exist on campus, there are other changes in the overall student population that are important for any advisor to understand. Some of these changes are addressed in Chapter Three, so only those changes most related to advising are addressed here: underpreparedness, identity development issues, shifts in attitudes, shifts in family dynamics, and increases in psychological and emotional damage.

Underpreparedness

College students have been identified as increasingly underprepared (Hansen, 1998; Levine & Cureton, 1998; Upcraft & Stephens, 2000). Seventy-three percent of college deans reported an increase in the last ten years in the proportion of students requiring remedial or developmental education (Levine & Cureton), with nearly one-third of all undergraduates reporting having taken a basic skills or remedial course in reading, writing, or math (Levine & Cureton). The increase in remedial course work and the needs of underprepared students is expected to continue expanding despite attempts by some systems of higher education to eliminate remedial courses from their curriculum (Woodard, Love, & Komives, 2000).

Identity Development Issues

Another problem for today's college students is the search for identity in an amorphous and unpredictable environment (Woodard et al., 2000). Although it is an issue throughout the life span, identity development is the central task of the traditional college years, yet Hersch (1998) pointed out that the most stunning change for adolescents today is their aloneness. The adolescents of the 1990s were more isolated and more unsupervised than those from other generations. This will provide significant challenges to the advisors who will work with these students when they arrive on college campuses where students are expected to be active and contributing members of a community. The challenges will include trying to connect with students who need the structure and contact of an advising relationship, yet who resist such a relationship due to a history of independence that may border on isolation.

Shifts in Attitudes

Levine and Cureton (1998) pointed out that the students of the late 1990s lived in an era very different from that of previous generations of college students. The students Levine and Cureton interviewed believed they were living in a deeply troubled nation and perceived large-scale problems all around them, from poverty, racism, and crime to environmental pollution and global conflict. The long-term impact of the tragic events of September 11, 2001, and continuing global conflicts will emerge over time, so advisors in the near future will need to be much more aware of potential shifts in attitudes and values among the college student population.

Shifts in Family Dynamics

Approximately one-quarter of freshmen in 1997 came from divorced families (Hansen, 1998), and almost one-third of all children lived in single-parent situations. This represents a 300 percent increase from 1972 (Hansen). Additionally, "students who themselves are divorced or single parents make up a significant part of our adult learner population" (Upcraft & Stephens, 2000, p. 77). These shifts in family dynamics will play a part in most advising relationships and may relate to increases in psychological and emotional damage.

Increase in Psychological and Emotional Damage

Gannon (1989) points out physical violence, sexual abuse, and alcohol and drug abuse continue to increase within families. Hansen (1998) remarks that violence among children and adolescents remains extremely high and that more than 25 percent of adult women report having been sexually assaulted during their childhood or as young women. Sixty percent of campuses surveyed by Levine and Cureton (1998) reported record use of psychological services and increases in eating disorders, drug abuse, alcohol abuse, and suicide attempts. Today's student population is dealing with significant levels of psychological and emotional damage. Advisors need to be aware of and prepared for this, since on most campuses advisors are the only professionals with whom students have one-on-one contact (Nutt, 2000).

Obviously, not all students are affected by these trends; however, individual and group advisors need to be sensitive to the fact that in addition to traditional developmental and learning needs, they may be working with students who are struggling with additional problems. The ability to make appropriate and sensitive referrals becomes that much more important.

Technology and Advising

As technology continues to evolve, the relationship between the various advising roles and technology will continue to grow in significance. For example, Penietz (1997) discovered that academic advising was the most essential student service for students enrolled in community college distance education programs. Sotto (2000) described a variety of forms of technology-based academic advising including synchronous advising, asynchronous advising, videoconferencing, computer chat, and e-mail. She also described how students can address some of their advising-related needs through the Internet. These include the ability to retrieve advising and registering policies and procedures, forms, and planners, as well as being able to use assessment or practice tests. Patankar (1998) described an Internet-based Academic Counseling Expert (ACE), which is a supplement to faculty advisors and saves many hours of faculty time. Treuer and Belote (1997) described how advisors of student organizations could encourage their organizations to use available technology to enhance their effectiveness. Their suggestions included using e-mail for quick access to the advisor or to address pressing needs, developing distribution lists to disseminate group information, creating web sites linked to the Office of Student Activities web site to communicate group activities and events, using the Internet to set up discussion groups, and, in general, using technology to attend to minor, business-related issues between formal meetings. Like all aspects of student affairs work, student affairs professionals involved in advising must seek to understand emerging technologies and how they can be used to improve advising practice and enhance students' developmental and learning outcomes.

Not surprisingly, there are both advantages and disadvantages to the technology-based advising services being developed. One of the largest advantages is accessibility. Technology allows access to advising services wherever and whenever a student has the need (Sotto, 2000). Information downloaded from official advising sites is the most accurate and up-to-date information, and some students prefer the anonymity offered by the technology. Not surprisingly, there are disadvantages as well. The largest single disadvantage has been the lack of a face-to-face interaction in most technology applications (e-mail, chat functions). While it is still possible to build rapport with an advisor (Sotto), the fact remains that important nonverbal and subverbal elements of communication are lost in most technology-based interactions. However, as technology continues to evolve, the issue of losing face-to-face interaction may become moot.

For example, Menlove, Hansford, and Lignugaris-Kraft (2000) described a teleconferencing system that is able to deliver voice and video, and therefore advising and mentoring, over the Internet to preservice teacher education students living at rural sites.

Another disadvantage of technology-based advising is that it differentially advantages those students with access to technology resources and those students who attend institutions able to keep up with the changes in technology and with the increased demands of technology needs by their students. As the cost of technology continues to drop, its accessibility will improve; however, advisors need to remain cognizant of the students with whom they might be losing touch due to students' inability to access the necessary technology.

Assessment of Advising

Assessing the effectiveness of advising continues to lag as a priority on most campuses (Habley & Morales, 1998). One of the primary purposes of assessment is to assist in the process of improving student learning outcomes. An effective assessment program related to the outcomes of the advising process needs to be implemented at both the individual advisor level as well as at the program or department level. While many elements and skills go into effective individual advising, Creamer and Scott (2000) identify accessibility, knowledge, and helpfulness as foundational elements. These can be added to the skill sets listed previously in this chapter: interpersonal skills, problem-solving skills, and the ability to apply student development theory. These attributes and skills should form the focus of the assessment process of individual advisors, which needs to be ongoing and not simply a one-time-per-year evaluation process. The purpose is to gather data from a variety of sources (students and peers) in order to provide advisors with quality feedback that allows them to shape their behavior and improve their skills.

Assessment at the program level is a much more complex process (Lynch, 2000), because it takes into account not only individual advisor work but the collective work and impact of the entire unit. Lynch recommends that units assess both the process of advising and the outcomes of advising (the influence that the individuals and program are having on student learning, behavior, and success) with the goal of enhancing effectiveness. Data can be collected through surveys, interviews, focus groups, and observation with the purpose of analyzing these data to provide information to the members of the program that will allow for the improvement of effectiveness. Techniques of program assessment are discussed in greater depth by Upcraft in Chapter Twenty-Six.

Advising the Institution: Internal Consultation

There are some similarities between advising groups and advising the institution in that the institution is a large, complex group, and internal consultants most often work with subgroups within the institution. Many of the same skills that underlie effective advising practice with student groups apply to the role of internal consultant. In fact, student organization advisors often act as consultants to the groups, as experts in providing training and as process consultants to diagnose, analyze, and address dysfunctional group processes. A significant difference is that an internal consultation tends to be issue or problem driven, rather than driven by long-term commitment to the growth and development of a particular group.

Consultation is a process that uses experts who employ their knowledge, advice, and expertise to assist organizations in addressing organizational problems. The types of problems typically addressed are those that inhibit organizational functioning or detract from student learning and development. While the use of external consultants in higher education is a growing phenomenon, it is important not to overlook the vital source of consultants already within the organization. Perhaps the most obvious reason to use internal consultants is the cost savings involved. Internal consultants also are familiar with the organization and may be aware of the concerns being addressed. Drawbacks to using internal consultants are that organizational members are sometimes more open and frank with people from outside the organization, and there may be political dynamics that influence the ability of an internal consultant to assist with the issue at hand. It is, therefore, wisest to use external consultants if there is a significant, intractable, systemic problem (such as racial conflict), while internal consultants can best assist in areas of organizational development, improvement, and problem solving.

The art and science of consulting has evolved during the past several decades. The former dominant form of consultation was the use of the expert consultant, or as Schein (1988) described it, the doctor-patient relationship. In this type of consultation, the consultant (virtually always external to the organization) works with the organization and applies solutions (medicine) to the problem (illness). Sometimes this works; however, more often than not the problem returns, or new, though similar, problems arise, and the consultant returns. This dynamic creates an amplifying cycle of increasing dependency of the organization on the consultant. Although declining in emphasis, there still are appropriate problems and situations in which an expert consultant can be of use to an organization. That is when the problem is clearly defined and involves a lack of knowledge or skill on the part of members of the organization. An expert consultant (either internal or external) takes on the role(s) of teacher and trainer. An example of internal expert consultation at work in higher education would be when academic affairs seeks to help faculty understand the needs of first-year students by employing expert consultation from student affairs professionals in the orientation program.

As the dominance of expert consultation has waned, two related and often overlapping forms of consulting have emerged as powerful tools to assist institutions: collaborative consultation and process consultation. It is these forms of consulting that most conform to the descriptions, assumptions, and practices of individual and group advising described earlier in this chapter.

Collaborative Consultation

Models of collaborative consultation have emerged from mental health consultation (Caplan, Caplan, & Erchul, 1994), special education (Idol, Nevin, & Paolucci-Whitcomb, 1993; Kampwirth, 1999), and other educational fields. Collaborative consultation diverges from expert consultation in that no one single expert is perceived as being able to address an institutional problem. The assumption in collaborative consultation is that institutional problems must be addressed by an interdisciplinary team of professionals, which includes internal staff members but can include external professionals as well. Professionals are selected for the team because of particular content or process expertise they hold. Responsibility is shared, and various talents and strengths are brought to bear on the issue at hand. Idol, Paolucci-Whitcomb, and Nevin (1987) defined collaborative consultation as "an interactive process that enables people with diverse expertise to generate creative solutions to mutually defined problems . . . and produces solutions that are different from those that the individual team members would produce independently" (p. 1).

An advantage of collaborative consultation is that multiple members of the institution help to shape strategies and are invested in the success of the results of the consulting effort and in helping to overcome institutional resistance. This is in contrast to one of the weaknesses of the expert consultation model, which is the difficulty in overcoming resistance to change on the part of institutional members. This is a challenge for both external and internal consultants. Crego (1996) points out that collaborative consultation is a way to transcend the traditional boundaries between departments, divisions, and roles that often block change from being implemented.

Process Consultation

Process consultation is the building of a helping relationship between the consultant and the members of the organization. It can be viewed as a series of steps taken by the consultant to involve members of the organization in defining and analyzing the problem at hand, developing a range of possible solutions, analyzing the solutions for value and potential obstacles, and identifying a solution. An important element of process consultation is the active part that the members of the organization take in solving the problem at hand. Process consultation is often used in combination with collaborative consultation. One of the underlying assumptions of process consultation is that many of the problems in organizational functions (issues of motivation, conflict, lack of teamwork, failure to produce desired outcomes) are the result of problematic or dysfunctional interpersonal communication and group processes (Schein, 1988). One of the goals of process consultation is to solve the current problem while uncovering the dynamics of the problem so that the members of the organization can identify for themselves how the problematic situation developed and persisted (Schein). Another goal is to have the consultation experience be a learning experience so that the members of the organization can come together, identify, and solve any related future problems that may arise.

The role of the consultant in process consultation is to observe the interactions that occur in the organization as it relates to the problems at hand. The consultant then provides feedback aimed at teaching group members to identify and diagnose the behaviors that either help or hinder the group's success and to take steps to correct the problems. This is precisely the kind of consultation that advisors provide to the students in the groups they advise. As Crego (1996) observed: "Student affairs personnel are often very good observers of group processes, able to point out patterns of group functioning to group members they are working with. Attending to how group members utilize feedback to improve their problem-solving capabilities will help the novice process consultant learn to effectively employ this role of observer and occasional intervener in group processes" (p. 369).

Skills and Competencies of Consultation

While the skills required of the different approaches to consultation vary, there are some competencies that are required of all consultants. These include the interpersonal skills and problem-solving skills mentioned in the individual advising section, as well as the skills related to motivation, group dynamics, and group development needed by group advisors. The skills reviewed in this section are working with fellow organizational members and data collection.

Working with Organizational Members

As indicated above, the internal organizational consultant has certain advantages over external consultants, the most significant being insider knowledge of the organization and initial access to organizational members. However, internal consulting is fraught with danger. The internal consultant must be able to engender trust on the part of members. For example, if the consultant is viewed as a pawn of the administration, the staff's willingness to be open and honest will be compromised. Trust building includes the ability to keep confidences (even after the period of consulting is finished), to maintain the integrity of the process, and to treat organizational members with respect. Working with organizational members also requires sensitivity to and knowledge of political processes occurring within the organization. Consultation often occurs within an environment of constrained resources, which engenders stress and conflict within an organization (which itself may be the reason why a consultant was identified in the first place). In such an environment, the internal consultant must be aware of the political dynamics that may be shaping the action within the organization. Such dynamics include the emergence of issue-specific interest groups and coalitions, the use of informal power (as opposed to positional authority), and diffused and decentralized decision making. The skills of negotiation, persuasion, and diplomacy become that much more important in such a highly politicized environment.

Data Collection: Interviews and Observation

Schein (1988) suggested a combination of interviewing and observation in the early part of any consulting process. While the focus of data collection will vary depending on the presenting problem, Schein was clear that the focus needs to be on the processes at work in the organization. These include communication processes, group roles, group task and maintenance functions, group problem solving, group decision making, group norms, leadership, authority, and other intergroup processes. Process consultation interviews can either be with individuals or focus groups. Interviews have an explicit purpose that is described to the participant(s); interviewers provide explanations about the purpose of the questions and the overall interview, and ask descriptive, structural, and contrast questions.

Observation used as data collection is different from merely watching something, which is often a passive experience (such as watching a sporting event or musical performance). Consultation-related observations are conducted with a focus and purpose. The consultant needs to look beyond the content of conversations and surface action of meetings and activities to the processes mentioned earlier. Observation "demands a complete commitment to the task of understanding" the group and its dynamics (Reeves Sanday, 1983, p. 20). The consultant must become part of the situation being observed and must focus on observing as an outsider and on trying to understand the situation from the perspective of an insider. Trying to identify with those being observed while trying to maintain an objective distance is an awkward dynamic (Reeves Sanday). Thus, while being able to empathize with those being observed is important, it is not enough. The consultant needs to be able to "record, categorize, and code what is being observed" (Reeves Sanday, p. 21). It is this information and the analysis of the information gathered from interviews and observations that the internal consultant brings to the group in order to analyze the problem at hand and work together to identify solutions and learn from the overall process.

Conclusion

Advising is a skill that is utilized by many different student affairs professionals and in a variety of contexts. No matter what the role and no matter which individuals or groups are being advised the practice of advising involves a focus on learning. Academic advisors encourage learning on the part of their advisees, group advisors encourage learning on the part of members of the groups they advise, and institutional advisors (or consultants) encourage learning on the part of institutional members. Quality advising requires individuals with appropriate skills and knowledge sets, and the willingness and ability to continually upgrade these skills and knowledge sets.

References

Beal, P. E., & Noel, L. (1980). *What works in student retention.* Iowa City, IA: American College Testing Program.

Bloland, P. A. (1967). *Student group advising in higher education* (Student Personnel Series No. 8). Washington, DC: American Personnel and Guidance Association.

Burley-Allen, M. (1995). *Listening: The forgotten skill.* New York: Wiley.

Caplan, G., Caplan, R. B., & Erchul, W. P. (1994). Caplanian mental health consultation: Historical background and current status. *Consulting Psychology Journal: Practice and Research, 46,* 2–12.

Creamer, D. G. (2000). Use of theory in academic advising. In V. N. Gordon & W. R. Habley (Eds.), *Academic advising: A comprehensive handbook* (pp. 18–34). San Francisco: Jossey-Bass.

Creamer, E. G., & Scott, D. W. (2000). Assessing individual advisor effectiveness. In V. N. Gordon & W. R. Habley (Eds.), *Academic advising: A comprehensive handbook* (pp. 339–348). San Francisco: Jossey-Bass.

Crego, C. A. (1996). Consultation and mediation. In S. R. Komives & D. B. Woodard (Eds.), *Student services: A handbook for the profession* (3rd ed., pp. 361–379). San Francisco: Jossey-Bass.

Crockett, D. S. (1978). Academic advising: Cornerstone of student retention. In L. Noel (Ed.), *Reducing the dropout rate* (New Directions for Student Services No. 3, pp. 29–35). San Francisco: Jossey-Bass.

Crockett, D. S. (1985). Academic advising. In L. Noel, R. Levitz, D. Saluri, & Associates, *Increasing student retention: Effective programs and practices for reducing the dropout rate* (pp. 244–263). San Francisco: Jossey-Bass.

DeCoster, D. A., & Brown, R. D. (1982). Mentoring relationships and the educational process. In R. D. Brown & D. A. DeCoster (Eds.), *Mentoring-transcript systems for promoting student growth* (New Directions for Student Services No. 19, pp. 5–17). San Francisco: Jossey-Bass.

Dunkel, N. W., & Schuh, J. H. (1998). *Advising student groups and organizations.* San Francisco: Jossey-Bass.

Frost, S. H. (1991). *Academic advising for student success: A system of shared responsibility* (ASHE-ERIC Higher Education Report No. 3). Washington, DC: George Washington University, School of Education and Human Development.

Gannon, J. R. (1989). *Soul survivors: A new beginning for adults abused as children.* Englewood Cliffs, NJ: Prentice Hall.

Gordon, V. N., & Steele, G. E. (1995). Toward a theory of academic advising. Paper presented at the National Academic Advising Association annual meeting, Nashville, TN.

Habley, W. R. (2000). Current practices in academic advising. In V. N. Gordon & W. R. Habley (Eds.), *Academic advising: A comprehensive handbook* (pp. 35–43). San Francisco: Jossey-Bass.

Habley, W. R., & Morales, R. H. (1998). *Current practices in academic advising: Final report on ACT's Fifth National Survey of Academic Advising* (National Academic Advising Association Monograph Series No. 6). Manhattan, KS: National Academic Advising Association.

Hansen, E. J. (1998). Essential demographics of today's college students. *American Association of Higher Education Bulletin, 51* (3), 3–5.

Hersch, P. (1998). *A tribe apart: A journey into the heart of American adolescence.* New York: Fawcett Columbine.

Hersey, P., & Blanchard, K. H. (1988). *Management of organizational behavior.* Englewood Cliffs, NJ: Prentice Hall.

Idol, L., Nevin, A., & Paolucci-Whitcomb, P. (1993). *Collaborative consultation* (2nd ed.). Austin, TX: Pro-Ed.

Idol, L., Paolucci-Whitcomb, P., & Nevin, A. (1987). *Collaborative consultation.* Rockville, MD: Aspen.

Johnson, D. W., & Johnson, F. P. (1991). *Joining together group theory and group skills.* Needham Heights, MA: Allyn & Bacon.

Kampwirth, T. J. (1999). *Collaborative consultation in the schools: Effective practices for students with learning and behavior problems.* Upper Saddle River, NJ: Merrill.

Levine, A., & Cureton, J. S. (1998). *When hope and fear collide: A portrait of today's college students.* San Francisco: Jossey-Bass.

Light, R. J. (2001). *Making the most of college: Students speak their minds.* Cambridge, MA: Harvard University Press.

Love, P. G., & Guthrie, V. (1999). *Understanding and applying cognitive development theory* (New Directions for Students Services No. 88). San Francisco: Jossey-Bass.

Lynch, M. L. (2000). Assessing the effectiveness of the advising program. In V. N. Gordon & W. R. Habley (Eds.), *Academic advising: A comprehensive handbook* (pp. 324–338). San Francisco: Jossey-Bass.

Menlove, R. R., Hansford, D., & Lignugaris-Kraft, B. (2000, March). Creating a community of distance learners: Putting technology to work. Paper presented at the conference Capitalizing on Leadership in Rural Special Education. (ERIC Document Reproduction Service, No. ED439890)

Napier, R. W., & Gershenfeld, M. K. (1987). *Group theory and experience.* Boston: Houghton Mifflin.

Nutt, C. L. (2000). One-to-one advising. In V. N. Gordon & W. R. Habley (Eds.), *Academic advising: A comprehensive handbook* (pp. 220–227). San Francisco: Jossey-Bass.

Patankar, M. (1998). A rule-based expert system approach to academic advising. *Innovations in Education and Training International, 35* (1), 49–58.

Penietz, B. (1997). Community college students' perceptions of student services when enrolled in telecourses. *Dissertation Abstracts International (UMI No. 9735008).*

Reeves Sanday, P. (1983). The ethnographic paradigm(s). In J. Van Maanen (Ed.), *Qualitative methodology* (pp. 19–36). Beverly Hills, CA: Sage.

Schein, E. H. (1988). *Process consultation: Its role in organization development* (2nd ed.). Reading, MA: Addison-Wesley.

Sotto, R. R. (2000). Technological delivery systems. In V. N. Gordon & W. R. Habley (Eds.), *Academic advising: A comprehensive handbook* (pp. 249–257). San Francisco: Jossey-Bass.

Treuer, P., & Belote, L. (1997). Current and emerging applications of technology to promote student involvement and learning. In C. M. Engstrom & K. W. Kreuger (Eds.), *Using technology to promote student learning: Opportunities for today and tomorrow* (New Directions for Student Services No. 78, pp. 17–30). San Francisco: Jossey-Bass.

Upcraft, M. L., & Stephens, P. S. (2000). Academic advising and today's changing students. In V. N. Gordon & W. R. Habley (Eds.), *Academic advising: A comprehensive handbook* (pp. 73–83). San Francisco: Jossey-Bass.

Winston, R. B., Jr., Miller, T. K., Ender, S. C., & Grites, T. J. (1984). *Developmental academic advising: Addressing students' educational, career, and personal needs.* San Francisco: Jossey-Bass.

Woodard, D. B., Jr., Love, P. G., & Komives, S. R. (2000). *Leadership and management issues for the new century* (New Directions for Students Services No. 92). San Francisco: Jossey-Bass.

Resources in Advising and Consulting

The National Academic Advising Association (NACADA) is the primary resource related to academic advising. Information is available at www.ksu.edu/nacada

Dunkel, N. W., & Schuh, J. H. (1998). *Advising student groups and organizations.* San Francisco: Jossey-Bass.

Forsyth, D. R. (1999). *Group dynamics* (3rd ed.). Stamford, CT: Wadsworth.

Gordon, V. N., & Habley, W. R. (Eds.). (2000). *Academic advising: A comprehensive handbook.* San Francisco: Jossey-Bass.

Holland, J. L. (1997). *Making vocational choices: A theory of vocational personalities and work environments.* Odessa, FL: Psychological Assessment Resources.

Schein, E. H. (1988). *Process consultation: Its role in organization development* (2nd ed.). Reading, MA: Addison-Wesley.

Super, D. (1990). *Career and life development.* San Francisco: Jossey-Bass.

CHAPTER TWENTY-FOUR

CONFLICT RESOLUTION

Saundra Lawson Taylor

University campuses, like any environment in which people come into contact with one another, are fraught with the possibility of conflict. Some see conflict as something to be avoided, but when dealt with effectively, conflict can be the mechanism through which learning and development take place.

Often, however, people on campus do not have the skills to effectively address conflict. One role of the student affairs professional is to practice and teach conflict resolution skills in order to help improve the student learning environment and to remove barriers to effective functioning for both individuals and groups (Aspy, 1989). This chapter offers a foundation for understanding conflict as well as a set of skills, tactics, approaches, and guidelines for the resolution of conflict. The chapter begins with a discussion of the definition of conflict followed by an exploration of the causes, levels, and consequences of conflict. Four theoretical perspectives (student development, organizational development, community development, and multiculturalism) are presented as frameworks for understanding the nature and complexities of conflict. Next, core skills in communication essential to helping resolve conflict are presented along with a set of resolution tactics that include intergroup dialogue, mediation, negotiation, and arbitration. Then, both the Ury, Brett, and Goldberg (1993) and Thomas-Kilman Five Modes of Conflict (1974) approaches to conflict resolution are discussed. Finally, ten basic guidelines for effective conflict resolution are presented; they are a synthesis from the extensive body of literature on conflict and from the practice of conflict resolution workshops with students, faculty, and staff in university settings.

Understanding Conflict

Defining conflict is the first step in understanding it. Only then is it possible to explore the causes of conflict, attitudes toward conflict, and levels of conflict.

Definitions of Conflict

Cohen, Davis, and Aboelata (1998) broadly define conflict as "a situation between two or more parties who see their perspectives as incompatible" (p. 4). Alternatively, conflict can be understood as a process of expressing dissatisfaction, disagreement, or unmet expectations with another person, group, or organization (Cohen et al., 1998).

Whether it is a construct or a process, conflict may further be defined as either substantive or emotional (Costantino & Merchant, 1996). In substantive cases the conflict may be centered on policies, practices, or competition for resources. If so, it may best be handled by problem solving, bargaining, or mediation by a third party. But if conflict is emotional (meaning that anger, distrust, resentment, fear, or rejection are involved), then it might best be resolved by working through feelings, restructuring perceptions, and using conciliation interventions by a third party. Situational (substantive) conflict and process (emotional) conflict are not mutually exclusive. Emotions may be involved in situational conflict, and situational issues may be involved emotional conflict. When this is the case, you first need to decide whether to first address the emotional issues or the situational issues.

People often use the term conflict and dispute interchangeably, but they are not synonymous (Costantino & Merchant, 1996). A dispute is one of the products of unresolved conflict. Conflicts are often intangible, vague, and ongoing, whereas disputes are concrete and tangible. If a conflict between two roommates is not resolved, for example, one may make a formal complaint against the other to the hall association. This escalates a conflict to the level of a dispute. Disputes involve issues and expectations for relief (Costantino & Merchant).

Causes of Conflict

What are the root causes of conflict? Among the causes are differences in values, style, and goals; scarce resources; organizational or environmental conditions; and differences in culture (C. J. Taylor, personal communication, 1974). Exhibit 24.1 offers examples of each of these root causes of conflict. Just as conflict may be some combination of substantive and emotional elements, it may have more than one single root cause.

Levels of Conflict

Conflict may also vary by level. Holton (1995) identified seven levels: pseudo-conflict, latent conflict, problems to solve, dispute, cry for help, fight or flight, and intractable. These are shown in Exhibit 24.2.

EXHIBIT 24.1. ROOT CAUSES OF CONFLICT.

Causes	Examples
Differences in values	One student co-chair values open communication and collaboration; the other values efficiency.
Differences in style and goals	One faculty member has the goal of bringing harmony to a departmental decision-making process; the other seeks a frank exchange of views.
Scarce resources	The campus is rich in student performance groups but short on well-equipped programming space.
Organizational or environmental conditions	A large and multilayered organization like a university can be prone to poor communication between departments.
Role ambiguity	A student paraprofessional, who is also a campus leader, takes a highly visible position in opposition to a new student affairs policy.
Cultural differences	The Hillel group and the Middle Eastern group disagree on whom to bring to campus to discuss peace in the Middle East.

EXHIBIT 24.2. LEVELS OF CONFLICT.

Level	Situation	Cause	Resolution
1. Pseudo-conflict	Appear to be no differences. *Examples:* task force, committee with specific charge and time frame (low emotion)	Unsuccessful communication, semantic difficulties, insufficient exchange of information	Clarify, define issues. No outside facilitation necessary.
2. Latent conflict	One party acknowledges the problem, and the other party denies or does not notice that a problem exists. *Examples:* marital issues, roommate problems (moderate emotion)	May be differences in values, style, goals, roles, or culture.	Person who perceives the problem discusses it with other party. A third party may be helpful by facilitating the communication process.
3. Problems to solve	All parties recognize that there are "differences." *Example:* supervisor and supervisee (moderate emotion)	May be differences in power, values, style, culture, role ambiguity.	Bring the two parties together to share problem and mutually solve it. Third party may be helpful.

(*Continued*)

EXHIBIT 24.2. LEVELS OF CONFLICT. (*CONTINUED*)

Level	Situation	Cause	Resolution
4. Dispute	Parties are in a destructive mode—need-centered, not problem-centered (high emotion).	Unresolved feelings, distrust.	Needs must be acknowledged before parties will work on resolution. Neutral third party intervention is critical.
5. Cry for help	Parties no longer can manage their dispute because they are out of control. Groups form sides and enlist aid of others outside the conflict (high emotion).	Long-standing impasse at communication due to differences in values, style, etc. Belief that conflict can't be resolved.	Need third party from outside of system to — establish firm ground rules — take over the guidance of conflict solution phase — build trust of the parties.
6. Fight or flight	Parties declare battle, strategize how to destroy each other. (emotion is charged, high)	Active fighting; parties believe their survival is threatened by other party.	Need third party intervention who must speak to individuals separately to — listen to personal needs — work through needs for understanding — restore civil conversation — build trust and respect.
7. Intractable	Parties are interested in sustaining conflict. Conflict is more important than its resolution. Parties talk negatively to anyone. (emotion is extremely high)	Long-standing conflict. May come from years of differences in values, goals, scarce resources.	Third party is necessary to bring justice to the situation, not just to defeat the enemy.

Source: Adapted from Holton (1995).

Understanding that there are levels of conflict can help the student affairs practitioner diagnose the best form of intervention and determine when a neutral third party would be most helpful. The goal is to intervene before conflict escalates to level 5 or above.

Consequences of Conflict

Another dimension of conflict complexity is consequences. Moore (1996) noted that conflict is unavoidable and is likely to be present in most human interactions.

When conflict is skillfully utilized, like an interesting puzzle, it may result in problem resolution and long-range benefit, including learning and development. Conflict is creative when it results in needed change: two charities that feed the poor compete for scare resources and find a way to join forces to triple the number of meals they can serve the homeless. Conflict, when creative, can result in new learning: two independent research groups meet to share findings and discover a new, unanticipated finding. Or creative conflict can lead to better use of new information: a professor in one university collaborates with a professor at a peer institution to bring new lecture material to each professor's course.

However, conflict can be destructive (Donohue & Kolt, 1992) when it results in unnecessary change—for example, when two groups decide to duplicate the efforts of the other. It is destructive when there is no learning, or when there is solidification of nonproductive behavior—for example, when two fraternities fight over who can out-drink the other. Additionally, conflict can be destructive when people are further apart (that is, when the attempt to deal with the conflict leads to an impasse and no resolution). Lastly, conflict can be destructive when resources are spent without results. For example, a unit elects to reorganize and add new staff positions to reconcile staff differences, but there is no change in the toxic work environment.

In summary, understanding the consequences of conflict broadens our grasp of the many underlying issues necessary to the successful resolution of conflict.

Theories, Skills, and Tactics for Addressing Conflict

The study of conflict as a concept gains meaning through the context of theories of personal growth, interpersonal interaction, organizational development, and the influence of multicultural perspectives. There are many theoretical frameworks from which to draw; those discussed below are the most useful in the student affairs arena.

Theories for Addressing Conflict

Student affairs practitioners can use four bodies of theory to better understand conflict: student development theory, organizational development theory, community development theory, and multiculturalism theory. As with most theoretical frameworks, a theory may be most helpful when used in combination with others as a way of better understanding the issue at hand.

Student development theory looks at conflict as an opportunity to better understand differences in a frame of reference of the individual. This perspective has evolved from the view that conflict is destructive and should be eliminated to the view that conflict promotes cohesiveness (Coser, 1956), maintains a balance of power between individuals (Blake, Shepard, & Mouton, 1964), generates creative approaches to problem solving (Hall, 1986), and facilitates change (Kolb & Glidden, 1986, as cited in McFarland, 1992). Conflict resolution, from the student development perspective, is an opportunity for personal growth and understanding. A student who has challenged her professor's grading of a paper discusses the assignment with the professor and comes to understand their differences, even though the professor does not change the grade.

Organizational development theory looks at the structure of the organization and the underlying assumptions that maintain the organization. Conflicts in an organization show up in a number of ways—through disputes, competition, sabotage, inefficiency, lack of productivity, low morale, and withholding knowledge (Costantino & Merchant, 1996). Conflict resolution work from an organizational development perspective focuses on understanding and changing the assumption of the organizational culture and finding ways to mediate or arbitrate to resolve differences.

Bolman and Deal (1984, 1997) propose four frames to understand organizations: structural, human resources, political, and symbolic. The structural frame looks at the patterns of expectations and exchanges among employees, supervisors, executives (internal), and external constituencies (customers, clients, students). Conflict in this set of interactions stems from such things as performance gaps as a result of deficiencies in the structure and are often resolved through restructuring. The human resources frame looks at the need of the employees (or students) and how to meet the needs in the work environment. Conflict arises when individuals disagree because of differences in needs. When conflict is high and resources are scarce, the dynamics of conflict, power, and self-interest regularly become dominant. Resolution occurs when individuals are encouraged to confront conflicts and promote improved relationships. The political frame views the organization from the arena of coalitions of various individuals and interest groups. From the political frame, conflict is a natural part of life. Change generates divisions and conflict among competing interest groups. The effective manager learns to build coalitions and establish arenas in which disagreements can be forged into workable pacts (Bolman & Deal, 1997). According to Bolman and Deal (1997), meaning, belief, and faith are central to the symbolic frame. Symbols express the organization's culture. Conflict in this frame occurs when the individual or group does not adhere to the norms of the culture, or when the behavior of an employee doesn't match the values expressed by the group. For example, two student clubs argue for limited funds but then join forces to increase their allocation and enhance their chances of both getting funded; they develop a shared vision and use conflict to arrive at meaning.

Community development theory looks at the group dynamics of differences and disputes. This approach focuses on the discovery of common ground; it also looks at social and cultural norms about nonviolent resolution. Violence prevention is the work of many in a community (Cohen et al., 1998). Workshops designed to teach anger management skills have taken on new importance as part of educational programs. This underscores a concern for nonviolence as a common value. In the community development theory, conflict resolution work focuses on intergroup dialogue to find common ground.

The theoretical framework of multiculturalism may also be useful in understanding the social and cultural norms underlying conflict (Myers & Finer, 1994). Making use of this framework requires being aware of one's own frame of reference as well as that of others, identifying and checking the other group members' assumptions, and paying attention to the variety of meanings assigned by different cultures to nonverbal behaviors (Pedersen, 1994).

Core Skills for Addressing Conflict

Conflict may have a variety of sources and levels and be viewed through several theoretical frameworks, and the choice of mode for addressing a particular conflict will be shaped by these variables. There are, however, some core or common skills that are essential in conflict management regardless of the nature of the conflict or the choice of style in addressing it.

Many of the skills related to resolving conflicts are those related to basic communication skills: active listening, clarifying statements made by others, paraphrasing for understanding, using empathy to build trust, as well as other counseling skills such as problem solving and evaluating options for effectiveness. It is important to note that communication behavior can create conflict, reflect conflict, and act as a means of productive or destructive resolution of conflict (Hocker & Wilmont, 1984).

Skills learned through leadership education programs also are useful. These may include summarizing, reframing comments to reduce negative perceptions of others' ideas, differentiating between issues or ideas and personality, and identifying power imbalances among group members that seem to be a barrier to clear communication.

The skill of establishing open and mutual trust is critical for conflict resolution (Deutsch, 1973; Doolittle, 1976; McFarland, 1992). McFarland writes about this approach as integrative conflict resolution. Trust is also essential for the maintenance of the relationship between the conflicted parties (Deutsch). Trust can be built through congruent verbal and nonverbal communication channels (Gahagan & Tedeschi, 1968; Satir, 1964).

Personal Characteristics. A number of personal characteristics are highly correlated with effective conflict resolution. Among these are mental toughness, assertiveness, flexibility, the ability to stand ground, and the ability to give and take to reach compromise (Donohue & Kolt, 1992; Fisher & Ury, 1981). Other personal characteristics correlated with effective conflict resolution are being consistent, empathic, and able to focus on the behavior rather than the person (Christiansen, 2001).

Tactics for Addressing Conflict

The core skills of conflict resolution (in the broader sense of the term) may be employed in a variety of tactics. Conflict resolution, intergroup dialogue, mediation, negotiation, and arbitration are among the tactics frequently employed in addressing conflict. Conflict resolution is the process by which disagreements, unmet expectations, or disputes are dealt with to the satisfaction of the parties involved in the conflict. The term *conflict resolution* suggests the possibility of finding an outcome that will be acceptable to the parties involved in the conflict.

Simon (1976) has written about the concept of satisficing solutions, which refers to a course of action that is considered to be "good enough" or adequate. In a conflict, the resolution that seems fair or meets the needs of some of a group would suffice. It is a form of compromise that allows parties to reconcile differences even though an optimal solution may not have been reached. For example, the university president and student body president disagree on the percentage of tuition increase. They find a satisficing solution by agreeing to a larger increase than the student body president wants, but it will go to improve student advising.

Intergroup dialogue is communication among and across a group of people who have a history of conflict or potential conflict; examples include dialogue between men and women, gays and heterosexuals, and people with and without disabilities (Schoem, Hurtado, Sevig, Chesler, & Sumida, 2001). The goals are to increase trust among members, develop creative solutions, and reinforce individual group members. Intergroup dialogue is a prerequisite for the resolution of conflict in group situations. Programs that focus on intergroup dialogue are based on the assumption that sustained and facilitated intergroup contact are necessary to promote and address better understanding, resolution of conflict, and the creation of a just and multicultural environment. Intergroup dialogue helps to challenge misconceptions and stereotypes, increase awareness of the self as a member of a social identity group, and give a more positive approach to exploring difficulties and potentially conflicting topics (Zúñiga & Sevig, 1997).

Mediation is "the intervention into a dispute or negotiation by an acceptable, impartial, and neutral third party who has no authoritative decision making power to assist disputing parties in voluntarily reaching their own mutually acceptable settlement of issues of dispute" (Moore, 1996, p. 4). The mediator or third party remains nonjudgmental in the effort to assist the parties in the conflict. The mediator helps the parties communicate more clearly with one another, identify misunderstandings or misconceptions, sort out multiple issues related to the conflict, and assist them to agree on which issues need attention.

Several authors and practitioners (Wing & Rifkin, 2001) have challenged the adherence to the concept of neutrality in mediation. They propose a different concept of mediation to deal with conflict related to racial identity of members of a group and oppression. They view mediation through the lens of social justice and conclude that the mediation process needs to be more focused on understanding the levels of racial identity with the goal of looking at the relationship between the dominant group and the subordinate group. Unlike traditional mediation, whose goal is to facilitate conflict at the individual level, the goal in a social justice model is to bring about a value-driven systemic change.

Negotiation is an exchange of information between parties that requires the parties to engage in a back-and-forth process with one goal to create questions and doubt in each other's mind about the information. Ultimately, a successful negotiation concludes with an acceptable outcome for both parties (Volpe, 1994).

Arbitration is an alternative approach to a court hearing. It is a private adjudication (Ury et al., 1993). It is used, like court, as a rights procedure in which the parties present arguments and evidence to a neutral third party who makes a binding decision.

Approaches to Conflict Resolution

Conflict resolution can be applied to disputes between two people as well as to those between and among groups. There are a number of different approaches to managing conflict that are built on different assumptions about the nature of conflict. For instance, some think that doing something is better than doing nothing at all, or that collaboration is always better than compromise (Moore, 2000). Moore suggests that these views are too linear and prescriptive.

The approaches of Ury et al. (1993) and Thomas and Kilman (1974) complement each other. These authors assume the situation (and the person's reaction to the situation) shapes the approach to the conflict, and that based on the situation, all approaches have value.

The Ury, Brett, and Goldberg Model

According to Ury et al. (1993), there are three dimensions to resolving conflict: dealing with interests (emotions), determining rights, and explicating power.

When dealing with interests (emotions), the focus is on parties' underlying needs, concerns, and issues—the things one cares about or wants. Conflict in this situation is need-centered. The person's needs take precedence over the problem. As an example, college roommates quarrel about the amount of time guests spend in their room. One roommate's underlying interest is to have no restrictions, while the other roommate wants no guests during the week. The two roommates have to look at reconciling differing interests. Mediation is an interest-based intervention in which a neutral third party assists the parties in understanding differing interests and in reaching agreements (Ury et al., 1993).

The second dimension focuses on determining who is right or what standards from law, contracts, or cultural norms influence the situation. These situations often require the use of objective criteria for agreement. The parties can develop what are fair standards and practices. As an example, the campus bookstore provides funding to support the student government. The student government wants an increase in the allocation. After much debate, students cite a long-standing contract between the two parties about profit sharing. Adhering to the terms of the contract allows both parties to resolve their differences and reach agreement on an increase in funding to the student government.

The third dimension is dealing with power—the ability to force others to accept the outcome you desire. This approach can be successful in situations where attempts at mediation and negotiation have failed. Exercising power may facilitate the short-term effect of getting more buy-in for a different outcome.

The focus of conflict resolution can shift from interests to rights to power. Ury et al. (1993) suggest that a focus on interests can resolve the problem underlying the conflict more effectively than can a focus on rights or power. This view is similar to identifying interpersonal conflicts. Ury et al. propose that dealing with interests generates a higher level of mutual satisfaction with outcomes than through determining rights or power. It also tends to produce better working relationships, less recurrence of the conflict, and fewer transaction costs. However, in some instances interest-based resolution cannot occur unless rights or power procedures are first employed to deal with a recalcitrant group or person. As an example, a student group may organize a demonstration on the steps of the administration building to get the president to discuss their demands. The president (or her representative) might first inform the protest leaders that, while peaceful and lawful protest will be respected, any action that interferes with the operation of the university is a violation of university (and, if applicable, municipal or state) laws and will result in arrests. Once the protest leadership acknowledges the information and pledges themselves to peaceful and lawful protest, then the president can begin a discussion with the protest leadership to explore an interest-based resolution.

Another issue is that interests can be so much in opposition that agreement is not possible. For instance, focusing on an interest cannot resolve a dispute between a pro-choice group and a right-to-life group about abortion information in the student health center.

Ury et al. (1993) suggest that in an effective system of resolving disputes, most conflicts are resolved through reconciling interests, some through determining who is right, and the fewest through determining who is the most powerful.

The Thomas-Kilman Model

In the Ury, Brett, and Goldberg model, identifying interest and working toward mutual agreement are necessary conditions for resolving conflict. Another complementary approach is to identify conflict situations and different styles to handle conflict. The Thomas-Kilman model, based on behaviors and situations, helps identify key competencies needed in dealing with conflict situations. Thomas and Kilman (1974) developed the Conflict Mode Instruction, a self-report instrument used in workshops on conflict, to help participants understand their approach to interpersonal conflict situations. It identifies five conflict-handling modes: competition, collaboration, compromise, avoidance, and accommodation. These styles are based on two dimensions of behavior: degree of assertiveness and degree of cooperativeness. The modes are defined as follows:

- *Competition.* You strive to satisfy your interest at the expense of others (forcing, arguing, pulling rank)
- *Collaboration.* You look for some way to satisfy both your interest and the other's (confronting disagreements and problem solving to find solutions)
- *Compromise (sharing).* You settle for partial satisfaction of your interest and partial satisfaction of others' interests (exchanging concessions, bargaining)
- *Avoiding.* You don't attempt to satisfy either your or the other's interest, side-stepping the issue (ignoring, passing the buck, delaying)
- *Accommodation.* You sacrifice your own interests in order to satisfy others' interest (conceding, taking pity)

All five modes are useful in some situations. For example, if the conflict situation poses an immediate threat, it is appropriate to use the competitive style to act quickly and deal with the emergency. If the conflict situation has been stalled, it is appropriate to use compromise as a way to move the parties to a solution. Each mode represents a set of useful social skills. Social wisdom recognizes, for example, that often "two heads are better then one" (collaborating). Other social conventions say, "kill your enemies with kindness" (accommodating), "split the difference" (compromising), "leave well enough alone" (avoiding), and "might makes right" (competing). The effectiveness of a given conflict-handling mode depends on the requirements of the specific conflict situation and the skill with which the mode is used.

Thomas and Kilman (1974) proposed that everyone is capable of using all five conflict-handling modes. They do not characterize anyone as having a single, rigid style of dealing with conflict. However, they suggest that a person uses some modes better than others and therefore tends to rely upon those modes more heavily than others, whether because of temperament or practice. The conflict behaviors that a person uses are therefore a result of personal predispositions and the requirements of the particular situations.

Basic Guidelines for Effective Conflict Resolution

In addition to understanding your styles of conflict resolution, ten basic guidelines can be synthesized from the literature on communication skills (Thomas & Kilman, 1974; Ury et al., 1993) to augment good conflict resolution skills.

1. *Understand perspective.* Put yourself in the other party's position and interest.
2. *Separate the person from the problem.* To do this you need to build a working relationship while separating the relationship from the substance of the problem.
3. *Focus on the interests of the parties, not the positions.* To facilitate this focus, identify specific interest(s), ask why and why not, and recognize there are typically multiple interests. It is important to acknowledge the other person's interest and discuss interests before you discuss the reasons for actions or behaviors. A helpful caution is to look forward, not backward; be concrete but flexible.
4. *Focus on behavior, not personality.* Be descriptive of what the party does (say "when you offer criticism . . . " rather than "you are a very critical person").
5. *Use empathy as a means to build trust, to increase your understanding of the other's interest, and to demonstrate sensitivity and care.*
6. *Be consistent, in both what you say and how you behave.* It is not helpful to speak of the importance of confidentiality and then tell others outside the group what other members have said.
7. *Take a realistic and positive approach.* Look for alternative explanations. Such a stance keeps communication open. You can model your desire for a mutually agreeable solution by looking for alternative explanations.

8. *Invent options for mutual gains by identifying the problem and defining approaches to reach resolution.* To achieve this you can seek an understanding of why the parties are reluctant to agree: Is it premature judgment, a search for a single answer, flawed assumptions? Don't be prescriptive; look for mutual gains. It is important to identify shared interest and dovetail differing interest. Be sure to look for preferences among multiple options.
9. *Insist on using objective criteria.* Identify what are fair standards and procedures. Avoid negativity by searching for objective criteria. Be open to reason and yield to principle, not to pressure.
10. *Be patient and respectful to establish a climate of mutual trust.*

These ten basic guidelines can help the student affairs practitioner navigate the levels of conflict and the framework of handling conflict. The real test comes in the practice of the guidelines in educational work settings.

Case Study

The following case gives an example of how conflict resolution style, communication skills, and intergroup dialogue interact to assist conflict resolution.

The president of a large public university recently announced a new contract with a large athletic sports apparel corporation for the shoes and uniforms of its athletic teams. The contract offered money for scholarships as well as unrestricted money for the university. An editorial in the student newspaper criticized the president for signing the contract. The criticism centered on the allegation that the athletic apparel corporation uses sweatshop labor to produce its products and that the university was, therefore, supporting sweatshop labor. The next day the president received a letter from a student organization demanding that he sign a letter condemning the corporation's business practices and calling for a cancellation of the contract. The president invited the student group to meet with him but indicated he would not take any action before the meeting. The group responded that they would have a protest in his office if he didn't meet their demands.

The students staged the protest in the foyer of the president's office suites. He spoke with them for over an hour and shared with them guidelines about appropriate protest behavior. One condition was that they not disrupt the business of his office. If that disruption occurred, they would be asked to leave by the campus police. Refusal to leave under these circumstances would result in arrests. The president allowed the students access to a conference room near his office for their meetings and for future discussions with him.

The students decided to stay overnight. The president consulted with his crisis management team (including the vice president for student affairs, chief of police, dean of students, chief attorney, and vice president for operations). The president invited three of his staff to assist him in being the liaison with the group so he could conduct the other business of the university. This team worked with the students to build their trust and to craft an agreement that both sides could accept. This process took five days and was taking a toll on the president and particularly his office staff.

The president proposed to establish a faculty-student task force to look at the issues regarding sweatshop involvement of the corporation. The student group was asked to select four of its membership to serve on the task force. The president asked the chair of the faculty to appoint four faculty to serve on the task force and to give him a report and recommendations about next steps. After obtaining the students agreements to this process, the students voluntarily left the president's suite.

Analysis

The president used avoidance to deal with the initial confrontation of the students. He bought time to build rapport and trust. He used his staff to build a negotiating team that could give him support and advice, and he employed a style of accommodation by allowing the students to stay in the suite. He used compromise to come to terms with the students regarding signing a letter, but the students shared in agreeing that they would withdraw all ultimatums in deference to the recommendations of the task force. Further, he used collaboration to forge an agreement regarding next steps and accelerated the negotiations as he saw the impact the sit-in was having on his staff and on his schedule. The president was aware of mounting criticism from outside the university that he was being too accommodating to the students. Through negotiations and the use of good communication skills, a mutually agreeable solution was found that moved the issue of demands to an action mode through the creation of the task force.

Conclusion

Learning to deal effectively with conflict is one of the most important and difficult skills a student affairs professional can develop. It is clear that conflict is part of the process of human interaction, and the goal is to become effective in dealing with and resolving conflict. It is useful to recall that key competencies (skills in conflict resolution, communication, mediation, negotiation, and arbitration) are teachable and are based on an understanding of the complexity and level of conflict and conflict resolution techniques. The five modes of conflict (compromise, accommodation, avoidance, competition, and collaboration) offer the student affairs practitioner tools to understand and effectively intervene in conflict situations. Further, the use of the three dimensions of conflict resolution—interest, rights, and power—facilitates conflict resolution. With these frameworks, the student affairs practitioner can become skilled in conflict resolution and interpersonal effectiveness.

References

Aspy, D. N. (1989). Can counselors apply their skills to real-life purposes? *Journal of Counseling and Development, 67,* 283.

Blake, R. R., Shepard, H. A., & Mouton, J. S. (1964). *Managing intergroup conflict in industry.* Houston, TX: Gulf.

Bolman, L. G., & Deal, T. E. (1984). *Modern approaches to understanding and managing organizations.* San Francisco: Jossey-Bass.

Bolman, L. G., & Deal, T. E. (1997). *Reframing organizations: Artistry, choice, and leadership* (2nd ed.). San Francisco: Jossey-Bass.

Christiansen, M. (2001, Oct. 30). *Under siege: Women in higher education building skills as conflict managers.* Workshop presented at the Way Up Conference for Women in Higher Education, Mesa, AZ.

Cohen, L., Davis, R., & Aboelata, M. (1998). Conflict resolution and violence prevention: From misunderstanding to understanding. *The Fourth R, 84,* 1–15.

Coser, L. A. (1956). *The functions of social conflict.* Glencoe, IL: Free Press.

Costantino, C. A., & Merchant, C. S. (1996). *Designing conflict management systems: A guide to creating productive and healthy organizations.* San Francisco: Jossey-Bass.

Deutsch, M. (1973). *The resolution of conflict: Constructive and destructive processes.* New Haven, CT: Yale University Press.

Donohue, W. A., & Kolt, R. (1992). *Managing interpersonal conflict.* Newbury Park, CA: Sage.

Doolittle, R. J. (1976). *Orientations to communication and conflict.* Reading, MA: Addison Wesley.

Fisher, R., & Ury, W. (1981). *Getting to yes.* Boston: Houghton and Mifflin.

Gahagan, J. P., & Tedeschi, J. T. (1968). Strategy and the credibility of promises in the Prisoner's Dilemma Game. *Journal of Conflict Resolution, 12,* 224–234.

Hall, J. (1986). A time for peace, a time for . . . conflict. *Manage, 39,* 32–34.

Hocker, R. G., & Wilmont, W. W. (1984). *Interpersonal conflict resolution.* Dubuque, IA: William C. Brown.

Holton, S. A. (1995). It's nothing new! A history of conflict in higher education. In S. A. Holton (Ed.), *Conflict management in higher education* (New Directions in Higher Education No. 92, pp. 11–18). San Francisco: Jossey-Bass.

McFarland, W. P. (1992). Counselors teaching peaceful conflict resolution. *Journal of Counseling and Development, 71,* 18–21.

Moore, C. W. (1996). *The mediation process: Practical strategies for resolving conflict* (2nd ed.). San Francisco: Jossey-Bass.

Moore, L. V. (2000). Managing conflict constructively. In M. J. Barr & M. K. Desler (Eds.), *The handbook of student affairs administration* (2nd ed., pp. 393–409). San Francisco: Jossey-Bass.

Myers, S., & Finer, B. (1994). *Mediation across cultures: A handbook about conflict and culture.* Amherst, MA: Amherst Educational Publishing.

Pedersen, P. (1994). *A handbook for developing multicultural awareness* (2nd ed.). Alexandria, VA: American Counseling Association.

Satir, V. M. (1964). *Conjoint family therapy: A guide to theory and technique.* Palo Alto, CA: Science and Behavioral Books.

Schoem, D., Hurtado, S., Sevig, T., Chesler, M., & Sumida, S. H. (2001). Intergroup dialogue democracy at work in therapy and practice. In D. L. Schoem & S. Hurtado (Eds.), *Intergroup dialogue: Deliberative democracy in school, college, community, and workplace* (pp. 1–21). Ann Arbor, MI: University of Michigan Press.

Simon, H. A. (1976). *Administrative behavior* (3rd ed.). New York: The Free Press.

Thomas, K. W., & Kilman, R. H. (1974). *Thomas-Kilman conflict mode instrument.* Tuxedo, NY: XICOM.

Ury, W., Brett, J. M., & Goldberg, S. B. (1993). *Getting disputes resolved: Designing systems to cut the costs of conflict.* Cambridge, MA: Program on Negotiation at Harvard Law School.

Volpe, M. (1994). CUNY dispute resolution consortium. *The Fourth R, 48,* 26.

Wing, L., & Rifkin, J. (2001). Racial identity development and the mediation of conflict. In C. Wijeyesinghe & B. Jackson III (Eds.), *New perceptions on racial identity development: A theoretical and practical anthology* (pp. 182–207). New York: University Press.

Zúñiga, X., & Sevig, T. D. (1997, Winter). Bridging the us/them divide through intergroup dialogues and peer leadership. *The Diversity Factor,* pp. 22–28.

CHAPTER TWENTY-FIVE

COMMUNITY BUILDING AND PROGRAMMING

Dennis C. Roberts

Students living out their conviction to service through volunteering on the campus and in the surrounding community. Campus activities that promote healthy lifestyle choices. Students acquiring knowledge and pushing the boundaries to discover new knowledge. Residence halls intentionally designed as places to complement classroom learning. Adult students enriching their lives through continuous learning. Distinguished alumni committed to leadership in work and public service.

Most student affairs administrators relish or envy working on a campus filled with learning opportunity and brimming with engaged students characterized by descriptions such as these. The reality is that most campuses can benefit from significant improvement of their campus climate, and the question is how can the ideal learning community be created?

The purpose of this chapter is to help student affairs professionals actualize a vision of a campus environment like that described above while respecting the unique culture and purpose of the campuses they serve. For the purposes of most professionals involved in student affairs administration, one of the key concepts that must be addressed if the campus is to have a rich learning culture is community.

How might we define community for a contemporary college or university setting? Is agreement achievable at many of the multiversities where the diversity of thought, background, and purpose varies so greatly? If there were an agreed, meaningful, and shared definition, could the process of how educators might foster a greater sense of community be prescribed? These questions have been a major part of student affairs administrators' struggle from the founding days of the field (Lloyd-Jones, 1989).

No matter how imperfect the concepts and models, they provide a framework of aspiration that is essential to our campuses. As has been conveyed in previous chapters, student affairs work is educational work, and the role of student affairs professionals is unique and purposeful in the context of higher education. While some of the curriculum of student affairs grants credit hours and grades, the majority of learning is in the noncredit experiences of students throughout the campus environment. Learning is seen in the encounters each student has with opportunities and programs designed to influence their learning. Student affairs programs have a profound impact on students' collegiate experiences, and it is the community that can be created through such programs that is the subject of this chapter.

The starting place for this chapter is a focus on the founding philosophy and theories of student affairs work and how this philosophy embraces the ideal of community. Different ideas of community will then be related to what we have come to recognize as "programming." A distinction will be made between conventional program development and community-building programming that serves other educational purposes. The outcomes one might expect are different, and it is important to recognize this in design, delivery, and evaluation. Once these purposes are defined, examples of programming in practice will be used to demonstrate what might be expected as student affairs administrators embark on or renew their work in community building through program implementation.

Origins of Community Building

As presented in Chapters Four and Five, the founders of student personnel work were interested in the environment of higher education and how it fostered learning and development. Early student personnel workers sought to complement or complete the educational experiences of students. They viewed students' educational experiences as including the acquisition of information or knowledge as well as maturational development. They would never have thought of themselves as standing apart from or being in competition with the curriculum.

Exploration of the historical context and documents at the time student personnel work emerged reveals some important philosophical underpinnings. Dewey (1923), a prominent educator in the early twentieth century, was instrumental in the thinking of trailblazers such as Lloyd-Jones (Evans & Reason, 2001). Lloyd-Jones' view of the emerging field of student personnel work was that it should be innovative and particularly attuned to the environment and culture of a campus as well as to the experiences of students. Lloyd-Jones was far ahead of her contemporaries at the time and remains as a source of innovative thinking among current student affairs professionals (Roberts, 1998). She saw student personnel work much like that of a cultural anthropologist, seeking to understand the dynamics of a living and working community. Lloyd-Jones and Smith (1954) advocated that student personnel workers should be attentive to student interests, should seek to connect to learning opportunities throughout the campus environment, and should intervene only to the extent that learning and personal development were enhanced. In essence, this description is indicative of a commitment to creating community among all those affiliated with the college or university.

The early twentieth century was dominated by the emergence of scientific method and positivist views of learning. Dewey (1923) saw this and countered with his views of democratic education. Lloyd-Jones and some of her colleagues followed Dewey by asserting that the emergence of specialization and objectification of learning would irreparably harm the holistic learning environments that had so powerfully shaped higher education in the United States up until that point. Lloyd-Jones likened the move toward specialized functions in education and student personnel work to that of industrial-era assembly lines; even while industrialization was at its zenith, Lloyd-Jones asserted that the transference of an assembly line mentality to learning would be disastrous. In the place of specialization and compartmentalization, Dewey and Lloyd-Jones advocated that education should be more experiential and inquiry based—democratic in its process and outcome.

Ultimately, Dewey's perspective was marginalized (Ehrlich, 1997), and the philosophy derived from him by Lloyd-Jones was abandoned when student personnel workers moved to the student services focus of the 1950s and 1960s (Evans & Reason, 2001). This resulted in a split in student affairs practice between the engaged and collaborative learning philosophy derived from Dewey and the service-provider view characteristic of the burgeoning campuses of the mid-twentieth century.

How programs are used to create community will vary depending on whether one endorses a positivist and service emphasis or an environmental and cultural view of student affairs administration.

Contrasting Philosophies and Purposes of Programming

The student service view characteristic of the 1950s, 1960s, and beyond was predictably bound in a historical context that made many student personnel professionals believe that learning was essentially a process of providing for students and treating them as if they were receptacles for knowledge. During this period, one might reasonably conclude that community was somewhat less important and that student service programming was something that was done for students, with professionals initiating programs conveying an expert notion of learning.

The cultural or democratic philosophy of learning that preceded the student services movement would exploit the relationships among faculty, staff, and students and would seek to use the grounded experiences of students as stimuli for learning. A program within this view could be one responding to a phenomenon on campus or in the community, it could be a program that students initiated with the support of staff, or it could be an experience deliberately designed to provoke reflection and learning among student participants. In this programmatic view, community could be the stimulus or the end product of the program and would have primary importance to student affairs administrators.

The schism of these two program models in student affairs lives on in today's practice. Neither view of programming is superior to the other. While historical analysis provides evidence that the origin of student affairs work is more aligned with democratic and engaged learning, there was, and continues to be, an appropriate role for more prescriptive programs in students' experiences. Understanding that there is a difference will have a profound impact on how programming is offered to students; a service approach will provide information, and an engaged learning perspective will involve students in the process of determining what should be learned and how. The point is that the latter has a much higher likelihood of fostering community among students.

Defining a Program

Programming frameworks and processes are available throughout a variety of functional specialties in student affairs work. What a student affairs professional might do in new student orientation, residence education, commuter affairs, fraternal organization advising, or in services to adult or special needs students will vary depending on the context and the need. However, some advice is available through generalizable models such as the one advocated by Saunders and Cooper (2001).

Program Development Model

In this generalized schema, programming "is a planned activity with individuals or student groups that is theoretically based and has as its intent the promotion of personal development and learning" (Saunders & Cooper, 2001, p. 310). Note that this definition makes no reference to an environmental or community outcome. The community outcome was not a concentration for Saunders and Cooper as it is in this chapter.

A programmatic intervention may include students in planning and implementation or it may not. In crises or other situations where an immediate response is essential, the number of faculty and staff involved in planning may be limited as well. The point is that these circumstances require the dissemination of information that is critical to others. Community building is not anticipated, or may not even be desired, as an outcome.

A specific example that may be an exception is the case of a campus crisis like an assault, fire, or death of a student. Many times campuses pull together in times like these to offer an immediate and soothing response, and this may look like "community." The positive and selfless response of others is more likely a representation of the community that was present before the incident even occurred. If there were no sense of connection or community, it would be highly unlikely that individuals would jump to fulfill one another's needs.

Programming is an intervention that requires integrating theory into planning and implementation, and it involves a number of steps and conditions (Saunders & Cooper, 2001). A brief summary is included in Exhibit 25.1.

The above conditions may inadvertently help to develop community among participants, but there is no focused intent to do so. Community-building programming might involve the very same end-result program. However, learners would be involved from the start. They would help shape the process, the promotion, and they would acquire reflective learner attributes and leadership abilities in the process.

EXHIBIT 25.1. SAUNDERS AND COOPER'S PROGRAM MODEL.

Planning:
- Select a planning team
- Identify conditions and constraints
- Obtain agreement on pedagogies
- Review the skills and preferences of facilitators
- Create or select activities
- Create an agenda for program sessions
- Identify referral resources

Implementation:
- Define responsibilities for implementation
- Make arrangements
- Establish the terms of collaboration
- Recognize that perfection is impossible
- Evaluate and redesign, if appropriate

Source: Saunders and Cooper (2001), pp. 333–335.

Community-Building Program Model

Building community necessitates that those in the community are involved. One has only to think of moments in one's own experience to realize that true community cannot be imposed or acquired from someone or something else. An example that may be instructive would be the moment when the campus is swept up in a thrilling athletic contest that resulted in winning the championship; students may or may not have been part of a true community under these circumstances. Those on the team, who had prepared, strategized, and played the game, were likely part of a community. Just being swept up in the exhilaration of victory would result in students being a part of campus spirit but perhaps not a true community. Community involves elements of responsibility, struggle, and sustainability (Peck, 1987).

In essence, the difference between program development and community-building programming is much like the distinction made by many contemporary theorists in regard to leadership (see also Chapter Twenty). The industrial era paradigm of leadership or management in the twentieth century assumed that leaders led because they knew what was in the best interest of the group and had special gifts that justified their taking charge. This is a prescriptive and expert view of leading.

Most contemporary leadership theorists advocate a view of leadership that is very different (Rost, 1991). Heifetz (1994) describes leadership as adaptive work among those seeking to address a mutual problem. Leadership then becomes a process of engaging with others to discover processes and knowledge required to resolve a specific dilemma. Applying the adaptive leadership model to programming on campus, the educator seeking to foster community-building programs will be a resource and participant with other learners rather than directing and controlling the process. By engaging students and involving them in addressing their own concerns, the capacities of the individuals in the group are enhanced and community is built among those working together (Komives, Lucas, & McMahon, 1998). The community-building program model is portrayed in Exhibit 25.2.

EXHIBIT 25.2. COMMUNITY-BUILDING PROGRAM MODEL.

Planning:
- Those interested in an idea join in the effort.
- Challenges and opportunities are identified.
- Multiple and related strategies are analyzed.
- Current capability and learning potential for planners are assessed.
- Resources are compiled from the network of extended supporters.
- Opportunities are prioritized based on the human, fiscal, and other material resources available.
- Responsibilities are distributed among the planners based on mutual agreement.

Implementation:
- Initiators take responsibility for getting things started and engage others as they are available.
- Resources are confirmed, reservations made, and tasks distributed.
- Collaboration and mutual work is expected.
- Participants recognize that perfection is impossible and rework as necessary.
- Evaluate and refine.
- Reflect and survey the learning acquired by those involved.

Outcomes:
- Those involved see themselves as responsible for what happens.
- The capacity of the community and the leadership to deal with issues it confronts is enhanced.
- Problem-solving becomes a natural and sustainable part of the community environment.
- Community health and vitality are created and maintained.

Source: Roberts (2001). © 2001 D. C. Roberts.

The above community-building program model is similar, yet different in important ways, from the previous model of Saunders and Cooper (2001). It bears significant similarity to the learning organization model of Senge (1990) and its translation to modern campuses (Brown, 1997). The point of the community-building program model is not to compete with other program development and delivery models but to draw explicit attention to a type of program that has the additional outcomes of leadership development, community capacity building, and sustainability.

Now that some philosophy is established as a foundation, what theories are available to help a student affairs administrator understand how to build community through programming?

Theories to Inform Community Building

A number of student development, cultural, and personality theories are addressed elsewhere in this book. This chapter relies on some theories that may be less familiar and less used by student affairs professionals. They are, nevertheless, important as one seeks to devise programs that build community. The theories that are included in the following brief synopses come from studies of group behavior, human development and inclusion, healthful communities, and leadership.

Group Behavior: Lewin

Lewin (1952) conducted some of his earliest studies on group process in an experiment designed to encourage housewives to consider alternative food sources in the family diet. The experiment was simple and straightforward; the willingness to change was measured among a group that was informed by an expert lecturer as compared to a group who mutually informed each other and discussed their views. The outcome was dramatic, and this led to much of the wisdom espoused today when the phrase "people support what they create" is used. Not only are participants more likely to accept change if they are part of conceiving it, the change that occurs is also much more sustainable over time.

The implication of this research is that programs that are simply informative, no matter how authoritative, are less likely to impact behavior and they will last for a shorter duration. The lessons:

- If an urgent issue needs attention and long-term impact is unnecessary, conventional programming is the best fit.
- If the change desired is to be embraced by a broad number of participants, and if the hope is to sustain the change, community-building programming is the best fit.

Mattering and Marginality: Schlossberg

Schlossberg's (1989) model of mattering and marginality defines how individuals respond to divergent experiences in their lives. The concept of mattering and marginality helps provides insight about students who, for whatever reason, see themselves as outside the circle of acquaintances with whom they would like to affiliate. The conditions Schlossberg suggests are critical in establishing environments that generate a belief that we matter are: attention, importance, ego-extension, dependence, and appreciation. Students feel marginalized when these conditions are not present; when this happens, they are less responsive to learning, they are preoccupied with belonging, and they are vulnerable to dropping out of a living group, organization, or out of learning entirely. The lessons to learn from Schlossberg are:

- If the information or idea advocated in a program is nonspecific or the need to know is not clearly understood, conventional programming is the easiest strategy.
- If the idea needs to be embraced deeply by individuals who seek or need to know, community-building programming is necessary to pull participants from potentially marginalized to mattering status.

Learning Community: Boyer

Boyer (1990) provided a very influential model of community when he challenged higher education to create communities that are purposeful, open, just, disciplined, caring, and celebrative. The Carnegie Foundation and Boyer believed that learning would be significantly enhanced if these attributes were present. In essence, these attributes define community. McDonald and his associates (2002) applied these conditions of community in several helpful case examples. These examples demonstrate that community building is possible and, indeed, very powerful. In his afterword, Parker Palmer proposed five experiential markers that can help determine whether real community exists or not (McDonald):

- I feel in community when I believe that I play a meaningful role in a shared educational mission, and others see me doing so.
- I feel in community when I am affirmed for the work I do on behalf of the shared mission if it contributes to that mission.
- I feel in community when I know that I can take creative risks in my work and sometimes fail.
- I feel in community when I am trusted with basic information about important issues relating to the shared mission.
- I feel in community when I have a chance to voice my opinion on issues relating to the shared mission or my part of it (pp. 182–183).

Additional lessons derived from Boyer's seminal work include:

- If community connection is only coincidental to learning, programs may be designed and implemented without attention to attributes such as purposefulness, openness, and caring.
- If a college or university seeks to deepen the connections among its students, faculty, and staff, specific initiatives should be undertaken to make sure that the community embraces and seeks to personify these same commitments.

Progression of Community: Peck

Peck (1987) provides invaluable insight on the progression of collections of people toward real community. While most groups resist the notion that building community is a difficult and arduous process, Peck retold persuasive stories of how groups with which he'd worked moved through stages of pseudocommunity, chaos, emptiness, and community. The natural tendency is for human beings to want to be in community with one another, but they may be unwilling to do the work to get there. The lessons:

- Community does not have to be part of every program initiative and may be a distraction from easier goals that require less substantive attention.
- Communities that accept and embrace diversity are, in many ways, stronger and more critical to our learning environments than those that are supportive and nurturing.
- Real community, although challenging and taxing to build, creates in the members deeper personal awareness, appreciation for each other, and tolerance for the chaos and uncertainty of life experience.

Healthy Community: Keeling and Berkowitz

Keeling (1998) and Berkowitz (1997, 1998) espouse essential ideas related to the healing potential in communities. Research is emerging that unhealthy environments result in individual marginalization, psychological distance, refusal to take responsibility for one's own actions, and ultimately a variety of illnesses. In two areas of deepest concern—the spread of HIV/AIDS infection and substance abuse—Keeling and Berkowitz suggest that the only way to counter the deep and systemic causes of these problems is to create open, healthful, and healing communities. The lessons provided by this powerful research and theory building is:

- If maintenance of existing systems and views is acceptable, conventional programming is the quickest and easiest way to achieve results.
- When deep and systemic solutions are needed, engaging students in creating healthy communities may be the primary, and perhaps only, way to address the concern.

Leadership Reconsidered: Astin and Astin

Pursuing a model of creating a healthy community requires one more essential element—community-building programs must engage a broad segment of the student community in order to build the leadership capacity necessary to bring about change. Astin and Astin (2000) worked over an extended period of time with other educators throughout the nation to conceptualize a shared and value-based commitment to leadership. In the latest piece in their emergent thinking, *Leadership Reconsidered: Engaging Higher Education in Social Change* (2000), students, faculty, and staff are encouraged to rethink how they view themselves and to consider the possibility that leadership must be accepted by all if the lofty objectives of higher education are to be achieved. The lessons:

- Conventional programs will convey knowledge that is knowable and that requires adherence in order for the information to be effective.
- Community-building programs require participants to consider the barriers and opportunities that are encountered when everyone assumes that they are equally capable of leadership. Participants are also encouraged to challenge the assumptions that others have of themselves, shifting toward a belief that they are effective and influential agents of change.

Special Conditions That Impact Community Building

There are any number of special conditions that might impact or influence efforts to build community. Three that might have particular importance on the modern college or university campus are the degree of involvement among its constituents, technology, and expectations of community.

Involvement

Astin (1993) and his associates have contributed some of the finest and most salient research and literature about the conditions that impact learning in higher education. His decades of research led to the conclusion that one of the most important variables was the degree to which students and other campus constituents were involved in the life of the campus. Spending time on tasks in learning and engaging with one's peers was found to be positively and strongly related to students' satisfaction with the college experience and with significant measures of educational attainment. The lesson is that, if learning is to be maximized, students have to be available to access the learning placed before them and they must have the time to reflect on and integrate those experiences.

Technology

Anyone who works in higher education would have to admit that one of the most important, if not the most important, aspects of their changing experiences with others has been technology. The prevalence of computers and other forms of technology both draws people together as well as pushes them apart. Though able to stay in contact via e-mail with students and colleagues involved in study abroad throughout the world on a daily basis, roommates debate their living conditions from the opposite sides of small rooms via laptop computers. While cell phones provide easy and immediate access to friends and loved ones, their presence in the hands of students in transit from class to class prohibits the exchange of casual hellos, smiles, and other human gestures. Technology can create cyber, networked, and microwave communities, but it can also divide those who share the same physical and learning space.

Community Expectations

One of the things that can positively influence community, and is especially related to the desire to increase the breadth, depth, and quality of involvement for all, is shared expectations. Whether implicitly or explicitly understood, models such as Boyer's (1990), Peck's (1987), and Schlossberg's (1989), all require some sharing of common expectation. Standards of how others are included or treated will heavily influence the degree to which all the members believe they are valued and benefit from their association. These influences must be recognized and fostered among those seeking to be a community.

Competencies Required

What competencies must student affairs administrators possess in order to work with theories and concepts like those described above? Effective programming of the kind described by Saunders and Cooper (2001) requires professional preparation in assessment, interpretation, planning, resource identification and utilization, and administration. This kind of programming also requires expertise in group communication and facilitation.

It is important to recognize that program development is an important part of any student affairs administrators' responsibilities. One of the key issues required to enhance effectiveness is the ability to determine when direct programming is the easiest and most expedient way of addressing an issue. Considering that program development that can be done by an individual or small group is easier to complete, a discerning judgment about the necessity to move quickly could preserve important resources for use in other initiatives.

In addition to the abilities identified above, the professional interested in engaging in community-building programming must have advanced skills in reflection, conceptualization, and collaboration. Probably above all insights or skills, student affairs professionals committed to community building must see themselves as full partners in the collegiate setting and must be comfortable with and be able to serve as catalysts for the learning and involvement of others. The capabilities named above related to community building are different from those possessed by the conventional programmer. While harder to cultivate, the community-building attributes can have tremendous pay-off in the capacity and potential that can be added to the community through their use.

The difficulty with community-building programs is that work is much less applied than one might be used to pursuing. There would likely be less direct involvement and less action-oriented behavior. However, serving in a more indirect and catalytic role is likely to help student affairs professionals relate more fully and meaningfully to the broader educational objectives of their college or university. By doing this, student affairs professionals augment the learning process so that all can experience powerful, holistic learning. The final implication is that the community-building professional is more likely to share many resources and stimulate changes in the environment that will become long-standing and permanent, regardless of the direct involvement by the individual over time. The shared ownership protects the initiative so that it becomes internalized and can be maintained. If a true learning organization approach is adopted, the subsequent students and educators who work on related issues will also see the need and promise of change when the time comes to pursue a new and different approach.

The community-building programmer becomes a somewhat unconventional and new kind of educator who works with and through faculty and students to achieve critical learning goals for the institution, as Lloyd-Jones and Smith (1954) suggested.

Examples in Practice

There are innumerable examples to illustrate how conventional and community-building programs can be conceived and implemented. It is also important to recognize that, for purposes of distinction, the following examples will be described as if they are discrete. Actual program implementation is seldom clearly either conventional or community building in its orientation. Most often there is overlap. Indeed, the overlap will hopefully increase as professionals become more aware of the educational potential and difference in design of each.

Community Service and Service Learning

One of the fastest growing areas of interest on many college campuses today is community service and service learning. Young and mature citizens have for years engaged in fundraising for economically depressed families, for illnesses that require more funding for research, and for funds to bolster the services of various community organizations. Today's college-age population is even more interested with 82 percent of them arriving on campus having completed some form of service in high school (Higher Education Research Institute, 2000). It is only natural that these students would want to continue their service involvement while they pursue collegiate studies. What can a campus do to reinforce and encourage this natural commitment among students?

A programmatic approach to supporting students' interest in service would include establishing an office to serve as a collection place and clearinghouse between agencies in the community needing help and students who are seeking to be of service. The role would primarily be one of assessing student interest, matching it with the needs, establishing cooperation with the community agency, and supporting the logistics necessary for students to get involved. In this programmatic approach, the staff and faculty serve as the experts in identifying the needs of the community, and they offer helpful assistance to students as they find a good fit for their interests. Students in such a model can make a tremendous difference by raising funds (charity/philanthropy) and by volunteering (performing necessary tasks for an agency) to help agencies that otherwise would not have the resources to get the job done. In this program model, students are satisfied, communities benefit through cheap or free labor, and the institution fulfills its civic service mission by placing students in service to the community.

In the community-building program approach to a similar need, the institution and student play very different roles. If community building were the intent of involving students in the community, students would be more involved in determining the critical needs that begged for their involvement. Students would work with student affairs program staff to assess both campus and external community capacity, and then decisions would be made about strategic initiatives that would be undertaken. Students would provide guidance to each other about how to get involved, issues to watch out for, how to establish a respectful working relationship, and coaching that would help students begin to understand the deeper issues behind the problem. Today's college campuses are exploding with interest in community service and service learning. Faculty who are eager to engage students more deeply in learning know that going where students' interests and hearts are will reap great benefit in learning. This form of service involvement builds the capacity of the individual, it informs the institution through being involved in the community, and it expands the potential of the community to remedy its own problems. Faculty, students, and community are mutual learners in the process of discovering solutions to persistent public problems.

Leadership Development

Most colleges and universities have developed leadership or promoted civic participation as part of their institutional mission from their founding. As leadership has grown in popularity as a critical educational outcome, the press to provide explicit leadership development opportunities has grown dramatically. Advocacy for comprehensive leadership program design (Roberts, 1981; Roberts & Ullom, 1989) calls for the provision of more than just an annual student leadership conference, workshop, or other isolated event. It challenges designers to cast the net wider to include a variety of program possibilities.

Any comprehensive leadership development program will begin with the institutional mission as it relates to developing leadership among students. The specific views of leadership as reflected in the institutional mission statement, subsequent planning documents, and critical constituent opinions would be considered. Once such an analysis of leadership development has been undertaken, planners would likely look at existing and potential new leadership development opportunities that could be orchestrated within a framework of serving multiple populations through multiple strategies and with multiple purposes being served. In many college and university settings, staff will conceive the comprehensive plan, even though student input may be solicited. If this is true, and it is coupled with a focus on students' acquisition of abilities and insights, the leadership development program is likely to be conventional in design and should be planned and implemented according to Saunders and Coopers' (2001) criteria.

A community-building program approach to comprehensive leadership programs would include critical aspects of design such as establishing institutional context and commitment just as above. In addition, a community-building approach will include institutional culture as a powerful dimension of leadership development. When a broad array of offerings are included in a series or framework, consistent and repeated messages will help to unify and will reinforce the common lessons communicated through the different activities and initiatives of the comprehensive program.

The Miami Leadership Commitment is a community-building program being implemented at Miami University. In this model, a common set of values was identified that provided the repeated messages about how the community views leadership. The vision "to develop the leadership potential in all for the global and interdependent world of the future" (Roberts, 2001, p. 77) requires broad cocurricular and curricular initiatives that complement and build on each other. This community-building program required that the coordinators actively share resources and that an emphasis be placed on giving the program away to anyone who was willing to collaborate. Such an approach drew unsolicited interest as it unfolded, and the capability of the program grew at every step in the process. The leadership development community was defined as a loose network of colleagues who valued similar things and who voluntarily chose to work together to learn from each other and to promote the importance of leadership development throughout the campus community. When the student, faculty, and staff creators of this program were involved in design, they gradually began to realize through the process that what they sought to accomplish in leadership development was really a cultural transformation of the campus. The ultimate objective, one that has community building in its purpose, was that all faculty, staff, and students would respect and take each other seriously and that by doing so, leadership potential would be cultivated in all.

Living-Learning Experiences

There are several different models for living-learning programs in residence halls on campuses that have at least a portion of their students living in residence. Possibilities include residential colleges, theme learning halls, first-year student interest groups, cluster courses, and others. Again, living-learning programs can be pursued either as conventional programs or they may embrace a community-building purpose.

In a conventional living-learning program approach, a planning team would be assembled and would likely include multiple constituencies such as students, faculty, and staff. The presumed purpose would be to enhance the climate in the residence halls by providing students the opportunity to focus on common purposes and educational goals. A living-learning program would allow students to have a choice in their place of residence and it would encourage participation in a mutual set of curricular and cocurricular experiences. Through placing students together around common interests and engaging them in work together, students would be much more likely to establish relationships and important connections with each other.

A community-building approach to living-learning would rely more on identification of mutual needs and interests of a variety of stakeholders. While students, faculty, and staff are likely to be involved in the conventional program approach, the community-building strategy would exploit the critical interests of a variety of those involved. The presumption of what themes or issues would be attractive to students would be supplemented by an analysis of the institution's core concerns and of student, faculty, and staff personal and social change concerns. The staff role in a community-building program would be different from a conventional program. If students are expected to engage fully and take responsibility for their own learning within the residential community, the residence staff would focus more on the group process and network of resources. There is considerable evidence that faculty on campuses are increasingly concerned about active engagement of students and that they are eager to enhance learning through partnerships that take learning into environments beyond the classroom. What is important in this kind of scenario is that faculty express their interests, couple them with student aspirations for living in a high quality and comfortable environment, and utilize the expertise of student affairs staff in planning and overseeing the initiative. A community-building approach to living-learning would be different in the depth of engagement, the inclusion of multiple concerns and interests, and it would define all as learners and collaborators working to enhance the capacity of the community to deal with the real living issues that they face on a daily basis.

Summary

Student affairs practice has a long history of attention to the complex dynamics that create learning and development among students in higher education. One of the more difficult dynamics is the tension between those scholars and practitioners advocating for different approaches to the role of a student affairs professional. There are those who believe that the greatest influence on learning is accomplished through environmental and cultural intervention. Scholars and practitioners committed to a service approach use more direct and prescriptive strategies. This chapter proposes that, while providing programs is an important responsibility, additional potential lies in designing programs that have the additional benefit of building community within and among groups and throughout the broader campus environment.

The purpose of this chapter was not to advocate for one approach over the other. It was simply to identify the different philosophical roots, the processes, and the purposes involved in each. Both approaches can be effective and can enhance learning, but it is important to know which is most likely to be appropriate to the specific circumstances one encounters.

Criteria for the design and implementation of programs are provided using the work of Saunders and Cooper (2001). A new model is offered that provides the opportunity to design community-building programs. Community-building programs have the potential to offer an additive effect that goes beyond those programs designed for the purpose of communicating information or addressing specific interests of students. These two models may be used for different purposes; informed professionals will look carefully at the opportunities and purposes they seek to achieve as they determine which model is most appropriate for their specific situation. Examples are provided to illustrate how one might approach programs using each of these models.

The program versus community-building program analysis may seem as if it is only common sense. However, how often do professionals actually analyze the degree to which the goal is simply providing a program versus fostering community on the campus? If the circumstances suggest that community building may be critical for the campus and the time can be taken, then what are the determining factors that enhance the potential for community-building success?

Programming that addresses a special need that is identified by a student affairs professional is an important responsibility in many circumstances. The potential of community-building programming is that student affairs professionals may rediscover their heritage as change agents, catalysts, and community builders. The roots of the student affairs profession provide a foundation and open student affairs administrators to campus roles that many may have been hesitant to claim.

References

Astin, A. W. (1993). *What matters in college: Four critical years revisited.* San Francisco: Jossey-Bass.

Astin, A. W., & Astin, H. S. (Eds.). (2000). *Leadership reconsidered: Engaging higher education in social change.* Battle Creek, MI.: W.K. Kellogg Foundation.

Berkowitz, A. D. (1997). From reactive to proactive prevention: Promoting an ecology of health on campus. In P. C. Rivers & E. R. Shore, *Substance abuse on campus: A handbook for college and university personnel* (pp. 119–139). Westport, CT: Greenwood Press.

Berkowitz, A. D. (1998). The proactive prevention model: Helping students translate healthy beliefs into healthy actions. *About Campus, 3* (4), 26–27.

Boyer, E. L. (1990). *Campus life: In search of community.* Lawrensville, NJ: Princeton University Press.

Brown, J. S. (1997). On becoming a learning organization. *About Campus, 1* (6), 5–10.

Dewey, J. (1923). *Democracy and education.* New York: Macmillan.

Ehrlich, T. (1997). Dewey versus Hutchins: The next round. In R. Orrill (Ed.), *Education and democracy: Re-imagining liberal learning in America* (pp. 225–262). New York: College Entrance Examination Board.

Evans, N. J., & Reason, R. D. (2001). Guiding principles: A review and analysis of student affairs philosophical statements. *Journal of College Student Development, 42*, 359–377.

Heifetz, R. A. (1994). *Leadership without easy answers.* Boston, MA: Harvard College.

Higher Education Research Institute. (2000). American freshman: National norms for fall 2001. Los Angeles: UCLA Graduate School of Education and Information Studies.

Keeling, R. P. (1998). HIV/AIDS in the academy: Engagement and learning in a context of change. *NASPA Leadership for a Healthy Campus Newsletter, 1.*

Komives, S. R., Lucas, N., & McMahon, T. R. (1998). *Exploring leadership for college students who want to make a difference.* San Francisco: Jossey-Bass.

Lewin, K. (1952). Group decision and social change. In G. E. Swanson, T. M. Newcomb, & E. L. Hartley (Eds.), *Readings in social psychology* (2nd ed., pp. 459–473). New York: Henry Holt.

Lloyd-Jones, E. M. (1989). Foreword. In D. C. Roberts (Ed.), *Designing campus activities to foster a sense of community* (New Directions for Student Services No. 48). San Francisco: Jossey-Bass.

Lloyd-Jones, E. M., & Smith, M. R. (1954). *Student personnel as deeper teaching.* New York: HarperCollins.

McDonald, W. M. (2002). *Creating campus community: In search of Ernest Boyer's legacy.* San Francisco: Jossey-Bass.

Peck, M. S. (1987). Stages of community-making. In M. S. Peck, *The different drum: Community making and peace* (pp. 86–106). New York: Simon & Schuster.

Roberts, D. C. (1981). *Student leadership programs in higher education.* Washington, DC: American College Personnel Association.

Roberts, D. C. (1998). Student learning was always supposed to be the core of our work—What happened? *About Campus, 3* (3), 18–22.

Roberts, D. C. (2001). Miami's leadership commitment. In C. L. Outcalt, S. K. Faris, & K. N. McMahon (Eds.), *Developing non-hierarchical leadership on campus: Case studies and best practices* (pp. 77–89). Westport, CT: Greenwood Press.

Roberts, D. C., & Ullom, C. (1989). Student Leadership Program Model. *NASPA Journal, 1,* 67–74.

Rost, J. (1991). *Leadership for the twenty-first century.* New York: Praeger.

Saunders, S. A., & Cooper, D. L. (2001). Programmatic interventions: Translating theory to practice. In R. B. Winston, D. G. Creamer, & T. K. Miller (Eds.), *The student affairs administrator: Educator, leader, and manager* (pp. 309–340). New York: Brunner-Routledge.

Schlossberg, N. K. (1989). Marginality and mattering: Key issues in building community. In D. C. Roberts (Ed.), *Designing campus activities to foster a sense of community* (New Directions for Student Services No. 48, pp. 5–15). San Francisco: Jossey-Bass.

Senge, P. M. (1990). *The fifth discipline: The art and practice of the learning organization.* New York: Doubleday.

CHAPTER TWENTY-SIX

ASSESSMENT AND EVALUATION

M. Lee Upcraft

Assessment is, quite simply, one of today's hottest issues in higher education and the student affairs profession, for many reasons. Assessment is becoming more important because it can be used to improve the quality of student services and programs, guide strategic planning, analyze cost effectiveness, justify student programs and services, assist in accreditation, and perhaps most importantly, guide decision making, policies, and practices. The purpose of this chapter is to introduce readers to some of the basic definitions surrounding the issue of assessment, provide some reasons to assess, offer a comprehensive assessment model for student affairs, outline steps in the assessment process, explore the ethics of assessment, and offer some advice to practitioners on assessment in student affairs.

Some Basic Definitions

One of the first problems encountered when discussing assessment is definitional. Too often, assessment is thought of as simply doing a survey or running a focus group. Some terms are used interchangeably (*assessment* and *evaluation*), some phrases are used incorrectly (statistics show . . .), and some terms are so vague as to not have any commonly accepted meaning (*quality* or *excellence*). Let's start with the term *assessment.* There are many definitions in the assessment and evaluation literature (Astin, 1991; Banta & Associates, 1993; Erwin 1991; Palomba & Banta; 1999, Rossi & Freeman, 1993), with no

Note: This chapter is a summary of issues discussed in greater detail in *Assessment Practice in Student Affairs: An Applications Manual* (Schuh, Upcraft, & Associates, 2001) and in *Assessment in Student Affairs: A Guide for Practitioners* (Upcraft & Schuh, 1996).

conclusive consensus among these scholars. For the purposes of this chapter, *assessment is any effort to gather, analyze, and interpret evidence, which describes institutional, divisional, or agency effectiveness* (Upcraft & Schuh, 1996, p. 18). Effectiveness includes not only assessing student learning outcomes but also assessing other important assessment indicators such as cost effectiveness, clientele satisfaction, clientele needs, professional standards, benchmarking, and institutional data bases. Assessment in student affairs is not restricted to students but may include other constituents within the institution such as the faculty, administration, and governing boards, and outside the institution, such as alumni, legislators, funding sources, and accreditation agencies.

One further clarification when using the term assessment: it does not include assessing individual student or other individual clientele outcomes, *except in the aggregate.* For example, while an institution may not want any information about why an individual student may persist to graduation, it may want to know why, in the aggregate, students drop out or graduate.

Assessment, however, must be contrasted with but also linked to *evaluation.* Here there is even less agreement among the experts. Again, for the purposes of this chapter, *evaluation is any effort to use assessment evidence to improve institutional, departmental, divisional, or institutional effectiveness* (Upcraft & Schuh, 1996, p. 19). While assessment describes effectiveness, evaluation uses these descriptions in order to improve effectiveness and determine progress toward objectives, goals, and benchmarks, however that might be defined by an institution. For example, determining why adult students have difficulty in making a successful transition to college is assessment. Using that assessment to make changes in policy and practice to ease adult students' transition to college is evaluation.

Another term also must be defined: *measurement. Measurement refers to the methods used to gather information for the purposes of assessment.* Typically, measurement methods are divided roughly into two not very discrete categories: *quantitative* and *qualitative.*

Quantitative methodologies assign numbers to objects, events, or observations according to some rule (Rossman & El-Khawas, 1987). Instruments with established psychometric properties are used to collect data; statistical methods are used to analyze data and draw conclusions. For example, the ability to predict college success might involve gathering all the quantifiable data about those variables which are thought to predict persistence and degree completion, such as high school grades, scores on standardized tests, involvement in high school activities, parents' education and income, and so on. These data might then be correlated with subsequent student behavior (dropping out or persisting) to determine which ones and in which combination best predict college success.

Qualitative methodologies, on the other hand, are detailed descriptions of situations, events, people, interactions, and observed behaviors; the use of direct quotations from people about their experiences, attitudes, beliefs, and thoughts; and the analysis of excerpts or entire passages from documents, correspondence, records, and case histories (Patton, 1990). For example, admissions personnel might want to interview students who persisted and those who dropped out to determine the extent to which their backgrounds and experiences might have contributed to their success or lack thereof. Variables that seem to predict college success but are difficult to measure (such as motivation) might be better understood through a qualitative approach. It should be pointed out that the selection of an assessment methodology might not be an either-or decision; in fact, there are many instances where the use of both methodologies is not only appropriate but also more powerful.

Another definition worth mentioning, although it will not be the focus of this chapter, is *research.* In the 1960s and 1970s, it was fashionable to use the term *student affairs research* to refer to assessment and evaluation efforts. This term proved to be confusing, particularly to faculty, who had a much narrower definition of research. When comparing research and assessment, Erwin (1991) argues that although they share many processes in common, they differ in at least two respects. First, assessment guides good practice, while research guides theory and conceptual foundations. Second, assessment typically has implications for a single institution, while research typically has broader implications for student affairs and higher education. I would add a third: assessment studies often cannot meet traditional social science research criteria in determining their rigor, viability, and worth. According to Cronbach (1982), while assessments use research methods, the central purpose of assessment differs from that of basic social science research because assessment is designed to fit different institutional and political contexts. He argued that many methods of social science research are ill-suited to assessment studies.

Upcraft and Schuh (2002) offer a series of modifications necessary to conduct viable and useful assessment studies, including:

- *Resource limitations:* Assessment studies are often modified because of limited money, as well as staff that lack the time or sufficient assessment expertise.
- *Time limitations:* Assessment studies often must meet much shorter time deadlines than research studies. Often, the window of opportunity to influence policy and practice may be as little as a month and rarely more than a year.
- *Organizational contexts:* Different organizational contexts may dictate different assessment approaches, even if the problems are the same. Further, the same organizations may vary over time, forcing modifications in an original assessment design.
- *Design limitations:* While assessment studies are conceived using the best possible designs, problems can arise as the project proceeds. Low response rates, useable samples that do not reflect the characteristics of the population, or poor attendance at focus groups may dictate modifications in the original design.
- *Political contexts:* As Schuh and Upcraft (2000) suggested, assessments almost always occur in a political context that must be taken into account in assessment designs. A study may never be done, discontinued in progress, or suppressed upon completion because the results may be politically or ideologically unacceptable to institutional leadership. (A fuller discussion of assessment politics appears later in this chapter.)

The question then becomes, when does a study become so modified that it should never be done, or discarded even if conducted? Rossi and Freeman (1993) argued that the assessment investigator must choose the best possible design, having taken into account the potential importance of the program, the practicality and feasibility of each design, and the probability that the design chosen will produce useful and credible results. Schuh and Upcraft (2001) add the caveat that all modifications must be clearly identified when an assessment study is published, cautioning all prospective audiences to take into account the study's various limitations as they decide what credence to give the study. Pat Terenzini, Senior Scientist at the Center for the Study of Higher Education at Pennsylvania State University, probably said it best: "In assessment, you start with the perfect design (recognizing that there really isn't any such animal), and then keep making modifications until you have a doable study" (P. Terenzini, personal communication, 1996). The failure to understand the differences between research and assessment does have enormous consequences for the credibility of assessment studies, particularly with faculty well-schooled in the tenets of social science research.

The Basic Question in Assessment: Why Are We Doing This Study?

The pressures on higher education institutions to demonstrate their effectiveness are continuing to mount. State legislatures and governors, the federal government, the general public, and students and their families are asking tough questions. What and how much does your college contribute to student learning? Do graduates know what you think they know and can they do what your degrees imply? How do you assure that? What do you intend for your students to learn? At what level are students learning what you are teaching? Is that the level you intend? What combination of institutional and student effort would it take to get to a higher level of student learning (Marchese, 1990)? Is your college accessible to *all* qualified students, regardless of gender, race, age, and demographic and background variables. Perhaps most importantly, as tuition increases at twice the rate of inflation, are students being shut out of education because they can't afford it, and if they can, are they getting a reasonable return on their considerable financial investment in higher education? In short, we can no longer ignore these questions. Assessment helps us answer them in more systematic and credible ways.

Student affairs is also under considerable pressure to demonstrate its importance and worth. In an era of declining resources and increased competition for what precious few resources are available, student affairs has come under the institutional fiscal microscope. Questions range from quality and efficiency to the ultimate question: Do we really need this service or program? So the first answer to the question Why are we doing this assessment? may be the very *survival* of our services, programs, and facilities. One might easily respond, "Isn't there a substantial body of research which demonstrates that students' out-of-class experiences contribute to their learning, personal development, academic achievement, and retention?" The answer is yes (See Kuh, Branch Douglas, Lund, & Ramin-Gyurnek, 1994, and Pascarella & Terenzini, 1991), but this fact often doesn't help for two reasons. First, this research is not well known among administrators and faculty and second, even if it is, the question of local applicability always arises. "Okay, so the research evidence shows that students who participate in service learning do better academically than nonparticipants, but is that true at our institution?" National studies may be more elegant in design, sophisticated in research techniques, and more lucid in the presentation and results, but locally produced studies, if well done, will have more impact on a particular campus. In this sense, *all assessment is local.*

In general, assessment efforts can and will demonstrate the effectiveness and worth of student services and programs, and show positive relationships between students' out-of-class experiences, use of student services and programs, and student learning, including academic achievement and retention. However, one should be prepared to deal with local results that may not be consistent with the findings of national studies, since students make their own environments based on interactions with their institutions (Baird, 1996). Further, even if there are local studies, which are consistent with national findings, policy and decision makers may choose to ignore this evidence for other reasons. Thus, *all assessment is a risk:* we can never be certain that local assessment studies will have the desired impact of demonstrating the worth of student services and programs or insuring their survival.

While survival may be the primary motivator for assessment in student affairs, there are other reasons. Even if it is demonstrated that student services and programs are essential and needed, a second answer to why we are doing a study may be to assess *quality.* Assessment can be a very powerful tool in linking goals to outcomes, helping define quality, and determining if quality exists in student affairs. It is a fundamental responsibility of student affairs to provide services, programs, and facilities that are of the highest quality. Assessment can help us determine if we have been successful in fulfilling that responsibility.

A third reason for assessment is to gauge *affordability and cost effectiveness.* The question often goes something like this: "Sure, this program or that service is needed, and there is evidence of its quality, but in an era of declining resources, can we afford it? Can we continue to fund it at current levels? Can we afford it at all?" Decisions to eliminate services and programs based on their affordability may have to be made, but other affordability questions abound. Might it be less expensive to outsource this service or program? Can this service or program generate income from fees? Can this service do more with less or less with less? And how do we know? Unfortunately, these decisions are often made without adequate assessment, in part because there are few if any cost-effectiveness models used in student affairs.

The fourth reason for assessment in student affairs is *strategic planning.* Strategic planning, according to Baldridge (1983), examines the big issues of an organization: its mission, purpose, long range goals, relationship to its environment, share of the market, and interactions with other organizations. Since many higher education institutions are seriously involved with strategic planning, it is important for student affairs to be an active and effective participant in this process. Assessment contributes to strategic planning by helping define goals and objectives and pointing to critical issues or problems that must be resolved successfully if the organization is to achieve its goals. Assessment is especially important in the early phases of strategic planning to identify strengths, weaknesses, and opportunities for the future. It is also critical in the later stages of planning, when evaluation of policies and programs occurs.

A fifth answer to the question, "why are we doing this study?" is to gain more information and insight into *policy development and decision making.* What evidence do we have to help us make a decision or develop or revise a policy? Assessment can provide systematic information, which can be critical in helping policy and decision makers make valid judgments about policy, decide on important issues, and make decisions about resource allocations. Making these kind of judgments based on systematic information is not only important within students affairs, it is also important to help student affairs influence policies and decisions within the institution and with stakeholders outside the institution, such as boards of control, legislatures, alumni, and the general public.

The sixth reason is *political.* Sometimes we must do assessment because someone or some institution of importance wants certain information, which makes it politically important to produce. It may be the president of the institution, a faculty governing group, an influential board of control member, an outspoken legislator, or a concerned alum. We must also be concerned about the political impact of our assessment findings. *All assessment is political;* thus assessment investigators must be attuned to the impact of their studies from the moment an assessment idea emerges. If one of the purposes of assessment is to influence policy and practice, then the political context within which decisions are made must be accounted for in the assessment process. (This issue is discussed in greater detail later in this chapter.)

Finally, assessment may be required for *accreditation.* According to the Commission on Higher Education's *Standards for Accreditation* (1992), one of the criteria for accreditation is outcomes or institutional effectiveness. "The deciding factor in assessing the effectiveness of any institution is evidence of the extent to which it achieves its goals and objectives. The necessity of seeking such evidence continually is inescapable; one of the primary hallmarks of faculty, administration, and governing boards is the skill with which they raise questions about institutional effectiveness, seek answers, and significantly improve procedures in the light of their findings" (pp. 17–18). This moves assessment from the "nice to have if you can afford it" category to the "you better have it if you want to stay accredited" category. Since student affairs is an active participant in the accreditation process, it will be required to contribute assessment evidence to this process.

Why are all these reasons important? Because the first step in the assessment process is to determine why a particular study needs to be done, and there may be one or several answers. Different assessment designs will be developed depending on the reason(s) the study is conducted. Too often, however, an assessment study is started without a clear idea of *why* it is being done thus often yielding results that are not useful to policy makers in addressing the problem that precipitated the study in the first place.

A Comprehensive Assessment Model for Student Affairs

Assuming that the why question has been answered, the next question is what should we do? Too often, an assessment study is planned without any real understanding of the options available. Upcraft and Schuh (1996) developed a comprehensive assessment model (revised in Schuh & Upcraft, 2001) that describes various types of assessment, and offers choices about which assessments are appropriate. The first component of this model is *keeping track of who uses student services, programs, and facilities.* How many clients use services, programs, and facilities, and how are they described by gender, race, ethnicity, age, class standing, residence, and other demographic variables? This component is very important, because if our intended clientele do not use our services, programs, or facilities, then our intended purposes cannot be achieved. However, sheer numbers do not tell us the whole story, especially if users or participants are not representative of our clientele. The quantity and distribution of users has important implications for policy and practice and must be assessed.

The second component of this model is *assessing student and other clientele needs.* The basic principle that we should meet the needs of our clientele is a good one and is well supported in the literature, but it often is not easy. There are many questions to be answered. What kinds of services, programs, and facilities do students and other clientele need, based on student and staff perceptions, institutional expectations, and research on student needs? How do we distinguish between wants and needs? How do we know if what we offer fits our clientele? Assessing student and other clientele needs can provide answers to these questions.

The third component of this model is *assessing student and other clientele satisfaction.* Of those persons who use our services, programs, and facilities, what is their level of satisfaction? What strengths and suggestions for improvement do they identify? Clientele satisfaction is important because if they are not satisfied, they won't use what we offer again, and they will not recommend them to friends and colleagues. We are also interested in clientele satisfaction because it gives us valuable information about how to improve our services, programs, and facilities.

The fourth component is assessing *campus environments and student cultures.* While assessing individual use, needs, and satisfaction is important, it is also critical to take a look at their collective perceptions of campus environments and student cultures within which they conduct their day-to-day lives. This component of the assessment model can help answer such questions as, what is the climate for women on this campus? What is the academic environment, both inside and outside the classroom? What is the overall quality of life in residence halls?

A fifth component is *assessing outcomes.* Of those persons who use our services, programs, and facilities, is there any effect on their learning, development, academic success, or other intended outcomes, particularly when compared with nonusers? Can programmatic interventions be isolated from other variables, which may influence outcomes, such as background, characteristics, and other experiences? These kinds of studies are very difficult to design, implement, and interpret, but in some ways they attempt to answer the most fundamental question of all: Is what we are doing having any effect, and is that effect the intended one? These studies are at once the most important we do, yet most difficult to conduct.

A sixth component is *comparable institutions assessment.* How does the quality of services, programs, and facilities compare with "best in class" comparable institutions? An important way of assessing quality is to compare one's institution to other institutions which appear to be doing a better job with a particular service, program, or facility, often described as benchmarking. One purpose would be to discover how others achieve their results and then to translate their processes to one's own environment. The key to this assessment component is to select comparable institutions which have good assessment programs, rather than relying on anecdotal or reputational information.

A seventh component of this model is *using nationally accepted standards to assess.* How do our services, programs, and facilities compare to accepted national standards, such as those developed by the Council for the Advancement of Standards for Student Services and Development Programs, various national and regional accrediting agencies, and professional organizations?

A final component, added to the model since the publication of *Assessment in Student Affairs,* is *assessing cost effectiveness.* Are the benefits students derive from what we offer worth the cost, and how do we know? There is very little guidance offered from existing student affairs literature, except at the crudest level of analysis: divide the cost of a service by the number of students using the service. Such an "analysis" is often fraught with so many methodological problems that its conclusions may be meaningless. Cost-benefit analysis is difficult and somewhat imprecise in a nonprofit, service-oriented organization but should be attempted nevertheless.

Steps in the Assessment Process

Too often, assessment studies are designed in a disorganized, helter-skelter way without any real thought to all aspects of the assessment process. For example, it is not unusual for assessment designers to pick an instrument first and then try to design a study around it, almost always resulting in an assessment disaster. What is needed is a much more systematic approach suggested by Schuh and Upcraft (2001), a step by step process that increases the likelihood that the assessment study will be done logically and thoroughly, producing viable results.

Step 1: Define the Problem

All assessment flows from an attempt to solve some problem, so establishing a clear and concise definition of the problem facing the student affairs practitioner is the first step in the assessment process. Another way of framing this step is to refer to my previous discussion of reasons for doing an assessment. The "why" determines what we do, how we do it, and how we use the results. Other questions that might help define the problem include:

- *What specific circumstances or situations are driving assessment efforts?* Examples might include low enrollments, consideration of a policy to protect students from being discriminated against on the basis of their race or sexual orientation, pressures to reduce budgets, commitment to improving services and programs, impending accreditation review, and so on.
- *What external pressures are driving assessment efforts?* Pressures external to student affairs might include: the general public (costs are rising more quickly than inflation), institutional boards of control (we need to increase minority enrollments), institutional leadership (there are too many problems arising from students abusing alcohol), alumni (the sinking feeling that student life just isn't what it used to be!), in-state supported institutions, legislatures, and governors (we need to cut state allocations by X percent), and accrediting agencies (assessment is required for reaccreditation).
- *What internal circumstances are driving assessment?* There is always a need to improve student services and programs, regardless of their quality, so improvement is a primary internal circumstance that drives assessment efforts. Other internally driven variables may include a concern that services and programs might not be meeting student needs or might not be equally accessible and used by all types of students. We may need to know more about whether or not our services and programs are achieving their intended outcomes, and if so, if they are being administered in cost effective ways.

Step 2: Determine the Purpose of the Study

As discussed above, assessment is the process of gathering, analyzing, and interpreting evidence (information). Given the particular problem identified in Step 1, what information do we need to help solve it? What information will be critical to responding to external and internal pressure to do assessment? The answers to these questions then become the basis for determining the purpose of the study. For example, if we need more information about student satisfaction with our health service, then we should conduct a study whose purpose is to measure that satisfaction.

Step 3: Determine Where to Get the Information Needed

Information can be retrieved from a wide variety of sources. The most obvious source is students or other clientele, but there are many other sources. Institutional or functional unit records may well contain valuable information needed to solve a problem. For example, if our concern is the differential use of services by underrepresented groups, an analysis of student usage by gender, race-ethnicity, age, disability, and other categories may provide all the information needed to verify the problem. Other sources of information might include institutional documents, student newspaper articles, and field observations.

Most student affairs assessment, however, focuses on gathering information directly from students, but they may not be the only sources of information. There may be others who might have insight into the problem, including staff, faculty, administrators, community leaders, or even the general public. It may seem obvious, but defining the population precisely is important because the conclusions drawn from a particular inquiry apply only to those studied in the first place.

Step 4: Determine the Best Assessment Method(s)

Another way of framing this step is to answer the question, what's the best way to get the information I need? Of course, the best assessment method depends on the purpose of the study. Basically we have three choices: quantitative methods, qualitative methods, or a combination of both. According to Patton (1990), qualitative methods focus on gathering information from interviews, observations, and documents, and they require much smaller samples than quantitative measures. Quantitative measures, on the other hand, include gathering data from a survey or other instrument and require much larger samples than qualitative methods. So the questions becomes, Given the information we need, what is the best way to retrieve it? Generally speaking, if we need information about *what* is going on, quantitative methods are more appropriate. If we need information about *why* something is going on, qualitative measures are more appropriate. Our experience has also taught us that a *combination of methods* may well best provide information to solve the problem that precipitated the study. For example, if one is studying the development of critical thinking in first year students, a pre- and posttest measure of critical thinking would tell us if such development did occur. Focus groups might best tell us why or why not.

Step 5: Determine Whom to Study

Having decided on the population to be studied, it is rarely possible to include the whole population in a study, regardless of the type of study chosen. Sometimes, however, if the population is narrowly defined, it is possible. But most often, a *sample* of the whole population must be selected in ways that insure that those selected are *representative* of that population according to some criteria. For quantitative studies, the most typical criteria are the demographics of the population, such as gender, age, race-ethnicity, disability, and others. In the collegiate setting, factors such as class standing, grades, place of residence, full-time or part-time enrollment, major field, and others may also be important. If the sample is, in fact, representative, then one can *generalize* with much more confidence to the whole population. In qualitative studies, however, although strict adherence to the representativeness is not required, it is still nonetheless important within general parameters.

Step 6: Determine How Data Will Be Collected

Data can be accessed in a wide variety of ways. Existing institutional data are often overlooked as a source for assessment. So every effort should be made to discover what, if any, existing data might be relevant to the study. But more often, additional data must be collected using mailed questionnaires, web-based questionnaires, telephone surveys, individual interviews, focus groups, and other data collection procedures. Each procedure has its strengths and limitations, but all are intended to get the desired number of participants in the study. For example, mailed questionnaires will often yield the fewest number of participants but more thorough information. Telephone surveys will yield a higher percentage of return but a limited amount of information. Individual interviews and focus groups require a more personal touch, and incentives such as food or token monetary compensation may be helpful. Whatever data collection procedures are chosen, they should be consistent with the purpose of the study and yield the optimum number of participants needed.

Step 7: Determine What Instrument(s) Will Be Used

The instrument(s) used to collect data depends on several factors, including which methodologies are chosen. For quantitative methodologies, an instrument must be chosen which yields results that can be statistically analyzed. Beyond that, we need to decide whether to use an already constructed instrument with appropriate psychometric properties and standardized norms, or a locally constructed instrument that may be more appropriate to our study but lacks validity, reliability, and other psychometric properties. Generally speaking, instruments available from any one of several national test publishing houses are preferable, if there is an opportunity to add locally developed items. But if the problem under study is unique to a particular campus, then test construction experts should be consulted when developing local instruments.

For qualitative methodologies, an interview protocol must be developed, consisting of standardized, open-ended questions that retrieve the information needed for the study. According to Patton (1990), an item is standardized when it is written out in advance *exactly* the way it is to be asked during the interview. Clarifications or elaborations should be included, as well as any probing questions. Variations among interviewers can be minimized, and comparisons across interviews can be made if the interview protocol is standardized. Open-ended means there are no prescribed answers (such as yes or no); respondents are free to provide any answer they choose. Although this may seem obvious, there should be a direct connection between the questions asked and the information needed to help solve the problem.

Step 8: Determine Who Should Collect the Data

At first glance, this question may not seem to matter much. Obviously, data should be collected by people who are competent to do so. But often the most qualified people are also those who have a vested interest in the outcome. This is less of a problem with quantitative methodologies, where bias is more likely to have occurred in the selection or development of the instrument. In qualitative methodologies, however, where the data is collected and filtered by those who conduct the study and record the data, bias becomes a much larger issue.

There is also the lingering problem of the "face credibility" of the study. Can we really trust a study that was done entirely by those with a vested interest in the outcome? On the other hand, can we really trust a study that was done entirely by outside experts who know little or nothing about the context and nuances of the study? In general, if the study and the people who are doing it have integrity, there is usually no problem with those who have a vested interest in the outcome being a part of the data collection process.

Step 9: Determine How the Data Will Be Analyzed

Analysis of quantitative data depends on the purpose of the study. Probably the most important first step is to determine if the respondents are, in fact, representative of the population to be studied. Then appropriate descriptive and inferential statistical analyses can be applied. Because most student affairs professionals lack the skills necessary about which statistical analyses are most appropriate and how to interpret statistically generated results, we recommend using statistical consultants familiar with social science research methodologies for both data analysis and interpretation.

Analysis of qualitative data is somewhat more consistent with the skills and abilities of student affairs professionals but still must be done in systematic ways, including listening to and searching for meaning in interview or focus group audio tapes or transcripts, and looking for themes, trends, variations, and generalizations. This process should be an inclusive one, with data gatherers collaborating with colleagues, students, and even subjects in the interpretation of the data.

Step 10: Determine the Implications of the Study for Policy and Practice

Too often, investigators are content with reporting the findings and conclusions of a study, leaving its implications for policy and practice to various audiences. We believe that in reporting assessment results, the implications of the study should be spelled out. Here we are clearly crossing over from assessment to evaluation. Remember that while assessment is the gathering and analyzing of information, evaluation is using assessment information to solve the problem that precipitated the study in the first place. What approaches to solving the problem should be considered in light of the findings? What policies or practices need to be revised, eliminated, or created because of the findings? There should be clear calls for action in assessment reports that motivate the reader to do something about the problem that precipitated the study.

Step 11: Report the Results Effectively

Once the findings have been reported and analyzed, and the implications for policy and practice identified, how do we report the results? In what form do we report the results? To whom should the study be reported? Should every stakeholder get the whole report? More studies end up filed under "I" for "Interesting" or gathering dust on someone's shelf because we fail to package results in ways that move decision makers to make changes based on the study. In fact, how a study is formatted and distributed may be more important than the results of the study. Probably the biggest mistake we make is to send the full report to all audiences and hope for the best.

There are several ways to overcome this problem. Multiple reports for multiple audiences are one way, highlighting the results most applicable to a particular audience. Executive summaries that summarize the study, its findings, and recommendations for policy and practice are also effective. Getting results to the "right" people (those who can do something about the problem studied) is also very important. Offering to discuss the results in greater detail in person may also be appropriate. Even going so far as to suggest how decision makers may make best use of the study is not out of the question. Clearly, if the purpose of the study is to solve a problem, then the report must not only report the results but how the results can be used to solve the problem.

We would again assert that these steps should be addressed for each study *before* the study is conducted. To be sure, as the study progresses, changes may have to be made, but a major impediment to good assessment is the lack of planning, and following these steps helps insure that the study will be a good one.

The Ethics of Assessment

A major concern in any assessment study is that the highest ethical standards guide the activity. As discussed earlier in this chapter, an assessment study may have to be modified in order to meet certain realities. Of course, one should never make compromises, engage in short cuts, or in any other way fail to uphold the highest ethical standards. Such standards are built upon commonly accepted statements of ethical principles, such as those promulgated by the American College Personnel Association and other professional organizations.

However, as Schuh and Upcraft (2001) have argued, working with subjects is at the heart of conducting assessment studies in an ethical way. This is not only an ethical requirement but a legal one as well. There are federal regulations governing the protection of human subjects that require an institution, through its Institutional Review Board (IRB, often referred to as the "human subjects committee"), to review assessment studies. Before anyone is permitted to collect data from subjects, an institution-based IRB, consisting of faculty members and administrators, must certify that the rights of subjects are protected. IRBs will require a written consent form from study participants which outlines the purpose of the study, the procedures involved, the sponsors, any potential benefits and risks involved, confidentiality parameters, compensation conditions (if any), a statement that expresses that the individual is participating willingly, and other issues. Individual campuses may vary in their approach to protecting the rights of participants, so it is essential that before conducting a study, assessment investigators consult with the chair of their local IRB to determine how federal and institutional regulations are applied.

Advice for Practitioners

1. *Understand and overcome barriers to assessment.* Unfortunately, understanding the importance of assessment and how to do assessment does not necessarily result in getting it done. There are many reasons why assessment doesn't get done. They include:

• *Lack of commitment from institutional leadership.* Sometimes there is little or no institutional commitment to assessment because the leadership of an institution doesn't have a commitment to it. It may be because the leadership doesn't understand the value of assessment, doesn't believe the institution has the expertise, is afraid of possible findings, or other reasons. Whatever the reasons, leaders must be shown that the benefits of assessment outweigh the risks, and that, on the whole, assessment can become an important problem-solving, policy development, and decision-making tool.

• *Lack of time.* Assessment requires a lot of staff time, if we subscribe to the principle that those affected by the assessment should be involved in it. Often, those staff members most resistant to assessment are those that are unwilling to take time away from their jobs or students to get involved in assessment. While this is an admirable point of view, it may also be somewhat short-sighted. For example, if the very existence of a service or program is being questioned, there may have to be some temporary reduction of direct service to ensure its continuance. The reality may be that staff does what is has to do in order to keep doing the things it wants to do.

• *Lack of money.* Assessment costs money. Sometimes funding for assessment comes from external sources, but most often the cost of assessment is expected to be covered within existing fiscal and human resources. Again, if the very existence of a program or service is being questioned, spending money to demonstrate its importance and impact is money well spent. The cost of assessment may well be, in the long run, of benefit to students.

• *Lack of expertise.* Too often we are intimidated by the lack of assessment technical expertise, particularly on statistical analysis and design. While this may be true, student affairs professionals may be more qualified than they think when is comes to qualitative approaches, especially individual interviews and focus groups. Most student affairs professionals claim some interpersonal and group skills that can readily apply to these data collection procedures. This barrier may be overcome through retraining of existing staff and students, hiring consultants on an as-needed basis with help on specific projects, and reconfiguring existing professional and staff positions to include assessment.

• *Fear of results.* As pointed out earlier in this chapter, all assessment is a risk. There is no guarantee that assessment will necessarily make us look good or yield positive results. For example, we know that generally speaking, living in residence halls is associated with persistence to graduation, even when other variables that contribute to that outcome are taken into account. What if an institution does a study that shows that there is no relationship, or worse yet, a negative relationship between living in residence halls and retention? In this instance, isn't the fear legitimate? It all depends on the reason the study was done in the first place. If it was to improve residence halls, then there is less risk than if it was to determine whether or not the institution should continue to have residence halls. The risk must be considered in light of the potential consequences. Put another way, can we live with all the possible results?

2. *Select qualified professionals to conduct studies.* In the eyes of many intended assessment audiences, the qualifications of the persons conducting the study may determine the study's credibility. On the one hand, some may argue that many studies can and should be done by student affairs professionals whose training and background includes assessment expertise. On the other hand, some would argue that a study is credible only if it is done exclusively by social science researchers or institutional research personnel, based on the questionable assumption that most, if not all, student affairs practitioners lack the necessary skills to conduct rigorous and unbiased studies. Schuh and Upcraft (2001) take the middle ground that some studies may, in fact, be conducted by student affairs practitioners if they have the appropriate education and training and if those studies meet acceptable standards. Other studies, whose designs and analyses may be more complex, require investigators with more assessment expertise. Either way, someone with assessment design and analysis expertise should review all assessment studies to ensure that these studies are rigorous, unbiased, and defensible.

3. *Develop strategies for ensuring maximum participation in assessment studies.* A frequent complaint of assessment investigators is the failure to generate acceptable response rates for quantitative studies. There are several strategies to improve response rates:

- *Consider data collection procedures.* Response rates may vary by the type of data collection procedures used. For example, generally speaking, telephone surveys and online data collection procedures may yield higher response rates than mailed surveys.
- *Consider incentives.* While monetary incentives often yield increased response rates, there are very few institutions that can afford such a strategy. Other incentives include gift certificates to campus food services or bookstores (thus keeping the money within the institution and encouraging students to become customers), lotteries (where legal), food at focus groups, and personal follow-up contacts.
- *Collect data in classes.* Response rates are often increased when assessment investigators cooperate with faculty to collect data in classes. But this typically requires taking class time (which faculty guard jealously), and the resulting sample may not be representative of the student population.

Two caveats: First, a low response rate may not necessarily doom a study. Statistical strategies may be used to deal with small samples. Second, a high response rate does not necessarily guarantee that the sample is representative of the population. Weighting responses by selected demographic characteristics (gender, age, race, ethnicity, and so on) may help overcome an unrepresentative sample.

4. *Make special efforts to ensure that participation in assessment studies is accessible to all students.* Too often, certain student groups are left behind in the assessment process. For example, racial-ethnic minorities are often underrepresented in higher education in general and thus assessment studies in particular. The same is often true of adult students, part-time students, commuters, and off-campus students. Special efforts must be made to make sure these groups are represented in assessment studies, including

sampling adjustments, special incentives to participate, collaboration with student organizations who represent these groups, and perhaps most important, making sure that instruments and interview protocol are sensitive to their perceptions and needs.

5. *Understand that all assessment is political.* As Schuh and Upcraft (2000) pointed out, too often, assessment studies are given initial attention and then forgotten, roundly criticized as hopelessly flawed and dismissed, or suffer the ultimate ignominy—being ignored completely. Of course, there are many reasons for these unintended results, but almost always the reason studies end up gathering dust on some policy maker's shelf is the failure of the assessment investigator to account for the institutional political context within which all assessment studies are conducted. Put another way, the challenge of the assessment investigator is to plan and conduct a study and report the results in ways that build support for its recommendations. These include:

- *Don't do a study nobody wants.* This may mean that some needed studies will never be started or completed because influential leaders fear the consequences of the findings.
- *Identify important constituents before the study is conducted.* This includes persons whose support will be needed to conduct and implement the study, as well as those who are likely to oppose the study or dispute the results.
- *Involve key constituents before the study is conducted.* If key constituents know about and have been given the opportunity to have input into the study, they are more likely to take the findings seriously.
- *Build support from senior leadership.* Because support from senior leadership is especially critical in implementing assessment results, their involvement is absolutely essential. Often this involves making leaders aware of the benefits of the study from a policy or public relations standpoint and the increasing role of assessment in the accreditation.
- *Build support among staff.* Student affairs staff themselves, for whatever reasons, sometime torpedo assessment studies, so it is important to involve them from the beginning in any assessment studies that may affect their jobs or careers.
- *Conduct a good study.* This advice may seem too obvious to mention, but the influence of a study may well rest upon its credibility with intended audiences. Credibility is, in part, determined by the quality of the study, the integrity of the design, and indications of the study's limitations.
- *Write a good report.* As discussed below, report formats are critical to the success of assessment studies in influencing policy and practice.

6. *Market assessment reports so that intended audiences are reached and influenced.* More than one well-done, credible assessment study has failed to have the intended influence because of the ineffective ways in which the results were reported and distributed. Upcraft and Schuh (1996) argue that the most common mistake assessment investigators make is to send a complete and comprehensive report (most often modeled after a typical academic thesis) to all intended audiences. Suskie (1992) suggests the following to ensure that assessment reports will have their intended impact:

- *Determine which audience or audiences should read and use the findings.* Depending on the study, potential audiences may include students, student affairs professional staff, faculty, the chief student affairs officer, other senior leadership, alumni, the local community, state legislatures, and the general public.

- *Write multiple reports for multiple audiences.* Briefer reports should be tailored to the needs and interests of the intended audiences. Reports to busy decision makers should be short, to the point, and no more than one page.
- *Write reports that are well organized, succinct, and attractive.* Reports should be written in ways that are readable, interesting, and engage the reader in the topic while at the same time insuring the integrity of the work.
- *Format the report properly.* Include a meaningful title, an executive summary, a statement of purpose, a summary of the design, a summary of results, and most importantly, recommendations for practice.
- *Write reports that are persuasive.* The likelihood that a report will be taken seriously is enhanced if there are hard hitting, succinct recommendations based on the findings. There are some researchers who believe their responsibility ends with reporting the findings of a study, leaving the implications of the study to decision makers. While that may be appropriate for research, it is a near-fatal mistake for assessment. Decision makers should be guided by the recommendations of an assessment study with the caveat that decision makers have the ultimate responsibility for deciding how assessment results will be used.

Conclusion

Assessment is not just another educational fad that will disappear when newer fads emerge. For the many reasons discussed in this chapter, assessment will continue to be integral to student affairs for the foreseeable future. But perhaps most importantly, assessment must be done because it is the best way to insure our professional, educational, and ethical commitment to high-quality student services, programs, and facilities for students.

References

Astin, A. W. (1991). *Assessment for excellence: The philosophy and practice of assessment and evaluation in higher education.* New York: MacMillan.

Baird, L. L. (1996). Learning from research on student outcomes. In S. R. Komives & D. B. Woodard, Jr. (Eds.), *Student Services: A handbook for the profession* (3rd ed., pp. 515–535). San Francisco: Jossey-Bass.

Baldridge, V. J. (1983). Strategic planning in higher education: Does the emperor have any clothes? In V. J. Baldridge (Ed.), *Dynamics of organizational change in education.* Berkeley, CA: McCutchan.

Banta, T. W., & Associates. (1993). *Making a difference: Outcomes of a decade of assessment in higher education.* San Francisco: Jossey-Bass.

Commission on Higher Education. (1992). *Standards for accreditation.*

Cronbach, L. J. (1982). *Designing evaluations of educational and social programs.* San Francisco: Jossey-Bass.

Erwin, T. D. (1991). *Assessing student learning and development: A guide to principles, goals, and methods of determining college outcomes.* San Francisco: Jossey-Bass.

Kuh, G. D., Branch Douglas, K., Lund, J. P., & Ramin-Gyurnek, J. (1994). *Student learning outside the classroom: Transcending Artificial Boundaries* (ASHE-ERIC Higher Education Report, volume 23, No. 8). Washington, DC: The George Washington University Press.

Marchese, T. J. (1990). Assessment's next five years. *Association of Institutional Research Newsletter,* Fall-Winter, 1–4, (Special Supplement).

Palomba, C. A., & Banta, T. W. (1999). *Assessment essentials: Planning, implementing and improving assessment in higher education.* San Francisco: Jossey-Bass.

Pascarella, E. T., & Terenzini, P. T. (1991). *How college affects students: Findings and insights from twenty years of research.* San Francisco: Jossey-Bass.

Patton, M. Q. (1990). *Qualitative evaluation and research methods* (2nd ed.) Newbury Park, CA: Sage.

Rossi, P. H., & Freeman, H. E. (1993). *Evaluation: A systematic approach* (5th ed.). Newbury Park, CA: Sage.

Rossman, J. E., & El-Khawas, E. (1987). *Thinking about assessment: Perspectives for presidents and chief academic officers.* Washington, DC: American Council on Education & American Association for Higher Education.

Schuh, J. H., & Upcraft, M. L. (2000). Assessment politics. *About Campus, 5* (4), pp. 14–21.

Schuh, J. H., Upcraft, M. L., & Associates. (2001). *Assessment practice in student affairs: An applications manual.* San Francisco: Jossey-Bass.

Suskie, L. A. (1992). *Questionnaire survey research: What works.* Resources for Institutional Research, Number Six. Tallahassee, FL: Association for Institutional Research.

Upcraft, M. L., & Schuh, J. H. (1996). *Assessment in student affairs: A guide for practitioners.* San Francisco: Jossey-Bass.

Upcraft, M. L., & Schuh, J. H. (2002). Assessment vs. research: Why we should care about the difference. *About Campus, 7* (1), pp. 16–20.

CHAPTER TWENTY-SEVEN

PROFESSIONALISM

D. Stanley Carpenter

Part Five of this book has focused on very complex competencies, large areas of endeavor requiring sophisticated human relations and presentation skills, detailed knowledge of theory and practice, and a mature attitude of respect for diversity and individualism in the context of community. Some of the competencies require quite specialized (such as assessment) or even governmentally regulated (such as counseling) knowledge and practice. The very term *competency* implies a level of understanding and confidence that must be reached before one can hope to perform at a satisfactory level. A person who masters any one of these broad areas, let alone all or most of them as student affairs workers frequently do, would be an extremely valuable employee. Competence in one's job or duties, however, is not enough.

Accordingly, this chapter will explore the area of professionalism, proceeding from the definition of a profession to a consideration of student affairs as a profession and some of the implications of such a designation. It will then move to a discussion of developing a professional identity and what professionalism means for individuals and organizations, followed by issues and challenges facing the field, tips for professionals, and a conclusion.

What Is a Profession?

The term *professional* has multiple meanings (for example, professional football player, a plumber who is a "real professional," even a professional criminal). Doing a job or activity well or for pay is not sufficient, however, to define a professional in a sociological sense. From the perspective of the sociology of occupations, a profession is a special kind of work. Brint (1993) suggested that recent work by occupational sociologists has concentrated in three schools of thought: a focus on traits necessary to define a profession, emphasis on the process(es) of professionalization, and a conception that the entire notion of professions is simply a societal construction. While each of these conceptions has been challenged in terms of elitism, power, and societal conflict (for a fuller treatment of criticisms, see Brint, 1993, and Friedson, 1986), elements of each of these views are widely thought to be useful and must be accounted for in a satisfactory theory or model. While seeking some middle ground, this chapter will rely upon a modified process model that offers analytical value while respecting Brint's (1993) theoretical concerns. Pavalko (1971) offered eight profession-occupation continua upon which it is possible to situate any job or type of work (See Figure 27.1).

The idea is that professions and occupations could be located along these continua. A profession, for example, should require a high degree of specialized knowledge and skill, should be based primarily upon a service motivation, should perform a crucial societal task(s), should require an extended preparation, and so on. Presumably, occupations become professions to the extent that they make movement along a significant number of the continua.

Distilling Pavalko and other researchers and writers, the appellation *profession* would seem to rest on three central themes (Carpenter, 1991). First, the members of a profession possess shared goals, for example the creation of an optimal learning environment for college and university students. Second, a professional community exists that supports its members and defines appropriate and inappropriate behaviors, resulting in more or less consistent rewards and punishments, formally and informally. Examples of this in student affairs are behaviors surrounding job searches, publishing,

FIGURE 27.1 THE OCCUPATIONAL-PROFESSIONAL MODEL.

Dimensions		Occupation		Profession
1. Theory, intellectual technique		Absent	⟷	Present
2. Relevance to social values		Not relevant	⟷	Relevant
3. Training period	A	Short	⟷	Long
	B	Non-specialized	⟷	Specialized
	C	Involves things	⟷	Involves symbols
	D	Subculture Unimportant	⟷	Subculture Important
4. Motivation		Self-interest	⟷	Service
5. Autonomy		Absent	⟷	Present
6. Commitment		Short term	⟷	Long term
7. Sense of community		Low	⟷	High
8. Code of ethics		Underdeveloped	⟷	Highly developed

Source: Adapted from Pavalko (1971).

and promotions. Third, a profession attends to socialization and regeneration, resulting in accepted practices with regard to adequate initial preparation for entry into the field and proper continuing education, as well as mentoring and sponsoring.

The reader is directed to a reconsideration of previous chapters in this book by Nuss (Chapter Four), Young (Chapter Five), and Fried (Chapter Six) in the context of professionalism. While a careful examination will show that it is possible to place student affairs work toward the profession end of each of the Pavalko criteria and to see elements of the three more general qualifications just proposed, it is easy to see that student affairs work does not fit perfectly. The following section, then, is an examination of student affairs as a profession.

Student Affairs Work as a Profession

The controversy about whether or not student affairs work has earned the status of profession is long and interesting. As early as 1949, Wrenn applied the then-current criteria for professional stature and found the field wanting. Shoben (1967) and Penney (1969) both sounded similarly unhopeful notes, but by 1980, Carpenter, Miller, and Winston (to which the reader is referred for a more complete treatment of this literature) called student affairs work an "emerging profession" (p. 21) based upon an analysis of sociological criteria suggested by Wilensky (1964). Winston, Creamer, Miller, and Associates (2001), upon updating the analysis, arrived at the same conclusion. That is, the field, while having made undeniable progress, is still emerging as a profession. This is not an unusual state of affairs. Other professions are also similarly situated, such as financial planning and development or fundraising work in higher education.

For a variety of good reasons, student affairs work may never fully qualify as a profession, but it may not matter in practice. Stamatakos (1981), among others, held that, profession or not, professional behavior was expected of student affairs practitioners on campus and by their peers. Indeed, much of the literature and most of the practices of student affairs in hiring, in professional development and associations, and in many other functions so closely mimic those of professions as to be indistinguishable. It may be that, as Blake (1979) suggested, it is more important simply to be professional than to claim to be so. Meanwhile, it may be useful to consider a notion of professionalism that would fit student affairs better, instead of trying to form the field to an uncomfortable model. In fact, the criticisms of traditional professions with regard to privilege, exclusivity, and power seem quite consonant with student affairs values (Young, 2001). Perhaps it is useful to posit a new kind of profession (for want of a better term). What is needed is a new form of professional community that recognizes the complexity of student affairs work settings, postindustrial institutions that defy characterization as traditional organizations. Models of professions, such as law or medicine that depend upon preparation standard monopolies and licensure, no longer seem adequate or appropriate.

Theory Base

The theory base of student affairs for the past three decades has been largely derived from psychology and counseling and is known as student development (Evans, 2001). But even this conception is open to challenge. When the field was largely service oriented, the most sophisticated models of management were applied (Blimling, 2001) and the values of "deeper teaching" were espoused (Lloyd-Jones & Smith, 1954). The framers of the *Student Personnel Point of View* (ACE, 1937) relied upon social science research techniques and findings, and thoughtful practitioners have always understood that elements of sociology, anthropology, philosophy, and many other fields are necessary for a complete understanding of practice. More recent forays into learning theory, whether one couches them as something new or simply fuller conceptions of student development, are adding to the picture, but we have always borrowed from many disciplines and have no one field to call our own. It can be argued that any complex field dealing with human behavior relies on multifaceted theory, but this begs the question. In student affairs, we will continue to be intellectually ecumenical, interdisciplinary eclectics searching for helpful research, theory, and practices. In keeping with our reverence for diversity and in view of an increasing emphasis on interdisciplinarity in all of higher education, we should embrace this truth.

Ambiguous Training and Entry Criteria

Brint (1993) suggests that a principal determinant of professional status is that entry into a field is contingent upon training and education exclusively provided by higher education. So it is in student affairs, but there is controversy surrounding the correct preparation (Winston & Creamer, 1997). While there are suggestions and some agreement concerning entry-level preparation, there is no consensus that one should have a master's degree from a program that follows the Council for the Advancement of Standards in Higher Education (CAS) standards (Miller, 1999). Indeed, such programs do not graduate enough new professionals every year to fill all the available positions, so such consensus would be an empty triumph. Winston et al. (2001) state "there is basic agreement that graduate education directly focused on working with students outside the classroom is appropriate and desirable, if not obligatory" (p. 30). This prescription largely applies to entry-level professionals, but Carpenter (1998) notes that even the most senior of student affairs positions can be obtained with no student affairs education or experience. Knowing this, Creamer and Associates (1992) suggested strong emphasis upon continuing professional education to bring all student affairs professionals up to speed, regardless of background or education. The good news about this approach is that it recognizes the reality of the field and allows for a healthy diversity of individuals and preparation profiles. The bad news is that if we cannot agree upon entry-level criteria, we may have trouble deciding upon what continuing education is needed. And in any case, there is no formal mechanism in the field for requiring such updating. Still, student affairs professionals practice in a variety of institutions and perform more and more complex and boundary-spanning functions, so the field may not be ill-served by a continuing ambiguity of preparation and professional education standards. New ideas bring energy, if not always direction.

Specialist Versus Generalist

An important question in student affairs is one's primary affiliation in terms of professional identity and affiliation. The field is composed of many different specializations, many of which, such as academic advising, financial aid, recreational sports, and others cross administrative, professional association, and disciplinary lines. Indeed, one can go from specialist to generalist (working in an office that has responsibility and reporting lines arising from several disparate functions) and back several times in a career. Each specialty has its own professional association, with all the trappings of a profession including journals, codes of ethics, and so on (see Chapter Fifteen). While there are umbrella organizations, they too are somewhat balkanized by specialty, while attempting to serve the needs of all. In fact, what may be considered a core function of student affairs on one campus, for example orientation, may not even be administratively housed in student affairs on another campus.

In addition, many student affairs divisions include such offices as legal advisor or health center. Professionals in these offices, characterized by Creamer and Associates (1992) as allied professionals, do not necessarily identify with student affairs at all and yet are critical to education for the whole student. Any useful conception of student affairs work as a profession must take into account these varied roles and their importance. Clearly, a "full" professional preparation (even if a consensus existed on what that means) would be inappropriate for a lawyer or a nurse or an accountant. Still, such professionals see students on campus and play large roles in their education. Hence, our notions of the words *profession* and *professional development* must have room for a variety of levels and circumstances. We must marshal resources for the continuing education of all student affairs professionals, no matter how they entered the field or with what background, appropriate to their needs and related to their roles and functions. A simplistic, linear model will not serve.

The Licensure Question

One of the cornerstones of traditional profession models is licensure, a governmentally sanctioned legal status accorded to some occupations, such as physicians, lawyers, and nurses. Licensure in itself is not enough to assure professional status as can be seen by the fact that cosmetologists, plumbers, and the like are also licensed, but when it is tied to elaborate preparation and peer-led sanctioning and disciplinary procedures, as well as legal recognition of professional opinion, licensure is a powerful tool. Student affairs work will not be a licensed activity in the foreseeable future. Principally, the field is simply too broad and undefined to lobby effectively, even if it wished to. Add to that the variegated theory base, labor market concerns (colleges and universities are unlikely to support a restriction on whom they can hire and are often exempted even from psychology and counseling licensure requirements already), and the variety of institutional administrative and reporting arrangements that exist on campuses, and one can readily see that organization of the field at the level required to gain legal sanction is doomed.

It is left to the individual professional and to the professional associations to provide definitions of full membership in the profession and what constitutes appropriate professional development. In keeping with the theme that diversity serves us well and that our variety rightly reflects our clients and institutions, this is probably a positive thing. However, recent efforts toward serious consensus on voluntary certification of preparation programs, quality assurance standards for practice, registry of professionals, and more formal continuing professional education give hope of preserving the desired flexibility while introducing needed structure in these critical areas (Carpenter, 1998; Creamer & Associates, 1992).

Tension Between Professional and Institutional Values

Birnbaum (1988) has noted the several differences between higher education organizations and traditional ones. One of the principal contrasts is the variety of professional cultures that dominate decision making in subsystems of colleges and universities. Each discipline has rules and mores, and these sometimes take precedence over institutional goals and regulations. Similarly, student affairs work and the various specialties therein have practices and cultures that dictate and suggest proper courses of action that may vary from institutional interests. In attempting to meet student needs in an ethical way, professionals may find themselves in conflict. After all, as members of the administration, student affairs practitioners owe allegiance to their employers; likewise, as professionals they must have some measure of autonomy in order to function effectively. Ideally, institutional missions and the interests of the student clients can be resolved amicably, but student affairs workers must sometimes walk a tightrope between the two. Any conception of student affairs professionalism must recognize this duality of interests.

A New Kind of Profession

Student affairs work needs to create a new form of interconnection, a professional community that benefits from the advantages the term implies, yet avoids the downsides. Our profession should be inclusive, not exclusive, and yet be able to define and encourage good practice and punish or sanction poor practice. We should recognize that all four of Blimling's (2001) communities of practice, student administration, student services, student development, and student learning, are valid modes and be versed in each, as appropriate to our job and our clients' needs. We should welcome theory and research from any quarter if it is helpful and not worry about who accomplished it. We should facilitate multiple entry modes into student affairs, as long as the individuals are qualified in ways appropriate to their setting and are willing to learn more about the field, while also rewarding excellence in professional preparation. We should celebrate the expertise of specialists and generalists and make it possible for the one to become the other at different career stages. We should continually be cognizant that without institutions our profession would not exist and hence work to make the missions of colleges and universities compatible with our understanding of what is best for students. In short, we must embrace ambiguity, in Komives' (2001) helpful and hopeful phrase, and inhabit all the gaps between what we might wish in terms of structure for our profession and what exists and is practical to accomplish now. We can and we should join together in a way that honors our core values of human dignity, equality, and community (Young, 1993), that brings together excellence and exploration, and that serves our students and institutions in the best way possible while celebrating differences in viewpoint and culture. We cannot be like the traditional professions; indeed, we do not wish to be. What we can do is exemplify a modern model of professions.

Developing a Professional Identity

It was suggested above that a profession possesses shared goals, a sense of community, and means of socialization and regeneration (Carpenter, 1991). It follows that members of the profession should be aware of these things and continually learn about and contribute to them. The process of doing so is professional development. Professional development begins with initial preparation, which leads to a career-long learning process. Miller and Carpenter (1980) suggested that professional development ought to conform to human development principles and derived five propositions:

1. Professional development is continuous and cumulative in nature, moves from simpler to more complex behavior, and can be described via levels or stages held in common.
2. Optimal professional development is a direct result of the interaction between the total person striving for professional growth and the environment.
3. Optimal professional preparation combines mastery of a body of knowledge and a cluster of skills and competencies within the context of personal development.
4. Professional credibility and excellence of practice are directly dependent upon the quality of professional preparation.
5. Professional preparation is a lifelong learning process (p. 84).

Allowing for the context of the piece, Miller and Carpenter are clearly describing a model of continuing professional education. Carpenter and Miller (1981) later reported on a study that clearly establishes the existence of three stages of professional development, the Formative, Application, and Additive stages.

The Formative Stage

The Formative stage is the time of training and orientation into the field. During this time, the young professional is principally concerned with learning and practicing professional knowledge and skills. The locus of control is largely external as the opinions of supervisors and professors are paramount in matters of professionalism such as ethics, quality and nature of practice, and values. Ideally, education and training provide preparation in theories of college student development, program design and implementation, organization development, assessment and evaluation, research design and implementation, interpersonal communication and facilitation, group dynamics, staffing practices, budget development and resource allocation, as well as theories about how gender, sexual orientation, ethnicity, and cultural background affect students and their environments (Winston et al., 2001).

Professional organizations are primarily seen as places for learning and for job placement and networking. Commitment to the field grows as the Formative professional gets closer to taking the first job. The Formative stage is a period of learning (Exhibit 27.1).

The Application Stage

The Application stage starts when the new professional obtains a position. At first, professional practice is much like graduate school in that supervisors and more experienced peers are looked to for advice and clues. Before long, though, situations arise requiring self-responsibility and presenting the opportunity to test out skills and knowledge learned in the training period. It is not long before the new professional figures out that theory, job descriptions, and handbooks do not contain everything needed to do a job. Experience is a good teacher, but the wise new professional continues to also keep up with newsletters and journals, attend in-service training and workshops, and goes to state, regional, and national conferences whenever possible, building on skills and knowledge and coming to acknowledge other professionals as a reference group. In fact, as time goes by opportunities are sought to team up in presentations of best practices, exemplary programs, and workshops on new techniques. Ethical questions are treated with care. Advice is sought, but gradually the person comes to trust his or her interpretations and even to share them with peers and with formative stage professionals and supervised students. Peer opinion and respect are important, but so is self-confidence.

After two to three years in the first job, the Application stage person is ready to consider further responsibility either on the same campus or another. A further commitment to student affairs as a field comes into play here, as do decisions about further education, moving toward more generalist or more specialist positions, and getting more middle management experience. This is a key point in a student affairs career. Actualizing these decisions, usually four to six years into the career, frequently signals a transition to the Additive stage. The Application stage is characterized by doing.

EXHIBIT 27.1. EXAMPLE DEVELOPMENTAL TASKS BY PROFESSIONAL STAGE.

Stage 1 Formative	Stage 2 Application	Stage 3 Additive
1. Getting enough education and/or skill training to obtain and hold a position in student affairs.	1. Beginning to apply the skills and competencies involved with student affairs practice.	1. Creating and devising new approaches to student development.
2. Tailoring learnings and experiences to meet the criteria and expectations of teachers or supervisors.	2. Learning to take responsibility for professional decisions.	2. Taking responsibility for the professional activities and ethics of one's administrative subdivisions and the professionals one supervises.
3. Attaining knowledge of the theory and skills necessary for facilitating the development of students.	3. Attaining the respect of the campus community.	3. Contributing to professional publications in order to share current thinking and practice techniques.
4. Reading journals and other professional publications in order to learn about the field and become aware of basic approaches.	4. Making a firm commitment to student affairs as a profession.	4. Interpreting the rationale of student affairs to the larger community.
5. Internalizing the values of student affairs professionals.	5. Applying established ethical standards in direct contact work with students.	5. Encouraging younger professionals to take responsibility for their own professional efforts, while still providing them with support, input, and feedback.
6. Attending regional and national conferences to make contacts and obtain a position.	6. Contributing to newsletters that report on current practices in specific student services.	6. Helping to welcome and orient young professionals to the field by "showing them the ropes" and encouraging the continued professional development of all colleagues.
	7. Taking part in in-service education, workshops, and other methods of gaining knowledge and skills to aid performance in one's current position.	7. Consulting with, directing, and/or supervising those responsible for accomplishing practical student development goals.
		8. Taking part in the leadership of local, regional and national professional associations.

Source: Adapted from Carpenter (1991).

The Additive Stage

In the Formative stage, one is responsible to others. In the Application stage, one is responsible for oneself. In the Additive stage, professionals take responsibility for others. As the name implies, sufficient expertise and experience have been gained to permit contributions to professional practice at an ever-increasing level. Additive professionals are those in policy making, supervisory, and professional mentorship roles. They write ethical rules and interpretations, and they are accountable for the behaviors and accomplishments of the professionals in their units or divisions. They continue their own professional development and create conditions to facilitate that of others. They are firmly committed to student affairs work as a profession and are active in association leadership, in staff development, in research and publishing, and in the campus community in a variety of ways. Additive professionals are leaders, they are role models and mentors, and they strive to be exemplars of the student affairs profession. Additive professionals contribute to the practice of the profession.

Individual Professional Practice

This cycle of professional development—learning, doing, and contributing—clearly is repeated throughout the career in a myriad of ways and with a variety of tasks. The idea here is that, as in human development, one activity predominates in a particular stage. Other themes also permeate professional practice.

Intentionality

Professional practice is intentional, theory- and research-based, carefully considered, and evaluated. The point of being a professional is to bring preparation and experience, guided by continual learning, into play in a complex way. We should know why and how we are doing the things we do. Good practice does not happen by accident. The student affairs literature is large and growing, increasingly composed of sophisticated quantitative and qualitative research studies. More and more institutions are conducting assessment activities for a variety of reasons. Taking advantage of all this information requires both the ability to understand it and the willingness and competence to put it into play in meaningful, timely ways. In short, professionals must have good initial preparation and then engage in career-long learning.

Intentionality means that professionals approach every interaction with students or other members of the campus community, every budget decision, and every meeting with a point of view, an overall understanding of the general and specific nature of missions and objectives. This point of view is a living thing, it changes and grows and becomes more refined with discussion, experience, assessment, and research.

Scholarship

Komives (1998) suggested that every student affairs professional should be a scholar-practitioner. Schroeder and Pike (2001) elaborated on three tiers of knowledge required of student affairs scholar-practitioners first proposed for institutional researchers by Terenzini (1993). They suggested that knowledge of theory and research about college students, technical knowledge (since professionals should do research as well as read it), and operational and contextual knowledge are all necessary to put what is known into practice as programs that will aid in student learning. Additionally, cognitive complexity is required, both to understand and distill the large amount of information available and to navigate the tough campus cultural minefields that must be taken into account when acting upon it. For a more complete consideration of the ethos of scholarship applied to student affairs work, the reader is referred to the special issue of the *Journal of College Student Development* on Student Affairs Scholarship Reconsidered (July/August, 2001).

Collaboration and Community

Student affairs professionalism is quintessentially about collaboration. When any professional runs into a serious problem, the solution to which is not obvious, the immediate reaction should be to consult colleagues. When a promising new program or approach is identified, the immediate reaction should be to share it with other offices and institutions. Colleagues help each other and do not compete with one another for personal gain. Professionals have an obligation to help one another work through tough issues and to encourage new and better practice.

Collaboration and community take on many forms. Mentoring, once thought to be a top-down, formal activity is now recognized to take place in many ways, large and small, formal and informal. Professionals in every stage mentor others who need the support and help, and it is not uncommon to see mentoring activities flowing from a "younger" professional to an "older" one in specific instances, such as technology or computer issues. The point is not the label that is used, but rather the attitude of sharing that characterizes student affairs work.

A less well-known and practiced form of professional community is peer review. Student affairs work has a history of peer review in conference presentations and in publication activity but not overtly in employment settings, other than supervisory relationships. Peer review is not about criticism but rather about recognition that every professional can always use help, another set of opinions about programs, work accomplished, and techniques applied. Peer review is a staple of many professions and greatly increases quality of practice. Student affairs workers should demand it and make themselves available when others want it.

Ethical Behavior

There are codes of ethics associated with every specialty in student affairs, as well as with the umbrella organizations. A professional is responsible for knowing the ethics that apply to his or her endeavors and following them closely. Student affairs practitioners often find themselves in complex and possibly compromising situations. Only by scrupulously attempting to find the ethical answer, in consideration of client, institution, and professional standards, will they act professionally. Further, student affairs professionals cannot stand idly by when they see colleagues violating ethical codes. Failure to speak up or take action at such times diminishes the profession. Ethics apply not only to interactions with students but also in collegial interactions and to job search and employment procedures. Finally, the topic of ethics should be a frequent and consistent theme in training, vision and mission discussions, and staff development activities on campus. See Chapter Six for a more complete treatment of ethical principles.

Professional Involvement and Development

Professionalism cannot be defined by an individual outside the context of the professional community. It follows that a professional must take an active part in collegial activities. In student affairs, that means three major activities.

First, one should be a member of appropriate professional associations, thereby benefiting from publications, conferences, colleague networks, and periodic renewal and development opportunities. But simple membership is not enough. By definition, if any professional is not allowing his or her voice to be heard by actively participating in committee work, in leadership, and in presentations and workshops, then the profession is the lesser for it. Student affairs workers believe in inclusion—they value it, almost demand it. There is an obligation to join the associations and to assist them as they do their work to the best of one's ability and resources.

The second obligation that accrues to professionals is to contribute to research and scholarship in the field. While this is less obviously necessary to quality practice than being a consumer of such writing and thinking, it is nonetheless necessary when one takes a larger view. There is no such thing as too much research or writing about best practices. The next piece written might be the one that sparks a revolution in residence hall community building or leadership development. Combinations of ideas with one another and with disparate settings are unpredictable. There is a clear professional duty to contribute to the literature and to present one's work whenever possible and to the extent it passes peer review.

The third obligation is related to the other two, but is arguably the most important of all. Each professional can most help the professional community by living up to his or her potential, by continuing to develop and learn in every way possible. It has been suggested in this chapter that professional development is a process similar to student or human development. One difference is that some aspects of those kinds of development are not transparent to the person involved. Such is not the case for professionals. Professional development should be an intentional process, no less important to understand and pursue diligently than our best work with students. After all, excellent practice depends upon constant preparation. Professionals must learn, do, and contribute throughout their careers. It is no one else's job. The responsibility belongs to each of us.

Professional Identity in Perspective

The professional has many obligations. There are duties to students to do the best job possible in an informed and ethical way. The institution calls on the professional to be accountable to mission and to be efficient with resources. The profession and colleagues make legitimate demands on time and talent and energy. But the ultimate obligation of a professional is to self. A person who is tired, tense, or stressed out for long periods of time clearly cannot do his or her best work. Since students need our optimal effort, it behooves us to get appropriate exercise, pay attention to health needs, and to attend to needs for recreation and renewal. Whether it is a hobby or a periodic trip or a visit to friends, mental and physical relaxation and rest are necessary.

Professional identity is important, even critical, but it is only one part of life. Professions are more than jobs, but they are no substitute for family, for friends, for community, for health, and spiritual concerns. Balance is required to be a good person and a better person will also be a more valuable professional.

Implications of Professionalism for Student Affairs Divisions and Other Organizational Units

The philosophy of the division should reflect the institutional mission, be shared by the professionals in the division, and be informed by the values of the larger profession. There should be a regular examination of the mission by all the professionals, along with students and others. The division provides a quality assurance function and allows evaluation of performance in a more comprehensive way than units or individuals. Units have the additional task of upholding the standards and best practices of their particular area of responsibility. The division also provides the venue for appropriate allocation of resources, with all units cooperating in setting priorities.

A good division has employees with the education and experience necessary to accomplish their jobs professionally. There is a commitment to hiring only people who are professionally qualified and encouraging continuing professional education and development with resources and with a supportive philosophy. Professional development should be linked to supervision and performance appraisal, with the goal of improving individual and overall practice (Winston & Creamer, 1997) (see Chapter Eighteen). Professional development and excellence of practice should be understood to include association leadership and research and scholarly activities. Discipline of professionals and others should be conducted humanely, fairly, and consistently.

A professional student affairs division is responsible for allocating sufficient resources for the purpose of assessment and studies related to accountability. Other units should participate actively, but some kind of overall picture is desirable. Planning and allocation of resources should be based upon data and best practices, and benchmarked against appropriate institutions and professional standards. Divisions should actively pursue quality assurance by comparing themselves to accreditation and other extant practice standards, such as those promulgated by the Council for the Advancement of Standards in Higher Education (CAS) (Miller, 1999).

The leadership of the division is responsible for the interaction of student affairs ideas with those of the larger institution, although individual professionals and units should have active "citizenship" roles as appropriate. The division has the obligation to convey student affairs professional knowledge in discussions of institutional mission, policy, and practice. In keeping with Evans (2001), the division and its members should take on the task of student advocacy as appropriate to institutional circumstance. Professionals in the division should be free to be student advocates and responsible social activists, and these activities should be supported by the division.

Issues and Challenges for Student Affairs Professionalism

Student affairs professionalism faces a number of issues and challenges in the years ahead. Some of those issues and challenges are discussed in this section.

Professional Preparation Standards

There are CAS standards for student affairs preparation programs, and Commission XII (Professional Preparation) of ACPA, the principal faculty voice in the profession currently, has adopted these standards in principle and is moving toward voluntary cooperation in implementing them among quality preparation programs. NASPA has also begun efforts in this area, but it is too early to report on the results. In keeping with the field's historic diversity and breadth, a voluntary registry of programs that follow professional standards would probably serve best at this point in time. Together with the self-assessment guides, these standards allow for a total program review in the context of a professional consensus on quality of practice. The self-study approach is a sensible arrangement that avoids many of the pitfalls of benchmarking, such as comparisons of dissimilar institutions and failure to recognize institutional history and uniqueness of mission. The goal of self-assessments using CAS standards is program and division improvement with expert guidance. This is contrasted with accreditation self-studies which often founder upon the rocks of unclear, inappropriate, cognitively and academically focused, and vague or global standards.

Registry, Certification, and Quality Assurance

If divisions and other units (Chapter Fifteen) and preparation programs are moving toward professional standards, then individual practitioners will not be far behind. It has been argued above that student affairs is well served by multiple modes of entry into the field and by including allied professionals in divisions and units. Indeed, any other conception would fail to recognize history, tradition, campus uniqueness, and focus upon the whole student. However, as more and more is known about how students learn and develop and how campuses can facilitate such growth, it is clear that ignoring such knowledge is at best unprofessional and at worst unethical (Pascarella & Whitt, 1999). Student affairs professionals need certain kinds of theory, knowledge, and skills. If they do not have appropriate initial preparation, then continuing professional education is a good supplement (Carpenter, 1998; Creamer & Associates, 1992). Even well-prepared professionals need such career-long learning in order to keep current, to retrain for other opportunities, or to simply enhance practice. Continuing professional education needs to be available in a variety of conference, campus, workshop, and individually oriented settings and modes, in an organized way, with purposeful, meaningful goals.

One good way to structure initial preparation and continuing education would be a voluntary registry or certification process for student affairs workers. For example, individuals with a master's degree from a CAS standards program would be immediately eligible, after a suitable period of practice, while persons with an unrelated degree would need to gain some continuing education credits at conferences, workshops, on campus, or in some other way. Allied professionals, who need to gain a more limited perspective on student affairs theory and research, could be registered at a different level or with fewer credits. Appropriate doctoral studies or other course work could be substituted for continuing education credits and so on. In order to stay registered, professionals would be responsible for updating their own skills and knowledge and providing evidence of such. The professional associations could offer such continuing professional education in an organized way at conferences and other settings and provide clearinghouses for the credits. At this writing, NASPA is seriously considering such a plan.

This is only one model. There are several others, but the important thing is that the field take action on the need for practitioners to continue learning throughout their careers. Only in this way can quality of performance be assured (Creamer & Associates, 1992).

Challenges to Student Affairs Professionalism

The first and most obvious challenge to student affairs on campus is the budget climate for higher education in the coming years (Schroeder & Pike, 2001; Woodard, 1998). Enrollments are booming, but resources are tight. Restructuring has become almost a catch phrase. The student affairs field is going to have to make a cogent case for its existence, and the best way to do this is to clearly articulate the centrality of our goals and objectives to institutional missions. It will not be enough to make claims of our ability to collaborate with faculty in the learning process. Faced with exigency, the faculty may choose to allocate scarce resources to themselves and go it alone or reorganize in such a way that our functioning and modes of educating are deemphasized or disappear entirely. Student affairs will need to marshal arguments resting upon research, assessment, and theory to demonstrate our value in enhancing student learning and development, attracting and retaining students, and creating a healthy campus climate for the entire college and university community.

Student consumerism and the general tenor of vocationalism in the curriculum also tend to restrict options for advisors and other student affairs workers. Students need help to work out their own decisions, to map their own lives. Increasingly, business interests, business practices, utilitarian views of curricula, and privatization are changing the nature and tone of campus-student interactions. Clearly, student affairs must do a good job of services, as well as programming and advising, or risk being replaced.

Along these same lines, technology, distance education modalities, and proprietary higher education seem to be making inroads into traditional and nontraditional student enrollments. As campuses embrace distance learning and technology, what happens to education for the whole student, a staple of student affairs work for over sixty years (Evans, 2001)? Even as we know more than ever about student learning and development, we risk returning to an exclusively services model, or worse, a service by remote control model. To be sure, there are attempts to serve distant students using student affairs theory and research (Schwitzer, Ancis, & Brown, 2001), but student affairs professionals need to address serious issues about what constitutes the best higher education available. The field needs to weigh in now about the true costs of expediency and convenience. Certainly, some student needs can be met by distance education and other forms, but there is a price to be paid and students, parents, and other stakeholders should be making informed decisions. Education-as-commodity, or more properly information-as-commodity, is simply a transactional medium and does violence to our values as educators.

Finally, the discussion of credentialing above deserves further mention as a challenge for the profession. Constrained finances, notions of consumerism, and expedient modes of information transfer may combine to make human development obsolete as an intentional goal of higher education. If that happens, student affairs will cease to exist as a profession. So, credentialing, the idea that there are appropriate avenues of professional preparation and development over the course of a career, is more than a turf battle or a way to assure employment and choke off competition. It is in some ways a battle for the soul of higher education, an operational implementation of holistic pedagogy. If professionals are not qualified to do the work that we espouse, they may not value it. The notion that senior student affairs officers can be hired without so much as a day of experience in our field should be troubling in the extreme. The credentialing movement is one way to do something about it, if we proceed carefully and with full awareness of its pitfalls.

Professionalism Redux

***P**reparation*—make yourself ready for the incredible journey of student affairs work in the best way possible. But never assume you are completely prepared because there is always more to learn.

***R**enewal*—Periodically revisit whatever it was that led you to the profession, whether it is mingling with resident students, attending programs, advising groups or individuals, or just walking around on campus. You will remember why you are there!

***O**bligation*—Always understand that you have obligations to students, to your employing organization, to your profession and colleagues and to yourself to act in ways consonant with professional and personal values.

***F**un*—Have it! If you aren't having it at work, figure out why and change it.

***E**verything counts*—Your behavior in preparation programs and assistantships, at conferences, in every student or colleague interaction. Someone is watching. Be able to be proud of what you have done.

***S**tudents*—Don't forget them, no matter what your job function. They are the reason our profession exists.

***S**hare*—Professionals don't compete, they share. They collaborate; they consult; they write; and they present and give workshops. They build fires that will warm others.

***I**ntention*—Know what you are trying to do. If you don't know what to do, find out through consultation or learning. If you still can't decide, don't do anything. Unintended consequences are frequently bad.

***O**verwhelmed*—You will feel that way sometimes. All professionals do, if they are trying hard enough. But you are doing important work. Do it well.

***N**urture*—Yourself, your students, your family, your colleagues.

***A**ltruism*—Keep it! It will sustain you through the shoals of life and career.

***L**earn*—Above all, learn all you can, all the time. Then do. Then contribute so that others can learn and do.

Conclusion

Professionals often try to establish and rely upon exclusive jurisdiction to solidify their claims to recognition. As has been shown, this model does not work well for student affairs for a variety of reasons. We are natural collaborators, by nature and by design. Collaboration promotes student growth and notions of seamless education, but it does not put professionals in a very good position to argue for professional values in disputes over goals, objectives, and missions. This is true of all professionals in organizations, in greater or lesser degree (Birnbaum, 1988), but this is not comforting when institutional policies contravene what student affairs practitioners know to be good educational practice. Precisely because we attempt to meet the needs of everyone and offend none, we sometimes fail to achieve our goals. Evans (2001) declares that it may be time to stop being quiescent and complacent and become student advocates and social activists. By doing so, we may more clearly stake out a role that is unique in the educational community. If we argue cogently, from theory and research, we may gain respect and new attention to our professional voice.

The cycle of student affairs professional development and growth is one of learning, doing, and contributing. What turns learning into doing and deeds into contributions is reflection. Schön (1987), Senge (1994), and many other authors have all noted the power of reflection to alter insights, to change practice, and to influence entire organizations. Indeed, the service learning model (Delve, Mintz, & Stewart, 1990) insists that reflection is a necessary component of complete learning for students (see Chapter Twenty-One); it is not less so for practitioners. Student affairs educators can get so caught up on doing and contributing that they forget to learn, lose perspective, and burn out temporarily or permanently. Reflection is the way out of the trap. The best professionals build time into their busy lives to stop and to notice and to live. This is reflection and it colors the world in amazing ways. Student affairs professional practice is best approached with wonder and awe and love. Reflection reminds us.

References

American Council on Education. (1937). *The student personnel point of view.* American Council on Education Studies Series (Series 1, Vol. 1, No. 3). Washington, DC: Author.

Birnbaum, R. (1988). *How colleges work: The cybernetics of academic organizations and leadership.* San Francisco: Jossey-Bass.

Blake, E. S. (1979). Classroom and context: An educational dialectic. *Academe, 65* (5), 280–292.

Blimling, G. S. (2001). Uniting scholarship and communities of practice in student affairs. *Journal of College Student Development, 42*, 381–396.

Brint, S. (1993). Eliot Friedson's contribution to the sociology of professions. *Work & Occupations, 20* (3), 259–279.

Carpenter, D. S. (1991). Student affairs profession: A developmental perspective. In T. K. Miller, R. B. Winston, Jr., & Associates (Eds.), *Administration and leadership in student affairs* (pp. 253–278). Muncie, IN: Accelerated Development.

Carpenter, D. S. (1998). Continuing professional education in student affairs. In N. Evans & C. E. Phelps Tobin (Eds.), *The state of the art of preparation and practice in student affairs: Another look* (pp. 159–176). Washington, DC: American College Personnel Association.

Carpenter, D. S., & Miller, T. K. (1981). An analysis of professional development in student affairs work. *NASPA Journal, 19*, 2–11.

Carpenter, D. S., Miller, T. K., & Winston, R. B. (1980). Toward the professionalization of student affairs. *NASPA Journal, 18*, 16–22.

Creamer, D. G., Carpenter, D. S., Forney, D. S., Gehring, D. D., McEwen, M. K., Schuh, J. H., et al. (1992). Quality assurance in college student affairs: A proposal for action by professional associations. In R. B. Winston, Jr., & D. G. Creamer (Eds.) *Improving staffing practices in student affairs* (pp. 353–367). San Francisco: Jossey-Bass.

Delve, C. I., Mintz, S. D., & Stewart, G. M. (1990). *Community service as values education* (New Directions for Student Services No. 50). San Francisco: Jossey-Bass.

Evans, N. J. (with Reason, R. D.). (2001). Guiding principles: A review and analysis of student affairs philosophical statements. *Journal of College Student Development, 42*, 359–377.

Friedson, E. (1986). *Professional powers.* Chicago: University of Chicago Press.

Komives, S. R. (1998). *The art of becoming a professional.* Paper presented at the annual conference of the American College Personnel Association, Miami, FL.

Komives, S. R. (2001). Linking student affairs preparation with practice. In N. J. Evans & C. E. Phelps Torbin (Eds.), *The state of the art of preparation and practice in student affairs: Another look* (pp. 177–200). Washington, DC: American College Personnel Association.

Lloyd-Jones, E., & Smith, M. (1954). *Student personnel work as deeper teaching.* New York: Harper.

Miller, T. K. (1999). *The CAS book of professional standards for higher education.* Washington, DC: Council for the Advancement of Standards in Higher Education.

Miller, T. K., & Carpenter, D. S. (1980). Professional preparation for today and tomorrow: In D. G. Creamer (Ed.), *Student development in higher education: Theories, practices, and future directions* (pp. 181–204). Washington, DC: American College Personnel Association.

Pascarella, E. T., & Whitt, P. T. (1999). Using systematic inquiry to improve performance. In G. S. Blimling & E. J. Whitt (Eds.), *Good practice in student affairs: Principles to foster student learning* (pp. 91–112). San Francisco: Jossey-Bass.

Pavalko, R. M. (1971). *Sociology of occupations and professions.* Itasca, IL: F. E. Peacock.

Penney, J. F. (1969). Student personnel work: A profession stillborn. *Personnel and Guidance Journal, 47,* 958–962.

Schön, D. A. (1987). *Educating the reflective practitioner.* San Francisco: Jossey-Bass.

Schroeder, C. C., & Pike, G. R. (2001). The scholarship of application in student affairs. *Journal of College Student Development, 42,* 342–355.

Schwitzer, A. M., Ancis, J. R., & Brown, N. (2001). *Promoting student learning and student development at a distance: Student affairs concepts and practices for televised instruction and other forms of distance learning.* Washington, DC: American College Personnel Association.

Senge, P. M. (1994). *The fifth discipline: The art and practice of the learning organization.* New York: Doubleday.

Shoben, E. J. (1967). *Career dynamics: Matching individual and organizational need.* Reading, MA: Addison-Wesley.

Stamatakos, L. C. (1981). Student affairs progress toward professionalism: Recommendations for actions (Pt 1 and 2). *Journal of College Student Personnel, 22,* 105–111, 197–206.

Terenzini, P. T. (1993). On the nature of institutional research and the knowledge and skills it requires. *Research in Higher Education, 34,* 1–10.

Wilensky, H. L. (1964). The professionalization of everyone? *American Journal of Sociology, 70,* 137–158.

Winston, R. B., Jr., & Creamer, D. G. (1997). *Improving staffing practices in student affairs.* San Francisco: Jossey-Bass.

Winston, R. B., Jr., Creamer, D. G., Miller, T. K., & Associates (Eds.). (2001). *The professional student affairs administer: Educator, leader, and manager.* New York: Brunner-Routledge.

Woodard, D. B., Jr. (1998). Societal influences on higher education and student affairs. In N. J. Evans & C. E. Phelps Tobin (Eds.), *The state of the art of professional preparation and practice in student affairs: Another look* (pp. 3–20). Washington, DC: American College Personnel Association.

Wrenn, C. G. (1949). An appraisal of the professional status of student personnel workers, Part I. In E. G. Williamson (Ed.), *Trends in student personnel work* (pp. 264–268). Minneapolis: University of Minnesota Press.

Young, R. B. (1993). Academic values and service conflicts. *Higher Education in Europe,* 12–19.

Young, R. B. (2001). A perspective on the values of student affairs and scholarship. *Journal of College Student Development, 42,* 319–337.

PART SIX

LAYING NEW FOUNDATIONS FOR THE FUTURE

Parts One through Five have presented an extensive scholarly review of the field of student affairs—its history and contemporary context, guiding values and philosophy, ethical and legal foundations, theoretical underpinnings, administrative structures, and core competencies. Each day, student affairs professionals apply this knowledge base to solving students' problems and helping them succeed. We stay current with the literature and research in the field by attending workshops and conferences, reading books, consulting professional journals, and discussing commissioned reports with our colleagues. It may seem at times that we suffer from "time famine," that it is impossible to devote the necessary time to reading and understanding the literature and research that informs our practice. As Carpenter stressed in Chapter Twenty-Seven, however, these sources of professional development are critical to maintaining a fresh perspective and developing creative approaches to meeting the challenges of our job. Thus this final part of the book addresses how the research and literature in the field informs our practice, how we might apply this to practice in collaborations across campus, and the likely future directions of the profession.

Much has been written on the outcomes of higher education; this literature requires careful analysis to assess what is useful and under what conditions. In Chapter Twenty-Eight, Len Baird provides an insightful discussion of research on student outcomes, framed around the following four reconceptualizations: students are viewed as an active and diverse rather than as a monolithic group; the college environment is viewed as a collection of evolving environments rather than a static and homogeneous milieu; student outcomes are seen as individually chosen rather than institutionally determined; and multiple pathways to understanding student outcomes are presented as alternatives to the dominant, positivistic approach. Baird concludes with an agenda for future research, based on his reconceptualized paradigm.

In Chapter Twenty-Nine, Charles Schroeder builds on all previous chapters to present a new chapter on using the lessons from theory and research to develop collaborations and partnerships that benefit students and their experience. The symbiotic recognition of the complexity of shared issues combined with the 1990s shift from rigid hierarchies to flexible, organic systems have supported exciting collaborations and new partnerships within and external to the college. Student affairs play a key role in being the boundary spanners and border crossers who can accomplish change in this way.

In Chapter Thirty, the editors focus on the student affairs practitioner's professional identity, using this perspective as a springboard to discussing the profession's future directions. The 1990s were the decade of institutional restructuring, resulting in organizations and professional roles that are more in tune with and responsive to their social context. It has been a time to refocus on undergraduate education—especially on the interconnectedness of student learning and development; a time to make use of those institutional practices that we know foster learning, development, and success. It has been time to understand the powerful transforming nature of future change drivers, such as the shifts in funding, multiculturalism, the redefinition of individual and social roles, technology, and globalization. These trends and change drivers will influence the practice of student affairs well into the twenty-first century. This chapter concludes with a discussion of these issues and trends that will continue to shape and redefine the practice of student affairs.

CHAPTER TWENTY-EIGHT

NEW LESSONS FROM RESEARCH ON STUDENT OUTCOMES

Leonard L. Baird

The Senior and Emerging Scholars of the American College Personnel Association were asked to identify the most important research questions for the profession (Komives in Pickering & Hansen, 2000). The group of scholars identified the following questions:

- What is the impact of technology on the nature and extent of student learning, both inside and outside the classroom?
- What educational practices encourage and discourage access and educational success for diverse groups of students? More specifically, what practices work well and work poorly in regard to student subgroups that differ by factors such as age, gender, race and ethnicity, sexual orientation, preferred learning style, and learning or physical disability? What experiences are distinctive for these subgroups that affect students' educational success?
- How do students move from attitudes of intolerance to acceptance and valuing of diversity? How do factors related to cognitive, social, relational, and racial identity development affect this aspect of development?
- What learning outcomes are associated with students' interactions with student affairs educators?
- How can we better assess campus climate in terms of support for underrepresented and marginalized students? What aspects of campus culture are particularly important influences on learning, retention, satisfaction, and educational success of given student subgroups?
- Do cultural, ethnic, racial, gender, and class dynamics differentially affect learning? What are the direct and indirect contributions of faculty and student affairs

educators to specific student outcomes such as student persistence, learning, commitment to citizenship, and satisfaction?

- Which forms of academic and student affairs divisional collaboration are the most effective in promoting students' academic and cognitive development?
- Which contemporary forms of teaching (for example, developmental, feminist, constructivist) most effectively promote deep learning? Do they work equally well for students with various ways of knowing, learning styles, intelligences, abilities, and cultural backgrounds?
- How, if at all, do the nature and outcomes of the experience of learning at a distance differ from those of face-to-face, residential instructional setting? How are successful collaborative partnerships designed, implemented, and sustained?
- What are the multiple conceptions of knowing, learning styles, learning abilities, intelligences, and levels of development that students possess? How do these mediate learning in particular and disciplines in general?
- To what extent are educators clear on the learning goals of their particular educational practices?
- Which out-of-class experiences are the most effective in promoting academic and cognitive learning outcomes?
- How do educators and students learn to participate effectively in creative controversy to consider multiple perspectives?
- What factors contribute to the widespread pattern of self-segregation among White students (Smith, 1993)? What types of interactions across racial and ethnic groups enable such conversations and contribute to students' educational success? How can desired educational outcomes of involvement in such conversations be enhanced? The process of racial identity has been described for various racial and ethnic groups, including Whites. How is growth to the more complex stages of racial identity (in which difference is valued) promoted? In what ways can this be integrated into the collegiate experience?

All of these questions are concerned with college outcomes in one way or another and deserve thoughtful research-based answers. To address these questions (and many others which have been proposed) with the care and scholarship they deserve requires reconsiderations of how colleges affect students with different histories and characteristics. This chapter describes these reconsiderations and outlines their consequences for the theory and practice of student affairs. It summarizes some findings from recent research on student outcomes, particularly concerning the effects of diversity and learning communities.

This new research and thinking has important consequences for the theory and practice of student affairs, today and into the future. This chapter describes those consequences in terms of four reconceptualizations of traditional viewpoints.

The first reconceptualization discards the traditional view of students as a monolithic group in favor of a new appreciation of students as active and diverse individuals. Students are increasingly seen as responsible actors who shape their own experience and choose the outcomes *they* value. They are also increasingly regarded as a diverse group, not only in terms of demographics (gender, age, ethnicity) but also in terms of personal characteristics (learning styles, psychosocial development, individual abilities). The impact of student diversity is seen in all the other reconceptualizations.

The second reconceptualization moves from a view of college environments as static and universal milieus to a concept of multiple environments that can best be understood by the different interactions they demand. Some environments foster academic achievement, some personal development, and some a sense of community. Student diversity and environmental diversity lead to the next reconceptualization.

The third reconceptualization involves understanding the different patterns of students' interactions with their college. Many of the past models of this interaction assume a homogeneity of the process. Recent work on understanding the role of cultures, social and cultural capital, and institutional functioning has broadened our conceptual underpinnings.

The fourth reconceptualization is from outcomes as institutionally chosen and social to outcomes as individually chosen and personal. Students bring their own agenda to campus, and it affects their choices and behaviors as much or more than the institution's plans for them. Increasingly, outcomes are seen less in terms of individual benefit and more in terms of social or community benefit. The search for viable, humane communities in our colleges and in our society is one example.

Each of these reconceptualizations has consequences for student affairs and the ways we work with students. The possibilities and limitations these consequences suggest for professional practice are outlined below. The goal is to help new professionals begin their work with a deeper understanding of how colleges interact with students and thus provide them with a greater understanding of appropriate actions.

It should be noted that the discussion of the issues in this chapter focuses on the four-year undergraduate experience, but many points apply to community college students as well (see the burgeoning literature on community college outcomes reported in the *Community College Journal of Research and Practice* and *Community College Review*). Likewise, many of the points also apply to graduate and professional students (see Anderson, 1998: Haworth, 1996, 2000).

The Growing Interest in Student Outcomes

Student affairs professionals, like most other professionals in higher education, are being called upon to pay greater attention to defining, assessing, and demonstrating students' progress toward academic and developmental outcomes. Although these goals have been discussed in much the same terms for more than a quarter of a century (for example, see Hartnett, 1971; Lawrence, Weathersby, & Patterson, 1970), they have increased salience in recent times because of the changing fiscal and political environment in higher education.

Thus student affairs professionals are involved not only in defining outcomes but also in using outcomes for assessment, evaluation, and research. (Assessment and evaluation are discussed in detail in Chapter Twenty-Six.) Although many of the outcomes that constituent groups are concerned with involve basic progress (time to degree completion, placement in the work force, passing rates on licensing exams), other outcomes involve learning and personal development (Smith & Mather, 2000). As Pickering and Hanson (2000) point out, these latter outcomes are especially important to student affairs professionals, since they are held accountable for students' personal development and increasingly play a large role in students' cognitive development as well. The domains of affective and character development have become almost the sole province of student affairs professionals. Thus the combination of public pressure for evidence of academic achievement and the traditional concern of student affairs with students' affective development means that student affairs professionals are often called upon to assume wide responsibility for a considerable range of outcomes. Furthermore, as the people who are usually most knowledgeable about campus climate, student affairs professionals play a critical role in "creating a culture where assessment improves learning" (Loacker & Mentkowski, 1993, p. 5). Finally, with their knowledge of student development theory, student affairs professionals can provide an anchor for the identification and assessment of student outcomes.

What Do We Know About Student Outcomes?

The large body of recent research, including Astin's (1993, 1999) many studies, can be thought of in terms of a rephrasing of Pascarella and Terenzini's (1991) analytic framework. First, students bring an enormous amount of prior experience and thinking with them to college. That is, students' lives have been shaped by their families, prior schooling, cultural backgrounds, neighborhoods, and peers. All of these influences affect their personalities, values, and readiness for college work. They also influence how students interact with their college and how much they can change. The implication for student affairs professionals is that they need to understand the backgrounds of the students they work with as well as their own assumptions.

Second, the degree to which students change varies by type of outcome. For example, students seem to have sizable gains in general verbal skills and critical thinking but only small changes in the value placed on intrinsic occupational rewards. The implication for student affairs professionals is that it may be realistic to expect programs and interventions to have positive effects in some areas but not in others.

Third, it appears that differences among colleges in prestige and resources are much less important than the structure, policy, and actions within colleges (Astin, 1993). This result provides cause for optimism among student affairs practitioners. That is, a college does not need to rank high in the *U.S. News and World Report* ratings or be extremely wealthy in order to create significant changes in students. The success of innovative colleges such as Alverno and Evergreen State are well known, but more traditional colleges, such as most of those described by Kuh, Schuh, Whitt, and Associates (1991), suggest that much can be done within familiar contexts.

Fourth, the influences on students' outcomes can differ, depending on the characteristics of students. These differences, termed *conditional effects* by Pascarella and Terenzini (1998), reflect the increasing diversity of students and the patterns of their interactions with their colleges, a point elaborated below. As an example Pascarella, Truckenmiller, Nora, Terenzini, Edison, and Hagedorn (1999) found that athletic participation had negative effects on the critical thinking scores of men, particularly football and basketball players, and no effects on the critical thinking of women athletes. Fraternity membership had negative effects on the cognitive development of White men but positive effects among Black men (Pascarella et al., 1999). The implication for student affairs professionals is that it is important to understand the processes with which students with different attributes interact with their colleges, discussed further in the section on reconsidering student-college interaction.

Fifth, the effects of college experiences can be lasting. This is increasingly important as colleges reaffirm their role as a part of the larger society and as they are called upon to demonstrate their social utility as institutions. Although many of the studies of the long-term effects of college are concerned with fairly simple outcomes, such as the income and voting habits of graduates, more evidence is accumulating that college experiences have enduring impacts on students' personalities, values, behaviors, and health. For student affairs professionals, this evidence supports their hope that what they do can leave a lasting mark on the lives of students.

Sixth, many new insights into the ways that students interact with their college experiences are emerging from the use of qualitative methods. Although the great majority of studies of student outcomes use quantitative designs, researchers such as Baxter Magolda (2000) have shown that a key aspect of college experiences is the meaning students make of them.

Finally, most studies of student outcomes show them to be influenced by multiple factors (Astin, 1993). These results suggest the importance of considering the varied aspects of the college experience that influence students and working with the related people and sections of the institution. For student affairs professionals this means working with professors, academic affairs administrators, institutional researchers, and others who can join in collaborative efforts to promote positive student outcomes.

Reconceptualizing Students

When we look at old movies that portray college students, a common picture emerges: college students are young; they major in liberal arts; they attend school full time; they are supported by their parents; and they are concerned with ideas as well as with success. Students are also portrayed as White, middle-class, and supportive of mainstream assumptions about the meaning of education. (The main character is also usually male.) This stereotypical conception of college students has permeated much of the thinking of academics as well; thus when faculty and administrators interact with students, they sometimes make assumptions that are far removed from reality.

This may result in a "chilly climate" for students who don't fit preconceived notions, to borrow Hall and Sandler's (1984) term.

The inaccuracy of these stereotypes has been pointed out by many authors who have reflected on the changing demographics in our educational system (see Chapters Two and Three). This structural diversity has many consequences. For example, Sagaria and Johnsrud (1991) discuss the increasing number of minority students on our campuses and the challenges they represent to traditional practice. Smith and Schonfeld (2000) provide information related to the status of minority students and institutional responses to them. The cultural diversity in our society also presents challenges to our institutions of higher education (Hurtado, Milem, Clayton-Pederson, & Allen, 1999). Even greater challenges may be presented by the increasing numbers of international students and recent immigrants in American colleges and universities. As Stewart (1993) points out, immigrants and the children of recent immigrants create potential crises as well as opportunities for colleges and universities.

The age of college students has also changed. Students over twenty-five years of age now make up more than a third of all college students nationally, and on many campuses they represent the majority of students. Likewise, the assumption that students attend school full-time has been increasingly eroded. If present trends continue, the majority of students will attend part-time in the near future. Women now represent the majority of all college students (National Center for Education Statistics, 1995), and projections suggest even larger numbers of women in college in the future. As various critics have pointed out, the increasing presence of women on campus presents a challenge to colleges and universities dominated by a male-oriented culture (for example, see Hackman, 1992; Kuk, 1990; Tidball, Smith, Tidball, & Wolf-Wendel, 1999). Finally, many more students with disabilities attended college in the last decade (Horn & Berktold, 1999). Obviously, the physical needs of students with disabilities challenge those who plan and manage the physical environment on campus; in addition, their psychological and social needs present a challenge to the concerned student affairs professional (Hill, 2000). Altogether, these demographic changes in U.S. college students mean that our institutions need to reexamine their traditional practices, their traditional definitions of outcomes, and their assumptions about the relationship between their practices and the outcomes they desire for students.

Students have not only changed in demographic terms; they have also mirrored changes in the general culture. As discussed by Levine and Cureton (1998), students increasingly report severe financial pressures, poor academic preparation for college, drug and alcohol abuse, and risky sexual practices. At the same time, entering students are more likely to be interested in ecological and social issues, if not traditional politics (Astin, 2000). The mixture of vocationalism, materialism, concern for the environment, and commitment to social justice seen on campus today indicates that students represent a complex mosaic of attitudes and values that are not simple to summarize. The possibility, emphasized in the popular press, that students are also uninspired, alienated, and irresponsible makes any uniform understanding of students even more difficult (Howe & Strauss, 2000). Likewise, the increasing pace of technological advances, which are usually adopted most eagerly by the younger segments of society, is altering our society in ways that may be difficult to quantify. Thus, college students cannot be thought of without recognizing a diversity that matches that of a multicultural and rapidly changing society. The most important consequence of all this for colleges is that the concept of a college education now has multiple meanings for students; thus the outcomes educators are concerned with must be equally diverse.

Further, as Evans, Forney, and Guido-diBrito (1998) have discussed, numerous recent attempts to understand the different forms of development among multiple groups of students, particularly those from minority ethnic and cultural backgrounds, has led to the realization that there are multiple paths of development that do not always lead to the same place. In addition, detailed attempts to understand the complexity of areas that were once thought to be uniform have led to additional recognition of diversity. For example, elaborations of Erikson's conception of identity have resulted in the development of separate models for sexual identity, cultural or ethnic identity, female identity, and ethical identity (King, 1994). An important consequence of these concepts is that rather different outcomes are appropriate for different groups of students. Thus a single model for defining and assessing outcomes is not only unwise but also, in the strictest sense, unfeasible.

To have an authentic assessment of outcomes, we need to understand how institutional goals interact with student goals. Students pursue a great variety of paths to reach the goals or outcome they aspire to achieve. Students' widely varying learning styles (Claxton & Murrell, 1987) and their preference for active, collaborative learning are often ignored by faculty (Bonwell & Eison, 1991; Johnson, Johnson, & Smith, 1991). Most fundamentally, the meaning students attach to institutional goals plays a large role in their progress (Baxter Magolda, 2000). This point is elaborated in the following sections, which reach related conclusions in our reconceptualizations of the college environment, patterns of interaction, and outcomes.

Reconceptualizing Campus Environments

The college environment has traditionally been seen to possess stable traits, such as size or emphasis on scholarship, that are different from student characteristics and that characterize institutions as a whole (Baird, 1988). (See Chapter Thirteen for a rich discussion of the college environment and Braxton's insights in Chapter Fourteen.) Thus, the college environment was thought of in static terms, as monolithic. The main task for researchers was to identify the environmental dimensions that separate different colleges in meaningful ways. Of the myriad ways in which campuses may differ, those most often identified as systematic differences with the potential to affect students' experiences were summarized by Baird (1990). These include "friendliness or cohesiveness of the student culture, warmth or quality of faculty-student relations, flexibility and freedom versus rigidity and control of the academic and other programs, overall rigor of academic standards, emphasis on personal expression and creativity, emphasis on research versus concern for undergraduate learning, importance of fun and big-time sports, and sense of a shared identity or mission. These are all important

aspects of the psychological climate as perceived by respondents in many studies" (p. 39).

As plausible as these dimensions are, research that has attempted to relate them to student change has been disappointing (Astin, 1993; Pascarella & Terenzini, 1991). For example, institutional prestige has been found to have few effects, once students' initial characteristics are taken into account (Terenzini & Pascarella, 1994). One explanation offered for these meager results is that they have been neglectful of theory (Baird, 1988). But when theories that are used to help explain students' cognitive and affective development are examined, few deal with the environment to any extensive degree (Rodgers, 1991). Further, those theories that do deal with the environment have been criticized for being so complex or general that they do not lead to useful distinctions or implementations (Huebner & Lawson, 1990).

Researchers have consequently rethought the assumption that the characteristics of colleges can be identified by means of statistical differentiation, or that studies of college characteristics should be based on psychological theories oriented toward the individual. Thus, researchers have turned to sociological approaches to the college environment (Weidman, 1989). Increasingly, studies have emphasized the importance of students' interactions with their institution and the institution's aggregate values, norms, and behavior (Pascarella & Terenzini, 1991). The greater attention given these more conceptual kinds of variables has also led to a greater recognition of the cultural approach to environments (see Tierney, 1990) and the use of qualitative methods (Denzin & Lincoln, 1994). Colleges are increasingly seen as coherent, if complex, wholes rather than summations of unconnected characteristics.

But even a cultural approach to environment can characterize institutions in static terms, offering the student an externally defined set of stimuli and pressures. In contrast, the kinds of theories described as "impact models" by Pascarella and Terenzini (1991) emphasize students' *interactions* with the environment. There have been several attempts to analyze the nature of these interactions. The work of Spady (1971), who emphasized the importance of students' social integration with their environment, led Tinto (1975) to develop a model of student interaction that describes its impact on student retention. Tinto's model describes how students enter the college environment with a particular background and set of characteristics that help determine their initial commitment to their educational goals and their institution. This commitment is increased or decreased by the extent to which students are integrated into the academic and social environment of their institution. Tinto's work, and the simultaneous use of statistical methods to test his ideas, led Pascarella (1985), among others, to propose more general impact models that apply to more criteria than retention and include two classes of variables missing from Tinto's model—institutional characteristics and the level of student effort (Davis & Murrell, 1993). Institutions with various characteristics are seen as varying in the degree to which they provide enabling situations and stimuli for student change and achievement. The key change in the models, however, is in the concept of student effort or involvement.

The empirical evidence suggests that integration and involvement have consistent effects. As summarized by Davis and Murrell (1993), the evidence about integration is impressive: "student-faculty interaction and academic integration exert a direct and important effect on persistence, intellectual and academic outcomes, and institutional loyalty. Peer relations appear to be important in enhancing persistence and personal development" (p. 58). "Involvement" has wide meaning and equally wide-ranging effects, but as Davis and Murrell emphasize, three areas stand out:

> Involvement with other students, with faculty, and with work. . . . Student-faculty contact is correlated with student satisfaction, college GPA, graduation, and enrollment in graduate school. Such interaction, even after controlling for most individual student differences, is positively associated with intellectual and personal growth. . . . The involvement of students with one another around social and academic topics promotes a wide range of positive outcomes, even after controlling for many individual and institutional differences. When students help one another on class projects, discuss assignments, participate in social organizations, or simply socialize with different kinds of people, good things follow. Students who are socially involved also make gains in general knowledge and intellectual skills and tend to be more satisfied with the college experience. . . . There are some kinds of involvement, especially those which take students away from their studies or isolate them from the campus environment, that appear to have a negative effect on college outcomes [pp. 59–60].

Astin (1993) reports that the single largest negative effect on degree completion is holding a full-time or part-time job off-campus. Working has a negative effect on other outcomes too, such as GPA, growth in cultural awareness, college satisfaction, and willingness to reenroll in college.

These results, combined with extensive analyses of Pace's College Student Experiences Questionnaire (1993), led Davis and Murrell (1993) to call for student responsibility, by which students recognize their own role in making the most of their education. Other research, most notably that of Kuh et al. (1991), has shown that institutional culture and climate play a large role in determining whether students are positively involved with their college. Such factors as a clear and consistent mission and philosophy, symbolic actions that celebrate interaction and involvement, events that socialize students to core institutional values, programs and physical spaces that promote interaction, and a variety of other policies and practices all promote involvement.

One key factor is respect and celebration of differences among students. This research suggests the power (and therefore the responsibility) of the institution to promote a culture that encourages involvement among all students. Another implication of the research on student integration, involvement, and effort is that students make their own environments based on their interactions with their institution. Thus, the college environment is constructed by a process of psychological and social negotiation between the institution and its students. The potential consequences of this idea are discussed in the concluding section.

Reconsidering Student-College Interactions

Most of the research on student outcomes has been based on assumptions, not only of homogeneity in the educational process (Pascarella & Terenzini, 1998) but also of homogeneity in the interactions of students with those processes. The most dominant ideas have centered on the degree of student involvement, social integration, and academic integration. That is, as summarized by Braxton (2000), colleges bring about changes in students in proportion to their involvement with the social systems of the colleges they attend. However, as Tierney (2000) and Rendon, Jalomo, and Nora (2000) have pointed out, this idea is often interpreted as the absorption of students into the dominant culture of the institution. Further, this dominant culture is usually a reflection of traditional, primarily White, upper- and middle-class values and perspectives. The diversity of students makes the conception problematical, and several researchers have proposed different models or conceptions that could lead to understanding the variety of ways in which students can interact with their institutions. These conceptions include a cultural perspective (Hurtado et al, 1999; Kuh & Love, 2000), a cultural capital perspective (Berger, 2000; Bourdieu, 1977), and institutional theory (Laden, Milem, & Crowson, 2000; Zucker, 1987).

Kuh and Love (2000) propose that the influence of colleges is "inversely related to the cultural distance between a student's culture(s) of origin and the cultures of immersion" (p. 204)—or college cultures. For some students the typical college's values, attitudes, beliefs, and assumptions are familiar, for others they require considerable adjustment. In some cases this adjustment is difficult because the institution's cultures are reflected in a "hidden curriculum" (Margolis, 2001). For example, many classes assume independent work, grading (valuing) students at different levels for specific achievements, and inflexible deadlines. Kuh and Love contend that finding an enclave, or group of supportive students, is important in developing a sense of belonging, which is necessary for successful adaptation. Such groups provide positive regard for the student as well as suggestions for coping strategies in dealing with the expectations of the institution. Often these groups are not the conventional ones; rather, they are composed of students and sometimes faculty with a cultural origin similar to the student's.

Rendon et al. (2000) also use a cultural perspective but place more emphasis on a critique of the assimilation or acculturation assumptions of some models of college impact. They challenge the assumption that students must adopt the culture of the institution in order to be successful. Instead, they discuss the concept of dual socialization in which it is not assumed that one culture is superior to the other. The work of "converging two worlds requires the use of cultural translators, mediators, and role models to (1) provide information and guidance that can help students decipher unfamiliar college customs and rituals, (2) mediate problems that arise from disjunctions between students' cultural traits and the prevailing campus culture, and (3) model behaviors that are amenable with the norms, values, and beliefs of the majority and minority cultures" (pp. 137–138).

In this process, support and encouragement from family and friends from the culture of origin is important. Research suggests that this support helps to "negate discriminatory experiences, enhance the social and academic integration of students, and positively affect students' commitments" (Rendon et al., p. 140). In addition cultural translators, mediators, and role models are needed to negotiate the expectations of colleges. Finally, this approach emphasizes the role of the validation of students.

A second emerging view emphasizing the role of social reproduction and cultural capital is presented by Berger (2000). Drawing on the analyses of Bourdieu (1971, 1977), a number of researchers have investigated the experiences that students from different socioeconomic classes bring to college and the effects of those experiences on their adaptation to college. For example, students who have always assumed they would go to college, received private music lessons, traveled broadly, attended a range of cultural events, and met prominent people come to college with very different perspectives from first-generation students who have needed to work to contribute to their families' incomes. These perspectives produce what Bourdieu terms a *habitus* or a "system of lasting, transposable dispositions which, integrating past experiences, functions at every moment as *a matrix of perceptions, appreciations, and actions*" (1971, p. 83). "In other words, people who live similar lifestyles because of their common level of access to capital develop a shared worldview as a result of common experiences and interaction. This habitus fosters a common representation of the world in a class-specific manner at a cognitive, taken-for-granted level" (Berger, 2000, p. 99). People from similar class backgrounds share a common habitus, and interactions with others from the same class tend to reinforce it. Thus, interactions with the peer group as well as teachers are important in the process of accumulating cultural capital.

The other major conception is that institutions vary in the extent to which they serve the interests of students from different classes. Thus, attendance at elite universities is part of the habitus of upper-class students, and these institutions promote the idea that attendance at them promises greater individual success. As a consequence, institutions vary in the extent to which their students come from different classes. The peer cultures of the institutions reflect the differing habitus of the students who attend. Likewise, faculty may tend to interact with students with different levels of cultural capital differently.

Connecting these ideas, Berger (2000) proposes several propositions based on the match between the students' and the colleges' levels of cultural capital. Although students with higher levels of cultural capital are expected to be more successful across all institutions, they are especially likely to be successful at colleges with high levels of cultural capital, becoming integrated into the academic and social systems of the institution. Likewise, students with lower levels of cultural capital are expected to be more successful and integrated at institutions with low cultural capital.

The third area of new theorizing on college outcomes is in institutional theory. Although much work in this field has focused on change and stability in organizations in response to the environments with which they interact, Laden et al. (2000) have made provocative suggestions for how it can be applied to student outcomes. They note that institutions develop shared social realities, values, assumptions, and routine behaviors and also note that institutions often have considerable discretion in the use of their resources. They suggest that researchers could learn a great deal by examining the colleges that are highly effective in affecting student outcomes, even when they might not be expected to, given their resources or prestige. In effect, the question is, "What would a college devoted to student success look like; what would its organization, budgets, curriculum, programs and habitual behaviors be?" An example of this kind of analysis is provided by Wolf-Wendel (2000) who studied five colleges with records of producing unusually high percentages of women graduates who went on to earn a doctorate or to be listed in *Who's Who.* The study found that the colleges had eight attributes: high academic expectations, a clear sense of mission and history, positive role models, a supportive and caring environment, leadership opportunities, opportunities to learn about oneself, a high-achieving peer culture, and student connection to their communities.

These three newer approaches to understanding student-institution interaction use different theoretical ideas, but they share the common perspective of analyzing the process as involving varied students and varied institutions. They also are greatly enriched by the use of qualitative methods. Understanding this variability through a theoretical lens can help student affairs professionals see the aspects of their own practices that help or hinder the progress of students.

Reconceptualizing Outcomes

For many years, outcomes were described with grandiose rhetoric like that found in college catalogs. In more recent times there have been attempts to make the goals of a college education more specific and, importantly, better related to specific educational programs. Dressell (1976) summarized the logic:

> If students are expected to develop a degree of independence in pursuit of learning, reach a satisfactory level of skill in communication, demonstrate sensitivity to their own values and those of their associates, become capable of collaborating with peers in defining and resolving problems, be able to recognize the relevance of their increasing knowledge to the current scene, and seek continually for insightful understanding and organization of their total educational experience . . . outcomes must be specifically stated. In addition, they must be made explicit in relation to learning experiences and by providing opportunities for demonstration of the developing behavior and for evaluation of it. Content, subject matter, and behavior are interrelated and must be so construed by teachers, students, and evaluators. This requires an interrelated trinity of conceptual statements defining the

objectives of operational statements, indicating how the behavior is to be evoked and appraised, and providing standards for deciding whether progress is evident and whether accomplishment is finally satisfactory" [p. 303].

Summarizing the thinking since Dressell's work, Winston and Miller (1994) found some commonality in outcome taxonomies across writers and groups as diverse as Howard Bowen (1977) and the Southern Association of Colleges and Schools (1992). According to Winston and Miller, eight "developmental themes" run through these taxonomies: academic development, cultural development, emotional development, intellectual development, moral development, physical development, development of purpose, and social-interpersonal development. Like Dressell, Winston and Miller emphasized the importance of making developmental goals specific, of linking them to specific curricular and cocurricular programs and developing methods for assessment that can be used to evaluate students' progress toward achieving these goals. As these authors suggest, the logic, the assessment methods, and even the goals themselves have remained much the same for many years. Indeed, as Pace (1993) suggests, there were many imaginative and diverse attempts to assess student movement toward desired outcomes in the 1930s.

How have these long-dormant concepts changed in recent times? Perhaps the most important change is in the nature of the goals, as opposed to their content. As both Schuh and Upcraft (2000) and Gardiner, Anderson, and Cambridge (1997) have suggested, colleges can reach general agreement on outcomes; however, outcomes have traditionally been thought of in individualistic terms and, paradoxically, as defined by the institution. There is a growing recognition of the importance of community-oriented outcomes and, again paradoxically, student individuality. The basic approach was to emphasize individual achievement in terms of "independence, self-reliance, self-motivation, personal responsibility, and other personal traits" (King, 1994, p. 414). The constellation of values that these outcomes reflect are deeply embedded in our culture (Boyer, 1987; Noddings, 1984). The consequence is that outcomes are thought of as involving individual success, to be assessed by individual measures and evaluated only in terms of individual achievement. Ironically, these outcomes have been regarded as so obvious that there has apparently been no effort to consider individual students' definition of them. Thus institutions have considered themselves as the natural and appropriate source of outcome goals. The college outlines student goals, defines their meaning for students, and decides on ways to assess student progress toward meeting them.

In contrast, it has been argued that the emerging society of the twenty-first century will require a set of skills and attitudes that are much more community-oriented and will be needed in both the workplace and in private life (Power, Higgins, & Kohlberg, 1989). As summarized by King (1994), these attributes include "interdependence and altruism, creating just and caring communities, showing compassion and respect . . . being productive, responsible, honest and compassionate members of many communities," and knowing that "being part of a community requires some degree of involvement and positive identification, and demonstrating that making individual sacrifices is sometimes necessary for the good of the community" (p. 414).

Thus, an emerging paradigm shift in our society may be from individualistic to community-oriented goals. Although the outcomes trends that such goals suggest are not widely recognized in most assessment schemes, they are part of many conceptions of liberal education (for example, see Heath, 1968; Oakley, 1992). Indeed, there has been much discussion among college presidents and administrators in recent years of the need to foster a sense of community in higher education.

One of the implications of a sense of community is respect both for individuals' personal goals and for their needs as members of various groups and subgroups (Jones, 1990). This perspective is important to many specific groups of students now entering higher education in increasing numbers (Rendon et al., 2000). As King (1994) points out, this "perspective is found among Asian/Pacific Americans, American Indians, African Americans, and Hispanic Americans, whose cultural experiences and values offer many insights for fostering community values on college campuses, as well as for preparing students to live and work effectively in a multicultural society" (p. 416). Thus, the stance for colleges and universities increasingly will be to work with students in defining their own goals as they consider their personal needs and plans and the definitions and outcomes of the institution. This process will involve a negotiation between student and institutional definitions of outcomes. An emerging role for student affairs professionals is to serve as negotiators or brokers between colleges and students so that both may make progress toward the goals they desire. The student affairs professional may then not only help students clarify what they desire from their collegiate experience but also help institutions develop a strategy for merging their desired outcomes with those of each student. The result should be a procedure that will appropriately recognize the needs of students and simultaneously reflect the responsibility of the institution to meet its stated goals. Individualized goals call for an equally individualized assessment and evaluation procedure that will provide evidence of students' progress toward attaining their personal goals and those of the institution. This would represent a major shift from the practice of defining outcomes solely in terms of the institution's desires to one where the student is recognized as a partner in defining the meaning of his or her education (Stark, 1991; Stark, Shaw, & Lowther, 1989). This approach has already been recommended for working with the increasing number of adults on our campuses (for example, see Schlossberg, Lynch, & Chickering, 1989). It also often entails the use of qualitative approaches to research.

The change in focus from individualistic to community-oriented outcomes necessitates a similar shift in our conception of the college experience. That is, as we emphasize community-oriented outcomes, we must also emphasize community-oriented processes. The educational approaches that match community-oriented outcomes are different from the traditional, individualistic approach. Not surprisingly, they emphasize collaboration, cooperation, and interaction. A movement toward these ideals can be seen in the concept of learning communities (Lenning & Ebbers, 1999). The orientations of learning communities, as contrasted to traditional communities, are summarized by Smith (1993).

Clearly, the outcomes emphasized in learning communities focus on students' definitions of their goals as well as on institutional definitions. Learning communities attempt to help students and institutions collaborate in making progress toward achieving their respective desired outcomes. One of the additional positive consequences of working toward the outcomes needed for learning communities is that students obtain skills needed for citizenship in our society. As listed by Morse (1989), these include an attitude of thoughtfully considering problems and issues and the ability to apply methods of logical reasoning and inquiry. Thus an emphasis on learning communities can be quite consistent with the traditional goals of a liberal education; and a major potential task for student affairs professionals is to help colleges become learning communities (Lenning & Ebbers, 1999; Matthews, Smith, McGregor, & Gabelnick, 1997).

Whatever the conception of outcomes, student affairs professionals should recognize the difficulties in defining and assessing them (Pickering & Hanson, 2000; Schuh & Upcraft, 2000). The technical problems are succinctly described by Banta and Associates (1993): "The issues of comparability, relevance, reliability, and sensitivity to change are but a few of the measurement problems that educators face in attempting to provide the evidence of learning and satisfaction that will serve the purposes of accountability and of improvement. . . . Indeed, student outcomes are so complex and multifaceted that we may never be able to derive simple linear cause-effect relationships between what the faculty and staff put into the college experience and what students take away" (p. 362).

Implications for Student Affairs Practice

The perspectives drawn from the research described above have numerous implications for student affairs professionals. Although the research is often complex, and an understanding of the web of interrelated influences on any outcome can become difficult to achieve, the findings do form a distinct pattern.

First, the diversity in students' cultural backgrounds, personal characteristics, approaches to learning, and developmental status leads to a wide variety in student educational goals. Further, the ways in which students can most effectively attain their goals also vary. Clearly, the extent to which students' goals mesh with those of their institution can have a powerful effect on what they learn and the ways they grow. The extent to which institutions help students integrate their goals with those of the institution also has a powerful impact. This implies that institutions must also change to meet the needs of the student. That is, progress toward academic and social integration, to use the terms used in the impact models, is a mutual process. Also, the extent to which institutional goals emphasize students' personal development and individuation influences student change. This process may be quite difficult for institutions committed to research. Student affairs professionals have particularly large challenges in such institutions.

Thus, because of the differences in students' characteristics and goals, the ways in which students change and interact with their environment are critical. Environments that lead to greater involvement and integration have been shown to be more effective than those that do not. Likewise, students play a large role in creating the environment they inhabit. Therefore, students bear a responsibility for the educations they attain. Colleges that respect and encourage students' individuality *and* responsibility for their own careers are not only more effective but are more satisfying places to study and teach (Kuh et al., 1991).

When we apply the approach of respect for students' individuality and responsibility to college outcomes, we see the importance of including personal development as well as intellectual outcomes (Winston & Miller, 1994). Research suggests that these kinds of outcomes are most affected by involvement with peers and faculty (Astin, 1993; Pascarella & Terenzini, 1991). Likewise, the most effective way to increase positive involvement is to create a college culture that promotes involvement (that is, to create learning communities).

However, it is important to recognize that involvement has been defined in many different ways and related to many different criteria (Hernandez et al., 1999). As Kuh and Love (2000) and Rendon et al. (2000) have pointed out, the connections between students and institutions may be established in very different ways among students from different cultures of origins. In particular, the need for negotiators between cultures and validation of students may be critical.

The consequences for student affairs professionals of these reconceptualizations are numerous. If the argument put forward in this chapter is correct, the implication is that student affairs professionals should attempt to create learning communities that encourage student involvement and engagement. They should do this by creating the conditions for an active student life, which includes serving as negotiators between students and the institution so that students can become co-creators of their educational outcomes. This role may be especially important for students whose culture of origin is distant from that of the college. These outcomes should include goals for personal development and recognition of students' individuality, based as much on or more than their approach to thinking and learning as on their background. The end result will be a culture of responsibility and mutual respect. To promote learning and development, institutions need to place the responsibility for students' education in students' own hands; at the same time, institutions have a responsibility to help students learn how to handle this responsibility. The best way to create such mutual responsibility is to create a culture that promotes the process of negotiating individual and institutional goals. Such a culture necessarily involves mutual respect.

Any such program of culture creation needs to pay special attention to the nontraditional students described at the beginning of this chapter. For many students, college is not the most important force in their lives. One goal should be to find ways to encourage positive involvement among all students, wherever that involvement takes place. Students who are supported at home or by external community members should be encouraged to reinforce these positive involvements. Involvement with the college should add to, not compete with, outside involvements. Another task for student affairs professionals is to create a culture where students can sort out their own commitments and find ways to integrate them synergistically.

This altered role for student affairs professionals means that they need to be as concerned with (and proficient at) shaping culture as they are with working with individual students (Hamilton, 1994; Hurtado et al., 1999). Also, they must often be the advocates for students' point of view, since students have relatively little power on most campuses. As Silverman (1980) asserts, "Our uniqueness as student personnel workers rests on our ability to fashion significant educational environments, using the resources, values, norms, and opportunities of the variety of constituencies on our campuses. To the extent that we are successful in our innovative work, we will be respected, not because of position, but as a result of the impacts we have on campus life. Truly, student personnel workers have the opportunities to be central figures for campus improvement in an era when resources must be perceived as newly combined rather than as new" (p. 12).

The complexity of these efforts underlines not only the importance of working with students but also the critical role of collaboration with others on the campus. The many discussions of the *Student Learning Imperative* (see Whitt, 1999) indicate the need for cooperative venture with academic affairs administrators and professors. Pickering and Hanson (2000) discuss the many issues in productive collaboration between student affairs and institutional researchers. Astin (1999) discusses how student affairs professionals can use national research results and research from other campuses to help students learn and develop. As noted earlier, it is useful to foster collaboration with the major elements of a campus. Research results almost always show that many aspects of college as well as students' backgrounds affect positive student outcomes. Thus working productively in a common effort is much more likely to yield successful results than working alone. Schroeder elaborates these points in Chapter Twenty-Nine. These conceptions are similar to those of the "learning organization," a concept promoted by Senge (1990) and widely discussed in the corporate arena.

Thus student affairs professionals can play a powerful, if unorthodox, role in their institution's life. As cocreators and maintainers of a culture of responsibility and respect, they can become the leaders of the emerging campuses of the new millennium.

Directions for Future Research

Although it is hazardous to project into the future, the reconceptualizations discussed in this chapter suggest some areas where more work is needed. Each reconceptualization suggests further work in theory, methods, and practice. It may be helpful to consider each reconceptualization in turn.

Students

The increased diversity of students presents challenges to traditional, monolithic conceptions of student development (Evans, Forney, & Guido-diBrito, 1998; King &

Howard-Hamilton, 2000). One theoretical question is whether multiple models of development are needed or whether existing models are so robust that they can encompass this diversity. If traditional models are to be used, how do they need to be altered? If multiple models are needed, on what personal qualities should they be based—age, cohort, gender, ethnicity, social class, or cultural background? Should they be "grand theories" concerned with the total person or "midlevel theories" to be used on particular aspects of development, such as ethnic or racial identity or adaptation to academic material? A major methodological challenge lies in finding ways to assess either reworked traditional models or new models (Perl & Noldon, 2000). Research on developing such methods and assessing the development of diverse groups of students is greatly needed. A major challenge for professional practice lies in finding ways to work with diverse kinds of students and ways to engage part-time, commuter, and older students with the life of the campus.

Environments

A much better theoretical basis is needed for understanding how environments are formed, sustained, and changed. Student affairs professionals might look to sociological theories based on conflict, exchange, or interactionist approaches (Turner, Beeghley, & Powers, 1995). These approaches are used extensively in sociological studies, on a wide variety of topics. Another methodological concern is the quality of the measures used to assess the nature of the colleges students attend, students' experiences within those colleges, and—perhaps most important—how students interact with and are affected by their college and experiences. Pace's *College Student Experiences Questionnaire* (1993) and Kuh's *National Survey of Student Engagement* (2000) provide excellent beginnings toward mapping and measuring how students interact with their institution, but much more work is needed, both conceptually and technically (Baird, 1988). In general, we need to pay much closer attention to measurement issues.

Student–College Interactions

A set of research issues concerns how to influence the formation, sustenance, and change of environments and cultures (Blimling, Whitt, & Associates, 1999). The very diversity of student bodies today creates challenges for the formation of new campus cultures. On the other hand, the forces of tradition and entropy make changing an existing campus culture difficult. Both areas need to be addressed in the years ahead.

Outcomes

A major challenge for outcomes theory lies in explicating the place of community in defining outcomes. Combining individually chosen outcomes within a community framework requires the reworking of philosophical ideas and psychological and sociological theory. This shift in thinking is mirrored in the challenge of assessing individually chosen outcomes and identifying and providing evidence on the development of communities (Smith & Mather, 2000). How can communities of learning really be created and sustained? How can the entropy and resistance of those segments of a campus that are committed to traditional ways of doing things be overcome?

Conclusion

In all of this, the people on campus—students, faculty, staff, and student affairs professionals—need to seek ways to come together as well as respect and affirm their differences. As Sanford (1962) wrote over forty years ago, that differentiation is an

> essential feature of development, in a college or in an individual. But it increases the necessity of integration, which must keep pace, if fragmentation is not to be the final outcome. One basis for unity in the college could be its concerted attempt to find rational solutions to its educational problems. Here at least is something that all teachers can discuss together; here is an intellectual inquiry in which all can take part. The more the college becomes diversified and the more it finds integration in this kind of intellectual cooperation, the more will it do to make its students as complex and as a whole as they are capable of becoming [p. 1033].

References

Anderson, M. (Ed.). (1998). *The experience of being in graduate school: An exploration* (New Directions in Higher Education No. 101). San Francisco: Jossey-Bass.

Astin, A. W. (1993). *What matters in college: Four critical years revisited.* San Francisco: Jossey-Bass.

Astin, A. W. (1994). *The American freshman: National norms for fall 1994.* Los Angeles: University of California, Higher Education Research Institute.

Astin, A. W. (1999). "Involvement in learning" revisited: Lessons we have learned. *Journal of College Student Development, 40,* 587–598.

Astin, A. W. (2000). The American college student: Three decades of change. In J. Loslo & B. L. Fife (Eds.), *Higher education in transition: The challenges of the new millennium* (pp. 7–27). Westport, CT: Bergin and Garvey.

Baird, L. L. (1988). The college environment revisited: A review of research and theory. In J. C. Smart (Ed.), *Higher education: Handbook for theory and research* (Vol. 4, pp. 1–52). New York: Agathon Press.

Baird, L. L. (1990). Campus climate: Using surveys of policy and understanding. In W. G. Tierney (Ed.), *Assessing academic climates and cultures* (New Directions for Institutional Research No. 68, pp. 35–46). San Francisco: Jossey-Bass.

Banta, T. W., & Associates. (1993). *Making a difference: Outcomes of a decade of assessment in higher education.* San Francisco: Jossey-Bass.

Baxter Magolda, M. B. (Ed.). (2000). *Teaching to promote intellectual and personal maturity: Incorporating students worldviews and identities into the learning process* (New Directions for Teaching and Learning No. 82). San Francisco: Jossey-Bass.

Berger, J. B. (2000). Optimizing capital, social reproduction, and undergraduate persistence. In J. M. Braxton (Ed.), *Reworking the student departure puzzle* (pp. 95–124). Nashville: Vanderbilt University Press.

Blimling, G. S., Whitt, E. J., & Associates (Eds.). (1999). *Good practice in student affairs: Principles to foster student learning.* San Francisco: Jossey-Bass.

Bonwell, C. C., & Eison, J. A. (1991). *Active learning: Creating excitement in the classroom.* Washington, DC: Association for the Study of Higher Education.

Bourdieu, P. (1971). Systems of education and systems of thought. In M.F.D. Young (Ed.), *Knowledge and control: New directions for the sociology of education* (pp. 189–207). London: Collier-MacMillan.

Bourdieu, P. (1977). *Outline of a theory of practice.* Cambridge: Cambridge University Press.

Bowen, H. R. (1977). *Investment in learning.* San Francisco: Jossey-Bass.

Boyer, E. L. (1987). *College: The undergraduate experience in America.* New York: Harper & Row.

Braxton, J. M. (Ed.) (2000). *Reworking the student departure puzzle.* Nashville: Vanderbilt University Press.

Claxton, C. S., & Murrell, P. H. (1987). *Learning styles: Implications for improving educational practices* (ASHE-ERIC Higher Education Report No. 4). Washington, DC: Association for the Study of Higher Education.

Davis, T. M., & Murrell, P. H. (1993). *Turning teaching into learning: The role of student responsibility in the collegiate experience* (ASHE-ERIC Higher Education Report No. 8). Washington, DC: George Washington University.

Denzin, N. K., & Lincoln, Y. S. (Eds.). (1994). *Handbook of qualitative research.* Newbury Park, CA: Sage.

Dressell, P. L. (1976). *Handbook of academic evaluation: Assessing institutional effectiveness, student progress, and professional performance for decision making in higher education.* San Francisco: Jossey-Bass.

Evans, N. J., Forney, D. S., & Guido-diBrito, F. (1998). *Student development in college: Theory, research and practice.* San Francisco: Jossey-Bass.

Gardiner, L., Anderson, D., & Cambridge, B. (1997). *Learning through assessment: A resource guide for higher education.* Washington, DC: American Association for Higher Education.

Hackman, J. D. (1992). What's going on in higher education? Is it time for a change? *Review of Higher Education, 16,* 10–16.

Hall, R., & Sandler, B. (1984). *The classroom climate: A chilly one for women?* Washington, DC: Project on the Status and Education of Women, Association of American Colleges.

Hamilton, S. J. (1994). Freedom transformed: Toward a developmental model for the construction of collaborative learning environments. In K. Bosworth & S. J. Hamilton (Eds.), *Collaborative learning: Underlying processes and effective techniques* (pp. 93–102). San Francisco: Jossey-Bass.

Hartnett, R. T. (1971). *Accountability in higher education: A consideration of some of the problems of assessing college impacts.* New York: College Entrance Examination Board.

Haworth, J. G. (1996). Assessment in graduate and professional education: Present realities, future prospects. In J. G. Haworth (Ed.), *Assessing graduate and professional education: Current realities, future prospects* (New Directions for Institutional Research No. 92, pp. 89–97). San Francisco: Jossey-Bass.

Haworth, J. G. (2000). Learning experiences that make a difference: Findings from a national study of doctoral education in the profession. Paper presented at the Annual Meeting of the Association for the Study of Higher Education, Sacramento, CA.

Heath, D. (1968). *Growing up in college.* San Francisco: Jossey-Bass.

Hernandez, K., et al. (1999). Analysis of the literature on the impact of student involvement on student development and learning: More questions than answers? *NASPA Journal, 36* (Spring), pp. 184–197.

Hill, J. (2000). *The policy book: Guidance for disability service providers.* Horsham, PA: LRP Publishers.

Horn, L., & Berktold, J. (1999). *Students with disabilities in postsecondary education: A profile of preparation, participation and outcomes.* Washington, DC: U.S. Department of Education, National Center for Educational Statistics.

Howe, N., & Strauss, B. (2000). *Millennials rising: The next great generation.* New York: Vintage Books.

Huebner, L. A., & Lawson, J. M. (1990). Understanding and assessing college environments. In D. Creamer & Associates (Eds.), *College development theory and practice for the 1990s* (pp. 54–63). Alexandria, VA: American College Personnel Association.

Hurtado, S., Milem, J., Clayton-Pederson, A., & Allen, W. (1999). *Enacting diverse learning environments: Improving the climate for racial/ethnic diversity in higher education.* (ASHE-ERIC Higher Education Report 26, No. 8). Washington, DC: George Washington University.

Johnson, D. W., Johnson, R. T., & Smith, K. A. (1991). *Cooperative learning: Increasing college faculty instructional productivity.* Washington, DC: Association for the Study of Higher Education.

Jones, W. T. (1990). Perspectives on ethnicity. In L. V. Moore (Ed.), *Evolving theoretical perspectives on students* (New Directions for Student Services No. 51, pp. 59–72). San Francisco: Jossey-Bass.

King, P. M. (1994). Theories of college student development: Sequences and consequences. *Journal of College Student Development, 35,* 413–421.

King, P. M., & Howard-Hamilton, M. F. (2000). Using student developmental theory to inform institutional research. In J. W. Pickering & G. R. Hanson (Eds.), *Collaboration between student affairs and institutional researchers to improve institutional effectiveness* (New Directions for Institutional Research No. 108). San Francisco: Jossey-Bass.

Kuh, G. D. (2000). *The national survey of student engagement: Conceptual framework and overview of psychometric properties.* Bloomington: Indiana University Center for Postsecondary Research and Planning.

Kuh, G. D., & Love, P. G. (2000). A cultural perspective on student departure. In J. M. Braxton (Ed.), *Reworking the student departure puzzle.* Nashville: Vanderbilt University Press.

Kuh, G. D., Schuh, J. H., Whitt, E. J., & Associates. (1991). *Involving colleges: Successful approaches to fostering student learning and development outside the classroom.* San Francisco: Jossey-Bass.

Kuk, L. (1990). Perspectives on gender differences. In L. V. Moore (Ed.), *Evolving theoretical perspectives on students* (New Directions for Student Services No. 51, pp. 25–36). San Francisco: Jossey-Bass.

Laden, B. V., Milem, J. F., & Crowson, R. L. (2000). New institutional theory and student departure. In J. M. Braxton (Ed.), *Reworking the student departure puzzle.* Nashville: Vanderbilt University Press.

Lawrence, B., Weathersby, G., & Patterson, V. W. (Eds.). (1970). *The outputs of higher education: Their identification, measurement, and evaluation.* Boulder, CO: Western Interstate Commission for Higher Education.

Lenning, O. T., & Ebbers, L. H. (1999). *The powerful potential of learning communities.* (ASHE-ERIC Higher Education Reports 26, No. 6). Washington, DC: George Washington University.

Levine, A., & Cureton, J. S. (1998). *When hope and fear collide: A portrait of today's college student.* San Francisco: Jossey-Bass.

Loacker, G., & Mentkowski, M. (1993). Creating a culture where assessment improves learning. In T. W. Banta & Associates, *Making a difference: Outcomes of a decade of assessment in higher education* (pp. 5–74). San Francisco: Jossey-Bass.

Margolis, E. M. (Ed.). (2001). *The hidden curriculum in higher education.* New York: Routledge.

Matthews, R. S., Smith, B. L., MacGregor, J., & Gabelnick, F. (1997). Creating learning communities. In J. G. Gaff & J. L. Ratcliff (Eds.), *Handbook of the undergraduate curriculum.* San Francisco: Jossey-Bass.

Morse, S. W. (1989). *Renewing civic capacity: Preparing college students for service and citizenship.* (ASHE-ERIC Higher Education, Report 8). Washington, DC: Association for the Study of Higher Education.

National Center for Education Statistics. (1995). *Digest of education statistics.* Washington, DC: U.S. Department of Health and Human Services.

Noddings, N. (1984). *Caring: A feminine approach to ethics and moral education.* Berkeley: University of California Press.

Oakley, F. (1992). *Community of learning: The American college and the liberal arts tradition.* New York: Oxford University Press.

Pace, C. R. (1993). Foreword. In T. W. Banta & Associates, *Making a difference: Outcomes of a decade of assessment in higher education.* San Francisco: Jossey-Bass.

Pascarella, E. T. (1985). College environmental influences on learning and cognitive development: A critical review and synthesis. In J. C. Smart (Ed.), *Higher education: Handbook of theory and research* (Vol. 1, pp. 1–62). New York: Agathon Press.

Pascarella, E. T., & Terenzini, P. T. (1991). *How college affects students: Findings and insights from twenty years of research.* San Francisco: Jossey-Bass.

Pascarella, E. T., & Terenzini, P. T. (1998). Studying college students in the 21st century: Meeting new challenges. *Review of Higher Education, 21,* 151–165.

Pascarella, E. T., Truckenmiller, R., Nora, A., Terenzini, P. T., Edison, M., & Hagedorn, L. S. (1999). Cognitive impacts of intercollegiate participation: Some further evidence. *Journal of Higher Education, 70,* 1–26.

Perl, E. J., & Noldon, D. F. (2000). Overview of student affairs research methods: Qualitative and quantitative. In J. W. Pickering & G. R. Hanson (Eds.), *Collaboration between student affairs and institutional researchers to improve institutional effectiveness* (New Directions for Institutional Research No. 108). San Francisco: Jossey-Bass.

Pickering, J. W., & Hanson, G. R. (Eds.). (2000). *Collaboration between student affairs and institutional researchers to improve institutional effectiveness* (New Directions for Institutional Research No. 108). San Francisco: Jossey-Bass.

Power, F. C., Higgins, A., & Kohlberg, L. (1989). *Lawrence Kohlberg's approach to moral education.* New York: Columbia University Press.

Rendon, L. I., Jalomo, R. E., & Nora, A. (2000). Theoretical considerations in the study of minority student retention in higher education. In J. M. Braxton (Ed.), *Reworking the student departure puzzle.* Nashville: Vanderbilt University Press.

Rodgers, R. F. (1991). Using theory in practice in student affairs. In T. K. Miller, R. B. Watson, Jr., & Associates (Eds.), *Administration and leadership in student affairs: Actualizing student development in higher education* (pp. 203–255). Muncie, IN: Accelerated Development.

Sagaria, M. A., & Johnsrud, L. K. (1991). Recruiting, advancing, and retaining minorities in student affairs: Moving from rhetoric to results. *NASPA Journal, 28,* 5–20.

Sanford, N. (1962). Research and policy in higher education. In N. Sanford (Ed.), *The American college: A psychological and social interpretation of the higher learning* (pp. 1009–1034). New York: Wiley.

Schlossberg, N. K., Lynch, A. Q., & Chickering, A. W. (1989). *Improving higher education environments for adults: Responsive programs and services from entry to departure.* San Francisco: Jossey-Bass.

Schuh, J. H., & Upcraft, M. L. (2000). *Assessment in student affairs: An applications manual.* San Francisco: Jossey-Bass.

Senge, P. M. (1990). *The fifth discipline: The art and practice of the learning organization.* New York: Doubleday.

Silverman, R. J. (1980). The student personnel worker as leading-edge leader. *NASPA Journal, 18,* 10–15.

Smith, B. L. (1993, Fall). Creating learning communities. *Liberal Education,* 32–39.

Smith, D. G., & Schonfeld, N. B. (2000). The benefits of diversity: What the research tells us. *About Campus, 5* (5), 16–23.

Smith, K. M., & Mather, P. C. (2000). Best practices in student affairs research. In J. W. Pickering & G. R. Hanson (Eds.), *Collaboration between student affairs and institutional researchers to improve institutional effectiveness* (New Directions for Institutional Research No. 108). San Francisco: Jossey-Bass.

Southern Association of Colleges and Schools. (1992). *Criteria for accreditation: Commission on colleges, 1992–1993 edition.* Decatur, GA: Author.

Spady, W. (1971). Dropouts from higher education: Toward an empirical model. *Interchange, 2* (3), 38–62.

Stark, J. S. (1991). *Student goals exploration user's manual: Institutional research guide.* Ann Arbor: University of Michigan Press.

Stark, J. S., Shaw, K. M., & Lowther, M. A. (1989). *Student goals for college and courses: A missing link in assessing and improving academic achievement.* Washington, DC: Association for the Study of Higher Education.

Stewart, D. W. (1993). *Immigration and higher education: The crisis and the opportunities.* New York: Lexington Books.

Terenzini, P. T., & Pascarella, L. T. (1994). Living with myths: Undergraduate education in America. *Change, 26,* 28–32.

Tidball, M. E., Smith, D. G., Tidball, C. S., & Wolf-Wendel, L. E. (1999). *Taking women seriously: Lessons and legacies for educating the majority.* American Council on Education/Oryx Press Series on Higher Education. Washington, DC: American Council on Education.

Tierney, W. G. (Ed.). (1990). *Assessing academic climates and cultures* (New Directions for Institutional Research No. 68). San Francisco: Jossey-Bass.

Tierney, W. G. (2000). Power, identity, and the dilemma of college student departure. In J. M. Braxton (Ed.), *Reworking the student departure puzzle.* Nashville: Vanderbilt University Press.

Tinto, V. (1975). Dropouts from higher education: A theoretical synthesis of recent research. *Review of Educational Research, 45,* 89–125.

Turner, J. H., Beeghley, L., & Powers, C. H. (1995). *The emergence of sociological theory* (3rd ed.). Belmont, CA: Wadsworth.

Weidman, J. (1989). Undergraduate socialization: A conceptual approach. In J. C. Smart (Ed.), *Higher education: Handbook of theory and research* (Vol. 5, pp. 289–322). New York: Agathon Press.

Whitt, E. J. (Ed.). (1999). *Student learning as student affairs work: Responding to our imperative.* Washington, DC: National Association of Student Personnel Administrators.

Winston, R. B., & Miller, T. K. (1994). A model for assessing developmental outcomes related to student affairs programs and services. *NASPA Journal, 32,* 2–19.

Wolf-Wendel, L. E. (2000). Women-friendly campuses: What five institutions are doing right. *Review of Higher Education, 23,* 319–345.

Zucker, L. G. (1987). Institutional theories of organization. *Annual Review of Sociology, 13,* 443–464.

CHAPTER TWENTY-NINE

USING THE LESSONS OF RESEARCH TO DEVELOP PARTNERSHIPS

Charles C. Schroeder

Colleges and universities across the country are being confronted with such major challenges as shifting demographics, increasingly diverse student populations, changing economic agendas, increased emphasis on access, affordability, and accountability, accusations of inefficiency, duplication and waste, a widening gap between ideal academic standards and actual student learning, and eroding public trust. In response to these challenges, widely heralded reports have presented clarion calls for reform of higher education (Boyer Commission on Educating Undergraduates in the Research University, 1998; Kellogg Commission on the Future of State and Land-Grant Universities, 1998, 2000; Wingspread Group on Higher Education, 1993). These reports highlight particular concerns regarding the fragmented and specialized curriculum, the lack of clarity about goals and purposes, and the importance of integrating out-of-class experiences with the educational mission of the institution. They emphasize the need to connect undergraduate academic experiences with student services, learning, and development. And, they all stress the importance of putting student learning first. The Kellogg Commission emphasized this theme in their 1998 report, *Returning to Our Roots: The Student Experience*: "As we understand the term, learning is not something reserved for classrooms or degreed programs. It is available to every member of the academic community, whether in the classroom or the administration building, the laboratory or the library, the residence halls or the performing arts center . . . learning is available to all and all serve learning" (p. 17).

Student affairs has responded to these challenges and the need to put student learning first by embracing three seminal documents: *The Student Learning Imperative* (SLI) (ACPA, 1994); *Principles of Good Practice for Student Affairs* (ACPA & NASPA, 1997); and *Powerful Partnerships: A Shared Responsibility for Learning* (AAHE, ACPA, & NASPA, 1998). These documents urge directing resources and efforts to facilitating student learning and development by creating learning-oriented student affairs divisions that collaborate with academic colleagues to create effective policies and programs. The primacy of forging strong educational partnerships was stressed by the authors of the Powerful Partnerships document: "Only when everyone on campus—particularly academic affairs and student affairs staff—share the responsibility for student learning will we be able to make significant progress in improving it . . . it is only by acting cooperatively in the context of common goals, that our accumulated understanding about learning is put to best use" (p. 1).

Enhancing student learning and success through effective educational partnerships is best achieved by applying important lessons from the research on student learning and institutional specific data (ACPA, 1994; ACPA & NASPA, 1997). By doing so, personnel in academic affairs and student affairs can significantly improve the quality of undergraduate education on their campuses.

The purpose of this chapter is to demonstrate methods for utilizing information from national research and campus-based assessments to enhance learning and development through collaborative partnerships. The first section provides a brief overview of the major themes gleaned from the literature on student learning and personal development and the institutional conditions that enhance learning and development, particularly collaborative efforts between student affairs and academic affairs. Obstacles and constraints to collaboration are described in the following section. Effective strategies for forging collaborative partnerships are then highlighted along with comprehensive examples that illustrate the impact of partnerships on student learning and success. The chapter concludes with a set of recommendations and implications for the future.

Although the primary focus of this chapter is on forging partnerships between academic and student affairs, other important partnerships may be developed using the lessons of research. These include partnerships within student affairs units, between student affairs and administrative units, campus-community partnerships, and so on. (Schroeder, 1999a).

Overview of Lessons Learned from Research on Student Learning

To significantly strengthen undergraduate education, stronger collaborations between academic affairs and student affairs offices on behalf of student learning are needed (Potter, 1999). The development of collaborative partnerships cannot, however, be based simply on good will and well-intentioned efforts; rather, it must be guided and informed by relevant knowledge from national research and institution-specific data. Timely and relevant data generated through systematic inquiry is especially beneficial in identifying important problems and opportunities of consequence that often lend themselves to a collaborative response. This section highlights major themes from the research on student learning and implications of the themes for enhancing practice through effective partnerships. For a more detailed discussion of research findings and their implications, review Chapter Twenty-Eight.

Because partnerships should be based on a shared vision of undergraduate education, it is essential to define potential learning outcomes that should result from their implementation. In recent years, researchers (Baxter Magolda, Terenzini, & Hutchings, 1999; Kuh, 1993; Pascarella & Terenzini, 1991; and Whitt, 1999) have delineated a number of learning outcome clusters which include the following:

- *Cognitive complexity*—reflective thought, critical thinking, quantitative reasoning, and intellectual flexibility.
- *Knowledge acquisition and application*—understanding knowledge from a range of disciplines and the ability to relate knowledge to daily life.
- *Humanitarianism*—an understanding and appreciation of human differences.
- *Interpersonal and intrapersonal competence*—a coherent, integrative constellation of personal attributes such as identity, self-esteem, confidence, integrity, and sense of civic responsibility.
- *Practical competence*—skills reflected in enhancing the capacity to manage one's personal affairs, to be economically self-sufficient, and vocationally competent.

To this list, Schuh and Upcraft (1998) added two additional outcomes:

- *Academic achievement*—ability to earn satisfactory grades.
- *Persistence*—ability to pursue a degree to graduation.

Baxter Magolda (1999) combined the preceding definitions of student learning into four broad dimensions—cognitive competence; intrapersonal competence; interpersonal competence; and practical competence—that in her view incorporates all the aspects of students' experiences. Utilizing these dimensions, Whitt and Miller (1999) describe aspects of students' out-of-class experiences associated with gains in each of these areas. For example, gains in cognitive competence are associated with such out-of-class experiences as: involvement in a learning community; involvement in campus clubs and organizations; involvement with diverse peers; involvement with peers in course-related activities (such as studying with others, talking with others about ideas presented in class, and so on); student-faculty interaction outside of class; and attending racial-cultural awareness workshops. Experiences associated with gains in interpersonal competence include: involvement in a volunteer service organization; social leadership roles; paraprofessional experiences (such as resident assistant); living on campus (especially in a living-learning residence); and interaction with persons of different races or ethnic backgrounds and of diverse perspectives. A variety of out-of-class experiences contribute to gains in intrapersonal competence: involvement in leadership roles; interaction with diverse peers and faculty; study abroad; and involvement in student organizations. In addition to the preceding experiences, work on or off campus contributes to gains in practical competence.

Important conclusions can be drawn from the literature on the impact of out-of-class experiences on student learning. Whitt and Miller (1999) highlight these as follows:

1. Out-of-class experiences are important for achieving learning outcomes; in fact, these experiences are far more important for students' cognitive development than most faculty and others have believed (Terenzini, Pascarella, & Blimling, 1996).

2. Some out-of-class experiences (such as fraternity and sorority membership, excessive socializing/TV watching, and alcohol and other drug abuse) have a negative impact on desired learning outcomes.
3. Students do learn by being involved; in fact, systematic and sustained engagement in educationally purposeful activities results in gains in each of the four dimensions.
4. Students learn from other people; indeed, the most powerful source of influence on student learning appears to be students' interpersonal interactions with peers, faculty, and others.
5. Learning experiences are cumulative and interrelated. According to Pascarella and Terenzini (1991), a majority of important changes that occur during college are probably the cumulative result of a set of interrelated experiences sustained over an extended period of time (p. 610).

There are a number of important lessons common to national studies on college impacts. First, students need to be engaged; they need to devote significant time and energy to intentionally structured, educationally purposeful activities. Second, learning environments should motivate and inspire students to interact frequently with peers, faculty, and others around compelling intellectual and social activities. And, such experiences should emphasize the importance of making connections—connections that enable coherence and the integration of diverse intellectual and social experiences. Finally, student-learning productivity is enhanced when learning experiences are mutually shaping and reinforcing, complimentary and cumulative over time (Terenzini et al., 1996).

The preceding lessons provide powerful implications for those interested in creating collaborative partnerships to enhance learning. From a structural perspective, ways must be found to promote integrative learning by minimizing the current organizational bifurcation of academic and student affairs. Present boundaries must be blurred to reflect the joint and synergistic effects of students' in- and out-of-class experiences on learning (Baxter Magolda et al., 1999). To accomplish this objective, student affairs, in partnership with faculty, need to couple more tightly the connections between the curriculum and out-of-class life (Kuh, Douglas, Lund, & Ramin-Gyurnek, 1994) to create seamless learning environments. Environments such as these bind together in a whole and continuous fashion what was once believed to be separate and distinct (for example, in-class and out-of-class, curricular and co-curricular) to achieve the seamless coat of learning proposed long ago by Whitehead (1929). Seamless environments link and align people, experiences, and resources in a mutually supporting, complementary fashion to achieve a variety of important learning outcomes. The creation of such environments requires high levels of collaboration so that organizational arrangements and processes can be linked and aligned appropriately (Bloland, Stamatakos, & Rogers, 1996; Schroeder, 1999b). Although more emphasis is being placed on collaboration today than ever before, a variety of obstacles and constraints have made forging educational partnerships, especially between academic affairs and student affairs, elusive and difficult to achieve.

Challenges to Collaboration

Fostering and sustaining effective collaborative partnerships is, first and foremost, hard work. Why? Because there are significant challenges that can serve as barriers to effective collaborative initiatives. In this section, the following challenges will be addressed: fundamental, deeply rooted cultural differences; lack of mutual understanding and respect; fragmented organizational structures; tyranny of custom; and lack of knowledge and a common vision of undergraduate education.

Fundamental Cultural Differences

Perhaps the greatest barriers to forging effective collaborative partnerships are fundamental, deeply rooted cultural differences that manifest themselves within contemporary colleges and universities (Engstrom & Tinto, 2000; Young, 1996). Indeed, today's university community no longer has a culture but rather several cultures, including the faculty, administrative, student affairs, and student cultures, each with its own proponents, dominant values, and expectations. Embedded within these cultures are mental models that reflect basic assumptions and beliefs that guide the thought and behavior of various individuals. Not surprisingly, members of different institutional cultures ascribe different values and meaning to student learning and what matters in undergraduate education (Kuh, 1993; Kuh & Whitt, 1988). Within the faculty culture, what is believed to be important in undergraduate learning is curriculum, teaching, and scholarship—activities that regularly occur within classrooms, laboratories, and studios. Principal activities for faculty include focusing on academic disciplines, facilitating students' intellectual development, and producing knowledge to advance their fields (Blake, 1979, 1996).

Many faculty are not only unaware, but also often disinterested in, students out-of-class activities. Similarly, people in student affairs are often just as disconnected to the academic life of faculty as faculty are to the professional roles and responsibilities of student affairs. At the core of the mental model for student affairs educators is the primacy of the formal cocurriculum and the importance of promoting student involvement in activities that are assumed to foster student development. Issues of importance to faculty—such as research, grants, and tenure—are not on the radar screen of most student affairs educators. Students—particularly traditional-age residential students—have a mental model that is not only opposite, but also often antagonistic, to those of the faculty and student affairs educators. At the core of the traditional-age student mental model is fitting in, being successful academically and socially, making friends, and finding ways to meet the increasingly high cost of their education. Finally, the new majority student (age twenty-five and older) has a mental model very different from the faculty, student affairs educator, or traditional-age students (Arnold & Kuh, 1999). Understanding different mental models is important because well-intentioned efforts to create partnerships often are derailed because of competing assumptions about what constitutes learning and effective undergraduate education (Kuh, 1997).

Not only are there deeply rooted, cultural differences *between* academic affairs and student affairs, similar differences exist *within* these cultures. Internal to the academic culture of faculty are any number of important subcultures. Professional schools, such as law, medicine, and engineering, have cultures quite different from those of arts and sciences. Similarly, the reliance on hard data and experimentation characterizing the natural sciences has no real counterpart in the speculations of the humanities faculty (Kellogg Commission, 2000). Furthermore, faculty disciplinary interests not only affect the way they approach their work but also have a direct impact on student affairs and faculty collaborations (Eimers, 2000).

Faculty are often iconoclastic thinkers in their own field who value creation and dissemination of knowledge and autonomy, whereas student affairs values holistic student development and collaboration. Faculty life is usually centered in the academic department, which arguably is the definitive locus of faculty culture, and faculty may view their department as the last bulwark against a hostile and confusing environment in which outsiders (student affairs administrators, politicians, board members, and so on) may make unreasonable demands and even threaten academic freedom (Lovett, 1994). Finally, institutional rewards for faculty, particularly at Carnegie I institutions, are based on research productivity, scholarship, and teaching rather than on collaborative initiatives with student affairs. Recent research (Kolins, 2000) has revealed, however, tremendous interest on the part of faculty, academic administrators, and student affairs educators in community colleges to collaborate on a range of important issues.

Just as fundamental cultural differences exist within academic affairs, similar differences are evident within student affairs organizations. Blimling (2001) posits four communities of practice in student affairs: student administration, student services, student development, and student learning. Each community operates from a different set of assumptions (mental models) and, as a result, place more or less emphasis on various purposes of student affairs. For example, those embracing the student administration community of practice view student affairs as managers of institutional resources to support students, with the primary outcomes of staff efforts being operational efficiency and effectiveness. In contrast, those that embrace the student learning community of practice view student affairs as an active partner with faculty in the learning mission with the primary outcomes being knowledge, information, skill development, and personal growth (Blimling). Although all communities of practice may exist within the same student affairs organization, one usually assumes primacy over the others.

Communities of practice within any field can play a critical role in embracing or rejecting collaborative initiatives, because: "Information out of the context of the organization's community cannot be integrated effectively. If organizations are forced to adopt a new system that is in conflict with the fundamental assumptions on which the community of practice is based, the organization will resist change. Organizational change that is out of context with the assumptions of the organization cannot succeed" (Blimling, 2001, p. 386).

The preceding quote may explain, at least in part, why many student affairs staff, as well as faculty, are reluctant to journey beyond their organizational boundaries and forge effective partnerships. If certain communities of practice do not place a high value on student learning and undergraduate education, then it is not surprising that members of these communities would be less likely to consider themselves as potential partners in the collaborative process.

Lack of Mutual Understanding and Respect

Because of the cultural differences previously noted, a lack of mutual understanding and respect often exists between the two groups on campus most committed to educating students. Inappropriate behavior, such as faculty-bashing on the part of student affairs educators, reflects biases about faculty as not working hard, caring enough about students, or being unresponsive to students' problems (Creeden, 1996). In contrast, some faculty bash student affairs educators because they view them as anti-intellectuals who create inappropriate cocurricular activities that distract students from the rigors of academic life. Clearly, understanding the biases and cultural norms of each group is essential to building mutual respect. Unless student affairs educators and faculty can acknowledge the unique role, responsibilities, and contributions of each group to the academic enterprise, there is little chance of initiating and sustaining successful partnerships (Blake, 1996).

Fragmented Organizational Structures

In response to burgeoning enrollments, rapid expansion of knowledge, proliferation of disciplines, and increasingly diverse student populations, institutions have attempted to address increased complexity through creating highly specialized, hierarchical organizations. Specialization, in turn, has led to compartmentalization and fragmentation, often resulting in what is popularly described as *functional silos* or *mine shafts.* The authors of a recent reform report put it this way: "Organizationally, we have created an intellectual landscape made up of mine shafts, where most of the mine workers are intent on the essential task of deepening the mine without giving much thought to the need to build corridors linking the shafts (and the miners). We have become so poorly connected that we have greatly fragmented our shared sense of learning, for both students and faculty" (Kellogg Commission, 2000, p. x).

Although functional silos and mine shafts can provide a sense of security, predictability, and comfort to their inhabitants, they often foster insular and self-referencing thinking. These vertical structures, though often effective at promoting interaction within functional units, create obstacles to interaction, coordination, and collaboration between and among units. Developing a shared vision and collective responsibility for that vision is very difficult when fragmentation and compartmentalization foster insularity. This is particularly apparent in student affairs divisions that have become isolated and estranged from the academic mission of their institutions (Bloland et al., 1996).

Tyranny of Custom

Many colleges and universities represented tightly coupled bureaucratic organizations that emphasize control and stability rather than innovation. Within these organizations, divisions and departments strive for certainty and predictability by creating systems to maintain balance and continuity (Schroeder, Nicholls, &

Kuh, 1983; Seymour, 1997). There is often great reluctance to changing established practices that may have worked well, whether or not they are working well currently. Even in the face of overwhelming challenges, many organizations hold fast to what is familiar and are unwilling to make appropriate, and even necessary, changes. Forging effective partnerships, however, requires overcoming this tyranny of custom. Seymour (1995) alludes to the potentially paralyzing influence of routine and conventional practices when he states, "Most organizations have shared assumptions that protect the status quo and provide few opportunities for learning. Standard operating procedures can become so institutionalized that competence becomes associated with how well one adheres to the rules" (p. 101). Overcoming the tyranny of custom, often expressed as an if-it-ain't-broke-don't-fix-it mentality, is a principal leadership challenge for those committed to forging effective educational partnerships.

Lack of Knowledge and Shared Vision of Undergraduate Education

As previously stated, cultural differences, fragmented organizational structures, lack of mutual understanding and respect, and the tyranny of custom can serve as barriers to creating, nurturing, and sustaining effective educational partnerships. For student affairs educators and faculty, another challenge is their lack of knowledge about various dimensions of student learning and environmental conditions that enhance or inhibit them. Both *The Student Learning Imperative* (SLI) (ACPA, 1994) and the *Principles of Good Practice for Student Affairs* (ACPA & NASPA, 1997) emphasize the centrality of the scholarship of application to effective practice. According to the SLI, student affairs policies and programs are based on promising practices from the research on student learning and institutional-specific data (p. 4). Similarly, the *Principles* document (ACPA & NASPA, 1997) states that good practice in student affairs uses systematic inquiry to improve student and institutional performance. Although these statements highlight the critical role that applied knowledge plays in enhancing individual and organizational learning, many, if not most, student affairs educators fail to utilize relevant knowledge gleaned from national research or local sources to inform program and policy debates on their campuses (Pascarella & Whitt, 1999). As Schroeder and Pike (2001) argue, student affairs educators must embrace the scholar-practitioner model if they are to realize the full educational potential of their work. Indeed, generating timely, systematic, and relevant information on problems of consequence is a key strategy for forging collaborative partnerships. Faculty, in particular, value well-designed research and are more willing to engage in collaborative initiatives if those initiatives are well informed by national, as well as locally generated, data.

Collaborative Partnerships: Strategies for Bridging the Great Divide

The process of developing an effective collaborative partnership, whether between or among people, or between units of student affairs and academic affairs, is complex and takes time, energy, and commitment. Before describing appropriate strategies, however, a few words of caution are appropriate. In recent years, collaboration has become quite fashionable in higher education and student affairs. And why not? Collaboration sounds right (Magolda, 2002). So faculty and student affairs administrators may blindly jump on the collaboration bandwagon without carefully considering the merits and liabilities of collaboration. Hence, the first question to ask is: Is collaboration appropriate? If the answer is yes, then the following should be helpful in fostering collaborative partnerships.

One of the initial challenges in partnership formation is to define the nature of partnerships, particularly with regard to distinguishing between the roles of cooperation and collaboration. Even though both are essential attributes of partnerships, too frequently the terms are used interchangeably when, in reality, they are different concepts. As suggested by Stein and Short (2001) cooperative ventures are often short-term with limited objectives, shorter time agreements, and less commitment and investment among participants. Collaborative ventures, in contrast, are often long-term in nature, involve considerable amounts of shared decision making and risk taking, require substantial commitments—to relations and shared learning—and investment on the part of collaborators, and are more likely to require common philosophical ground as participants work to design agreed upon goals and objectives. Mutually constructing shared purposes, challenging one's mental models, and creating high degrees of interdependence and reciprocity are also hallmarks of collaborative partnerships (Engstrom & Tinto, 2000). This approach is in stark contrast to a variety of traditional working groups within higher education—committees, councils, task force, and so on—that are often characterized by cordial and cooperative behaviors, but whose members rarely view themselves as highly invested co-creators, generating something new and innovative from the enterprise. In authentic partnerships, collaborators share work, planning, goal setting, decision making, and problem solving, as well as vision, philosophy, values, and ideas.

Obviously, simply understanding the theoretical underpinnings of collaborative partnerships is insufficient to actually create them. The following strategies gleaned from the literature (Schroeder, 1999a, 1999b; Schroeder, Minor, & Tarkow, 1999a, 1999b; Schuh & Whitt, 1999; Westfall, 1999) can be very useful in guiding the creation of effective partnerships.

1. Collaborative partnerships are usually most successful when they are developed from a common reference point or common purpose—a shared vision of undergraduate education, an important institutional problem (such as poor retention and graduation rates), or a major triggering event (such as accreditation review, budget crisis, externally imposed undergraduate education mandates, and so on). Since organizations and individuals are motivated by opportunities that respond to their self-interests, an initial challenge is identifying important issues or problems of consequence that concern or affect members of the potential partnership. Schroeder (1999a) and Fried (1999) provide lists of relatively common campus problems that lend themselves to a collaborative response.

2. Once common issues or problems are identified, it is necessary to identify potential partners who have a common commitment to addressing the issues, an understanding of relevant campus operations, and the authority to institute and

support changes. It is also essential to determine the primary, as well as ancillary, stakeholders that are central to the partnership and can contribute to it by sharing their expertise and insights. Because effective relationships are the glue that hold partnerships together, it is important to build trust, understanding, and commitment among and between key stakeholders early on in the formation process.

3. Successful partnerships usually involve cross-functional teams, joint planning, and implementation and assessment of mutually agreed upon outcomes. Since collaboration, by definition, involves the co-creation of something new and innovative, processes must be developed that involve all stakeholders in the design and implementation of the project. It is very important to create a sense of team, identify common goals and values, and use these as a foundation upon which to plan and implement the group's vision. Communicating constantly and sharing all relevant information in a timely, comprehensive fashion is equally important as communicating with those who are not directly involved in the partnership but may be impacted later in the process. Also, partners must recognize and accept conflict and differences as natural conditions of collaborative initiatives. As Magolda (2001) suggests, collaborative teams are lightning rods for conflict because they provide space for diverse individuals to interact. Accepting, rather than repressing, conflict is an important consideration for those who desire healthy collaborative communities.

4. Effective partnerships often require new perspectives, such as thinking and acting systemically by linking, aligning, and integrating a variety of resources (human, fiscal, and so on) to achieve desired results. Although potential partners may have an interest in, and a commitment to, solving an important problem of consequence to their institution, they often come from widely variant functions and orientations; hence, it is vitally important to help everyone develop a comprehensive understanding of the effort as a whole and the potential benefits of the project. Early on, opportunities must be created for partners to learn about each other's roles, responsibilities, values, and philosophy and discuss how these affect the planning process as well as desired outcomes for the project. Although it may be time consuming, it is critical to understand the concerns of potential partners early in the partnership development process.

5. Effective partnerships may also require participants to step out of their comfort zones, challenge prevailing assumptions, and take reasonable risks; hence, it is important to recognize early on the distinctive cultural and mental model differences represented in the group (Engstrom & Tinto, 2000). Utilizing relevant assessment information throughout the collaborative partnership process is often a critical strategy in helping participants to take reasonable risks and have faith that the whole will be greater than the sum of the current parts.

6. Successful partnerships usually require senior administrators in academic and student affairs to be strong champions and advocates for innovation and change, and they must make visible their commitment to developing, nurturing, and sustaining partnerships. According to Kuh and Banta (2000), senior leaders must articulate the rationale and benefits of collaboration and consistently expect, encourage, and reward it. Advocacy and championing, however, do not always have to come from the top—directors, mid-management leaders, new professionals, and others can also

become champions of change. The critical element, in all situations, is that advocacy must be systematic and sustained, for without such support, collaborative efforts are often doomed to fail.

7. Accept the fact that building collaborative partnerships is hard work that necessitates perseverance and tenacity in pursuit of goals. Collaborative partnerships often require inordinate investments of human capital—time, energy, and expertise—and these investments rarely result in immediate success. Furthermore, building collaborative partnerships are not discrete events but rather continuous journeys requiring long-term perspectives and ongoing processes that build trust, respect, and openness.

The preceding strategies can be applied to collaborative initiatives at the macro or micro levels within an organization (Schroeder, 1999a). A critical point to keep in mind, however, is that student affairs educators must model collaborative behavior on a regular and systematic basis before they can expect their academic colleagues to cross the great divide and join them in the creation of partnerships. Finally, because student affairs has been criticized as being goal free and data averse (Marchese, 1994), combining knowledge from the national research with institution-specific data is a critical strategy in enlightening institutional stakeholders about the nature of problems that lend themselves to a collaborative response. The following section highlights ways of using relevant data and best practices to design and implement a variety of partnerships that enhance student learning, student success, and undergraduate education outcomes.

Examples of Effective Collaborative Partnerships

The design and implementation of successful collaborative partnerships are not only driven by clear strategies but also by national and institutionally specific data. Results from important national studies have been used to create the *Seven Principles of Good Practice in Undergraduate Education* (Johnson Foundation, 1987) and the *Principles of Good Practice for Student Affairs* (ACPA & NASPA, 1997)—documents that can be invaluable in guiding collaborative initiatives. This section demonstrates the use of various principles by illustrating two comprehensive examples of successful partnerships: improving student learning and success through learning communities and using institutional data on student learning patterns to improve the teaching learning process.

Improving Student Learning and Success Through Learning Communities

A central tenant of *The Student Learning Imperative* (SLI) is, "the key to enhancing learning and personal development is not simply for faculty to teach more and better, but also to create conditions that motivate and inspire students to devote time and energy to educationally-purposeful activities, both in and outside the classroom" (ACPA, 1994, p. 1).

What are these conditions that motivate and inspire students to become more engaged with the academic and cocurricular dimensions of their experience? According to the Johnson Foundation (1987), the following seven principles of good practice represent conditions that foster learning and development: student-faculty contacts, cooperation among students, active learning, prompt feedback, time on tasks, high expectations, and diverse ways of learning. These conditions are often regarded as key elements in the design of learning communities.

During the early years of the learning community movement, these principles were focused primarily on the formal, curricular aspect of students' experiences, particularly in community colleges where learning communities were initially developed. For example, Gabelnick, MacGregor, Matthews, and Smith (1990) define learning communities as curricular structures that link different disciplines around common themes or questions. They give greater coherence to the curriculum and provide students and faculty with a vital sense of shared inquiry. Because this definition focuses on curricular structures and student-faculty interaction in classrooms, the models make no attempt to integrate cocurricular experiences with curricular objectives, thereby creating seamless learning environments. Astin (1985) addressed this issue by defining learning communities as "small subgroups of students . . . characterized by a common sense of purpose . . . that can be used to build a sense of group identity, cohesiveness and uniqueness that encourages continuity and the integration of diverse curricular and co-curricular experiences" (p. 161).

Although learning communities can take various forms, it is clear from the literature (Love, 1999; MacGregor, 1991; Tinto, 1997; Tinto & Goodsell, 1993) that they make major contributions to enhancing the quality of student and faculty experiences by: providing opportunities to integrate courses in an interdisciplinary manner; helping students form social networks among their peers; increasing student involvement; improving student performance; increasing student retention; providing opportunities for faculty development; shifting the focus to student learning outcomes; and encouraging educators to rethink the ways in which students are taught.

The preceding knowledge was critical in addressing a number of long-standing concerns at the University of Missouri-Columbia including: poor retention and graduation rates, low occupancy rates in the residence halls, lack of coherence and integration within general education courses, and overall concerns about students' lack of engagement in the academic enterprise. These issues served as triggering events to create an educational partnership between the college of arts and sciences, residential life, the registrar's office, the campus writing program, and the offices of the vice-chancellor for student affairs and provost to design residential learning communities. These learning communities would: substantially enhance academic achievement, retention, and educational attainment for freshmen; make the campus psychologically small by creating peer reference groups for new students; purposefully integrate curricular and cocurricular experiences through the development of seamless learning environments; provide a venue for enabling admitted students to register early for their fall classes; and encourage faculty to integrate ideas, concepts, content, writing, assessment, and research from their various disciplines, thereby enhancing general education outcomes for students.

Building on Astin's (1985) definition of learning communities and utilizing models of Freshman Interest Groups (FIGs) originally developed at the Universities of Oregon and Washington, cross-functional teams composed of academic administrators, faculty, and student affairs educators, designed residentially-based, Freshmen Interest Groups to accomplish these objectives (Schroeder, Minor, & Tarkow, 1999b). These learning communities: are organized around general education academic themes; enroll between fifteen and twenty-two students in three common, general education courses; and assign these students to live together on the same floor of a residence hall. Each FIG also has a peer advisor who lives with the students and cofacilitates a one-hour weekly pro-seminar with a faculty or staff member. The peer advisor also organizes various activities directly linked to the academic theme of the FIG including service learning activities, field trips, and guest speakers on topics related to the FIG.

The FIG program was formed with the belief that student learning and success could be enhanced by: facilitating students' *incorporation* into university life and culture, encouraging *involvement* in educationally purposeful activities in and out of class, promoting effective *interaction* with faculty and peers, and assisting students in *integrating* diverse academic and campus experiences. Results from six years of systematic assessment show that these objectives were achieved (Pike, 1996; Pike, Schroeder, & Berry, 1997). These findings were communicated throughout the institution and, as a result, provided leverage for substantially expanding the learning community program. A collaboration initiative that started with fewer than a dozen Freshmen Interest Groups has now developed into 125 residential learning communities involving more than 3,600 students.

This partnership was very successful because it was created around a set of problems that key stakeholders really cared about and that senior leaders advocated. Cross-functional teams, operating from a common vision and shared goals, provided opportunities for ongoing dialogue, cooperation, and collaborative planning. Finally, the incorporation of important findings from the national research and locally sponsored assessment initiatives were also key ingredients that contributed to the success.

Using Institutional Data on Student Learning Patterns to Improve the Teaching-Learning Process

Numerous national reports have highlighted an increasing disparity between faculty and students and, between teacher and learner. The learning process itself suffers as a consequence, both in and outside the classroom. New perspectives are needed to respond to this challenge. For example, how can student affairs educators contribute to improving the quality of the academic experience for today's students? What can they do to help bridge the gap between students and faculty? These questions, along with concerns for improving students' academic performance, retention, and graduation rates, were the catalysts for creating a partnership at Saint Louis University between the offices of the vice president for student development, student life studies, the counseling center, and the English department to help bridge the gap between students and faculty. A primary strategy for nurturing and sustaining this partnership was the use of institution-specific data to enhance understanding of the teaching-learning process.

The office of student life studies, a department within the division of student development, created the TRAILS (Tracking Retention and Academic Integration by Learning Styles) project in the mid-1980s. The primary purpose of the project was to manage, in a systematic and longitudinal manner, information on the academic performance of students with certain learning styles and preferences (as measured by the Myers-Briggs Type Indicator [MBTI]). The project's objectives included: providing academic deans and faculty institutional data on how students' characteristics are related to choice of major, academic aptitude, academic performance in specific curricular and program areas, and attrition; and providing student development professionals a mechanism for building bridges with academic colleagues in the service of students (Kalsbeek, 1989).

The TRAILS research identified learning styles by administering the MBTI on an annual basis to entering students. A cumulative database monitored semester by semester students' choice of major, grade point average, and attrition patterns. Statistical analyses uncovered paths of predictable performance for certain types of learners. As a result, the project offered insights into how some cognitive and noncognitive personality variables affected students' academic integration as measured by their grades and persistence. Unlike typical institutional research efforts that describe general characteristics of the *total* student population, the TRAILS project was designed to provide faculty with information about *their* students. As such, TRAILS information was shared in college and departmental meetings, faculty development workshops, faculty senate retreats, and academic advisor training sessions. TRAILS data were particularly useful in helping faculty understand that their concerns about students were often the result of natural differences in students' learning patterns rather than defects or deficiencies in students' themselves. TRAILS data indicated, for example, that the dominant student learning pattern at the university was the concrete active pattern (Extroverted Sensing on the MBTI). Students who exhibit this pattern perform best in learning situations characterized by direct, concrete experience, moderate-to-high degrees of structure, and a linear, step-by-step approach to learning.

National data, as well as TRAILS specific data, revealed that three-quarters of the faculty, conversely, exhibit a teaching style that not only is opposite of, but often antagonistic to, that of the concrete active learner. The faculty style is referred to as abstract reflective (Introverted Intuition on the MBTI), and faculty who exhibit this style prefer the global to the particular; are stimulated by the realm of concepts, ideas, and abstractions; love learning for learning's sake; and assume that students, like themselves, need a high degree of autonomy in their work (Davis & Schroeder, 1982; Schroeder, 1993).

The preceding information was used as a compelling stimulus to engage faculty in a range of conversations about how to improve the teaching-learning process on campus. Faculty in the School of Nursing at Saint Louis University utilized the data to redesign courses and pedagogical approaches for first-year students. In addition, the English department chairperson and counseling center director invited selected arts and sciences faculty to a seminar series on the role of personality type and writing processes. Over a number of sessions, the faculty began to see the connections between the role that learning styles play in the writing process. They also applauded the rare opportunity to meet with colleagues from other disciplines to wrestle with important pedagogical issues with student affairs consultants who served as experts on the learning process. As a result, faculty incorporated their new learning in the redesign of writing assignments in their courses.

There are many important lessons that can be learned from this collaborative venture, but four, in particular, stand out. First, this effort was successful because it was driven by systematic, timely, and relevant information on changing student characteristics, particularly as those characteristics impacted the quality of teaching and learning on campus. Secondly, these data were directly related to concerns faculty faced with their students, thereby connecting with a primary motivation for creating collaborative initiatives—responding to individuals' self-interest. Third, student affairs staff with the most credibility with faculty—counseling psychologists—facilitated the partnership. Finally, by becoming experts on the diversity of learner characteristics exhibited by today's students, student affairs professionals were able to share their expertise to help faculty design instructional methods that responded effectively to this diversity.

Conclusions and Recommendations

The recent flood of major reports on the status of higher education has provided unique opportunities, and even obligations, for student affairs educators to work collaboratively with their faculty colleagues to improve the quality of undergraduate experiences on their campuses. Achieving this objective is based on the assumption that optimum student learning cannot occur if the institutional components involved in that learning are separated from one another by structure or commitments of both (Kuh, 1996; Terenzini et al., 1996). Institutions that are starting to foster collaboration and cross-functional dialogue between personnel in student affairs and academic affairs are beginning to respond to the challenge posed by Terenzini and Pascarella (1994): "Organizationally and operationally, we have lost sight of the forest. If undergraduate education is to be enhanced, faculty members, joined by academic and student affairs administrators, must devise ways to deliver undergraduate education that are as comprehensive and integrated as the ways that students actually learn. A whole new mind set is needed to capitalize on the interrelatedness of the in- and out-of-class influences on student learning and the functional interconnectedness of academic and student affairs divisions" (p. 32).

Creating collaborative partnerships, however, presents significant challenges—challenges that require new forms of educational and conceptual leadership on the part of student affairs educators. For example, although higher education has experienced profound changes during the past four decades, even more dramatic change is on the way. Undergraduates at the nation's colleges will increase by 2.6 million by 2015, and of this increase, 2 million, or roughly 77 percent, will be students of color. When dramatic demographic shifts such as these are combined with other major societal changes—such as shifts in family values, an increasingly interdependent global economy, an aging population and the complexities associated with an ongoing technological revolution—it is clear that institutions will be challenged, as never before, to provide high quality undergraduate experiences under very difficult conditions. Meeting this challenge will require not only focusing more attention and effort on student learning but on organizational learning as well. To thrive in an environment such as this, student affairs educators must become transformational leaders. They must know and understand the latest theory and research about college students, know how to use theory and process models to enhance professional practice, and know how to engage in unit-specific assessments that generate timely and relevant information for solving problems of consequence to their divisions and institutions. Clearly, they must embrace the scholar-practitioner model (Schroeder & Pike, 2001) to insure, not only their vitality, but also the vitality of their institutions.

Students affairs divisions and academic departments exist for one primary reason—so that student can learn. Although the learning objectives may differ among and between various institutional agents, learning remains at the core. Despite our common objectives, however, the notion that we might improve student learning by crossing the great divide and forging effective partnerships has somehow eluded us. Instead, we usually focus our efforts exclusively within our organizational boundaries, thereby reinforcing the myth that well-intentioned, yet fragmented and uncoordinated efforts, will produce the kinds of learning and success we desire for our students. Now, more than ever, we need to solve this age old part-whole problem (Plater, 1998) through the creation of collaborative partnerships committed to undergraduate education reform. Partnerships such as these will optimize the system through creating seamless learning environments where what has traditionally been separated—curriculum and cocurriculum—will now be linked, aligned, and integrated with the whole. In the process, we might just create collaborative campus cultures—cultures in which people continually expand their capacity to create the results they truly desire, where new and expansive patterns of thinking are nurtured, where collective aspiration is set free, and where people are continually learning how to learn together (Senge, 1990). The challenge, you see, is not only about connecting the fragmented pieces of the student experience; it is also about connecting us.

References

American Association of Higher Education, American College Personnel Association, and National Association of Student Personnel Administrators. (1998). *Powerful partnerships: A shared responsibility for learning.* Washington, DC: American Association of Higher Education, American College Personnel Association and National Association of Student Personnel Administrators.

American College Personnel Association. (1994). *The student learning imperative: Implications for student affairs.* Washington, DC.: American College Personnel Association.

American College Personnel Association and National Association of Student Personnel Administrators. (1997). *Principles of good practice for student affairs.* Washington, DC: American College Personnel Association and National Association of Student Personnel Administrators.

Arnold, K., & Kuh, G. D. (1999). What matters in undergraduate education? Mental models, student learning, and student affairs. In E. J. Whitt (Ed.), *Student learning and student affairs work:*

Responding to our imperative (pp. 11–34). Washington, DC: National Association of Student Personnel Administrators.

Astin, A. W. (1985). *Achieving educational excellence.* San Francisco: Jossey-Bass.

Baxter Magolda, M. (1999). Defining and redefining student learning. In E. J. Whitt (Ed.), *Student learning and student affairs work: Responding to our imperative* (pp. 35–50). Washington, DC: National Association of Student Personnel Administrators.

Baxter Magolda, M., Terenzini, P. T., & Hutchings, P. (1999). Learning and teaching in the 21st century: Trends and implications for practice. In C. S. Johnson & H. Cheatem (Eds.), *Higher education trends for the next century: A research agenda for student success* (pp. 20–29). Washington, DC: American College Personnel Association.

Blake, E. S. (1979). Classroom and context: An educational dialectic. *Academe, 65,* 280–292.

Blake, E. S. (1996). The yin and yang of student learning in college. *About Campus, 1* (4), 4–9.

Blimling, G. S. (2001). Uniting scholarship and communities of practice in student affairs. *Journal of College Student Development, 42*, 381–396.

Bloland, P. A., Stamatakos, L. C., & Rogers, R. R. (1996). Redirecting the role of student affairs to focus on student learning. *Journal of College Student Development, 37*, 217–226.

Boyer Commission on Educating Undergraduates in the Research University. (1998). *Reinventing undergraduate education: A blueprint for America's research universities.* New York: The Carnegie Foundation for the Advancement of Teaching.

Creeden, J. E. (1996). Student affairs biases as a barrier to collaboration: A point of view. *NASPA Journal, 26*, 60–63.

Davis, M., & Schroeder, C. C. (1982). New students in liberal arts colleges: Threat or challenge? In J. Watson & R. Stevens (Eds.), *Pioneers and pallbearers: Perspectives on liberal education* (pp. 147–168). Macon, GA: Mercer University Press.

Eimers, M. T. (2000). The discipline affiliation of faculty: Understanding the differences and the implications of student affairs and faculty collaboration. *About Campus, 5* (6), 12–18.

Engstrom, C., & Tinto, V. (2000). Developing partnerships with academic affairs to enhance student learning. In M. J. Barr, M. K. Desler, & Associates, *The handbook of student affairs administration* (2nd ed., pp. 425–452). San Francisco: Jossey-Bass.

Fried, J. (1999). Two steps to creative campus collaboration. *AAHE Bulletin, 52* (2), 10–12.

Gabelnick, F., MacGregor, J., Matthews, R. S., & Smith, B. L. (Eds.). (1990). *Learning communities: Creating connections among students, faculty, and disciplines* (New Directions for Teaching and Learning No. 41). San Francisco: Jossey-Bass.

Johnson Foundation. (1987). *Seven principles of good practice in undergraduate education.* Racine, WI: Johnson Foundation.

Kalsbeek, D. H. (1989). Linking learning style theory with retention research: The trails project. *Association of Institutional Research Professional File, 32,* 1–8.

Kellogg Commission on the Future of State and Land-Grant Universities. (1998). *Returning to our roots: The student experience.* Washington DC: National Association of State Universities and Land-Grant Colleges.

Kellogg Commission on the Future of State and Land-Grant Universities. (2000). *Returning to our roots: Toward a coherent campus culture.* Washington, DC: National Association of State Universities and Land-Grant Universities.

Kolins, C. A. (2000, Winter-Spring). An appraisal of collaboration: Assessing perceptions of chief academic and student affairs officers at public two-year colleges. *Student Development in the Two-Year Colleges, 14,* 9–12.

Kuh, G. D. (1993). In their own words: What students learn outside the classroom. *American Educational Research Journal, 30*, 277–304.

Kuh, G. D. (1996). Guiding principles for creating seamless learning environments for undergraduates. *Journal of College Student Development, 37*, 135–148.

Kuh, G. D. (1997, June). *Working together to enhance student learning inside and outside the classroom.* Paper presented at the annual AAHE Assessment and Quality Conference, Miami, FL.

Kuh, G. D., & Banta, T. W. (2000). Faculty/student affairs collaboration on assessment—lessons from the field. *About Campus, 4* (6), 4–11.

Kuh, G. D., Douglas, K. D., Lund, J. P., & Ramin-Gyurnek, J. (1994). *Student learning outside the classroom: Transcending artificial boundaries* (ASHE/ERIC Higher Education Report No. 8). Washington, DC: The George Washington University.

Kuh, G. D., & Whitt, E. J. (1988). *The invisible tapestry: Culture in American colleges and universities* (ASHE/ERIC Higher Education Report No. 1). Washington, DC: The George Washington University.

Love, A. G. (1999). What are learning communities? In J. H. Levine (Ed.), *Learning communities: New structures, new partnerships for learning* (pp. 1–8). Columbia, SC: University of South Carolina, National Resource for the First-Year Experience and Students in Transition.

Lovett, C. (1994). Assessment, CQI, and faculty culture. In American Association of Higher Education, *CQI 101: A first reader for higher education* (pp. 140–149). Washington, DC: American Association for Higher Education.

MacGregor, J. (1991). What differences do learning communities make? *Washington Center News, 6* (1), 4–9.

Magolda, P. M. (2001). Border crossings: Collaboration struggles in education. *Journal of Educational Research, 94,* 346–358.

Magolda, P. M. (2002, March). *Overcoming obstacles to successful collaboration.* Paper presented at the annual ACPA National Conference, Long Beach, CA.

Marchese, T. (1994, March). *Assessment.* Paper presented at the annual meeting of the American College Personnel Association, Indianapolis, IN.

Pascarella, E. T., & Terenzini, P. T. (1991). *How college affects students: Findings and insights from twenty years of research.* San Francisco: Jossey-Bass.

Pascarella, E. T., & Whitt, E. J. (1999). Using systematic inquiry to improve performance. In G. S. Blimling & E. J. Whitt (Eds.), *Good practice in student affairs: Principles to foster student learning* (pp. 91–112). San Francisco: Jossey-Bass.

Pike, G., Schroeder, C. C., & Berry, T. (1997). Enhancing the educational impact of residence halls: The affects of residential learning communities on first-year college experiences and persistence. *Journal of College Student Development, 38,* 609–621.

Pike, G. A. (1996). A student success story: Freshman interest groups at the University of Missouri, Columbia. Unpublished report. *University of Missouri-Columbia Student Life Studies Abstracts, 1.*

Plater, W. N. (1998). So why aren't we taking learning seriously? *About Campus, 3* (5), 9–14.

Potter, D. L. (1999). Where powerful partnerships begin. *About Campus, 4* (2), 11–16.

Schroeder, C. C. (1993). New students/new learning styles. *Change, 25* (4), 21–26.

Schroeder, C. C. (1999a). Collaboration and partnerships. In C. S. Johnson & H. Cheatem (Eds.), *Higher education trends for the next century: A research agenda for student success* (pp. 43–50). Washington, DC: American College Personnel Association.

Schroeder, C. C. (1999b). Forging educational partnerships that advance student learning. In G. S. Blimling & E. J. Whitt (Eds.), *Good practice in student affairs: Principles to foster student learning* (pp. 133–157). San Francisco: Jossey-Bass.

Schroeder, C. C. (1999c). Partnerships: An imperative for enhancing student learning and institutional effectiveness. In J. H. Schuh & E. J. Whitt (Eds.), *Creating successful partnerships between academic and student affairs* (New Directions for Student Services No. 87, pp. 5–18). San Francisco: Jossey-Bass.

Schroeder, C. C., Minor, F. D., & Tarkow, T. A. (1999a). Freshman Interest Groups: Partnerships for Promoting Student Success. In J. H. Schuh & E. J. Whitt (Eds.), *Creating successful partnerships between academic and student affairs* (New Directions for Student Services No. 87, pp. 37–50). San Francisco: Jossey-Bass.

Schroeder, C. C., Minor, F. D., & Tarkow, T. A. (1999b). Learning communities: Partnerships between academic and student affairs. In J. H. Levine (Ed.), *Learning community: New structures,*

new partnerships for learning (pp. 52–69). Columbia, SC: National Resource Center for the First-Year Experience and Students in Transition.
Schroeder, C. C., Nicholls, G., & Kuh, G. (1983). Exploring the student affairs rainforest: Testing assumptions and taking risks. In G. Kuh (Ed.), *Understanding student affairs organizations* (pp. 51–65). San Francisco: Jossey-Bass.
Schroeder, C. C., & Pike, G. (2001). The scholarship of application in student affairs. *Journal of College Student Development, 42*, 342–355.
Schuh, J. H., & Upcraft, L. (1998). Facts and myths about assessment in student affairs. *About Campus, 3* (5), 2–8.
Schuh, J. H., & Whitt, E. J. (Eds.). (1999). *Creating successful partnerships between academic and student affairs* (New Directions for Student Services No. 87). San Francisco: Jossey-Bass.
Senge, P. M. (1990). The leaders' new work: Building learning organizations. *Sloan Management Review, 32* (1), 7–23.
Seymour, D. (1995). *Once upon a campus: Lessons for improving quality and productivity in higher education.* Washington, DC: American Council on Education.
Seymour, D. (1997). Charting a future for quality in higher education. *About Campus, 2* (1), 4–10.
Stein, R. B., & Short, P. M. (2001). Collaboration in delivering higher education programs: Barriers and challenges. *The Review of Higher Education, 24*, 417–436.
Terenzini, P. T., & Pascarella, E. T. (1994). Living with myths: Undergraduate education in America. *Change, 26* (1), 28–32.
Terenzini, P. T., Pascarella, E. T., & Blimling, G. S. (1996). Students' out-of-class experiences and their influence on learning and cognitive development: A literature review. *Journal of College Student Development, 37*, 149–162.
Tinto, B. (1997). Classrooms as communities: Exploring the educational character of student persistence. *The Journal of Higher Education, 68* (6), 599–623.
Tinto, B., & Goodsell, A. (1993). Freshman interest groups and the first-year experience: constructing student communities in a large university. *Journal of the Freshman Year Experience, 6* (1), 7–28.
Westfall, S. B. (1999). Partnerships to connect in- and out-of-class experiences. In J. H. Schuh & E. J. Whitt (Eds.), *Creating successful partnerships between academic and student affairs* (New Directions for Student Services No. 87, pp. 51–62). San Francisco: Jossey-Bass.
Whitehead, A. N. (1929). *The aims of education and other essays.* New York: Free Press.
Whitt, E. J. (Ed.). (1999). *Student learning and student affairs work: Responding to our imperative.* Washington, DC: National Association of Student Personnel Administrators.
Whitt, E. J., & Miller, T. E. (1999). Student learning outside the classroom: What does the research tell us? In E. J. Whitt (Ed.), *Student learning and student affairs work: Responding to our imperative* (pp. 51–62). Washington, DC: National Association of Student Personnel Administrators.
Wingspread Group. (1993). *An American imperative: Higher expectations for higher education.* Racine, WI: Johnson Foundation.
Young, R. D. (1996). Guiding values in philosophy. In S. Komives & D. Woodard (Eds.), *Student services: A handbook for the profession* (3rd ed., pp. 83–105). San Francisco: Jossey-Bass.

CHAPTER THIRTY

SHAPING THE FUTURE

Dudley B. Woodard, Jr., and Susan R. Komives

Whether it is 1983, 1993, 2003, or 2013, there will always be issues! Our colleague, Bud Thomas, observes that we always have at least three levels of issues facing us at any given moment:

- *Ongoing issues*—These are inherent in the nature of the higher education enterprise and should not surprise us, as they are always with us. They include exuberant crowds after winning basketball games, student suicide attempts, budget cuts, cheating, and hiring freezes. All are sadly predictable. Good practice in student affairs work leads us to protocols to handle these ongoing challenges, because we know they will occur.
- *Issues unique to a particular campus*—The issues that grow out of the context of a particular campus might include the increasing number of adjunct faculty, a high number of students with disabilities, problems with teaching assistant unions, or the need to create senior transition courses.
- *Issues and trends on the national scene*—These emerge often, but they may seem distant. They may affect your campus soon, however. They may develop at an aspirational peer institution, in the social or global agenda, in pending federal legislation, or in cases before the courts. Difficult as it is, every student affairs worker is professionally, even ethically, obliged to try and foresee new trends, issues, and events and decide how to react if they occur.

Much of this book has been devoted to the first two categories, and our goal has been to help professionals anticipate these issues and build competency to approach those daily challenges in our work on our particular campuses. This chapter will focus on the third category of issues and examine developing trends and themes that influence our work now and in the future. We start with a description of broad societal trends followed by a discussion of the major change drivers in higher education. These trends and change drivers set the context for focusing on themes in student affairs. The concluding section offers future directions, assertions, and advice to professional leaders shaping the future.

Societal Trends

Forecasting the future and analyzing trends are risky ventures. With this caveat in mind, we now venture into a discussion of societal trends that will influence higher education and individual campus trends. Examine each of these trends, and others that come to mind, by asking "How might this trend influence my specific expertise areas, my campus, and my students?" Then go to the next step and ask "What can we do (in my office, in the profession, with like-minded colleagues) to take initiative to influence the direction this trend should take in our work?"

Among the many trend analysts and forecasters in the United States, the United Way's Strategic Institute (Morrison, 1992: United Way of America, 1989;) has distilled from several sources those issues that are likely to have a strong influence on the nation's human and social systems. In 1989 and in a 1992 revision, institute analysts identified nine forces they called "change drivers"—"profound influences upon our shared experience" (1989, p. 1). Each of these forces has direct and indirect implications for higher education, and each can help us understand the changes we see now in higher education and frame ways to deal with them in the next decade.

The Aging U.S. Population

"Baby Boomers" (born between 1946 and 1964) account for four out of every ten Americans. They have been the "demographic engine driving social change" since they were born (Spain, 1997, p. 3). Boomers and those over eighty years of age are the fastest-growing segments of the aging population (Morrison, 1992). This has many implications for those whose careers are in health services, geriatrics, adult care programs, continuing education, and leisure education. The late twentieth-century life experience of this aging population will lead to a restructuring of the life course. Instead of three phases of work (preparation, employment, retirement), the process now involves more work-life career changes. At the stage of retirement-age, many now find transitions to new jobs and careers, part-time jobs, or various forms of self-employment (Quadagno, 2001). Short-term return to college, notably community colleges, will fulfill a need for updating and preparing for these transitions.

The Mosaic Society

Americans are increasingly diverse, and a broadened base of diverse Americans is seeking higher education experiences. In contrast to the maturation change driver, this change driver acknowledges the high growth rates among diverse populations (such as Latino) and the increase in the college-going youth in these groups. The development of diversity and the need for services for diverse students has gained the attention of student affairs professionals for the last three decades and continues to deserve attention. Access to campus is not enough; chilly climate issues continue to challenge diverse students. White students come to campus more aware of the diverse world they live in, yet traditional-age students remain in need of skills to relate to those different from themselves. Curriculum transformation continues to be essential in all fields in order to adequately to address diverse needs and views on campus. The challenge is to develop a common purpose and a sense of community within the mosaic campus.

Redefinition of Individual and Social Roles

As the public sector tightens its fiscal belt and reexamines social service programs that have been in place for decades, we are seeing a similar reexamination of what Americans should expect from their institutions of higher education. American colleges and universities are asking themselves what they must do differently. As a result, self-help groups now abound on campus. Support groups provide expertise that was only available in the past from professionals, and community service has become a meaningful way for institutions to span boundaries that might have blocked needed societal resources in the past.

Globalization

Satellite communications and other technology bring distant wars, earthquakes, and political upheaval into our living rooms. Our interdependence is unquestioned, and students need to learn cross-cultural skills to understand and function alongside those with differing expectations, values, and world views. American college programs and services must have international links. Too often we rely on limited study abroad programs, often available only to the privileged, to address this need. Restrictive policies on immigration and student visas will change the export of graduate education through limitations in international student access. At a time when global leadership in science leads directly to economic leadership, the United States will expand its role in international economic development (Morrison, 1992).

Economic Restructuring

Our system of taxation and issues regarding the emerging global economy are leading to new views on national and personal financial health. Campus finances and students' ability to finance their education are equally affected. Loans are taking a major role in students' financing of education, leading even more to the question, "Can I afford the debt even if the long-term rate of return is beneficial?" The reorganization and restructuring taking place on most campuses will result in profound and fundamental changes in organizational structures and academic and support programs. There will be continued competition for federal and state dollars from K–12 education, health care, law enforcement, national security, and corrections. Confidence in large conglomerate organizations is diminished in the face of the 2001 scandals (such as those of Enron, Tyco, and Worldcom), resulting in a more critical and skeptical work force.

Personal and Environmental Health

The environmental movement is a growing cultural norm. More Americans are willing to make the connection between their personal behavior (such as smoking and drunk driving) and risks to their own health and the health of the ecosystem. Campuses must follow, modeling new environmental practices. We should support policy reforms in such areas as alcohol and drug use and campus immunizations. Campus employees continue to seek a quality of life along with economic well-being; campus environments will increasingly be seen as renewing, healthy places to work (such as having recreation centers, cultural events, and collaborative norms). Telecommuting and other flexible workplace concepts must no longer be the privilege of bosses and white-collar campus employees (such as faculty and department heads) but should also be offered to room assignment clerks and other support staff.

Redefinitions of Family and Home

Single-parent families, extended families, and domestic-partner arrangements have distinct needs that are still not addressed by programs and services designed around the traditional family model. Too many campuses still only allow one data "field" in the student's official record for a parent or guardian, so the student with two primary families (including stepparents) cannot get official materials regularly mailed or e-mailed to both. Further, things that used to be done only in the home, like caring for children, are now done externally, and things that used to be done externally, like seeing a movie, shopping, banking, working, and attending college, can now be done at home. The Boomer parents of today's traditional students will continue to seek more input in their students' education. The spouse, children, and parents of adult students need to be involved, and various services need to be offered for them.

Rebirth of Social Activism

Renewed civic activism to address school violence, youth crime, drugs, unethical business practices, and environmental safety is evidence of an increasingly concerned citizenry. Civic engagement will increase in the context of increasingly heated debates over civil liberties and governmental intervention. Protest and citizen involvement are accepted even in the most conservative sectors of society. The focus on school reform will continue to keep America's attention on the role of youth and education at all levels in societal development and economic development. Youth affirm their belief that shared civic problems should be addressed by citizens and civic groups instead of large institutions such as government (Hart Research Associates for Public Allies, 1998). The mid-1990s' heightened willingness to get involved, combined with the national disaster of September 2001, strengthened the development of civic leadership, community service, and civic engagement. Campuses must be models of civic engagement by how constituents are included (faculty, students) and by how they engage with local and regional concerns.

The Information-Based Economy

Our postindustrial world is increasingly based in cyberspace. An information-based economy potentially welcomes everyone regardless of sex or ethnicity because it is based on intellectual activity and not physical strength or skin color. Still, we must address the gender and class imbalance on the Internet. Universities should teach and expect computer literacy of all students, faculty, and staff. Campus information systems need to be easily and equally accessible. Information technologies will make distance learning and distance meetings easier. The question of support for student learning and development in distance learners remains largely unaddressed.

The Impact of Technology

The 1990s were vividly marked by one word: technology. Most of us started the 1990s with little e-mail, no mass use of the Internet, limited use of cell phones, no Palm Pilots, and no voice mail. The ways we work together has changed dramatically. The advantages of being able to send targeted e-mails or cell calls to large groups of students stand alongside the disadvantages of people sending e-mails to their office mates instead of interacting with them face-to-face. We know lives are being changed, but changes have been driven more by a "Madison Avenue" approach rather than a thoughtful educational approach. Technological marvels will continue, but what is our role in determining who is served and who benefits from these technological changes?

Higher Education Trends

Much of the literature on trends during the last decade (Boyer Commission, 1998; Kellogg Commission on the Future of State and Land-Grant Universities, 2001; Newman, 2000; Woodard, Love, & Komives, 2000) suggests that the major national trends and issues important to student advisors have remained fairly constant during the last decade and will continue driving change in the foreseeable future. Several of these trends mirror larger societal trends but reflect the themes and challenges directly facing higher education. These trends are described below, and the reader is asked to reflect on these trends in the context of the larger societal trends described above.

National Imperative

The national imperative is about who and how we serve diverse populations of students. A deeply rooted core value of higher education is education for the benefit of society—increasing access and success while serving students in a variety of contexts.

According to Newman (2000), the role of higher education is "the socialization of students, providing social mobility through access, and keeping universities as homes of disinterested scholarship in the pursuit of truth" (p. 3). In this country, we are fortunate to have an array of diverse higher education options, but we need to rethink how we can build on these options and create new ones so that higher learning is open, accessible, affordable, and flexible (Kellogg Commission, 2001). The borders of higher education are not physical walls but walls in our imagination. Clearly, it is a national imperative for higher education to educate the future work force. Futurists Popcorn and Hanft (2001) project that in the near future more than half of Americans will be working in jobs which do not exist now. Future job titles reflect the processes of connecting humans with each other and with the meaning making needed in this information explosion: bioinformationists, experimental therapy experts, hospitalists, social network analysts, personal career coaches, and whisperers. As illustrated in Exhibit 30.1, these careers highlight the shift from the way things have been to the needs of the workforce. The dynamic, explicit role in work force development has to be acknowledged by higher education (Association of Governing Boards, 2001). Meeting the needs of an educated work force is an essential element of nation building.

Learning and Development

Somewhere along the way, for many reasons, we lost our focus on the fundamental role of higher education, which is—the education of the whole person. The Kellogg Commission Report *Returning to Our Roots* (2001) describes several foundational principles as a way to think about redefining learning communities of the twenty-first century: "(1) [O]ur institutions must become genuine learning communities, supporting and inspiring faculty, staff, and learners of all kinds; (2) our learning communities should be student centered, committed to excellence in teaching and to meeting the legitimate needs of learners, wherever they are, whatever they need, whenever they need it; and (3) our institutions should emphasize the importance of healthy learning environments that support students, faculty, and staff with the facilities, support, and resources they need to make this vision a reality" (pp. 1–2). Recent attention to learning outcomes was fueled in great part by the accountability movement but converged with the

EXHIBIT 30.1. MISMATCH BETWEEN EDUCATION AND THE WORKPLACE.

Traditional Education	Workplace Requirements
• Facts	• Problem solving
• Individual effort	• Team skills
• Passing a test	• Learning how to learn
• Achieving a grade	• Continuous improvement
• Individual courses	• Interdisciplinary knowledge
• Receiving information	• Interacting and processing information
• Technology separate from learning	• Technology integral to learning

Source: Transforming Higher Education in the 21st Century, ACE/Kellogg Meeting, July 13, 1999.

examination of teaching processes so that even Research I universities were asking, "How can we be a student-centered research university?" (Boyer Commission, 1998). Even many colleges that have always been proud teaching institutions have had to examine the effect that focusing on learning brings to the teaching process. Research universities continue to face the biggest challenges in transforming the undergraduate experience. Instead of trying to clumsily adopt liberal arts colleges' strategies, they need to use their strengths and offer an inquiry-based undergraduate experience (Boyer Commission, 1998). Sadly, too many undergraduates are treated like "guests at the banquet who pay their share of the tab but are given leftovers" (p. 37).

Financial Stress and the Marketplace

Financial stress in higher education is and will continue to be a reality for the foreseeable future. The competition for state and federal dollars has intensified, resulting in a shifting of resources away from higher education. This trend will continue well into the twenty-first century and will force most public and private institutions to look for other sources of revenue and develop new practices such as outsourcing and partnering with industry. The increasing reliance on market-driven decisions, however, has the potential to undermine the basic mission of our colleges and universities and disenfranchise populations of students who cannot afford to pay the escalating costs of an education. In an increasingly market-driven scenario, scholarship "free from vested interest" (Press & Washburn, 2000, p. 4) becomes purchased scholarship for profit, and the socializing of students for societal roles becomes the training of students for jobs. This Faustian tangle with the marketplace has the potential to make knowledge a purchased commodity rather than a means in the pursuit of truth for the benefit of all people (Press & Washburn).

Accountability

Accountability in the context of higher education is usually viewed in two ways as stewardship of money or program performance. Higher education has come under intense scrutiny for its perceived mismanagement of public and private sources of funds. Legislators, funding agencies, parents, and donors are requiring institutions to demonstrate fiscal soundness and that the monies entrusted to higher education lead to the desired outcomes. Several state legislatures have tied annual funding to performance-based outcomes. These outcomes frequently are learning outcomes measured by standardized tests or other measurable outcomes such as graduation rates and job placement. Accountability measures will continue to influence how we organize and accomplish our work.

Sustaining Transformational Change

Transformational change is ongoing, deep, pervasive, and profound. It "alters the culture of the institution by changing select underlying assumptions and institutional behaviors, processes, and products" (Eckel, Hill, & Green, 1998, p. 3). This makes it hard to imagine new structures, processes, and settings, and to develop the accountability models needed to assess transformational change and "put in place structures to promote, sustain, and reward these changes" (Moses, 2001, p. 2). As professionals, we need to generate a vision to create the future because "if we don't become the architects of change, we will become its victims" (Kellogg Commission, 2001, p. 1). The challenge is how to collaboratively transform our institutions "when conditions are constantly changing, resources are light, expectations are high, and options are limited" (Kellogg Commission, p. 1).

Technology

Technology holds the promise of closing the digital divide, increasing cost efficiencies by educating greater numbers of students, and transforming our work. But it is uncertain what the ultimate impact technology will have on teaching and learning (Moses, 2001, p. 9). Several studies suggest that distance learning, for example, doesn't lose much money, but it doesn't generate much either (Carr, 2001, p. 41). The challenge for the student affairs professional is to understand the role of technology and how to use it to enhance the learning and work environment, reduce costs, and meet the challenges it poses. Some of these challenges are (1) issues associated with less face-to-face interaction; (2) measuring learning outcomes; (3) assessing cost benefits of technology; (4) increasing rather than eliminating the digital divide; and (5) creating and applying the use of technology rather than adapting to the manufacturers' suggested use (Moses).

Globalization

It is important for student affairs professionals to understand and experience the educational and economic changes taking place globally. Our students are preparing themselves to live in a global community and expect an educational experience supportive of this objective. So we must develop global awareness, see different worldviews as a shared interest, and use technology to bring global learning to campus. As Dalton (1999) points out: "Any attempt to understand the past, present, and future mission and role of student services in the United States must recognize the considerable influence of higher education traditions and practices in other countries" (p. x).

As we settle into the twenty-first century, the question is not whether these are major drivers of change but rather how we can harness our understanding of these issues and trends to create learning and working environments which are responsive to the needs of society. Tierney (1998) admonishes us to "rethink and restructure what we do rather than seeking new managerial fixes" (p. 3). The same seems true for student affairs. We need to step back and reexamine our core values and beliefs and rethink and restructure what we do in the context of these trends and issues while staying anchored by our core beliefs and values.

Student Affairs Themes and Issues

Change efforts do not fail so much from a lack of vision or commitment; change efforts fail because individuals do not identify and understand influential change drivers and future opportunities. Moreover, the process for accomplishing change is usually ill-defined. So it is important to our profession that we create our own future and not leave it simply to chance. This requires knowledge of the existing, changing, and likely future condition of higher education. Thus far, we have described both societal and higher education trends. In this section, we augment these trends by describing them in terms of the dominant themes embedded in the previous chapters.

In 1997, the American College Personnel Association (ACPA) Senior Scholars requested statements of policy initiatives, trends, and issues from higher education associations. The responses were classified into eight themes: (1) access for diverse students; (2) affordability; (3) teaching and learning; (4) technology; (5) work environment; (6) collaborations and partnerships; (7) accountability; and (8) role of the federal government (Trends Analysis Project, 1997). In 2001, Love and Yousey did a discourse analysis of the field to determine to what degree these eight trends were a focus of student affairs professionals. They found that four issues were common, (1) learning, (2) diversity, (3) collaboration, and (4) technology, but Love and Yousey (2001) did not find student affairs professionals discussing issues of rising costs in higher education or the role of the federal government. Moreover, two topics discussed by student affairs professionals were not included in the Senior Scholars trends: student affairs issues such as professional development and professional organizations and social issues such as race, gambling, and risky behaviors.

A similar discourse analysis, albeit simpler, was done for the chapters in this book. In other words, what are the authors saying are the major trends and issues that will influence and shape our professional preparation programs and practice? The results reflected similarities between author themes and the themes identified by the Senior Scholars and Love and Yousey (2001): access and diversity, learning communities, costs, and restructuring. There were also themes unique to student affairs, such as professionalism and the use of multiple and alternative frames for reflection about practice. Collectively, these are a rich source of data that we can use to help create the vision and practice for our future as a profession. Read them with this in mind.

Anchors

The basic professional foundational tenets repeated throughout the book are these:

- History informs our practice and our sense of mission. We can learn much from the pioneers in our profession, and we need to pay attention to landmark events, which will help us maintain a sense of purpose and direction.
- The core values of caring, development of the whole person, and community have served as our navigational system for more than a century.

- The values of equality, justice, fairness, helping others, and responsibility are deeply rooted in our practice.
- Access is a bedrock principle. Everyone should have an opportunity to advance the development of his or her skills, values, and knowledge.

Purpose

In defining the purpose of the profession, many authors used phrases like the following:

- Our role is to understand how students develop and learn and help create purposeful environments that stimulate growth.
- We help prepare students for civic, career, and leadership roles in a complex world—a raison d'etre for attending to student learning and conditions which enhance learning.
- We must find ways to facilitate student learning in a variety of contexts and share these understandings with faculty and decision makers.

Change

The challenge of change was a recurring theme:

- Change is not an event with a beginning, middle, and end. Rather change "is an ongoing organic process in which one change triggers another. Often in unexpected places, and through which an interrelationship of the component parts leads to an unending cycle" (Eckel, Hill, Green, & Mallon, 1999, p. 1).
- Change may not be predictable but neither is it a mystery or random.
- Change is a way of life. Rather than adapting to change, we should be helping to generate and influence change anchored in our core values but reflective of a changing context.
- We should watch globally and observe locally for clues to changes within student populations, societal needs, and the economy.

Learning and Development

Perhaps the theme discussed most was our emerging role in helping to design and assess purposeful learning environments:

- The profession has evolved from an in loco parentis and service orientation to a developmental and learning orientation. This is a profound shift in terms of understanding our role in learning in collaboration with faculty.
- Student affairs professionals have a clear responsibility to assist in designing powerful learning environments and assessing and evaluating outcomes of those efforts.
- We need to learn more about what actually influences learning and development—especially the influence of culture on learning.

- Understanding student intentions helps us evaluate what role the institution plays to support or inhibit student achievement.

Multiple Frames

Several authors commented on how important it is to use multiple frames or to draw on multiple sources of data to analyze and reflect on different situations and challenges:

- Theory informs practice, and it is important to reflect about theory in terms of how it informs practice, who benefits, and how and by whom theory was derived.
- Developmental theory, learning theory, retention theory, organizational theory, environmental theory, and student characteristics, values, and attitudes help give us a more complete understanding of students, behavior, and structure and governance process.
- No one theory can help us understand the complex behavior of organizations and individuals. Multiple theoretical windows help form more accurate interpretations of events and actions.

Alternative Frames

Some authors suggested the use of alternative frames to help us think more creatively and broadly about who our students are and how best to help them:

- We approach most of our work with a Western perspective, and we need to stretch and see what we can learn about learning and student development from a non-Western perspective. In other words, we need to understand other ways of thinking and knowing.
- Thinking and research has been dominated by psychological paradigms and positivistic assumptions, but other theoretical or ways of knowing are now beginning to illuminate the work of student affairs.
- There is a clear emphasis on efficiency and outcomes. An alternate view is that these efforts lead to a bureaucratizing of practice and reflect the goals of the privileged.
- We need more than a management fix to meet some of the current challenges in student affairs. We need to think about transformative change—profound, real change, not incremental change.
- We have lost sight of who we serve and the why by focusing on the how—the process.

Professionalism and Competencies

Finally, it was clear throughout the book that there is no substitute for basic competency in a broad range of skills necessary for effective practice:

- Some authors expressed concerns about the future of the profession of student affairs. The question is not about survival but rather how we will remain anchored

by our core beliefs and values while rethinking what we do to address a constantly changing landscape and needs of a changing clientele.
- It is not student affairs' job to create powerful learning environments; it is a partnership with faculty and other vested parties.
- If we continue to dance with the marketplace, we will lose our privileged status as institutions involved in pursuit of truth and knowledge for the benefit of all (Newman, 2000).

These themes, trends, and issues, taken together, serve as a wonderful segue into thinking about the future of student affairs and how to shape and create that future.

Future Directions, Assertions, and Advice

The preceding observations about the changing landscape, emerging societal trends, and themes from our authors all provide challenges to current practice. The robust student affairs profession is well grounded in philosophies, values, research, theory, and practices that become a foundation to leadership in changing times. It is not sufficient for us to merely adapt or respond to these changes. We must build, create, initiate, and lead.

Promoting Good Practices

Good practices in student affairs must continue to be the goal of all professional staff. The Council for the Advancement of Standards continues to do strong work to renew expectations of us in our daily work. ACPA and NASPA have advanced a set of good practices that are designed to affirm student learning and development (Blimling & Whitt, 1999).

Good practice in student affairs:

- Engages students in active learning
- Helps students develop coherent values and ethical standards
- Sets and communicates high expectations for learning
- Uses systematic inquiry to improve student and institutional performance
- Uses resources effectively to achieve institutional missions and goals
- Forges educational partnerships that advance student learning
- Build[s] supportive and inclusive communities (pp. 14–19)

We support and affirm these practices. The ideas advanced in this book and reflections on the good practices noted above lead us to several assertions.

Assertions for Future Practices

Building, creating, initiating, and leading in the coming decade means reflecting on some new assertions about student affairs work:

Student affairs professionals are everywhere. No longer is student affairs work done only in the division of student affairs. Professional student affairs work happens in such places as advising offices within academic colleges, in academic and career support services of athletics departments, and in student employment offices of the physical plant. Even the alumni affairs office is working with former students. The twofold challenge of this realization is to make sure that staff with appropriate professional credentials are hired into these positions (for example, the career center in the college of engineering needs professional career counselors) and to create new cross-functional teams to connect these professionals from across campus regardless of their reporting channels. Now that many student affairs professionals are hired other than in divisions of student affairs, the need for a campuswide professional community and for interfunctional collaboration is keen.

Student affairs professionals challenge our mental models about who our students are. Professionals have long advanced the inclusion of diverse students and their diverse perspectives. Indeed, we have been the champions of multiculturalism and inclusion and carried the banner to all segments of our institutions. What was labeled "political correctness" in the early 1990s shifted to "educationally correct" by the close of the decade. But we still often think of students as campus-based undergraduates. We have to broaden our view of which students get our attention and even our services. Graduate and professional students are largely ignored in student affairs practice; distance learners struggle from afar, aided by web pages but limited in direct services; and adult students continue to find little recognition of their time schedules and multiple roles such as raising children and caring for ill and aging parents.

Student affairs professionals work collaboratively. Today's organizations need new relational ways of leading (Allen & Cherrey, 2000). Many authors in this book assert the imperative of identifying shared campus issues (such as retention to the first-year student experience) and come together from various units to address these issues. Collaboration recognizes the contributions of diverse shareholders and building stronger interventions across the environment. Not only must we work collaboratively, we must cease all practices that create unhealthy work environments and dysfunctional work families. There is no place in a caring profession for hurtful behaviors or unethical practices.

Student affairs professionals assertively challenge the environment to enrich the student experience. Student affairs continues to be the moral voice of the campus (Barr, 1983), raising the right questions, expecting offices and policies to be responsive to all students, and continually raising awareness of how the environment (such as about the culture, the human aggregates, policies and procedures, and physical elements) influences student success. Any hands-off practices that pretend athletics, student employment, or off-campus student behavior is not our concern must be challenged.

Student affairs professionals recognize there is no substitute for research and scholarship to inform practice. The theoretical frames and conceptual models student affairs professionals bring to any campus or student issue are rich and meaningful. The research that helps us prove or understand important phenomena is profound. Far too many "professionals" do not draw on these bases to guide and ground their practice; all professionals need to hold each other to higher standards and expect professional staff to bring that knowledge to the table.

Student affairs professionals need to know if our work matters. This is a corollary to the point above but is presented separately here to encourage all professionals and their offices to engage in regular assessment, research, and program evaluation to know if and how what we do matters. Staff specialists might help each unit with this important goal, or individual staff in each unit should have it in their job descriptions to do these studies. Hire people who can do research, want to do research, and enjoy that activity for any opening that may arise in the staff. Expect research of new employees and retrain continuing staff if necessary.

Student affairs professionals harness technology toward educational outcomes. Reaching more students more effectively is a wonderful contribution of technology. However, we need to be vigilant that it remains a cost effective tool; it is accessible to students, staff, and faculty; and its uses are well conceived and desired outcomes are assessed.

Student affairs professionals must be proactive change agents. One important dimension to empowerment is self-empowerment. Individually and as a profession, student affairs staff must claim their place in the academy and freely assert and work toward changes that benefit the student experience. Too many staff still behave as second-class members of the academy, whine, feel victimized, and wait to be asked to be included. While strategies may vary in different environments, practice strategies such as Schroeder presents in Chapter Twenty-Nine and clearly working toward shared institutional goals supported by theory, research, and assessment information must be the norm of practice.

Getting Down to Advice

As the authors in this book assert, effective student affairs practice in the next decade will be required to do some things differently and to start doing some new things. We challenge readers in three domains to reconsider their work with students, with the campus environment, and with the profession. These small pieces of advice bring some of the themes and assertions to life. We challenge you to think of the many diverse ways you can create a future for your students and for student affairs practice on your campus that is wise, informed, and upholds the best traditions of our profession.

Students. In addition to the myriad of best practices to respond to the ever-changing complex world of the student experience, we suggest a focus on these arenas.

- Expand practice to include graduate and professional students. It is time we got concerned about the retention, progress toward degree, quality of experience, skill development like teaching, and leadership skills of graduate students. We need to promote collaborations, partnerships and cross-functional work with the student affairs staff in medical schools and law school programs. A corollary is to work with graduate students as faculty-in-training to help them understand student learning and teaching practices that promote learning (Boyer Commission, 1998).

- Expand all practices to include distance learners. We need to provide leadership on how local agencies and local community colleges may have an enhanced role in partnering with four-year institutions in supporting distance learners to the completion of their degree work. Focus groups of distance learners are one way to determine what would be helpful.
- Raise your awareness of student needs in all the new markets your campus is exploring (such as international collaborations and cross-institutional joint degree programs). Reach out to all units expanding the scope of their programs to assess student needs and aid in designing programs and interventions to help those students be successful.
- Promote new language. It is time we stopped labeling older learners, students of color, and distance learners as the "nontraditional" students. These students are the new majority. In any case, the root of the term "nontraditional" still values the "traditional" as the norm. Perhaps we should just use the term "students."
- Develop meaningful interventions to promote lifelong learning. Integral to lifelong learning is a keen awareness of self-authorship (Baxter Magolda, 2001; Kegan, 1994) and the related processes of learning to construct knowledge. It is unlikely higher education will change the nature of degrees comprised of credit hours earned, but support for competency-based opportunities and degree requirements that include application and synthesis (like group projects and community interventions) teach to lifelong learning. In addition to teaching students to critique what they access on the web, engage in problem-based learning, and truly work on the processes of understanding and applying knowledge, institutions need to also provide learning supports for alumni. Campus web pages might provide latest practices and recommended literature in areas of office expertise (such as leadership or health education).

The Campus Environment. Our campuses need student affairs professionals to engage across the environment as boundary spanners. The skills that promote collaboration and facilitate diverse voices coming together to change practices are important contributions in times of rapid change:

- Sustain transformative change. It is not enough to try new strategies, but to sustain those new approaches takes new processes, new training, clear expectations, and perhaps different reward systems.
- Truly internationalize the student experience. Beyond study abroad, use technology creatively such as cross-cultural experiences that are web-based or through video conferencing. Find ways to link students from different cultures using desktop computer interactive software.
- Foster coalitions, alliances, and collaborations everywhere. Just about everything we do would benefit from the involvement of professionals in other offices as well as other shareholders like students. Inviting others into our work and offering support to other offices' activities spans the chasms on campus and develops a culture of trust and collaboration. Consider what services could be offered through

consortiums, partnerships with local agencies, and with public schools. Readers will want to track the American Council of Education's Changing Enterprises Project which tracks cross-institutional collaborations.
- Redesign entry-level jobs. It is unconscionable that many campuses still offer new masters' staff subpoverty-level incomes. We must insist on professional livable wages, focus on developmental supervision, and build practices that target new employees for development and retention in the field. As Pogo noted, "we have met the enemy and he is us." Most of the practices that devalue entry-level student affairs employees come from the culture of student affairs itself.

The Profession. Beyond our individual campus, we need to grapple with some profound issues to advance our work in the academy and in support of the national agenda by taking these steps:

- Prepare new professionals with adaptive perspectives. Graduate preparation programs and entry staff development programs must promote competencies in multiframing, intergroup dialogue skills, boundary spanning, organization renewal, staff renewal, leading in a networked world, and collaborative teamwork. This preparation and professional orientation is learned both through graduate study and in developmental supervision and mentoring on the job. It is essential that supervisors of new professionals are prepared for these roles.
- Be realistic. There will always be financial stress, people who do not understand or appreciate the nature of student affairs, and faculty that have the central role as campus educators. Anticipate it, get over it, and shape the environment with unique contributions.
- Inform the national higher education agenda. Professional associations have to do more than the internal work to serve members. All associations must find strategies to influence state and federal policy, perhaps through partnerships with other associations such as AACC, HACU, ACE, or AACC. Few current student affairs associations are actively leading in the national student agenda.
- Engage in serious dialogue about creating one student affairs generalist association. There needs to be a strong central voice within and external to higher education. ACPA, NASPA, and other partners need to engage in serious discussion about creating a *new* voice for student affairs work in postsecondary education, preferably with an international focus.

Conclusion

In *Megatrends 2000,* futurists Naisbitt and Aburdene (1990) observe: "The most exciting breakthroughs of the 21st century will occur not because of technology but because of an expanding concept of what it means to be human" (p. 16). In times of biotechnological advance when science *can* clone humans, the question becomes *should* we? What does it mean to be human? Indeed, the challenges of the next decade will focus on what it means to be human beings together in many shared contexts. What does it mean to be *in community* with each other? What is a community of scholars? What is a learning community? What is our shared obligation toward youth? What does it mean to construct a life in common?

It means we must focus on the human agenda. This should be the primary focus for all we do today. The leaders who gathered at Wingspread at the beginning of the last decade (Wingspread Group, 1993) shaped a reflective time in higher education in the 1990s. Refocusing on the role of higher education and the public good, these leaders wondered what our society needs from higher education. They concluded that it needs stronger, more vital forms of community. It needs an informed and involved citizenry. "It needs graduates able to assume leadership roles in American life. It needs a competent and adaptable workforce. It needs high-quality undergraduate education producing graduates who can sustain each of these goals. It needs more first-rate research pushing the boundaries of human knowledge and less research designed to lengthen academic resumes. It needs an affordable, cost-effective educational enterprise offering lifelong learning. Above all, it needs a commitment to the American promise—the idea that all Americans have the opportunities to develop their talents to the fullest. Higher education is *not* meeting these imperatives" (p. 2).

No one strategy could address all these needs in every type of institution. But the *American Imperative* report called for three areas of focus that would help reshape the role of postsecondary institutions. It proposed that institutions take values more seriously, put student learning first, and create a nation of learners. We have made great progress on each of these three challenges, yet each still applies to the next decade as we explore that human agenda.

The trends and themes we have emphasized in this chapter and throughout the book continue to reflect the challenges of the *American Imperative* report. Thinking about trends requires making space in our busy lives for reflection. It means recognizing that this reflection is not a luxury after all the pressing work is done or only practiced at the annual retreat, but an essential value and an important element of our work. Making meaning of trends and applying that meaning to the human agenda must be a priority.

In his book *Servant Leadership,* Greenleaf (1977) notes that reflection and foresight are essential in organizational life; indeed in the future it might be considered an ethical violation not to have acted responsibly when one could have taken prudent action. It is essential that all professionals learn to individually reflect on their lived experience in practice and find mechanisms for staff meetings to regularly reflect together.

The importance of tracking campus trends, national trends, and societal issues is profound. Being proactive means wondering together what trends will influence the student experience and engaging with that trend to shape its future direction. Partners of good will abound across campus and in the community who share a commitment to getting ahead of these anticipated issues. It is no longer sufficient for student affairs staff to just "put out fires," although that role is a persistent, essential one and always will be with us. We must instead capture campus energy and help direct it toward enhancing the student experience in every way possible. We must proactively bring the best of our scholarship and competence to address campus issues in collaborative ways. We hope this book has helped you find new ways your own work might make such a contribution.

References

Allen, K. E., & Cherrey, C. (2000). *Systemic leadership: Enriching the meaning of our work.* Washington, DC: American College Personnel Association and National Association of Campus Activities.

Association of Governing Boards of Universities and Colleges (2001). *Ten public policy issues for higher education in 2001 and 2002.* Washington, DC: Association of Governing Boards of Universities and Colleges. Available at www.agb.org/about13.cfm.

Barr, M. J. (1983, March). *Presidential address.* Annual meeting of the American College Personnel Association. Baltimore.

Baxter Magolda, M. B. (2001). *Making their own way: Narratives for transforming higher education to promote self-development.* Sterling, VA: Stylus Publishing.

Blimling, G. S., & Whitt, E. (Eds.). (1999). *Good practice in student affairs: Principles to foster student learning.* San Francisco: Jossey-Bass.

Boyer Commission on Educating Undergraduates in the Research University (1998). *Reinventing undergraduate education: A blueprint for America's Research Universities.* SUNY Stony Brook. Available at www.naples.cc.stonybrook.edu/Pres/boyer.nsf/.

Carr, S. (2001, Feb. 16). Is anyone making money on distance education? *The Chronicle of Higher Education,* A41–43.

Dalton, J. (1999). The significance of international issues and responsibilities in the contemporary work of student affairs. In J. Dalton (Ed.), *Beyond borders: How international developments are changing student affairs practice* (New Directions for Student Services No. 86, pp. 3–11). San Francisco: Jossey-Bass.

Eckel, P., Hill, B., & Green, M. (1998). *On change: En route to transformation.* American Council on Education Occasional Paper Series. Washington, DC: American Council on Education.

Eckel, P., Hill, B., Green, M., & Mallon, B. (1999). *On change: Reports from the Road: Insights on Institutional Change.* American Council on Education Occasional Paper Series. Washington, DC: American Council on Education.

Greenleaf, R. (1977). *Servant leadership.* Mahwah, NJ: Paulist Press.

Hart Research Associates for Public Allies. (1998). *New leadership for a new century: Key findings from a study on youth, leadership, and community service.* Available at www.publicallies.org/poll.htm.

Kegan, R. (1994). *In over our heads: The mental demands of modern life.* Cambridge, MA: Harvard University Press.

Kellogg Commission on the Future of State and Land-Grant Universities. (2001). *Returning to our roots.* Washington, DC: National Association of State Universities and Land-Grant Colleges. Available at www.nasulgc.org.

Love, P. G., & Yousey, K. (2001). Gaps in the conversation: Missing issues in the discourse of the student affairs field. *Journal of College Student Development, 42,* 430–446.

Morrison, J. L. (1992). What lies ahead: A decade of decision. *On the Horizon.* Available at www.horizon.unc.edu/projects/OTH/prev_default.asp.

Moses, Y. T. (2001, June). Scanning the environment. *AAHE Bulletin, 53* (10), 7–9.

Naisbitt, J., & Aburdene, P. (1990). *Megatrends 2000: Ten new directions for the 1990s.* New York: William Morrow.

Newman, F. (2000). Saving higher education's soul. The Futures Project: Policy for higher education in a changing world. *Change,* Sept.-Oct., 16–23.

Popcorn, F., & Hanft, A. (2001). *Dictionary of the future.* New York: Hyperion.

Press, E., & Washburn, J. (2000). The kept university. *Atlantic Monthly.* March, 39–54.

Quadagno, J. (2001). *A future I would welcome.* Commission on the Future, Florida State University. Available at www.fsu.edu/~future/quadagnol.html.

Spain, D. (1997). *Societal trends: The aging baby boom and women's increased independence.* Report for the Federal Highway Administration. Available at www.cta.ornl.gov/npts/1995/Doc/SocTrends.pdf.

Tierney, W. G. (Ed.). (1998). *The responsive university: Restructuring for high performance.* Baltimore: The Johns Hopkins University Press.

United Way of America. (1989). *What lies ahead: Countdown to the 21st century.* Alexandria, VA: Author.

Wingspread Group on Higher Education. (1993). *An American imperative: Higher expectations for higher education.* Racine, WI: Johnson Foundation.

Woodard, D. B. Jr., Love, P., & Komives, S. R. (2000). *Leadership and management issues for a new century.* (New Directions for Student Service No. 92). San Francisco: Jossey-Bass.

EPILOGUE

A look back over the first century of student affairs work leaves us with a proud connection to our field which is well grounded in a rich history, with robust scholarly literature, meaningful philosophy and values, professional colleagues, and a campus and national agenda for change to enrich the student experience. This will be our last edition of this book. Along with our authors, we wanted to capture this first century in this epilogue and challenge you to build the next century of meaningful transformation to ensure higher education stays focused on students and their experience.

Professional Identity and Historical Perspectives

Erikson (1968) proposed that individuals need to look to their "conceptual ancestors" to help them define and understand their identity, and John Thelin reminds us that we can learn much from the pioneers in our profession. Perhaps people can discover their professional identity in the same manner. Who are the conceptual ancestors of student affairs from the past three hundred years? You have been introduced to them throughout this book. In Chapters Four and Five, Nuss and Young described some of the pioneer deans of men and women, the seminal professional statements in the field, and several professional organizations that provided structure and direction to the emerging profession of student affairs. The 1937 and 1949 *Student Personnel Point of View* (American Council on Education, 1937/1994) and the guidelines published by the Council for Advancement Standards in Higher Education have had an enormous shaping influence on our profession.

The doctrine of in loco parentis was the guiding philosophy of early student affairs professionals; although it is no longer legally viable, it is still visible in the ethic of care that permeates the field. Ethical practices are clearly expected and, as Fried explains in Chapter Six, promoted in our student affairs cultures. Barr (1988) describes how the law dramatically redefined students' relationship with their institution, especially the *1967 Joint Statement on Rights and Freedoms of Students* and federal statutes such as Titles VI and IX of the Civil Rights Act and Section 504 of the Rehabilitation Act. McEwen (Chapters Eight and Ten), Evans (Chapter Nine), King (Chapter Eleven), Strange (Chapter Thirteen), and Braxton (Chapter Fourteen) all discussed the profound influence of the student development movement that began in the 1960s, and Baird (Chapter Twenty-Eight) chronicled the attendant research and theory on the influence of the college environment on student outcomes. These theories and research efforts have led to a deeper understanding of student development, the interactive relationship between students and the collegiate environment, and the outcomes of the undergraduate experience. The events, concepts, and individuals briefly mentioned above represent a sampling of the richness and diversity of our conceptual ancestors. They symbolize Erikson's (1968) epigenetic principle—the many facets of student personnel work that have emerged to form the functioning whole we call student affairs.

Transformation of the Profession

The history and development of the student affairs profession has been both rapid and controversial. Student affairs functions exist on all campuses and have enjoyed significant growth during the last four decades. During this same time, however, the identity of the profession has been at times heatedly debated, ranging from discussions as to whether the field is truly a profession to debates about professional accreditation, certification, registry, and licensing. As Carpenter illustrates in Chapter Twenty-Seven, the field is in the process of becoming a credible profession, anchored in an identifiable philosophy based on guiding principles, a rich and diverse literature, a recognized body of theory (much of it based on research performed in the last thirty-five years), practice guided by ethical principles, and energetic professional associations working on behalf of both students and student affairs professionals. We are engaged in what Young (1994) calls the profession's "laying stone on sacred stone" (p. 7).

A Philosophy Based on Guiding Principles

The principles of the profession have withstood the test of time and guided us through substantial change (Woodard, 1990). Individuals like Thomas Arkle Clark, appointed dean of men at the University of Illinois in 1901, and Evelyn Wright Allen, appointed dean of women at Stanford in 1910, were pioneers in the emerging profession then known as student personnel work. For these two ground-breaking professionals there was no coherent institutional philosophy or purpose to guide their work. Clark said, "I had no specific duties, no specific authority, no precedence either to guide me or to handicap me. . . . My only chart was that of the action of the Board of Trustees which said I was to interest myself in the individual student" (Fley, 1979, p. 37). These professionals were left to decide for themselves how to handle the student service functions of their time. They, along with many others, helped shaped the events that led up to the 1937 *Student Personnel Point of View.* This pioneering document gave the profession its soul. Its second paragraph expands on the many aspects of student development that continue to deserve the attention of professionals in higher education: "This philosophy imposes upon educational institutions the obligation to consider the student as a whole, the student's intellectual capacity and achievement, emotional make-up, physical condition, social relationships, vocational aptitudes and skills, as well as moral and religious values, economic resources, aesthetic appreciation" (American Council on Education, 1937/1994, p. 68).

An overriding goal of the profession has always been to further the development of the student as an individual. This guiding principle and others identified by Nuss (Chapter Four) and Young (Chapter Five) have been reaffirmed throughout the history of student affairs. Even if the politics of some foundational statements and professional projects were controversial at the time, the core of their content affirmed the professional values and philosophies of student affairs and the impact of our work on the student experience.

In addition to the *Student Personnel Point of View,* the field has been immensely shaped by such thoughtful pieces as the following:

- *Student Development Services in Postsecondary Education* by the Council of Student Personnel Associations (COSPA, 1975/1994)
- *A Perspective on Student Affairs* by the National Association of Student Personnel Administrators (1987)
- Various foundation- and association-sponsored studies, such as *Campus Life: In Search of Community* (Carnegie Foundation for the Advancement of Teaching, 1990), *College: The Undergraduate Experience in America* (Boyer, 1987), the 1993 *American Imperative* report of the Wingspread Group, and the series of reports by the NASULGC/Kellogg Commission on the Student Experience (2001)
- The National Institute of Education's report *Involvement in Learning* (Study Group on the Condition of Excellence in American Higher Education, 1984) and the 1967 and 1992 versions of the *Joint Statement on Student Rights and Freedoms*
- Pivotal early projects like the ACPA's *Tomorrow's Higher Education,* which resulted in such pieces as Brown's *Student Development in Tomorrow's Higher Education: A Return to the Academy* (1972) and Miller and Prince's *The Future of Student Affairs* (1976)
- Recent works such as *The Student Learning Imperative* (American College Personnel Association, 1994, 1996), *Reasonable Expectations,* commissioned by the National Association of Student Personnel Administrators (Kuh, Lyons, Miller, & Trow, 1995), *Powerful Partnerships* (a joint project of AAHE, ACPA, and NASPA, 1998), and ACPA and NASPA's *Good Practices* (Blimling & Whitt, 1999)
- Reports of various research projects, including *Involving Colleges* (Kuh, Schuh, Whitt, & Associates, 1991), *What Matters in College* (Astin, 1993), *How College Affects*

Students (Pascarella & Terenzini, 1991), the 1999 ACPA Senior Scholars report: *Higher Education Trends for the Next Century* (Johnson & Cheatham, 1999)

These works speak to the importance of focusing on student development and student learning; emphasizing student rights; encouraging students to take responsibility for their own learning and personal development; affirming the uniqueness, worth, and dignity of all students; respecting others regardless of individual differences such as race, gender, sexual orientation, class, ability, or beliefs; and supporting the creation and maintenance of a caring and collaborative community based upon common purposes. These goals embody the enduring principles of our profession, principles that have transcended generations and remain our navigational system.

A Rich and Diverse Literature

Research and scholarship in the field of student affairs has come into its own during the last twenty-five years. The sheer volume of published research and books written on matters pertaining to the profession is quite impressive. A review of Pascarella and Terenzini's *How College Affects Students* (1991) attests to the amount of research undertaken since the publication of Feldman and Newcomb's *The Impact of College on Students* (1969). So much more literature has emerged in the 1990s that Pascarella and Terenzini's update to the 1991 publication will be published in the early 2000s. Books such as Rentz's *Student Affairs: A Profession's Heritage* (1994); Astin's *What Matters in College* (1993); Strange and Banning's *Educating by Design* (2001); Winston, Creamer, and Miller's (2001) *The Professional Student Affairs Administrator;* Barr and Upcraft's *New Futures for Student Affairs* (1990); Barr and Desler's *The Handbook of Student Affairs Administration* (2000); Evans, Forney, and Guido-DiBrito's *Student Development in College* (1998); Blimling and Whitt's *Good Practice in Student Affairs* (1999); Upcraft and Schuh's (1996) *Assessment in Student Affairs;* the Jossey-Bass New Directions in Student Services series; and the expanded number of generalist and professional journals and magazines related to student affairs attest to the field's explosive growth. Numerous research grants and nationally funded projects over the past thirty-five years have produced a rich and varied body of research and scholarship in student affairs, both from student affairs practitioners and from teaching professionals.

We must acknowledge that not all of our literature and published research is of equal quality, and not all of what is useful finds its way into practice. We are encouraged that our field is now concentrating on needed critiques of its professional practices, promoted by the almost simultaneous publication of such reform-minded works as Bloland, Stamatakos, and Rogers's *Reform in Student Affairs* (1994) and the series of five articles in Caple's capstone issue of the *Journal of College Student Development* (1994), led by Strange's piece "Student Development: The Evolution and Status of an Essential Idea" (1994), along with Woodard, Love, and Komives' exploration of myths and heresies in a later book on *Leadership and Management Issues for a New Century* (2000). Informed critique will serve to enhance and advance our work in the twenty-first century.

A Growing Body of Theory

Our understanding of student development has been advanced by a growing body of theory on student learning and success, allowing us to respond confidently to the rapidly changing world of higher education. Early student development theory and retention models were unidimensional in their approach. As many authors in this book have explained, they were skewed toward a traditional-age, White, male perspective, both in their initial conception and because of the subjects used in studies to validate them. Since the 1960s and 1970s, however, the paradigm of student development has been stretched and reframed. Researchers and theorists have helped us understand multiple views of student development, including the notions that retention is not about integration into the dominant culture and that dominant modes of teaching do not connect with all learners.

Informed Practice

Over the past thirty-five years, student affairs professionals have been outspoken advocates of civil rights, student rights, and inclusive campus practices. They have often functioned as the moral conscience of the campus. Sometimes this has brought criticism of their being too "politically correct." A more accurate description is that student affairs professionals are "educationally correct," dedicated to upholding the principle of inclusion for all students. Student affairs divisions are proudly the most diverse units on campus, reflecting the principles of the profession in their hiring policies. Not all campus environments achieve this match between intentions and results. These principles are reflected in other aspects of student affairs work as well; student affairs professionals have consistently promoted and used authentic and ethical processes in our daily practice as we advocate for students.

Professional Organizations

The growth, strength, and contributions of the many national student affairs organizations have been amazing. These professional associations have produced statements of ethical practice, sponsored research, and advanced continued professional development through national, regional, and local conferences as well as through special workshops and institutes. Student affairs associations have published a significant amount of literature, often on neglected topics such as fiscal management; gay, lesbian, and bisexual student issues; and the needs of international students. Interassociation collaboration is laudable and perhaps best evidenced by the Council for the Advancement of Standards. Current work on quality assurance continues to raise important issues regarding preparation and practice (Creamer et al., 1992; NASPA, 2002). Various student affairs organizations have also assumed national leadership roles on such issues as financial aid, student right-to-know acts, campus safety and violence prevention, community service, and drug and substance abuse programming.

In Reflection

We are proud to be working with you to do this important work. Students deserve caring professionals challenging, guiding, and advocating for them in higher education. As counselors, administrators, environment managers, and above all as educators, we will continue to enrich the student experience in higher education for the next century. We do this best when we address the human agenda that binds all of us together. Student affairs work may be the most rewarding on campus largely because we have a collegial community who truly care about each other and value the precious relationships we have on campus and in our larger professional community. What we *do* will always matter, but who we *are* matters even more. We have been blessed with the wonderful authors who have shared themselves in this book, with the graduate students who helped us present these ideas to you, and with each other. We hope that each of you have a rewarding professional friendship like we have found in doing this book and other projects together. While we leave the fifth edition to others, we are grateful that we have been able to share ourselves at the turn of this century with you.

Susan R. Komives
University of Maryland

Dudley B. Woodard, Jr.
University of Arizona

References

AAHE, ACPA, NASPA. (1998). *Powerful partnerships: A shared responsibility for learning.* Washington, DC: American Association for Higher Education, American College Personnel Association, National Association of Student Personnel Administrators. Available at www.naspa.org.

American College Personnel Association. (1994). *The student learning imperative: Implications for student affairs.* Washington, DC: Author.

American College Personnel Association (1996). Student learning imperative. *Journal of College Student Development, 37,* 118–122.

American Council on Education. (1994). The student personnel point of view. In A. L. Rentz (Ed.), *Student affairs: A profession's heritage* (pp. 66–77). Lanham, MD: University Press of America.

Astin, A. (1993). *What matters in college: Four critical years revisited.* San Francisco: Jossey-Bass.

Barr, M. J., & Associates. (1988). *Student services and the law.* San Francisco: Jossey-Bass.

Barr, M. J., & Desler, M. K. (Eds.). (2000). *The handbook of student affairs administration* (2nd ed.). San Francisco: Jossey-Bass.

Barr, M. J., & Upcraft, M. L. (Eds.). (1990). *New futures for student affairs.* San Francisco: Jossey-Bass.

Blimling, G. S., & Whitt, E. (Eds.). (1999). *Good practice in student affairs: Principles to foster student learning.* San Francisco: Jossey-Bass.

Bloland, P. A., Stamatakos, L. C., & Rogers, R. R. (1994). *Reform in student affairs.* Greensboro, N.C.: ERIC Counseling & Student Services Clearinghouse.

Boyer, E. (1987). *College: The undergraduate experience in America.* New York: Harper & Row.

Brown, R. (1972). *Student development in tomorrow's higher education: A return to the academy.* Alexandria, VA: American College Personnel Association.

Caple, R. B. (Ed.). (1994). *Journal of College Student Development, 35* (1–6).

Carnegie Foundation for the Advancement of Teaching. (1990). *Campus life: In search of community.* Princeton, NJ: Princeton University Press.

Council of Student Personnel Associations. (1994). Student development services in postsecondary education. In A. L. Rentz (Ed.), *Student affairs: A profession's heritage* (American College Personnel Association Media Publication No. 40, 2nd ed., pp. 390–401). Lanham, MD: University Press of America. (Original work published 1975)

Creamer, D., Winston, R. B., Jr., Schuh, J. H., Gehring, D. D., McEwen, M. K., Forney, D. S., Carpenter, D. S., & Woodard, D. B. (1992). *Quality assurance in college student affairs: A proposal for action by professional associations.* Report prepared for the American College of Personnel Administrators.

Erickson, E. H. (1968). *Youth and crisis.* New York: Norton.

Evans, N. J., Forney, D. S., & Guido-DiBrito, F. (1998). *Student development in college: Theory, research, and practice.* San Francisco: Jossey-Bass.

Feldman, K. A., & Newcomb, T. M. (1969). *The impact of college on students.* San Francisco: Jossey-Bass.

Fley, J. (1979). Student personnel pioneers: Those who developed our profession. *NASPA Journal, 17,* 23–39.

Johnson, C. S., & Cheatham, H. E. (Eds.). (1999). *Higher education trends for the next century: A research agenda for student success.* Washington, DC: American College Personnel Association.

Kellogg Commission on the Future of State and Land-Grant Universities (2001). *Returning to our roots.* Washington, DC: National Association of State Universities and Land-Grant Colleges. Available at www.nasulgc.org

Kuh, G. D., Lyons, J., Miller, T. K., & Trow, J. (1995). *Reasonable expectations.* Washington, DC: National Association of Student Personnel Administrators.

Kuh, G. D., Schuh, J. H., & Whitt, E. J. (Eds.). (1991). *Involving colleges: Successful approaches to fostering student learning and development outside the classroom.* San Francisco: Jossey-Bass.

Miller, T. K., & Prince, J. (1976). *The future of student affairs.* San Francisco: Jossey-Bass.

National Association of Student Personnel Administrators. (1987). *A perspective on student affairs.* Washington, DC: NASPA.

National Association of Student Personnel Administrators. (1992). *Student rights and freedoms: Joint statement on the rights and freedoms of students.* Washington, DC: NASPA.

National Association of Student Personnel Administrators. (2002). *A national registry for student affairs administrators.* Available at www.naspa.org.

Pascarella, E. J., & Terenzini, P. T. (1991). *How college affects students.* San Francisco: Jossey-Bass.

Rentz, A. L. (1994). *Student affairs: A profession's heritage* (2nd ed.). Lanham, MD: American College Personnel Association & University Press of America.

Strange, C. C. (1994). Student development: The evolution and status of an essential idea. *Journal of College Student Development, 35,* 399–412.

Strange, C. C., & Banning, J. H. (2001). *Educating by design: Creating campus learning environments that work.* San Francisco: Jossey-Bass.

Study Group on the Condition of Excellence in Higher Education. (1984). *Involvement in learning: Realizing the potential of American higher education.* Washington, DC: National Institute of Education.

Upcraft, M. L., & Schuh, J. H. (1996). *Assessment in student affairs: A guide for practitioners.* San Francisco: Jossey-Bass.

Wingspread Group on Higher Education. (1993). *An American imperative: Higher expectations for higher education.* Racine, WI: Johnson Foundation.

Winston, R. B., Jr., Creamer, D. G., & Miller, T. (2001). *The professional student affairs administrator: Educator, leader, and manager.* Philadelphia: Brunner/Routledge.

Woodard, D. B., Jr. (1990). *Tenacious tenets of an involving learning environment.* Paper presented at the annual Region IV-East meeting of the National Association of Student Personnel Administrators, Pheasant Run, IL.

Woodard, D. B. Jr., Love, P., & Komives, S. R. (2000). *Leadership and management issues for a new century* (New Directions for Student Services No. 92). San Francisco: Jossey-Bass.

Young, J. H. (1994). Laying stone on sacred stone: An educational foundation for the future. *Educational Record, 75* (1), 7–12.

RESOURCE A: NASPA'S STANDARDS OF PROFESSIONAL PRACTICE

The National Association of Student Personnel Administrators (NASPA) is an organization of colleges, universities, agencies, and professional educators whose members are committed to providing services and education that enhance student growth and development. The association seeks to promote student personnel work as a profession which requires personal integrity, belief in the dignity and worth of individuals, respect for individual differences and diversity, a commitment to service, and dedication to the development of individuals and the college community through education. NASPA supports student personnel work by providing opportunities for its members to expand knowledge and skills through professional education and experience. The following standards were endorsed by NASPA at the December 1990 board of directors meeting in Washington, DC.

1. *Professional Services.* Members of NASPA fulfill the responsibilities of their position by supporting the educational interests, rights, and welfare of students in accordance with the mission of the employing institution.

2. *Agreement with Institutional Mission and Goals.* Members who accept employment with an educational institution subscribe to the general mission and goals of the institution.

3. *Management of Institutional Resources.* Members seek to advance the welfare of the employing institution through accountability for the proper use of institutional funds, personnel, equipment, and other resources. Members inform appropriate officials of conditions which may be potentially disruptive or damaging to the institution's mission, personnel, and property.

4. *Employment Relationship.* Members honor employment relationships. Members do not commence new duties or obligations at another institution under a new contractual agreement until termination of an existing contract, unless otherwise

agreed to by the member and the member's current and new supervisors. Members adhere to professional practices in securing positions and employment relationships.

5. *Conflict of Interest.* Members recognize their obligation to the employing institution and seek to avoid private interests, obligations, and transactions which are in conflict of interest or give the appearance of impropriety. Members clearly distinguish between statements and actions which represent their own personal views and those which represent their employing institution when important to do so.

6. *Legal Authority.* Members respect and acknowledge all lawful authority. Members refrain from conduct involving dishonesty, fraud, deceit, and misrepresentation or unlawful discrimination. NASPA recognizes that legal issues are often ambiguous, and members should seek the advice of counsel as appropriate. Members demonstrate concern for the legal, social codes, and moral expectations of the communities in which they live and work even when the dictates of one's conscience may require behavior as a private citizen which is not in keeping with these codes/expectations.

7. *Equal Consideration and Treatment of Others.* Members execute professional responsibilities with fairness and impartiality and show equal consideration to individuals regardless of status or position. Members respect individuality and promote an appreciation of human diversity in higher education. In keeping with the mission of their respective institution and remaining cognizant of federal, state, and local laws, they do not discriminate on the basis of race, religion, creed, gender, age, national origin, sexual orientation, or physical disability. Members do not engage in or tolerate harassment in any form and should exercise professional judgment in entering into intimate relationships with those for whom they have any supervisory, evaluative, or instructional responsibility.

8. *Student Behavior.* Members demonstrate and promote responsible behavior and support actions that enhance personal growth and development of students. Members foster conditions designed to ensure a student's acceptance of responsibility for his/her own behavior. Members inform and educate students as to sanctions or constraints on student behavior which may result from violations of law or institutional policies.

9. *Integrity of Information and Research.* Members ensure that all information conveyed to others is accurate and in appropriate context. In their research and publications, members conduct and report research studies to assure accurate interpretation of findings, and they adhere to accepted professional standards of academic integrity.

10. *Confidentiality.* Members ensure that confidentiality is maintained with respect to all privileged communications and to educational and professional records considered confidential. They inform all parties of the nature and/or limits of confidentiality. Members share information only in accordance with institutional policies and relevant statutes when given the informed consent or when required to prevent personal harm to themselves or others.

11. *Research Involving Human Subjects.* Members are aware of and take responsibility for all pertinent ethical principles and institutional requirements when planning any research activity dealing with human subjects. (See *Ethical Principles in the Conduct of Research with Human Participants,* Washington, DC: American Psychological Association, 1982.)

12. *Representation of Professional Competence.* Members at all times represent accurately their professional credentials, competencies, and limitations and act to correct any misrepresentations of these qualifications by others. Members make proper referrals to appropriate professionals when the member's professional competence does not meet the task or issue in question.

13. *Selection and Promotion Practices.* Members support nondiscriminatory, fair employment practices by appropriately publicizing staff vacancies, selection criteria, deadlines, and promotion criteria in accordance with the spirit and intent of equal opportunity policies and established legal guidelines and institutional policies.

14. *References.* Members, when serving as a reference, provide accurate and complete information about candidates, including both relevant strengths and limitations of a professional and personal nature.

15. *Job Definitions and Performance Evaluation.* Members clearly define with subordinates and supervisors job responsibilities and decision-making procedures, mutual expectations, accountability procedures, and evaluation criteria.

16. *Campus Community.* Members promote a sense of community among all areas of the campus by working cooperatively with students, faculty, staff, and others outside the institution to address the common goals of student learning and development. Members foster a climate of collegiality and mutual respect in their work relationships.

17. *Professional Development.* Members have an obligation to continue personal professional growth and to contribute to the development of the profession by enhancing personal knowledge and skills, sharing ideas and information, improving professional practices, conducting and reporting research, and participating in association activities. Members promote and facilitate the professional growth of staff and they emphasize ethical standards in professional preparation and development programs.

18. *Assessment.* Members regularly and systematically assess organizational structures, programs, and services to determine whether the development goals and needs of students are being met and to assure conformity to published standards and guidelines such as those of the Council for the Advancement of Standards for Student Services/Development Programs (CAS). Members collect data which include responses from students and other significant constituencies and make assessment results available to appropriate institutional officials for the purpose of revising and improving program goals and implementation.

RESOURCE B: ACPA'S STATEMENT OF ETHICAL PRINCIPLES AND STANDARDS

American College Personnel Association Standing Committee on Ethics

Preamble

The American College Personnel Association (ACPA) is an association whose members are dedicated to enhancing the worth, dignity, potential, and uniqueness of each individual within post-secondary educational institutions and thus to the service of society. ACPA members are committed to contributing to the comprehensive education of the student, protecting human rights, advancing knowledge of student growth and development, and promoting the effectiveness of institutional programs, services, and organizational units. As a means of supporting these commitments, members of ACPA subscribe to the following principles and standards of ethical conduct. Acceptance of membership in ACPA signifies that the member agrees to adhere to the provisions of this statement.

This statement is designed to address issues particularly relevant to college student affairs practice. Persons charged with duties in various functional areas of higher education are also encouraged to consult ethical standards specific to their professional responsibilities.

Use of This Statement

The principal purpose of this statement is to assist student affairs professionals in regulating their own behavior by sensitizing them to potential ethical problems and by providing standards useful in daily practice. Observance of ethical behavior also benefits fellow professionals and students due to the effects of modeling. Self-regulation is the most effective and preferred means of assuring ethical behavior. If, however, a professional observes conduct by a fellow professional that seems contrary to the provisions of this document, several courses of action are available.

Initiate a private conference. Because unethical conduct often is due to a lack of awareness or understanding of ethical standards, a private conference with the professional(s) about the conduct in question is an important initial line of action. This conference, if pursued in a spirit of collegiality and sincerity, often may resolve the ethical concern and promote future ethical conduct.

Pursue institutional remedies. If private consultation does not produce the desired results, institutional channels for resolving alleged ethical improprieties may be pursued. All student affairs divisions should have a widely-publicized process for addressing allegations of ethical misconduct.

Contact ACPA Ethics Committee. If the ACPA member is unsure about whether a particular activity or practice falls under the provisions of this statement, the Ethics Committee may be contacted in writing. The member should describe in reasonable detail (omitting data that would identify the person[s] as much as possible) the potentially unethical conduct or practices and the circumstances surrounding the situation. Members of the Committee or others in the Association will provide the member with a summary of opinions regarding the ethical appropriateness of the conduct or practice in question. Because these opinions are based on limited information, no specific situation or action will be judged "unethical." The responses rendered by the Committee are advisory only and are not an official statement on behalf of ACPA.

Request consultation from ACPA Ethics Committee. If the institution wants further assistance in resolving the controversy, an institutional representative may request on-campus consultation. Provided all parties to the controversy agree, a team of consultants selected by the Ethics Committee will visit the campus at the institution's expense to hear the allegations and to review the facts and circumstances. The team will advise institutional leadership on possible actions consistent with both the content and spirit of the ACPA Statement of Ethical Principles and Standards. Compliance with recommendations is voluntary. No sanctions will be imposed by ACPA. Institutional leaders remain responsible for assuring ethical conduct and practice. The consultation team will maintain confidentiality surrounding the process to the extent possible.

Submit complaint to ACPA Ethics Committee. If the alleged misconduct may be a violation of the ACPA Ethical Principles and Standards, the person charged is a member of ACPA, and the institutional process is unavailable or produces unsatisfactory results, then proceedings against the individual(s) may be brought to the ACPA Ethics Committee for review. Details regarding the procedures may be obtained by contacting the Executive Director at ACPA Headquarters.

Ethical Principles

No statement of ethical standards can anticipate all situations that have ethical implications. When student affairs professionals are presented with dilemmas that are not explicitly addressed herein, five ethical principles may be used in conjunction with the four enumerated standards (Professional Responsibility and Competence, Student Learning and Development, Responsibility to the Institution, and Responsibility to Society) to assist in making decisions and determining appropriate courses of action.

Ethical principles should guide the behaviors of professionals in everyday practice. Principles, however, are not just guidelines for reaction when something goes wrong or when a complaint is raised. Adhering to ethical principles also calls for action. These principles include the following.

Act to benefit others. Service to humanity is the basic tenet underlying student affairs practice. Hence, student affairs professionals exist to (a) promote healthy social, physical, academic, moral, cognitive, career, and personality development of students; (b) bring a developmental perspective to the institution's total educational process and learning environment; (c) contribute to the effective functioning of the institution; and (d) provide programs and services consistent with this principle.

Promote justice. Student affairs professionals are committed to assuring fundamental fairness for all individuals within the academic community. In pursuit of this goal, the principles of impartiality, equity, and reciprocity (treating others as one would desire to be treated) are basic. When there are greater needs than resources available or when the interests of constituencies conflict, justice requires honest consideration of all claims and requests and equitable (not necessarily equal) distribution of goods and services. A crucial aspect of promoting justice is demonstrating an appreciation for human differences and opposing intolerance and bigotry concerning these differences. Important human differences include, but are not limited to, characteristics such as age, culture, ethnicity, gender, disabling condition, race, religion, or sexual/affectional orientation.

Respect autonomy. Student affairs professionals respect and promote individual autonomy and privacy. Students' freedom of choice and action are not restricted unless their actions significantly interfere with the welfare of others or the accomplishment of the institution's mission.

Be faithful. Student affairs professionals are truthful, honor agreements, and are trustworthy in the performance of their duties.

Do no harm. Student affairs professionals do not engage in activities that cause either physical or psychological damage to others. In addition to their personal actions, student affairs professionals are especially vigilant to assure that the institutional policies do not: (a) hinder students' opportunities to benefit from the learning experiences available in the environment; (b) threaten individuals' self-worth, dignity, or safety; or (c) discriminate unjustly or illegally.

Ethical Standards

Four ethical standards related to primary constituencies with whom student affairs professionals work—fellow professionals, students, educational institutions, and society—are specified.

1. *Professional Responsibility and Competence.* Student affairs professionals are responsible for promoting students' learning and development, enhancing the understanding of student life, and advancing the profession and its ideals. They possess the knowledge, skills, emotional stability, and maturity to discharge responsibilities

as administrators, advisors, consultants, counselors, programmers, researchers, and teachers. High levels of professional competence are expected in the performance of their duties and responsibilities. They ultimately are responsible for the consequences of their actions or inaction.

As ACPA members, student affairs professionals will:

1.1. Adopt a professional lifestyle characterized by use of sound theoretical principles and a personal value system congruent with the basic tenets of the profession.

1.2. Contribute to the development of the profession (e.g., recruiting students to the profession, serving professional organizations, educating new professionals, improving professional practices, and conducting and reporting research).

1.3. Maintain and enhance professional effectiveness by improving skills and acquiring new knowledge.

1.4. Monitor their personal and professional functioning and effectiveness and seek assistance from appropriate professionals as needed.

1.5. Represent their professional credentials, competencies, and limitations accurately and correct any misrepresentations of these qualifications by others.

1.6. Establish fees for professional services after consideration of the ability of the recipient to pay. They will provide some services, including professional development activities for colleagues, for little or no remuneration.

1.7. Refrain from attitudes or actions that impinge on colleagues' dignity, moral code, privacy, worth, professional functioning, and/or personal growth.

1.8. Abstain from sexual harassment.

1.9. Abstain from sexual intimacies with colleagues or with staff for whom they have supervisory, evaluative, or instructional responsibility.

1.10. Refrain from using their positions to seek unjustified personal gains, sexual favors, unfair advantages, or unearned goods and services not normally accorded those in such positions.

1.11. Inform students of the nature and/or limits of confidentiality. They will share information about the students only in accordance with institutional policies and applicable laws, when given their permission, or when required to prevent personal harm to themselves or others.

1.12. Use records and electronically stored information only to accomplish legitimate, institutional purposes and to benefit students.

1.13. Define job responsibilities, decision-making procedures, mutual expectations, accountability procedures, and evaluation criteria with subordinates and supervisors.

1.14. Acknowledge contributions by others to program development, program implementation, evaluations, and reports.

1.15. Assure that participation by staff in planned activities that emphasize self-disclosure or other relatively intimate or personal involvement is voluntary and that the leader(s) of such activities do not have administrative, supervisory, or evaluative authority over participants.

1.16. Adhere to professional practices in securing positions: (a) represent education and experiences accurately; (b) respond to offers promptly; (c) accept only those positions they intend to assume; (d) advise current employer and all institutions at which applications are pending immediately when they sign a contract; and (e) inform their employers at least thirty days before leaving a position.

1.17. Gain approval of research plans involving human subjects from the institutional committee with oversight responsibility prior to initiation of the study. In the absence of such a committee, they will seek to create procedures to protect the rights and assure the safety of research participants.

1.18. Conduct and report research studies accurately. They will not engage in fraudulent research nor will they distort or misrepresent their data or deliberately bias their results.

1.19. Cite previous works on a topic when writing or when speaking to professional audiences.

1.20. Acknowledge major contributions to research projects and professional writings through joint authorships with the principal contributor listed first. They will acknowledge minor technical or professional contributions in notes or introductory statements.

1.21. Not demand co-authorship of publications when their involvement was ancillary or unduly pressure others for joint authorship.

1.22. Share original research data with qualified others upon request.

1.23. Communicate the results of any research judged to be of value to other professionals and not withhold results reflecting unfavorably on specific institutions, programs, services, or prevailing opinion.

1.24. Submit manuscripts for consideration to only one journal at a time. They will not seek to publish previously published or accepted-for-publication materials in other media or publications without first informing all editors and/or publishers concerned. They will make appropriate references in the text and receive permission to use if copyrights are involved.

1.25. Support professional preparation program efforts by providing assistantships, practica, field placements, and consultation to students and faculty.

As ACPA members, preparation program faculty will:

1.26. Inform prospective graduate students of program expectations, predominant theoretical orientations, skills needed for successful completion, and employment of recent graduates.

1.27. Assure that required experiences involving self-disclosure are communicated to prospective graduate students. When the program offers experiences that emphasize self-disclosure or other relatively intimate or personal involvement (e.g., group or individual counseling or growth groups), professionals must not have current or anticipated administrative, supervisory, or evaluative authority over participants.

1.28. Provide graduate students with a broad knowledge base consisting of theory, research, and practice.

1.29. Inform graduate students of the ethical responsibilities and standards of the profession.

1.30. Assess all relevant competencies and interpersonal functioning of students throughout the program, communicate these assessments to students, and take appropriate corrective actions including dismissal when warranted.

1.31. Assure that field supervisors are qualified to provide supervision to graduate students and are informed of their ethical responsibilities in this role.

2. *Student Learning and Development.* Student development is an essential purpose of higher education, and the pursuit of this aim is a major responsibility of student affairs. Development is complex and includes cognitive, physical, moral, social, career, spiritual, personality, and educational dimensions. Professionals must be sensitive to the variety of backgrounds, cultures, and personal characteristics evident in the student population and use appropriate theoretical perspectives to identify learning opportunities and to reduce barriers that inhibit development.

As ACPA members, student affairs professionals will:

2.1. Treat students as individuals who possess dignity, worth, and the ability to be self-directed.

2.2. Avoid dual relationships with students (e.g., counselor/employer, supervisor/best friend, or faculty/sexual partner) that may involve incompatible roles and conflicting responsibilities.

2.3. Abstain from sexual harassment.

2.4. Abstain from sexual intimacies with clients or with students for whom they have supervisory, evaluative, or instructional responsibility.

2.5. Inform students of the conditions under which they may receive assistance and the limits of confidentiality when the counseling relationship is initiated.

2.6. Avoid entering or continuing helping relationships if benefits to students are unlikely. They will refer students to appropriate specialists and recognize that if the referral is declined, they are not obligated to continue the relationship.

2.7. Inform students about the purpose of assessment and make explicit the planned use of results prior to assessment.

2.8. Provide appropriate information to students prior to and following the use of any assessment procedure to place results in proper perspective with other relevant factors (e.g., socioeconomic, ethnic, cultural, and gender-related experiences).

2.9. Confront students regarding issues, attitudes, and behaviors that have ethical implications.

3. *Responsibility to the Institution.* Institutions of higher education provide the context for student affairs practice. Institutional mission, policies, organizational structure, and culture, combined with individual judgment and professional standards, define and delimit the nature and extent of practice. Student affairs professionals share responsibility with other members of the academic community for fulfilling the institutional mission. Responsibility to promote the development of individual students and to support the institution's policies and interests require that professionals balance competing demands.

As ACPA members, student affairs professionals will:

3.1. Contribute to their institution by supporting its mission, goals, and policies.

3.2. Seek resolution when they and their institution encounter substantial disagreements concerning professional or personal values. Resolution may require sustained efforts to modify institutional policies and practices or result in voluntary termination of employment.

3.3. Recognize that conflicts among students, colleagues, or the institution should be resolved without diminishing appropriate obligations to any party involved.

3.4. Assure that information provided about the institution is factual and accurate.

3.5. Inform appropriate officials of conditions that may be disruptive or damaging to their institution.

3.6. Inform supervisors of conditions or practices that may restrict institutional or professional effectiveness.

3.7. Recognize their fiduciary responsibility to the institution. They will assure that funds for which they have oversight are expended following established procedures and in ways that optimize value, are accounted for properly, and contribute to the accomplishment of the institution's mission. They also will assure equipment, facilities, personnel, and other resources are used to promote the welfare of the institution and students.

3.8. Restrict their private interests, obligations, and transactions in ways to minimize conflicts of interest or the appearance of conflicts of interest. They will identify their personal views and actions as private citizens from those expressed or undertaken as institutional representatives.

3.9. Collaborate and share professional expertise with members of the academic community.

3.10. Evaluate programs, services, and organizational structures regularly and systematically to assure conformity to published standards and guidelines. Evaluations should be conducted using rigorous evaluation methods and principles, and the results should be made available to appropriate institutional personnel.

3.11. Evaluate job performance of subordinates regularly and recommend appropriate actions to enhance professional development and improve performance.

3.12. Provide fair and honest assessments of colleagues' job performance.

3.13. Seek evaluations of their job performance and/or services they provide.

3.14. Provide training to student affairs search and screening committee members who are unfamiliar with the profession.

3.15. Disseminate information that accurately describes the responsibilities of position vacancies, required qualifications, and the institution.

3.16. Follow a published interview and selection process that periodically notifies applicants of their status.

4. *Responsibility to Society.* Student affairs professionals, both as citizens and practitioners, have a responsibility to contribute to the improvement of the communities in which they live and work. They respect individuality and recognize that worth is not diminished by characteristics such as age, culture, ethnicity, gender, disabling condition, race, religion, or sexual/affectional orientation. Student affairs professionals work to protect human rights and promote an appreciation of human diversity in higher education.

As ACPA members, student affairs professionals will:

4.1. Assist students in becoming productive and responsible citizens.

4.2. Demonstrate concern for the welfare of all students and work for constructive change on behalf of students.

4.3. Not discriminate on the basis of age, culture, ethnicity, gender, disabling condition, race, religion, or sexual/affectional orientation. They will work to modify discriminatory practices.

4.4. Demonstrate regard for social codes and moral expectations of the communities in which they live and work. They will recognize that violations of accepted moral and legal standards may involve their clients, students, or colleagues in damaging personal conflicts and may impugn the integrity of the profession, their own reputations, and that of the employing institution.

4.5. Report to the appropriate authority any condition that is likely to harm their clients and/or others.

RESOURCE C: ACPA'S POLICIES AND PROCEDURES FOR PROCESSING COMPLAINTS OF ETHICAL VIOLATIONS

American College Personnel Association Standing Committee on Ethics

Section A: General

1. The American College Personnel Association (ACPA) is an association whose members are dedicated to enhancing the worth, dignity, potential, and uniqueness of each individual within post-secondary educational institutions and thus to the service of society. ACPA members are committed to contributing to the comprehensive education of the student, protecting human rights, advancing knowledge of student growth and development, and promoting the effectiveness of institutional programs, services, and organizational units. As a means of supporting these commitments, members of ACPA subscribe to the Statement of Ethical Principles and Standards. Acceptance of membership in ACPA signifies that the member agrees to adhere to the provisions of this Statement.

2. The purpose of this document is to facilitate the work of the Ethics Committee by specifying the procedures for processing cases of alleged violations of the Statement of Ethical Principles and Standards, codifying options for sanctioning members, and stating appeal procedures.

Section B: Ethics Committee Members

1. The Ethics Committee is a standing committee of ACPA. The Committee consists of twelve (12) members. Four (4) members are appointed annually, serving for three (3) year terms. The members shall consist of two (2) representatives of the commissions, two (2) representatives of the state divisions, two (2) representatives of the Executive Council, and six (6) at large members. All members shall be chosen by the ACPA President in consultation with the Chair of the Ethics Committee. The

Ethics Committee will be guided by all the standard procedures of ACPA including the Affirmative Action Policy, in conducting its business.

2. The Chair of the Ethics Committee is appointed biannually by the ACPA President-Elect and serves a term of two (2) years as Chair. The Chair must have served on the Ethics Committee for at least one (1) year subsequent to the formation of ACPA as an independent organization.

Section C: Role and Function

1. The role of the Ethics Committee is to assist in the resolution of conflicts among members of ACPA. The Committee also is responsible for:

A. educating the membership as to the Statement of Ethical Principles and Standards;

B. periodically reviewing and recommending changes in the Statement of Ethical Principles and Standards of ACPA as well as the Policies and Procedures for Processing Complaints of Ethical Violations;

C. receiving and processing complaints of alleged violations of the Statement of Ethical Principles and Standards; and

D. receiving and processing questions.

2. The Ethics Committee itself will not initiate any ethical violation charges against an ACPA member. The Ethics Committee will allow non-members to bring allegations of unethical conduct to the attention of the Ethics Committee. The Ethics Committee has the authority to determine if the charges have merit and to respond to charges which are determined to have merit.

3. In processing complaints about alleged ethical misconduct, the Ethics Committee will compile a factual account of the dispute in question and make the best possible recommendation for the resolution of the case. The Ethics Committee, in the imposition of sanctions or discipline, shall do so only for cause, shall only take the degree of disciplinary action that is reasonable, shall utilize these procedures with objectivity and fairness, and in general shall act only to further the interests and objectives of ACPA and its membership.

4. All formal allegations of ethical misconduct will be reviewed by a Hearing Panel. Hearing Panels shall consist of five (5) members chosen by the Chair. In addition, the Chair will serve on all Hearing Panels as presiding officer and a non-voting member. Members of the Ethics Committee who have a personal interest in any case will be excluded from serving on the panel which hears the case. The findings of all Hearing Panels are understood to represent the Ethics Committee as a whole.

5. The Chair of the Ethics Committee and/or any ACPA Executive Director (or his/her designee) may consult with ACPA legal counsel at any time.

Section D: Responsibilities of Committee Members

1. The members of the Ethics Committee must be conscious that their position is extremely important and sensitive and that their decisions involve the rights of many

individuals, the reputation of the student affairs profession, and the careers of the members. The Committee members have an obligation to act in an unbiased manner, to work expeditiously, to safeguard the confidentiality of the Committee's activities, and to follow procedures that protect the rights of individuals involved.

Section E: Responsibilities of the Chair

1. In addition to the above guidelines for members of the Ethics Committee, the Chair, in conjunction with Headquarters staff and Hearing Panels, has the responsibilities of:

A. receiving (via Headquarters) complaints that have been certified for membership status of the accused;

B. notifying the complainant and the accused of receipt of the case;

C. notifying the members of the Ethics Committee of the case;

D. presiding over the meetings of the Committee;

E. preparing and sending (by certified mail) communications to the complainant and accused member on the recommendations and decisions of the Committee; and

F. arranging for legal advice with assistance and financial approval of the ACPA Executive Director.

Section F: Complaints

1. All correspondence, records, and activities of the Ethics Committee will remain confidential.
2. The Ethics Committee will not act on anonymous complaints nor will it act on complaints known to be currently under civil or criminal investigation.
3. The Ethics Committee will act only on those cases where the accused is a current member of ACPA or was a member of ACPA at the time of the alleged violation.

Section G: Submitting Complaints—Procedures for ACPA Members

1. The procedures for submission of complaints to the Ethics Committee are as follows:

A. If feasible, the complainant should discuss with utmost confidentiality the nature of the complaint with a colleague to see if he/she views the situation as an ethical violation.

B. Whenever feasible, the complainant is to approach the accused directly to discuss and resolve the complaint.

C. In cases where a resolution is not forthcoming at the personal level, the complainant shall prepare a formal written statement of the complaint and shall submit it to the Ethics Committee. Action or consideration by the Ethics Committee may not be initiated until this requirement is satisfied.

D. Formal written complaints must include a statement indicating the behavior(s) that constituted the alleged violation(s), the date(s) of the alleged violation(s), and the Standard(s) which the person making the charges believes has (have) been violated. The written statement must also contain the accused member's full name and complete address. Any relevant supporting documentation may be included with the complaint.

E. All complaints that are directed to the Ethics Committee should be mailed to the Ethics Committee, c/o The ACPA Executive Director, One Dupont Circle, Suite 360-A, Washington, DC 20036–1110. The envelope must be marked "CONFIDENTIAL." This procedure is necessary to ensure the confidentiality of the person submitting the complaint and the person accused in the complaint.

Section H: Submitting Complaints—Procedures for Non-ACPA Members

1. The Ethics Committee will permit a non-ACPA member to bring allegations of unethical conduct to the attention of the Ethics Committee. Ordinarily this non-member will be a colleague, student, or client of an ACPA member who believes that the ACPA member has acted unethically.
2. In such cases, the complainant shall contact the ACPA Executive Director (or his/her designee) and outline, in writing, those behaviors he/she feels were unethical in nature.
3. The Executive Director will forward to the complainant the Statement of Ethical Principles and Standards and the Policies and Procedures for Processing Complaints of Ethical Violations. Complainant will follow the procedures outlined in Section G1 C and D above. The Ethics Committee has the authority to determine if the charges have merit and to respond to charges which are determined to have merit.

Section I: Processing Complaints

1. When complaints are received at Headquarters, the ACPA Executive Director (or his/her designee) shall: (a) check on the membership status of the accused, (b) acknowledge receipt of the complaint within ten (10) working days after it is received at Headquarters, and (c) consult with the Chair of the Ethics Committee within ten (10) working days after the complaint is received in Headquarters to determine whether it is appropriate to proceed with the complaint. If the Director (or his/her designee) and Chair determine it is inappropriate to proceed, the complainant shall be so notified. If the Director (or his/her designee) and Chair determine it is appropriate to proceed with the complaint, they will identify which Standard(s) are applicable to the alleged violation. A formal statement containing the Standard(s) that were allegedly violated will be forwarded to the complainant for his/her signature. This signed statement will then become a part of the formal complaint.
2. Once the formal complaint has been compiled (as indicated above), the Chair of the Ethics Committee shall do the following:

A. Direct a letter to the accused member informing the member of accusations lodged against him/her, including copies of all materials submitted by the complainant, asking for a response, and request that relevant information be submitted to the Chair within thirty (30) working days, and

B. Inform the complainant in writing that the accused member has been notified of the charges.

3. The accused is under no duty to respond to the allegations, but the Ethics Committee will not be obligated to delay or postpone its review of the case unless the accused so requests, with good cause, in advance. Failure of the accused to respond should not be viewed by the Ethics Committee as sufficient grounds for taking disciplinary action.

4. The Chair will choose five (5) members of the Ethics Committee to serve as the Hearing Panel for the case.

5. Once the Chair has received the accused member's response or the thirty (30) days have elapsed, the Chair shall forward to the members of the Hearing Panel legal counsel's opinion (if applicable), staff verification of membership status, allegations, and responses, and direct the Hearing Panel to review the case and make recommendations for its disposition within 90 days of receipt of the case.

6. The Ethics Committee Chair may ask the President of ACPA to appoint an investigating committee at the local or state level to gather and submit relevant information concerning the case to the Hearing Panel.

Section J: Available Options

1. After reviewing the information forwarded by the Chair, the Hearing Panel has the authority to:

A. dismiss the charges, find that no violation has occurred or that the allegation is frivolous, and dismiss the complaint; or

B. find that the practice(s) in which the member engaged that is (are) subject of the complaint, is (are) unethical, notify the accused of this determination, and request the member to voluntarily cease and desist in the practice(s) without impositions of further sanctions; or

C. find that the practice(s) in which the member engaged, that is (are) the subject of the complaint, is (are) unethical, notify the accused of this determination, and impose sanctions.

Section K: Appropriate Sanctions

1. The Hearing Panel may consider extenuating circumstances before deciding on the penalty to be imposed. If the Hearing Panel finds that the accused has violated the Statement of Ethical Principles and Standards and decides to impose sanctions, the Hearing Panel may take any of the following actions:

A. issue a reprimand with recommendations for corrective action, subject to review by the Hearing Panel; or

B. place the member on probation for a specified period of time subject to review by the Hearing Panel; or

C. suspend eligibility for membership in ACPA for a specified period of time, subject to review by the Hearing Panel; or

D. expel the member from ACPA permanently.

Section L: Consequences of Sanctions

1. Neither a reprimand nor probation carry with it a loss of membership rights or privileges.
2. A suspended member forfeits the rights and privileges of membership only for the period of his/her suspension.
3. In the event a member is expelled from ACPA membership, he/she shall lose all rights and privileges of membership in ACPA and its divisions permanently. The expelled member shall not be entitled to a refund of dues already paid.
4. If the member is suspended or expelled, and after any right to appeal has been exhausted, the Ethics Committee will notify any appropriate licensing board(s) of the disciplined member's status with ACPA. Notice also will be given to the ACPA State Divisions of which the disciplined party is a member, the complainant, and other organizations appropriate given the member's professional affiliations. Such notice shall only state the sanctions imposed and the sections of the Statement of Ethical Principles and Standards that were violated. Further elaboration shall not be disclosed.
5. Should a member resign from ACPA or fail to renew his/her membership after a complaint has been brought against him/her and before the Hearing Panel has completed its deliberations, that member is considered to have been expelled from ACPA for failure to respond to an allegation of ethical misconduct under consideration by the Ethics Committee.
6. Annually the Ethics Committee will publish a list of all suspended and expelled members in an official publication.

Section M: Hearings

1. At the discretion of the Hearing Panel, a hearing may be conducted when the results of the Hearing Panel's preliminary determination indicate that additional information is needed. The Chair shall schedule a formal hearing on the case and notify both the complainant and the accused of their right to attend.

Section N: Hearing Procedures

1. Purposes of Hearings. The purposes for which hearings shall be conducted are: (a) to determine whether a breach of the Statement of Ethical Principles and Standards has occurred, and (b) if so, to determine what disciplinary action should be taken by ACPA. If a hearing is held, no disciplinary action will be taken by ACPA until after the accused member has been given reasonable notice of the hearing and the specific charges raised against him/her and has had the opportunity to be heard and to present evidence in his/her behalf. The hearings will be formally conducted. The Hearing Panel will be guided in its deliberations by principles of basic fairness and professionalism and will keep its deliberations as confidential as possible, except as provided herein.
2. Notice. At least forty-five (45) working days before the hearing, the accused member should be advised in writing of the time and place of the hearing and of the

charges involved. Notice shall be given either personally or by certified or registered mail and shall be signed by the Committee Chair. The notice should be addressed to the accused member at his/her address as it appears in the membership records of ACPA. The notice should include a brief statement of the complaints lodged against him/her and should be supported by the evidence. The accused is under no duty to respond to the notice, but the Hearing Panel will not be obligated to delay or postpone its hearing unless the accused so requests in writing, with good cause, in advance. Failure of the accused to appear at the hearing should not be viewed by the Hearing Panel as sufficient grounds for taking disciplinary action.

3. Conduct of the Hearing.

A. Accommodations. The Hearing Panel shall provide a private room in which to conduct the meetings and no observers shall be permitted. The location of the hearing shall be determined at the discretion of the Committee taking into consideration the convenience of the Committee and the parties involved.

B. Presiding Officer. The Chair of the Ethics Committee shall preside over the hearing and deliberations of the Hearing Panel. In the event the Chair or any other member of the Hearing Panel has a personal interest in the case, he/she shall withdraw from the hearing and deliberations and shall not participate therein. The Hearing Panel shall select from among its members a presiding officer for any case in which the Chair has excused him/herself. At the conclusion of the hearing and deliberation of the Hearing Panel, the Chair shall promptly notify the accused and complainant of the Hearing Panel's decision in writing.

C. Record. A record of the hearing shall be made and preserved, together with any documents presented as evidence, at Headquarters for a period of three (3) years following the hearing decision. The record may consist of a summary of testimony received or a verbatim transcript at the discretion of the Hearing Panel.

D. Right to Counsel. The parties shall be entitled to have counsel present to advise them throughout the hearing but the counsel may not participate beyond advising. Legal Counsel for ACPA may also be present at the hearing to advise the Hearing Panel and may respond only to questions of procedure.

E. Witnesses. Either party shall have the right to call witnesses to substantiate his/her version of the case. The Hearing Panel shall also have the right to call witnesses it believes may provide further insight into the matter before the Hearing Panel. Witnesses shall not be present during the hearings except when they are called upon to testify. The presiding officer shall allow questions to be asked of any witness by the opposition or members of the Hearing Panel and shall ensure that questions and testimony are relevant to the issues in the case. The presiding officer has the right to determine when sufficient information has been heard, may limit witnesses, and determine when to stop testimony. Witnesses shall be excused upon completion of their testimony. All expenses associated with witness or counsel on behalf of the parties shall be borne by the respective parties.

F. Presentation of Evidence.

1. The presiding officer shall present the charge(s) made against the accused and briefly describe the evidence supporting the charge(s).

2. The complainant or a member of the Hearing Panel shall then present the case against the accused. Witnesses who can substantiate the case shall testify and answer questions of the accused and the Hearing Panel.
3. If the accused has exercised the right to be present at the hearing, he/she shall be called upon last to present any evidence which refutes the charges against him/her. This includes the presentation of witnesses as in Subsection E above. The accused member has the right to refuse to make a statement in his/her behalf. The accused will not be found guilty simply for refusing to testify. Once the accused chooses to testify, however, he/she may be questioned by members of the Hearing Panel or the complainant.
4. The Hearing Panel will endeavor to conclude the hearing expeditiously.
5. The accused has the right to be present at all times during the hearing and to challenge all of the evidence presented against him/her.

G. Evidence. The Hearing Panel is not a court of law and is not required to observe the rules of evidence that apply in the trial of lawsuits. Consequently, evidence that would be inadmissible in a court of law may, at the Hearing Panel's discretion, be admissible at the hearing if it is relevant to the case and probative on a relevant issue. The Hearing Panel will not receive evidence or testimony for the purpose of supporting any charge that was not set forth in the notice of the hearing or that is not relevant to the issues of the case.

4. Burden of Proof. The burden of proving a violation of the Statement of Ethical Principles and Standards is on the complainant and/or the Hearing Panel. It is not up to the accused to prove his/her innocence of any wrong-doing. Although the charge(s) need not be proved "beyond a reasonable doubt," the Hearing Panel will not find the accused guilty in the absence of substantial and credible evidence to sustain the charge(s).

5. Deliberation of the Hearing Panel. After the hearing is completed, the Hearing Panel shall meet in a closed session to review the evidence presented and reach a conclusion. The Hearing Panel shall be the sole trier of fact and shall weigh the evidence presented and judge the credibility of the witnesses. The act of a majority of the members of the Hearing Panel shall be the decision of the Hearing Panel.

6. Decision of the Hearing Panel. The Hearing Panel will first resolve the issue of the guilt or innocence of the accused. Applying the burden of proof in paragraph 4 above, the Hearing Panel will vote by secret ballot, unless the members of the Hearing Panel consent to an oral vote. In the event a majority of the members of the Hearing Panel do not find the accused guilty, the charges shall be dismissed and the parties notified. If the Hearing Panel finds the accused has violated the Statement of Ethical Principles and Standards, it must then determine what sanctions to impose in accord with Section K.

Section O: Appeal Procedures

1. Appeals will be heard only in such cases wherein the appellant presents new evidence which would have affected the outcome of the original hearing or can

demonstrate that a procedural error has occurred which can be shown to have had an adverse effect on the outcome.

A. The Appeals Committee will be composed of three (3) people: the past President, a member of the Ethics Committee who did not serve on the Hearing Panel, and another member of the Executive Committee chosen by the current President in consultation with the Chair of the Ethics Committee. ACPA Counsel and the Executive Director shall be available as consultants to the Appeals Committee.

B. The appeal with supporting documentation must be made in writing within sixty (60) working days by certified mail to the ACPA Executive Director and indicate the basis upon which it is made. If the member requires a time extension, he/she must request it in writing by certified mail within thirty (30) working days of receiving the decision by the Ethics Committee. The extension will consist of ninety (90) working days beginning from that request.

C. The Appeals Committee shall review all materials considered by the Ethics Committee.

D. Within thirty (30) working days of this appeal, the members on the Appeals Committee shall submit to the President of ACPA a written statement giving their opinion regarding the decision of the Hearing Panel.

E. Within fifteen (15) working days of receiving this opinion, the President of ACPA will reach a decision based on the considered opinions of the Appeals Committee from the following alternatives:

1. support the decision of the Hearing Panel, or
2. reverse the decision of the Hearing Panel.
3. The parties to the appeal shall be advised of the action in writing.

Section P: Records

1. Records of the Ethics Committee and the Appeals Committee shall remain at Headquarters and be confidential except for use by the Ethics Committee.

NAME INDEX

C

D

E

F

G

K

L

T

U

V

W

Y

Z

SUBJECT INDEX

B

C

D

G

J

M

N

O

P

Q

R

T